THE MICRO ECONOMY TODAY

THE MICRO ECONOMY TODAY

BRADLEY R. SCHILLER
The American University

RANDOM HOUSE
New York

First Edition

98765432

Library of Congress Cataloging in Publication Data

Schiller, Bradley R., 1943–
The micro economy today.

Together with The macro economy today comprises a 2 vol. ed. of: The economy today. 2nd ed.
Includes index.
1. Microeconomics. I. Title.
HB172.S36 1983 338.5 82-25487
ISBN 0-394-33167-2

Manufactured in the United States of America

Design by Betty Binns Graphics/Martin Lubin

Charts by Rino Dussi

Cover design by Leon Bolognese

Cover art by Ronald F. Hall

PREFACE

At first blush, microeconomics seems so much less important than macroeconomics. Micro is concerned, after all, with the decisions and behavior of individual workers, families, firms, and markets. Macro, on the other hand, focuses on the big picture—the collective (aggregate) behavior of all market participants. The great policy debates all seem to be about the macro problems of inflation, unemployment, and economic growth. In this context, knowledge of individual decision making seems so much less significant than an understanding of our collective behavior.

This first impression is highly misleading, however. To begin with, microeconomics is the foundation of all macroeconomics. Macro outcomes are the result of millions of individual decisions. If these decisions are not understood, then knowledge of macroeconomics is necessarily incomplete. The result may be bad macro policy. The situation is much like driving a car. Most of the time you can get along just knowing the (macro) principles of accelerating, steering, and braking. But when something goes wrong, you need to know how the car really works. Why did it fail to accelerate or slow down on time? Why is it veering off the road? To answer these questions, someone must look under the hood.

Recent debates about supply-side economics have encouraged more people to look under the economy's hood. The emphasis of supply-side economics is on individual decision making. Supply-Siders argue that greater incentives are the key to increased work effort, more savings and investment, and greater productivity. From the supply-side perspective, improved macro outcomes—particularly less unemployment and inflation—are possible only if these micro incentives are included in the design of economic policies.

Not everyone accepts the supply-side prescriptions for macro problems. But there is now a much greater recognition of the role micro behavior plays in macro outcomes.

Microeconomics is also important in its own right. The well-being of individuals is of direct concern to society, independently of macro implications. Two societies, identical in every other respect except their different distributions of income, are not viewed similarly. People *do* care about the distribution of income, even in the absence of macro problems. This concern is manifest in continuing debates about tax reform, budget cuts, welfare programs, and recent changes in social security. The reason these debates are so intense and so protracted is that no one wants a smaller slice of the economic pie.

This text seeks to satisfy two related goals. First, it tries to convey the dimensions of our microeconomic problems. For example, the distribution of income is described before the trade-offs between equity and efficiency that redistributions may involve are examined. The nature and severity of pollution are assessed before the economic incentives to pollute are analyzed. Likewise, the nature and extent of profits are described before the text examines the forces and decisions that create profits. And a whole chapter is devoted to examples of market power that illustrate the principles of monopoly, oligopoly, and monopolistic competition.

The justification for this descriptive material is the notion that you must get a person's attention before you can teach anything. That notion leads to the second goal of the text: to teach the basic principles of microeconomics. Writing style and topical illustrations facilitate the goal. In addition, however, the text provides clear, step-by-step development of basic concepts. Instead of being encyclopedic, the text concentrates on the exposition of core principles. The aim here is to teach economic principles in a way that maximizes retention—through the use of real-world examples, basic concepts, and careful, readable explanations.

REAL-WORLD APPLICATIONS

The emphasis on real-world applications is apparent throughout. Chapter 1 sets the tone, by illustrating the concept of opportunity cost with the Reagan defense build-up. In later chapters price elasticity is illustrated by airfare cuts, increased gasoline taxes, and excise taxes on liquor. An extended discussion of the pocket-calculator industry is used to introduce the concept of competition. Competition emerges as a dynamic force characterized by a rapid rate of firm entry, unrelenting pressure on prices and profits, and a tendency toward product and cost innovation. Students following the decline of calculator prices from $200 (in 1972) to under $6 (in 1982) should develop a keen appreciation of what competition is all about. The dynamics of a competitive market are further illustrated with video games, personal computers, and Atlantic City casinos. An Appendix to Chapter 7 shows the same kind of competitive forces at work in agriculture and assesses the consequences for farm technology, employment, prices, and income.

The competitive dynamics of the electronic-calculator industry provide the foundation for analysis of alternative market structures. By assuming various barriers to entry and other noncompetitive practices, the calculator industry is transformed into a monopoly (Chapter 8) and an oligopoly (Chapter 9); then its current structure of monopolistic competition (also Chapter 9) is examined. In each case, direct comparisons of behavior and outcomes in alternative market structures are highlighted. The implications for our economic welfare, antitrust activity, and government regulations are emphasized. The AT&T and IBM antitrust cases are used to illustrate the different principles at work.

Chapter 10 provides another unique chapter for an introductory text. No new theory is presented in this chapter. Instead, it surveys the actual behavior of familiar U.S. firms. Firms possessing substantial market power (high market share) are first identified, by name. The concentration ratios used here refer to individual product markets (e.g., tennis balls), not the more traditional (and much less meaningful) industry classifications (e.g., rubber products). The noncompetitive practices of these and other firms are then described in considerable detail and illustrated with many news clippings. Examples include price fixing (Arkansas milk producers, Cleveland supermarkets), monopoly patents (Prince tennis rackets), and product differentiation (designer jeans). This chapter should add color to the more theoretical discussions of market structure contained in Chapters 7–9.

Considerable space is devoted to labor markets. Again, both competitive behavior and noncompetitive behavior are described. Unionism and employer power (monopsony) are portrayed as significant influences on market outcomes. Specific unions (the Baseball Players Association, the United Mine Workers, the UAW) and employers are identified, and their behavior assessed. Labor-market outcomes (wages and employment) are seen as the result of both competitive forces and institutional barriers. Of special interest here are the discussions of robotics and the high salaries paid to some college football coaches.

THEORETICAL DEVELOPMENT

The real-world applications make the learning process more interesting and ultimately more successful. Careful development of basic theory is not sacrificed along the way, however. Chapter 4 illustrates the careful sequence in which basic concepts are first introduced with a real-world example, then defined, then explained and illustrated in a variety of ways. Particularly useful is the way that tables and graphs are interrelated with parallel notation. Notice on page 89, for example, how the rows of the demand schedule are reflected in points on the demand curve. Consistent use of color and broken lines for shifts of curves (e.g., in Figure 4.4, p. 91) also facilitates comprehension.

The theory of the firm is introduced with full-length chapters on costs (Chapter 5) and profits (Chapter 6). In Chapter 5, money costs are explicitly related to real production functions, so that students get a meaningful sense of where costs originate. This treatment greatly facilitates the later discussion of the distinction between economic costs and accounting costs.

The distinction between economic and accounting costs re-emerges in Chapter 6, where the concept of profits is examined. The chapter starts by contrasting the very different views of profits held by the public, accountants, and economists. Then the economic concept of profits is explained and illustrated. The changing relationships of profits, prices, and costs are described in detail. As a result, students are apt to be comfortable with the concepts of cost and profits by the time they start examining production and investment decisions.

THE ISSUE CHAPTERS

The balance of theory and applications is also maintained in the issue chapters. The distinguishing feature of these chapters is that they tend to focus on a small number of principles already introduced in the core chapters. Chapter 17, for example, examines the perplexing issue of welfare vs. "workfare," with references to both labor-supply theory (Chapter 11) and negative-income-tax experiments. In Chapter 16, externalities are portrayed as the core of our pollution problems. And marginal productivity theory is contrasted with "comparable worth" and the perspectives of "radical" economists in assessing discrimination in Chapter 18.

INTERNATIONAL TOPICS

The final section of the text focuses on international subjects. International trade and finance receive substantial attention, in recognition of their growing influence on our economic performance. In each case, the motivations for trade and finance are discussed at length. The market mechanism is then related to those motivations. Finally, the sources of resistance to free trade and finance are identified as constraints on policy decisions. In the process, David Ricardo's theories and vested economic interests are both viewed as important determinants of trade flows. One story about Franco-American trade in wheat and wine weaves through the trade and finance chapters, helping to drive home the intrinsic relationships of trade and finance.

STUDENT LEARNING AIDS

It is hoped that the style and approach of *The Micro Economy Today* will motivate students to learn and remember basic economics. To facilitate this process, the text also offers a variety of pedagogical features.

Textual learning aids

To facilitate comprehension and retention, each chapter contains the following learning aids:

CHAPTER PREVIEW Each chapter begins with a narrative introduction to the content and purpose of the chapter. Each preview highlights basic questions to be answered and relates them to previous chapters.

RUNNING GLOSSARY Definitions of key terms are provided in the margins, to facilitate retention and quick review. Definitions are repeated in successive chapters where they are relevant, in recognition of the fact that students do not remember basic terms after only one "lesson." All of these terms are compiled into a complete glossary, with chapter references, at the end of the book.

FULLY ANNOTATED GRAPHS AND TABLES All graphs and tables in the text are accompanied by self-contained captions. These reinforce the in-text discussions and facilitate quick review. In addition, as mentioned above, the content of related schedules and graphs is explicitly synchronized with the aid of labeled rows (in schedules) and dots (on graphs). Color is used in tables and graphs throughout to highlight new or important concepts.

SELF-CONTAINED EXAMPLES The text makes considerable use of shaded boxes to illustrate key points of the text. Some of these are designed to highlight a basic concept (e.g., *ceteris paribus*). Others are illustrative digressions and include newspaper and magazine clippings, public-opinion polls, or short summaries of related material. The use of shaded boxes clearly distinguishes all of this material from the flow of the basic text.

POLICY IMPLICATIONS Every theory chapter contains a brief discussion of a specific policy implication. These sections reinforce the basic theoretical presentations by underscoring the use of the principles introduced in the chapter.

NARRATIVE SUMMARIES Chapter summaries highlight basic points and principles in brief, sequenced paragraphs.

KEY-TERM REVIEW Each chapter ends with a list of key terms for quick review. These lists include all terms contained in the running glossary of the chapter.

DISCUSSION QUESTIONS Four or five discussion questions are provided at the end of each chapter. These relate directly to basic principles covered in the chapter and can be used for student review, class discussion, or homework assignments.

NUMERICAL PROBLEM Almost every chapter concludes with one numerical problem. These test the student's ability to solve typical exam-type problems. Answers are at the end of the *Instructor's Resource Manual.*

Study Guide

There are several supplements available to accompany the text itself. From the student's perspective, the most important of these is the *Study Guide,* prepared by Professors Lawrence Ziegler of the University of Texas (Arlington) and Michael Tansey of Rockhurst College. Each chapter of the *Study Guide* contains the following features:

QUICK REVIEW Key points in the text chapter are restated at the beginning of each *Study Guide* chapter. These reviews are parallel to and reinforce the chapter summaries provided in the text.

LEARNING OBJECTIVES The salient lessons of the text chapters are noted at the outset of each *Study Guide* chapter. These objectives focus the student's study and help to assure that key points will not be overlooked. The objectives are keyed to the exercises in the *Study Guide* to help reinforce learning.

KEY-TERM REVIEW Early in each chapter the student is asked to match definitions with key terms. This relatively simple exercise is designed to refresh the student's memory and provide a basis for subsequent exercises.

TRUE-FALSE QUESTIONS Twenty or so true-false questions are provided in each chapter. These questions have been class-tested to assure their effectiveness in highlighting basic principles.

MULTIPLE-CHOICE QUESTIONS Approximately fifteen multiple-choice questions are also provided. These questions generally allow only one answer and also focus on basic principles.

PROBLEMS AND APPLICATIONS Each chapter of the *Study Guide* contains one or two real-world problems. These problems require the student to complete graphs, tables, or simple algebraic solutions.

COMMON ERRORS In each chapter of the *Study Guide,* errors that students frequently make are identified. The bases for those errors are then explained, along with the correct principles. This unique feature is very effective in helping students discover their own mistakes.

ANSWERS Answers to *all* problems, exercises, and questions are provided at the end of each chapter. These answers make the *Study Guide* self-contained, thus allowing students to use it for self-study.

INSTRUCTOR'S AIDS

We have tried to make the learning process easier for teachers as well as students. To this end, Professors Virginia Owen and Alan Dillingham (Illinois State University) have prepared an *Instructor's Resource Manual.* In addition, Professor Michael Ellis (North Texas State University) has compiled a *Test Bank* of multiple-choice questions.

Instructor's Resource Manual

The purpose of the *Instructor's Resource Manual* is to provide a ready source of lecture and discussion material for classroom teaching. To this end, it offers a variety of material, including:

CHAPTER OUTLINE The first section of each chapter briefly summarizes the material under the text's major headings. Instructors can duplicate this section for students as an aid in studying.

TEXT EXPANSION The second section of each chapter highlights subjects that often require special attention, giving many interesting examples for classroom discussion.

CONTROVERSIAL ISSUES The third section of each chapter, "Take a Stand," describes a controversial issue associated with the theory presented in the text. Chapter 2 of the text, for example, discusses the basic elements of supply and demand. The *Resource Manual* discusses the pros and cons of regulating the price of natural gas, drawing on the text and a recent news article. No resolution of the issue is offered. "Take a Stand" is intended to start a classroom discussion or to form the basis for essay-type questions.

NEWS UPDATE The fourth section of each *Resource Manual* chapter provides a summary and analysis of a recent economics event. The core of the "News Updates" is drawn from *The Wall Street Journal, Business Week,* or similar publications. The news summary is supplemented by a brief analysis that ties the story directly to the content of the text.

SUPPLEMENTARY RESOURCES The final section of each chapter serves two separate functions. First, it provides a list of audio-visual and printed materials that can be readily obtained for class use. Second, it provides references for additional lecture material or student assignments.

Test Bank

The *Test Bank* includes approximately 50 multiple-choice questions for each text chapter. Each question has been classified according to its level of difficulty. There are three levels. The first requires the simple recall of facts, names, or definitions. The second level of question is analytical, requiring greater comprehension and an understanding of functional relationships. The third level, the most difficult, demands a thorough comprehension of theory and a high degree of analytical reasoning.

About half of the *Test Bank* questions are cross-referenced directly to the learning objectives in the *Study Guide.* Midterms and comprehensive final examinations are also available in the *Test Bank.* The entire *Test Bank* is available on computer tape.

Overhead transparencies

Over 100 of the key tables and graphs in the text have been reproduced as overhead masters. These are made available to users by the publisher.

A COMPLETE TEACHING PACKAGE

We have tried to assemble a complete teaching package for classroom use. In the process we have introduced several unique text features, including the chapters concerned with economic problems; the liberal use of news stories and other supplementary materials; the use of a running glossary; and an explicit, simultaneous introduction to both theory and institutions. In the *Study Guide* we have introduced the "Common Errors" section and a greater emphasis on learning basic definitions, the *Instructor's Resource Manual* features the "Take a Stand" section, as well as "News Updates." We have tried to present all of the material in a lively manner that stimulates student interest.

Have we succeeded in producing a new and effective teaching package? We hope so. The real test will be administered by students who use this text. Success will be measured in terms of increased student interest in the economy today and a better understanding of how it works.

ACKNOWLEDGMENTS

The Micro Economy Today has been improved by the suggestions of many users and reviewers. Walter Johnson (University of Missouri), Carl Austermiller (Oakland Community College), and Walter Nicholson (Amherst College) were particularly generous with their time in reviewing the text in its various stages. In addition to them, I would like to thank publicly the following reviewers: Robert Costrell (University of Massachusetts), Herbert J. Eskowitz (Northeastern University), Donald Farness (Oregon State University), Roger Frantz (San Diego State University), William Gunther (The University of Alabama), Alan Mandelstamm (Virginia Polytechnic Institute), Henry McCarl (The University of Alabama in Birmingham), Herbert Milikien (American River College), Dan Morgan (University of Texas at Austin), Martha Olney (University of California, Berkeley), Arthur Peterson (Middlesex County College), Michael Tansey (Rockhurst College), Robert Thomas (Iowa State University), and Lawrence Ziegler (University of Texas at Arlington).

In addition to the reviewers' advice, this book has benefited greatly from the assistance and encouragement of many people. Foremost among these is Paul Shensa, who marshaled all the resources and people required to create this teaching package. Elaine Romano was one of those people and did a meticulous job of editing the entire package. My own efforts were invaluably assisted by Anita Janks, who never hesitated to go the proverbial extra mile, and several research assistants, including Franklin Armstrong, Colin Gibson, Kati Ho, and Ann Levin.

BRADLEY R. SCHILLER
The American University
December 1982

CONTENTS IN BRIEF

CONTENTS

SECTION I

BASICS

CHAPTER 1

AN OVERVIEW

Public-opinion polls suggest that Americans worry more about the economy than anything else. The outlook for jobs, prices, taxes, government spending, and interest rates is always at the forefront of public concern. A Gallup poll taken in April 1982 illustrates this concern. When asked what the country's most important problem was, 44 percent of the population cited unemployment. Almost everyone else worried about other aspects of the economy, such as inflation (24 percent), high interest rates (11 percent), and budget cuts (7 percent).[1] Very few people cited noneconomic problems. Even more remarkable is the response to a Gallup poll taken in October 1943. That poll asked people what they thought the greatest problem facing the country would be in the year ahead. At that time the nation was deeply involved in World War II. Nevertheless, most Americans thought jobs and economic readjustment would be our greatest problems. Little concern was expressed for the prospects of peace.[2]

For many people, of course, concern for the economy goes no further than the price of gasoline or the fear of losing a job. Many others, however, are becoming increasingly aware that their job prospects and the prices they pay are somehow related to national trends in prices, unemployment, and economic growth. Although few people think in terms of price indexes, graphs, or economic cy-

[1] *The Gallup Poll,* April 25, 1982.
[2] George H. Gallup, *The Gallup Poll: Public Opinion 1935–1971* (New York: Random House, 1972), vol. 1, p. 410.

ECONOMICS UP, RELIGION DOWN

In 1981 *Psychology Today* asked the Gallup Organization to survey the worries and hopes of Americans—to find out how Americans *feel* about themselves and the country. The results were striking. At the top of the list of personal concerns was the hope for a better standard of living and the fear of a worse one. With respect to national issues, economic stability and a cure for inflation ranked at the top of America's hopes. By contrast, moral and religious concerns (e.g., "social decay," "integrity in politics," "public morality," "brotherhood") were hardly even expressed. As compared to earlier surveys, these opinions reflected a sharp increase in the concern for economic issues and a lessening of religious concerns.

Source: *Psychology Today*, September 1981.

cles, most have learned to recognize the importance of certain economic phenomena. And that is why so many people worry about such abstractions as unemployment rates, inflation, and economic growth.

Despite the widespread concern for the economy, few people really understand how it works. You can hardly blame them. For one thing, the very dimensions of the economy tend to obscure its relevance. The annual output of our economy is now measured in trillions of dollars. For those of us who rarely see a $100 bill, it is difficult to comprehend such figures. The significance of billion-dollar changes in output is easily lost on people who are trying to figure out how to pay this month's rent.

Despite the seeming irrelevance of "the economy," it is very much a part of our everyday lives. We spend much of our lives working to produce the goods and services that flow from our factories and offices. We spend a good part of the remaining time consuming those same goods and services. And during much of the time left over, we worry about what to produce or consume next. Even such simple things as reading this book, going to school, and lying on the beach can be described as economic activities.

Interest in the workings of the economy will develop only as we begin to see some immediate stake in its performance. The loss of a job, for example, can rivet one's attention on the causes of unemployment. A tuition increase may start you thinking about the nature and causes of inflation. And high rents can start you thinking about the demand for housing in relation to its supply.

What we seek to determine, then, is not simply whether we are involved in the economy—a fact nearly everyone can accept with a shrug—but more important, how we are involved and where our interests lie. How can we reduce pollution, eliminate poverty, improve the quality of life? How can we provide jobs for everyone who wants to work? How can you increase your income? To answer such questions, we need to understand the relationship between the workings of the economy and our individual pursuits. We also need to know how our individual and collective actions help shape the course of economic events. To this end, later chapters will focus on two key questions: (1) How does the economy function, and (2) How do our private and public actions affect the course of economic

"Meaningless statistics were up one-point-five per cent this month over last month."

Drawing by Dana Fradon; © 1977 The New Yorker Magazine, Inc.

events? Of special interest will be the potential for public policy to improve the performance of the economy. Each chapter of the text concludes with a section on policy implications.

THE ECONOMY IS US

It may be useful to begin our study of the economy by recognizing a very basic relationship, namely, that *the economy is us.* "The economy" is simply an abstraction that refers to the sum of all our individual production and consumption activities. What we collectively produce is what the economy produces; what we collectively consume is what the economy consumes. In this sense, the concept of "the economy" is no more difficult than the concept of "the family." If someone tells you that the Jones family has an annual income of $22,000, you know that the reference is to the collective earnings of all the Joneses. Hence, when someone reports that the nation's income exceeds $3 trillion per year—as it now does—we should recognize immediately that the reference is to the sum of our individual incomes. If we work fewer hours or get paid less, family income and national income are both reduced. Hence to understand the economy is to understand our own economic behavior, both individually and collectively.

The same relationship between individual behavior and aggregate behavior applies to specific outputs as well. If we as individuals insist on driving cars rather than walking or taking public transportation, the economy will produce millions of cars each year and consume vast quantities of oil. In a slightly different way, the economy produces and consumes billions of dollars of military hardware to satisfy our desire for national defense. In each case, the output of the economy reflects the collective efforts and demands of the 230 million individuals who participate in the economy. In these very tangible dimensions, the economy is truly us.

We may not always be happy with the output of the economy, of course. But we cannot deny the essential relationship between individual and collective action. If the highways are clogged and the air is polluted as a consequence of our transportation choices, we cannot blame someone else for our predicament. If we are disturbed by the size of our military arsenal, we must still accept responsibility for our choices (or nonchoices, if we failed to vote). In either case, we continue to have the option of reallocating our efforts or rearranging our priorities. We can create a different outcome the next day, month, or year.

THE NATURE OF ECONOMIC CHOICE

Because individual decisions directly affect the economy, it is important that we understand the nature of our choices. Why, for example, do we choose private cars, instead of public buses, or more armaments instead of more swimming pools? Why, indeed, don't we choose both, in sufficient quantities to satisfy all our desires?

factors of production: Resource inputs used to produce goods and services; for example, land, labor, capital.

One basic constraint on our production and consumption choices is a scarcity of resources. In order to produce anything, we need resources, or factors of production. **Factors of production** are the inputs—land, labor, and capital (buildings and machinery)—we use to produce final goods and services (output). To produce this textbook, we needed paper, printing presses, a building, and lots of labor. To produce the education you are getting in this class, we need not only a textbook, but a classroom, a teacher, and a blackboard as well. Without factors of production, we simply cannot produce anything.

Unfortunately, the quantity of available resources is limited. We cannot produce everything we want in the quantities we desire. Resources are scarce, relative to our desires. This fact forces us to make difficult choices. The building space we use for this class cannot be used to show Charlie Chaplin movies at the same time. Your professor cannot lecture (produce education) and repair a car simultaneously. Likewise, the more labor and machinery used to dig holes in the ground for missiles, the less is available to dig holes for swimming pools. Hence the more missiles we build, the less of other goods and services we can produce at the same time. This classic "guns vs. butter" problem is illustrated in the accompanying news clipping. The article indicates some of the goods we could have produced with the resources allocated to production of military goods.

Opportunity costs

The dilemma of guns vs. butter typifies our economic problem. ***Because our resources are limited, we are compelled to choose among goods and services.*** Even the time you spend reading this book illustrates the problem. The labor time you devote to reading this book reduces the amount of time you have for other activities. You could be sleeping, watching television, or using your time in

Looting the Means of Production

SOUTH WELLFLEET, MASS. — . . . The way that an economy uses its capital—its production resources—is a crucial determinant of its productivity and economic well-being.

The United States has "achieved" its present state of industrial deterioration by assigning to the military economy large quantities of machinery, tools, engineers, energy, raw materials, skilled labor, and managers. . . .

This looting of the means of production on behalf of the military economy can only be accelerated as a consequence of the unprecedented size of the war budgets advocated by the Reagan Administration.

The vital resources that constitute a nation's capital fund cannot be enlarged by waving a budgetary wand. Neither can manufacturing facilities be multiplied by ever richer subsidies to the managers of military industry. Basic machinery, skilled labor, engineers and scientists—all are finite in number and difficult to increase.

The concentration of capital on the military portends sharply diminished opportunity for a productive livelihood for most Americans. Clearly, a choice must be made as to where these resources will be used.

The accompanying list of trade-offs illustrates the kinds of choices that the Reagan Administration and the Congress are now making with their budget and tax plans, intended or not.

—Seymour Melman

Seven percent of the military outlays from fiscal 1981 to 1986	$100 billion	the cost of rehabilitating the United States' steel industry so that it is again the most efficient in the world
The cruise-missile programs	$11 billion	the cost of bringing the annual rate of investment in public works to the 1965 level
Two B-1 bombers	$400 million	the cost of rebuilding Cleveland's water-supply system
The Navy's F-18 fighter program	$34 billion	the cost of modernizing America's machine-tool stock to bring it to the average level of Japan's
Two nuclear-powered aircraft carriers	$5.8 billion	the cost of converting 77 oil-using power plants to coal, saving 350,000 barrels of oil per day
The cost overrun, to 1981, of the Army's UH-60A helicopter program	$4.7 billion	the annual capital investment for restoring New York City's roads, bridges, aqueducts, subways and buses
One nuclear (SSN-688) attack submarine	$582 million	the cost of 100 miles of electrified rail right-of-way

some other way. The true cost of reading this book, then, is the most enjoyable activity you could have pursued in the same amount of time but had to sacrifice in order to complete this reading assignment. As long as you continue to read this book, you are sacrificing the *opportunity* to use your time in other ways. This sacrifice is your **opportunity cost** of reading these pages.[3] Similar costs are associated with all activities.

opportunity cost: The most desired goods or services that are forgone in order to obtain something else.

Opportunity costs exist in all situations where available resources are not abundant enough to satisfy all our desires. In all such situations, we must make hard decisions about how to allocate our scarce resources among competing uses. Because our wants and desires generally exceed our resources, ***everything we do involves an opportunity cost.***

Opportunity costs are relevant not only to personal decision making, but also to the decisions of an entire economy. Consider the guns vs. butter dilemma again. The news clipping indicates that the production of a nuclear attack submarine uses land, labor, and capital worth $582 million. That same quantity of resources could build 100 miles of electrified railroad (or thousands of other things). But those resources cannot be used to produce *both* goods at once. Hence, if we choose to build the sub, we forsake the opportunity of building an additional 100 miles of railroad. Forgone railroads become the *opportunity cost* of building more nuclear attack subs. If we make the opposite choice—that is, build more railroads and fewer subs—then the forgone subs would be the opportunity cost of the additional railroads. The opportunity cost of anything is the forgone alternative.

The concept of opportunity cost is basic to economic decision making. Indeed, **economics** itself has often been defined as the study of how to allocate scarce resources so as to attain the greatest satisfaction. The study of economics focuses on "getting the most from what we've got"—on making the *best* use of our scarce resources. In these terms, reading this book right now represents the *best* use of your time if it ultimately yields greater satisfaction (from higher grades, if nothing else) than any other use of the same time. Production of additional nuclear submarines represents the *best* use of society's resources only if the additional subs are more highly valued than any other goods or services that could be produced with the same factors of production.

economics: The study of how best to allocate scarce resources among competing uses.

PRODUCTION POSSIBILITIES

The opportunity costs implied by our every choice can be easily illustrated. Imagine for the moment that labor (workers) is the only factor of production used to produce either submarines or railroads and that no other goods are desired. Although other factors of production (land, machinery) are also needed in actual production, ignoring them for the moment does no harm. Let us assume further

[3] By the way, if you continue reading, we can conclude that you expect the benefits of doing this homework to exceed their opportunity cost, and thus that doing your homework will be "worthwhile."

that we have a total of 1,000 workers (labor) available in a given year, and that they can be used to produce either subs or railroads. Our initial problem is to determine how many subs or railroads can be produced in a year under such circumstances.

Before going any further, notice how opportunity costs will affect our answer. If we choose to employ all 1,000 of our workers in the production of nuclear submarines, then no labor will be available to build railroads. In this case, forgone railroads would become the opportunity cost of a decision to use all our resources in the production of submarines.

We still do not know how many submarines could be built with 1,000 workers or exactly how many railroads would be forgone by such a decision. To get these answers, we must know a little more about the production process involved; specifically, how many workers are required to build a nuclear sub or a railroad.

For the sake of convenience, we shall assume that 200 workers are needed to build either a submarine or a small railroad in a year. As we have only 1,000 workers available, the *maximum* number of subs we *could* build in one year is five. But we would then have no labor available for the production of railroads. Hence a decision to produce five subs per year implies a choice of no new railroads. In other words, the opportunity cost of five subs is the five railroads that could have been built with the same amount of labor, but were not.

production possibilities: The alternative combinations of final goods and services that could be produced in a given time period with all available resources and technology.

Table 1.1 summarizes the hypothetical choices, or **production possibilities,** that we confront in this case. Row *A* of the production-possibilities schedule shows the consequences of a decision to produce submarines only. With 1,000 workers available and a labor requirement of 200 workers per sub, we can build a *maximum* of five subs per year. By so doing, however, we use up all our available resources, leaving nothing for railroad construction. If we want more railroads, we have to cut back on submarine construction: this is the essential choice we must make.

The remainder of Table 1.1 describes the full range of choices that confront us. By cutting back the rate of sub production from five to four subs per year (row *B*), we reduce labor use from 1,000 workers to 800. The remaining 200 workers are then available for other

TABLE 1.1 PRODUCTION POSSIBILITIES SCHEDULE
(for one year)

So long as resources are limited, their use entails an opportunity cost. In this case, resources (labor) used to produce nuclear submarines cannot be used to produce railroads at the same time. Hence forgone railroads are the opportunity cost of additional subs. If all of our resources were used to produce subs (row A), no railroads could be built.

		Submarines								*Railroads*		
	Total available labor	*Number of subs*	×	*Labor needed per sub*	=	*Total labor required for subs*	*Labor not used for subs*	÷	*Labor needed per rail-road*	=	*Number of potential railroads*
A	1,000	5		200		1000	0		200		0
B	1,000	4		200		800	200		200		1
C	1,000	3		200		600	400		200		2
D	1,000	2		200		400	600		200		3
E	1,000	1		200		200	800		200		4
F	1,000	0		200		0	1000		200		5

FIGURE 1.1 A LINEAR PRODUCTION-POSSIBILITIES CURVE

A production-possibilities curve describes the various combinations of final goods or services that could be produced in a given time period with available resources and technology. It represents a "menu" of output choices an economy confronts. Point *B* indicates that we could produce a *combination* of four submarines and one railroad per year. By giving up one sub, we could produce a second railroad, and thus move to point *C*. Points *A*, *D*, *E*, and *F* illustrate still other output combinations that could be produced. This curve is a graphic illustration of the production-possibilities schedule provided in Table 1.1.

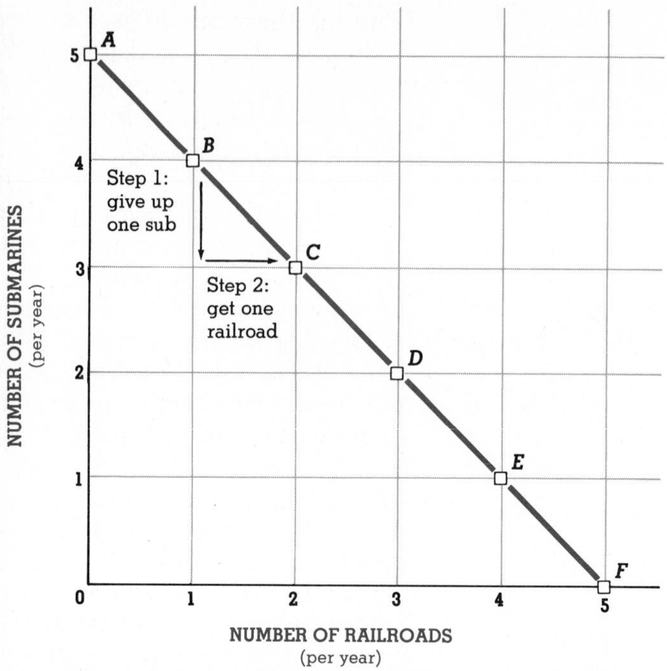

uses, including railroad construction. If we in fact employ these workers to lay rails, we can build one new railroad per year. In this case, we end up with four new subs and one new railroad per year. What is the opportunity cost of that railroad? Clearly it is the one additional submarine that we could have built but did not, in order to make factors of production (labor) available for railroad construction.

As we proceed down the rows of Table 1.1, the nature of opportunity costs becomes apparent. Each additional railroad built implies the loss (opportunity cost) of one nuclear submarine. Likewise, every sub built implies the loss of one railroad.

These trade-offs between railroads and submarines are illustrated in the production-possibilities curve of Figure 1.1 Each point on the curve depicts a particular combination of railroads and submarines that we could produce if we so chose, using all available resources (labor in this case) and technology.

Notice in particular how points *A* through *F* in Figure 1.1 represent the choices described in each row of Table 1.1. At point *A*, we are producing five subs per year and no railroads. As we move from point *A* to point *B*, we are decreasing submarine production from five to four subs per year, while increasing railroad construction from zero to one. This is precisely what Table 1.1 depicts. A production-possibilities curve, then, is simply a graphic summary of production possibilities, as described in Table 1.1. The purpose of the table and the graph is to illustrate the hard choices we must make among alternative goods and services—and the implied opportunity costs of each choice.

In summary, the production-possibilities curve illustrates two essential principles:

- There is a limit to the amount we can produce in a given time period with available resources and technology. (Scarcity is a fact of life.)
- We can obtain additional quantities of any desired good only by reducing the potential production of another good. (Opportunity costs are always present.)

Increasing opportunity costs

Although Figure 1.1 illustrates the principles of scarcity and opportunity costs, it depicts an overly optimistic view of our production possibilities. When we reduce the rate of output of one good in order to get more of another, we have to reallocate factors of production from one industry to another. In order to get more railroads, for example, we have to take workers out of nuclear submarine construction and put them to work laying rails. No magic wand is available to transform nuclear subs into railroads. Instead, the rails must be laid with the same factors of production that would otherwise be used in submarine production. As a consequence, ***our ability to alter the mix of output depends in part on the capability of factors of production to move from one industry to another.***

As we contemplate the possibilities of moving resources from one industry to another, two issues arise. First, can the resources be moved? Second, how efficient will the resources be in a new line of production?

In our example, it is probably safe to assume that workers can move from submarine construction to railroad construction. We have made this kind of move after every war. But it is also likely that some efficiency will be lost in the process. Workers who have been constructing submarines for several years will probably not be as adept at building railroads. As a result, we will not be able to "transform" subs into railroads so easily. Instead, we may discover that sooner or later more than 200 former submarine workers will be required to construct one railroad. That is, the opportunity cost of one new railroad will be more than one potential sub.

One reason for this higher opportunity cost is the different skills required for submarine and railroad construction. Both industries need welders, for example. But in railroad construction a weld must be secure, not necessarily airtight. The welds on nuclear subs, on the other hand, must be completely airtight, or the sub may never resurface. So when we start to move welders out of nuclear submarine construction and into railroad development, we will move the worst welders first. That will minimize our losses in submarine production while increasing our output of railroads. As we continue moving labor from sub production to railroad construction, the remaining sub builders are likely to be the least adept at laying rails or the most adept at building subs. If we nevertheless continue to shift resources, one of two things will probably happen. Either we will get less railroad output for each additional worker employed in rail construction or we will sacrifice more sub output for each worker taken out of submarine construction. In either case, we are likely to get

TABLE 1.2 INCREASING OPPORTUNITY COSTS

Resources are not perfectly adaptable from one industry to another. As a consequence, we are unlikely to get one additional railroad for every sub given up. Instead, opportunity costs *increase*. Notice that we get two railroads for the first sub given up (row *A* to row *B*) but only one railroad for the second sub given up (row *B* to row *C*). The third sub is "transformed" into only 0.8 railroad. These increasing opportunity costs bend the production-possibilities curve outward, as in Figure 1.2.

		Submarines					Railroads	
	Total labor available	*Output of subs*	× *Labor needed per sub*	= *Total labor required for subs*	*Labor not used for subs*	*Potential output of railroads*		*Change in output*
A	1,000	5	200	1,000	0	0		
							>	2.0
B	1,000	4	200	800	200	2.0		
							>	1.0
C	1,000	3	200	600	400	3.0		
							>	0.8
D	1,000	2	200	400	600	3.8		
							>	0.7
E	1,000	1	200	200	800	4.5		
							>	0.5
F	1,000	0	200	0	1,000	5.0		

fewer railroads for each potential sub given up. The opportunity cost of railroads increases as more railroads are produced.

Increasing opportunity costs are illustrated in Table 1.2. We still have 1,000 workers available, all of whom are initially employed in submarine production (row *A*). When we cut back submarine production to only four per year (row *B*) we release 200 workers for railroad construction, as before. Now, however, those first 200 workers are assumed to be capable of producing two railroads (rather than only one, as in Table 1.1).

This high rate of submarine-to-railroad transformation does not last long. When sub production is cut back from four to three per year, another 200 workers are made available for railroad construction (row *C*). But now railroad output increases by only one, from two to three roads per year. Hence we are getting fewer railroads for each sub given up. The opportunity cost of railroads is increasing.

This process of increasing opportunity costs continues. By the time we give up the last sub (row *F*), railroad output increases by only 0.5. Hence we get only half a railroad for the last sub given up.

Increasing opportunity costs alter the shape of the production-possibilities curve. The linear "curve" in Figure 1.1 suggested that factors of production could be moved effortlessly from one industry to another. In reality, such transformations are more difficult, and the production-possibilities curve will usually bend outward, as in Figure 1.2.

Figure 1.2 is based on Table 1.2. Suppose that we start out again at point *A*, using all our labor to produce five nuclear submarines per year, leaving no resources for railroad construction. We then decide (Step 1) to reduce the rate of submarine construction in order to free resources for railroad production. According to Table 1.2, we can produce two railroads per year with the labor initially taken out of submarine production. Thus Step 2 takes us to point *B*, where we produce four subs and two railroads per year.

Suppose that we continue to alter the mix of output by reducing the rate of submarine construction further, from four to three subs per year (Step 3). How many additional railroads can we produce with the released labor? According to Table 1.2, we can obtain only

FIGURE 1.2 A CURVED (NONLINEAR) PRODUCTION-POSSIBILITIES CURVE

The production-possibilities curve bends outward—is actually curved—because resources are not perfectly adaptable from one industry to another. As a consequence, the opportunity costs of a good increase as more of it is produced. In this case, we get two railroads (Step 2) by giving up the fifth submarine (Step 1). When we give up the next sub (Step 3), however, we get only one additional railroad (Step 4). Each additional railroad "costs" more submarines.

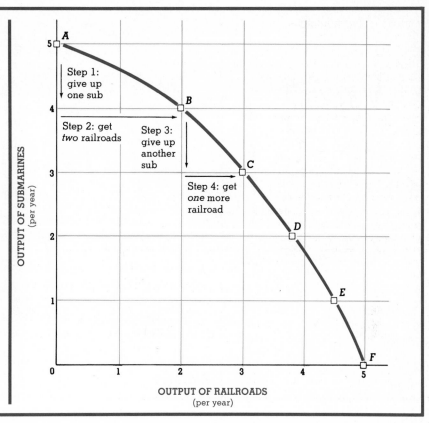

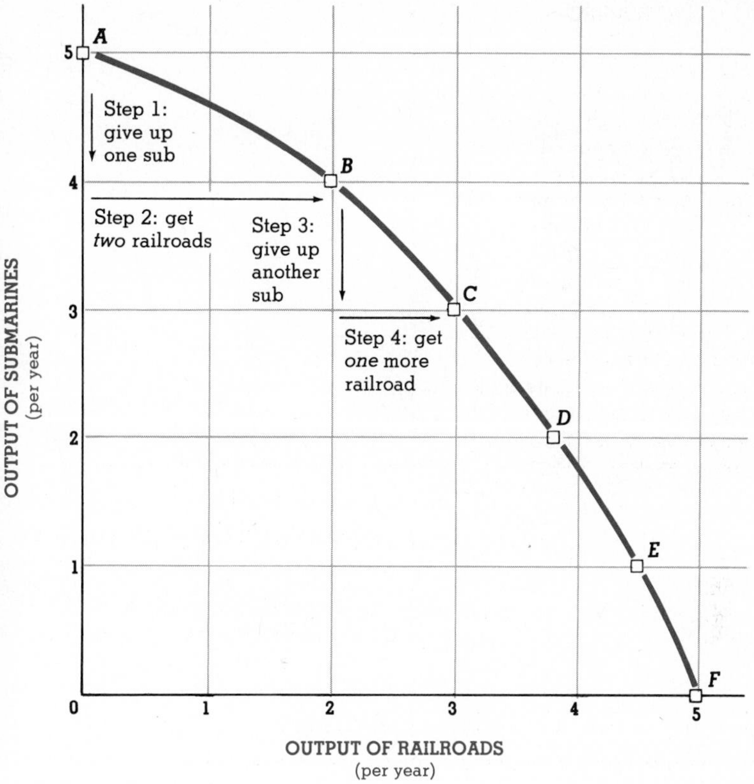

one more railroad per year with the additional labor (Step 4). Hence the opportunity cost of a railroad has risen. The newest (third) railroad "cost" one sub, whereas we earlier obtained *two* railroads by forgoing one sub (i.e., one railroad previously cost only half a nuclear submarine).

Nonlinear production-possibilities curves like the one in Figure 1.2 are so universal that they have become a basic "law" of economics, the **law of increasing opportunity costs.** According to this law, we must give up ever-increasing quantities of other goods and services in order to get more of a particular good.

law of increasing opportunity costs: In order to get more of any good in a given time period, society must sacrifice ever-increasing amounts of other goods.

The law of increasing opportunity costs is not based solely on the limited versatility of individual workers. In most production processes, some amount of land and capital works with labor. If they had to, railroad workers could lay rails with picks, shovels, and sledgehammers. The construction of nuclear submarines requires much more capital, of far greater complexity. Hence the productivity of workers moved from the railroad industry to nuclear submarine construction depends on how much capital equipment we supply them with. With little capital—or the wrong kind of capital—they won't be able to produce many nuclear submarines. Accordingly, our ability to alter the mix of output does not depend on the talents of individual workers alone. It also depends on the adaptability of land and capital and the availability of each in the right proportions.[4]

[4] A more complete discussion of the basis for increasing opportunity costs (diminishing returns) is provided in Chapter 5.

"There's no such thing as a free lunch."

Points inside and outside the curve

Points X and Y in Figure 1.3 illustrate two additional combinations of submarines and railroads. One of these combinations is unattainable, however, while the other is undesirable. Consider point X, which represents a combined output of five submarines and two railroads per year. Point X is clearly better than point A, because it includes just as many subs and two more railroads. It appears, in other words, that by moving from point A to point X we could get two additional railroads *without* giving up any potential submarines. Unfortunately, point X lies *outside* our production possibilities and thus is beyond our grasp. In order to produce five nuclear submarines per year, we have to use *all* our available resources and technology, leaving none to produce railroads. Hence we cannot have five new submarines every year *and* two new railroads; point X represents an unattainable output combination. In fact, ***all output combinations that lie outside the production-possibilities curve are unattainable with available resources and technology.***

Point Y represents a very different situation. At point Y, three submarines and two railroads are being produced each year. This output combination is easily attainable with our available resources and technology. But if we produced at point Y, we would be wasting resources. Either some labor is completely idle (unemployed) or workers are not employed efficiently (underemployed). This is evident from the fact that we could produce at point C, with one more railroad and no fewer submarines each year. Or we could move to point B and have one more sub and no fewer railroads. By choosing to stay at point Y, we would be forsaking the opportunity to use all

FIGURE 1.3 POINTS INSIDE AND OUTSIDE THE CURVE

Points outside the production-possibilities curve (e.g., point *X*) are unattainable with available resources and technology. Points inside the curve (e.g., point *Y*) represent the incomplete use of available resources. Only points on the production-possibilities curve (e.g., *A*, *B*, *C*) represent maximum use of our production capabilities.

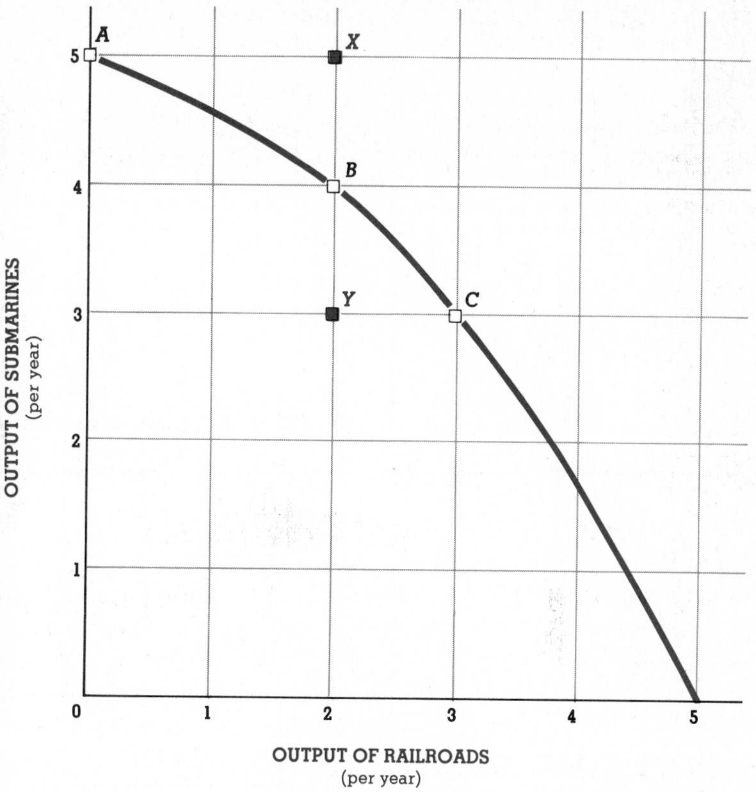

our resources to the fullest, in effect giving up potential output for nothing in return. So long as either more submarines or more railroads (or any other good) are desired, it is wasteful to leave workers idle when they could be producing one of those goods. Thus point *Y*, and ***all points inside the production-possibilities curve, are undesirable because they imply the waste (nonuse) of available resources.*** The significance of unemployment, for individuals and the economy, is discussed in Chapter 5 of *The Macro Economy Today*.

Growth and technology

The production possibilities illustrated in Figure 1.3 are not fixed for all time. As time passes, we will acquire more resources and improve our knowledge of how to use them. Fifty years ago, no one even knew what a nuclear submarine was. Advances in both nuclear technology and submarine design since that time have made nuclear submarines both feasible and familiar. In other words, our technology has improved. As a result, we can produce more subs today than we could fifty or even five years ago, with the same quantity of resources.

Over time, the quantity of resources available for production has also increased. Each year our population grows a bit, thereby enlarging the number of potential workers. Our stock of capital equipment has increased even faster. In addition the *quality* of our labor and capital resources has improved, as a result of more education (labor) and better machinery (capital).

FIGURE 1.4 INCREASING PRODUCTION POSSIBILITIES

A production-possibilities curve is based on *available* resources and technology. If more resources or better technology become available, production possibilities will increase. This is illustrated by the *shift* from PP_1 to PP_2.

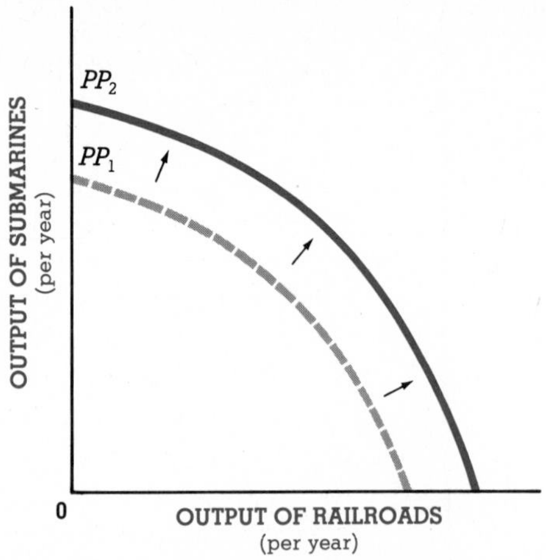

economic growth: An increase in output (real GNP); an expansion of production possibilities.

All of this adds up to an ever-increasing capacity to produce goods and services. This is illustrated in Figure 1.4 by the outward *shift* of the production-possibilities curve. Before the appearance of new resources or better technology, our production possibilities were limited by the curve PP_1. ***With more resources or better technology, our production possibilities increase.*** This greater capacity to produce is represented by curve PP_2. This outward shift of the production-possibilities curve is the essence of **economic growth.** As we shall see in later chapters (especially Chapter 5), much of our recent growth has come from continuing improvements in technology.

HOW CHOICES ARE MADE

However promising the prospects for growth may be, we still have to contend with our current production constraints. At any point in time there is still a limit to how much we can produce. The fact that those limits may expand in future years does not make our current choices any easier. Each year we still have to choose some mix of output that is consistent with our existing production possibilities. Choosing WHAT to produce is one of our most important economic decisions.

Our menu of choices is illustrated by the prevailing production-possibilities curve. Because those points that lie *outside* the production-possibilities curve are unattainable and those *inside* the curve are undesirable, only those points on the curve represent our immediate choices. But which of these many points should we choose? What goods and services should the economy produce?

Although the consequences of alternative output choices can be illustrated with a production-possibilities curve, the curve itself says nothing about the reasons for choosing one combination of goods and services over another. Why do we choose fewer railroads and more nuclear submarines? Or, for that matter, why do you choose—and it is a choice!—to do more homework and get less sleep? If we are really to understand economic outcomes, we have to know more than just what the choices (and associated opportunity costs) are. We also have to know how we, individually and collectively, make such choices.

The market mechanism

market mechanism: The use of market prices and sales to signal desired outputs (or resource allocations).

The actual choices individual consumers and firms make are expressed for the most part in market purchases and sales. The use of the **market mechanism** to express your desires is as familiar as grocery shopping. If you desire ice cream and have sufficient income, you simply buy ice cream. Your purchases act as a signal to producers that ice cream is desired. By expressing the ability and *willingness to pay* for ice cream, you are effectively telling ice cream producers that their efforts are going to be rewarded. If enough consumers feel the same way you do—and are able and willing to pay the price of ice cream—ice cream producers will produce more ice cream.

The same kind of interactions influence the choice we must make between houses and cars. There are many alternative combinations of houses and cars that we *could* produce. But we must choose only one. How do we express our preference? Consumers may express their preference for houses simply by purchasing houses, that is, by expressing a willingness to pay for such output. Similarly, consumers who would prefer to see more new cars can express their desires by buying cars. In this way, the debate over cars versus houses boils down to a question of who is willing and able to pay the most for the available factors of production. If potential homeowners are willing to pay more for our limited resources than are potential drivers, then more houses will be supplied. Why? Simply because suppliers will provide those products that offer the highest profit.

Thus ***the essential feature of the market mechanism is the price signal.*** If you want something and have sufficient income, you buy it. If enough people do the same thing, the total sales of that product will rise, and perhaps its price as well. Producers, seeing sales and prices rise, will be inclined to increase production. To do so, they will attempt to purchase a larger share of our available resources, and use them to produce the goods we desire. No direct communication between us and the producer is required; market sales and prices convey the message and direct the market, much like an "invisible hand." Although producers and sellers have a variety of reasons for offering their wares, and consumers have myriad motives for buying, prices are used as a common means of communication. It is this price or market mechanism that translates the disparate interests and desires of our 230 million selves into a producing and consuming whole. From this perspective, the price system is a very efficient method of communication.

MARKET IMPERFECTIONS The details of the price system are reserved for Chapter 2. Before looking at those details, we should note some potential problems associated with the market mechanism. The first of these problems concerns equity. Use of the price system presumes allegiance to certain standards of fairness. In particular, reliance on prices as a mechanism for distributing goods and resources implies that we believe such a distribution is "fair." For example, goods and services distributed through the market mechanism go disproportionately to those with the greatest ability to pay. Whether this system of allocation is "fair" depends on how one views the distribution of wealth and income and the nature of the goods to be divided up. It is at least conceivable that the efficiency of the price system may conflict with standards of equity or fairness, necessitating difficult policy choices. Medical and legal assistance provided for the poor, not to mention public schools, illustrate departures from the price mechanism prompted by our concern for equity.

Another problem that strikes at the very heart of the market mechanism is that some very valuable things are not priced. Clean air, for example, is something nearly everyone (smokers and nonsmokers alike) considers precious. Nevertheless, it is difficult to imagine how we could *buy* clean air, much less reserve the cleanest air for those who are most eager and able to purchase it. Air, unlike video tapes or soap, cannot be packaged and marketed. Hence to leave the quality of the air we breathe to the determination of the market mechanism is like tightening one's own noose. The final outcome is foreseeable, but not necessarily desirable. Just breathing in New York City, Los Angeles, or Chicago can be dangerous to your health. The economic forces that actually *encourage* pollution are discussed in Chapter 16.

Clean air is not alone among unpackageable and unmarketable goods. On the contrary, the list of such goods is long, including such diverse products as national defense, traffic congestion, and the vibrations from your next-door neighbor's stereo. In every such case, some sort of interactions among us operate outside the market mechanism: benefits or costs are being exchanged without direct payment. These kinds of interactions are referred to as **externalities.**

externalities: Costs (or benefits) of a market activity borne by a third party; the difference between the social and private costs (benefits) of a market activity.

Externalities violate the basic market dictum that everything must be packaged, marketed, and exchanged for a negotiated price. Consequently, the production and consumption of such goods must often be controlled by other mechanisms. These mechanisms may be public laws (such as those against pollution), taxes (to pay for common defense), or threats against neighbors (to muffle their stereos). In almost all cases, we seek to alter market choices by intervening directly in the production or consumption process. The nature of externalities, and policy responses to them, are discussed at length in Chapters 3 and 16.

Planned economies

Although the United States relies heavily on the market mechanism to make basic economic decisions, there are alternative ways of making the same kinds of choices. One such alternative is centralized decision making, as practiced in such socialist countries as the Soviet Union, China, and Cuba. In socialist economies, the decisions of government planners substitute for the decisions of individual consumers and business firms. For example, we rely on the decisions of millions of individual consumers and a few automobile companies to determine how many American cars will be produced each year.

By contrast, the level of automobile production in the Soviet and Chinese economies is determined by the decisions of government planners.

Countries that rely heavily on centralized decision making for resolution of basic economic questions are referred to as "planned" or "command" economies. Countries that rely primarily on market behavior to make basic economic choices are often referred to as "market economies."

The mixed economy

The U.S. economy is not a purely market economy, of course. As we have already noted (and can observe daily), the government often intervenes in the market to control externalities (antipollution laws and penalties) and to redistribute income (through income taxes and transfer payments). The use of both market-directed signals and non-market directives is the hallmark of a **mixed economy** like our own.

mixed economy: An economy that uses both market and nonmarket signals to allocate goods and resources.

Our heavy reliance on the market mechanism is based on its efficiency in allocating resources and goods in accordance with consumer preferences. At the same time, our apparent commitment to government intervention reflects the judgment that market outcomes are not always best. The market mechanism is only a means to an end, not an end in itself. When we find the mechanism or the outcomes incompatible with our visions of the good and proper life, we can and do seek to change them. Such considerations explain why we formulate public policies to reduce unemployment, to slow the rate of inflation, to foster economic growth, and to redistribute incomes. If the market mechanism could itself ensure fulfillment of these goals, economic policy would be unnecessary, and possibly counterproductive.

We should not embrace market interference too hastily, however. We have no assurance that public policy is *capable* of improving our economic performance or that such policy will be properly implemented at the appropriate time. That is to say, nonmarket signals are imperfect, too. Accordingly, we cannot assume that all our economic problems are attributable to the market mechanism or that public policy will always provide a solution. On the contrary, experience has taught us that the truly difficult part of economic policy making is deciding whether or not to interfere with market outcomes. Further, if we decide to interfere, we still have to determine just what kind of action is likely to bring about desired results. This continuing dilemma will be emphasized throughout the remainder of this book. In the final chapter, we shall also examine how planned socialist economies resolve the same dilemma.

WHAT ECONOMICS IS ALL ABOUT

Understanding how various economies work is the basic purpose of studying economics. We seek to know how an economy is organized, how it behaves, and how successfully it achieves its basic objectives. Then, if we are lucky, we try to discover better ways of attaining those same objectives.

Ends vs. means

Economists do not formulate an economy's objectives. Instead, they focus on the *means* available for achieving given *goals*. In 1978, for example, the U.S. Congress identified "full employment" as a major economic goal. The Congress then directed future presidents (and their economic advisers) to formulate policies that would enable us to achieve full employment.

Other major economic goals of our economy include:

- Price stability
- Economic growth
- An equitable distribution of income

In each case, the goal is formulated through the political process. The economist's job is to help design policies that will allocate resources in ways that best achieve these goals. The nature and significance of our major economic goals are discussed in Chapter 15 in this book and Chapters 5 and 6 of *The Macro Economy Today*. The rest of the book is concerned with the means available for attaining them.

Macro vs. micro

macroeconomics: The study of aggregate economic behavior, of the economy as a whole.

microeconomics: The study of individual behavior in the economy, of the components of the larger economy.

The study of economics is typically divided into two parts: macroeconomics and microeconomics. Macroeconomics focuses on the behavior of an entire economy—the "big picture." In macroeconomics we worry about such national goals as full employment, control of inflation, and economic growth, without worrying about the well-being or behavior of specific individuals or groups. The essential concern of **macroeconomics** is to understand and improve the performance of the economy as a whole.

Microeconomics is concerned with the details of this "big picture." In microeconomics we focus on the individuals, firms, and government agencies that actually comprise the larger economy. Our interest here is in the behavior of individual economic actors. What goals do they have? How can they best achieve them with their limited resources? How will they respond to various incentives and opportunities?

A primary concern of macroeconomics, for example, is to determine the impact of aggregate consumer spending on total output, employment, and prices. Very little attention is devoted to the actual content of consumer spending or its determinants. Microeconomics, on the other hand, focuses on the specific expenditure decisions of individual consumers and the forces (tastes, prices, incomes) that influence those decisions.

The distinction between macro- and microeconomics is also reflected in discussions of business investment. In macroeconomics we want to know what determines the aggregate rate of business investment and how those expenditures influence the nation's total output, employment, and prices. In microeconomics we focus on the decisions of individual businesses regarding the rate of production, the choice of factors of production, and the pricing of specific goods.

The distinction between macro- and microeconomics is a matter of convenience. In reality, macroeconomic outcomes depend on micro behavior and micro behavior is affected by macro outcomes. Hence one cannot fully understand how an economy works until one understands how all the participants behave and why they behave as they do. But just as you can drive a car without knowing how its engine is constructed, you can observe how an economy runs without completely disassembling it. In macroeconomics we observe that the car goes faster when the accelerator is depressed and that it slows when the brake is applied. That is all we need to know in most situations. There are times, however, when the car breaks down. When it does, we have to know something more about how the pedals work. This leads us into micro studies. How does each part work? Which ones can or should be fixed?

Our interest in microeconomics is motivated by more than our need to understand how the larger economy works. The "parts" of the economic engine are people. To the extent that we care about the welfare of individuals in society, we have a fundamental interest in microeconomic behavior and outcomes. In this regard, we examine the goals of individual consumers and business firms, seeking to explain how they can maximize their welfare in the economy. In microeconomics, for example, we spend more time looking at which goods are produced, who produces them, and who receives them. In macroeconomics we tend to focus only on how much is produced, or how many people are employed in the process.

Theory and reality

The distinction between macroeconomics and microeconomics is one of many simplifications we make in studying economic behavior. The economy is much too vast and complex to describe and explain in one course (or one lifetime). Accordingly, we focus on basic relationships, ignoring annoying detail. In so doing, we isolate basic principles of economic behavior, then use those principles to predict economic events and formulate economic policies. What this means is that we formulate theories, or *models*, of economic behavior, then use those theories to evaluate and design economic policy.

Because all economic models entail simplifying assumptions, they never *exactly* describe the real world. Nevertheless, the models may be useful. If our models are *reasonably* consistent with economic reality, they may yield good predictions of economic behavior. Likewise, if our simplifications do not become distortions, they may provide good guidelines for economic policy.

Our theory of consumer behavior assumes, for example, a distinct relationship between the price of a good and the quantity people buy. As prices increase, people buy less. In reality, however, people *may* buy *more* of a good at increased prices, especially if those high prices create a certain "snob appeal" or if prices are expected to increase still further. In predicting consumer responses to price increases, we typically ignore such possibilities by *assuming* that the price of the good in question is the *only* thing that changes. This assumption of "other things remaining equal (unchanged)" (in Latin, ***ceteris paribus***) allows us to make straightforward predictions. If instead we described consumer responses to increased prices in any and all circumstances (allowing everything to change at once), every prediction would be accompanied by a bookful of exceptions and qualifications.

ceteris paribus: **The assumption of "everything else being equal," of nothing else changing.**

Although the assumption of *ceteris paribus* makes it easier to formulate economic theory and policy, it also increases the risk of error. Obviously, if other things do change in significant ways, our predictions (and policies) may fail. But, like weather forecasters, we continue to make predictions, knowing that occasional failure is inevitable. In so doing, we are motivated by the conviction that it is better to be approximately right than to be dead wrong.

Policy

Politicians cannot afford to be quite so complacent about predictions, however. Policy decisions must be made all the time. And a politician's continued survival may depend on being more than approximately right. Economists can contribute to those policy decisions by offering measures of economic impact and predictions of economic behavior. But in the real world, those measures and predictions will always contain a substantial margin of error. That is to say, economic policy decisions are always based on some amount of uncertainty. Even the best economic minds cannot foretell the future.

Even if the future were known, economic policy could not rely completely on economic theory. There are always political choices to be made. The choice of more submarines or more railroads, for example, is not an economic decision. Rather it is a sociopolitical decision based in part on economic trade-offs (opportunity costs). The "need" for more subs or more railroads must be expressed politically. Ends versus means again. Political forces are a necessary ingredient in economic policy decisions. That is not to say that all "political" decisions are right. It does suggest, however, that economic policies may not always conform to economic theory. In Chapter 14 of *The Macro Economy Today* we explore the interaction of policy and theory, highlighting those forces that contribute to disappointing economic performance.

Controversy

One last word of warning before you go further. Economics claims to be a science, in pursuit of basic truths. We want to understand and explain how the economy works without getting tangled up in subjective value judgments. This may be an impossible task. First of all, it is not clear where the truth lies. For over 200 years economists have been arguing about what makes the economy tick. None of the competing theories have performed spectacularly well. Indeed, few economists have successfully predicted major economic events with any consistency. Even annual forecasts of inflation, unemployment, and output are regularly in error. Worse still, there are never-ending arguments about what caused a major economic event long after it has already occurred. In fact, economists are still arguing over the causes of the Great Depression of the 1930s!

The most persistent debate in economics has focused on the degree to which the government can improve the economy's performance. Two hundred years ago, Adam Smith convinced most of the world that the economy worked best when it was left alone. In the throes of the Great Depression, the British economist John Maynard Keynes forced people to rethink that conclusion. He convinced people that active government intervention in the marketplace was the only way to ensure economic growth and stability. For nearly 30 years his theory dominated the economics profession and public policy. A decade of disappointing economic performance ended Keynes' overwhelming dominance. The 1970s were fraught with repeated recessions, slow growth, and high inflation. "Supply-siders" and "monetarists" laid much of the blame on Keynesian theory. Specifically, they argued that we got into economic trouble because we permitted too much government intervention. Excessive government intervention had stifled the market mechanism, they claimed; Keynes' call for active government policy had to be rejected. This view has had a formative influence on the policies of the Reagan administration.

In part, this enduring controversy reflects diverse sociopolitical views on the appropriate role of government. Some people think a big public sector is undesirable, even if it improves economic performance. But the controversy has even deeper roots. There are still important gaps in our understanding of the economy. We know how much of the economy works, but not all of it. We are adept at identifying all the forces at work, but not always successful in gauging their relative importance. In point of fact, we may *never* find an absolute truth, because the inner workings of the economy can change over time. When economic behavior changes, our theories must be adapted.

Modest expectations

In view of all these debates and uncertainties, you should not expect to learn everything there is to know about the economy today in this text or course. Our goals are more modest. We want to develop a reasonable perspective on economic behavior, an understanding of basic principles. With this foundation, you should acquire a better view of how the economy works. Daily news reports on economic events should make more sense. Congressional debates on tax and budget policies should take on more meaning. Who knows? You may even develop some insights useful for running a business or planning a career.

SUMMARY

- Scarcity is a basic fact of economic life. Available resources (factors of production) are scarce in relation to our desires for goods and services.
- Scarcity necessitates difficult choices. Factors of production (resources) used to produce one output cannot simultaneously be used to produce something else. Accordingly, we must forsake the opportunity to produce alternative goods or services when we choose to produce something else.
- A production-possibilities curve illustrates the kinds of opportu-

nity costs an economy confronts. It shows the alternative combinations of final goods and services that could be produced in a given time period with available resources and technology.

- The bent shape of the production-possibilities curve reflects the law of increasing opportunity costs. This law states that increasing quantities of any good can be obtained only by sacrificing ever-increasing quantities of other goods.
- Production possibilities expand (shift outward) when additional resources or better technologies become available. This is the essence of economic growth.
- The market mechanism facilitates the actual choice of output combinations. Consumers indicate their preference for specific outputs by expressing an ability and a willingness to pay for desired goods. Their actual purchases act as signals to producers, who in turn assemble factors of production and produce the desired outputs.
- The market mechanism does not work efficiently when externalities exist, that is, when market interactions between two parties impose costs or benefits on third parties. Market outcomes may also conflict with accepted standards of equity. In both cases, some kind of nonmarket intervention is often desired.
- A mixed economy relies on a combination of market signals and nonmarket intervention to allocate goods and services. The critical problem for both economic theory and public policy is to determine the mix of market and nonmarket directives that will best fulfill our social and economic goals.
- The study of economics focuses on the broad question of resource allocation. Macroeconomics is concerned with allocating the resources of an entire economy to achieve aggregate economic goals (e.g., full employment). Microeconomics focuses on the behavior and goals of individual market participants.

Terms to remember

Define the following terms:

factors of production
opportunity cost
economics
production possibilities
law of increasing opportunity costs
economic growth
market mechanism
externalities
mixed economy
macroeconomics
microeconomics
ceteris paribus

Questions for discussion

1. What opportunity costs did you incur in reading this chapter?
2. If you read four more chapters of this text today, would your opportunity costs (per chapter) increase? Explain.
3. How does the concept of opportunity cost help explain the maxim "There is no such thing as a free lunch"?
4. If all consumers desire clean air, why doesn't the market mechanism produce it?

Problem

POTENTIAL WEEKLY OUTPUT COMBINATIONS, USING ALL RESOURCES

	Pianos	*Stereos*
A	10	0
B	9	1
C	7	2
D	4	3
E	0	4

Assume that the schedule at the left describes the production possibilities confronting an economy. Using the information from the table:

(*a*) Draw the production possibilities curve. Be sure to label each alternative output combination (*A* thru *E*).

(*b*) Calculate and illustrate on your graph the opportunity cost of producing one stereo per week.

(*c*) What is the cost of producing a second stereo? What accounts for the difference?

(*d*) Which point on the curve is the most desired one? How will we find out?

(*e*) What would happen to the production-possibilities curve if additional factors of production became available? Illustrate.

APPENDIX

USING GRAPHS

Economists like to draw graphs. In fact, we didn't even make it through the first chapter without a few graphs. The purpose of this appendix is to look more closely at the way graphs are drawn and used.

The basic purpose of a graph is to illustrate a relationship between two things, or *variables*. Consider, for example, the relationship between grades and studying. In general, we expect that additional hours of study time will lead to higher grades. Hence we should be able to see a distinct relationship between hours of study time and grade-point average.

Suppose that we actually surveyed all of the students taking this course with regard to their study time and grade-point averages. The resulting information can be compiled in a table such as Table A.1.

TABLE A.1 HYPOTHETICAL RELATIONSHIP OF GRADES TO STUDY TIME

Study time (hours per week)	*Grade-point average*
16	4.0 (A)
14	3.5 (B+)
12	3.0 (B)
10	2.5 (C+)
8	2.0 (C)
6	1.5 (D+)
4	1.0 (D)
2	0.5 (F+)
0	0 (F)

According to the table, students who don't study at all can expect an F in this course. To get a C, the average student apparently spends eight hours a week studying. All those who study sixteen hours a week end up with an A in the course.

These relationships between grades and studying can also be illustrated on a graph. Indeed, the whole purpose of a graph is to summarize numerical relationships.

We begin to construct a graph by drawing horizontal and vertical boundaries, as in Figure A.1. These boundaries are called the *axes* of the graph. On the vertical axis we measure one of the variables; the other variable is measured on the horizontal axis.[1]

In this case, we shall measure the grade-point average on the vertical axis. We start at the *origin* (the intersection of the two axes) and count upward, letting the distance between horizontal lines represent half (0.5) a grade point. Each horizontal line is numbered, up to the maximum grade-point average of 4.0.

The number of hours each week spent doing homework is measured on the horizontal axis. We begin at the origin again, and count

[1] The vertical axis is often called the *Y*-axis; the horizontal axis the *X*-axis.

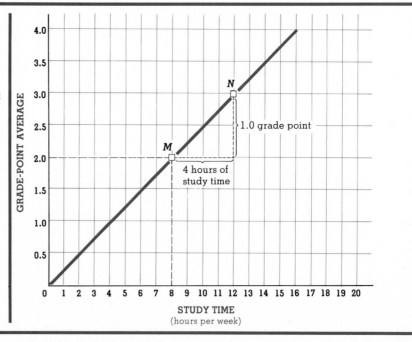

FIGURE A.1 THE RELATIONSHIP OF GRADES TO STUDY TIME

The upward (positive) slope of the curve indicates that additional studying is associated with higher grades. The average student (2.0, or C grade) studies 8 hours per week. This is indicated by point *M* on the graph.

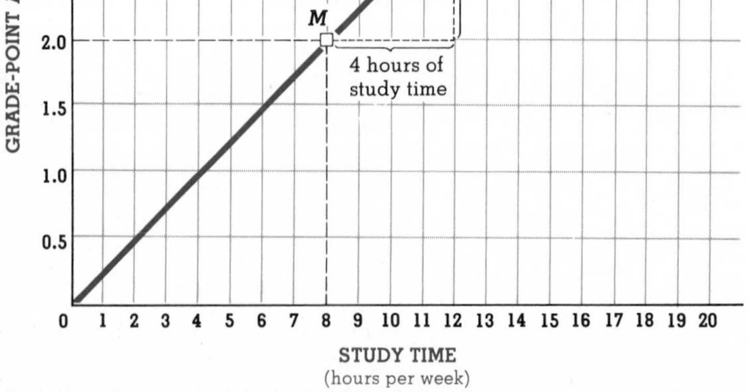

to the right. The *scale* (numbering) proceeds in increments of one hour, up to twenty hours per week.

When both axes have been labeled and measured, we can begin to illustrate the relationship between study time and grades. Consider the typical student who does eight hours of homework per week and has a 2.0 (C) grade-point average. We illustrate this relationship by first locating eight hours on the horizontal axis. We then move up from that point a distance of 2.0 grade points, to point *M*. Point *M* tells us that eight hours of study time is typically associated with a 2.0 grade-point average.

The rest of the information in Table A.1 is drawn (or plotted) on the graph in the same way. To illustrate the average grade for people who study twelve hours per week, we move upward from the number 12 on the horizontal axis until we reach the height of 3.0 on the vertical axis. At that intersection, we draw another point (point *N*).

Once we have plotted the various points describing the relationship of study time to grades, we may connect them with a line or curve. This line (curve) is our summary. In this case, the line slopes upward to the right, that is, it has a *positive* slope. This slope indicates that more hours of study time are associated with *higher* grades. Were higher grades associated with *less* study time, the curve in Figure A.1 would have a *negative* slope (slope downward from left to right).

Slopes

The upward slope of Figure A.1 tells us that higher grades are associated with increased amounts of study time. That same curve also tells us *how much* grades tend to rise with study time. According to point *M* in Figure A.1, the average student studies eight hours per week and earns a C (2.0 grade-point average). In order to earn a B (3.0 average), students apparently need to study an average of twelve hours per week (point *N*). Hence an increase of four hours of study time per week is associated with a one-point increase in grade-point average. This relationship between *changes* in study time and *changes* in grade-point average is expressed by the steepness, or *slope*, of the graph.

The slope of any graph is calculated as:

$$\text{Slope} = \frac{\text{vertical distance between two points}}{\text{horizontal distance between two points}}$$

In our example, the vertical distance between points *M* and *N* represents a change in grade-point average. The horizontal distance between these two points represents the change in study time. Hence the slope of the graph between points *M* and *N* is equal to

$$\text{Slope} = \frac{3.0 \text{ grade} - 2.0 \text{ grade}}{12 \text{ hours} - 8 \text{ hours}} = \frac{1 \text{ grade point}}{4 \text{ hours}}$$

In other words, a four-hour increase in study time (from eight to twelve hours) is associated with a one-point increase in grade-point average (see Figure A.1).

Linear vs. nonlinear curves

In Figure A.1, the relationship between grades and studying is represented by a straight line, that is, a *linear* curve. A distinguishing feature of linear "curves" is that they have the same (constant) slope throughout. In this case, it appears that *every* four-hour increase in study time is associated with a one-point increase in average grades. (By how much do grades tend to rise when study time increases from twelve to sixteen hours? Show this relationship in Figure A.1.) Were the relationship between study time and grades not constant, the line in Figure A.1 would be curved rather than straight; it would be a nonlinear curve.

Causation

Figure A.1 itself does not guarantee that your grade-point average will rise by one point if you study four more hours per week. In fact, the graph drawn in Figure A.1 does not prove that additional study ever results in higher grades. The graph is only a summary of empirical observations. It says nothing about cause and effect. It could be that students who study a lot are also smarter to begin with. If so, then less able students might not get higher grades if they studied harder. In other words, the *cause* of higher grades is debatable. At best, the empirical relationship summarized in the graph may be used to support a particular theory (e.g., that it pays to study more). Graphs, like tables, charts, and other statistical media, rarely tell their own story; rather, they must be "interpreted" in terms of some underlying theory or expectation.

CHAPTER 2

SUPPLY AND DEMAND

Every country must make certain choices about the dimensions of its economy. The United States makes them, the Soviet Union and China make them, even smaller countries such as Burundi and New Zealand make them. Not only are the basic questions always the same, but they are also quite simple:

- WHAT goods and services should the economy produce?
- HOW should they be produced?
- FOR WHOM should they be produced?

Although the questions asked are strikingly similar, the ways countries go about resolving these questions and the choices that result vary widely. In the People's Republic of China and the Soviet Union, these questions are answered for the most part by the government. In the United States, a great deal of decision-making authority is vested in individual workers, consumers, and business people. Each of these people enters the decision-making process by participating in the **markets** for factors of production and final products.

market: Any place where individuals buy or sell resources or products.

The U.S. economy is not a purely market economy, of course. As we noted in Chapter 1, many production, consumption, and income-distribution questions are decided outside the market mechanism.[1] Income taxes, public-welfare programs, and state univer-

[1] Nor are the Soviet and Chinese economies purely "command economies"; both permit some market-type activity. Accordingly, most economies are really "mixed," that is, a unique combination of market and nonmarket activities. The Soviet and Chinese economies are discussed further in Chapter 21 in *The Macro Economy Today.*

sities, for example, did not emerge from private production and consumption decisions made in the marketplace. Nor are the regulatory activities of the Food and Drug Administration, the Public Health Service, or the Environmental Protection Agency maintained by market decisions. These economic decisions and activities are handled collectively in the political arena, outside the marketplace. Nevertheless, a great deal of economic activity in the United States is fashioned by decisions that individuals and firms make in the marketplace. Thus, if we know how the market mechanism operates, we can understand a lot about the way the U.S. economy works. We begin in this chapter by looking at the purpose of market transactions, then examine the nature of the decisions that emerge.

MARKET PARTICIPANTS

Over 230 million individual consumers, nearly 12 million business firms, and tens of thousands of government agencies participate directly in the U.S. economy. Fortunately, we can summarize much of this activity by classifying market participants into three distinct groups—consumers, business firms, and government agencies—and analyzing their goals and behavior.

Their goals

Individual consumers, business firms, and government agencies participate in the market in order to achieve certain goals. Consumers strive to maximize their own happiness by purchasing the most satisfying bundle of goods and services with their available incomes. For their part, businesses try to maximize profits by using the most efficient combination of resources to produce the most profitable products. Finally, government agencies are assigned the responsibility of maximizing the general welfare by using available resources to produce desired public goods and services and to redistribute incomes. That is not to say that government agencies are always faithful to this responsibility. Narrow bureaucratic concerns and vested economic or political interests can easily substitute for maximization of the general welfare. In every case, however, it is reasonable to assume that government activity (like private market activity) is directed toward a specific goal.[2]

Their constraints

The tendency of all participants in the economy to try to maximize something, be it profits, private satisfaction, or social welfare, is not their only common trait. Another element common to all participants is their *limited resources*. You and I cannot buy everything we desire; we simply don't have enough income. As a consequence, we must make *choices* among available products, always hoping to get the most satisfaction for the few dollars we have to spend. Likewise, business firms and government agencies must decide how *best* to use their limited resources to maximize profits or public welfare.

[2] We shall explore these issues further in Chapters 3 and 14.

Specialization and exchange

Our desire to maximize the returns on our limited resources leads us to participate in the market, buying and selling various goods and services. Our decision to participate in these exchanges is prompted by two considerations. First, most of us are incapable of producing everything we desire to consume. So we must rely on others to supply us with some desired goods and services. Second, even if we *could* produce all our own goods and services, it would still make sense to specialize, producing only one product and trading it for other desired goods and services.

Suppose you were capable of growing your own food, stitching your own clothes, building your own shelter, and writing your own textbooks. Even in these idyllic circumstances, it would still make sense to decide how *best* to expend your limited time and energy, and to rely on others to fill in the gaps. If you were *most* proficient at growing food, you would be best off spending your time farming. You could then exchange some of your food output for the clothes, shelter, and books you desired.[3]

Our economic interactions with others are thus necessitated by two constraints:

- Our absolute inability as individuals to produce all the things we need or desire
- The limited amount of time, energy, and resources we possess for producing those things we could make for ourselves

Together, these constraints lead us to specialize and interact. Most of the interactions that result take place in the market.

MARKET INTERACTIONS

Figure 2.1 provides a summary of the kinds of interactions that occur among market participants. Note first of all that we have identified three separate groups of participants, each containing many individuals. In the rectangle marked "Consumers" we have grouped all 230 million consumers in the United States. In the "Business firms" box we have grouped all of the various business enterprises that buy and sell goods and services. The third participant, "Governments," includes the many separate agencies of the federal government, as well as state and local governments.

The two markets

factor market: Any place where factors of production (e.g., land, labor, capital) are bought and sold.

A second feature of Figure 2.1 is its identification of two kinds of markets, product markets and factor markets. In **factor markets,** factors of production are exchanged. Specifically, market participants buy or sell land, labor, or capital that can be used in the production process.[4] When you go looking for work, for example, you are making a factor of production—your labor—available to producers. The producers will hire you—purchase your services in the

[3] A more formal proof of the basis for specialization and exchange—the theory of comparative advantage—is provided in Chapter 19.

[4] Factor markets are also called "*resource markets*"; "resources" and "factors of production" are often used synonymously.

FIGURE 2.1 MARKET INTERACTIONS

Market participation is motivated by the desire to maximize personal utility (consumers), profits (business firms), or the general welfare (governments). Business firms participate in markets by supplying goods and services to product markets and purchasing factors of production in factor markets. Individual consumers participate in the marketplace by supplying factors of production (*e.g.*, their own labor) and purchasing final goods and services. Federal, state, and local governments also participate in both factor and product markets.

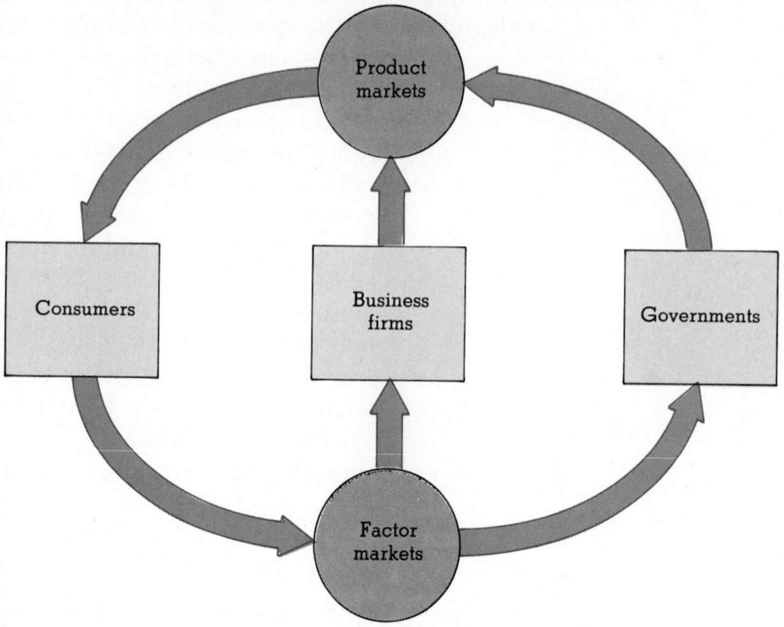

product market: Any place where finished goods and services (products) are bought and sold.

factor market—if you are offering the skills they need at a price they are willing to pay. The same kind of interaction occurs in factor markets when the government seeks to employ workers or any other factors of production (land, machinery) that are available.

Interactions within factor markets are only half the story, of course, as both Figure 2.1 and everyday experience quickly confirm. At the end of a hard day's work consumers enter the grocery store (or bar) to purchase desired goods and services, that is, to buy *products*. In this context, consumers again interact with business firms, this time purchasing goods and services those firms have produced. These interactions occur in **product markets.**

In addition to business firms, governments also supply goods and services to product markets. The consumer rarely buys national defense, schools, or highways directly; instead, such purchases are made indirectly, through taxes and government expenditure. In Figure 2.1, the arrows running from the government through product markets to consumers serve to remind us, however, that all government output is intended "for the people." In this sense, the government acts as an intermediary, buying factors of production and providing certain goods and services consumers desire.

In Figure 2.1 the arrow connecting product markets to consumers emphasizes the fact that consumers, by definition, do not supply products. To the extent that individuals produce goods and services, they do so within the government or business sector. An individual who is a doctor, a dentist, or an economic consultant functions in two sectors. When selling services in the market, this person is regarded as a "business"; when away from the office, he or she is regarded as a "consumer." This distinction is helpful in emphasizing the role of the consumer as the final recipient of all goods and services produced.

Locating markets

Although we may speak of two kinds of markets, it would be a little foolish to go off in search of the product and factor markets. Neither a factor market nor a product market is a single, identifiable structure. The term "market" simply refers to any place where an economic exchange occurs—where a buyer and seller interact. The exchange may take place on the street, in a taxicab, over the phone, in the mail, or through the classified ads of the newspaper. In some cases, the market used may in fact be quite distinguishable, as in the case of a retail store, the Chicago Commodity Exchange, or a state employment office. But whatever it looks like, ***a market exists wherever and whenever an exchange takes place.*** The market is simply a place or medium where buyer and seller get together; which market they are in depends on what they are buying or selling.

Money and exchange

While Figure 2.1 is a useful summary of market activities, it does neglect one critical element of market interactions: money. Each of the arrows depicted in the figure actually has two dimensions. Consider again the arrow linking consumers and product markets. It is drawn in only one direction because consumers, by definition, do not provide goods and services directly to product markets. But they do provide something: money. If you want to obtain something from a product market, you must offer to pay for it with money (typically, cash or check). Thus consumers *exchange* money for goods and services in product markets. This basic exchange of money for goods is depicted in Figure 2.2.

The same kinds of exchange occur in factor markets. When you go to work, you are exchanging a factor of production (your labor) for money, typically a paycheck. Here again, the path connecting consumers to factor markets really goes in two directions, one of real resources, the other of money. Notice in Figure 2.2 that consumers receive wages, rent, and interest for the labor, land, and capital they bring to the factor markets. Indeed, nearly every market transaction

FIGURE 2.2 MARKET EXCHANGES

Most market transactions involve an *exchange* of real goods or resources for money (income). When products or factors of production flow in one direction, income flows in the other. *Note:* government revenues are typically not obtained directly from product sales, but instead indirectly from taxes (see Chapter 3).

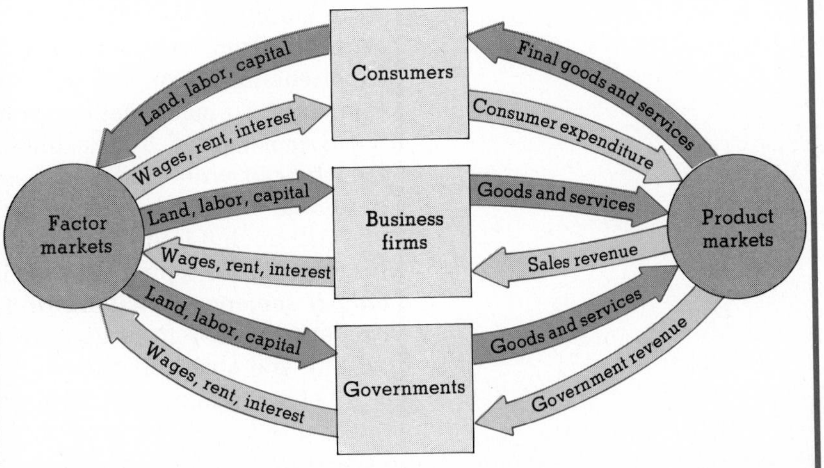

involves an exchange of money for goods (in product markets) or resources (in factor markets).[5]

Supply and demand

supply: The ability and willingness to sell (produce) specific quantities of a good at alternative prices in a given time period (*ceteris paribus*).

demand: The ability and willingness to buy specific quantities of a good at alternative prices in a given time period (*ceteris paribus*).

Because all market transactions actually have two dimensions, it is convenient to have names for both. We call these dimensions—the two sides of each market transaction—**supply** and **demand.**

Whether one is on the supply side or the demand side of any particular market transaction depends on the nature of the exchange, not on the people or institutions involved. Consumers may both demand goods and services and supply labor or other resources. As noted earlier, we are *supplying* resources to the market when we look for a job, that is, offer our labor in exchange for money. By contrast, we are *demanding* goods when we shop in a supermarket, that is, when we are prepared to offer money in exchange for something to eat. Business firms may *supply* goods and services in product markets at the same time that they are *demanding* factors of production in factor markets.

MARKET FORCES

Although the concepts of supply and demand are useful for explaining what's happening in the marketplace, we are not yet ready to summarize the zillions of transactions that are occurring daily in both factor and product markets. Recall that ***every market transaction involves an exchange and thus some element of both supply and demand.*** Then just consider how many exchanges you alone undertake in a single week, not to mention the transactions of the other 230 million or so consumers among us. Clearly, the daily volume of market transactions is staggering; to keep track of so much action, we will need to summarize the activities of many individuals.

Individual demand

We can begin to understand how market forces work by looking more closely at the behavior of a single market participant. Let us start with Tom, a sophomore at Clearview College. Tom is currently experiencing the torment of writing a paper for his English composition class. To make matters worse, Tom's professor has insisted on *typed* papers, and Tom cannot type with his fingers much better than he can write with his toes. Under the circumstances, Tom is desperate for a typist.

Although it is apparent that Tom has a strong *desire* for a typist, his *demand* for typing services is not yet evident. ***A demand exists only if someone is willing and able to pay for the good,*** that is, exchange money for a good or service in the marketplace. Is Tom willing and able to pay for typing?

Let us assume that Tom has some income and is willing to

[5] In the rare cases where one good is exchanged directly for another, we speak of *barter* exchanges.

TABLE 2.1 TOM'S DEMAND SCHEDULE

A demand schedule indicates the quantities of a good a consumer is able and willing to buy at alternative prices (*ceteris paribus*). This demand schedule indicates that Tom would buy five pages of typing per semester if the price of typing were $3.50 per page (row *D*). If typing were less expensive (rows *E–I*). Tom would purchase a larger quantity.

	Price of typing (per page)	*Quantity of typing demanded (pages per semester)*
A	$5.00	1
B	4.50	2
C	4.00	3
D	3.50	5
E	3.00	7
F	2.50	9
G	2.00	12
H	1.50	15
I	1.00	20

spend some of it to get his English paper typed. Under these assumptions, we can claim that Tom is a participant in the *market* for typing services.

But can we say anything about his demand? Surely Tom is not prepared to exchange *all* his income for the typing of a single English paper. After all, Tom *could* use his income to buy more desirable goods and services; to give up everything for the typing of just one paper would imply an extremely high **opportunity cost.** It would be more reasonable to assume that there are *limits* to the amount Tom is willing to pay for any given quantity of typing. These limits will be determined by how much income Tom has to spend and how many other goods and services he must implicitly forsake in order to pay for typing services. If the price of typing exceeds these limits, Tom may end up typing all or part of the paper himself.

opportunity cost: The most desired goods or services that are forgone in order to obtain something else.

We assume, then, that when Tom starts looking for a typist, he has in mind some sort of **demand schedule** like that described in Table 2.1. According to row *A* of this schedule, our tormented English compositionist is willing and able to pay for the typing of only one page per semester if he must pay $5 per typed page. At such an outrageous price, he will have only the first page of his paper typed professionally and will peck out or print the remaining pages himself. That way, the paper will make a good first impression, and Tom won't have to sacrifice so many other goods and services for his paper.

demand schedule: A table showing the quantities of a good a consumer is willing and able to buy at alternative prices in a given time period (*ceteris paribus*).

At lower prices, Tom would behave differently. According to Table 2.1, Tom would get more pages typed if the price of typing were less. At lower prices, he would not have to give up so many other goods and services for each page of professional typing and would be more *willing* to have his paper typed. The reduced opportunity costs implied by lower typing prices increase the attractiveness of professional typing. Indeed, we see from row *I* that Tom is willing to have 20 pages per semester typed professionally—an entire paper—if the price per page is as low as $1.

Notice that the demand schedule doesn't tell us anything about *why* this consumer is willing to pay specific prices for various amounts of typing. Tom's expressed willingness to pay for typing may reflect a desperate need to finish his paper, a lot of income to spend, or a relatively small desire for other goods and services. All the demand schedule tells us is what the consumer is *willing and able* to buy, for whatever reasons.[6]

Also observe that the demand schedule doesn't tell us how many pages of typing the consumer will *actually* buy. Table 2.1 simply states that Tom is *willing and able* to pay for one page of typing per semester at $5.00 per page, for two pages at $4.50 each, and so on. How much typing he purchases will depend on the actual price of typing in the market. Until we know that price, we cannot tell how much typing will be purchased. Hence ***"demand" is an expression of consumer buying intentions, of a willingness to buy, not a statement of actual purchases.***

demand curve: **A curve describing the quantities of a good a consumer is willing and able to buy at alternative prices in a given time period (*ceteris paribus*).**

A convenient summary of buying intentions is provided by the **demand curve,** a graphical illustration of the demand schedule. The demand curve in Figure 2.3 tells us again that this consumer is willing to pay for only one page of professional typing per semester if the price is $5.00 per page (point *A*), for two if the price is $4.50 (point *B*), for three pages at $4.00 a page (point *C*), and so on. Once we know what the market price of typing actually is, a quick look at the demand curve tells us how much typing this consumer will buy.

Ceteris paribus

The demand curve in Figure 2.3 has only two dimensions—quantity demanded (on the horizontal axis) and price (on the vertical axis). This seems to imply that the amount of typing demanded depends *only* on the price of typing. This is surely not the case. A consumer's demand for any product depends on a variety of forces, including:

- Tastes (desire for this and other goods)
- Price (of this particular good)
- Income (of the consumer)
- Other goods (their availability and price)
- Expectations (for income, prices, tastes)

If Tom didn't have to turn in a typed English composition, he would have no taste (desire) for typing services and thus no demand. If he had no income, he would not have the ability to pay and thus would still be out of the typing market. Other goods shape the opportunity cost of typing, while expectations for income, grades, and graduation prospects would all influence his willingness to buy typing services.

If demand is in fact such a multidimensional decision, how can we reduce it to only two dimensions? This is one of the most common tricks of the economics trade. To simplify their models of the world, economists focus on only one or two forces at a time and *assume* nothing else changes. We know a consumer's tastes, income, other goods, and expectations all affect the decision to buy typing services. But we want to focus on the relationship between quantity demanded and price. That is to say, we want to know what

[6] Some of the economic, sociological, and psychological forces that influence consumer desires are discussed in Chapter 4.

FIGURE 2.3 A DEMAND CURVE

A demand curve expresses the quantity of a good a consumer is willing and able to buy at alternative prices. Each point on the curve refers to a specific quantity that will be demanded at a given price. If, for example, the price of typing were $3.50 per page, this curve tells us the consumer would purchase five pages per semester (point *D*). If typing cost $3 per page, seven pages per semester would be demanded (point *E*). This particular curve is based on the demand schedule in Table 2.1.

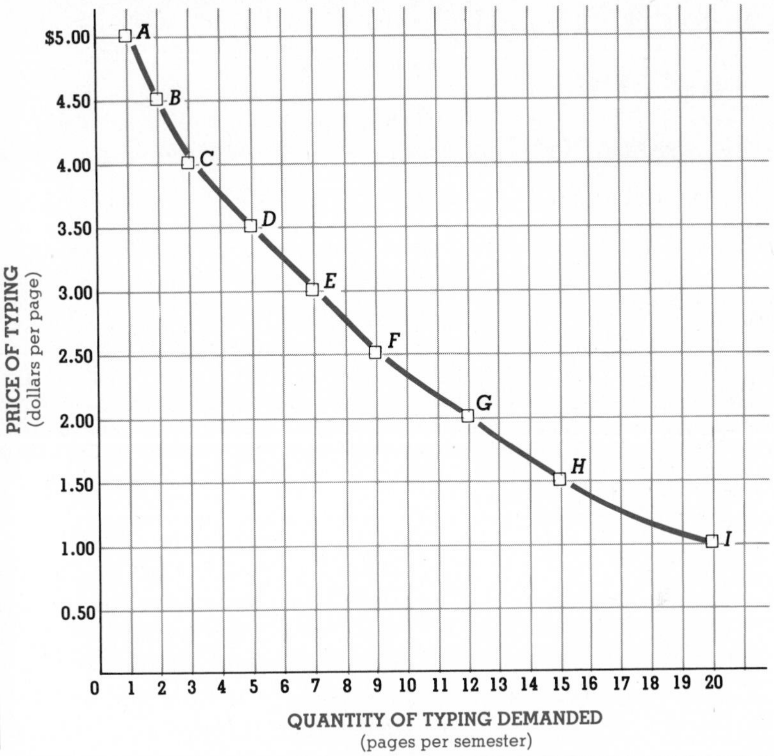

independent influence price has on consumption decisions. To find out, we must isolate the one determinant, price, and assume all other determinants of demand remain unchanged. Formally, this assumption is referred to by the Latin expression ***ceteris paribus*** ("all other things remaining equal").

ceteris paribus: The assumption of "everything else being equal," of nothing else changing.

The *ceteris paribus* assumption is not as farfetched as it may seem at first. In the short run, people's tastes, income, and expectations do not change very much. Also, the prices and availability of other goods remain fairly constant. Hence a change in the price of a product may be the only thing that prompts a change in quantity demanded.

Other determinants of demand *do* change, of course, particularly as the time frame is expanded. Accordingly, the demand schedule and curve remain unchanged only so long as these other influences are constant. Were Tom's income to increase, he might be willing to buy *more* typing at every price. In this case, the entire demand curve would have to be redrawn. Such *shifts* of the demand curve are examined later in this chapter.

Market demand

What we can say about demand for typing on the part of one harassed English major we can say about the demand of all other market participants. That is to say, we can identify the demand for typing services associated with every student at Clearview College (or, for that matter, with all 230 million consumers in the United States). Some students, of course, have no need or desire for profes-

Dentists Urged to Go Back to Using Gold

When the price of gold zoomed up, dentists cut back sharply on their use of the precious metal for bridges, inlays and crowns. . . .

And that has set off a sharp debate in the dental profession. Health issues are involved along with economies. While gold's price soared, dentists wanted cheaper materials, and foundries turned out hundreds of alternative alloys from silver and from base metals such as nickel, chrome and cobalt.

Are the substitutes as good as gold? Or risky? Dentists are trying to resolve those questions.

A Cautious Stand

The American Dental Association says in a cautious comment that the best of the new alloys are "as satisfactory as gold, although no long-term studies have been made as to relative durability."

The new alloys are substantially cheaper. Though the price of gold has fallen to $415 an ounce or so from the high of $875, which it reached for only a day in January 1980, gold reconstructive work on a tooth can add $100 or so to a dental bill.

In 1980, the 136,000 dentists in the U.S. used 341,000 ounces of gold, less than half the 706,000 ounces they used in 1978. "That's a fast drop," says Louis Calisti, director of dental-care management at Boston University's Goldman School of Graduate Dentistry.

—Roger Lowenstein

sional typing and are not willing to pay anything for such services: they do not participate in the typing market. Other students have a desire for such services but not enough income to pay for them; they, too, are excluded from the typing market. A large number of students, however, not only have a need (or desire) for typing services but are also willing and able to purchase such services, either because their incomes are sufficient or because typing prices are comparatively low. How much income is "sufficient" and what price is regarded as "low" will depend on the attitudes, experiences, and opportunity costs of each person.

What we start with in product markets, then, is many individual demand curves. Can we make enough sense out of these curves to say anything in general about the market demand for typing services at Clearview College? What we really need is some way to add up all the individual demand curves to produce a single **market demand** for typing.

market demand: The total quantities of a good or service people are willing and able to buy at alternative prices in a given time period; the sum of individual demands.

Fortunately, it is possible to combine all the individual demand curves into a single market demand for typing services, and the aggregation process is no more difficult than simple arithmetic. In fact, simple arithmetic is all that's needed, once you know the buying intentions of all consumers. Suppose you would be willing to buy one page of typing per semester at a price of $8 per page. George, who is desperate to make his English essays at least *look* good, would buy two at that price; and I would buy none, since I only grade papers, and needn't type the grades. What would our combined (market) demand for typing services be at that price? Clearly, our individual inclinations indicate that we would be willing to buy a total of three pages of typing per semester if the price were $8 per page. Our combined willingness to buy—our collective market demand—is nothing more than the sum of our individual demand schedules. The same kind of aggregation can be performed for all consumers, leading to a summary of the total market demand for typing services at Clearview College.

What is nice about a market-demand concept is that it permits us to ignore some of the idiosyncrasies of our friends and neighbors.

With thousands of students at Clearview College, the typing market is large. Accordingly, we don't have to consider whether George's roommate will move out if he starts doing his own typing, or whether you will buy more typing if you win the state lottery. Regardless of the personal virtues that you, George, and George's roommate possess, the market demand for typing services will be little affected by these great moments in your lives. In so large a market, the demand for typing services tends to be more stable and predictable than the demands of the separate individuals who participate in that market. In still larger markets—say, the total U.S. market for typewriters—the predictability of market demand is important to the business people and bureaucrats who make output and price decisions.

We cannot completely ignore the factors that mold and shape the buying habits of individual consumers, however. First of all, we are likely to be as interested in the welfare and happiness of specific individuals as in the dimensions of the whole market. Second, and more important for the purposes of economic forecasting or policy formulation, we must recognize that if enough consumers change their buying intentions, then the market demand will change. Hence, if we want to change the market demand for typing, we have to know what motivates individual consumers of typing services.

Market supply

market supply: The total quantities of a good that sellers are willing and able to sell at alternative prices in a given time period (*ceteris paribus*); the combined willingness of all market suppliers to sell.

Everything we have said about market demand applies with equal force to the concept of market supply. **Market supply** is simply the total quantity of a good that *all* potential sellers are *willing* and *able to sell* at alternative prices. Thus the market supply of typing services at Clearview College is the number of typed pages all professional typists at Clearview, taken together, are prepared to produce (type) per semester, at various prices. Similarly, the "supply of labor" is equal to the amount of labor willingly supplied each year by millions of individual workers at particular wage rates. The "supply of automobiles" is equal to the number of cars produced per year at various prices by General Motors, Ford, and other automakers. The "supply of wheat" is the number of bushels willingly brought to market each year at various prices by a million farmers.

Like market demand, ***market supply is an expression of sellers' intentions, of the ability and willingness to sell, not a statement of actual sales.*** My next-door neighbor may be *willing* to sell his 1972 Ford Pinto for $8,000, but it is most unlikely that he will ever find a buyer at that price. Nevertheless, his *willingness* to sell his car at that price is part of the *market supply* of used cars. The significance of these various intentions for market prices and sales is examined next.

PROFESSIONAL TYPING COMPANY. Dissertations, theses, manuscripts. $1/page. Campus pickup. Jane Davis, 840-8854.

PROF. TYPING-$1.00 page, exp. Cathy 498-6672.

Computer-scripted dissertations, texts, papers. Perfect. $2 per page. Anita 686-2479

24-hour service [4 typists] Masters theses, term papers, etc. Professionally typed and corrected. 653-2880.

THE ACTION IN PRODUCT MARKETS

We can use the concepts of market supply and market demand to determine the quantity of goods and services that will be exchanged in each market. The same concepts can be used to determine the

TABLE 2.2 THE MARKET DEMAND SCHEDULE FOR TYPING

Market demand represents the combined demands of all market participants. To determine the total quantity of typing demanded at any given price, we add up the separate demands of the individual consumers. Row G of this schedule indicates that a *total* quantity of 39 pages per semester will be demanded at a price of $2 per page.

	Price per page	Quantity demanded (pages per semester) Tom	+	George	+	Lisa	+	Me	=	Total demand
A	$5.00	1		4		0		0		5
B	4.50	2		6		0		0		8
C	4.00	3		8		0		0		11
D	3.50	5		11		0		0		16
E	3.00	7		14		1		0		22
F	2.50	9		18		3		0		30
G	2.00	12		22		5		0		39
H	1.50	15		26		6		0		47
I	1.00	20		30		7		0		57

price at which the goods and services will be bought and sold. Consider, for example, the interplay of supply and demand in the Clearview College typing *market*. As we noted earlier, not all students will desire typing services; even fewer will be able and willing to purchase such services. Nevertheless, so long as *some* students are willing and able to pay for typing, we can speak of a *demand* for typing. We can then use arithmetic to construct a market demand curve based on the willingness to pay expressed by all persons.

The market demand curve

Table 2.2 provides the basic market demand schedule for a situation in which only four people participate on the demand side of the market. Figure 2.4 illustrates the same market situation with demand curves. The four individuals who participate in the market demand for Clearview College typing obviously differ greatly, as suggested by their respective demand schedules. Tom has to turn in several papers each semester, has a good income, and is willing to purchase typing services. His demand schedule is portrayed in the first column of Table 2.2 (and is identical to the one we examined in

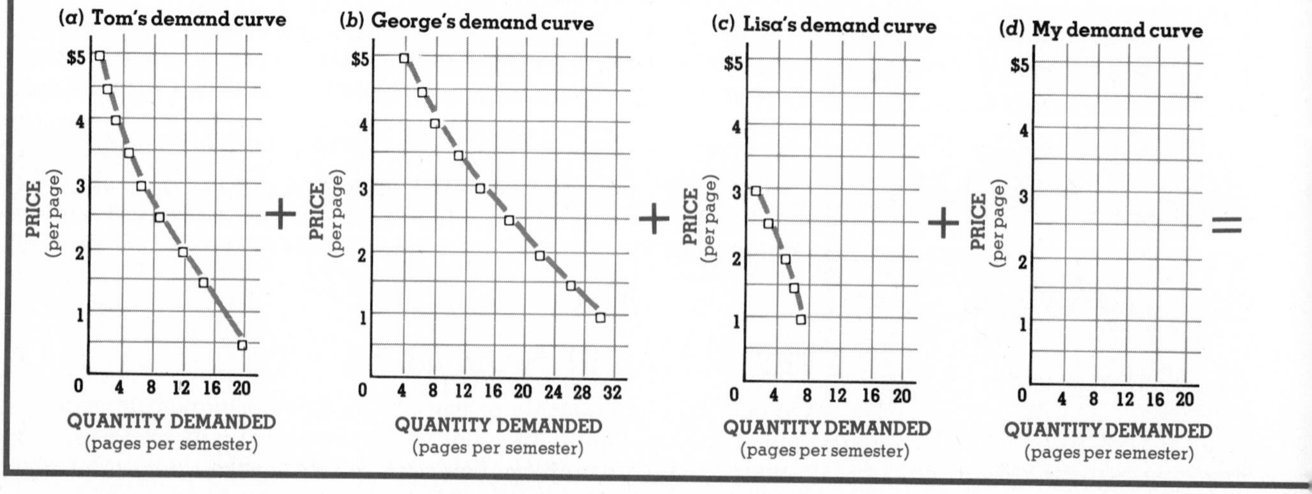

Table 2.1). George, as we already noted, is desperate to improve the appearance of his papers and is willing to pay for typing services, even at relatively high prices. His demand schedule is summarized in the second column under "Quantity demanded" in Table 2.2. The third consumer in this market is Lisa. She has a very limited budget and can do her own typing if she must, and so is not willing to buy any typing at higher prices. As prices drop below \$3.50 per page, however, her demand schedule indicates that she will get some of her work professionally typed. Finally, there is my demand schedule (the fourth column under "Quantity demanded" in Table 2.2), which confirms that I really don't participate in the local typing market.

The differing personalities and consumption habits of Tom, George, Lisa, and me are expressed in our individual demand schedules and associated curves, as depicted in Table 2.2 and Figure 2.4. To determine the *market* demand for typing from this information, we simply add up these four separate demands. The end result of this aggregation is, first, a *market* demand schedule (the last column in Table 2.2) and, second, the resultant *market* demand curve (the curve in Figure 2.4e). These market summaries describe the various quantities of typing that Clearview College students are *willing and able* to purchase each semester at various prices.

How much typing will be purchased each semester? Knowing how much typing Tom, George, Lisa, and I are willing to buy at various prices doesn't tell you how much we are actually going to purchase. To determine the actual consumption of typing services, we have to know something about prices and supplies. What is the price of typing in this market, and who sets it?

The market supply curve

To understand how the going price for typing is established, we will focus on the activities of the three people who offer typing services at Clearview College. None of these three entrepreneurs is willing to type for less than \$1 a page; they reason that their leisure time is worth more than that. As a consequence, no typing services are

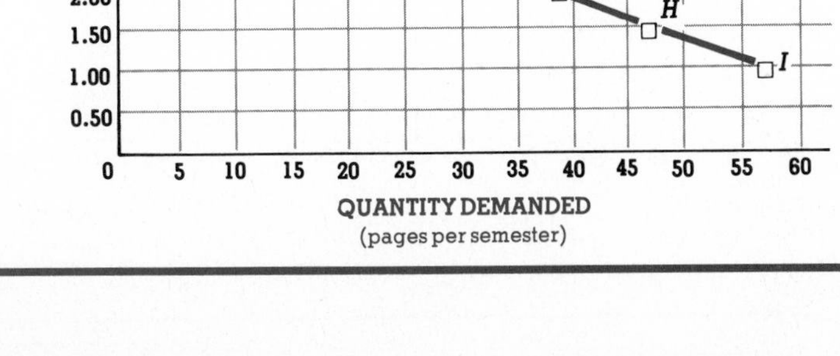

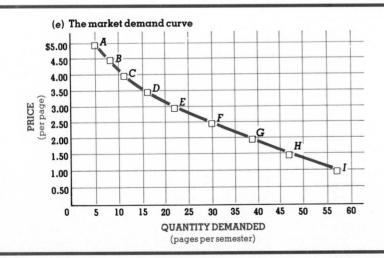

FIGURE 2.4 CONSTRUCTION OF THE MARKET DEMAND CURVE

The market demand curve expresses the *combined* demands of all market participants. At a price of \$3 per page, the total quantity of typing demanded would be 22 pages per semester (point *E*): 7 pages demanded by Tom, 14 by George, and 1 by Lisa.

TABLE 2.3 THE MARKET SUPPLY SCHEDULE FOR TYPING SERVICES

Market supply represents the *combined* willingness to sell of all individual sellers (producers). In this case, the total quantity supplied to the market at alternative prices depends on the ability and willingness of three individual sellers to sell. If typing can be sold at $4 per page (row *h*), a total of 130 pages per semester will be offered.

	Price per page	Quantity supplied (pages per semester) Don	+ Lynn	+ Terry	= Total market
j	$5.00	46	54	48	148
i	$4.50	45	51	44	140
h	$4.00	44	47	39	130
g	$3.50	39	43	32	114
f	$3.00	34	32	24	90
e	$2.50	25	23	14	62
d	$2.00	17	15	7	39
c	$1.50	11	9	0	20
b	$1.00	6	4	0	10
a	$0.50	0	0	0	0

available at prices under $1 per page. Prices must be at least high enough to compensate sellers for their opportunity costs, in this case, the leisure or study time given up in order to type.

At a price of $1 per page, two typists are able and willing to forsake some leisure or study time and offer typing services. As row *b* of Table 2.3 indicates, Don is *willing* to type six pages per semester if the price is only $1 per page. Lynn is able and willing to type four pages per semester at that price. Clearly there won't be much professional typing activity at Clearview College if the price for typing is only $1 per page.

At higher prices per page, typing becomes more attractive. As prices rise above $1 per page, typists are receiving more income for the leisure or study time they give up; that is, the *relative* attractiveness of typing improves. Accordingly, when the price of typing is $2 per page (row *d*), it is not surprising that a third typist enters the market. At this higher price, both Don and Lynn are also willing to supply larger quantities of typing, as their demand schedules indicate.

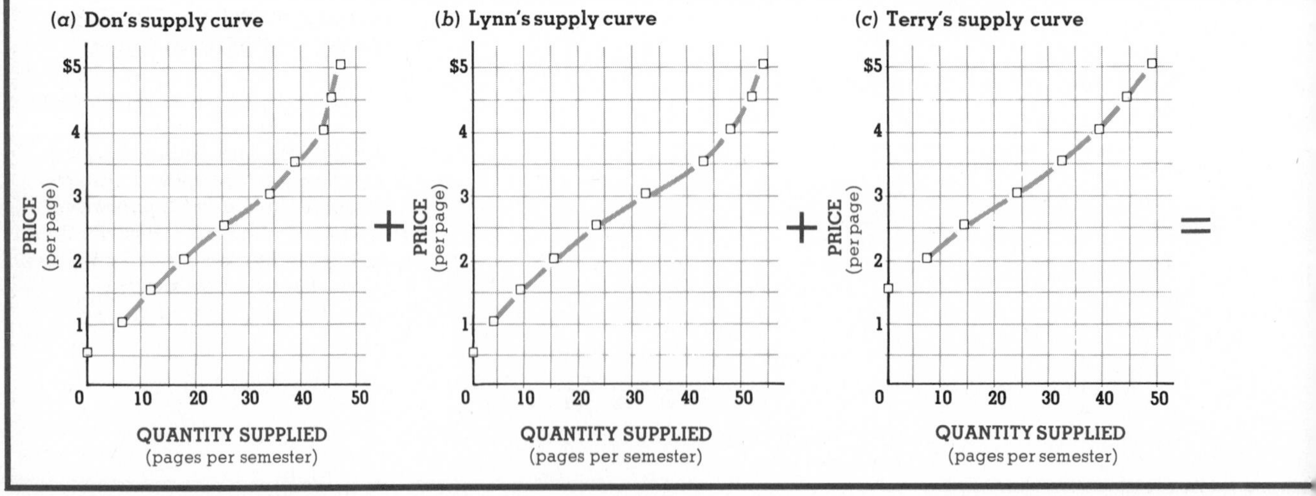

If typing services could be sold at very high prices, Don, Lynn, and Terry would be willing to sacrifice substantial amounts of leisure time for their typing. Hence the quantity of typing supplied to the Clearview College market would rise.

The various inclinations of Don, Lynn, and Terry are reflected in their respective supply schedules. We can combine these schedules into a single *market* supply schedule in the same way that we constructed a market demand schedule. Table 2.3 details the quantity of typing that Don, Lynn, and Terry would be able and *willing to sell* at various prices. Figure 2.5 illustrates this information with supply curves. Notice how each point on the supply curve corresponds to a particular row of Table 2.3. As should be apparent by now, the market supply curve is conceptually the same kind of thing as an individual's (or firm's) supply curve, except that it includes the behavior and intentions of more people (or firms).

EQUILIBRIUM

equilibrium price: The price at which the quantity of a good demanded in a given time period equals the quantity supplied.

We can now determine the price and quantity of typing being sold at Clearview College without going to the campus and interviewing all the students. A market supply curve and a market demand curve are all we require. All we need do is bring the two curves together, as in Figure 2.6. The market supply curve expresses the *ability and willingness* of Don, Lynn, and Terry to sell typing at various prices. The market demand curve illustrates the *ability and willingness* of Tom, George, Lisa, and me to buy typing at those same prices. When we put the two curves together, we see that ***only one price and quantity are compatible with the existing intentions of both buyers and sellers.*** This **equilibrium** occurs at the intersection of the two curves. Once it is established, typing will cost $2 per page. At that price, Don, Lynn, and Terry will sell 39 pages of typing per semester—the same amount that Tom, George, and Lisa wish to buy at that price.

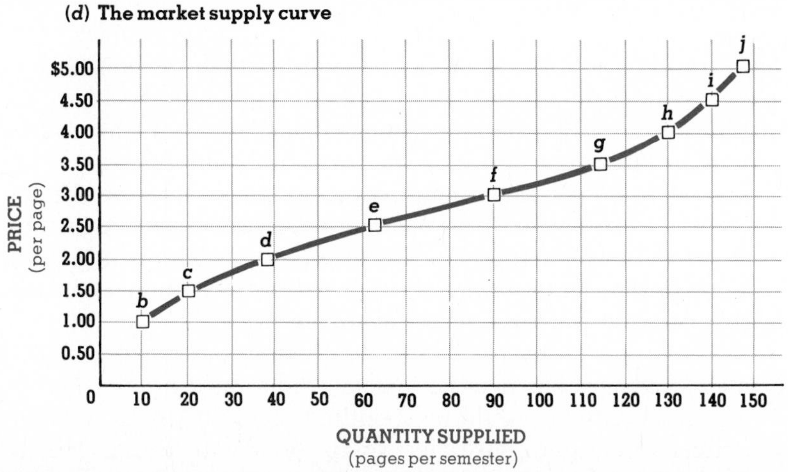

FIGURE 2.5 CONSTRUCTION OF THE MARKET SUPPLY CURVE

The market supply curve indicates the *combined* sales intentions of all market participants. If the price of typing were $2.50 per page (point e), the *total* quantity of typing supplied would be 62 pages per semester. This quantity is determined by adding together the individual responses (supply curves) of Don, Lynn, and Terry.

FIGURE 2.6 THE TYPING MARKET

The equilibrium price and quantity are determined by the intersection of the market supply and demand curves. The equilibrium price is the only price at which the quantity demanded equals the quantity supplied. In this case, the equilibrium price is $2 per page. At that price, 39 pages of typing are supplied and demanded per semester.

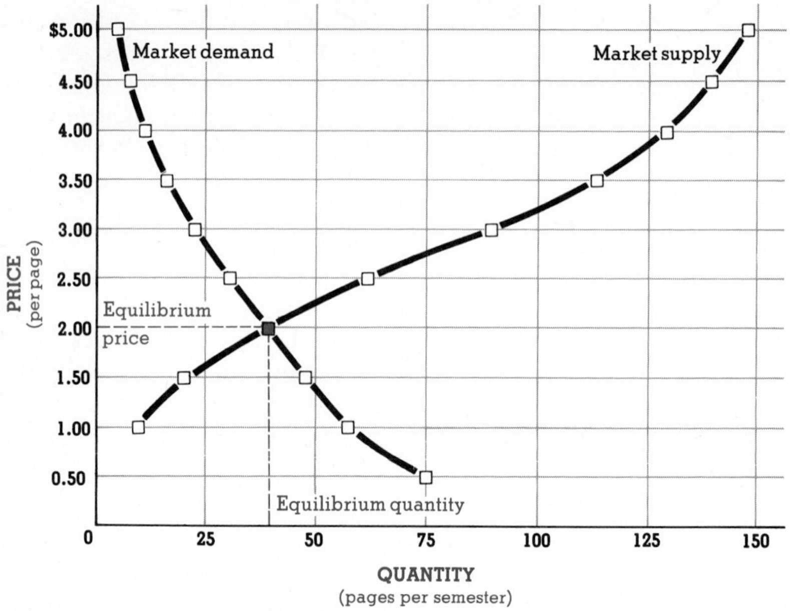

An important characteristic of the equilibrium price is that it is not determined by any single individual. Rather it is determined by the collective actions of many buyers and sellers, each acting out his or her own demand or supply schedule. It is this kind of impersonal price determination that gave rise to Adam Smith's characterization of the market mechanism as "the invisible hand." In attempting to explain how the market mechanism works, the famed nineteenth-century economist noted a certain feature of market prices. The market behaves *as if* some unseen force (the invisible hand) were examining each individual's supply or demand schedule, then selecting a price that assured an equilibrium. In practice, of course, the process of price determination is not so mysterious; rather it is a simple process of trial and error.

Surplus and shortage

Suppose for the moment that Don, Lynn, and Terry believed that typing could be sold for $2.50 per page rather than the equilibrium price of $2.00, and offered it only at this higher price. From the demand and supply schedules depicted in Table 2.4 (themselves taken from Tables 2.2 and 2.3) we can readily foresee the consequences. At $2.50 per page, Don, Lynn, and Terry would be offering more typing services than Tom, George, and Lisa were willing to buy at that price. Thus a **market surplus** of typing services would exist, in the sense that more typing was offered for sale (supplied) than students cared to purchase at the available price.

market surplus: The amount by which the quantity supplied exceeds the quantity demanded at a given price; excess supply.

As Table 2.4 indicates, at a price of $2.50 per page, a market surplus of 32 pages per semester exists. Under these circumstances, Don, Lynn, and Terry would be spending many idle hours at their typewriters, waiting for customers to appear. Their waiting will be in vain, because the quantity of typing demanded will not increase

TABLE 2.4 MARKET DEMAND AND SUPPLY

Only at the equilibrium price of $2 is the quantity demanded equal to the quantity supplied. At higher prices, a market surplus exists—the quantity supplied exceeds the quantity demanded. At prices below equilibrium, a market shortage exists.

Price per page	*Quantity supplied (pages per semester)*		*Quantity demanded (pages per semester)*
$5.00	148	market surplus	5
4.50	140		8
4.00	130		11
3.50	114		16
3.00	90		22
2.50	62		30
2.00	39	equilibrium	39
1.50	20	market shortage	47
1.00	10		57

until the price of typing falls. That is the clear message of the demand curve. The tendency of quantity demanded to increase as price falls is illustrated in Figure 2.7 by a movement along the demand curve from point X to lower prices and greater quantity demanded. As we move down the market demand curve, the desire for typing does not change, but the quantity people are able and willing to buy increases. Indeed, a basic implication of the downward-sloping demand curve is that *one can stimulate sales of a product by lowering its price.*

A very different sequence of events would occur if someone were to spread the word initially that typing services were available at only $1.50 per page. Tom, George, and Lisa would be standing in line to get their papers typed, but Don, Lynn, and Terry would not be willing to supply the quantity desired at that price. As Table 2.4 confirms, at $1.50 per page, the quantity demanded (47 pages per

FIGURE 2.7 MARKET SURPLUS OR SHORTAGE

Only at the equilibrium price ($2) is the quantity demanded equal to the quantity supplied. At higher prices (e.g., $2.50), the quantity supplied will exceed the quantity demanded. This imbalance is called a market surplus (excess supply). At lower prices, a market shortage (excess demand) will exist; the quantity demanded will exceed the quantity supplied.

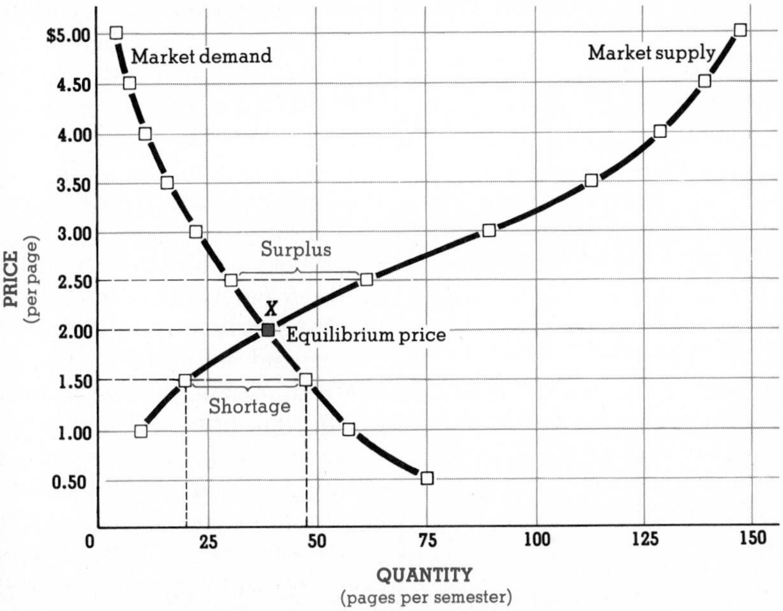

Fed up with the food fight

Forced to queue endlessly for supplies, the Poles are boiling

It is 4 a.m. The sun will not rise for almost three hours, but already the line has begun to form in front of the austere, dimly lit shop. A panel truck pulls up to the rear entrance, and two burly workers, their white smocks spattered with red stains, deliver their precious cargo: a day's supply of meat. Within three hours, the choicest cuts—pork chops, ham, boneless beef—will be gone. The late arrivals will have to make do with sausage, soup bones or chicken. Or perhaps nothing at all. . . .

The government officially maintains that the average Pole spends four hours queuing up each day. That estimate drew derisive laughter from most shoppers. Says one retired woman: "I spend half my time in lines. I do all the shopping for my daughter and her family." Indeed, the elderly are one of the Polish family's most valuable assets, since they have more free time for waiting in line. . . .

With the state-run supply system on the verge of collapse, most Poles must turn to alternate sources for food and other scarce items. Those with friends or relatives abroad may get some of what they need via parcel post. Others resort to barter: a mechanic might trade two quarts of motor oil to a salesgirl for a pound of coffee; in Silesia, the miners are reportedly trading coal to farmers for meat. For exorbitant prices, or hard Western currency, almost anything can be gotten on the black market. Sample prices: blue jeans, $180; one pint of vodka, $24.

More affordable to the average Pole are the so-called free markets, which the government traditionally has ignored. These extralegal bazaars are operated as private enterprises by farmers or nimble entrepreneurs who offer abundant quantities of fruits and vegetables at prices slightly higher than the state stores. A free-market egg costs about 40¢, for example, compared with 30¢ for one in a state store. The more wealthy city dweller may drive out into the country and buy meat directly and illegally from a farmer. One Gdansk bureaucrat admits that he and a neighbor buy whole pigs and then salt the meat down in barrels. Such stratagems have become so common that the government last month prohibited the sale of meat outside state stores. Reason: farmers were refusing to sell their pigs to the government at the official price of $1.30 per lb. when they could get half again as much from individuals.

market shortage: **The amount by which the quantity demanded exceeds the quantity supplied at a given price; excess demand.**

semester) would greatly exceed the quantity supplied (20 pages per semester). In this situation, we may speak of a **market shortage,** that is, an excess of quantity demanded over quantity supplied.

When a market shortage exists, not all consumer demands can be satisfied. In other words, some people who are *willing* to buy typing at the going price ($1.50) will not be able to do so. To assure themselves of sufficient typing, Tom, George, Lisa, or some other consumer may offer to pay a *higher* price, thus initiating a move up the demand curve of Figure 2.7. The higher prices offered will in turn induce Don, Lynn, and Terry to type more, thus ensuring an upward movement along the market supply curve. Thus a higher price tends to call forth a greater quantity supplied, as reflected in the upward-sloping supply curve. Notice, again, that the *desire* to type has not changed; only the quantity supplied has responded to a change in price.

What we observe, then, is that ***whenever the market price is set above or below the equilibrium price, either a market surplus or a market shortage will emerge.*** To overcome a surplus or shortage, buyers and sellers will change their behavior, that is, the prices charged or paid and the quantities demanded or sold. Only at the *equilibrium* price will no further adjustments be required. The equilibrium price is the only price at which the amount consumers are willing to buy equals the amount producers are willing to sell. We can count on market participants to find this equilibrium.

Business firms can discover equilibrium market prices in the same way. If they find that consumer purchases are not keeping up with production, they may conclude that their price is above the equilibrium price. They will have to get rid of their accumulated inventory. To do so they will have to lower their price (by a Grand End-of-Year Sale, perhaps) or convince consumers (via advertising) that they have underrated a most indispensable product. In the happy situation where consumer purchases are outpacing production, a firm might conclude that its price was a trifle too low and give it a nudge upward. Or it might expand production facilities. In any case, the equilibrium price can be established after a few trials in the marketplace.

SHIFTS IN DEMAND

We can anticipate that the collective actions of buyers and sellers will quickly establish an equilibrium price for any product. We should not regard any particular equilibrium price as permanent, however. The equilibrium price established in the Clearview College typing market, for example, was the unique outcome of specific demand and supply schedules. Those schedules themselves were based on our *ceteris paribus* assumption of "all other things remaining equal." Specifically, we assumed that the "taste" (desire) for typing was given, as were consumers' incomes, the price and availability of other goods, and expectations. But any of these other deter-

CETERIS PARIBUS: MOVEMENTS VS. SHIFTS

A demand curve is constructed on the assumption that all determinants of demand other than price are given (i.e., constant). It tells us how the quantity demanded of a good will change in response to a change in the price of that good. The demand curve is a reliable predictor of consumers' behavior so long as underlying tastes, incomes, costs of other goods, or expectations do not change. As long as *ceteris paribus* (other things remain equal), the quantity demanded will move up or down the demand curve in response to changes in price.

But other things do not remain equal forever: tastes, incomes, and opportunity costs do change. When they do, the entire demand curve will *shift* to a new position. As a consequence, the quantity demanded of a good may change even if the price of the good does not.

The quantity demanded of a good may change, then, in response to one of two factors:

- A change in the price of that good, which causes a movement along the existing demand curve
- A change in underlying tastes, income, other goods, or expectations, which causes a *shift in the demand curve*

On the supply side, too, changes in the quantity supplied may result from movements along an existing supply curve or shifts of that curve. We thus distinguish between "changes in supply" (a shift) and "changes in quantity supplied" (which result from a movement or shift).

FIGURE 2.8 A SHIFT IN DEMAND

A rightward shift of the demand curve indicates that consumers are willing to buy a larger quantity at every price. As a consequence, a new equilibrium is established (point *Y*), at a higher price and greater quantity. A shift of the demand curve occurs only when the assumption of *ceteris paribus* is violated.

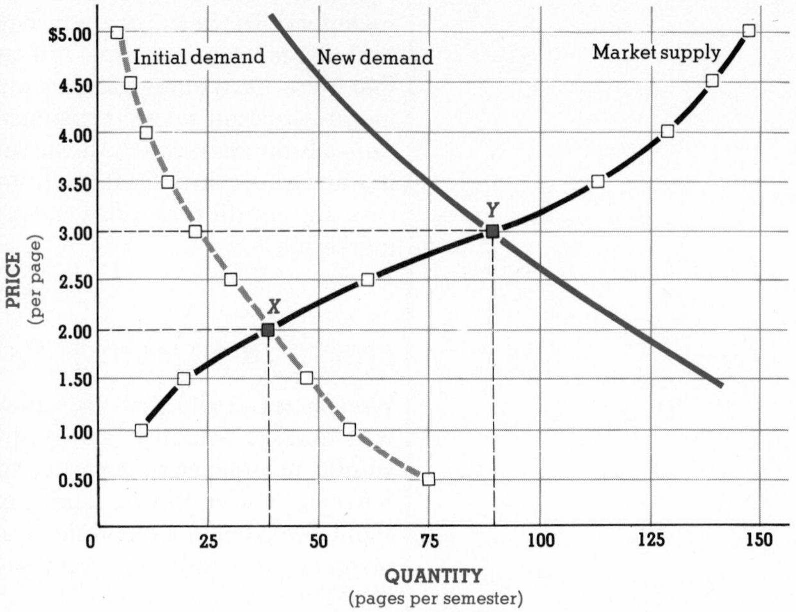

shift in demand: A change in the quantity demanded at any (every) given price.

minants of demand could change. When they do, the demand curve has to be redrawn. Such a **shift in** the **demand** curve will lead to a new equilibrium price and quantity. Indeed, ***the equilibrium price will change whenever the supply or demand curve shifts.***

We can illustrate how equilibrium prices change by taking one last look at the supply and demand curves that characterize the Clearview College typing market. Our original supply and demand curves, together with the resulting equilibrium (point *X*), are depicted in Figure 2.8. Now suppose that the professors at Clearview begin assigning additional papers and homework, all of which must be typed. The increased need (desire) for typing services will affect market demand. Tom, George, and Lisa (but not I) are suddenly willing to buy more typing at every price than they were willing to before. That is to say, the *demand* for typing has increased. We can represent this increased demand by a rightward shift of the market demand curve, as illustrated in Figure 2.8.

Note that the new demand curve intersects the (unchanged) market supply curve at a new price (point *Y*): the equilibrium price is now $3 per page. This new equilibrium price will persist until either the demand curve or the supply curve shifts again.

The kinds of price changes we are describing here are quite common. Indeed, equilibrium prices change as often as significant changes occur in the behavior of buyers or sellers. A few moments in a stockbroker's office or a glance through the stock pages of the daily newspaper should be testimony enough to the fluid character of market prices. If thousands of stockholders decide to sell IBM shares tomorrow, you can be sure that the market price of that stock will drop.

In any large market, of course, a change of outlook on the part of any single buyer or seller may have little effect on the market. Were I to sell my two shares of IBM stock, the market price could probably withstand the onslaught, since thousands of shares are exchanged every day. In a product market with many buyers and sellers, many people have to change their behavior at the same time and in the same way before market prices are affected. On the other hand, if there are only a few buyers or sellers, then the action of any one of them may have a significant impact on market prices and sales.

THE ACTION IN FACTOR MARKETS

Once the action in product markets is understood, the action in factor markets begins to look familiar. Indeed, the factor and product markets function in much the same way with the same participants; only the goods and services being exchanged differ. In the factor market, the things being exchanged are intended for use in production processes. Land, timber, machinery, oil, and labor are salient examples of basic resources, although we might also include steel, grains, coal, and other resources that are bought primarily for production purposes.

Because factor markets operate like product markets, the analysis of product markets can be duplicated to explain what's happening in factor markets. The largest factor market is the one for labor. Its behavior is discussed in Chapters 11–13.

POLICY IMPLICATIONS: LAISSEZ FAIRE

The action in the marketplace is intriguing in that so much can happen with no fixed program or direction. The flows of goods and services moving between consumers and businesses in our examples are completely determined by the independent choice made by each buyer or seller. The prices at which goods and services are exchanged are also determined by the interactions of many independent individuals. Moreover, the individual participants need not be familiar with the way the **market mechanism** works. They have only

market mechanism: The use of market prices and sales to signal desired outputs (or resource allocations).

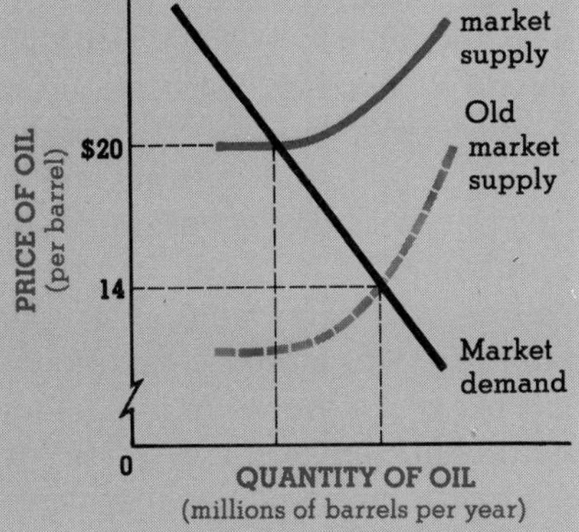

A SHIFT IN THE SUPPLY OF OIL

In 1979 the Organization of Petroleum Exporting Countries (OPEC) announced that it was no longer willing to sell oil for the existing price of approximately $14 per barrel. Henceforth, OPEC decreed, oil would be supplied to the market only at prices above $20 per barrel. This change in the willingness to sell implied a *shift* of the market supply curve, leading to higher prices and smaller sales. The impact of this shift on the world economy is discussed in Chapter 16 of *The Macro Economy Today*.

to follow their own inclinations, buying and selling resources or products as their own incomes and desires dictate.

The highly mechanical nature of the market mechanism has some advantages. First of all, all the participants in our markets can do their own thing and we will still see some sort of coherent action. That is to say, a distinct set of prices, a distinct volume and distribution of products, and a recognizable volume and distribution of resources will be generated by the forces of market supply and demand. In that sense, the market is able to resolve the basic questions of WHAT to produce, HOW to produce it, and FOR WHOM it should be produced with no guidance from external forces.

Not only is some distinct set of economic outcomes generated in the marketplace, but all participants in the market have been able to maximize their respective profits or satisfactions. This is not to say that Tom, George, Lisa, and the rest of the students in our imaginary typing market are in a constant state of euphoria as a result of their market activity. It does mean, though, that each person has got as much satisfaction or profit as is attainable from the resources he or she possesses. Tom and George, for example, would be happier if they had more income or if the price of typing were lower. Given small allowances and their inability to alter market prices, however, the buying and consuming choices they have made represent the best they can do under current conditions. In other words, this is an *optimum* situation. How do we know? Because Tom and George and everybody else in our little drama have had (and continue to have) absolute freedom to make their own purchase and consumption decisions. And also because we assume that sooner or later they will make the choices they find most satisfying.[7]

Accordingly, the market mechanism suggests a situation in which the economy can function and in which all individuals can achieve some satisfaction. What is especially noteworthy is that society's scarce resources end up being devoted to the production of goods and services in greatest demand. This demand is expressed by the *willingness* of market participants to pay for various goods. Moreover, the output gets distributed on the same basis. That is to say, FOR WHOM is determined by the amount of purchasing power each individual is willing and able to give up in order to acquire particular goods.

These features of the market mechanism can be translated readily into policy guidelines. In a word, these features suggest that individuals and the marketplace should be left alone to pursue their own interests. From this perspective, there is no need or justification for market intervention on the part of government or any other body. The price mechanism alone permits people and businesses to achieve the greatest amount of satisfaction possible; government intervention might only disrupt that outcome.

laissez faire: The doctrine of "leave it alone," of nonintervention by governments in the market mechanism.

This particular policy implication is the foundation of the **laissez faire** doctrine, the doctrine of "leave it alone." Since its development by Adam Smith in 1776, it has had a profound impact on the way the economy functions and what government does (or doesn't do). Laissez faire continues to be a major plank in what is

[7] The dynamics of individual choices are discussed in Chapters 4–11.

commonly regarded as the conservative platform of American politics.

One cannot dispute the mechanical precision with which the market mechanism works. Prices do in fact serve to allocate goods and factors of production in accordance with people's expressed market wishes. We can note, however, that the fulfillment of individual pursuits does not always create as much satisfaction as might be attainable. As we observed earlier (and will discuss further in Chapter 3), many public goods will not be produced in the absence of some collective, even coercive, effort. Yet nearly everyone obtains some satisfaction from public goods, be they national defense, highways, police officers and fire fighters, or the administration of justice. Hence, if everyone does his or her own thing exclusively, each individual and society as a whole may be getting less satisfaction from available resources than might otherwise be the case.[8]

Someone who has little income available with which to obtain goods or services may also be disenchanted with the doctrine of laissez faire. In a laissez faire world, the amount of food, shelter, and entertainment you can get is limited by the amount of income you possess. If you have little wealth or talent to begin with, you are not going to get much satisfaction or profit, no matter how cleverly you deploy your resources. On the other hand, if you inherited particularly good genes or fortunes, you are likely to reap a good deal of satisfaction and profit in the market. Hence those persons who possess more things to exchange ("dollar votes") are treated better in the market.[9]

Finally, those who possess significant control over productive resources are in a position to alter market outcomes in their own interest. If only one individual owns all the typewriters on campus, then the market supply of typing will be determined by that person's willingness to supply. It will not be determined by the interactions of a lot off independent producers. In such a case, the single producer is likely to tip the scale of profits and satisfaction in his favor.

The way the market treats various individuals and groups is the subject of many subsequent chapters. We shall also consider how various configurations of wealth and power may affect the way the economy works, the kinds of goods we produce, the resources we use, and the incomes we receive. Knowing how things work does not completely answer the question of how things *should* work. That will remain a question for individual and collective resolution.

SUMMARY

- Individual consumers, business firms, and government agencies participate in the marketplace by offering to buy or sell goods and services or factors of production. Participation is motivated by the

[8] The problem of *externalities*, noted in Chapter 1, is further explored in Chapters 3 and 16.

[9] This particular feature of market economies has been a prime consideration in the rejection by socialist economies (especially China and the Soviet Union) of the market mechanism in favor of centralized planning. The economics of planned economies are discussed in Chapter 21 of *The Macro Economy Today*.

desire to maximize utility (consumers), profits (business firms), or the general welfare (government agencies).

- All interactions in the marketplace involve the exchange of either factors of production or finished products among consumers, businesses, and government. Although the actual exchanges can take place anywhere, we may say that they take place in product markets or factor markets, depending on what is being exchanged.
- People who are willing and able to buy a particular good at some price become part of the market demand for that product. All those who are willing and able to sell that good at some price are part of the market supply. Total market demand or supply is the sum of individual demands or supplies.
- The quantity of goods and services or factors of production that is actually exchanged in each market will depend on the behavior of all buyers and sellers, as summarized in market supply and demand curves. At the point where the two curves intersect, an equilibrium price—the price at which the quantity demanded equals the quantity supplied—will be established.
- A distinctive feature of the equilibrium price and quantity is that it is the only price-quantity combination that is acceptable to buyers and sellers alike. At higher prices, sellers supply more than buyers are willing to purchase (a market surplus); at lower prices, the amount demanded exceeds the quantity supplied (a market shortage). Only the equilibrium price clears the market. At that price, everyone who is willing to buy may do so, and everyone who wants to sell at that price may do so.
- Should either market supply or demand change (shift), a new equilibrium price will be established. Supply and demand curves shift whenever the assumption of *ceteris paribus* (unchanged income, tastes, etc.) is violated.
- The market mechanism is a device for establishing prices and product and resource flows. As such, it may be used to answer the basic economic questions of WHAT to produce, HOW to produce it, and FOR WHOM. Whether or not these answers are accepted—and laissez faire prevails—will depend in part on our views of the underlying distribution of incomes ("dollar votes") and the prevalence of externalities.

Terms to remember

Define the following terms:

market
factor market
product market
supply
demand
opportunity cost
demand schedule
demand curve
ceteris paribus
market demand
market supply
equilibrium price
market surplus
market shortage
shift in demand
market mechanism
laissez faire

Questions for discussion

1. In our story of Tom, the nontypist confronted with a typing assignment, we emphasized the great urgency of his desire for typing services. Many people would say that Tom had an "absolute need" for typing, and was therefore ready to "pay anything" to get his paper typed. If this were true, what shape would his demand curve have? Why isn't this realistic?

2. If Tom were to type the paper himself, would his opportunity costs thereby be eliminated (and typing thus become a "free" good)?

3. How were the basic economic questions of WHAT to produce and FOR WHOM decided in the Clearview College typing market?

4. Word-processing machines make typing easier and improve the appearance of the final product as well. How have word processors altered the supply and demand for typing services?

5. Can you explain the practice of "scalping" tickets for major sporting events in terms of market shortages? How else might tickets be distributed?

Problem

Given the following data, (1) construct market supply and demand curves and identify the equilibrium price; and (2) identify the amount of shortage or surplus that would exist at a price of $4:

Participant	*Quantity demanded or supplied (price or per week)*				
A. Demand side	**$5**	**$4**	**$3**	**$2**	**$1**
Al	1	2	3	4	5
Betsy	0	1	1	1	2
Casey	2	2	3	3	4
Daisy	1	3	4	4	6
Eddie	1	2	2	3	5
Market total	—	—	—	—	—
B. Supply side					
Alice	3	3	3	3	3
Butch	7	5	4	4	2
Connie	6	4	3	3	1
Dutch	6	5	4	3	0
Ellen	4	2	2	2	1
Market total	—	—	—	—	—

CHAPTER 3

THE PUBLIC SECTOR

Not all goods and services produced in the economy pass through product markets, at least not in the conventional way. On the contrary, a vast array of goods and services is produced in the *public sector*, by federal, state, and local governments. These goods are not sold directly to consumers, but instead are paid for through taxes. Among such goods and services are national defense, public schools, highways, courts of law, fire fighters, and sanitation workers. The production of goods in the public sector accounts for nearly one-fifth of our total output.

In view of the public sector's substantial contribution to total output, we cannot begin to know how the U.S. economy answers the basic questions of WHAT to produce, HOW to produce it, and FOR WHOM to produce it until we examine the nature and dimensions of public-sector activity. The purposes of this chapter are, first, to describe the general dimensions of public-sector activity, then to determine why we rely on governments rather than on the market mechanism for so much production. As we shall see, much of what the government produces cannot be produced efficiently by the private sector.

FEDERAL EXPENDITURE

In fiscal year 1983 the federal government spent nearly $800 billion. We can begin to appreciate the dimensions of public-sector activity by looking at the ways in which all this revenue is spent.

The federal budget

fiscal year (FY): The twelve-month period used for government accounting purposes; begins October 1 and ends September 30.

A complete accounting of federal expenditures is contained in the federal budget. At the beginning of each year, the president, with the assistance of the Office of Management and Budget (OMB) and the many agencies of the federal government, prepares a statement of desired expenditures for the next **fiscal year,** which begins on October 1. The president then submits this budget to Congress for review and approval. After amending the proposed budget to its own liking, the Congress returns it to the president, with authorization to begin spending federal money. In February 1982, for example, President Reagan submitted his proposed fiscal year 1983 (FY 1983) budget to Congress. The Congress then reviewed his proposals, revised them, and ultimately gave the president permission (budget authorization) to spend nearly $800 billion in the fiscal year beginning October 1, 1982.

The complete budget of the U.S. government is a document over four inches thick and weighing nearly five pounds. A brief summary of its contents is provided in Table 3.1.

Expenditures on goods and services

Much of the federal budget is devoted to the purchase of goods and services. In FY 1983, for example, the federal government spent over $200 billion on national defense, nearly $20 billion on transporta-

TABLE 3.1 PROJECTED FEDERAL EXPENDITURES, FISCAL 1983 (billions of dollars)

The federal government spent nearly $800 billion in fiscal 1983. Half of this ($407 billion) was for goods and services. The rest represents transfers to individuals ($276 billion), general aid to state and local governments ($6.7 billion), and interest payments ($96 billion). All of these expenditures influence our collective answers to the questions of WHAT, HOW, and FOR WHOM to produce.

Expenditures		*Amount*
A. *Goods and services*		
National defense	$221.1	
Transportation	19.6	
Education, training, and social services	21.6	
Commerce and housing	1.6	
International affairs	12.0	
Science, space, and technology	7.6	
Energy	4.2	
Natural resources and environment	9.9	
Agriculture	4.5	
Community and regional development	7.3	
Administration of justice	4.6	
Health	78.1	
Veterans' services	10.0	
General government	5.0	
Total purchases of goods and services		$407.1
B. *Income transfers*		
Social security	$175.6	
Federal employees' retirement benefits	21.1	
Public assistance	42.5	
Unemployment insurance	22.6	
Veterans' benefits	14.4	
Total income transfers		$276.2
C. *General aid to state and local governments*		6.7
D. *Interest* (net)		96.4
E. *Total expenditures*		$786.4

Source: Fiscal 1983 estimates. Office of Management and Budget.

FIGURE 3.1 GOVERNMENT IN THE MARKETPLACE

The public sector is a major participant in both factor and product markets. Federal, state, and local governments hire labor, capital, and land in factor markets. They use these resources to produce goods and services for consumers (taxpayers).

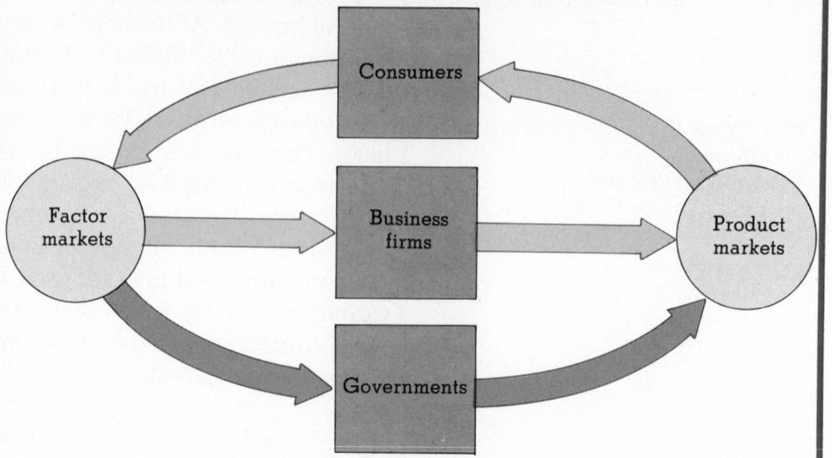

tion, and over $4 billion on the administration of justice (Table 3.1). In many cases—for example, the purchase of new weapons—these expenditures look just like any other purchases in product markets. In reality, however, the government itself typically *produces* the good or service in question. The judges and clerks who comprise the federal judicial system, for example, are employed by the U.S. government to "produce" $4.6 billion worth of "administration of justice." Similarly, the 2 million men and women who serve in the armed forces are employed to "produce" national defense. Although the federal government directly pays for such goods and services, the government's basic role is really to produce these outputs for the use of consumers.

The role of government as a producer of final products is emphasized in Figure 3.1 by the heavy arrows connecting the government and consumers to the product market. Even in those cases where the federal government appears to be buying a final product, such as a new weapons system, such **"intermediate goods"** are simply used to produce something else, such as "national defense." What consumers receive as a finished product is national security, not a new weapons system.

intermediate goods: Goods or services purchased for use as input in the production of final goods or services.

In order to produce all the goods summarized in Table 3.1, the federal government must have access to factors of production. These resources may be purchased directly in factor markets, as in the case of labor employed in the armed forces or the halls of justice. Or they may be purchased indirectly, as when the government pays a building contractor to build a highway or government building. In either case, ***expenditures of the federal government imply vast command over our available resources and thus our decisions on* WHAT *to produce and* HOW *to produce it.*** An indication of how many of our resources the public sector commands is provided in Table 3.2. The resource shown here is labor. What we see is that the public sector *directly* employs one out of every six workers and indirectly hires another 8 million. These workers are not available, therefore, for the production of private goods.

Income transfers

income transfers: Payments to individuals for which no current goods or services are exchanged; for example, social security, welfare, and unemployment benefits.

Although the federal government is the single largest participant in U.S. product and factor markets, expenditures on goods and services account for only half of the federal budget. A large fraction of the budget represents **income transfers** to individuals. Transfers are income payments for which no current services or goods are exchanged.

The most familiar income transfers (and the second largest single item in the U.S. budget) are social security benefits. More than 36 million Americans receive social security checks every month. Most of these individuals are retired; others are either disabled or the children of workers who died before retirement. As Table 3.1 indicates, over $175 billion was spent on social security benefits in fiscal 1983.

Individuals are eligible for social security retirement benefits after reaching a certain age (62 or 65) and having worked a minimum number of years. The benefits themselves are paid for by taxes imposed on those who are still working. Thus social security retirement benefits transfer income from those who are currently working to those who are retired. By altering the distribution of income in this way, ***income transfers help determine* FOR WHOM *our output is produced.*** In this case, the income transfers help to ensure that retired individuals will continue to receive some of our current output.

Welfare benefits and unemployment insurance benefits also alter the distribution of income (and output). In the case of welfare benefits, income is transferred to those who are poor in order to enable them to purchase a greater quantity of goods and services.[1] Unemployment benefits serve the same income-transfer purpose but are distributed to those who are unable to find work, regardless of their other income or wealth. In all of these cases, the income transfers are not paid in return for any current product or service. Rather, they represent an explicit attempt to alter the distribution of income, and hence of access to goods and services.

State-local aid

The third expenditure category depicted in Table 3.1 is "General aid to state and local governments," an expenditure that totaled $6.7 billion in 1983. But this figure is a gross understatement of actual aid

[1] The welfare system is examined in detail in Chapter 17.

TABLE 3.2 EMPLOYMENT RESULTING FROM GOVERNMENT PURCHASES, 1980
(in millions of persons)

The public sector directly employs nearly one out of every six workers. The jobs of another 8 million people are directly dependent on government purchases. State and local governments account for most of this employment.

Government	*Direct employees*	*Indirect employees (in private sector)*	*Total*
Federal	**4.2**	**3.5**	**7.7**
State and local	**12.1**	**4.5**	**16.6**
Total	**16.3**	**8.0**	**24.3**

Source: *Employment and Training Report of the President,* 1981.

categorical grants: Federal grants to state and local governments for specific expenditure purposes.

because one-fifth of federal expenditures for goods and services are made through state and local governments. For example, Table 3.1 indicates that the federal government spent nearly $10 billion on natural resources and environment. But one-fifth of this amount was simply given to local communities for the construction of sewage treatment plants. The local governments actually purchased or built the sewage plants; the federal government only provided the necessary revenue. Accordingly, control over WHAT to produce was maintained by the federal government, but local governments exercised some judgment on HOW to produce it.

This "strings-attached" nature of most federal aid is the distinguishing feature of **categorical grants.** Funds bestowed on state and local governments in the form of categorical grants have to be used for specific purposes. If a city government needs street lighting but federal grants are available only for sewage treatment or job training, the city must choose between one of the latter or do without federal aid. Categorical grants cannot be shifted from one use to another.

In fiscal 1983 the federal government gave over $80 billion to state and local governments in the form of categorical grants (including those for welfare benefits, Medicaid, schools, and highways). These intergovernmental transfers appear in the federal budget (Table 3.1) as expenditures on the specific items Congress instructed state and local governments to buy.

The $6.7 billion that does appear in the FY 1983 federal budget as "general aid to state and local governments" represents a different kind of federal assistance. Since 1972, some federal aid to state and

How U.S. aid pie gets divvied up

A new report on federal aid to state and local governments discloses some prime targets for President Reagan's program to reduce government spending.

The study shows the distribution, state by state, of some 90.1 billion in Washington's tax dollars for job-training plans, urban and community-development grants, highway construction, child-nutrition programs, medicaid and other purposes in 1980.

For an idea of just how heavily state and local governments rely on federal aid—

	Per Capita Aid
Alaska	$1,114
Vermont	690
South Dakota	634
Wyoming	620
Montana	609
New York	539
North Dakota	524
New Mexico	507
Rhode Island	500
Massachusetts	498
West Virginia	481
Hawaii	474
Oregon	464
Maine	461
Mississippi	459
Delaware	459
Maryland	433
Georgia	430
Wisconsin	427
Michigan	420
Nevada	413
Idaho	410
Arkansas	408
Minnesota	406
Alabama	402
Washington	400
U.S. AVERAGE	**398**
Kentucky	398
Illinois	388
Utah	386
New Jersey	379
Pennsylvania	375
New Hampshire	375
Connecticut	369
California	367
Louisiana	367
Tennessee	366
Oklahoma	347
Nebraska	346
Kansas	343
Missouri	342
South Carolina	339
Colorado	339
Iowa	337
Virginia	329
North Carolina	325
Ohio	316
Arizona	302
Indiana	290
Florida	289
Texas	274

revenue sharing: Federal aid to state and local governments without stringent restrictions on its use.

local governments has been given with few or no strings attached.[2] Such **revenue sharing** is typically given for a very broadly stated purpose ("block grants" or "special revenue sharing") or for no stated expenditure purpose at all ("general revenue sharing"). In either case, state and local governments not only get to dip into the federal treasury but acquire some independent influence on the mix of output, that is, the issue of WHAT to produce. The recipients of general revenue sharing include all 50 states and more than 38,000 cities, counties, towns, townships, Indian tribes, and Alaskan native villages.

In 1982 President Reagan proposed a further departure from categorical grants. His "New Federalism" would turn over revenue *sources* to the states, not just a share of collected revenues. In the process, the states would acquire more direct control over the level and contents of their budgets.

Interest

interest: payments made for the use of borrowed money.

The last major expenditure category in the federal budget consists of **interest** payments. Federal expenditures usually exceed federal revenues. As a consequence, the U.S. government must borrow money to finance its purchases. Like all borrowers, the U.S. government pays interest on its debts. At the beginning of 1983 the total debt of the U.S. government was over $1 trillion, requiring interest payments of over $96 billion in fiscal 1983.[3]

STATE AND LOCAL EXPENDITURE

Although the federal government exercises substantial influence over the basic issues of WHAT to produce, HOW to produce it, and FOR WHOM, state and local governments also have a role to play. There are 80,171 government units in the United States, most of them at the state and local levels. To some extent, the power of state and local governments to alter the mix of output or distribution of income is easily overlooked. The fragmented nature of such decision making makes the size of individual state and local expenditures relatively small. City, school-district, and township budgets are calibrated in millions of dollars, not billions; even state budgets rarely exceed the billion-dollar level by any significant amount. By contrast, the federal budget is measured in hundreds of billions of dollars. From this perspective, public power at the national level appears to dwarf power at state and local levels.

The forest, in this case, is definitely obscured by the trees. When the fiscal activities of the 50 states, 3,000 counties, 18,000 cities, 17,000 townships, 21,000 school districts, and 21,000 special dis-

[2] Once before, in 1837, the federal budget surplus was so large that $28 million was distributed to the states, with no restrictions attached. But this no-strings-attached bonanza came to a halt when the depression of 1838 wiped out the federal surplus. The State and Local Fiscal Assistance Act of 1972 made "revenue sharing" a more permanent feature of the government budget.

[3] The public debt and its impact on the economy are discussed further in Chapter 9 of *The Macro Economy Today.*

FIGURE 3.2 DIRECT PUBLIC PURCHASES OF GOODS AND SERVICES

The government share of total expenditures in the economy has been relatively constant since World War II (at 20 percent). Within the public sector, state and local governments have acquired increasing control over the decisions of WHAT, HOW, and FOR WHOM to produce. By contrast, the federal share of total expenditures on goods and services has actually declined.

Source: U.S. Census Bureau; Office of Management and Budget.

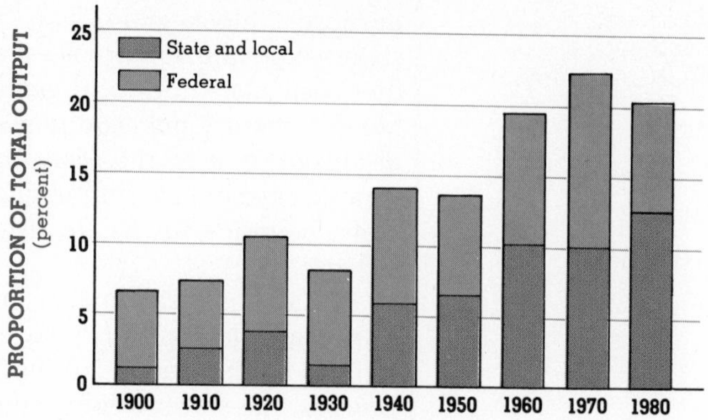

tricts are combined, a very different perspective on state and local power is achieved. ***In terms of direct purchases of goods and services, state and local outlays exceed federal outlays.*** State and local governments also employ far more people than does the federal government (Table 3.2). This phenomenon should not come as a great surprise—after all, you see a traffic cop or state college professor more often than you see a census taker or Washington bureaucrat.

The aggregate size of state and local budgets and employment rolls is sufficient introduction to the potential of these government units to influence WHAT is produced, HOW it is produced, and FOR WHOM. As Figure 3.2 illustrates, this state and local influence is growing, whereas the share of the federal government in total output has fallen since 1960. If the "New Federalism" results in more state and local autonomy, these trends will accelerate.

How the money is spent

opportunity cost: The most desired goods or services that are forgone in order to obtain something else.

In the light of so much state and local spending—so much influence on output, employment, prices, and the distribution of income—it seems reasonable to ask what we are getting from all this expenditure. **Opportunity costs** are involved here. The resources now commanded by state and local governments could be put at the disposal of the federal government or even at the disposal of the private sector (us taxpayers). Our collective answers to the questions of WHAT, HOW, and FOR WHOM would surely be changed in either case. What kinds of goods and services are purchased or provided by state and local governments?

Table 3.3. provides an overview of the content of state and local expenditure. Education accounts for 40 percent of state and local budgets. State governments tend to split their school expenditures between higher education (state colleges and universities) and state aid to local school systems. For their part, local governments focus nearly all education expenditures on elementary and secondary school systems. States devote other large portions of their resources to highways and welfare programs. At the local level, noneducation expenditures tend to be concentrated on police protection, health services, fire protection, and streets.

TABLE 3.3 STATE AND LOCAL EXPENDITURES, FISCAL 1980

Most direct state expenditures (excluding transfers to local governments) are for education, welfare programs, and highways. Local governments also spend more on education than anything else.

Expenditures	*State governments (in millions)*	*Percent*	*Local governments (in millions)*	*Percent*
Education	$35,251	25.3	$97,960	44.6
Highways	20,661	14.1	12,650	5.6
Public welfare	33,242	23.0	12,310	5.5
Health and hospitals	15,666	10.9	16,507	7.0
Natural resources	4,124	2.8	1,385	0.6
Housing and urban renewal	331	0.2	5,731	2.5
Airports	360	0.2	2,141	0.9
Social insurance	2,001	1.3	7	—
Interest	6,763	4.7	7,984	3.5
Police, courts, prisons	6,272	4.3	13,668	6.0
Fire protection	—	—	5,718	2.5
Sanitation and sewage	—	—	12,880	5.8
Other	19,047	13.2	34,680	15.5
Total	$143,718	100.0	$223,621	100.0

Source: U.S. Department of Commerce.

TAXATION

Whatever we may think of any specific government expenditure, we must recognize one basic fact of life: we pay for government spending. In real terms, the cost of government spending can be measured by the private goods and services that are forsaken when the public sector takes command over factors of production. Factors of production used to produce national defense or schools cannot be used at the same time to produce private goods or services.

The opportunity costs of public spending are not always apparent, as we don't directly hand over our factors of production to the government. Instead, we give the government part of our income in the form of taxes. Those dollars are then used to buy factors of production or goods and services in the marketplace. Thus ***the primary function of taxes is to transfer command over resources (purchasing power) from the private sector to the public sector.*** When we pay taxes, we give the public sector increased control over WHAT to produce, HOW, and FOR WHOM.

Federal taxes

As recently as 1902, much of the revenue collected by the federal government came from taxes imposed on alcoholic beverages. The federal government did not have authority to collect income taxes. As a consequence, *total* federal revenue in 1902 was only $653 million.

INCOME TAXES All of that has changed. The Sixteenth Amendment to the U.S. Constitution, enacted in 1913, granted the federal government authority to collect income taxes. The government now collects over $300 *billion* in that form alone. In fact, although the federal government still collects taxes on alcoholic beverages, the

TABLE 3.4 FEDERAL REVENUES, FISCAL 1983
(in billions of dollars)

Taxes transfer purchasing power from the private sector to the public sector. The largest federal tax is the individual income tax. The second largest source of federal revenue is the social security tax.

Source	*Amount*
Individual income taxes	$304.5
Social security taxes	222.5
Corporate income taxes	65.3
Excise taxes	41.7
Other	32.1
Total	$666.1

Source: Office of Management and Budget estimates.

progressive tax: A tax system in which tax rates rise as incomes rise.

individual income tax has become the largest single source of government revenue (see Table 3.4).

In theory, the federal income tax is designed to be **progressive**, that is, to take a larger *fraction* of high incomes than of low incomes. In 1982, for example, tax rates imposed on single taxpayers ranged from as little as 14 percent of incomes of under $3,000 to 50 percent on incomes in excess of $100,000. Thus an individual with a very high income not only was supposed to pay more dollars in taxes, but was also expected to pay a larger *fraction* of his or her income in taxes.[4]

The progressive nature of the federal income tax is designed to distribute the tax burden on the basis of *ability to pay*. It has had another and largely unintended effect, however. During periods of inflation, all incomes tend to rise. As they do, people are pushed into higher tax brackets and end up paying higher tax rates. In the proc-

[4] In reality, however, the federal income tax is not nearly so progressive as it appears, because the tax laws include myriad provisions that permit individuals to "shelter" income that otherwise would be taxed at very high rates. The federal income tax system is discussed further in Chapter 15.

"I can't find anything wrong here, Mr. Truffle . . . you just seem to have too much left after taxes."

GRIN AND BEAR IT by George Lichty. © Field Enterprises, Inc., 1978. Courtesy of Field Newspaper Syndicate.

bracket creep: The movement of taxpayers into higher tax brackets (rates) as nominal incomes grow.

ess, the federal government gets an increasing share of total income. This phenomenon, often referred to as **bracket creep,** was partly overcome by the Economic Recovery Act of 1981. That act indexed tax *rates* to inflation, beginning in 1985. Thereafter, federal income tax rates will be adjusted downward when inflation pushes incomes up. This will prevent the federal government from automatically increasing its share of total output when prices and incomes rise.

SOCIAL SECURITY TAXES The second major source of federal revenue is the social security tax. As we noted earlier, people now working transfer part of their earnings to retired workers by making "contributions" to social security. There is nothing voluntary about these "contributions," however, because they take the form of mandatory payroll deductions.[5] In FY 1983 each worker paid 6.7 percent of his or her wages to social security and employers contributed an equal amount.[6] As a consequence, the government collected over $220 billion.

CORPORATE TAXES The federal government taxes the profits of corporations as well as the incomes of consumers. But there are far fewer corporations than consumers and their profits are small in comparison to total consumer income. In fiscal 1983, the federal government collected less than $70 billion in corporation income taxes, despite the fact that it imposed a tax rate of 46 percent on corporate profits.

EXCISE TAXES The last major source of federal revenue is excise taxes. Like the early taxes on whiskey, excise taxes are sales taxes imposed on specific goods and services. The federal government taxes not only alcoholic beverages ($10.50 per gallon) but also gasoline ($0.04 per gallon), cigarettes ($4.00 per thousand), telephone service (1 percent), and a variety of other goods and services. Such taxes not only discourage production and consumption of these goods—by raising their price, and thereby reducing the quantity demanded—but also raise a substantial amount of revenue.

State and local revenues

State and local governments also levy taxes on consumers and businesses. In general, cities and other local units of government depend heavily on property taxes—taxes levied on the value of homes and other real property. State governments, on the other hand, rely heavily on sales taxes (see Figure 3.3). Although nearly all states and many cities also impose income taxes, effective tax rates are so low (averaging less than 2 percent of personal income) that income tax revenues are much less than sales and property tax revenues.

regressive tax: A tax system in which tax rates fall as incomes rise.

One feature of state and local tax structures is important to note. State and local taxes tend to be **regressive;** that is, they take a larger share of income from the poor than from the rich. Consider a 4-percent sales tax, for example. It might appear that a uniform tax rate

[5] Not all workers participate in social security; government employees, for example, may instead choose a separate public retirement system.

[6] This tax rate is imposed on the first $32,400 of income; both the tax rate and the income ceiling increase each year.

FIGURE 3.3 STATE AND LOCAL TAX SOURCES

State governments get half of their tax revenue from sales taxes. By contrast, local governments depend heavily on property taxes.

Source: U.S. Department of Commerce.

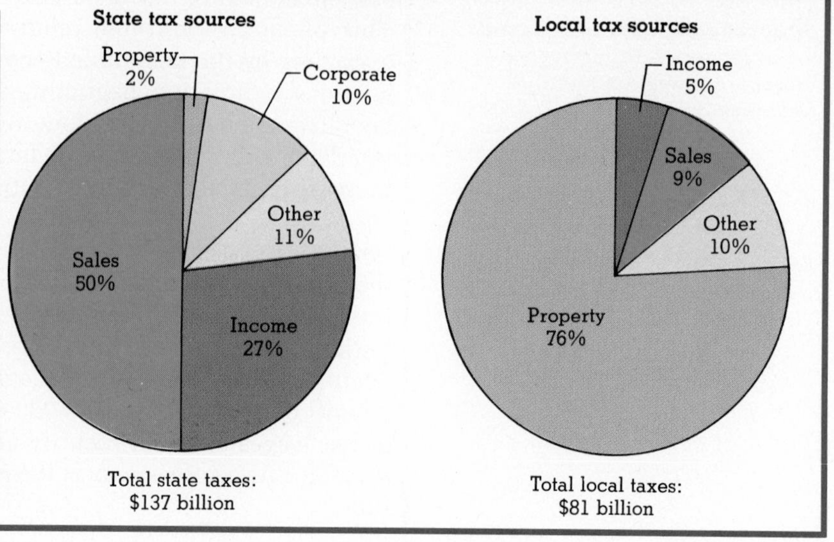

like this would affect all consumers equally. But this is not the way it works. People with lower incomes tend to spend most of their income on goods and services. Thus most of their income is subject to sales taxes. By contrast, a person with a high income can afford to save part of his or her income and thereby shelter it from sales taxes. A family that earns $20,000 and spends $15,000 of it on taxable goods and services, for example, pays $600 in sales taxes when the tax rate is 4 percent. In effect, then, they are handing over 3 percent of their *income* ($600 ÷ $20,000) to the state. By contrast, the family that makes only $6,000 and spends $5,800 of it for food, clothing, and shelter pays $232 in sales taxes in the same state. Their total tax is smaller, but it represents a much larger *share* (3.9 versus 3.0 percent) of their income.

Local property taxes exhibit the same feature. They are regressive, because poorer people devote a larger portion of their incomes to housing costs. Property taxes directly affect housing costs. Hence a larger share of a poor family's income is subject to property taxes. According to the Advisory Council on Intergovernmental Relations, a family earning $50,000 a year devotes only 2.5 percent of its income to property taxes, whereas a family earning $5,000 pays out 4.6 percent of its income in property taxes.[7]

FEDERAL AID State and local governments also get substantial revenue from nontax sources. The federal role in distributing money to state and local governments has already been noted. In 1983 federal grants and revenue sharing provided over one-fifth of all state and local revenues. But federal aid is slowing. In fact, federal grants to state and local governments have begun to decline, reversing an upward trend of many decades. The New Federalism, to be discussed in a moment, would reduce federal grants still further.

[7] State lotteries are also regressive, since lower-income people spend a higher fraction of their income on lottery tickets. Fifteen states use lotteries to raise revenues.

user charge: Fee paid for the use of a public-sector good or service.

USER CHARGES The third major source of state and local revenues consists of **user charges.** The tuition that college students (or their parents) pay for attending a state university or community college is a familiar user charge, and generates billions of dollars in state and local revenues. But tuition fees never cover the full costs of maintaining public colleges. Part of the costs of providing higher education are borne by all state taxpayers, whether or not they attend college. Public hospitals and highways are financed in the same way, with users paying part of the costs directly and all taxpayers paying the remaining costs through state and local taxes. Hence user charges are not identical to market prices, because they are not intended to cover the full costs of supplying a particular good.

FUNCTIONS OF THE PUBLIC SECTOR

In view of the large share of our income we give to federal, state, and local governments, we have the right to ask what purposes are served by such a large public sector. The high opportunity cost attached to all this public activity should be evident to taxpayers, in the form of the income (and implied access to goods and services) given up to finance public expenditures. Do we need such a large public sector? Can't the private sector produce the same goods and services, maybe even at less cost? What economic functions does the public sector fulfill?

Public goods

market mechanism: The use of market prices and sales to signal desired outputs (or resource allocations).

In Chapter 2 we emphasized the unique capability of the **market mechanism** to signal consumer demands for various goods and services. By offering to pay higher prices for some goods, we express our collective answer to the question of WHAT to produce. However, the market mechanism works efficiently only if the benefits of consuming a particular good or service are available only to the individuals who purchase that product.

Consider doughnuts, for example. When you eat a doughnut, you get the satisfaction from its taste and your fuller stomach, that is, you derive a private benefit. No one else reaps any significant benefit from your consumption of a doughnut: the doughnut you purchase in the market is yours alone to consume. Accordingly, your decision to purchase the doughnut will be determined by your anticipated satisfaction as well as your income and opportunity costs.

Most of the goods and services produced in the public sector are different from doughnuts—and not just because doughnuts look, taste, and smell different from nuclear submarines. When you buy a doughnut, you effectively exclude others from consumption of that product. If Dunkin' Donuts sells a particular pastry to you, it cannot supply the same pastry to someone else. If you devour it, no one else can. In this sense, the transaction and product are completely private.

The same exclusiveness is not characteristic of national defense. If you buy a nuclear submarine to patrol the Pacific Ocean, there is no way you can exclude your neighbors from the protection your submarine provides. Either the submarine deters would-be attackers or it doesn't. In the former case, both you and your neighbors survive happily ever after; in the latter case, we are all blown away together. In that sense, you and your neighbors either consume or don't consume the benefits of nuclear submarine defenses *jointly*. There is no such thing as exclusive consumption here. The consumption of nuclear defenses is a communal feat, no matter who pays for them. Accordingly, national defense is regarded as a **public good** or product, in the sense that consumption by one person does not preclude consumption of the same good by another person. By contrast, a doughnut is a private good, because once I eat it, nobody else can have it.

public good: A good or service whose consumption by one person does not exclude consumption by others.

THE FREE-RIDER DILEMMA The "communal" nature of public goods leads to a real dilemma. If you and I will *both* benefit from nuclear defenses, which one of us should buy the nuclear submarine? I would prefer, of course, that *you* buy it, thereby providing me with protection at no direct cost. Hence I may profess no desire for nuclear submarines, secretly hoping to take a **"free ride"** on your market purchase. Unfortunately, you, too, have an incentive to conceal your desire for national defenses, and neither one of us may step forward to demand nuclear submarines in the marketplace. As a consequence, we will both be defenseless.

free rider: An individual who reaps direct benefits from someone else's purchase (consumption) of a public good.

Police and fire protection also exhibit this free-rider phenomenon. If your neighbors pay for improved police and fire services, you will benefit from their purchases even if you don't contribute a penny. Would-be burglars are apt to be deterred from both your house and your neighbors' houses by the presence of more police on the street. By the same token, your house is in less danger of fire if your neighbor's house is protected. In both these cases, your neighbors are unable to confine all the benefits of their expenditure to themselves. Consumption of these goods is nonexclusive—that is, public. Even streets and highways have the characteristics of public goods. Although we could theoretically restrict the use of streets and highways to those who paid for them, a toll gate on every corner would be exceedingly expensive and impractical. Here again joint or public consumption appears to be the only feasible alternative.

To the list of public goods we could add the administration of justice, the regulation of commerce, and the conduct of foreign relations. These services—which cost tens of *billions* of dollars and employ thousands of workers—provide benefits to everyone, no matter who pays for them.

The free riders associated with public goods upset the customary practice of paying for what you get. If I can get all the highways, defenses, and laws I desire without paying for them, I am not about to complain. I am perfectly happy to let you pay for the services while all of us consume them. Of course, you may feel the same way. Why should you pay for these services if you can consume just as much of them when your neighbors foot the whole bill? It might be regarded as selfish or unseemly not to pay your share of the cost of providing public goods, but you would be better off in a material sense if you spent your income on doughnuts, letting others pick up the tab for public services.

Because the familiar link between paying and consuming is broken, public goods cannot be peddled in the supermarket. People are reluctant to buy what they can get free, a perfectly rational response for a consumer who has limited income to spend. Hence, if public goods were marketed like private goods, everyone would wait for someone else to pay. The end result might be a total lack of public services. Accordingly, we cannot rely on the market mechanism to allocate resources to the production of such goods, no matter how much they might be desired.

The failure of the market mechanism to signal the desire for public goods necessitates some form of nonmarket payment mechanism. Passing the hat would be one way, but a highly unstable means of support, as most churches and charities will attest. Compulsory taxation elicits a more dependable response and is the more traditional means of payment. Recognizing that everyone benefits from public services, we require everyone to help pay the bill.

WHAT to produce

The nonmarketability of public goods not only requires the presence of governments but complicates production decisions as well. Our basic economic problem is to allocate resources to their most desired uses. But now there is no obvious way to decide WHAT to produce. Consumers do not have the opportunity to buy public goods directly. As a result, they cannot reveal their preferences in the same way that they do for private goods, through the mechanism of market demand.

In addition to deciding *whether* to produce specific public goods, we must also decide how much of any public good to produce. Dunkin' Donuts and other private producers choose the level of output that maximizes profits. A clear and concise set of decision-making rules is available for them. But what about government? If public goods can't be peddled in the supermarket, then they don't have any market price. Hence output levels cannot be determined by market sales. Instead, decisions on what to produce in the public sector must be guided by objectives and rules other than those that apply to private producers. What are the relevant guidelines and how are they expressed?

BALLOT-BOX ECONOMICS The traditional method for communicating consumption desires for public goods is through the ballot box. If you are concerned about the size of the military establishment or upset about the conduct of foreign relations, you have the option of expressing your feelings by electing different public officials. You could also demonstrate in the streets, withhold taxes, or mobilize others to some form of protest or affirmative action, but these forms of expression can land you in jail. As a consequence, public investment and production decisions are likely to be influenced by voting patterns. Some people have even suggested that the variety and volume of public goods are determined by the most votes, just as the variety and volume of private goods are determined by the most dollars. Thus governments choose that level and mix of output (and related taxation) that seem to command the most votes.[8]

Sometimes the link between the ballot box and output decisions is very clear and direct. State and local governments, for example, are often compelled to get voter approval before building another highway, school, housing project, or sewage plant. *Bond referendums* are direct requests by a government unit for the authority and purchasing power to expand the production of particular public goods. In 1980, for example, governments sought voter approval for $2.9 billion of new borrowing to finance public expenditure. Eighty percent of those requests were approved.

Although the direct link between bond referenda and spending decisions is important, it is more the exception than the rule. Bond referenda account for less than 1 percent of state and local expenditures. As a consequence, voter control of public spending is much less direct. Although federal agencies must get authorization from Congress for all expenditures, consumers get a chance to elect new congressmen only every two years. Much the same is true at state and local levels. Hence voters are in the position of dictating the general level and pattern of public expenditures but have little direct influence on everyday output decisions. In this sense, the ballot box is a poor substitute for the market mechanism.

Even if the link between the ballot box and allocation decisions were stronger, the resulting mix of output might not be optimal. A "democratic" vote, for example, might yield a 51 percent majority for approval of new local highways. Should the highways then be built? The answer is not obvious. After all, a large minority (49 percent) of the voters have stated that they don't want resources used in this way. If we proceed to build the highways, we will make those

[8] In the absence of unanimity, this means that some people will end up paying for public goods and services they do not want. The majority will thus benefit at the expense of the minority, a familiar consequence of democratic rule. Is there any other way to share the costs of public goods and services?

BALLOT-BOX ECONOMICS: A SAMPLING OF 1980 BOND REFERENDA

- **Arizona: Phoenix-area residents approved $30 million to build new flood-resistant highway bridges.**
- **California: Voters approved $285 million for the expansion of state and local parks.**
- **Maine: Voters said no to funds for improved court facilities but agreed to spend $7 million for energy conservation and school buildings.**
- **New Jersey: Voters approved $350 million to improve the state's water supply.**
- **New York: Voters approved $500 million for new prisons.**
- **Rhode Island: Voters approved $88 million for sewage treatment facilities.**
- **Texas: Voters rejected a plan to set aside surplus tax revenues for water projects.**
- **West Virginia: Voters rejected a request for $750 million to improve state highways.**

people worse off. Even the voters who voted *for* the highways may end up worse off, depending on how the benefits and costs of the highway are distributed and what other opportunities exist. The basic dilemma is really twofold. We do not know what the real demand for public goods is, and votes alone do not reflect the intensity of individual demands. Moreover, real-world decision making involves so many choices that a stable consensus is impossible.

BENEFIT-COST ECONOMICS It is sometimes suggested that benefit-cost analysis provides a way out of this public-choice dilemma. The principles of benefit-cost analysis are straightforward. A public project is desirable only to the extent that it promises to yield some benefits (or utility). But all public projects involve some costs. Hence a project should be pursued only if it can deliver a satisfactory *ratio* of benefits to costs. Otherwise we would not be making very good use of our limited resources. In general, we would want to pursue those projects with the highest benefit-cost ratio. They will maximize the amount of utility we get from the resources we devote to the public sector.

Although the principles of benefit-cost analysis are simple enough, they are deceptive. How are we to measure the potential benefits of improved police services, for example? Do we simply estimate the number of robberies and murders prevented, calculate the worth of each, and add up the benefits? And how are we supposed to calculate the worth of a saved life? By a person's earnings? value of assets? number of friends? And what about the increased sense of security people have when they know the police are patrolling in their neighborhood? Should this be included in the benefit calculation? Some people will attach great value to this service; others will attach little. Whose values should we use?

When we are dealing with (private) market goods and services, we can gauge the benefits of production by the amount of money consumers are willing to pay for some particular output. In the case of public goods, however, we must make crude and highly subjective guesstimates of the benefits yielded by a particular output. Accordingly, benefit-cost analyses are valuable only to the extent that they are based on broadly accepted perceptions of benefits (or costs). In those cases, however, voting systems work well, too. In practice, consensus on the value of benefits is hard to reach, and benefit-cost calculations are subject to great controversy.[9]

Externalities

Although the free-rider phenomenon explains most public-sector activity, it does not explain all government expenditure. The government also regulates much private-sector production and consumption, particularly as they relate to the environment. The Environmental Protection Agency, for example, sets "clean air" and "clean water" standards that force private consumers and producers to limit their pollution. How is such governmental regulation to be explained?

[9] The *Study Guide* accompanying this text contains a detailed application of benefit-cost economics.

externalities: Costs (or benefits) of a market activity borne by a third party; the difference between the social and private costs (benefits) of a market activity.

The explanation for many governmental restrictions on HOW to produce lies in the phenomenon of **externalities.** Externalities are the costs or benefits of a market activity borne by a third party, that is, someone other than the immediate producer or consumer. When you go for a drive in your car, for example, you pollute the air with your car's emissions. All of the people who breathe that air are harmed by your consumption. In this respect, they suffer indirect, or "spillover," costs from your market activity.

Externalities represent a "market failure" in the sense that they are not reflected in market prices. When you drive your car, you pay only for gasoline and car maintenance; you do not pay for the health damage inflicted on others by the noise and pollutants your car emits. In this sense, the market mechanism fails to signal the true costs of driving. Specifically, the market price of driving understates its social cost, and you end up driving too much (the lower the price, the greater the quantity demanded). Moreover, the third parties who suffer from your pollution have no means of collecting medical costs from you.

To redress this inequity, the government must intervene in the marketplace and limit either your driving or the kind of car you drive. As a result, the government has established a regulatory bureaucracy (Environmental Protection Agency) to set and enforce pollution standards.[10] This kind of government regulation also occurs in medicine (Food and Drug Administration), job safety (Occupational Safety and Health Administration), air travel safety (Federal Aviation Administration), and auto liability insurance (state insurance commissions).

Externalities may also be beneficial. Education, for example, enriches not only the individual who goes to school but also the student's community. Basic literacy assures a better-informed electorate and a more viable democracy. Higher education often stimulates scientific and humanitarian discoveries that improve the well-being of millions of people. Educators also like to think that educated people make better neighbors! In these respects, the *social* benefits of education generally exceed the *private* benefits reaped by those who attend school: education generates beneficial externalities.

Goods and services that exhibit substantial external benefits fit our definition of *public goods.* A public good is one whose benefits cannot be captured by the purchaser(s) alone; all benefit if one benefits. Hence public goods, by definition, yield externalities.

FOR WHOM to produce

Although the free-rider phenomenon and externalities explain most public-sector production and regulatory activity, they do not explain all government expenditure. Government budgets are used to alter the market's answers to the questions not only of WHAT to produce and HOW, but also FOR WHOM. The power to alter the distribution of goods and services lies in the income-redistribution activities of governments. As we observed in Tables 3.1 and 3.3, government

[10] The mechanisms used to control pollution are discussed at length in Chapter 16.

budgets include substantial *income transfers.* On what grounds can these transfers be justified?

In our discussion of the market mechanism (Chapter 2), we observed that the market distributes goods and services according to people's *ability and willingness to pay.* But our ability to pay depends on the amount of income we have to spend. As a consequence, the market mechanism tends to answer the basic question of FOR WHOM to produce by distributing a larger share of total output to those with the most income. Although this result may be efficient, it is not necessarily equitable. Individuals who are aged or disabled, for example, may be unable to earn much income, yet still are regarded as "worthy" recipients of goods and services. In such cases, we use income transfers as a mechanism for altering the distribution of income and thus changing the market's answer to the basic question of FOR WHOM goods are produced.

To some extent, public income-redistribution efforts can also be explained by the theory of public goods. If the public sector did not provide help to the aged, the disabled, the unemployed, and the needy, what would they do? Some might find a little extra work, but many would starve, even die. Others would resort to private solicitations or criminal activities to fend off hunger or death. This would mean more beggars and muggers on the streets. In nearly all cases, the general public would be beset with much of the burden and consequences of poverty and disability, either directly or through pangs of conscience. Because the sight or knowledge of hungry or sick neighbors is something most people seek to avoid, the elimination of poverty creates some satisfaction for a great many people.

But even if the elimination of poverty were a common objective, it could be accomplished by individual action. If I contributed heavily to the needy, then you and I would both be relieved of the burden of the poor. We could both walk the streets with less fear and better consciences. Hence you could benefit from my expenditure, just as was possible in the case of national defense. In this sense, the relief of misery is a *public* good. Were I the only taxpayer to benefit substantially from the reduction of poverty, then charity would be a private affair. As long as income support substantially benefits the public at large, then income redistribution is a *public good,* for which public funding is appropriate. There is therefore an *economic* rationale for public income-redistribution activities. To this rationale one can add such moral arguments as seem appropriate.[11]

Stabilization

Another major function of public-sector expenditure is to stabilize the economy. The federal government, in particular, attempts to stabilize the total volume of spending in the economy at a level that is consistent with our production possibilities. That is to say, the federal government uses its vast tax and expenditure powers to help

[11] Current income-redistribution efforts do not benefit the poor alone. The middle class receives a large share of income transfers, particularly from social security. Further discussion of income-redistribution policies is contained in Chapters 15 and 17.

keep the economy producing at some point on its production-possibilities curve. The mechanisms used for this purpose and their impact on the U.S. economy are the subject of Chapters 7–13 of *The Macro Economy Today*.

POLICY IMPLICATIONS: TAXPAYER REVOLT

If we think only of the goals of public goods, externalities, and income redistribution, or of the need for economic stabilization, nearly all public-sector activity appears to be justified. Yet in recent years taxpayers have expressed increasing reluctance to support public-sector activity. The hallmark of the "taxpayer revolt" was California's Proposition 13, which was overwhelmingly accepted by California voters in June 1978. Proposition 13 forced local governments in California to reduce property taxes by an average of nearly 60 percent. In 1980, voters in Massachusetts approved Proposition 2½, which put an upper limit of 2.5 percent on local property tax rates. Missouri and Montana also passed limits on tax rates. At the national level, Congress approved the Economic Recovery Act of 1981, which reduced federal tax rates by 25 percent and indexed future tax rates to inflation.

At first blush, the tax revolt appears to be just another expression of people's understandable reluctance to part with their income. The origins and impact of that revolt may go much deeper, however. The taxes people pay are used by governments to purchase scarce resources. As a consequence, fewer resources are available for the production of private goods and services. The more policemen or schoolteachers employed by the public sector, the fewer workers available to private producers and consumers. Similarly the more typewriters, pencils, and paper consumed by government agencies, the fewer accessible to individuals and private companies. In other words, ***everything the public sector does involves an opportunity cost.***

When assessing government's role in the economy, then, we must consider not only what governments do, but also what we give up to allow them to do it. The theory of public goods tells us only

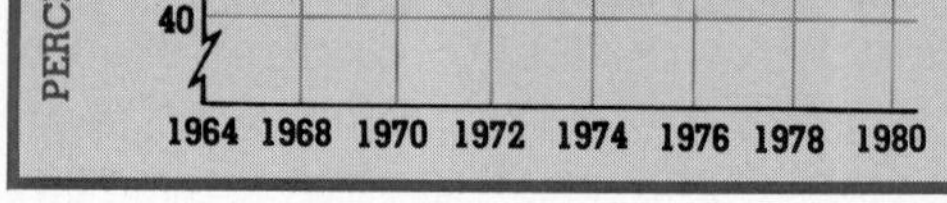

RISING DOUBTS ABOUT GOVERNMENT WASTE

Question: **Do you think that people in government waste a lot of the money we pay in taxes, waste some of it, or don't waste very much of it?**

Source: PUBLIC OPINION © American Enterprise Institute for Public Policy Research, 1981. Reprinted with permission.

A SHIFT OF RESPONSIBILITIES: THE NEW FEDERALISM

In his 1982 State of the Economy message to Congress, President Reagan proposed a major shift in the respective roles of federal, state, and local governments. Arguing that "a wide range of federal activities can be more appropriately and efficiently carried out by the states," he proposed:

- *A swap.* The federal government would assume all costs and responsibility for Medicaid. In exchange, the states would take full responsibility for food stamps and welfare (AFDC). In 1982 the federal government paid roughly 60 percent of AFDC and Medicaid costs and all food-stamp costs. All three programs were administered by state and local governments.
- *A turnback.* The federal government would abandon 61 specific grant programs, allowing the states to pick them up. These would include education and training programs, child nutrition, social services, noninterstate highways, mass transit, community development, and vocational education.
- *A trust fund.* For the first eight years of the turnback, states would receive federal revenues from a trust fund. The fund itself would be financed from federal excise taxes and windfall profits taxes on oil. The federal taxes and trust fund would be eliminated by 1991, leaving states free to impose their own taxes.

neighbor" by cutting back local spending. Welfare is a classic example. The extent of poverty is more a reflection of national economic forces than of state or local circumstances. In this sense, the number of people who apply for welfare aid is beyond state and local control. By denying aid, however, states can encourage poor people to go elsewhere in search of assistance. Thus the New Federalism may encourage states to shirk their share of national responsibilities. The basic problem here is the free-rider dilemma that afflicts all public goods. The solution requires a careful sorting out of state, local, and federal responsibilities.

SUMMARY

- Federal, state, and local governments all participate extensively in the economy, thereby helping answer the basic questions of WHAT to produce, HOW to produce it, and FOR WHOM. Altogether, the public sector absorbs roughly one-fifth of total resources and output.
- For the most part, government production activities focus on public goods. These are goods and services that benefit consumers generaly, no matter who pays for them. Unlike private goods, public goods (e.g., national defense) cannot be packaged and sold to individual consumers, because consumption by one person does not preclude consumption of the same good by another.
- The public-goods nature of most government activities complicates the question of WHAT to produce. Production decisions cannot

be made on the basis of dollar votes (market demand), as public goods encourage free riders to conceal their demand for public goods. Instead, public production decisions are usually made in the political arena, via general elections and specific tax and spending referenda. Benefit-cost analysis can also be used to guide public production decisions, but it requires difficult and often highly subjective estimates of related benefits and costs.

▪ The presence of harmful externalities also necessitates government intervention. Where the costs of a market activity are borne in part by third parties, the market mechanism fails to signal the true social cost of that activity. In such cases, the government intercedes to alter consumption and production patterns.

▪ Governments also redistribute incomes. Public income transfers are essentially a mechanism for altering the market's answers to the question of FOR WHOM to produce. By taking income from some people in the form of taxes and bestowing it on others, the government alters our access to goods and services.

▪ Guidelines for choosing the right mix and level of government activity can be constructed from the concept of opportunity costs. The transfer of resources from the private sector to the public sector is accomplished through the imposition of taxes. In assessing the level of those taxes, we must compare the benefits of public-sector production with those obtainable from the private production or consumption that must be given up to support it.

▪ The New Federalism entails a shift of both revenue sources and program responsibilities from the federal government to the states.

Terms to remember

Define the following terms:

fiscal year
intermediate goods
income transfers
categorical grants
revenue sharing
interest
opportunity cost
progressive tax
bracket creep
regressive tax
user charges
market mechanism
public good
free rider
externalities
production possibilities

Questions for discussion

1. Why should taxpayers subsidize public colleges and universities? What benefits do they receive from someone else's education?

2. If you abhor tennis, should you be forced to pay local taxes that are used to build and maintain public tennis courts? What if you don't like national defense; should you be able to withhold the part of your taxes that pays for it? What would happen if everyone followed this rationale?

3. Could local fire departments be privately operated, with services sold directly to customers? What problems would be involved in such a system?

4. In what ways do governments affect our collective answer to the basic question of HOW to produce? Can you give specific examples?

Problem

Suppose that the following table describes the spending behavior of individuals at various income levels.

Income	*Total spending*	*Sales tax*	*Sales tax paid as percent of income*
$ 1,000	$ 1,000	______	______
2,000	1,800	______	______
3,000	2,400	______	______
5,000	3,500	______	______
10,000	6,000	______	______
100,000	40,000	______	______

Assuming that a sales tax of 10 percent is levied on all purchases, calculate:

(*a*) The amount of taxes paid at each income level
(*b*) The fraction of income paid in taxes at each income level
Is the sales tax progressive or regressive in relation to income?

SECTION II

MICROECONOMICS

Microeconomics is concerned with the little pieces of the economy—the individual consumers, workers, business firms, and unions that keep the economy moving. The basic objective of **microeconomics** is to explain the behavior of all these market participants. Why do consumers buy goods and services? What determines which goods they will buy and in what quantities?

microeconomics: The study of individual behavior in the economy, of the components of the larger economy.

With respect to business firms, microeconomics focuses on the specific decisions people make. These decisions include the choice of how much output to produce, how to produce it, and at what prices to sell it. In microeconomics we also study how decisions to buy, build, or lease factories and machinery are made by business people.

Virtually all of these issues discussed in microeconomics are also discussed in macroeconomics. The difference is the level of abstraction. In **macroeconomics,** we tend to view the economy from afar. We seek the "big picture" and don't really concern ourselves with all the messy details.

macroeconomics: The study of aggregate economic behavior, of the economy as a whole.

Microeconomics takes a much closer look. In microeconomics we want to know how things really work. Why is it that total investment tends to rise when interest rates drop? What business decisions are affected by interest rates and in what ways? Why does consumer spending tend to increase when incomes rise? In macroeconomics we satisfy ourselves with the observation that such responses are common and thus predictable. In microeconomics we want to know *why* these responses are typical. By examining the determinants of behavior, we also hope to be better prepared to predict *changes* in market behavior. Such information not only satisfies intellectual curiosity, but can be of great value to people who want to sell goods or, for that matter, to tax them.

One must also understand the origins of market behavior to assess the general desirability of having a market system in the first place. Most of us become familiar with only one economic system, namely, the U.S. economy. As a result, we learn to accept its virtual inevitability, without ever really understanding *how* it is different or what advantages or disadvantages it has. In microeconomics we take a closer look at how the **market mechanism** works. How is it that the basic economic questions of WHAT to produce, HOW, and FOR WHOM can be resolved without a finely detailed master plan? What do we gain or lose by letting market signals like prices and profits determine the basic outcomes of our economy? How are such decisions made in countries where central government planning dominates? Are countries like the Soviet Union and China, which rely heavily on central planning, more efficient or in any other way better off? To answer these questions we need to know how the market mechanism affects producer and consumer decisions, and what central planners would do instead. This requires a much closer inspection of market activity than macroeconomics undertakes.

market mechanism: The use of market prices and sales to signal desired outputs (or resource allocations).

Even if we satisfy ourselves that the market mechanism works best, we still have to worry about how well it works in different situations. In 1982 the U.S. Department of Justice acted to break up the largest private corporation in the United States, AT&T, but declined to take any action against another corporate giant, IBM. Why did the Justice Department feel the need to act against one corporation but not the other? In what ways were consumers affected by these decisions? To answer these questions—and to understand government antitrust activity—we need to know how market outcomes are affected by corporate size, power, and behavior. Microeconomics examines these questions.

A lot of attention in microeconomics is devoted to the welfare of the individual market participants. We want to know why some people are richly rewarded for their market activity while others receive little. We also want to know how the level and distribution of income would change with different economic circumstances or shifts in government policy.

This section of the text starts with a closer look at consumer behavior (Chapter 4), then proceeds to look at producer behavior. There is more than just theory in these pages. The behavior of actual industries (e.g., electronic calculators) and firms are described. Chapter 10 provides a close look at the power and behavior of some of the largest U.S. corporations. Chapter 13 offers a similarly close view of specific labor unions.

Part C provides detailed discussions of three major microeconomic issues. These include pollution (Chapter 16), welfare and poverty (Chapter 17), and discrimination (Chapter 18). The final chapters examine our economic relationships with the rest of the world.

PART A
PRODUCT MARKETS

CHAPTER 4

THE DEMAND FOR GOODS

Americans love to go shopping. Consumer purchases of goods and services now exceed *$2 trillion* annually. This amounts to an *average*, or per capita, expenditure of nearly $8,000 for every man, woman, and child in the United States. On a per capita basis, this is five times as much as we consumed in 1929, and also about five times as much as the rest of the world spends today.

A major concern of microeconomics is to explain all of this activity. What drives us to department stores, grocery stores, and every Big Sale in town? How do we decide which goods to buy, and in what quantities? These are the kinds of questions that attract not only economists, but also sociologists, psychiatrists, advertisers, and just about everyone who owns or manages a business. Economists hope that their answers to such questions will both explain what is happening in product markets now and predict what will happen in the future.

In this chapter we shall briefly survey American consumption patterns, then try to develop explanations of consumer behavior. As we shall observe, the actual purchase of a good is the culmination of a series of decisions involving tastes, prices, income, expectations, and the availability of different goods. Once we have examined those decisions, we will be able to predict consumer responses to changes in the price of a good or other market influences. The emphasis here will be on the individual consumer, that is, on microeconomics.

PATTERNS OF CONSUMPTION

Figure 4.1 provides a quick summary of how the average consumer dollar is spent. Forty-six cents out of the typical consumer dollar is devoted to housing, including everything from rent and repair to utility bills and grass seed. Another seventeen cents out of every dollar is spent on food. Thus, nearly two-thirds of all consumer spending is for food and shelter.

The other large items in our shopping bag are transportation (car purchases and maintenance, gasoline, bus fares) and clothing. These items are followed by medical care, entertainment, and an assortment of other goods and services.

Table 4.1 provides an even closer look inside the average shopping bag. The average U.S. consumer purchases 298 eggs a year—slightly less than one per day. We also consume, on average, 220 pounds of meat each year, and 121 pounds of potatoes. Indeed, when all our food consumption is added up, it comes to 1,500 pounds of food per year for the average person! Small wonder that diet plans and health spas are so popular. In addition, we consume nearly 37 gallons of booze a year, while trying to maintain a sense of sobriety with 9.4 pounds of coffee. We also smoke an average of 3,104 cigarettes each year. (Think how many the smokers smoke!)

Not all our consumer expenditures are related to food, of course. Food expenditures account for less than one-fifth of our total purchases. The variety of consumer items ranges from the practical to the useless, from the familiar to the bizarre. The list of consumer goods also grows longer daily, with over 100 new products introduced each week.

FIGURE 4.1 HOW THE CONSUMER DOLLAR IS SPENT

Consumers spend their incomes on a vast array of goods and services. This figure summarizes those consumption decisions, by showing how the average consumer dollar is spent. The goal of economic theory is to explain and predict these consumption choices.

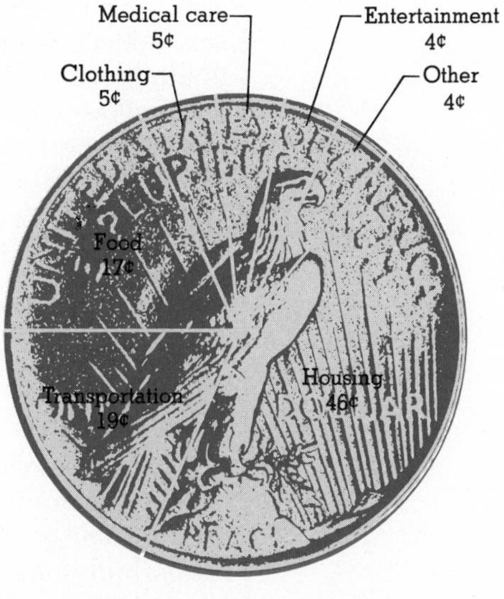

TABLE 4.1 THE ANNUAL SHOPPING LIST

This table shows the quantities of some familiar products consumed by the average American in a single year. What determines how much of each good consumers buy?

Item	*Annual consumption per capita*
Beer	**32 gallons**
Distilled spirits	**2.0 gallons**
Wine	**2.5 gallons**
Milk	**28 gallons**
Eggs	**298**
Beef and veal	**130 pounds**
Pork	**62 pounds**
Potatoes	**121 pounds**
Coffee	**9.4 pounds**
Cigarettes	**3,104**
Refrigerators	**1 per 38 persons**
Television sets	**1 per 14 persons**
Automobiles	**1 per 17 persons**
Gasoline	**476 gallons**

Source: U.S. Departments of Commerce and Agriculture.

DETERMINANTS OF DEMAND

Why do we buy and consume so many goods and services year in and year out? Do our materialistic appetites know any limits? What leads us to buy some goods while rejecting others?

The sociopsychiatric explanation

As one might expect, psychiatrists and psychologists have had a virtual field day formulating explanations of our behavior in the supermarket. Sigmund Freud was among the first to describe us poor mortals as bundles of subconscious (and unconscious) fears, complexes, and anxieties. From a Freudian perspective, we strive for ever higher levels of consumption to satisfy basic drives for security, sex, and ego gratification. Like the most primitive of people, we seek to clothe and adorn ourselves in ways that assert our identity and worth. We eat and smoke too much because we need the oral gratifications and security associated with mother's breast. Self-indulgence, in general, creates in our minds the safety and satisfactions of childhood. Oversized homes and cars provide us with a source of warmth and security remembered from the womb. On the other hand, we often buy and consume some things we expressly don't desire, just to assert our rebellious feelings against our parents (or parent substitutes). In Freud's view, it is the constant interplay of these id, ego, and superego drives that motivates us to buy, buy, buy.

Sociologists have provided still more explanations for our consumption behavior. Lloyd Warner and David Riesman, for example, have noted our yearning to stand above the crowd, to receive recognition from the masses. For those of truly exceptional talents, such recognition may come easily. But for the ordinary person, recognition may depend on conspicuous consumption. A larger car, a newer fashion, a more exotic vacation become expressions of identity that provoke recognition, even social acceptance. Thus, we strive for ever higher levels of consumption—so as to *surpass* the Joneses, not just to keep up with them.

Not *all* consumption is motivated by ego or status concerns, of course. Some food is consumed for the sake of self-preservation, some clothing for warmth, and some housing for shelter. Once our incomes exceed minimum subsistence levels, however, the potential for discretionary spending grows. Spending on nonnecessities is obviously more susceptible to the dictates of personality and social interaction. At current and ever rising levels of American affluence, the theories of psychiatrists and sociologists take on increasing relevance.

The economic explanation

As perceptive as sociopsychiatric theories of consumer behavior are, they tell only part of the story. They shed light on why consumers *desire* certain goods, but desire is only the first step in the consumption process. To acquire goods and services, one must be willing and able to *pay* for one's wants. Producers won't give you their goods just because you want to satisfy your Freudian desires. They want money in exchange for their goods. Hence prices and income are just as relevant to the consumption decision as are more basic desires and preferences.

demand: The ability and willingness to buy specific quantities of a good at alternative prices in a given time period (*ceteris paribus*).

In explaining consumer behavior, then, economists focus on the demand for goods and services. **Demand** entails the *willingness and ability to pay* for goods and services. Many people with a strong desire for a Rolls-Royce have neither the ability nor the willingness actually to buy it; they do not *demand* Rolls-Royces. Similarly, there are many rich people who are willing and able to buy goods they only remotely desire; they *demand* all kinds of goods and services.

To say that someone *demands* a particular good, then, means that he or she is able and willing to buy it at some price(s). As suggested above, ***desire alone is not sufficient to create demand. Instead, an individual's demand for a specific product is determined by:***

- TASTES (desire for this and other goods)
- PRICE (of this particular good)
- INCOME (of the consumer)
- EXPECTATIONS (for income, prices, tastes)
- OTHER GOODS (their availability and prices)

In the remainder of this chapter we shall examine these determinants of demand. Our objective is not only to explain consumer behavior, but also to see (and predict) how consumption patterns change in response to *changes* in tastes, prices, income, the prices or availability of other goods, or expectations. Subsequent chapters will examine the nature of producer supply.

THE DEMAND CURVE

Tastes: the role of utility theory

The first determinant of demand is *taste,* or desire. Economists generally don't concern themselves with the origins of tastes; we leave that explanation to psychologists and sociologists. We simply assume that a person must have a taste for a good—must expect to derive some satisfaction from it—even to consider buying it. This is an eminently reasonable assumption.

It is also reasonable to assume that the more pleasure a product gives us, the higher the price we would be willing to pay for it. If the oral sensation of buttered popcorn at the movies really turns you on, you're likely to be willing to pay dearly for it. If you have no great taste or desire for popcorn, they might have to give it away before you'd eat it. Thus, there exists a positive relationship between our expected pleasure (tastes) and our willingness to pay for something. Economists focus on that relationship, leaving the question of why we desire certain goods and services to the explorations of other social scientists.

utility: The pleasure or satisfaction obtained from a good or service.

total utility: The amount of satisfaction obtained from entire consumption of a product.

marginal utility: The change in total utility obtained from an additional (marginal) unit of a good or service consumed.

TOTAL VS. MARGINAL UTILITY Economists use the term **utility** to refer to the expected pleasure, or satisfaction, obtained from goods and services. We also make an important distinction between total utility and marginal utility. **Total utility** refers to the amount of satisfaction obtained from your *entire* consumption of a product. By contrast, **marginal utility** refers to the amount of satisfaction you get from consuming the last (i.e., "marginal") unit of a product.

DIMINISHING MARGINAL UTILITY The concepts of total and marginal utility explain not only why we buy popcorn at the movies, but also why we stop eating it at some point. Even people who love popcorn (i.e., derive great utility from it), and can afford it, don't eat endless quantities of popcorn. Why not? Presumably because the thrill diminishes with each mouthful. The first box of popcorn may bring sensual gratification, but the second or third box is likely to bring a stomachache. We express the phenomenon by noting that the marginal utility of the first box is higher than the additional or marginal utility derived from the second box of popcorn.

The behavior of popcorn connoisseurs is not abnormal. Generally speaking, the amount of additional utility we obtain from a product declines as we continue to consume it. The third pizza is not so desirable as the first, the sixth beer not so satisfying as the fifth, and so forth. Indeed, this phenomenon of diminishing marginal utility is so nearly universal that economists have fashioned a law around it. The **law of diminishing marginal utility** states that each successive unit of a good consumed yields less *additional* utility.

law of diminishing marginal utility: The marginal utility of a good declines as more of it is consumed in a given time period.

The law of diminishing marginal utility does *not* say that we won't like the third box of popcorn, the second pizza, or the sixth beer; it just says we won't like them as much as the ones we've already consumed.[1] This expectation is illustrated in Figure 4.2. Notice in Figure 4.2*a* that total utility continues to rise as we consume the first five boxes (ugh!) of popcorn. But total utility increases by smaller and smaller increments. Each successive step in Figure

[1] Note also that time is important here: if the first pizza was eaten last year, the second pizza may now taste just as good. The law of diminishing marginal utility is most relevant to short time periods.

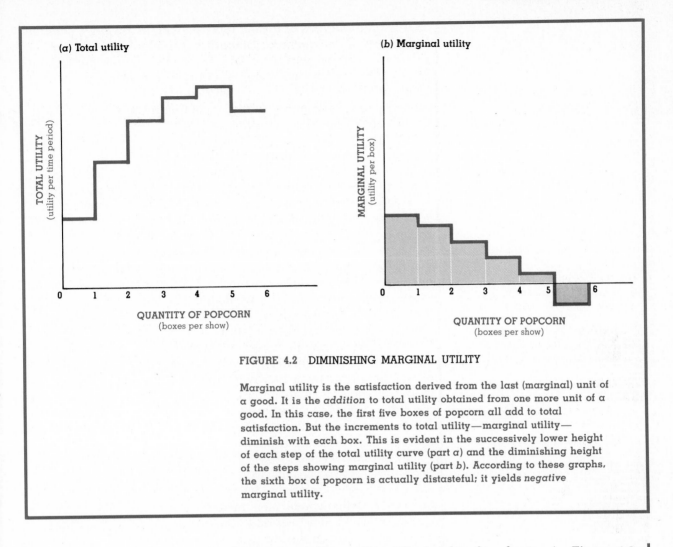

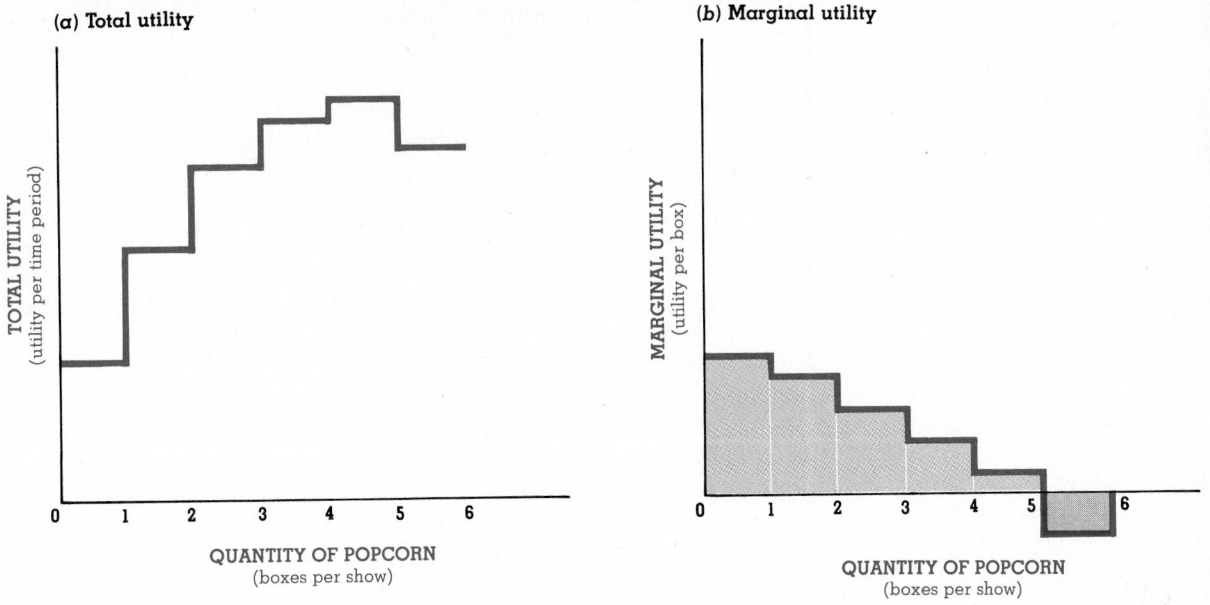

FIGURE 4.2 DIMINISHING MARGINAL UTILITY

Marginal utility is the satisfaction derived from the last (marginal) unit of a good. It is the *addition* to total utility obtained from one more unit of a good. In this case, the first five boxes of popcorn all add to total satisfaction. But the increments to total utility—marginal utility—diminish with each box. This is evident in the successively lower height of each step of the total utility curve (part *a*) and the diminishing height of the steps showing marginal utility (part *b*). According to these graphs, the sixth box of popcorn is actually distasteful; it yields *negative* marginal utility.

4.2*a* is a little smaller. The height of each step in Figure 4.2*a* represents *marginal* utility—the increments to total utility. *Marginal* utility is clearly diminishing. Nevertheless, because marginal utility is still positive, total utility must be increasing. The *total* utility curve keeps rising.

The height of each step in Figure 4.2*a* is also illustrated in Figure 4.2*b*. Here we show marginal utility only. Again we observe that marginal utility is diminishing but still positive as we consume the first five boxes of popcorn.

The situation changes with the sixth box of popcorn. According to Figure 4.2, the good sensations associated with popcorn consumption are completely forgotten by the time the sixth box arrives. Nausea and stomach cramps dominate. Indeed, the sixth box is absolutely *dis*tasteful, as reflected in the downturn of total utility (Figure 4.2*a*) and the negative value for marginal utility (Figure 4.2*b*).

Not every good ultimately gives off negative marginal utility. And it's clear that people won't desire those increments of a good that detract from total satisfaction. Yet the more general principle of diminishing marginal utility is experienced daily. That is to say,

additional quantities of a good tend to yield increasingly smaller increments of satisfaction. Total utility continues to rise, but at an ever slower rate as more of a good is consumed. For our purposes, it does not matter whether marginal utility can be measured (it cannot), just so long as it declines with continued consumption of a good. There are exceptions to the law of diminishing marginal utility, but not many. (Can you think of any?)

Price: a constraint on desire

In product markets, no matter how much marginal utility a particular good or service promises, you won't get any unless you're willing to *buy* that product. In other words, we must distinguish our *desire* for a product from our *demand* for that product. Our demand for a good is an expression of our ability and willingness to buy it at some price(s).

How much of a certain good we are willing to buy at any particular price depends not only on its marginal utility (an expression of our "taste"), but also on our income, our expectations, and the prices of alternative goods and services. Rather than try to explain all these forces at once, however, let us focus on the relationship between the *price* of the good and the amount of it we are willing to buy. This simplification is common to economic analysis. If we want to focus on the relationship between any two phenomena (e.g., price and consumption), we momentarily ignore everything else. This doesn't mean that other forces are unimportant, just that we want to proceed one step at a time. In effect, we are assuming that everything else is constant, or unchanging. This assumption is typically referred to by its Latin term, ***ceteris paribus***.

***ceteris paribus*: The assumption of "everything else being equal," of nothing else changing.**

Notice how we used *ceteris paribus* in our definition of demand. Demand refers to a person's readiness to buy a good at some price(s), given that person's tastes and income, the person's expectations, and the prices of other goods. Were these other determinants of demand to change, we have no assurance that the person would continue to be willing to buy, at the old price(s) or any other.

We can explain the two-dimensional relationship between demand for a product and its price with the help of utility theory. In fact, it is an easy step from the law of diminishing marginal utility to the law of demand.

Recall our earlier observation that the willingness to pay is directly related to utility; the more utility a product delivers, the more a consumer will be willing to pay for it. But we have also noted that

KICKING THE COFFEE HABIT

In early 1976, the price of coffee more than doubled, to over $4 per pound, when a frost in Brazil destroyed most of the coffee crop. Consumers responded to this sudden and dramatic price increase by cutting back on coffee drinking, often switching to tea or other beverages. In other words, *the quantity of coffee demanded decreased when its price increased*. The coffee habit was not easy to kick, however: the quantity of coffee demanded fell by only 17 percent when the price of coffee doubled. This modest change in drinking habits did not reflect a reduced *desire* for coffee on the part of consumers, but instead an increase in the cost of satisfying that desire.

TABLE 4.2 THE DEMAND SCHEDULE OF A POPCORN CONSUMER

Consumers are generally willing to buy larger quantities of a good at lower prices. This demand schedule illustrates the specific quantities demanded at alternative prices. If popcorn sold for 25 cents per ounce, the typical consumer would buy 12 ounces per show (row *F*). At higher prices, less popcorn would be consumed.

	Price (per ounce)	*Quantity demanded (ounces per show)*
A	$0.50	1
B	0.45	2
C	0.40	4
D	0.35	6
E	0.30	9
F	0.25	12
G	0.20	16
H	0.15	20
I	0.10	25
J	0.05	30

quantity demanded: The amount of a product a consumer is willing and able to buy at a specific price in a given time period (*ceteris paribus*).

law of demand: The quantity of a good demanded in a given time period increases as its price falls (*ceteris paribus*).

demand schedule: A table showing the quantities of a good a consumer is willing and able to buy at alternative prices in a given time period (*ceteris paribus*).

marginal utility *diminishes* as increasing quantities of a product are consumed. This suggests that consumers will be willing to pay progressively less for additional quantities of a product. The moviegoer who is willing to pay 50 cents for that first mouth-watering ounce of buttered popcorn may not be willing to pay so much for a second or third ounce. The same is true for the second pizza, the sixth beer, and so forth. *With given income, taste, expectations, and prices of other goods and services,* ***people are willing to buy additional quantities of a good only if its price falls.*** In other words, as the marginal utility of a good diminishes, so does our willingness to pay. This inverse relationship between the **quantity demanded** of a good and its price is referred to as the **law of demand**.

The law of demand is illustrated by the **demand schedule** of Table 4.2 and the downward-sloping demand curve of Figure 4.3. Notice that in Table 4.2 the quantity demanded rises as price falls. When popcorn is selling for 50 cents an ounce (row *A*), the typical moviegoer buys only one ounce per show. At reduced prices, how-

FIGURE 4.3 THE DEMAND CURVE OF A POPCORN CONSUMER

A downward-sloping demand curve expresses the law of demand: the quantity of a good demanded increases as its price falls. People buy more popcorn at low prices than at high prices. Notice that points *A* through *J* on the curve correspond to the rows of the demand schedule (Table 4.2).

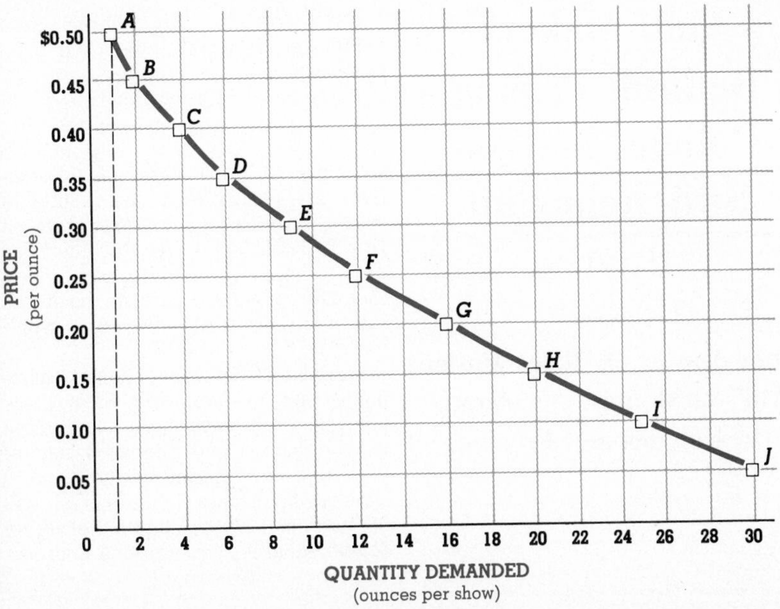

ever, the quantity demanded increases. At a price of 45 cents per ounce (row *B*), the average moviegoer demands two ounces per show; at 40 cents an ounce, the quantity demanded jumps to four ounces per show.

The tendency of quantity demanded to rise as price falls is also seen in Figure 4.3. According to the demand schedule (Table 4.2), the typical moviegoer is willing to buy only one ounce of popcorn per show when it sells for 50 cents per ounce; this is illustrated by point *A* on the **demand curve.** At 45 cents per ounce (point B), the quantity demanded increases to two ounces per show. The remainder of the demand curve expresses the law of demand, as detailed in Table 4.2. The most important characteristic of the demand curve is its downward slope. ***The demand curve slopes down to the right, in accordance with the law of demand.***

demand curve: A curve describing the quantities of a good a consumer is willing and able to buy at alternative prices in a given time period (*ceteris paribus*).

The law of demand and the law of diminishing marginal utility tell us nothing about why we crave popcorn or why our cravings subside. They do describe much of our behavior, however. Accordingly, the theory of demand can be used to predict our responses to changing prices: prediction of larger amounts of popcorn consumed at low prices than at high prices is a pretty safe bet. Moreover, such a prediction is easily tested, unlike most theories of motivation. How can we prove or reject the notion that we eat popcorn to satisfy needs for security or autoerotic titillation? To prove that prices influence consumer behavior, we need only raise or lower the price of popcorn.

SHIFTS OF THE DEMAND CURVE

A demand curve tells us how consumers respond to a change in the price of a particular good or service, *ceteris paribus*. But other things

Auto Makers Rethink Pricing Policies to Woo Still-Reluctant Buyers

They Brake on Rises Posted On '82 Models, Accelerate On Rebates and Freebies

DETROIT—The Big Three auto makers are in a tizzy over their pricing strategies.

At General Motors Corp., a high-level debate is raging over whether the company priced its 1982 models too high. At Ford Motor Co., executives are poring over the results of recent price experiments for clues on how to boost sales. And at Chrysler Corp., financial officials are hoping that their decision to trim back the size of their price increase won't backfire.

Slowly and painfully, the auto companies are reevaluating their price policies. They have begun to gamble on the heavy and repeated use of price-discount gimmicks. Customers showing up in showrooms this fall will be barraged by salesmen heralding $1,000 rebates, free options and cut-rate auto loans. They will even see some 1982 cars at 1981 prices.

Deterrent to Sales

Detroit is reacting to growing evidence that soaring sticker-prices, which have pushed the average price of a new car to $10,000, are primarily responsible for keeping car sales in the doldrums. So far in the young 1982 model year, sales are running 35% behind last year's depressed levels, and auto company financial results remain disastrous.

A recent University of Michigan survey found that "high price" is the main reason why more consumers than ever are simply deciding not to buy a new car. . . .

—John Koten and Amanda Bennett

don't remain equal forever: tastes, income, expectations, and the prices of other goods do change. When they do, the demand curve will change as well.

A change in tastes

Suppose for the moment that roasted pumpkin seeds became immensely popular. Perhaps pumpkin-seed roasters could convince consumers that pumpkin seeds fight tooth decay, thus eliminating the necessity of brushing your teeth. If roasted pumpkin seeds really caught on, how would popcorn sales be affected?

Before pumpkin seeds became popular, we saw that the average moviegoer was willing to buy six ounces of popcorn per show at a price of 35 cents per ounce. This relationship was illustrated by point *D* in Figure 4.3 and is illustrated again by point *D* on the "initial demand" curve in Figure 4.4. Now, however, we have to contend with a change in tastes. Once moviegoers start turning on to roasted pumpkin seeds and off popcorn, the willingness to buy popcorn will diminish. Specifically, we shall assume that after tastes change, the typical moviegoer will buy only two ounces of popcorn per show, rather than six, at a price of 35 cents per ounce. This new quantity demanded is represented by point *P* in Figure 4.4.

Similar reductions in quantity demanded occur at other prices. Before the pumpkin-seed craze, 12 ounces of popcorn were demanded at a price of 25 cents (point *M*). Now only 4 ounces are demanded at that price (point *N*). These and other changes cause a

FIGURE 4.4 A SHIFT IN DEMAND

If consumer tastes turn from popcorn to pumpkin seeds, consumers will be less willing to pay for popcorn than they used to be. That is to say, the quantity of popcorn demanded at any particular price will decline. In such a case, the demand curve *shifts* to the left. Initially, consumers purchased six ounces of popcorn per show at 35 cents an ounce (point *D*). After tastes change, consumers buy only two ounces at that price (point *P*). Nevertheless, the demand curve still slopes downward because consumers can still be persuaded to buy a third or fourth ounce if the price of popcorn drops far enough.

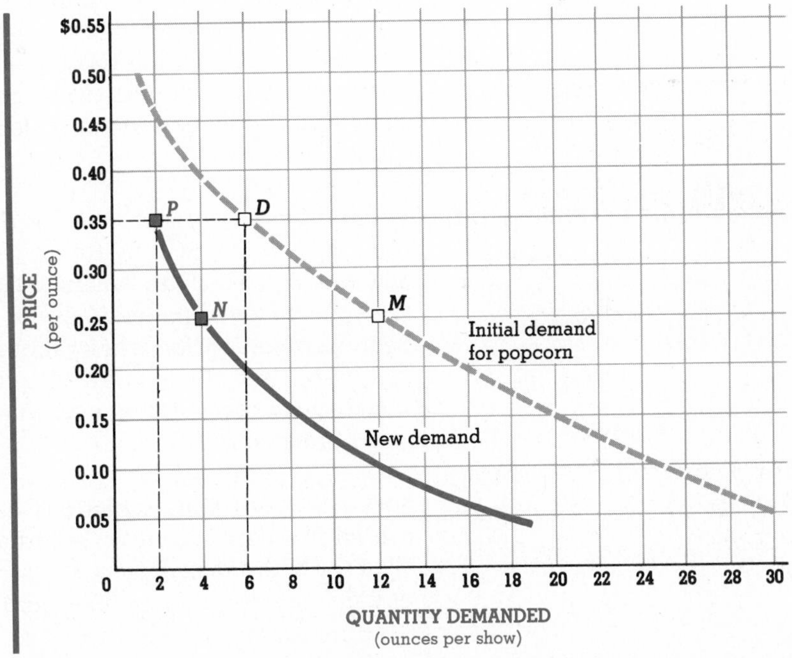

shift in demand: A change in the quantity demanded at any (every) given price.

shift in demand—the popcorn demand curve shifts to the left. As a result of the change in tastes, people demand a smaller quantity of popcorn at each and every price.

An increased taste for popcorn would shift the demand curve to the right, indicating that moviegoers were willing and able to increase their purchases of popcorn at all prices. Such a favorable shift might occur if popcorn were discovered to be a cure for acne or if movie theaters started selling beer.

A change in income

Changes in a consumer's income have the same kind of effect on demand curves as do changes in taste. Poor people may have a great taste for popcorn at the movies but still consume little of it. By contrast, a rich person may be *willing and able to buy* lots of hot buttered popcorn even if he gets only minimal gratification from it. Hence, we may assert that *the shape and position of the demand curve depend on income as well as on taste.* Should a consumer's income change, the relevant demand curve will probably *shift.* Thus, the leftward shift of the demand curve depicted in Figure 4.4 could also express a fall in demand due to a reduction in the income of the average moviegoer.[2] (What would happen to the demand curve if income *increased?*)

A change in expectations

A demand curve may also shift if a consumer *expects* a change in income. College seniors, for example, often step up their spending for goods and services as soon as they are reasonably certain of obtaining a postgraduation job. Anticipating a rise in income in the near future, they increase the quantity they demand in the present. Whenever income expectations change, demand curves tend to shift.

Expectations also affect consumer responses to prices. If consumers expect prices to rise tomorrow, they may increase their purchases today (before the price goes up). That is to say, price expectations also influence consumer behavior.

A change in other goods

Finally, we note again that the demand for popcorn or any other product is influenced by the prices and availability of other goods and services. This was evident in our turn to pumpkin seeds. Before the appearance of pumpkin seeds, everyone ate popcorn. Similarly, people's demand for typewriters shifted significantly when word-processing machines were introduced. The demand for conventional typewriters shifted even further to the left when the price of word processors fell.

SUBSTITUTES AND COMPLEMENTS Changes in the prices of other goods can shift a demand curve in either direction. Once people have a taste for both roasted pumpkin seeds and popcorn, their consumption decisions will be influenced by the respective prices of the two

[2] In some cases, a reduction in income will cause an *increase* in demand. Such goods are called "inferior" goods (potatoes and plain white bread are examples).

FIGURE 4.5 A CHANGE IN THE PRICES OF OTHER GOODS

The curve D_1 represents the initial demand for popcorn, given the prices of other goods. Those other prices may change, however. If a reduction in the price of another good (pumpkin seeds) causes a reduction in the demand for this good (popcorn), the two goods are substitutes. In this case, popcorn demand shifts to the left, to D_2.

If a reduction in the price of another good (e.g., Pepsi) leads to an *increase* in the demand for this good (popcorn), the two goods are complements. In this case, popcorn demand shifts to the right, to D_3.

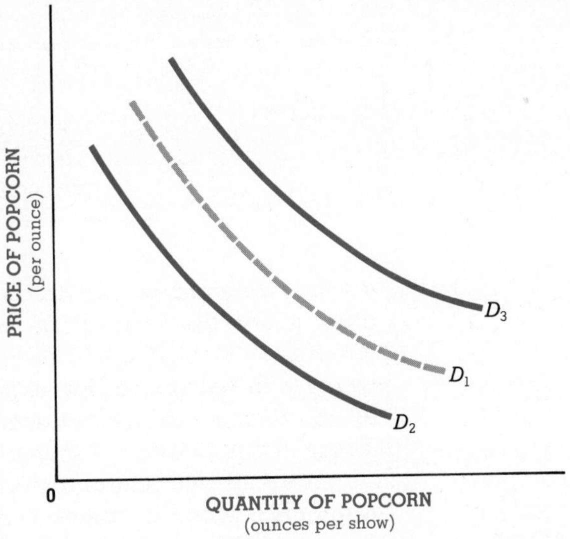

substitute goods: Goods that substitute for each other; when the price of good X rises, the quantity of good Y demanded increases (*ceteris paribus*).

complementary goods: Goods frequently consumed in combination; when the price of good X rises, the quantity of good Y demanded falls (*ceteris paribus*).

goods. If pumpkin seeds become cheaper, people will be less willing to buy popcorn. As a consequence, the demand curve for popcorn will shift to the left.

Popcorn and pumpkin seeds are called **substitute goods,** because a fall in the price of one leads to a decrease in the demand for the other. Substitute goods are used *instead* of each other.

Other goods are used *with* each other. Suppose the price of Pepsi fell at movie theaters. What would happen to the demand for popcorn? Would people demand larger or smaller quantities of popcorn at a given price? Experience suggests that the demand curve for popcorn would shift to the *right*. A reduction in Pepsi prices leads to an *increase* in the demand for popcorn. Pepsi and popcorn are **complementary goods.**

The distinction between substitute goods and complementary goods is illustrated in Figure 4.5. Note that the price of one good and the demand for the other move in the *same* direction for substitute goods. (A *decrease* in pumpkin-seed prices causes a *decrease* in popcorn demand.) In the case of complementary goods (e.g., Pepsi and popcorn, cream and coffee), the price of one good and the demand for the other move in opposite directions. This helps explain why American consumers cut back on car purchases when the price of gasoline jumped in 1979 and 1980.

Movements vs. shifts

To understand consumer behavior, it is essential to distinguish shifts of a demand curve from movements along that demand curve. A demand curve for a particular product is constructed on the basis of given tastes, income, expectations, and the prices of other goods. It tells us how a consumer will respond to a change in the price of that good, *ceteris paribus*. Thus ***consumer responses to changes in the price of a particular good are illustrated by movements along***

TABLE 4.3 THE TERMINOLOGY OF DEMAND

A change in:	*implies:*
quantity demanded	**a movement along a demand curve, in response to a change in price, *ceteris paribus*.**
demand	**a shift of the demand curve, in response to a change in tastes, income, expectations, or the prices of other goods.**

a given demand curve. But if the tastes, income, expectations, or other goods that underlie a particular demand curve change, the curve itself will be altered. That is to say, ***consumer responses to changes in income, tastes, expectations, or the price or availability of other goods are illustrated by shifts of the demand curve.*** These distinctions are summarized in Table 4.3.

Were all the determinants of demand changing repeatedly, an economist would be almost helpless in trying to predict consumer behavior. We would not be completely helpless, however, if we could at least identify some of the salient factors that give a demand curve its particular shape. As long as we know, for example, that the demand for popcorn depends to some extent on demand for pumpkin seeds, we can better predict when and how the popcorn demand curve will shift. Such knowledge still leaves us without a satisfactory theory of motivation, but it does enable us to keep up better with consumer expenditure patterns.

CHOOSING AMONG PRODUCTS

The dilemma of choosing between pumpkin seeds and popcorn is an example of a basic decision we make daily. As consumers, we are always choosing from among available products. It is not simply a question of how much popcorn to buy at alternative prices (the demand curve), but also whether to buy something else besides popcorn. In other words, the existence of other products gives us a *choice*. When we purchase popcorn, we are not only giving up income for popcorn but also relinquishing the opportunity to buy something else with that same income. In other words, consuming popcorn (or any other good) entails distinct **opportunity costs.** On what basis do we make such choices?

opportunity cost: The most desired goods and services that are forgone in order to obtain something else.

Marginal utility vs. price

The economic explanation for consumer choice builds on the theory of marginal utility and the law of demand. On the basis of utility theory, we expect people to prefer those products that give them greater utility to others (or at least those they think will give greater utility). Suppose you have a choice between buying a Coke and playing a video game. The first proposition of consumer choice simply states that if you think a Coke will be more satisfying than playing a video game, you will prefer to buy the Coke. Hardly a revolutionary proposition.

The second postulate of consumer-choice theory takes into account the market prices of the goods we desire. Although you may prefer to drink a Coke rather than play a video space game, one play of a video game is cheaper than a Coke. Under these circumstances, your budget may win out over your desires, and you may forgo the Coke. There is nothing irrational about playing a video game instead of buying a Coke when you have a limited amount of income to spend. On the contrary, ***rational behavior requires one to compare the anticipated utility of each expenditure with its cost,*** and to choose those products that promise to provide the most pleasure for the amount of income available.

Suppose your desire for a Coke is one and a half times as great as your desire to play a video game. In economic terms, this means that the marginal utility of the first Coke is 1.5 times as high as the marginal utility of the first space game. Which one should you consume? At first glance, the answer seems obvious. But what if a Coke costs 50 cents, while one play on a video game costs only 25 cents? In this case, you must pay *two* times as much for a Coke that gives only 1.5 times as much pleasure. This is not a good deal. You could get more utility per dollar by playing video games.

The same kind of principle explains why some rich people drive around in Fords rather than shiny new Mercedeses. The marginal utility (*MU*) of driving a Mercedes is substantially higher than the *MU* of driving a Ford. A nice Mercedes, however, costs about four times as much as a basic Ford. Hence Ford delivers more for the money. Specifically, Ford yields more *marginal utility per dollar spent.* The key to consumer choice is to compare the marginal utilities of different goods with their respective prices. In general, ***the consumer should choose that good which delivers the most marginal utility per dollar.***

Utility maximization

This basic principle of consumer choice is easily illustrated. Suppose you have $1.50 to spend on a combination of Cokes and video games, the only consumer goods available. Your objective, as always, is to get the greatest satisfaction possible from this limited income. That is to say, you want to maximize the *total* utility attainable from the expenditure of your income. The question is how to do it. What combination of Cokes and games will maximize the utility you get from $1.50?

We have already assumed that the marginal utility of the first Coke is 1.5 times as high as the *MU* of the first video game. This is reflected in the second line of Table 18.4. The *MU* of the first video-game play has been set arbitrarily at 10 utils. We don't need to know whether 10 utils is a real thrill or just a bit of amusement. Indeed, the concept of "utils," or units of utility, has little meaning by itself; it is only a useful basis for comparison. In this case, we want to compare the *MU* of the first game with the *MU* of the first Coke. Hence we set the *MU* of the first game at 10 utils and the *MU* of the first Coke at 15 utils. The first Coke is 1.5 times as satisfying as the first video space game ($MU_{\text{Coke}} = 1.5\ MU_{\text{game}}$).

TABLE 4.4 MAXIMIZING UTILITY

Q: **How can you get the most satisfaction (utility) from $1.50 if you must choose between buying Cokes that cost 50 cents and video games that cost 25 cents each?**

A: **By drinking one Coke and playing four video games. See text for explanation.**

	Amount of utility (in units of pleasure)			
	From Cokes		From video games	
Quantity consumed	*Total*	*Marginal*	*Total*	*Marginal*
0	0	0	0	0
1	15	15	10	10
2	23	8	19	9
3	25	2	26	7
4	25	0	31	5
5	22	−3	34	3
6	12	−10	35	1

The remainder of Table 4.4 indicates how marginal utility diminishes with increasing consumption of a product. Look at what happens to the good taste of Coke. The marginal utility of the first Coke is 15; but the *MU* of the second Coke is only 8 utils. Once you've quenched your initial thirst, a second Coke still tastes good but is not nearly so satisfying as the first one. A third Coke yields even less marginal utility, and a fourth one none at all ($MU = 0$). A fifth or sixth Coke would make your teeth rattle and cause other discomforts—its marginal utility is actually negative.

Video games also conform to the law of diminishing marginal utility. However, marginal utility doesn't decline quite so rapidly in the consumption of electronic space games. The second game is almost as much fun ($MU = 9$) as the first ($MU = 10$). It's not until you have played several games that you realize you don't stand a chance of breaking the previous high score. At that point you begin to feel the tension and enjoy the game less. By the sixth game, marginal utility is fast approaching zero.

With these psychological insights to guide us, we can now determine how best to spend $1.50. What we are looking for is that combination of Cokes and video games which *maximizes* the total utility attainable from an expenditure of $1.50. We call that combination **optimal consumption,** that is, the mix of goods that yields the most utility for the available income.

optimal consumption: **The mix of consumer purchases that maximizes the utility attainable from available income.**

We can start looking for the optimal mix of consumer purchases by assessing the utility of spending the entire $1.50 on video games. At 25 cents per play, we could "buy" six games. This would give us *total* utility of 35 utils (see Table 4.4).

You might also want to consider spending all your income on Cokes. With $1.50 to spend, you could buy three Cokes. However, this would generate only 25 utils of total utility. Hence, if you were forced to choose between three Cokes and six games, you would pick the games.

Fortunately, we do not have to make such awful choices. In reality, we can buy a *combination* of Cokes and video games. This complicates our decision making (with more choices) but also permits us to attain still higher levels of total satisfaction.

To reach the peak of satisfaction, consider spending your \$1.50 in three 50-cent increments. How should you spend the first 50 cents? If you spend it on a Coke, you will get 15 utils of satisfaction. On the other hand, 50 cents will buy your first *two* video games. The first game has a *MU* of 10 and the second game adds another 9 utils to your happiness. Hence by spending the first 50 cents on games, you reap 19 utils of total utility. This is superior to the pleasures of a first Coke and is therefore your first purchase.

Having played two space games, you now can spend the second 50 cents. How should it be spent? Your choice now is that first Coke or a third and fourth video game. That first unconsumed Coke still promises 15 utils of real pleasure. By contrast, the *MU* of a third video game is 7 and the *MU* of a fourth game only 5 utils. Together, then, the third and fourth games will increase your total utility by 12 utils while a first Coke will give you 15 utils. You should spend the second 50 cents on a Coke.

The decision on how to spend the remaining half dollar is made the same way. The final choice is either a second Coke (*MU* = 8) or the third (*MU* = 7) and fourth (*MU* = 5) video games. The two games together offer more marginal utility and are thus the correct decision.

After working your way through these calculations, you will end up drinking one Coke and playing four video games. Was it worth it? Do you end up with more total utility than you could have gotten from any other combination? The answer is yes. The *total* utility of one Coke (15 utils) and four games (31 utils) amounts to 46 units of utility. This is significantly better than the alternatives of spending your \$1.50 on Cokes alone (total utility = 23) or games alone (total utility = 35). In fact, the combination of one Coke and four games is the *best* one you can find. Because this combination maximizes the total utility of your income (\$1.50), it represents *optimal consumption.*

The essence of utility maximization, then, lies in comparisons of marginal utilities and prices. If a dollar spent on product X yields more marginal utility than a dollar spent on product Y, we should buy product X. To use this principle, of course, we have to know the amounts of utility obtainable from various goods and be able to perform a little arithmetic. By doing so, however, we can be assured of getting the greatest satisfaction from our limited income.

ELASTICITY

The dilemma posed by the choice between Coke and video games illustrates the complexity of the relationship between consumer choices and product prices. The decision to buy a particular product is not based solely on the pleasure or utility anticipated from its consumption—that is, on how much the consumer wants it. There are many products we greatly desire but do not buy. Nor is the decision to buy based on price alone; we pass up thousands of inexpensive products every day. To understand consumer choices fully, we have to consider not only the anticipated utility and price of a particular good, but also a consumer's income, expectations, and the util-

FINDING YOUR OPTIMAL CONSUMPTION

The basic rule for utility maximization is to purchase that good next which delivers the most *marginal utility per dollar.* Marginal utility per dollar is simply the *MU* of the good divided by its price: $MU \div P$.

From Table 4.4 we know that a first Coke has an *MU* of 15 and a price of 50 cents. It thus delivers a marginal utility per dollar of

$$\frac{MU_{\text{first Coke}}}{P_{\text{Coke}}} = \frac{15}{0.50} = 30$$

On the other hand, the first video game has a marginal utility of 10 and a price of 25 cents. It offers a marginal utility per price of

$$\frac{MU_{\text{first game}}}{P_{\text{game}}} = \frac{10}{0.25} = 40$$

From this perspective, the first video game is a better deal than the first Coke and should be purchased.

Optimal consumption implies that the utility-maximizing combination of goods has been found. If this is true, you cannot increase your total utility by trading one good for another. There is no unpurchased good that offers a higher marginal utility per dollar. Moreover, there is no good in your shopping bag that offers less *MU* per price. If there were, you would trade it in for a preferred good. Hence we conclude that all goods included in the optimal consumption mix yield the *same* marginal utility per dollar. We know we have reached maximum utility when

$$\frac{MU_x}{P_x} = \frac{MU_y}{P_y}$$

where x and y represent any two goods included in our consumption.

ity and prices of alternative goods. In other words, the *ceteris paribus* assumption that underlies demand curves covers a lot of potential influences on consumer choice.

Price elasticity of demand

Despite the multiple influences that shape consumption decisions, demand curves are useful tools. Over short periods of time, tastes, income, and expectations do not change much. As a consequence, the *price* of a good is likely to have the greatest immediate impact on the quantity demanded. For this reason, we often need to know quite precisely how consumers will respond to a change in a product's price.

By itself, the law of demand tells us that the quantity demanded will go down if price goes up. But it does not tell us by *how much* quantity demanded will fall when price rises. Yet this is the kind of information needed by a producer who is trying to decide whether to increase prices. Will an increase in the price of popcorn cause a big

Liquor Lobby Rallies to Fight 'Sin Tax' Rise

WASHINGTON—Back to the bad old days of bootleg liquor?

That is just one of the gloomy consequences foreseen by the nation's liquor lobby if President Reagan were to go along with his advisers' proposal to sharply increase federal excise taxes on alcohol.

Other nasty results of higher liquor costs, the lobby warns, could include plant closings and layoffs, a rise in antipathy among blue-collar drinkers toward the Grand Old Party and a decline in state liquor revenue. Higher liquor taxes might even raise prices to the point where some thrifty Americans are scared onto the wagon, lobbyists for the liquor, wine and beer industry contend.

Although probably overstated, these dire warnings seem to have had an effect. President Reagan still hasn't disclosed his position, but it appears that in his State of the Union message tonight, he will decline to follow the urgings of his advisers to as much as double excise taxes on some liquor products.

The Distilled Spirits Council of the United States (Discus), which represents most of the nation's distillers, has attacked the proposed tax increases in a letter to the President, a 10-page "white paper." . . . The organization figures that doubling the tax would raise retail prices by $2 to $3 a bottle on a fifth of liquor, which, in turn, could cut consumption by 20% to 25% a year. That could mean losses of $4 billion a year to an industry whose sales have been essentially flat for five years, Discus says.

The hard-liquor industry feels put upon in other ways, too. Federal excise taxes on distilled spirits already are much higher than those on beer and wine, Discus says. And, in 1980, for the first time, more wine than hard liquor was sold in the U.S. Discus is worried that higher prices would exacerbate the trend.

—Laurie McGinley

drop in sales or only a small decline? How high a price can the theater manager charge for popcorn without losing all of his gratification-seeking customers? What price will bring in the highest total receipts?

Such concerns are not unique to profit-hungry theater managers. In 1982 President Reagan's advisers urged him to raise excise taxes on cigarettes, liquor, and gasoline. The objective of the proposed tax increases was to raise government revenues. In the process, however, the prices of these products would have gone up and their sales would have declined. Reagan concluded that the resulting decline in sales, output, and employment would be too great and decided against such tax hikes.

Even Communists have to worry about the law of demand. In socialist economies such as the Soviet Union and China, the prices of goods are typically set by central planners. In setting prices, the central planners must consider how consumption will vary with different prices. If the price of wheat is set too low, the quantity demanded may exceed available supplies and consumer demand will not be met. On the other hand, if the price of wheat is raised too high, the quantity demanded may fall so far that the nutritional well-being of the population is threatened.

price elasticity of demand: The percentage change in quantity demanded divided by the percentage change in price.

The central question in all these decisions is the response of quantity demanded to a change in price. The ***response of consumers to a change in price is measured by the price elasticity of demand.*** Specifically, the **price elasticity of demand** refers to the percentage change in quantity demanded divided by the percentage change in price, that is,

$$\text{Price elasticity } (E) = \frac{\text{percentage change in quantity demanded}}{\text{percentage change in price}}$$

According to the law of demand, when price increases (decreases), the quantity demanded decreases (increases). Since price and quantity demanded always move in opposite directions, the price elasticity of demand (E) is always negative. However, E is typically expressed in absolute terms (without the minus sign).

A NUMERICAL EXAMPLE To get a feel for the concept of elasticity, let us return to the popcorn counter at the movies. We have already observed that consumers respond to reductions in the price of popcorn by demanding larger quantities of it. At a price of 45 cents an ounce (point B in Figure 4.6), for example, the average moviegoer demands two ounces of popcorn per show. At the lower price of 40 cents per ounce (point C), the quantity demanded jumps to four ounces per show.

We can summarize this response with the price elasticity of demand. To do so, we have to calculate the *percentage* changes in quantity and price. Consider the percentage change in quantity first. In this case, the change in quantity demanded is 4 ounces − 2 ounces = 2 ounces. The *percentage* change in quantity is therefore:

$$\text{Percentage change in quantity} = \frac{2}{q}$$

The problem is to transform the denominator q into a number. Should we use the quantity of popcorn purchased *before* the price reduction, that is, $q_1 = 2$? Or should we use the quantity purchased *after* the price reduction, that is, $q_2 = 4$? To avoid confusion, econo-

FIGURE 4.6 GAUGING ELASTICITY

From the downward-sloping demand curve, we know that a price reduction will lead to an increase in quantity demanded. The price *elasticity of demand* (E) is *a measure* of that response. In this case, demand for popcorn is elastic (E = 5.65) between points B and C: quantity demanded increases by a much larger *percentage* than price falls (see text for calculation).

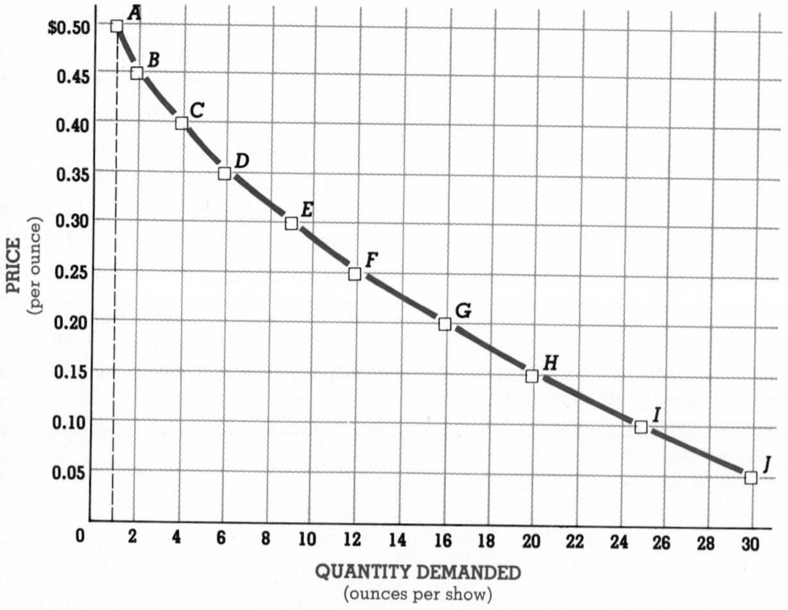

mists prefer to use the *average* quantity in the denominator.[3] The average quantity is simply:

$$\text{Average quantity} = \frac{q_1 + q_2}{2} = \frac{2 + 4}{2} = 3 \text{ ounces}$$

We can now complete the calculation of the percentage change in quantity demanded. It is:

$$\begin{array}{l}\text{Percentage change in}\\\text{quantity demanded}\end{array} = \frac{q_1 - q_2}{\dfrac{q_1 + q_2}{2}} = \frac{2}{3} = 0.667$$

Popcorn sales increased by an average of 67 percent when the price of popcorn was reduced from 45 cents to 40 cents per ounce.

The computation of the percentage change in price is similar. We first note that the price of popcorn fell by 5 cents (45¢ − 40¢). We then compute the *average* price of popcorn as:

$$\begin{array}{l}\text{Average price}\\\text{of popcorn}\end{array} = \frac{p_1 - p_2}{2} = \frac{45 + 40}{2} = 42.5 \text{ cents}$$

This is our denominator in calculating the percentage price change. Using these numbers, we see that

$$\begin{array}{l}\text{Percentage change}\\\text{in price}\end{array} = \frac{p_1 - p_2}{\dfrac{p_1 + p_2}{2}} = \frac{5}{42.5} = 0.118$$

The price of popcorn fell by 11.8 percent.

Now we have all the information required to compute the price elasticity of demand. In this case,

$$E = \frac{\begin{array}{c}\text{percentage change}\\\text{in quantity}\end{array}}{\begin{array}{c}\text{percentage change}\\\text{in price}\end{array}} = \frac{q_1 - q_2}{\dfrac{q_1 + q_2}{2}} \div \frac{p_1 - p_2}{\dfrac{p_1 + p_2}{2}} = \frac{0.667}{0.118} = 5.65$$

What have we learned from all these calculations? Have we gotten anything useful? Fortunately, the answer is yes. The computed elasticity of demand is a very useful number. It says that the consumer response to a price reduction will be extremely large. Specifically, the quantity of popcorn consumed will increase 5.65 times as fast as price falls. A 1 percent reduction in price brings about a 5.65 percent increase in purchases. The theater manager can therefore boost popcorn sales greatly by lowering price a little. Central planners would view such a high elasticity of demand as signaling the need for great caution in abruptly changing the price of wheat.

ELASTIC VS. INELASTIC In general, we categorize goods according to their relative elasticity—whether E is larger or smaller than 1. If E is larger than 1, demand is *relatively elastic* in the immediate price range. If E is less than 1, we say demand is relatively *in*elastic. In that

[3] This procedure is referred to as the *arc* (midpoint) elasticity of demand. If a single quantity and price are used in the denominator, we refer to the *point* elasticity of demand.

TABLE 4.5 ELASTICITY ESTIMATES

Price elasticities vary greatly. When the price of gasoline increases, consumers reduce their consumption only slightly. When the price of fish increases, however, consumers cut back their consumption substantially. These differences reflect the availability of immediate substitutes, the prices of the goods, and the amount of time available for changing behavior.

Type of elasticity	*Estimate*
Relatively elastic ($E > 1$)	
Airline travel, long run	**2.4**
Fresh fish	**2.2**
New cars, short run	**1.2–1.5**
Unitary elastic ($E = 1$)	
Private education	**1.1**
Radios and televisions	**1.2**
Shoes	**0.9**
Relatively inelastic ($E < 1$)	
Cigarettes	**0.4**
Coffee	**0.3**
Gasoline, short run	**0.2**

Source: Compiled from Hendrick S. Houthakker and Lester D. Taylor, *Consumer Demand in the United States, 1929–1970* (Cambridge: Harvard University Press, 1966); and F. W. Bell, "The Pope and Price of Fish," *American Economic Review*, December 1968.

case, the percentage change in quantity demanded is less than the percentage change in price; that is, consumers are not very responsive to price changes. Notice in Table 4.5, for example, the relatively low elasticity of demand for coffee and cigarettes. When the prices of these products increase, consumers don't reduce their consumption very much. In the extreme case, when quantity demanded does not respond at all to a change in price—people are willing and able to buy the same (unchanged) quantity of a good no matter how high its price goes—the price elasticity of demand is zero. Varying degrees of elasticity are illustrated in Figure 4.7.

FIGURE 4.7 DEGREES OF ELASTICITY

These various demand curves illustrate different responses to a price increase from p_1 to p_2. In each case, the initial quantity demanded at price p_1 is q_1. In part *a* when price rises to p_2, no output is sold (quantity demanded drops to zero); the demand curve is perfectly elastic. In part e quantity demanded does not change at all; people continue to buy the quantity q_1 even when price goes up. In that case, demand is completely inelastic. Between these two extremes consumer response may be relatively elastic (part *b*), unitary elastic (part c), or relatively inelastic (part *d*).

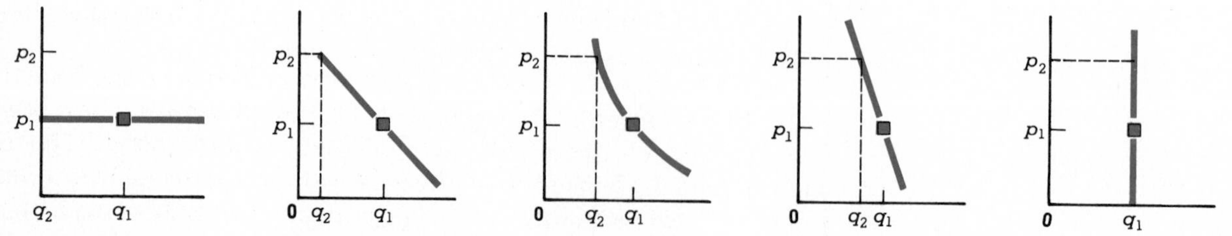

(*a*) Perfectly elastic $E=\infty$ **(*b*) Relatively elastic $E>1$** **(c) Unitary elastic $E=1$** **(d) Relatively inelastic $E<1$** **(e) Perfectly inelastic $E=0$**

FIGURE 4.8 ELASTICITY AND TOTAL REVENUE

Total revenue is equal to the price of the product times the quantity sold. It is illustrated by the area of the rectangle formed by $p \times q$. The shaded rectangle illustrates total revenue ($1.60) at a price of 40 cents and a quantity demanded of four. When price is increased to 45 cents, the rectangle and total revenue shrink because demand is relatively elastic in that price range.

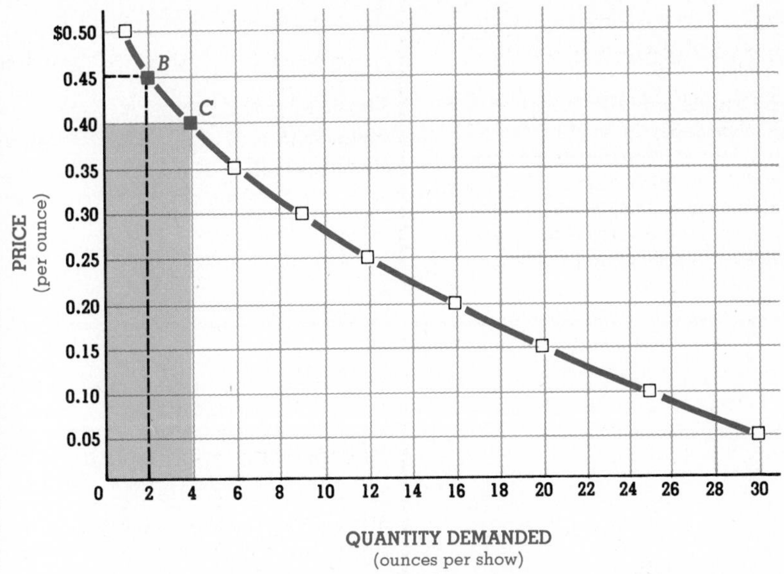

Price elasticity and total revenue

total revenue: The price of a product multiplied by the quantity sold in a given time period; $p \times q$.

The concept of price elasticity is useful for destroying the popular misconception that producers often charge the "highest price possible." Except in the very rare case of completely inelastic demand, this notion makes no sense. Indeed, higher prices may actually *lower* total sales revenue.

The **total revenue** of a seller is the amount of money received from product sales. It is determined by the quantity of the product sold and the price at which it is sold. If the price of popcorn is 40 cents per ounce and only four ounces are sold, total revenue equals $1.60 per show. This total revenue is illustrated by the shaded rectangle in Figure 4.8. (Recall that the area of a rectangle is equal to its height [*p*] times its width [*q*].)

Now consider what happens to total revenue when the price of popcorn is increased. From the law of demand, we know that an increase in price will lead to a decrease in quantity demanded. Hence it is not apparent whether total revenue will rise or fall. The change in total revenue depends on *how much* quantity demanded falls when price goes up. This brings us back to the concept of elasticity.

Suppose we raised popcorn prices again, from 40 cents back to 45 cents. What happens to total revenue? At 40 cents per box, four ounces are sold (see Figure 4.8) and total revenue equals $1.60. If we increase the price to 45 cents, only two ounces are sold and total revenue drops to 90 cents. In this case, an increase in price leads to a decrease in total revenue. The new and smaller total revenue is illustrated by the dotted rectangle in Figure 4.8.

Price increases don't always lower total revenue, of course. If demand were relatively *in*elastic ($E < 1$), a price increase would

TABLE 4.6 PRICE ELASTICITY OF DEMAND AND TOTAL REVENUE

The impact of higher prices on total revenue depends on the price elasticity of demand. Higher prices result in higher total revenue only if demand is relatively inelastic. If demand is relatively elastic, *lower* prices result in *higher* revenues.

If demand is:	*and price increases, total revenue will:*	*If price decreases, total revenue will:*
Elastic ($E > 1$)	**decrease**	**increase**
Inelastic ($E < 1$)	**increase**	**decrease**
Unit-elastic ($E = 1$)	**not change**	**not change**

lead to higher total revenue. The possible outcomes of a price change are summarized in Table 4.6.

Once we know the price elasticity of demand, we can predict quite accurately how consumers will respond to changing prices. By the same token, we can also predict what will happen to the total revenue of the seller. The elasticity of demand we calculate, however, applies to a specific range of prices only. The demand for popcorn or any other product may be highly elastic at one price level but relatively inelastic at much different prices, as Figure 4.9 illustrates.[4] Finally, elasticity, like the demand curve itself, is subject to the vagaries of changing tastes, changing incomes, and changes in the prices or availability of alternative goods. All of these potential changes are ignored when we calculate elasticity along a given demand curve.

Determinants of elasticity

The price elasticity of demand is influenced by all of the determinants of the demand curve. Table 4.5 indicated the actual price elasticity for a variety of familiar goods and services. These large differences in elasticity are explained by several factors. One of them is *price*. If the price of an item is very high in relation to one's income, then price changes will be important. Airline travel and new cars, for example, are quite expensive, so even a small percentage change in their prices could have a big impact on a consumer's budget (and consumption decisions). By contrast, coffee is so cheap

[4] Thus elasticity is not equal to the slope of the demand curve. A linear demand curve has a constant slope but a changing elasticity.

DELTA AIRLINES: PRICES DOWN, REVENUES UP

In 1978 major airlines offered fare discounts in order to boost traffic. The average fare on Delta flights was reduced by 4 percent in the fourth quarter of 1978 (some fares were reduced greatly, others not at all). In response, revenue passenger miles increased by 21 percent. In other words, the quantity demanded increased by a much larger percentage than average air fares fell. This high elasticity of demand led to a 16 percent increase in Delta's total revenue.

FIGURE 4.9 THE PRICE ELASTICITY OF DEMAND

The concept of price elasticity can be used to determine whether kids will spend more money on bubble gum when its price rises, an issue of continuing concern to bubble-gum producers. The answer to this question is yes and no, depending on how high the price goes.

Notice in the table and the graph that total revenue rises when the price of bubble gum increases from 1 cent to 2 cents, and again to 3 cents. At low prices, the demand for bubble gum is relatively inelastic: price and total revenue move in the same direction. As the price of bubble gum continues to increase, however, total revenue starts to fall. As the price is increased from 3 cents to 4 cents, total revenue drops. At higher prices, the demand for bubble gum is relatively elastic: price and total revenue move in opposite directions. Hence the price elasticity of demand depends on where one is on the demand curve; *that is,* at which price-and-quantity combination one starts.

Price of bubble gum ×	*Quantity demanded* =	*Total revenue*	
$0.01	100	$1.00	Low elasticity (total revenue rising as price increases)
0.02	90	1.80	
0.03	70	2.10	
0.04	50	2.00	High elasticity (total revenue falling as price increases)
0.05	25	1.25	
0.06	10	0.60	
0.07	6	0.42	

(a) The demand curve

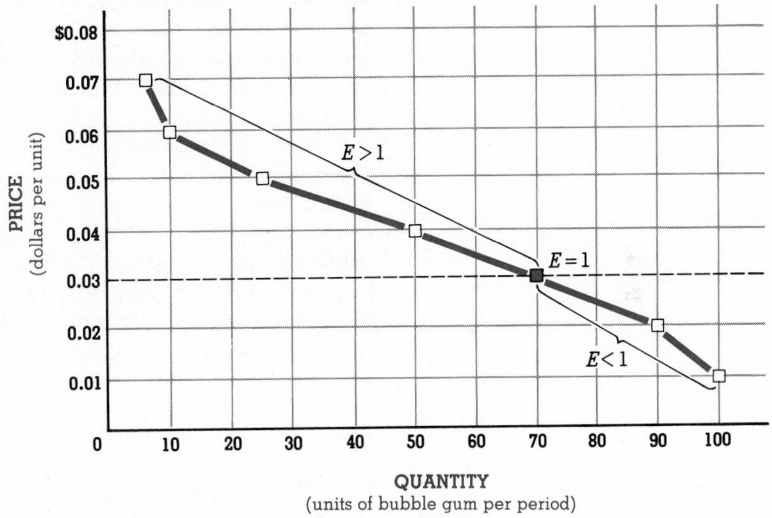

(b) Total revenue

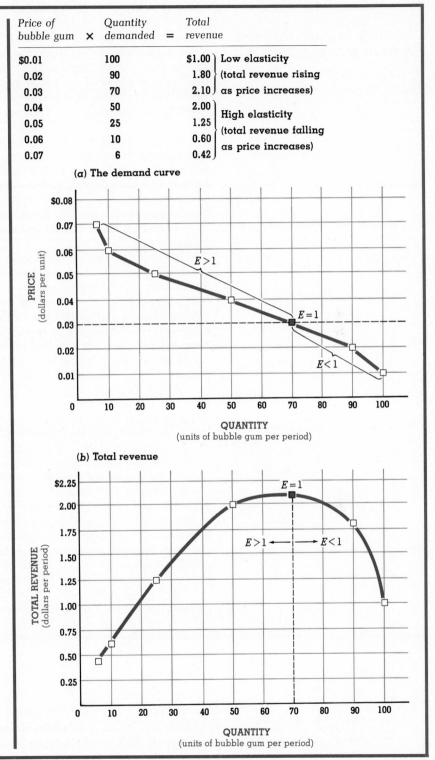

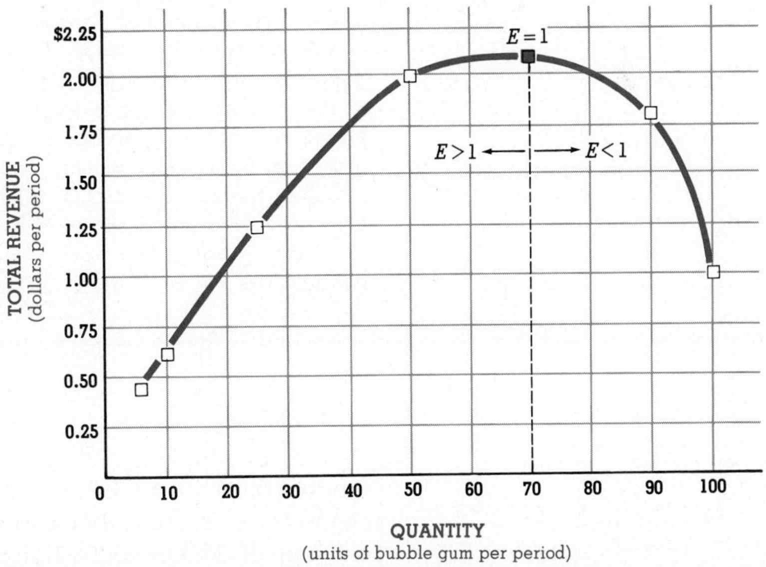

for most people that even a large percentage change in price is of little real significance.

A second determinant of elasticity is the *availability of substitutes.* The high elasticity of demand for fish reflects the fact that consumers can always eat chicken, beef, or pork if fish prices rise.

RAISING THE D.C. GAS TAX: A LESSON IN ELASTICITY

Like many local governments, the District of Columbia is perennially short of revenues. In an effort to raise additional revenue, Mayor Marion Barry of Washington, D.C., decided in early 1980 to increase the city's tax on gasoline. On August 6, 1980, the city government raised the gas tax to 18 cents per gallon, from the previous level of only 10 cents per gallon. The higher gas tax raised the retail price of gasoline by 8 cents, to $1.60 per gallon.

The mayor and city council thought the higher gas tax would be an easy way to increase city revenue. First of all, the difference of a few pennies a gallon would hardly be noticed, they reasoned, especially since gasoline prices were already so high. Second, much of the increased tax would be paid by tourists and suburbanites rather than city residents. Finally, a few pennies a gallon would generate lots of revenue, since District gas stations were then selling 16 million gallons a month.

The D.C. Department of Finance and Revenue had heard about the law of demand, of course. But it thought the reduction in quantity demanded (gasoline sales) would be very small in relation to the gas-tax increase. After all, U.S. motorists had reduced their gasoline consumption only slightly when OPEC had *tripled* the price of gasoline. Economists had consistently estimated the price elasticity of demand for gasoline to be very low (see Table 4.5).

Unfortunately, the District's projections were grossly in error. In August 1980, gasoline sales in the nation's capital fell from 16 million gallons per month to only 11 million. Ten gas stations closed down and more than 300 service-station workers were laid off. Realizing his mistake, Mayor Barry asked the city council to repeal the higher gas tax in November, just four months after it was introduced.

The price elasticity of demand for D.C. gasoline obviously turned out to be much higher than the city had thought. How did the city make such a mistake? Evidently the leaders forgot about the *price and availability of other goods*. True, the price elasticity for gasoline is generally quite low. But motorists in the D.C. area can buy gasoline in the District itself or in the neighboring states of Virginia and Maryland. Hence there are readily available substitutes for D.C. gasoline. By driving just another mile or so, a motorist can buy gasoline not subject to D.C. taxes. When the price of D.C. gasoline went up, motorists responded by doing just that. The ready availability and lower price of gasoline in Maryland and Virginia doomed the hopes of the D.C. government for increased revenues.

On the other hand, most cigarette smokers cannot imagine any other product that could substitute for a cigarette. As a consequence, when cigarette prices rise, smokers do not reduce their purchases very much at all. The price elasticity of demand for cigarettes is very low.

Finally, *time* affects the price elasticity of demand. Car owners cannot switch to coal-fired autos every time the price of gasoline goes up. In the short run, consumers are stuck with their gasoline-drinking automobiles and can only vary the amount of driving they do. Even that can't be varied much, however, unless one relocates one's home or job. Hence the quantity of gasoline demanded doesn't drop much immediately when gasoline prices increase. In the short run, the elasticity of demand for gasoline is quite low. With more time to adjust, however, consumers can buy more fuel-efficient cars, relocate homes or jobs, and even switch fuels. As a consequence, the long-run price elasticity of demand for gasoline is higher than the short-run elasticity.

POLICY IMPLICATIONS: CAVEAT EMPTOR

No discussion of consumer demand would be complete without consideration of the role that advertising plays in shaping our consumer behavior. As we noted earlier, psychiatrists see us as complex bundles of basic drives, anxieties, and layers of consciousness. They presume that we approach the market and all external things with confused senses of guilt, insecurity, and ambition. Economists, on the other hand, regard the consumer as the rational *homo economicus,* conversant with his or her wants and knowledgeable about how to satisfy them. In reality, however, we do not always know what we want or which products will satisfy us. This uncertainty creates a vacuum into which the advertising industry has eagerly stepped.

The efforts of producers to persuade us to buy, buy, buy are as close as the nearest television, radio, magazine, or billboard. Much advertising (including product labeling) is intended to provide information about existing products or to bring new products to our attention. A great deal of advertising, however, is also designed to exploit our senses and lack of knowledge. Recognizing that we are guilt-ridden, insecure, and sex-hungry, advertisers offer us pictures and promises of exoneration, recognition, and love; all we have to do is buy the right product. The attitude is summed up nicely by the preachments of a major perfume seller: "Promise her anything, but give her Arpège." To the extent that our social and psychological needs remain unsatisfied, the sales potential is unlimited.

One of the favorite targets of advertisers is our sense of insecurity. Thousands of products are marketed in ways that appeal to our need for identity, most often by creating a specific identity image for each product. Thousands of brand images are designed to help the consumer answer the nagging question "Who am I?" The answers, of course, vary. *Playboy* magazine says I'm a virile man of the world; Marlboro cigarettes say I'm a rugged individualist who enjoys "man-sized flavor." All users of Tide detergent are neat and worthy homemakers, whereas all Virginia Slims cigarette smokers are liberated women. The right bourbon or scotch is reserved for the successes among us, of either sex.

Other needs and drives are equally susceptible to the blandishments of promoters. Those who fear rejection can find solace and confidence in the right mouth freshener or deodorant; exhibitionist urges can be sublimated with the right bra (or no bra). A measure of immortality may be achieved through insurance plans that will exercise our wishes and control in our absence. On the other hand, eternal youth can be preserved with a proper mix of vitamin supplements, face lotions, and laxatives. Some products even appeal to a variety of needs simultaneously, such as the low-calorie ice cream sundae, which satisfies the craving for self-indulgence while allaying our sense of guilt.

Are wants created?

It does not appear reasonable to identify the blandishments of advertisers as the origin of our needs and desires. In the first place, the dynamics of personality structure and social interaction give rise to generalized drives and needs that operate in any economic context. Even members of the most primitive tribes, uncontaminated by the seductions of advertising, encrusted themselves with rings, bracelets, and pendants. These adornments demonstrated their worth and status, and alternately satisfied and denied the urges of Freud's id, ego, and superego. Second, advertising has grown to massive proportions only in the last three decades, but regular increases in consumption spending have taken place throughout recorded history. Accordingly, on both conceptual and historical grounds, it is a mistake to attribute the growth of consumption to the persuasions of advertisers.

This is not to say that advertising has necessarily made us happier or directed consumption into preferred channels. Although advertising cannot be charged with creating our needs, it does provide specific (if not necessarily correct) outlets for satisfaction of those needs. The objective of all advertising is to alter the choices we make. Just as product images are used to attract us to particular commodities, so are pictures of hungry, ill-clothed children used to persuade us to give money to charity. In the same way, public-relations gimmicks are employed to sway our votes for public servants. In the case of consumer products, advertising seeks to increase tastes for particular goods and services and therewith our willingness to pay. ***A successful advertising campaign is one that shifts the demand curve to the right,*** inducing consumers to increase their purchases of a product at every price (see Figure 4.10). Advertising may also

FIGURE 4.10 THE IMPACT OF ADVERTISING ON A DEMAND CURVE

Advertising seeks to increase our taste for a particular product. If our taste (the product's perceived utility) increases, so will our willingness to buy. The resulting change in demand is reflected in a rightward shift of the demand curve, often accompanied by diminished elasticity.

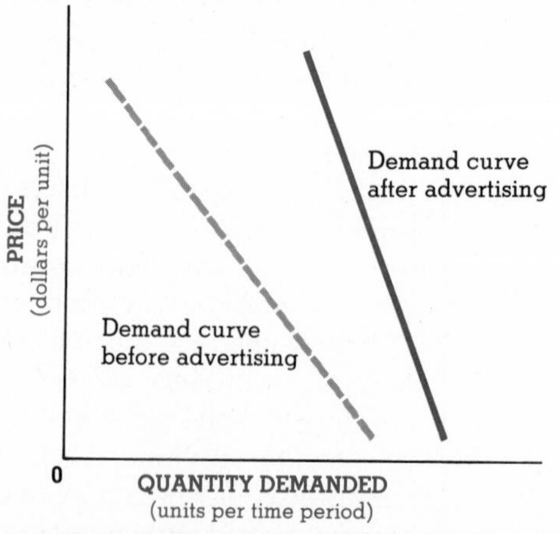

MILLER LITE: AN ADVERTISING SUCCESS

In January 1975 Miller Brewing Company set out to change the tastes of U.S. beer drinkers. It introduced Miller Lite, a low-calorie beer. Many other companies had produced low-calorie beers and failed. But Miller was convinced it could succeed. Other companies had directed their sales pitches to diet-conscious people and had ignored the mass of beer drinkers. In introducing its new beer, Miller emphasized that Lite tasted as good as regular beer but simply contained fewer calories. In its advertising, Miller used macho sports figures and other celebrities to emphasize that Lite was *real* beer, not a diet drink for sissies. As one analyst noted, "The typical beer drinker is not dietetically oriented, but when he sees a football player drinking this low-calorie beer, he figures he shouldn't be ashamed to drink it." Miller spent nearly $10 million per year to get this message across.

The results of the advertising campaign were phenomenal. Sales of Miller Lite skyrocketed and Miller Brewing moved up from fifth place to second place in total U.S. beer sales. In the wake of Miller's success, all other brewers were forced to introduce their own low-calorie beers to satisfy the new tastes of American drinkers. In the process, the demand for regular beer shifted to the left, while the demand for light beers shifted to the right.

make the demand curve less elastic, thus reducing consumer responses to price increases. By influencing our choices in this way, advertising alters the distribution of our consumption expenditures, if not their level.

SUMMARY

- In their role as consumers, Americans purchase roughly $2 trillion worth of goods and services each year. On a per capita basis, we consume nearly five times as much as the rest of the world.
- Our desires for goods and services originate in the structure of personality and social dynamics, and are not explained by economic theory. Economic theory focuses on *demand*, that is, our ability and willingness to *pay* for goods.
- The determinants of individual consumer demand include tastes, price, income, expectations, and the price and availability of other goods.
- Our demand for goods is dependent on the expectation of satisfaction, or *utility*. We will be willing to buy a product only if it increases our total utility.
- Marginal utility measures the additional satisfaction obtained from consuming one more unit of a good. The law of diminishing marginal utility says that the more of a product we consume, the smaller the increments of pleasure we tend to derive from additional units of it.
- The law of diminishing marginal utility translates readily into the law of demand, which asserts that we will buy increasing quantities

of a product as its price falls. That is, an inverse relationship exists between quantity demanded and price. This law is graphically illustrated by a downward-sloping demand curve.

- The shape and position of any particular demand curve depend on a consumer's income, tastes, expectations, and the price and number of substitute and complementary goods. Should any of these things change, the assumption of *ceteris paribus* will no longer hold and the demand curve will *shift,* indicating that a different quantity will be demanded at any given price.
- In choosing among alternative goods and services, a consumer compares the prices and anticipated satisfactions that they offer. To maximize utility with one's available income—to achieve an optimal mix of goods and services—one has to get the most utility for every dollar spent. To do so one must compare relative prices and pleasures, and choose those goods that offer the most pleasure per dollar.
- The price elasticity of demand is a numerical measure of consumer response to a change in price (*ceteris paribus*). It equals the percentage change in quantity demanded divided by the percentage change in price. Elasticity depends on the relative price of a good, the availability of substitutes, and time.
- Advertising seeks to change consumer tastes, and thus the willingness to buy. If tastes do change, the demand curve will shift.

Terms to remember

Define the following terms:

demand
utility
total utility
marginal utility
law of diminishing marginal utility
ceteris paribus
quantity demanded
law of demand
demand schedule
demand curve
shift in demand
substitute goods
complementary goods
opportunity cost
optimal consumption
price elasticity of demand
total revenue

Questions for discussion

1. Is it possible to have a great taste for French cooking and still eat at McDonald's? What is the relationship of tastes, income, prices, and consumer behavior in this case?

2. If status anxieties create a need for a shiny new Statusmobile, will our car purchases still be affected by income or prices?

3. It has been suggested that a consumer can get the most satisfaction from expenditures by buying a mix of goods such that the marginal utility of the last dollar spent on each good is equal to the marginal utility of the last dollar spent on every other good. Is this suggestion correct? Can you prove it?

4. What is the effect of Schlitz beer advertisements on your total consumption of beer? Your demand for Budweiser?

5. What is the price elasticity of demand for gasoline in Washington, D.C. (see p. 106)? for Delta flights (see p. 104)? What accounts for these elasticities?

Problem

The following figures summarize someone's demand for ice cream:

Price per cone:	**$0.50**	**$0.40**	**$0.30**	**$0.20**	**$0.10**
Cones demanded per day:	**1**	**2**	**4**	**6**	**9**

Using this information,

(a) Draw the demand curve.
(b) Indicate the change in quantity demanded as the price of ice cream drops from 50 to 40 cents.
(c) Calculate the price elasticity of demand for this change.
(d) Calculate the price elasticity of demand for a change in price from 30 to 20 cents.
(e) Explain the difference in the price elasticities calculated for *c* and *d*.

CHAPTER 5

THE COSTS OF PRODUCTION

Although consumers desire to buy a vast array of goods and services, and are willing to pay for that privilege, it is not so obvious how or why their desires can be fulfilled. If consumers are to buy digital watches, designer jeans, and video cassette players, somebody must agree to produce and sell these goods. Knowledge of consumer behavior will not in itself enable us to understand how product markets work. Like all markets, product markets have two sides, one of demand, the other of supply. **Supply** refers to the willingness and ability to sell (produce) goods and services at different prices.

supply: The ability and willingness to sell (produce) specific quantities of a good at alternative prices in a given time period (*ceteris paribus*).

In this chapter we shall begin to explore the supply side of product markets. Our inquiry begins with a quick survey of who's who on the supply side, then examines the nature of production costs. Our major objective in this chapter is to determine the costs of producing desired goods. In Chapter 6 we shall look at how producers' supply decisions are affected by these costs.

WHO'S WHO IN BUSINESS

We can begin our exploration of the supply side of product markets by observing who actually supplies goods and services in the United States. At the present time, more than 14 *million* business firms produce and supply the goods and services we demand (see Table 5.1). Among these firms are more than 218,000 grocery stores, 216,000

TABLE 5.1 NUMBER AND TYPES OF BUSINESS FIRMS, BY INDUSTRY

Millions of business firms supply goods and services to U.S. product markets. They are organized as proprietorships, partnerships, or corporations. Most proprietorships are found in agriculture, services, and retail trade.

	Proprietorship		*Partnership*		*Corporation*		*Total*	
Industry	*Number (thousands)*	*Percent of industry*	*Number (thousands)*	*Percent of industry*	*Number (thousands*	*Percent of industry*	*Number (thousands*	*Percent of industry*
Agriculture, forestry, fishing	3,177	94	121	4	66	2	3,364	100
Mining	71	63	22	20	19	17	112	100
Construction	994	78	69	5	215	17	1,278	100
Manufacturing	224	46	28	6	231	48	483	100
Transportation, public utilities	385	79	17	3	85	18	487	100
Wholesale trade	307	53	29	5	238	42	574	100
Retail trade	1,862	76	164	7	433	17	2,459	100
Financial, insurance, real estate	895	50	476	26	433	24	1,804	100
Services	3,303	82	227	6	516	12	4,046	100
	11,346*	77	1,153	8	2,242*	15	14,741*	100

*Sums do not total because businesses not allocable to individual industries are included.

Source: U.S. Department of Commerce, *Statistical Abstract of the United States*, 1981.

gas stations, and 111,000 purveyors of alcoholic beverages. Among them also are a handful of giant computer firms that provide the machinery for counting and classifying the millions of other firms.

Most people think all U.S. business firms are corporations. This is far from the truth. Corporations account for only 15 percent of all business firms. Much more common are the other two forms of business enterprise, proprietorships and partnerships. The primary distinction among these three forms lies in their ownership characteristics. A single proprietorship is a firm owned by one individual. A partnership is owned by a small number of individuals. A corporation is typically owned by many individuals (stockholders)—even hundreds of thousands.

One consequence of different ownership structures is reflected in the disparate size of proprietorships, partnerships, and corporations. In general, the more people you can get to invest in a firm, the larger its potential size. As a rule, corporations tend to be much larger than the other two forms because they bring together the financial resources of more individuals. Single proprietorships are typically quite small, because few individuals have vast sources of wealth or credit. The typical proprietorship has less than $10,000 in assets, whereas the average corporation has assets in excess of $1

FIGURE 5.1 U.S. BUSINESS FIRMS: NUMBERS VS. SIZE

Proprietorships (individually owned companies) are the most common form of American business firm. Corporations are so large, however, that they account for most business sales and assets. Although only 15 percent of all firms are incorporated, corporations control 87 percent of all sales and 95 percent of all assets.

Source: U.S. Department of Commerce (1980 data).

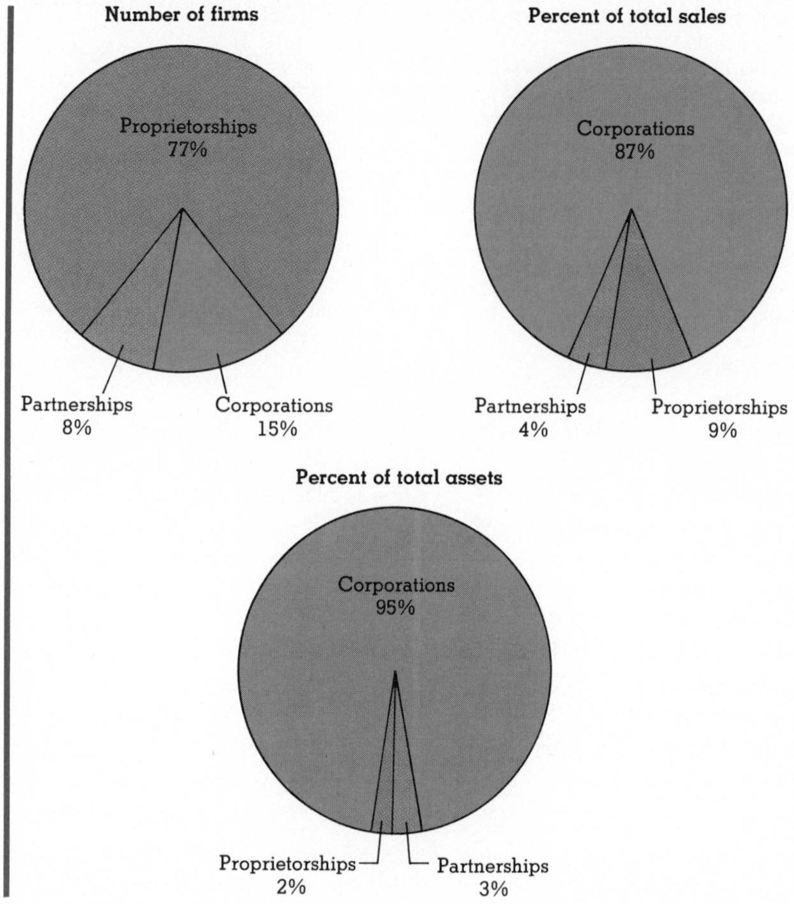

million. As a result of their size, corporations dominate market transactions, accounting for 87 percent of all business sales.

We can describe who's who in the business community, then, in two very different ways. In terms of numbers, the single proprietorship is the most common type of business firm in America. Proprietorships are particularly dominant in agriculture (the family farm), retail trade (the corner grocery store), and services (your dentist). In terms of size, however, the corporation is the dominant force in the economy (see Figure 5.1). The four largest nonfinancial corporations in the country (AT&T, Exxon, GM, Mobil) alone have more assets than *all* the 11 million proprietorships represented in Table 5.1. Just one of the four, General Motors, commands over $40 billion in assets and $60 billion in sales, and employs more than 600,000 workers (and pays its president four times as much as we pay the president of the country). Even in agriculture, where corporate entities are still comparatively rare, the few "agribusiness" corporations are so large as to dominate many thousands of small farms. Some of the consequences of corporate size, especially in regard to economic and political power, are discussed in Chapters 8–10.

THE PRODUCTION FUNCTION

No matter how large a business is or who owns it, all businesses confront one central fact: it costs something to produce goods. To produce corn, a farmer needs land, water, seed, equipment, and labor. To produce fillings, a dentist needs a chair, a drill, some space, and labor. Even the "production" of educational services (e.g., this economics class) requires the use of labor (your teacher), land (on which the school is built), and some capital (the building and blackboard). In short, unless you are producing unrefined, unpackaged air, you need some **factors of production,** that is, resources that can be used to produce a good or service.

factors of production: Resource inputs used to produce goods and services; for example, land, labor, capital.

Resource costs

The first inklings of what costs are should be evident already. If factors of production are needed to produce goods, then the amount needed of such factors must be a basic measure of cost. The costs of production are, in fact, measured in terms of the value of these factors. As always, ***we gauge the value of the resources used in the production of one good by their opportunity costs,*** that is, the other goods and services that could have been produced with the same resources. The costs of this class are thus measured in the first instance by the amount of land, labor, and capital it requires. The *value* of these resources is measured in terms of the goods and services forgone when we "produce" this class.

The essential question for production is how many resources are actually needed to produce a given product. The answer depends on our technological know-how and how we organize the production process. At any moment, however, there is sure to be some minimum amount of resources needed to produce a good. Or, to put it another way, there will always be some *maximum* amount of output attainable from a given quantity of resources. These limits to our production of any good are reflected in the **production function.** The production function tells us the maximum amount of good X producible from various combinations of factor inputs. With one chair and one drill, a dentist can fill a maximum of 32 cavities per day. With two chairs, a drill, and an assistant, a dentist can fill up to 55 cavities per day.

production function: A technological relation expressing the maximum quantity of a good attainable from different combinations of factor inputs.

A production function, then, is a technological summary of our ability to produce a particular good.[1] Table 5.2 provides a partial glimpse of one such function. In this case, the desired output is designer jeans, as produced by University Jeans Corporation. The essential inputs in the production of jeans are: land, labor (seamstresses), and capital (a factory and sewing machines). With these inputs, a person can buy denim by the yard, cut and sew it, and sell fancy jeans to status-conscious consumers.

As in all production endeavors, we want to know how many pairs of jeans we can produce with our available resources. We shall

[1] By contrast, the production-possibilities curve discussed in Chapter 1 expresses our ability to produce various *combinations* of goods, given the use of *all* our resources. The production-possibilities curve summarizes the output capacity of the entire economy. A production function describes the capacity of a single firm.

TABLE 5.2 THE PRODUCTION OF JEANS (pairs per day)

A production function tells us the maximum amount of output attainable from alternative combinations of factor inputs. This particular function tells us how many pairs of jeans we can produce in a day with a given factory and varying quantities of capital and labor. With one sewing machine and one seamstress, we can produce a maximum of 15 pairs of jeans per day, as indicated in the second column of the second row. To produce more jeans, we need more labor and/or more capital.

Capital input (sewing machines per day)	*Labor input (workers per day)*							
	0	**1**	**2**	**3**	**4**	**5**	**6**	**7**
0	0	0	0	0	0	0	0	0
1	0	15	34	44	48	50	51	46
2	0	20	46	64	72	78	81	80
3	0	21	50	73	82	92	99	102

assume that the factory is already built, with fixed space dimensions. The only inputs we can vary are labor (the number of seamstresses per day) and additional capital (the number of sewing machines we lease per day).

As you would expect, the quantity of jeans we can produce depends on the amount of labor and capital we employ. The purpose of the production function in Table 5.2 is to tell us just *how much* output can increase as we employ more factors of production.

Consider the simplest option, that of employing no labor or capital (the upper left corner of Table 5.2). An empty factory cannot produce any jeans; maximum output is zero per day. The lesson here is quite simple: no inputs, no outputs. Even though land, capital (an empty factory), and even denim are available, some essential labor and capital inputs are missing, and jeans production is precluded.

Suppose now we employ some labor (a seamstress) but do not lease any sewing machines. Will output increase? Not according to the production function. The first row of Table 5.2 illustrates the consequences of employing labor without any additional capital equipment. Without sewing machines, the seamstresses cannot make jeans out of denim. Maximum output remains at zero, no matter how much labor is employed in this case.

productivity: Output per unit of input; for example, output per labor-hour.

The dilemma of seamstresses without sewing machines illustrates a more general principle of production. ***The* productivity *of any factor of production depends on the amount of other resources available to it.*** Industrious, hard-working seamstresses cannot make designer jeans successfully without sewing machines.

We can increase the productivity of seamstresses by providing them with machines. The production function again tells us by *how much* jeans output could increase if we leased some sewing machines. Suppose we leased just one machine per day. Now the second row of Table 5.2 is the relevant one. It says jeans output will remain at zero if we lease one machine but employ no labor. If we employ one machine *and* one worker, however, the jeans will start rolling out the front door. Maximum output under these circumstances (row 2, column 2) is 15 pairs of jeans per day. Now we're in business!

The remaining columns of row 2 tell us how many additional jeans we can produce if we hire more workers, still leasing only one sewing machine. Conversely, if we read down any column of Table 5.2 we can see how jeans output could increase if we leased more sewing machines, with a given number of seamstresses. For example, with one machine and two seamstresses, maximum output is 34 pairs per day. If we lease an additional machine but hire no additional workers, maximum output jumps to 46 pairs per day.

Efficiency

The production function summarized in Table 5.2 underscores the essential relationship between resource *inputs* and product *outputs*. It also provides a basic introduction to economic costs. To produce 46 pairs of jeans per day, we need two sewing machines, two seamstresses, a garage, and the denim itself. All of these inputs comprise the resource cost of producing that many jeans. Were we to produce 46 jeans with another combination of inputs—for example, one machine and slightly more than three workers per day—the value of those inputs would be our basic measure of cost.

Another essential feature of Table 5.2 is that it conveys the *maximum* output of jeans producible from particular input combinations. The standard seamstress and sewing machine, when brought together at University Jeans Corporation, can produce *at most* 15 pairs of jeans per day. They could also produce a lot less. Indeed, a careless cutter can waste a lot of denim. A lazy or inattentive one will not keep the sewing machines humming. As many a producer has learned, actual sales (output) can fall far short of the limits described in the production function. Indeed, jeans output will reach the levels of Table 5.2 only if the jeans factory operates with relative **efficiency**. This requires getting *maximum* output from the resources used in the production process.

efficiency: Maximum output of a good from the resources used in production.

We can always be inefficient, of course. This merely means getting less output than possible for the inputs we use. But this is not a desirable situation, however comfortable it might be for the seamstresses in question. To a factory manager, it means less output for a given amount of input (cost). To society as a whole, inefficiency implies a waste of resources. If seamstresses are not performing up to par, society is either (1) getting fewer jeans than it should for the resources devoted to jeans production or (2) giving up too many other goods and services in order to get a desired quantity of jeans. From a social (economy-wide) perspective, labor is one of our scarce resources. When we allocate some of it to sewing jeans, we are forsaking the opportunity to use it to produce something else. The seamstresses that represent a payroll cost to the University Jeans Corporation also represent an **opportunity cost** to society. If they don't function efficiently, we all end up with fewer goods than possible.[2]

opportunity cost: The most desired goods or services that are forgone in order to obtain something else.

[2] Inefficiency in the production of any good implies that the economy is operating *inside* our production-possibilities frontier, rather than on it; see pp. 14–15.

Although we can always do worse than the production function suggests, we cannot do better, at least in the short run. The production function represents the best we can do with our current technological know-how. For the moment, at least, there is no better way to produce a specific good. As our technological and managerial capabilities increase, however, we will attain higher levels of productivity. These advances in our productive capability will be represented by new production functions.[3] These new functions will then define the new and higher limits of efficiency, at least until new technologies are discovered.

MARGINAL PRODUCTIVITY

short run: The period in which the quantity (and quality) of some inputs is fixed, that is, cannot be changed.

Let us step back from the threshold of scientific advance for a moment and return to University Jeans Corporation. Forget about possible technological breakthroughs in jeans production (e.g., electronic sewing machines, robot seamstresses) and concentrate on the economic realities of our modest endeavor. In the **short run,** we are stuck with existing technology. We are also encumbered with commitments to some factors of production. In particular, suppose we have already committed ourselves not only to the lease of the factory but also to the lease of only one sewing machine. Under these circumstances, there is only one input we can vary in order to get more jeans output. That variable input is labor. We need to focus, then, on the relationship between jeans output and additional quantities of labor.

As we noted before, a factory and sewing machine without seamstresses produce no jeans. This was observed in Table 5.2 (second row, first column) and is now illustrated by point *A* in Figure 5.2. Only after we employ a seamstress do jeans start appearing. By placing just one seamstress in the factory we can produce 15 pairs per day. This possibility is represented by point *B*. At this point, *total* output is 15 pairs per day.

marginal physical product *(MPP)*: The change in total output associated with one additional unit of input.

Another way of viewing this situation is to note that total output has *increased* by 15 pairs when we employ the first seamstress. This is called the **marginal physical product** of that first seamstress, that is, the *increase* in total output that results from employment of one more unit of (labor) input. Without that first seamstress we get zero output; with her, we get 15 pairs of jeans per day.

Marginal physical product provides a basic measure of how desirable additional seamstresses are. Consider the impact of hiring more seamstresses. According to Table 5.2, with one seamstress we can get 15 pairs per day, with two seamstresses we can get 34 pairs. Potential output more than doubles! Whereas the *marginal* physical product of the first seamstress was only 15 pairs, a second seamstress increases total output by 19 pairs. This is represented by point *c* on the marginal physical product curve in Figure 5.2 and also by the rise in the total output curve (to point *C*).

[3] From an economy-wide perspective, technological advances are illustrated by outward shifts of the production-possibilities curve; see p. 16.

FIGURE 5.2 MARGINAL PHYSICAL PRODUCT

Marginal physical product is the *increase* in total output that results from employing one more unit of input. The second unit of labor, for example, increases *total* output from 15 (point *B*) to 34 (point C). Hence the *marginal* output (*MPP*) of the second worker is 19 pairs of jeans (point c). What is the *MPP* of the third seamstress? What happens to *total* output when she is hired?

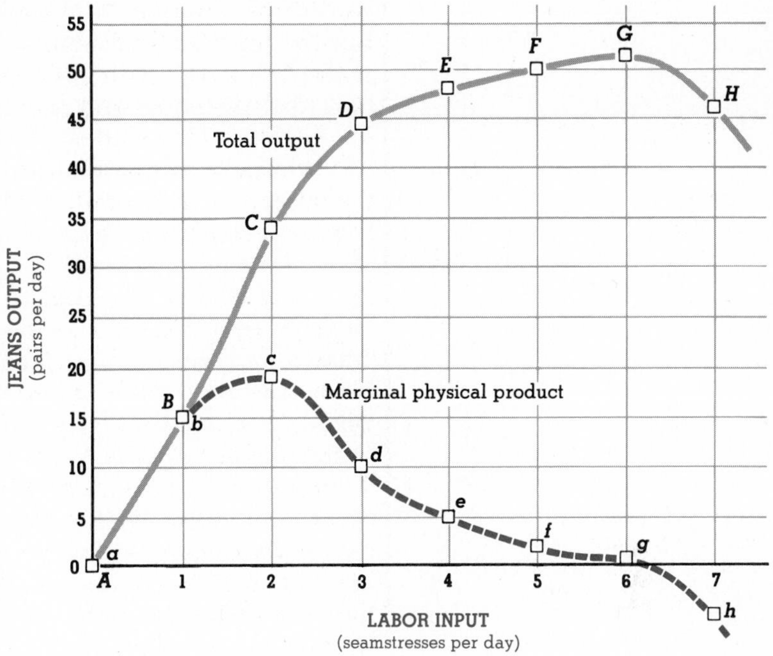

The higher *MPP* of the second seamstress raises a question about the first seamstress. Why was her *MPP* lower? Was she lazy? Is the second seamstress faster, less distracted, or harder working?

The higher *MPP* of the second seamstress is not explained by superior talents or effort. We assume, in fact, that all "units of labor" are equal, that is, one seamstress is just as good as another.[4] Their different marginal products are explained by the structure of the production process, not by their respective abilities. The first seamstress had not only to sew jeans but also to unfold bolts of denim, measure the jeans, sketch out the patterns, and cut them to approximate size. She spent a lot of time going from one task to another. Despite her best efforts (we're assuming she is working efficiently), she simply could not do everything at once.

A second seamstress greatly changes this situation. With two workers, less time is spent running from one task to another. While one seamstress is measuring and cutting, the other can continue sewing. This improved ratio of labor to other factors of production results in the large jump in total output. The superior *MPP* of the second seamstress is not unique to her; it would have occurred even if we had hired the seamstresses in the reverse order. What matters is the amount of other factors of production each unit of labor must work with.

[4] In reality, seamstresses do differ greatly in energy, talent, and diligence. These differences can be eliminated by measuring units of labor in *constant-quality* units. A seamstress who works twice as hard as everyone else would count as two *quality-adjusted* units of labor.

Diminishing returns

Unfortunately, these large increases in output cannot be maintained as still more workers are hired. Look what happens when a third seamstress is hired. Total jeans production continues to increase. But the increase from point *C* to point *D* in Figure 5.2 is only 10 pairs per day. Hence the *MPP* of the third seamstress (10 pairs) is *less* than that of the second (19 pairs). Marginal physical product is *diminishing.* This is illustrated by point *d* in Figure 5.2.

What accounts for this decline in *MPP*? The answer again lies in the ratio of labor to other factors of production. A third seamstress begins to crowd our facilities. We still have only one sewing machine. Two people cannot sew at the same time. As a result, some time is wasted as the seamstresses wait for their turns at the machine. Even if they split up the various jobs, there will still be some "downtime," since measuring and cutting are not so time-consuming as sewing. In this sense, we cannot make full use of a third worker. The relative scarcity of other inputs (capital and land) constrains the marginal physical product of labor.

Resource constraints are even more evident when a fourth seamstress is hired. Total output does increase again, but the increase this time is very small. With three workers, we got 44 pairs of jeans per day (point *D*); with four workers, we get a maximum of 48 pairs (point *E*). Thus the marginal physical product of the fourth seamstress is only 4 pairs of jeans. A fourth seamstress really begins to strain our productive capacity to the limit. There simply aren't enough machines to make productive use of so much labor.

The situation gets downright comical if a seventh seamstress is hired. Now the seamstresses are getting in each other's way, arguing, and wasting denim. Total output actually falls when a seventh seamstress is hired! In other words, the *MPP* of the seventh seamstress is *negative,* as reflected in point *h* of Figure 5.2 and the downturn in the total output curve (from 51 to 46 pairs of jeans).

LAW OF DIMINISHING RETURNS The problem of crowded facilities applies to most production processes. In the short run, a production process is characterized by a fixed amount of available land and capital. Typically, the only factor that can be varied in the short run is labor. Yet ***as more labor is hired, each unit of labor has less capital and land to work with.*** This is simple division: the available facilities are being shared by more and more workers. At some point, this begins to matter. When it does, marginal physical product starts to decline. This eventuality is so common that it is the basis for another law: the **law of diminishing returns.** This law says that the marginal physical product of any factor of production (e.g., labor) will begin to diminish at some point as more of it is used in a given production setting.

law of diminishing returns: The marginal physical product of a variable factor declines as more of it is employed with a given quantity of other (fixed) inputs.

RESOURCE COSTS

The law of diminishing returns has important implications for the costs of production. The economic cost of a product is measured by the value of the resources needed to produce it. What we have seen here is that those resource requirements increase. Each additional seamstress produces fewer and fewer jeans. In effect, then, each additional pair of jeans produced uses more and more labor.

Suppose that we are employing one sewing machine and one seamstress again, for a total output of 15 pairs of jeans per day. How much labor are we using *per pair*? The answer is one-fifteenth of a seamstress' day, that is, 0.067 units of labor.

Marginal cost

marginal cost: The increase in total cost associated with a one-unit increase in production.

In order to increase total output, we need more labor, that is, a second seamstress. When we employ that second seamstress, output increases by 19 pairs. To get these additional 19 pairs, we did not lease more space or machines, but instead just hired one more unit of labor. Hence an increase in labor and denim costs is the only extra, or marginal, cost of those additional jeans. **Marginal cost** refers to the *increase* in total costs required to get one additional unit of output. In this case, we are only interested in labor and denim costs, since no additional land or capital is required to increase output. Since we need one more unit of labor to get 19 additional pairs of jeans, we can say that 1 ÷ 19, or 0.053 units of labor, is the amount of labor input required to produce *one* more pair of jeans. That labor cost plus the price of the denim itself comprises the marginal cost of additional jeans.

Notice that the marginal labor cost of jeans production declines when the second seamstress is hired. Marginal cost falls from 0.067 units of labor (plus denim) per pair to only 0.053 units of labor per pair. It costs less labor *per pair* to use two seamstresses rather than only one. This is a reflection of the increased *MPP* of the second seamstress. ***Whenever* MPP *is increasing, the marginal cost of producing a good must be falling.*** This is illustrated in Figure 5.3.

Unfortunately, as we observed a moment ago, marginal physical product typically declines. As it does, the marginal costs of production rise. In this sense, each additional pair of jeans becomes more expensive—it uses up more and more labor per pair. This inverse relationship between *MPP* and marginal cost is illustrated in Figure 5.3. The third seamstress has an *MPP* of 10 pairs, as illustrated by point *d* in Figure 5.3*a*. The marginal labor input of these extra 10 pairs is thus 1 ÷ 10, or 0.10 units of labor. In other words, one-tenth of a seamstress' daily effort goes into each pair of jeans. This additional labor cost *per unit* is illustrated by 1/*d* in Figure 5.3*a*.

Increasing marginal cost is as common as diminishing returns. Indeed, increasing marginal costs are typically caused by declining *MPP*. These increasing costs are not the fault of any person or factor, but simply a reflection of the resource constraints found in any established production setting (i.e., existing and limited plant and equipment). Nevertheless, they imply that increased output of any good from existing facilities will drive up the economic cost of that good. To keep costs from rising, we would have to discover new and improved production technologies or build better production facilities. These are *long-run* possibilities, however, and not available for short-run cost savings. In the *short run*, the quantity and quality of land and capital are fixed, and we can vary only their intensity

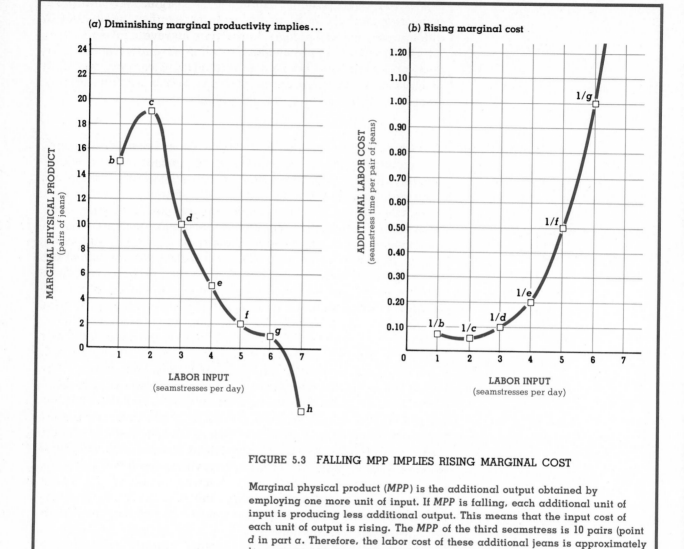

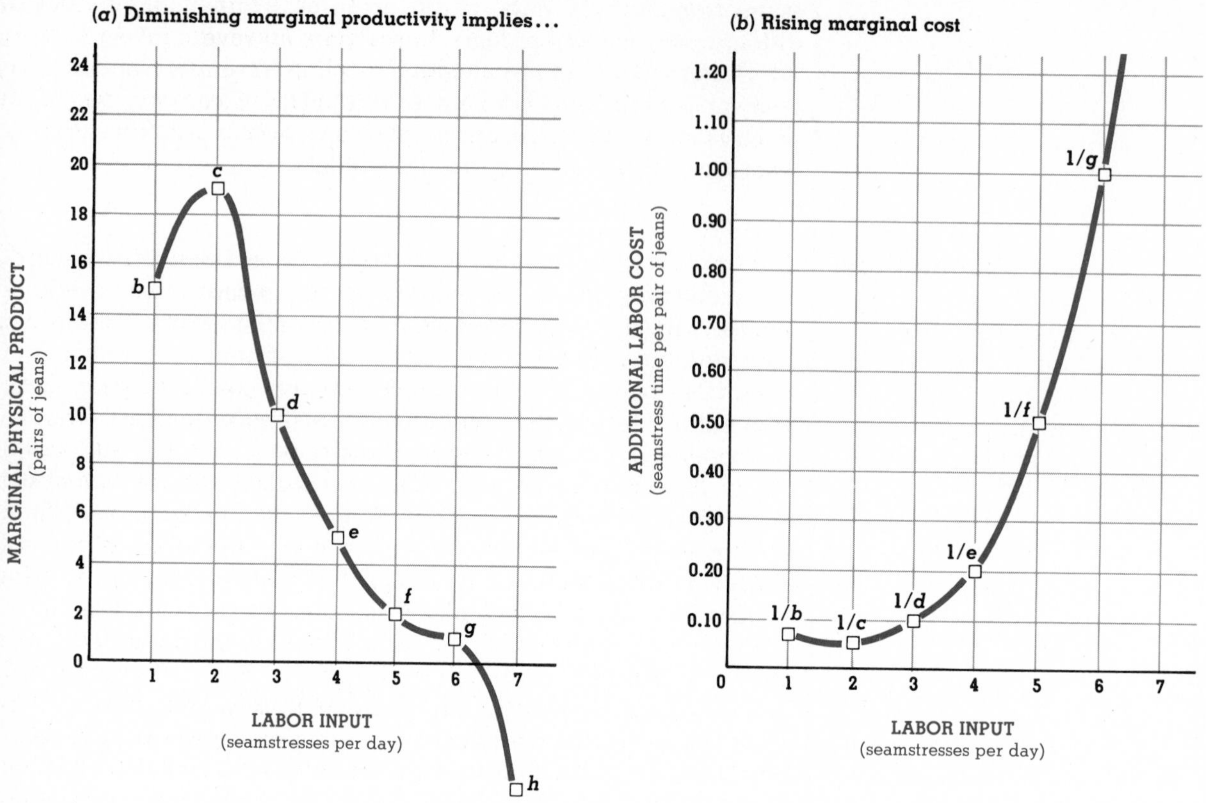

FIGURE 5.3 FALLING MPP IMPLIES RISING MARGINAL COST

Marginal physical product (*MPP*) is the additional output obtained by employing one more unit of input. If *MPP* is falling, each additional unit of input is producing less additional output. This means that the input cost of each unit of output is rising. The *MPP* of the third seamstress is 10 pairs (point *d* in part *a*. Therefore, the labor cost of these additional jeans is approximately $^{1}/_{10}$ unit of labor per pair (point 1/*d* in part *b*).

of use (e.g., with more or fewer seamstresses). It is in this context that we keep running into diminishing marginal returns and rising marginal costs.

DOLLAR COSTS

This entire discussion of diminishing returns and marginal costs may seem a bit alien. After all, we are interested in the costs of production, and costs are typically measured in *dollars,* not such technical notions as *MPP* or whatever. A jeans producer needs to know how many dollars it costs to keep jeans flowing; he doesn't want a lecture on marginal physical product. Can't we provide any useful answers?

A jeans manufacturer need not study marginal physical products, or even the production function. He can confine his attention to dollar costs. The dollar costs he observes, however, are directly related to the underlying production function. To understand why his costs rise—and how they might be reduced—some understanding of the production function is necessary. In this section we shall translate production functions into dollar costs.

Total cost

total cost: The market value of all resources used to produce a good or service.

The **total cost** of producing a product includes the market value of all the resources used in its production. To determine these costs, we simply identify all the resources used in production and their value, then add everything up.

In the production of jeans, these resources included land, labor, and capital. Table 5.3 identifies these resources, their unit values, and the total costs associated with their use. This table is based on maximum output of 15 pairs of jeans per day, with the use of one seamstress and one sewing machine. The rent on the factory is $100 per day, a sewing machine costs $20 per day, the wages of a seamstress are $80 per day. We shall assume University Jeans Corporation can purchase bolts of denim for $30 apiece, each of which provides enough denim for 10 pairs of jeans. In other words, one-tenth of a bolt ($3 worth of material) is required for one pair of jeans. We shall ignore any other potential expenses.[5] With these assumptions, the total cost of producing 15 pairs of jeans per day amounts to $245.

fixed costs: Costs of production that do not change when the rate of output is altered; for example, the cost of basic plant and equipment.

Total costs will, of course, change as we alter the rate of production. But not all costs increase. On the contrary, some costs don't increase at all when output is increased. These are **fixed costs** in the sense that they do not vary with the rate of output. The factory lease is an example. Once you lease a factory, you are obligated to pay for it, whether you use it or not. The person who owns the factory wants $100 per day, whether you produce any jeans or not. Even if you produce no jeans, you are still going to have to pay the rent. That is the essence of fixed costs.

The leased sewing machine is another example of a fixed cost. When you rent a sewing machine, you must pay the rental charge. It doesn't matter whether you use it for a few minutes or all day long—the rental charge is fixed at $20 per day.

[5] One cost we are ignoring is profit. Traditionally, "normal" profits are counted as a cost of production. The concept of profit is explored in Chapter 6.

TABLE 5.3 THE TOTAL COSTS OF PRODUCTION
(total cost of producing 15 pairs of jeans per day)

The total cost of producing a good equals the market value of all the resources used in its production. In this case, we have assumed that the production of 15 pairs of jeans per day requires resources worth $245.

Resource	*Price*	*Total cost*
1 factory	$100 per day	$100
1 sewing machine	20 per day	20
1 seamstress	80 per day	80
1.5 bolts of denim	30 per bolt	45
Total		$245

FIGURE 5.4 THE COSTS OF JEANS PRODUCTION

Total costs include both fixed and variable costs. Fixed costs must be paid even if no output is produced (point *A*). Variable costs start at zero and increase with the rate of output. The total cost of producing 15 pairs of jeans (point *B*) includes $120 in fixed costs (rent on the factory and sewing machines) and $125 in variable costs (denim and wages). Total cost rises as output increases because additional variable costs must be incurred.

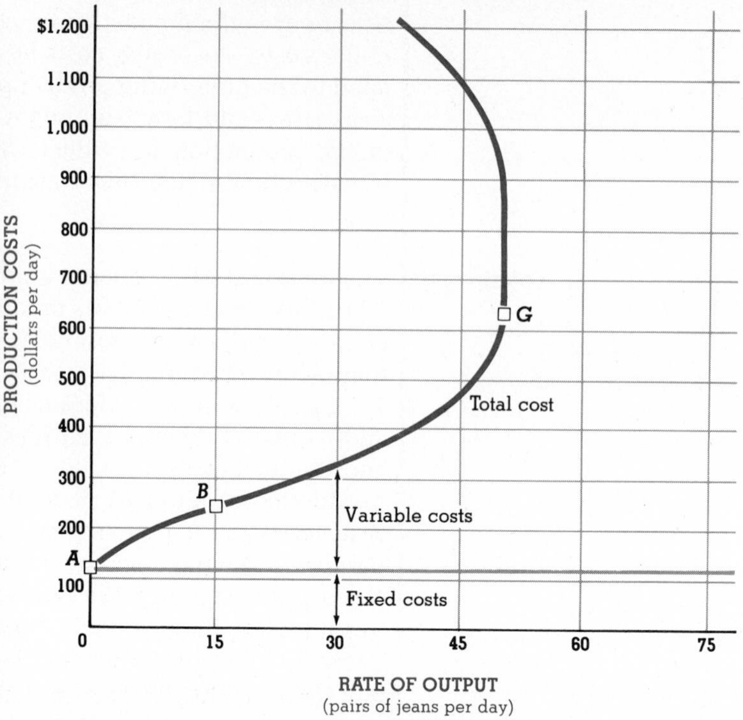

variable costs: Costs of production that change when the rate of output is altered; for example, labor and material costs.

Labor costs are another story altogether. The amount of labor employed in jeans production can be varied easily. If we decide not to open the factory tomorrow, we can just call Suzy Seamstress and tell her to take the day off. We will still have to pay rent, but we can cut back on wages. On the other hand, if we want to increase daily output, we can also get additional seamstresses easily and quickly. Labor, then, is regarded as a **variable cost** in this line of work, that is, a cost that varies with the rate of output.

The denim itself is another variable cost. Denim not used today can be saved for tomorrow. Hence, how much we "spend" on denim today is directly related to how many jeans we produce. In this sense, the cost of denim input varies with the rate of jeans output.

Figure 5.4 illustrates how these various costs are affected by the rate of production. On the vertical axis are the associated costs of production, in dollars per day. Notice that the total cost of producing 15 pairs per day is still $245, as indicated by point *B*. This figure consists of $120 of fixed costs (factory and sewing-machine rents) and $125 of variable costs ($80 in seamstress wages and $45 for denim). If we increase the rate of output, total costs will rise. ***How fast total costs rise depends on variable costs only,*** however, since fixed costs remain at $120 per day.

With one sewing machine and one factory, there is an absolute limit to daily jeans production. The capacity of a factory with one machine is roughly 51 pairs of jeans per day. If we try to produce more jeans than this by hiring additional seamstresses, our total costs will rise, but not our output. Recall that the seventh seamstress had a *negative* marginal physical product (Figure 5.2); she actually reduced total output. In fact, we could fill the factory with seamstresses and drive total costs sky-high. But the limits of space and one sewing machine do not permit output in excess of 51 pairs per day. This limit to productive capacity is represented by point *G* on the total-cost curve. Further expenditure on inputs will increase production costs but actually reduce output.

Although there is no upper limit to costs, there is a lower limit. If output is reduced to zero, total costs only fall to $120 per day, the level of fixed costs. This is illustrated by point *A* in Figure 5.4. As before, there is no way to avoid fixed costs in the short run.

Average costs

average total cost (*ATC*): Total cost divided by the quantity produced in a given time period.

average fixed cost (*AFC*): Total fixed cost divided by the quantity produced in a given time period.

average variable cost (*AVC*): Total variable cost divided by the quantity produced in a given time period.

Often there is an interest in the cost per pair of jeans, that is, in average total costs. **Average total cost (ATC)** is simply total cost divided by the rate of output. At an output of 15 pairs of jeans per day, total costs are $245. The average cost of production is thus $16.33 per pair ($245 ÷ 15).

Figure 5.5 shows the level and composition of average total costs for various rates of output. Row *J* of the table, for example, again indicates the fixed, variable, and total costs of producing 15 pairs of jeans per day. Fixed costs are still $120; variable costs are $125. Thus the total cost of producing fifteen pairs per day is $245.

The rest of row *J* shows the average costs of jeans production. These figures are obtained by dividing each total (columns 2, 3, and 4) by the rate of output (column 1). At an output rate of 15 pairs per day, **average fixed cost (AFC)** is $8 per pair, **average variable cost (AVC)** is $8.33, and *average* total cost (*ATC*) equals $16.33. *ATC*, then, is simply the sum of *AFC* and *AVC*, that is,

$$\text{ATC} = \text{AFC} + \text{AVC}$$

At this relatively low rate of output, fixed costs are a large portion of total costs. The rent paid for the factory and sewing machine works out to $8 per pair. This high average fixed cost accounts for nearly one-half of total average costs. This suggests that it is pretty expensive to lease a factory and sewing machine to produce only 15 pairs of jeans per day. To reduce average costs, we must make fuller use of our leased plant and equipment.

Notice what happens to average costs when the rate of output is increased to 20 pairs per day. Average fixed costs are cut by a third, to only $6 per pair. This sharp decline in *AFC* results from the fact that total fixed costs ($120) are now spread over much more output. Even though our rent has not dropped, the *average* fixed cost of producing jeans has.

As jeans output is increased from 15 to 20 pairs per day, *AVC* falls as well. *AVC* includes the price of denim purchased and labor costs. The price of denim is unchanged, at $3 per pair ($30 per bolt). But per-unit *labor* costs have fallen, from $5.33 to $4.50 per pair. Thus the reduction in *AVC* is completely due to the greater productivity of a second seamstress. To get 20 pairs of jeans, we had to employ a second seamstress part-time.[6] In the process, the marginal physical product of labor rose, and *AVC* fell.

[6] We are assuming a seamstress' time is divisible, that is, she can be hired for less than a full day.

FIGURE 5.5 AVERAGE COSTS

Average total costs (*ATC*) in column 7 equal total cost (column 4) divided by the rate of output (column 1). Since total costs include both fixed (column 2) and variable (column 3) costs, *ATC* equals *AFC* (column 5) plus *AVC* (column 6). This relationship is also illustrated in the graph below. The *ATC* of producing 15 pairs per day (point *J*) equals $16.33, the sum of *AFC* ($8.00) and *AVC* ($8.33).

	(1) Rate of output	(2) Fixed costs	+	(3) Variable costs	=	(4) Total costs	(5) Average fixed cost	+	(6) Average variable cost	=	(7) Average total cost
H	0	$120		$ 0		$120	—		—		—
I	10	120		85		205	$12.00		$ 8.50		$20.50
J	15	120		125		245	8.00		8.33		16.33
K	20	120		150		270	6.00		7.50		13.50
L	30	120		240		360	4.00		8.00		12.00
M	40	120		350		470	3.00		8.75		11.75
N	50	120		550		670	2.40		11.00		13.40
O	51	120		633		853	2.35		12.80		15.15

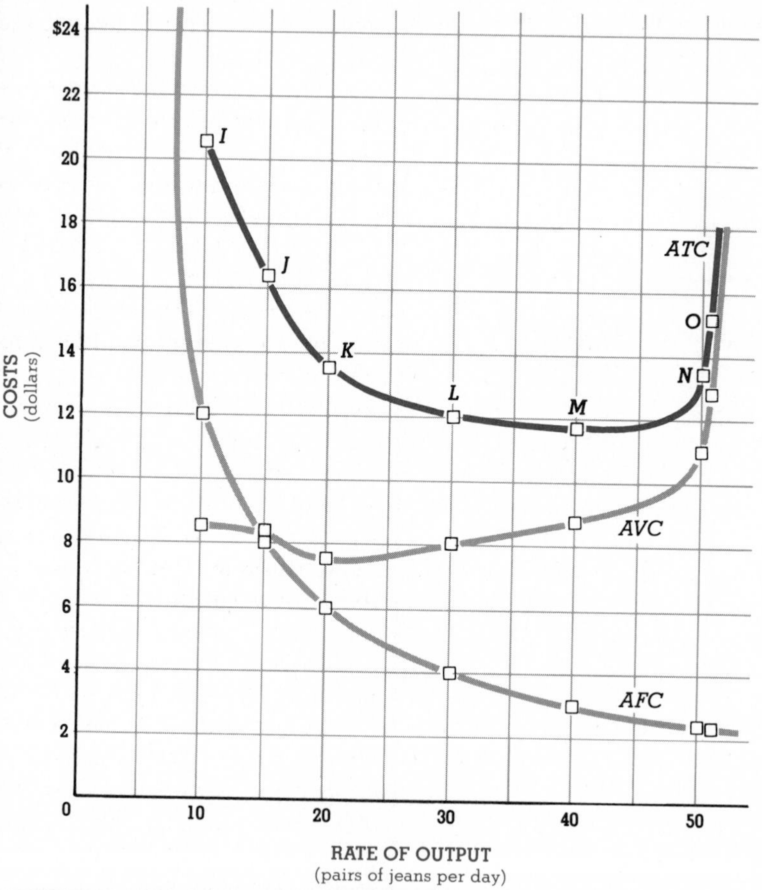

With both *AFC* and *AVC* falling, *ATC* must decline as well. In this case, *average* total costs fall from $16.33 per pair to $13.50. This is reflected in row *K* of the table as well as in point *K* on the *ATC* curve in Figure 5.5.

FALLING *AFC* If we increase production beyond 20 pairs of jeans per day, *AFC* will continue to fall. Recall that

$$AFC = \frac{\text{total fixed cost}}{\text{total output}}$$

The numerator is fixed (at $120 in this case). Increases in output enlarge the denominator. Hence any increase in output will lower average fixed cost.

RISING *AVC* The steady decline of *AFC* is not matched by declining *AVC*. On the contrary, *AVC* tends to start rising quite early in the expansion process. Look at column 6 of the table in Figure 5.5. After an initial decline, *AVC* starts to increase. At an output of 20 pairs, *AVC* is $7.50. At 30 pairs, *AVC* is $8.00. By the time the rate of output reaches 51 pairs per day, *AVC* is $12.80.

The rise in* AVC *is another reflection of diminishing returns in the production process. We have been through all this before. As output expands, each unit of labor has less land and capital to work with. Marginal physical product falls. As it does, labor costs *per pair of jeans* rise, pushing up *AVC*.

U-SHAPED *ATC* The steady decline of *AFC*, when combined with the typical increase in *AVC*, results in a U-shaped pattern for average *total* costs. In the early stages of output expansion, the large declines in *AFC* tend to outweigh any increases in *AVC*. As a result, *ATC* tends to fall. Notice that *ATC* declines from $20.50 to $11.75 as output increases from 10 to 40 pairs per day. This is also illustrated in Figure 5.5 with the downward move from point *I* to point *M*.

The battle between falling *AFC* and rising *AVC* takes an irreversible turn soon thereafter. When output is increased from 40 to 50 pairs of jeans per day, *AFC* continues to fall (row N in the table). But the decline in *AFC* (−60 cents) is overshadowed by the increase in *AVC* (+$2.25). Once rising *AVC* dominates, *ATC* starts to increase as well. *ATC* increases from $11.75 to $13.40 when jeans production expands from 40 to 50 pairs per day.

This and further increases in average total costs cause the *ATC* curve in Figure 5.5 to start rising. The initial dominance of falling *AFC*, combined with the later resurgence of *AVC*, is what gives the *ATC* curve its characteristic U shape.

MINIMUM AVERAGE COST The bottom of the U is an important point. Point *M* in Figure 5.5 represents *minimum* average total costs. This rate of production (40 pairs of jeans per day) represents the most efficient use of our sewing machines, factory, and labor. Any other rate of production alters the balance between *AFC* and *AVC* and increases average total costs. By producing exactly 40 pairs per day, we minimize the amount of land, labor, and capital used per pair of jeans. For University Jeans Corporation, point *M* represents least-cost production—the lowest-cost jeans. For society as a whole, point *M* also represents lowest possible opportunity cost, that is, we are minimizing the sacrifice of resources implied by the production of a pair of jeans. We are maximizing the amount of resources left over for the production of other goods and services.

As attractive as point *M* is, you should not conclude that it is everyone's dream. As we shall discuss at length in Chapter 6, the primary objective of producers is to maximize their *profits*. This is not necessarily the same thing as minimizing *costs*. In fact, the two objectives rarely coincide. Nevertheless, minimum average cost re-

TABLE 5.4 RESOURCE COMPUTATION OF MARGINAL COST

Marginal cost refers to the value of the additional inputs needed to produce *one* more unit of output. To increase daily jeans output from 15 to 16 pairs, we need 0.053 units of labor and one-tenth of a bolt of denim. These extra inputs cost $7.24.

Resources used to produce 16th pair of jeans	*Market value*	*Marginal cost*
0.053 units of labor	**0.053 × $80/day**	**$4.24**
0.1 bolt of denim	**0.1 × $30**	**3.00**
		$7.24

mains an important economic objective for society. In subsequent chapters we shall see how these different objectives are reconciled.

Marginal cost

One final cost concept is important. Indeed, this last concept is probably the most important one for production. It is *marginal cost.* We have already encountered this concept in our discussion of resource costs. There we noted that marginal cost refers to the value of the resources needed to produce *one* more unit of a good. To produce *one* more pair of jeans, we need the denim itself and a very small amount of additional labor. These are the extra or added costs of increasing output by one pair of jeans per day. To compute the dollar value of these marginal costs, we could determine the market price of denim and labor, then add them up. Table 5.4 provides an example. In this case, we calculate that the additional or **marginal cost** of producing a sixteenth pair of jeans is $7.24. This is how much *total* costs will increase if we decide to expand jeans output by one pair per day (from 15 to 16).

marginal cost: The increase in total cost associated with a one-unit increase in production.

Table 5.4 emphasizes the links between resource costs and dollar costs. However, there is a much easier way to compute marginal cost. Marginal cost refers to the change in total costs associated with one more unit of output. Accordingly, we can simply observe *total* dollar costs before and after the rate of output is increased. The difference between the two totals equals the *marginal* cost of increasing the rate of output. This technique is obviously much easier for jeans manufacturers, who don't know much about marginal resource utilization but have a sharp eye for increases in total dollar costs. It's also a lot easier for economics students, of course. But they have an obligation to understand the resource origins of marginal costs and the potential causes of rising or falling marginal costs. As we noted before, diminishing returns in production cause marginal costs to increase as the rate of output is expanded. Hence the marginal cost curve generally slopes upward, as in Figure 5.6.

A cost summary

By now we have enough curves to put together a summary of production costs. This summary is provided in Figure 5.7. As before, we are concentrating on a short-run production process, with fixed quantities of land and capital. In this case, however, we have abandoned the University Jeans Corporation and provided hypothetical

FIGURE 5.6 THE MARGINAL COST CURVE

Marginal cost (*MC*) is the increase in *total* costs resulting from a one-unit increase in the rate of production. *MC* is the additional cost of producing one more unit. These hypothetical numbers indicate that total costs increase from $25 to $34 when a fifth unit is produced (compare rows *u* and *t*). Hence the *MC* of the fifth unit is $9, as illustrated by point *u* on the marginal cost curve. The *MC* curve generally rises (as a consequence of the law of diminishing returns).

	Rate of output	*Total cost*	*Marginal cost*
p	0	$10	
q	1	13	3
r	2	15	2
s	3	19	4
t	4	25	6
u	5	34	9
v	6	48	14
w	7	68	20
x	8	98	30

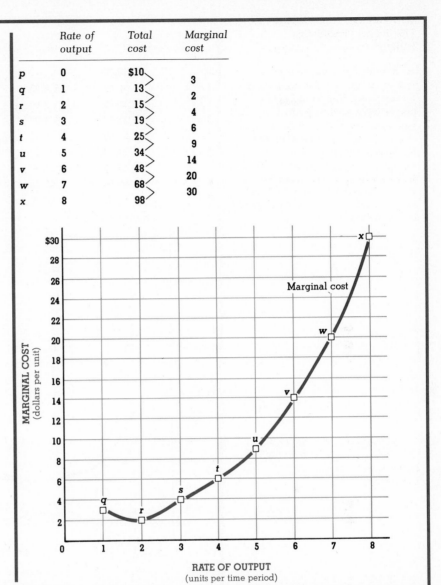

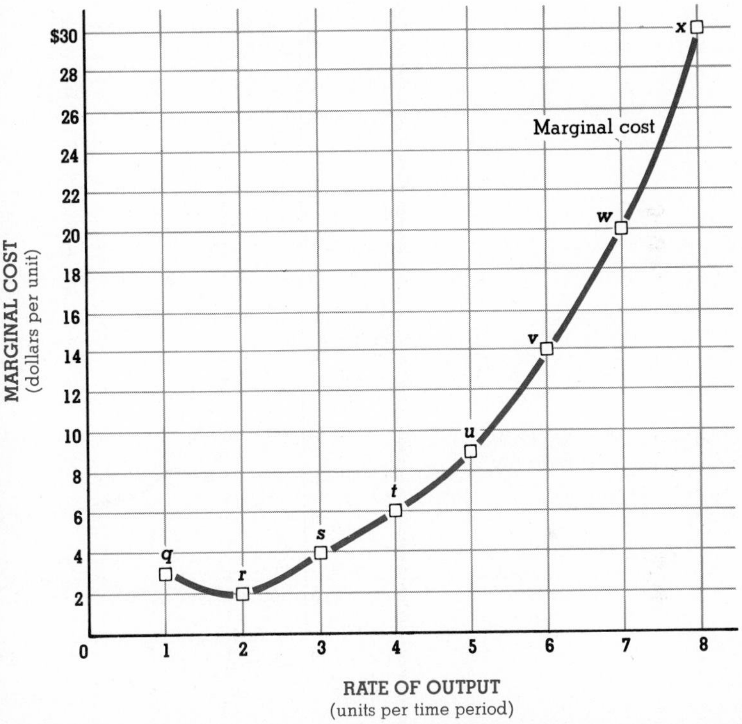

costs for an idealized production process. The purpose of these figures is to provide a more general view of how the various cost concepts relate to each other. Note that *MC*, *ATC*, *AFC*, and *AVC* can all be computed from total costs. All we need, then, is the first two columns of the table and we can compute and graph all the rest of the cost figures.

The centerpiece of Figure 5.7 is the U-shaped *ATC* curve. What is of special significance is its relationship to marginal costs. Notice that ***the* MC *curve intersects the* ATC *curve at its lowest point*** (point *m*). This will always be the case. So long as the marginal cost of producing one more unit is less than the existing average cost, average costs must fall. Thus average costs decline as long as the marginal cost curve lies below the average cost curve, as to the left of point *m* in Figure 5.7.

FIGURE 5.7 BASIC COST CURVES

With total costs and the rate of output, all other cost concepts can be computed. The resulting cost curves have several distinct features. The *AFC* curve always slopes downward. The *MC* curve typically rises, sometimes after a brief decline. The *ATC* curve has a U shape. And the *MC* curve will always intersect both the *ATC* and *AVC* curves at their lowest points (*m* and *n*, respectively)

Rate of output	*TC*	*MC*	*ATC*	*AFC*	*AVC*
0	$10.00	—	—	—	—
1	13.00	$ 3.00	$13.00	$10.00	$ 3.00
2	15.00	2.00	7.50	5.00	2.50
3	19.00	4.00	6.33	3.33	3.00
4	25.00	6.00	6.25	2.50	3.75
5	34.00	9.00	6.80	2.00	4.80
6	48.00	14.00	8.00	1.67	6.33
7	68.00	20.00	9.71	1.43	8.28
8	98.00	30.00	12.25	1.25	11.00

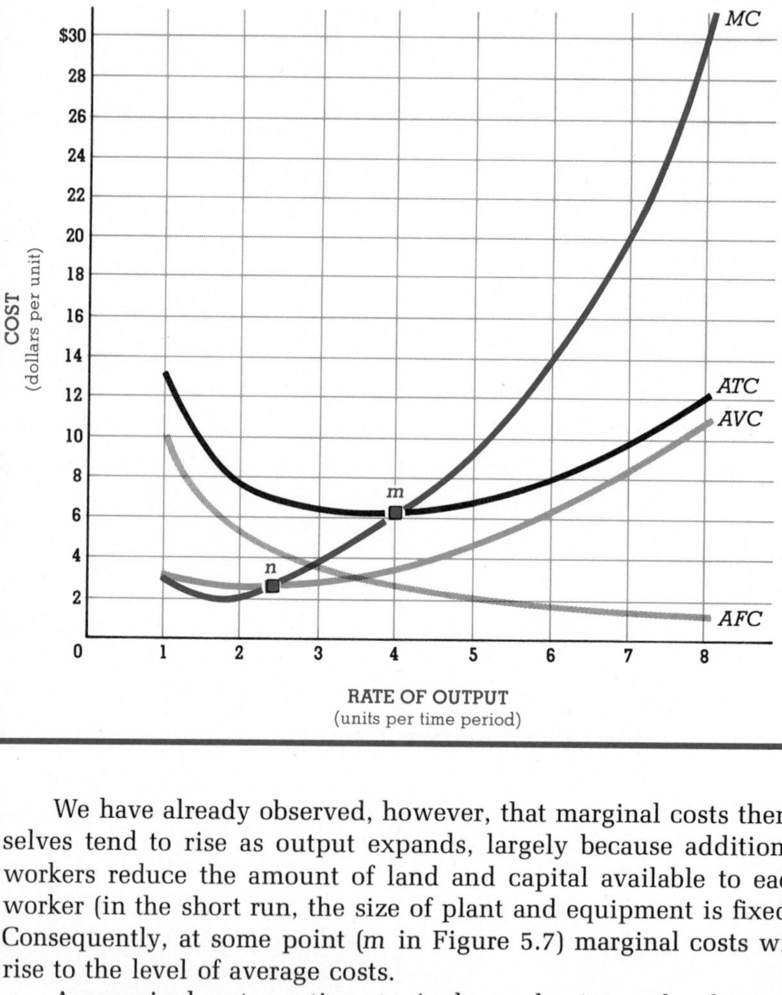

We have already observed, however, that marginal costs themselves tend to rise as output expands, largely because additional workers reduce the amount of land and capital available to each worker (in the short run, the size of plant and equipment is fixed). Consequently, at some point (*m* in Figure 5.7) marginal costs will rise to the level of average costs.

As marginal costs continue to rise beyond point *m*, they begin to pull average costs up, giving the average cost curve its U shape. Average costs increase whenever marginal costs exceed average costs. This is the case to the right of point *m*, since the marginal cost curve always lies above the average cost curve in that part of Figure 5.7.

To visualize the relationship between marginal cost and average cost, imagine computing the average height of people entering a room. If the first person who comes through the door is six feet tall, then the average height of people entering the room is six feet at that point. But what happens to average height if the second person entering the room is only three feet tall? *Average* height declines because the last (marginal) person entering the room is shorter than the previous average. Whenever the last entrant is shorter than the average, the average must fall.

The relationship between marginal costs and average costs is also similar to that between your grade in this course and your grade-point average. If your grade in economics is better (higher) than your other grades, then your overall grade-point average will rise. In other words, a high *marginal* grade in economics will pull your *average* grade up. If you don't understand this, your grade-point average is likely to fall.

ECONOMIC VS. ACCOUNTING COSTS

An essential characteristic of the cost curves we have observed is that they are based on *real* production relationships. The dollar costs we compute are a direct reflection of underlying resource costs, that is, the land, labor, and capital used in the production process. Not everyone counts this way. On the contrary, accountants and business people typically count dollar costs only and ignore any resource use that doesn't result in an explicit dollar cost.

Return to University Jeans Corporation for a moment to see the difference. When we computed the dollar cost of producing 15 pairs of jeans, we noted the following resource inputs:

1 factory rent	@	$100
1 machine rent	@	20
1 seamstress	@	80
1.5 bolts of denim	@	45
Total cost		$245

The total value of the resources used in the production of 15 pairs of jeans was thus $245. But this figure need not conform to *actual* dollar costs. Suppose the owner of University Jeans decided to sew jeans himself. Then he would not have to hire a seamstress or pay $80 per day in wages. *Dollar* costs would drop to $165 per day. This figure would be the focus of attention for the producer or his accountant. They would assert that the cost of producing jeans had fallen.

Economic cost

An economist would draw no such conclusions. The essential *economic* question is how many *resources* are used to produce jeans. This has not changed. One unit of labor is still being employed at the factory. That unit of labor is not available for the production of other goods and services. Hence society is still paying $245 for jeans, whether the owner of University Jeans writes checks in that amount or not. We really don't care *who* sews jeans—the essential point is that someone (i.e., a unit of labor) does.

The same would be true if University Jeans owned its own factory rather than rented it. If the factory was owned rather than rented, the owner probably would not write any rent checks. Hence accounting costs would drop by $100 per day. But society would not be saving any resources. The factory would still be in use for jeans production and therefore unavailable for the production of other goods and services. The economic (resource) cost of producing 15 pairs of jeans would still be $245.

economic cost: The value of all resources used to produce a good or service; opportunity cost.

The distinction between an economic cost and an accounting cost is essentially one between resource and dollar costs. *Dollar cost* refers to the actual dollar outlays of a producer; it is the lifeblood of accountants. **Economic cost,** in contrast, refers to the dollar value of all resources used in the production process; it is the lifeblood of economists. ***Economic and accounting costs will diverge whenever any factor of production is not paid an explicit wage (or rent, etc.).***[7]

LONG-RUN COSTS

All of our discussion thus far has been confined to short-run production costs. The short run is characterized by a commitment to plant and equipment. A factory, an office building, or some other plant and equipment have been leased or purchased: we are stuck with *fixed* costs. In this context, our objective is to make the best use of those fixed costs by choosing the appropriate rate of production.

long run: A period of time long enough for all inputs to be varied (no fixed costs).

The long run opens up a whole new range of options. In the long run, we have no lease or purchase commitments. We are free to start all over again, with whatever scale of plant and equipment we desire. There are no fixed costs in the **long run.**

Long-run average costs

The opportunities available in the long run include building a plant of any desired size. Suppose we still wanted to go into the jeans business. In the long run, we could build or lease any size factory we wanted and could lease as many sewing machines as we desired. Figure 5.8 illustrates three choices: a small factory (ATC_1), a medium-sized factory (ATC_2), and a large factory (ATC_3). As we observed earlier, it is very expensive to produce lots of jeans with a small factory. The ATC curve for a small factory (ATC_1) starts to head straight up at relatively low rates of output. In the long run, we would lease or build such a factory only if we anticipated a continuing low rate of output.

The ATC_2 curve illustrates how costs might fall if we leased or built a medium-sized factory. With a small-sized factory, ATC becomes prohibitive at an output of 50 to 60 pairs of jeans per day. A medium-sized factory can produce these quantities at lower cost. Moreover, ATC continues to drop as jeans production increases in the medium-sized factory. At least for a while. Even a medium-sized

[7] The distinction between economic and accounting costs is also referred to as the difference between implicit costs (all costs) and explicit costs (only those paid).

FIGURE 5.8 LONG-RUN COSTS WITH THREE OPTIONS

Long-run cost possibilities are determined by all possible short-run options. In this case, there are three options of varying size (ATC_1, ATC_2, and ATC_3). In the long run we would choose that option which yielded the lowest average cost for any desired rate of output. The solid portion of the curves (*LATC*) represents these choices.

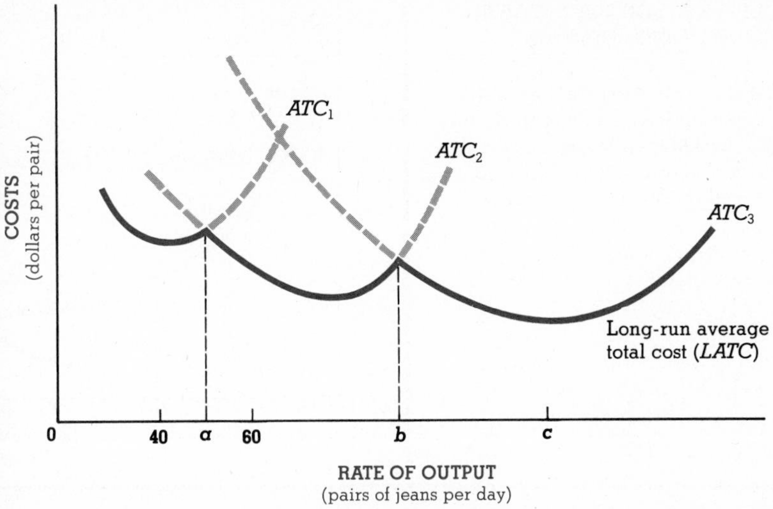

factory must contend with resource constraints and therefore rising average costs: its *ATC* curve is U-shaped also.

If we expected to sell really large quantities of jeans, we would want to build or lease a large factory. Beyond the rate of output *b*, the largest factory offers the lowest average total cost. There's a risk in leasing such a large factory, of course. If our sales don't live up to our high expectations, we will end up with very high fixed costs and thus very expensive jeans. Look at the high average cost of producing only 60 pairs of jeans per day with the large factory (ATC_3).

In choosing an appropriate factory, then, we need to know how many jeans we expect to sell. Once we know our expected output, we can easily pick the right-sized factory. It will be the one that offers the lowest *ATC* for that rate of output. In this case, the decision is pretty easy. If we expect to sell fewer jeans than *a*, we will choose the small factory. If we expect to sell jeans at a rate between *a* and *b*, we will select a medium-sized factory. Beyond rate *b*, we will want the largest factory. These choices are reflected in the solid part of the three *ATC* curves. The "curve" created by these three segments constitutes our long-run cost possibilities. ***The long-run cost curve is just a summary of our best short-run cost possibilities.***

We might confront more than three choices, of course. There is really no reason we couldn't build a factory to any desired size. In the long run we face an infinite number of scale choices, not just three. The effect of all these choices is to smooth out the long-run cost curve. Figure 5.9 depicts the long-run curve that results. Each rate of output is most efficiently produced by some size (scale) of plant. That sized plant indicates the minimum cost of producing a particular rate of output. Its corresponding short-run *ATC* curve provides one point on the long-run *ATC* curve.

Long-run marginal costs

Like all average cost curves, the long-run (*LATC*) curve has its own marginal cost curve. The long-run marginal cost (*LMC*) curve is not a composite of short-run marginal cost curves. Rather, it is computed

FIGURE 5.9 LONG-RUN COSTS WITH UNLIMITED OPTIONS

If plants of all sizes can be built, short-run options are infinite. In this case, the *LATC* curve becomes a smooth U-shaped curve. Each point on the curve represents lowest-cost production for a plant size best suited to one rate of output. The long-run *ATC* curve has its own *MC* curve.

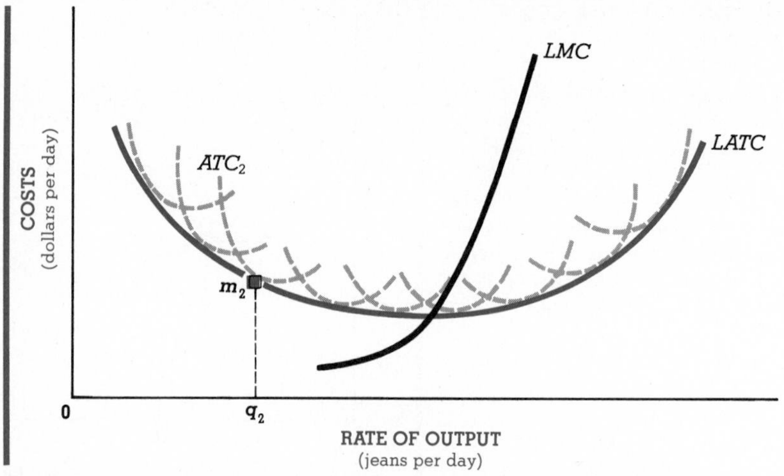

on the basis of the costs reflected in the long-run *ATC* curve itself. We won't bother to compute those costs here. We will note, however, that the long-run *MC* curve—like all *MC* curves—intersects its associated average cost curve at its lowest point.

ECONOMIES OF SCALE

In reality, a producer is not confined to the choice of only *one* plant. A producer can use either one large plant or several smaller ones to produce the same output. Suppose the output level *c* was desired in Figure 5.8. The producer would never try to produce such a high rate of output with a single small plant (ATC_1). But it might be desirable to produce that rate of output with *several* small plants rather than one large one (ATC_3). In this case, the producer must compare the *minimum ATC* associated with different plant sizes

Notice what happens to *minimum ATC* in Figure 5.8 when the size (scale) of the factory changes. When a medium-sized factory (ATC_2) replaces a small factory (ATC_1), minimum average cost drops (the bottom of ATC_2 is below the bottom of ATC_1). This implies that a jeans producer who wants to minimize costs should build one medium-sized factory rather than try to produce the same quantity with two small ones. In this situation, **economies of scale** exist: larger facilities reduce minimum average costs.

economies of scale: Reductions in average costs that come about through increases in the size (scale) of plant and equipment.

Larger production facilities do not always result in cost reductions. Suppose a firm has the choice of producing the quantity Q_m from several small factories or from one large, centralized facility. Centralization may have three different impacts on costs. These are illustrated in Figure 5.10. In each of the three illustrations, we see the average total cost (*ATC*) curve for a typical small firm or plant and the *ATC* curve for a much larger plant producing the same product. Figure 5.10*a* depicts a situation in which there is no economic advantage to centralization of manufacturing operations, because a large plant is no more efficient than a multitude of small plants. The critical focus here is on the *minimum* average costs attainable for a

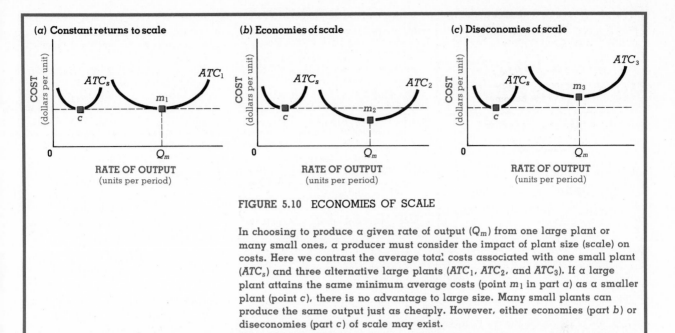

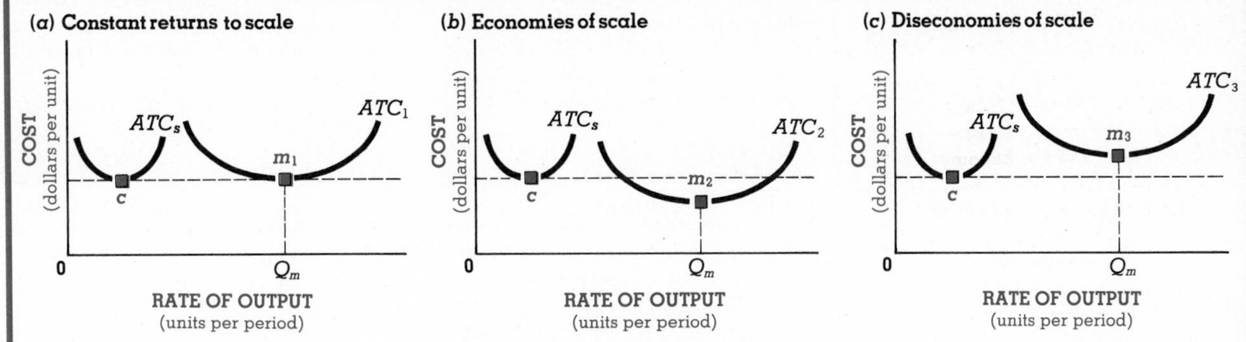

FIGURE 5.10 ECONOMIES OF SCALE

In choosing to produce a given rate of output (Q_m) from one large plant or many small ones, a producer must consider the impact of plant size (scale) on costs. Here we contrast the average total costs associated with one small plant (ATC_s) and three alternative large plants (ATC_1, ATC_2, and ATC_3). If a large plant attains the same minimum average costs (point m_1 in part *a*) as a smaller plant (point *c*), there is no advantage to large size. Many small plants can produce the same output just as cheaply. However, either economies (part *b*) or diseconomies (part *c*) of scale may exist.

constant returns to scale: Increases in plant size do not affect minimum average cost; minimum per-unit costs are identical for small plants and large plants.

given rate of output. Note that the lowest point on the smaller plant's *ATC* curve (point *c*) is no higher or lower than the lowest point on the larger firms's *ATC* curve (point *m*). Hence it would be just as cheap to produce the quantity Q_m from a multitude of small plants as it would be to produce Q_m from one large plant. Thus increasing the size (or *scale*) of individual plants will not reduce minimum average costs: this is a situation of **constant returns to scale.**

Figure 5.10*b* illustrates the situation in which a larger plant is able to attain a lower minimum average cost than a smaller plant. That is, economies of scale (or "increasing returns to scale") exist. This is evident from the fact that the larger firm's *ATC* curve falls *below* the dotted line in the graph (m_2 is less than *c*). The greater efficiency of the large factory might come from any of several sources. A large factory, for example, might be able to enjoy greater specialization of labor, with each worker becoming expert in a particular skill. By contrast, a smaller establishment might have to use the same individual(s) to perform several functions, thereby reducing productivity at each task. Also, some kinds of machinery may be economical only if they are used to produce massive volumes,[8] an opportunity only very large factories have. Finally, a large plant might acquire a persistent cost advantage through the process of learning by doing. That is, its longer experience and greater volume of output may translate into improved organization and efficiency.

But even though large plants may be able to achieve greater efficiencies than smaller plants, there is no assurance that they actually will. In fact, increasing the size (scale) of a plant may actually *reduce* operating efficiency, as depicted in Figure 5.10*c*. Workers

[8] That is to say, the machinery itself may be subject to economies of scale.

Some Firms Fight Ills of Bigness by Keeping Employe Units Small

At 3M Plants, Workers Have Flexibility, Involvement —And Their Own Radios

ST. PAUL, Minn.—For a company with some 87,000 employes and annual sales in excess of $6 billion, Minnesota Mining & Manufacturing Co. spends a lot of time "thinking small."

"We are keenly aware of the disadvantages of large size," says Gordon W. Engdahl, the company's vice president for human resources and its top personnel officer. "We made a conscious effort to keep our units as small as possible because we think it helps keep them flexible and vital," he says. "When one gets too large, we break it apart. We like to say that our success in recent years amounts to multiplication by division."

Mr. Engdahl's comment is no conceit. 3M's average U.S. manufacturing plant employs just 270 people, and management groups as small as five guide the fortunes of the company's numerous household, industrial and scientific products. In the 1970s, its sales and earnings grew almost fourfold, while its U.S. work force increased by 40%.

3M's record stands in sharp contrast to a mostly overlooked trend developing over the past 15 years or so: the declining role of large companies in this country's employment picture. . . .

The Inefficiencies of Size

Not all of the mechanisms behind these developments are clear, and some surely are complex. Observers note that many of the biggest companies of the 1970s were manufactureres that suffered from heightened foreign competition and the related swing of the U.S. economy toward "service" functions. . . .

Increasingly, however, blame for the laggard performance of many large corporations is focusing on their structures and entrenched ways of doing things. A growing body of opinion has it that the "economies of scale" made possible by bigness often are more than nullified by organizational rigidities and bottlenecks.

"More companies seem to be showing concern that their neat organization charts don't always reflect reality and certainly don't, in themselves, overcome the tensions between autonomy and control that get worse with size," says Larry E. Grejner, a professor of organizational behavior at the University of Southern California's School of Business Administration.

—Frederick C. Klein

may feel alienated in a plant of massive proportions and feel little commitment to productivity. Moreover, a large plant may offer greater opportunities to slack off without getting caught. For these reasons and others, a large plant may require more intensive managerial supervision, which would raise production costs. Indeed, even a decentralized supercorporation may find that the managerial efforts required to coordinate a multitude of separate plants raise average costs above those of the smaller firm. These kinds of situations, wherein minimum average costs rise as the scale of operations increases, are referred to as "diseconomies of scale."

In evaluating long-run options, then, we must be careful to recognize that ***efficiency and size do not necessarily go hand in hand.*** Some firms and industries may be subject to economies of scale, but others will not be. Bigger is not always better.

POLICY IMPLICATIONS: PRODUCTIVITY IMPROVEMENTS

All of the cost concepts discussed in this chapter have been derived from the production function. That function, describing our productive capabilities, has been taken as a technological fact of life. It represents the *best* we can do, given our state of technological and managerial knowledge. In the real world, however, the best is always getting better. Science and technology are continuously advancing. So is our knowledge of how to organize and manage our

FIGURE 5.11 IMPROVEMENTS IN PRODUCTIVITY REDUCE COSTS

Advances in technological or managerial knowledge increase our productive capability. This is reflected in upward shifts of the production function (part *a*) and downward shifts of production cost curves (part *b*).

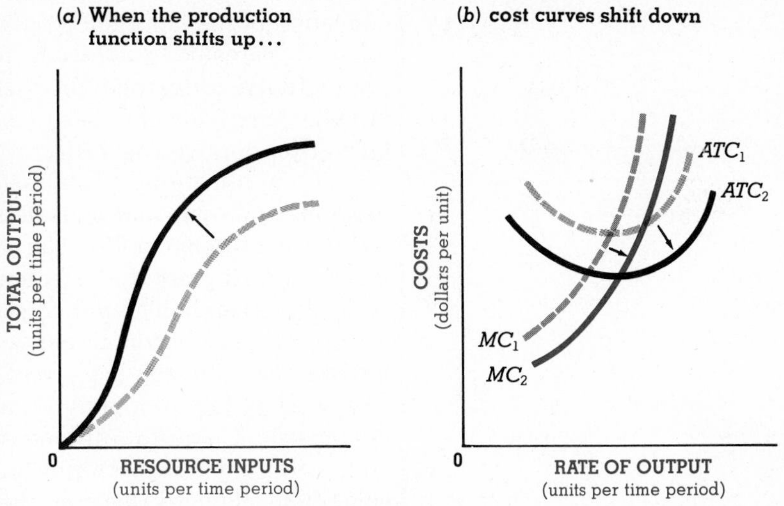

resources. These advances keep *shifting* our production functions upward: more can be produced with any given quantity of inputs. In the process, the costs of production shift downward. This is illustrated in Figure 5.11 by the downward shifts of the *MC* and *ATC* curves. These downward shifts imply that we can get more of the goods and services we desire with available resources.

Table 5.5 indicates the historical importance of productivity improvements in the U.S. economy. From 1948 to 1973, total output grew at just less than 4 percent per year. Less than half of this growth was due to increased use of labor and capital, that is, more inputs. The rest of our growth came from improvements in technology, management, and the quality of our labor. Advances in knowledge

TABLE 5.5 THE SOURCES OF U.S. GROWTH, 1948–73

From 1948 to 1973 total output grew by 3.87 percent annually. More than half of this growth was due to improvements in our technological and managerial capabilities. These advances in productivity have made it possible to produce more output at less cost.

Source	*Percentage contribution to output growth*
More inputs	
additional labor	**27.6**
additional capital	**18.3**
	45.9
Productivity advances	
education of labor	**10.6**
advances in knowledge	**28.7**
improved resource allocation	**7.8**
economies of scale	**8.3**
	55.4
Miscellaneous	**−1.3**
	100.0

Source: Edward F. Denison, *Accounting for Slower Economic Growth: The United States in the 1970s* (Washington, D.C.: Brookings Institution, 1979).

are credited with over one-fourth of our economic growth. Greater education of the labor force (quality improvements) contributed another 10 percent. In addition, reallocation of resources from low-productivity industries to high-productivity industries boosted growth. Finally, economies of scale accounted for 8 percent of our greater productive capability.

The implication of this historical experience is that future reductions in growth and costs depend on further advances in productivity. Government policy can and does play an important role in this regard. At present, the federal government pays for 47 percent of all basic research. The public sector is also responsible for most of our educational system. Finally, the government helps establish the institutional climate (e.g., regulations, standards) for U.S. businesses. How fast productivity advances thus depends not only on the persistent inquiries of lone scientists and managers, but also on how well the public sector encourages or impedes research and development. Edward Denison, the source of Table 5.5, sees potential problems here. From 1973 to 1976, the rate of growth declined significantly. Denison and others attribute much of this slowdown in productivity to government regulation, particularly rules governing workplace safety and environmental protection.[9] Others point to the sharply higher costs of energy that occurred after 1973 and the resulting changes in investment and production behavior. For the most part, however, the causes of the productivity slowdown remain a mystery. Solving that mystery may provide insights for greater productivity improvements in the future.

SUMMARY

- A production function indicates the maximum amount of output that can be produced with different combinations of inputs. It is a technological relationship and changes (shifts) when new technology or management techniques are discovered.
- The contribution of an input to total output is measured by its marginal physical product (*MPP*). This is the amount by which *total* output increases when one more unit of the input is employed. The productivity of any input depends on technology and the amount of other resources it has to work with.
- The *MPP* of a factor tends to decline as more of it is employed in a given production facility. Diminishing returns are attributable to the declining ratio of other inputs to the one factor that is being used in greater quantity.
- Marginal cost is the increase in total cost that results when output is increased by one unit. Marginal cost increases whenever marginal physical product diminishes.

[9] The costs and benefits of environmental policies are discussed in Chapter 16.

- Not all costs go up when the rate of output is increased. Fixed costs (e.g., space and equipment leases) do not vary with the rate of output. Only variable costs (e.g., labor and material) go up when output is increased.

- Average total cost (*ATC*) equals total cost divided by the quantity of output produced. *ATC* declines whenever marginal cost (*MC*) is less than average cost and rises when *MC* exceeds it. The *MC* and *ATC* curves intersect at minimum *ATC* (the bottom of the U). That intersection represents least-cost production.

- The economic costs of production include the value of *all* resources used. Accounting costs typically include only those dollar costs actually paid (explicit costs).

- In the long run there are no fixed costs; the size (scale) of production facilities can be varied. The long-run *ATC* curve indicates the lowest cost of producing output with facilities of appropriate size.

- Economies of scale refer to reductions in minimum average cost attained with larger plant size (scale). If minimum *ATC* rises with plant size, diseconomies exist.

- Historically, advances in technology and the quality of our inputs have been the major source of economic growth. These advances have shifted production functions upward and pushed cost curves down.

Terms to remember

Define the following terms:

supply	**total cost**
factors of production	**fixed costs**
production function	**variable costs**
productivity	**average total cost (*ATC*)**
efficiency	**average fixed cost (*AFC*)**
opportunity cost	**average variable cost (*AVC*)**
short run	**economic cost**
marginal physical product	**long run**
law of diminishing returns	**economies of scale**
marginal cost	**constant returns to scale**

Questions for discussion

1. What is the marginal cost of enrolling one more student in your class? What are the fixed and variable costs associated with "production" of students?

2. Suppose all your friends offered to help wash your car. Would marginal physical product decline as more friends helped? Why, or why not?

3. Owner-operators of small gas stations rarely pay themselves an hourly wage. Does this practice reduce the economic cost of dispensing gasoline?

4. Supermarkets have replaced small grocery stores in many areas, in large part because of the lower costs they achieve. What kind of economies of scale exist in supermarkets? Why doesn't someone build one colossal supermarket and drive costs down further?

Problem Complete the following table and graph the marginal cost and average total cost curves.

Rate of output	*Total cost*	*Marginal cost*	*Average fixed cost*	*Average variable cost*	*Average total cost*
0	$100				
1	110				
2	130				
3	165				
4	220				
5	300				

CHAPTER 6

PROFITS AND THE SUPPLY DECISION

The production of goods and services entails real costs. In view of these costs, we should not expect business firms simply to give us the goods and services we desire. At a minimum, they will want to be paid enough to recover the costs of production. Ideally, they would like to be paid something *more* than the costs of production, so as to benefit from their efforts. Such is the nature of a business. Like most of us, people who create and maintain production units are motivated by self-interest. Even though they *could* supply us with goods "at cost," they want more. In general, they will be *willing* to produce the goods and services we desire only when they get their "just rewards." The **supply** of goods requires both the ability and the willingness to produce.

supply: The ability and willingness to sell (produce) specific quantities of a good at alternative prices in a given time period (*ceteris paribus*).

In this chapter we shall examine the nature of the supply decision. The central motivator here is profits. We shall first look at the nature of profits and who gets them. We shall then look at how profits are earned and how the quest for profits influences supply decisions.

THE PROFIT MOTIVE

The market mechanism answers the basic question of FOR WHOM to produce by distributing goods and services on the basis of ability to pay. To the extent that people who own a business want a share of total output, they must acquire an income that can be used to buy the consumer goods they desire. *Owning* plant and equipment is not enough. To generate a current flow of income, one must *use* that plant and equipment to produce goods. When sold, those goods generate the income business owners need for their own consumption desires. ***The basic incentive to produce is the promise of income.***

profit: The difference between total revenue and total cost.

Whereas the monetary incentives for motivating workers are usually expressed in terms of wages and salaries, returns to the efforts of a business are commonly referred to as profits. **Profit** is the difference between the total revenues of a firm and its total costs. It is the "residual" that is received by the owners of a business. The recipient of that residual may be the single owner of a corner grocery store or it may be the group of stockholders who collectively own a large corporation. In either case, it is the promise (hope?) of some residual profit that motivates people to own and operate a business.

Other motivations

Profit is not the only thing that motivates producers. Like the rest of us, producers also worry about social status and crave recognition. Hence they are most willing to take on production responsibilities for those products or services that command most acceptance or prestige. Producers will also be more willing to make the leisure and consumption sacrifices required by production if business people are generally held in high regard by the rest of society. That is to say, producers will work for less profit if we reward them with high status.[1]

Psychological influences are also important in motivating producers. People who have a need to feel important, to control others, or to demonstrate achievement are likely to be easily drafted for the job of producing goods. On the other hand, some people are lured into business by a relentless need to be "their own man," to confirm their independence and freedom. Owners of small businesses are especially prey to this motivation. Many small businesses are maintained by people who gave up 40-hour weeks, $20,000 incomes, and a sense of alienation in exchange for 80-hour weeks, $15,000 incomes, and a sense of identity.

Additional motivations for producing arise from the structure of many production units. The ownership of large corporations tends to be fragmented among thousands of individual stockholders, most of whom have never even seen corporate headquarters. At the same time, the people who manage the corporation's business on a day-to-day basis may have little or no stock in the company. As a consequence, the possibility arises that the self-interests of owners and of managers may conflict. Corporate managers who have little or no ownership rights are likely to be at least as interested in their own jobs, salaries, and self-preservation as in the profits that accrue to the owners. Such "technocrats," as John Kenneth Galbraith of Harvard has labeled them, may seek to mollify owners with a steady flow of profits rather than maximum profits at any given point in time. To

[1] The People's Republic of China has experimented with this trade-off between monetary and social incentives. A comparison of Chinese, Soviet, and American incentive systems is provided in Chapter 21 of *The Macro Economy Today*.

FIGURE 6.1 U.S. BUSINESS PROFITS, 1960–81

The level of corporate profits is highly sensitive to economic conditions, particularly the level of business activity (total output). Total corporate profits fell sharply in 1970, 1974, and 1980, all years of economic decline (recession).

Source: U.S. Department of Commerce.

the extent that their salaries depend on corporate size or sales—as they usually do—corporate managers may show more interest in corporate growth than in corporate profits. If these efforts reduce the flow of profits below some minimum acceptable to owners, however, the corporation may start looking for new managers. Hence the level of profits must still be an object of concern.

PROFITS OF U.S. BUSINESS

Public perceptions

Although profits might be a necessary inducement for producers, most consumers feel that profits are too high (see box). And they may be in many cases. But most consumers do not have any idea how much profit U.S. businesses receive or which firms get the lion's share. We start, then, with a quick survey of profit experiences in U.S. businesses.

Reported profits

U.S. corporations reported profits of $233 billion in 1981. As Figure 6.1 illustrates, 1981 was a fairly good year for U.S. corporations; profits in 1980 had been much lower. Included in this total were the profits of American Telephone & Telegraph, IBM, and some other truly huge corporations, as well as substantial losses for a few major firms (see Table 6.1).

Figure 6.2 provides a glimpse of how profits are distributed across U.S. industries. The emphasis here is not on total profits in dollars but on the profit *rate*, in percentages. The profit rate is expressed in two ways: as a percentage of sales and as a percentage of net worth. The first rate indicates how many cents of each sales dollar represents profits. This is the rate discussed in the public-opin-

TABLE 6.1 THE BIG MONEY MAKERS AND LOSERS

U.S. corporations reported total profits of $233 billion in 1981. Included in this total were the huge profits of some corporations and sizable losses of others. Some of the largest winners and losers are shown here.

Big winners	*Profits*
AT&T	**$7,026,390,000**
Exxon	**5,567,481,000**
IBM	**3,308,000,000**
Mobil	**2,433,000,000**
Standard Oil of California	**2,380,000,000**
Big losers	*Losses*
Ford	**$1,060,100,000**
Chrysler	**475,600,000**
Kaiser Steel	**437,455,000**
International Harvester	**393,128,000**
Lockheed	**288,800,000**

Source: *Fortune Magazine.*

CORPORATE PROFITS: PUBLIC OPINION VS. REALITY

Most consumers—including college students—think profits are far higher than they really are. This misperception is revealed in public-opinion surveys that ask what percentage of each sales dollar represents after-tax profits. The average responses in recent years are noted below. They reveal that the American public thinks profits are six or seven times higher than they really are. The perceptions of college students are even more exaggerated: the average college student thinks 45 cents out of each sales dollar goes to profits!

	1971	*1973*	*1975*	*1976*	*1979*	*1981*
Mean public estimate of profit per sales dollar:	**28.0¢**	**28.0¢**	**33.0¢**	**29.0¢**	**32.0¢**	**31.0¢**
Actual after-tax profit per sales dollar:	**4.5¢**	**5.1¢**	**5.2¢**	**4.4¢**	**5.2¢**	**4.8¢**

In view of these misperceptions, it is hardly surprising that most Americans think business profits are too high. In a series of public-opinion polls about the level of profits, more and more consumers have said business profits are too high. Fewer than 10 percent of the public has ever thought profits were too low. The question and responses are noted below:

Q: Do you think business as a whole is making too much profit, a reasonable profit, or not enough profit?

A:	*1965*	*1969*	*1973*	*1976*	*1979*	*1981*
Too much profit	**24%**	**38%**	**35%**	**50%**	**51%**	**51%**
Reasonable profit	**58**	**47**	**50**	**37**	**38**	**37**
Not enough profit	**6**	**4**	**3**	**9**	**8**	**8**
No opinion	**12**	**11**	**12**	**4**	**3**	**4**

Source: Opinion Research Corporation and Gallup.

FIGURE 6.2 PRETAX PROFIT RATES IN SELECTED INDUSTRIES, 1981

Profits are often measured in relation to total sales revenue or invested capital. In either case, there is great variability across industries. Even within a single industry, some firms do well while others earn little or no profit.

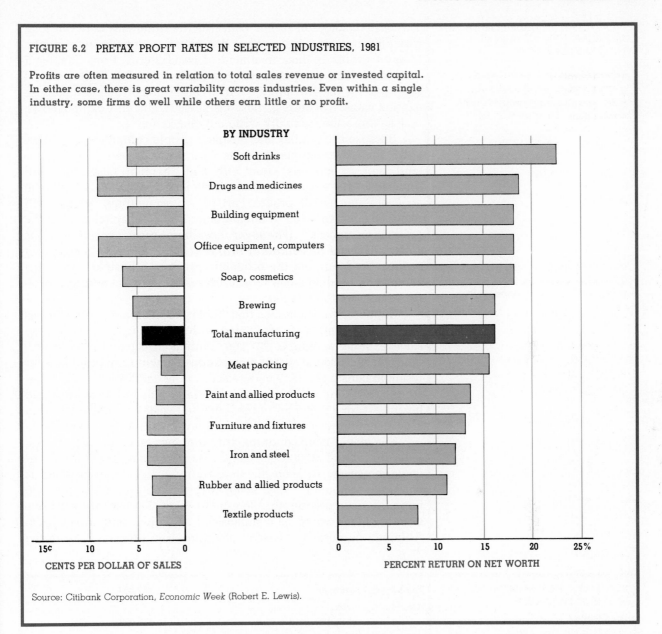

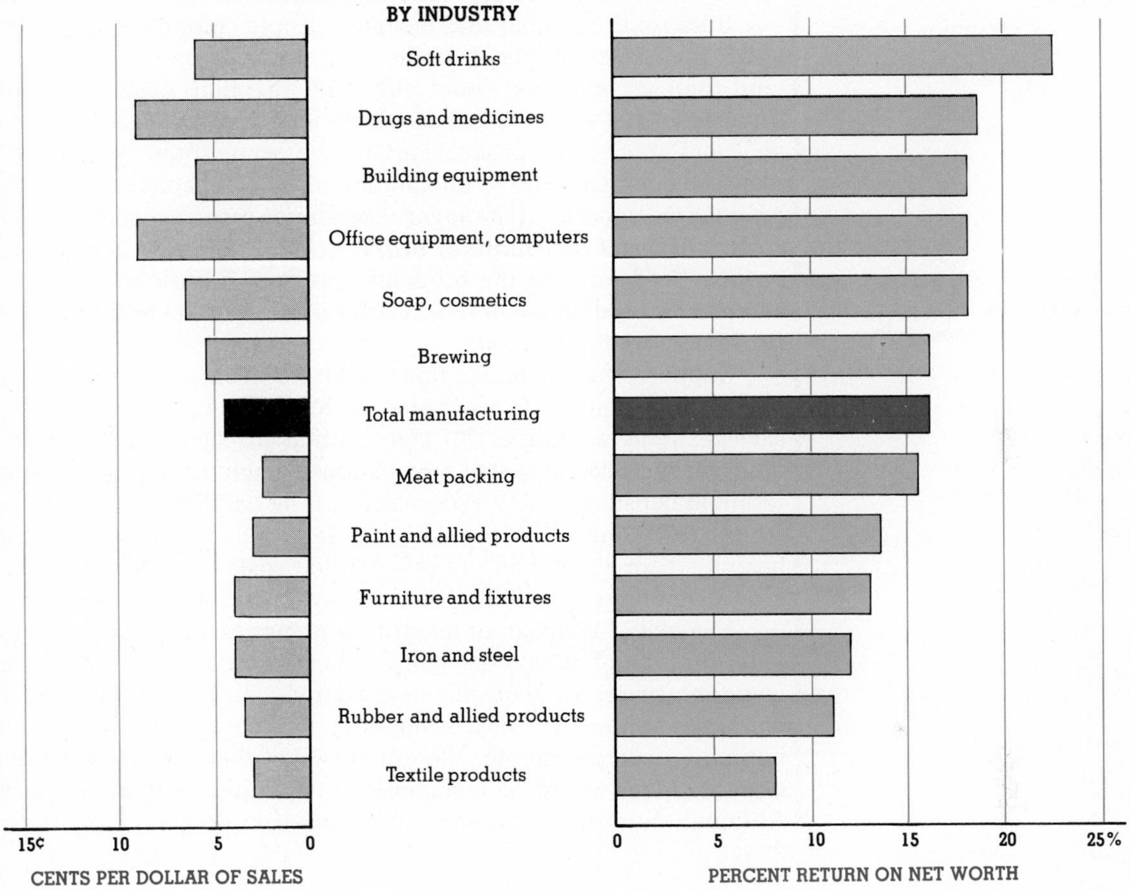

Source: Citibank Corporation, *Economic Week* (Robert E. Lewis).

ion surveys noted on the previous page. The second rate expresses profits as a percentage of the value of the firm's net assets, that is, its "investment" in the business. On either measure, the soft drink, computer, and office equipment industries score quite well.

ECONOMIC VS. ACCOUNTING PROFITS

Public perceptions of profits and reported corporate profits are clearly very different. Ironically, economists' computations of profits coincide with neither. Economists calculate profits differently from the way everyone else does.

Economic profits

economic cost: The value of all resources used to produce a good or service; opportunity cost.

economic profit: The difference between total revenues and total economic costs.

The basic concept of profits concerns the difference between total revenues and total costs. What distinguishes economists' calculations of profits is their treatment of costs. Recall from Chapter 5 how economists compute costs. **Economic cost** refers to the value of *all* resources used in production, whether or not they are paid an explicit wage. By contrast, most businesses count only explicit costs, that is, those they actually write out checks for.

Because economists and business people compute costs differently, their calculations of profits must differ as well. If businesses (and their accountants) count only *paid* (explicit) costs, they will understate true costs. This incomplete accounting of costs leads to an *over*statement of profits. Part of the accounting "profit" will really be compensation to unpaid land, labor, or capital used in the production process. ***Whenever economic costs exceed explicit costs, observed (accounting) profits will exceed true (economic) profits.*** To determine the **economic profit** of a business, we must subtract all implicit factor returns from observed "net returns"; profits, if any, are the residual.

Suppose, for example, that Table 6.2 accurately summarizes the revenues and costs associated with a local drugstore. Monthly sales revenues amount to $27,000. Explicit costs paid by the owner-manager include the cost of merchandise bought from producers for resale to consumers ($17,000), wages to the employees of the drugstore, "rent" and utilities paid to the landlord, and local sales and business taxes. When all of these explicit costs are subtracted from total revenue, we are left with a *net revenue* of $6,000 per month.

The owner-manager of the drugstore may be quite pleased with a net revenue of $6,000 per month. He is working hard for this income, however. To keep his store running, the owner-manager is working ten hours per day, seven days a week. This adds up to 300 hours of labor per month. Were he to work this hard for someone else, his labor would be compensated explicitly, with a paycheck. Although he doesn't choose to pay himself in this way, part of the

TABLE 6.2 THE COMPUTATION OF ECONOMIC PROFIT
(per month)

To calculate economic profit, we must take account of *all* costs of production. The economic costs of production include the implicit (opportunity) costs of the labor and capital a producer contributes to the production process. The net revenues of a business take into account only explicit costs paid by the owner.

Total (gross) revenues	$27,000
less explicit costs:	
Cost of merchandise sold	$17,000
Wages to cashier, stock, and delivery help	2,500
Rent and utilities	800
Taxes	700
Total explicit costs	$21,000
Net revenue	$ 6,000
less implicit costs:	
Wages of owner-manager, 300 hrs. @ $10 per hour	$ 3,000
Return on inventory investment, 10% per year on $120,000	1,000
Total implicit costs	$ 4,000
Economic profit	$ 2,000

net returns of the drugstore nevertheless represent a return for his labor. Hence we compute his implicit wages by noting that he would earn $10 per hour in the best alternative job. Multiplying this wage rate ($10) by the number of hours he works in the drugstore (300), we see that the implicit return for his labor is $3,000 per month.

We also observe that he has used his savings to purchase inventory for the store. He purchased the goods on his shelves for $120,000, and they represent his capital investment in the business. If he had invested his savings in some other business, he could have earned a return of 10 percent per year. This opportunity cost is used to determine the implicit return to his capital investment. In this case, the implicit return amounts to $12,000 per year (10 percent × $120,000), or $1,000 per month.

To calculate the "economic profit" generated by the corner drugstore, we subtract all implicit factor payments (costs) from net revenue. The residual in this case amounts to $2,000 per month. That is the drugstore's economic profit.

"Normal" profits are an economic cost. Note that when we compute the drugstore's economic profits, we include a measure of the opportunity costs of the owner's capital. Specifically, we assumed that his funds would have reaped a 10 percent return somewhere else. In effect, we have assumed that a standard, or "normal," rate of return is 10 percent. Rather than investing in a drugstore, the owner could have earned a 10 percent return on his funds by investing in a fast-food franchise, video games, a steel plant, or some other production activity. By choosing to invest in a drugstore instead, the owner was seeking a *higher* return on his funds—an *above-average* return. Had he not succeeded, he would have had no *economic* profits. In other words, economic profits represent an above-average return—something over and above "normal profits."

Our treatment of "normal" returns as an economic cost leads to a startling conclusion: on average, economic profits are zero. Only firms that reap *above-average* returns can claim economic profits. If some firms are above the average, other firms must be below the average. In other words, the economic profits (above-average returns) of some firms are offset by the economic losses (below-average returns) of other firms. This seemingly strange perspective on profits emphasizes the opportunity costs of all economic activities. ***A productive activity is "profitable" only if it earns more than its opportunity cost.***

Sources of profit

Naturally, everyone in business wants to earn an economic profit. But relatively few people can stay ahead of the pack. To earn economic profits, a business must see opportunities that others have missed, discover new products, find new and better methods of production, or take above-average risks. In fact, economic profits are often regarded as a reward to entrepreneurship, the ability and willingness to take risks, to organize factors of production, and to produce something society desires. From this perspective, profit represents a return to an intangible but vitally important "fourth factor of production."

Cubist profits

Ideal Toy rebounds with Rubik

Lionel A. Weintraub, 61, chairman of Ideal Toy Corp., has yet to figure out the solution to Rubik's cube. But he's having no trouble figuring out the bottom-line effect of the cube, which has put his company squarely in the black. Ideal Toy, headquartered in Hollis, New York, expects to sell more than ten million cubes in the fiscal year that ends on January 29, 1982, boosting revenues by $40 million to an estimated $210 million. Earnings will reach an all-time high of at least $9 million, a wide swing from a net loss of $15.5 million in the previous fiscal year.

Ideal Toy stumbled onto its salvation. Weintraub picked up the U.S. rights to manufacture Rubik's cube (named for its inventor, Ernö Rubik, a Hungarian architecture professor) two years ago, after several big American toy makers turned it down. He hasn't always been so lucky. His company's Evel Knievel line of toys bombed when the stuntman was jailed for beating a former press agent with a baseball bat. But the cube, Weintraub says, "is like Frisbee. It will be around forever."

Consider the local drugstore again. People in the neighborhood clearly desire such a drugstore, as evidenced by its substantial sales revenue. But why should anyone go to the trouble and risk of starting and maintaining one? In calculating the profits of the drugstore, we noted that the owner-manager *could* earn $3,000 in wages by accepting a regular job plus $1,000 per month in returns on capital by investing in an "average" business. Why should he take on the added responsibilities and risks of owning and operating his own drugstore?

The inducement to take on the added responsibilities of owning and operating a business is the potential for profit, the "extra" income over and above nominal factor payments. In the absence of such additional compensation, few people would want to make the extra effort required. From this perspective, the potential for profit is a major source of economic activity and growth.

Although entrepreneurship is an important source of economic profits—and economic losses!—it is not the only explanation for above-average returns. Some firms command above-average returns through their control of specific processes, products, or markets. The most familiar situation is a monopoly, exclusive production of a particular product by one firm. In such cases, a firm may continue to earn economic profits simply because no other firms are allowed to produce the same good or sell it at lower prices. In this case, profits are less a reward to entrepreneurship than a tribute to market power.

In the chapters that follow, we shall examine the origins of profits more closely. We shall be especially concerned with assessing the potential for profits in markets dominated by market power (e.g., monopolies) and those in which competition thrives. First, however, we shall look more carefully at how profits are actually determined.

PROFITS, PRICES, AND COSTS

Prices and profits

Profits are directly related to the prices producers charge for their output. But the relationship is not as simple as most people think. High prices do not necessarily mean high *profits.* If this isn't immediately obvious to you, try selling ice cream cones at $4 apiece outside the student union. You're apt to find that you have the highest

law of demand: The quantity of a good demanded in a given time period increases as its price falls (*ceteris paribus*).

price in town and the lowest profit. Remember the **law of demand?** It says that ice cream lovers buy fewer cones at high prices than at low prices. Even if you are the only ice cream seller in sight, you are not likely to sell many cones at $4 apiece. If there are other ice cream vendors around, the situation will be even worse. Indeed, you may not sell *any* ice cream if your price is higher than theirs.

The first thing a producer has to consider, then, is how the price charged will affect sales. Is the firm the only producer of the good, or are many other firms selling the same good? Does the firm have to charge the "prevailing" price? Or can the price be raised or lowered? What impact would a different price have on unit sales?

Prices and total revenue

total revenue: The price of a product multiplied by the quantity sold in a given time period; $p \times q$.

Your brief introduction to the ice cream market should provide convincing evidence that the quantity sold rarely increases when price rises. But it is still possible for **total revenue** to rise when price is increased. As we observed in Chapter 4, the critical question is not whether the demand curve slopes downward—as it almost always does—but rather *how much* the quantity demanded increases when the price falls. In particular, the impact of a change in price on total revenue depends on the price elasticity of demand (see Table 6.3).

Consider the case of meat prices and sales. When the Safeway store prices its sirloin steaks at $3.95 per pound, it is able to sell 200 pounds of steak per day. Total revenue—price times quantity sold—equals $790 ($3.95 × 200) in this case.

What would happen to total revenue if Safeway Stores were to raise the price of steak to $4.40 a pound? Would consumers continue to buy 200 pounds of steak a day? If they did, total revenue would rise to $880 a day (200 pounds × $4.40 per pound). But this outcome is most unlikely, because it suggests a completely vertical (perfectly inelastic) demand curve. A more likely result is that consumers will reduce their steak purchases as the price of steak rises, switching instead to other meats, poultry, or fish. Sales volume will drop below 200 pounds per day, and total revenue will be less than $880. How far sales drop depends on the **price elasticity of demand** for steak. Total revenue will actually fall below the original $790 if demand is elastic in this price range. ***Total revenue will rise when price is increased only if demand is relatively inelastic.***

price elasticity of demand: The percentage change in quantity demanded divided by the percentage change in price.

The dependence of total revenues on the price elasticity of de-

TABLE 6.3 PRICE, ELASTICITY, AND TOTAL REVENUE

Higher prices do not necessarily lead to higher profits. In fact, higher prices do not even ensure increased revenues. The response of total revenue to a change in price depends on the price elasticity of demand. If demand is perfectly elastic ($E = \infty$), the firm can sell all it produces at the current price.

	Response to price increase		*Response to price reduction*	
Degree of elasticity	*Quantity demanded*	*Total revenue*	*Quantity demanded*	*Total revenue*
$E = 0$	no change	rises	no change	falls
$E < 1$	falls	rises	rises	falls
$E = 1$	falls	no change	rises	no change
$E > 1$	falls	falls	rises	rises
$E = \infty$	falls	falls to zero	rises	infinite

Apple Computer Sets Expansion of Facility

CUPERTINO, Calif.—Apple Computer Inc. said it will spend $25 million to expand its manufacturing and test plant in Singapore.

The maker of personal computers said the plant, which opened in July, would be increased to 273,000 square feet from 133,000 square feet.

The project is expected to begin in about four months and the company said it hopes to have it completed in 1½ to two years.

mand came as a shock to many airlines. During the early 1960s, airline traffic was growing rapidly and profits were high. Then some wild-eyed airline executive got the idea of increasing output (and revenue) by enlarging the planes. The Boeing 707, with a capacity of 189 passengers, was replaced by the 747, with a capacity of 490. Did sales keep pace? No. The airlines had erroneously assumed that they could sell a far greater number of seats at the existing (high) fares. What they got was a lot of empty seats, tremendous losses, and a lesson in the price elasticity of demand. It took at least five years for the airlines to recover, and then only with the help of reduced-rate fares. And it was not until 1978, when bargain fares became commonplace, that jumbo planes began to fill up. Unfortunately, the airlines started raising prices significantly shortly after that. Once again they got stuck with empty seats and had to reintroduce "bargain" fares. The price elasticity of demand for air travel remained high.

We should also note, however, that in some situations additional output *can* be sold at virtually unchanged prices. You can sell another 100 shares of IBM stock, another 1,000 textbooks, or another 100,000 bushels of wheat with very little effect on prices. In these cases, the additional quantity offered for sale is so small in relation to total sales that the demand curve may be characterized as *completely* elastic (horizontal) in the relevant price range. Increased sales in these cases contribute directly to increased revenues. Even in these cases, however, a point will be reached where additional sales can be made only at lower prices. How far away that point is depends on the size of the added output in relation to total sales or consumption. With 600 million shares of IBM available, 750,000 copies of introductory economics texts for sale, and 1½ billion bushels of wheat produced annually, the added sales contemplated here will hardly affect prices at all.

These interactions of product prices and sales lead to a few simple observations. *A producer who seeks to improve total revenues by increasing the price of his product must consider the impact of the price change on sales.* By the same reasoning, *a producer who wishes to improve total revenues by expanding output must take into account the effect of increased output on product prices.* What is required in both cases is some knowledge of the price elasticity of consumer demand.

Sales and costs

Just as sales vary with price (or price with output), so too do costs vary with sales. This relationship is perhaps the most obvious of all. Unless you are selling unrefined, unpackaged air, anything you sell is going to cost something to produce. Each textbook produced costs a certain amount for paper, printing, binding, and labor; each bushel of wheat uses up a certain amount of land, fertilizer, harvesting, and packaging. Even another passenger on an airplane costs something for additional fuel, food, and service. In general, then, we may conclude that ***additional output is obtainable only at greater cost,*** and profitability depends in part on how fast costs rise with output.

marginal cost: The increase in total cost associated with a one-unit increase in production.

In Chapter 5 we examined how costs vary with the rate of output. The central force in production decisions is **marginal cost.**

total cost: The market value of all resources used to produce a good or service.

Marginal cost measures the *change* in **total cost** asociated with a change in output. It is the *added* cost of producing one more unit of a good. In deciding whether to expand the rate of output, a producer needs to consider what will happen to costs. Even if additional units of output could be sold, the marginal cost of producing them may be too high.

LONG-RUN VS. SHORT-RUN DECISIONS

short run: The period in which the quantity (and quality) of some inputs is fixed, that is, cannot be changed.

It may be evident by now that the road to profits is not an easy one. Successful producers must be able to juggle prices, sales, revenues, and costs. They must know how these concepts relate to each other and what will happen to profits in the process. In the remainder of this chapter we shall examine the techniques of successful profit maximizers. To simplify matters, we shall concentrate on **short-run** decisions.

The short-run production decision

production decision: The selection of the short-run rate of output (with existing plant and equipment).

In the short run, producers are saddled with fixed costs. They have already bought or leased basic plant and equipment. This was the situation of the Universal Jeans Corporation in Chapter 5. Its problem was to make the best possible use of fixed facilities (leased factory and sewing machines). In this short-run context, the primary concern is to operate the plant at its most profitable rate of output. Choosing the short-run rate of output is called the **production decision.** The right production decision is the one that maximizes the profits attainable with the firm's available plant and equipment.

The long-run investment decision

long run: A period of time long enough for all inputs to be varied (no fixed costs).

investment decision: The decision to build, buy, or lease plant and equipment to start or expand a business.

Producers without any fixed-cost commitments have a broader range of options. They are not confined to selecting a single rate of output for existing facilities. Instead, they have the option of selecting different facilities, or even none at all. In the **long run,** there are no fixed commitments and thus no fixed costs. In this context, firms can make a fundamental **investment decision,** that is, a decision about whether to build, buy, or lease basic plant and equipment. The news clipping on the preceding page summarizes a recent investment decision made by Apple Computer. By expanding its production facilities, Apple incurred larger fixed costs. It did so because it anticipates continued growth of demand for personal computers. In the following analysis of supply behavior, we shall first discuss a firm's production decision, then look at these less frequent but very basic investment decisions.[2]

MAXIMIZING SHORT-RUN PROFITS

The best single rule for maximizing profits in the short run is this: never produce anything that costs you more than it brings in. By

[2] In Chapters 7 and 12 we shall also examine the *efficiency decision*, involving the long-term choice of production processes and related cost curves.

following this simple rule, a producer is likely to make the right production decision. We shall see how this rule works, first by looking at the revenue side of production ("what it brings in"), then at the cost side ("what it costs").

The horizontal demand curve

The first thing a producer must determine is whether a change in the rate of output will affect the price of the good sold. In other words, does the producer have the power to change the product's price? To most people, the obvious answer would seem to be yes. But our brief experience trying to sell $4 ice cream cones should raise some doubts. A producer can, of course, put higher price tags on his output. But there is no assurance that those goods can be sold. Two kinds of situations might preclude sales at higher prices.

Government regulation could preclude sales at higher prices. A utility company, for example, cannot charge prices above those approved by the state utility commission. The telephone company, many railroads, and international airlines also confront price ceilings that limit their power to change prices. In this context, the firm need not worry about what price to charge; the primary concern is to find that rate of output which maximizes profits at the regulated price.

Short-run prices are effectively constant in other contexts as well. Recall the ice cream dilemma. If the student union is surrounded by ice cream vendors charging $2 per cone, you cannot sell much ice cream at $4 per cone. The presence of other vendors pretty much precludes sales at higher prices. In fact, if your ice cream is no different from anyone else's and there are lots of other vendors nearby, you will be compelled to charge the prevailing price of $2 per cone (or sell no ice cream). From this perspective, price is constant; producers can only adapt their rate of output to that price. This kind of situation is characteristic of **competitive firms.** They have no power to raise the price of their output. Moreover, such firms can sell their entire output at the prevailing market price, so they have no incentive to charge a lower price. For competitive firms, the demand curve appears to be *horizontal*, as in Figure 6.3. The demand curve is *perfectly elastic* over the relevant range of output.

competitive firm: A firm without market power, with no ability to alter the market price of the goods it produces.

In Chapter 7 we shall take a closer look at the nature of compet-

FIGURE 6.3 HORIZONTAL DEMAND

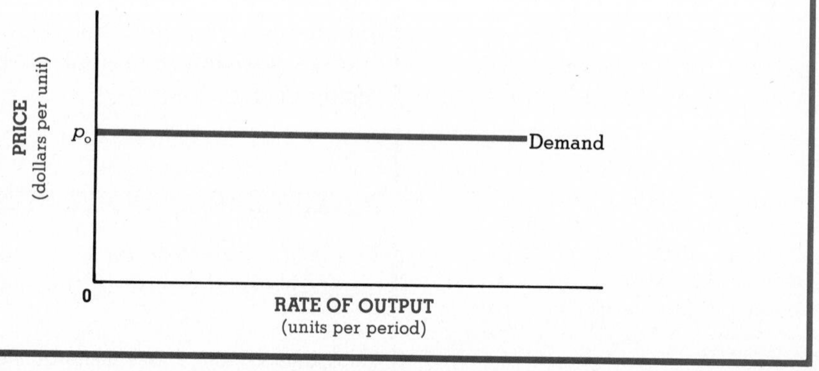

A single firm often cannot raise the price of its product and continue to sell its output. On the other hand, it may be able to sell its entire output at the prevailing price. In the short run, such firms confront a constant price. This is illustrated by the horizontal demand curve at the price p_0. An individual firms objective is to find the rate of output that maximizes profits at this price.

itive firms. We shall also examine the behavior of firms that are noncompetitive, in the sense that they *can* raise their prices and continue to sell their output. For the moment, however, we shall focus on a trait common to both: the quest for maximum profit.

Marginal revenue

In making a production decision, we are searching for the most profitable rate of output from existing plant and equipment. This implies looking at all possible short-run rates of output. In each case, we want to know if *one more* unit of output would increase our profits. In making this decision, we need to know what that additional unit of output will bring in, that is, how much it adds to the total revenue of the firm. *Total revenue* is the sum of money a firm takes in from *all* of its production. It is equal to the average price of output multiplied by the quantity sold:

$$\underset{(TR)}{\text{Total revenue}} = \underset{(p)}{\text{price}} \times \underset{(q)}{\text{quantity}}$$

marginal revenue: The change in total revenue that results from a one-unit increase in the quantity sold.

The contribution to total revenue of an additional unit of output is called **marginal revenue.** Marginal revenue is the *change* in total revenue that occurs when the rate of output is increased by one unit. To calculate marginal revenue, we can just compare the total revenues received before and after a one-unit increase in the rate of production: the *difference* between the two totals equals marginal revenue.

When the price of a product is constant, the computation of marginal revenue is even simpler. Suppose we are actually selling ice cream cones at a constant price of $2 apiece. In this case, a one-unit increase in sales (one more cone) increases total revenue by $2. This is illustrated in Table 6.4. Notice that ***as long as the price of a product is constant, price and marginal revenue are one and the same thing.***

This is not always the case. Often additional output can be sold only if price is reduced. In these situations, price is not constant and marginal revenue and price are no longer equal. We shall look at these situations a bit later.

Marginal cost

Knowing what marginal revenue is leaves us just one step away from applying the simple rule for profit maximization: never produce anything that costs more than it brings in. We already know what

TABLE 6.4 TOTAL AND MARGINAL REVENUE

Marginal revenue *(MR)* is the *change* in total revenue associated with the sale of one more unit of output. A third ice cream cone increases total revenue from $4 to $6; *MR* equals $2. If the price is constant (at $2 here), marginal revenue equals price.

Quantity sold		*Price per unit*		*Total revenue*	*Marginal revenue*
0	×	$2	=	$ 0	
					$2
1	×	2	=	2	
					2
2	×	2	=	4	
					2
3	×	2	=	6	
					2
4	×	2	=	8	
					2
5	×	2	=	10	

one more unit brings in; all we need to do now is look at its cost.

The added cost of producing one more unit of a good is its *marginal* cost. Figure 6.4 summarizes the marginal costs associated with the production of brass doorknobs.

The production of brass doorknobs requires a certain set of tools and equipment that can be leased for $10 a day on a long-term basis. Once leased, these tools and equipment become part of fixed costs; they must be paid for no matter how many doorknobs are produced.[3] In addition, labor and material (primarily brass) must be purchased to produce the doorknobs. Obviously, the quantity of labor and brass varies with the number of doorknobs produced. These are *variable costs*. *Marginal costs* in this case are the cost of the added labor and brass needed to produce *each* additional doorknob.

According to Figure 6.4, marginal costs tend to increase when doorknob production is increased. Like most production processes, doorknob manufacture takes place in an existing plant that is equipped with a certain amount of tools and machinery. To increase output in the short run, more labor is hired to use that (fixed) plant and equipment. As the number of workers increases, however, each worker has fewer tools and machines to work with. In other words, the existing (fixed) plant and equipment must be shared by an ever

[3] Whether one should lease this equipment in the first place is an investment decision.

FIGURE 6.4 THE COSTS OF BRASS DOORKNOB PRODUCTION

Marginal cost is the increase in total cost associated with a one-unit increase in production. When the production of brass doorknobs expands from two to three per day, total costs increase by $9 (from $22 to $31 per day). The marginal cost of the third knob is therefore $9, as illustrated by point *D* in the graph below.

	Rate of output (knobs per day)	*Total cost (per day)*	*Marginal cost (per unit)*	*Average cost (per unit)*
A	0	$10	—	—
B	1	15	$ 5	$15.00
C	2	22	7	11.00
D	3	31	9	10.33
E	4	44	13	11.00
F	5	61	17	12.20

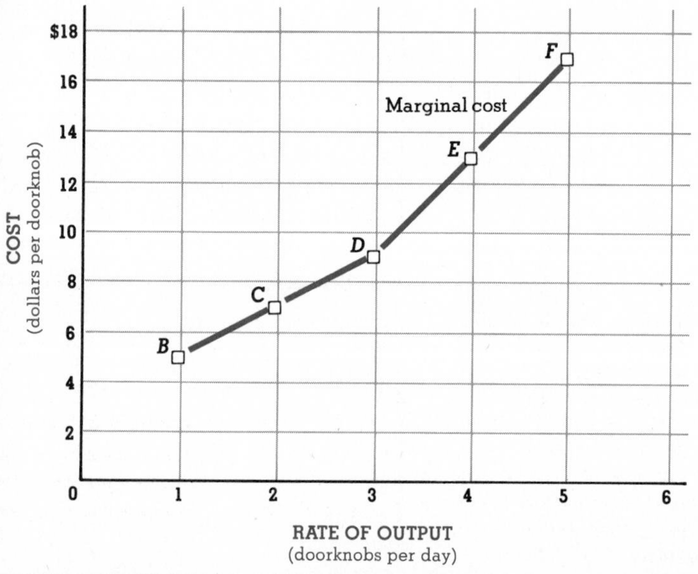

law of diminishing returns: The marginal physical product of a variable factor declines as more of it is employed with a given quantity of other (fixed) inputs.

larger (variable) number of workers. Eventually, this situation reflects the **law of diminishing returns.** As marginal product diminishes, marginal cost increases. The upward-sloping *MC* curve of Figure 6.4 illustrates this phenomenon.

The production decision

We are now in a position to make a production decision. The rule about never producing anything that costs more than it brings in can now be stated in more technical terms. What an additional unit of output brings in is its marginal revenue (*MR*); what it costs is its marginal cost (*MC*). Therefore, we do not want to produce an additional unit of output if its *MC* exceeds *MR*. If *MC* exceeds *MR*, we are spending more to produce that extra unit than we are getting back: total profits will decline if we produce it.

The opposite is true when *MR* exceeds *MC*. If an extra unit brings in more revenue than it costs to produce, it is adding to total profit. Total profits must increase in this case. Hence we want to expand the rate of production whenever *MR* exceeds *MC*.

profit-maximization rule: Produce at that rate of output where marginal revenue equals marginal cost.

Since we want to expand output when *MR* exceeds *MC* and contract output if *MR* is less than *MC*, the profit-maximizing rate of output is easily found. ***Short-run profits are maximized at that rate of output where* MR = MC.** The **profit-maximization rule** is summarized in Table 6.5.

Figure 6.5 illustrates the application of our profit-maximization rule in the production of brass doorknobs. We shall assume that the prevailing price of brass doorknobs is $13 apiece. At this price we can sell all the knobs we can produce, up to our short-run capacity. Knobs cannot be sold at a higher price, because lots of producers make doorknobs and sell them for $13. If we try to charge a higher price, consumers will buy their knobs from other producers. Hence the demand curve facing this one firm is horizontal at the price of $13. ***Whenever the price of a firm's product is constant in the short run, marginal revenue and price are identical.*** Thus the horizontal demand curve confronting this producer of doorknobs also represents marginal revenues.

The costs of producing brass doorknobs were already examined in Figure 6.4. The key concept illustrated here is marginal cost. The *MC* curve slopes upward, in conventional fashion.

Also depicted in Figure 6.5 are the total revenues, costs, and profits of alternative production rates. Study the table first. Notice first of all that the firm loses $10 per day if it produces no doorknobs (row *A*). At zero output, total revenue is zero ($p \times q = 0$). However,

TABLE 6.5 SHORT-RUN PROFIT-MAXIMIZATION RULES

The relationship between marginal revenue and marginal cost dictates short-run production decisions. Profits are maximized at that rate of output where *MR* = *MC*.

If	*Then*
$MR > MC$	increase output rate
$MR = MC$	maintain output rate (profits maximized)
$MR < MC$	decrease output rate

FIGURE 6.5 MAXIMIZATION OF PROFITS WITH CONSTANT PRICES

Knowing the marginal cost and marginal revenue associated with each doorknob, we can easily determine the most profitable rate of output. The table and graph show the desired rate of brass doorknob production. Profits are at a maximum at that rate of output where marginal revenue equals marginal cost. In this case, profit maximization occurs at an output of four doorknobs per day.

	(1) Number of doorknobs (per day)	(2) Price	(3) Total revenue	(4) Total cost	(5) Total profit	(6) Marginal revenue	(7) Marginal cost
A	0	—	0	$10.00	−$10.00	—	—
B	1	$13.00	$13.00	15.00	− 2.00	$13.00	$ 5.00
C	2	13.00	26.00	22.00	+ 4.00	13.00	7.00
D	3	13.00	39.00	31.00	+ 8.00	13.00	9.00
E	4	13.00	52.00	44.00	+ 8.00	13.00	13.00
F	5	13.00	65.00	61.00	+ 4.00	13.00	17.00

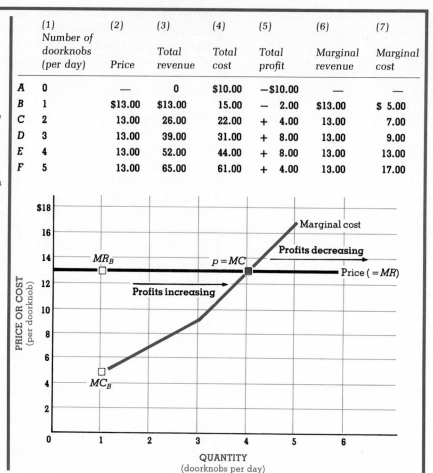

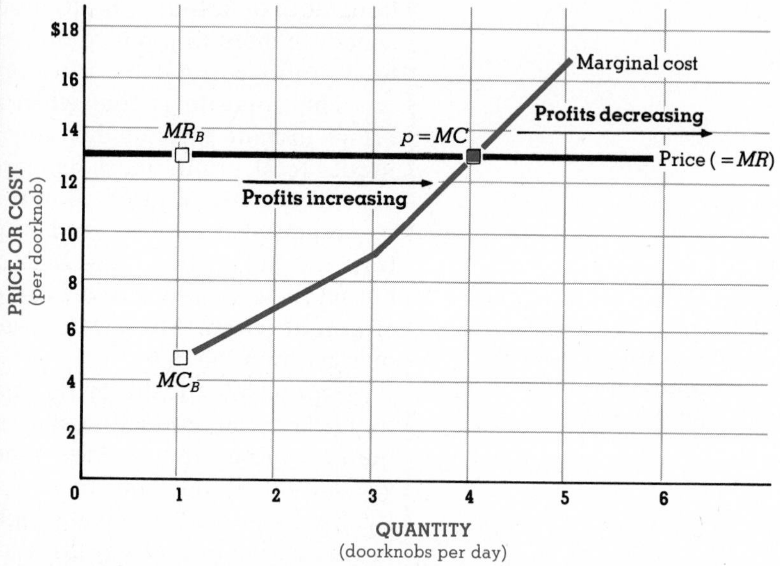

the firm must still contend with fixed costs of $10 per day. Total profit—total revenue minus total cost—is therefore *minus* $10; the firm incurs a loss.

Row *B* of the table shows how this loss is reduced when one doorknob is produced per day. The production and sale of one doorknob per day brings in $13 of total revenue (column 3). The total cost of producing one knob per day is $15 (column 4). Hence the total loss associated with an output rate of one knob per day is $2 (column 5). This may not be what we hoped for, but it is certainly better than the $10 loss incurred at zero output.

The superiority of producing one knob per day rather than zero is also evident in columns 6 and 7 of row *B*. The first doorknob produced has a *marginal revenue* of $13. Its *marginal cost* is only $5. Hence it brings in more added revenue than it costs to produce. Under these circumstances—whenever *MR* exceeds *MC*—output should definitely be expanded.

The excess of *MR* over *MC* for the first unit of output is also illustrated by the graph in Figure 6.5. Point MR_B ($13) lies above MC_B ($5); the *difference* between these two points measures the contribution that first doorknob makes to the total profits of the firm. In this case, that contribution equals $13 − $5 = $8; and production losses are reduced by that amount when the rate of output is increased from zero to one knob per day.

So long as* MR *exceeds* MC, *further increases in the rate of output are desirable. Notice what happens to profits when the rate of output is increased from one to two doorknobs per day (row *C*). The *MR* of the second knob is $13; its *MC* is $7. Therefore it *adds* $6 to total profits. Instead of losing $2 per day, the firm is now making a profit of $4 per day. The second unit of daily output has improved the situation considerably.

The firm can make even more profits by expanding the rate of output further. Look what happens when the rate of output reaches three doorknobs per day (row *D* of the table). The marginal revenue of the third knob is $13; its marginal cost is $9. Therefore the third knob makes a $4 contribution to profits. By increasing its rate of output to three doorknobs per day, the firm doubles its total profits.

This firm will never make huge profits. The fourth unit of output has a *MR* of $13 and a *MC* of $13 as well. It does not contribute to total profits, nor does it subtract from them. The fourth unit of output represents the highest rate of output the firm desires. At the rate of output where *MR* = *MC*, total profits of the firm are maximized.[4]

Notice what happens if we expand output beyond four doorknobs per day. The *MR* of the fifth doorknob is $13; its *MC* is $17. The fifth knob costs more than it brings in. If we produce that fifth doorknob, total profit will decline by $4. The fifth unit of output makes us worse off. This eventuality is evident in the graph of Figure 6.5; at the output rate of five knobs per day, the *MC* curve lies above the *MR* curve. The lesson here is clear: ***output should not be increased if* MC *exceeds* MR.**

The outcome of the production decision is illustrated in Figure 6.5 by the intersection of the *MR* and *MC* curves. At this intersection, *MR* equals *MC* and profits are maximized. If we produced less, we would be giving up potential profits. If we produced more, total profits would also fall.

Adding up profits

To reach the right production decision, we have relied on *marginal* revenues and costs. Having found the desired rate of output, however, we may want to take a closer look at the profits we are accumulating. We could, of course, content ourselves with the statistics in the table of Figure 6.5. But a picture would be nice, too, especially if it reflected our success in production. To draw that picture, we can use either *total* revenue and cost curves or *average* revenue and cost curves. Figure 6.6 illustrates both approaches.

Figure 6.6*a* depicts *total* revenues and costs at various rates of

[4] In this case, profits are the same at output levels of three and four. Given the choice between the two levels, most firms will choose the higher level. By producing the extra unit of output, the firm increases its customer base. This not only denies rival firms an additional sale but also provides some additional "cushion" when the economy slumps. Also, corporate size may connote both prestige and power (more on this later). In any case, the higher output level defines the limit to maximum-profit production.

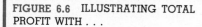

FIGURE 6.6 ILLUSTRATING TOTAL PROFIT WITH . . .

Total profits can be computed as *TR* − *TC*, as in part *a*. Or they can be computed as profit *per unit* (*p* − *ATC*) multiplied by the quantity sold. This is illustrated in part *b* by the shaded rectangle. To find the profit-maximizing rate of output, we could use either of these graphs or the *MR* and *MC* curves of Figure 6.5.

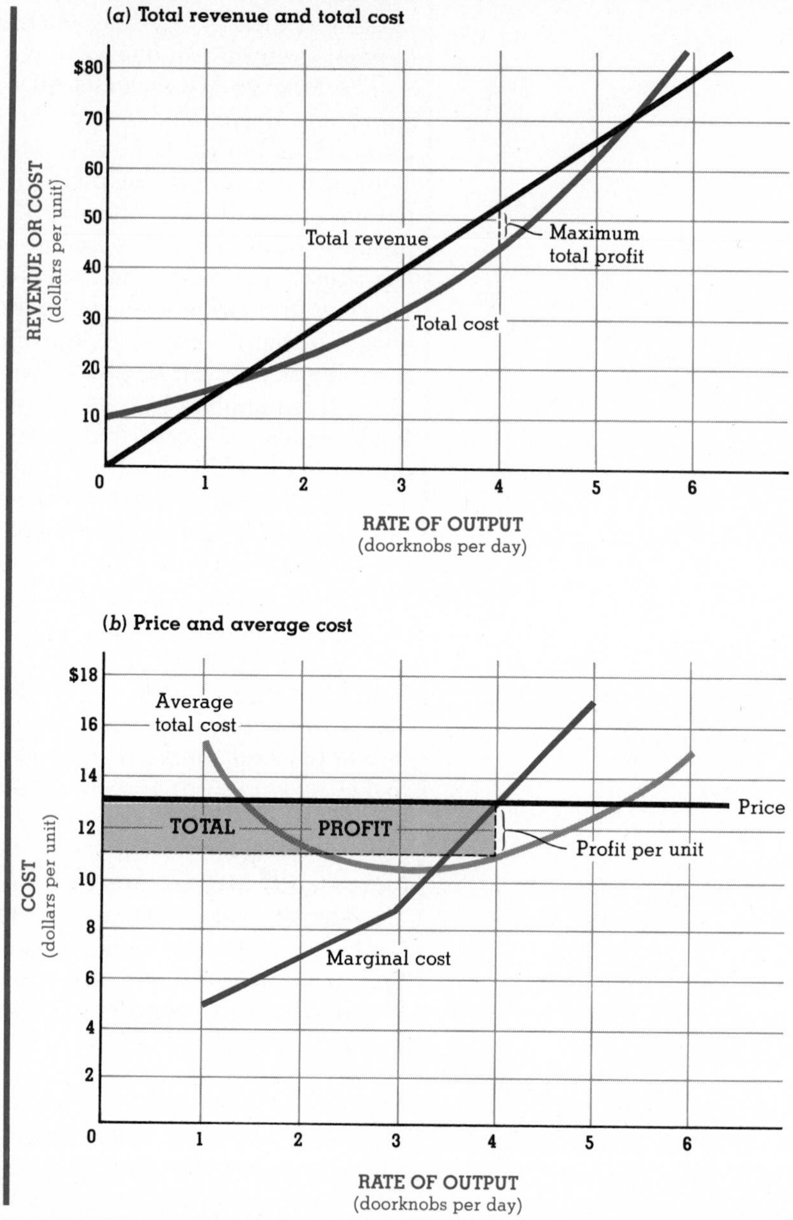

output. Recall that all brass doorknobs are sold at the prevailing price of $13 each. Hence total revenue equals $q \times \$13$. The resulting *TR* curve is a straight line. The total cost (*TC*) curve in Figure 6.6*a* starts above the total revenue line, dips below it, then rapidly overtakes it again. This is a reflection of the fact that marginal costs are initially low but rise quite rapidly as output expands.

Total profits are represented in Figure 6.6*a* by the vertical distance between the total revenue and total cost curves. This is a straightforward interpretation of our definition of total profits, that is, total profits = *TR* − *TC*. The vertical distance between the *TR* and *TC* curves is maximized at the output of four doorknobs per day.

Our success in producing brass doorknobs can also be illustrated by *average* revenue and costs. Total profit is equal to *average* profit per unit multiplied by the number of units produced. Profit *per unit*, in turn, is equal to price *minus* average total cost, that is,

$$\text{Profit per unit} = p - ATC$$

The price of brass doorknobs is illustrated in Figure 6.6*b* by the price line at $13. The average cost of producing brass doorknobs is illustrated by the *ATC* curve. Like the *ATC* curve we encountered in Chapter 5, this one has a U shape. Therefore, the *difference* between price and average cost—profit per unit—is illustrated by the vertical distance between the price and *ATC* curves. At four doorknobs per day, for example, profit per unit equals $13 − $11 = $2.

To compute *total* profits, we note that

$$\begin{aligned}\text{Total profits} &= \text{profit per unit} \times \text{quantity}\\ &= (p - ATC) \times q\end{aligned}$$

In this case, the four doorknobs generate a profit of $2 each, for a *total* profit of $8 per day. *Total* profits are illustrated in Figure 6.6*b* by the shaded rectangle. (Recall that the area of a rectangle is equal to its height [profit per unit] multiplied by its width [quantity sold].)

Profit per unit not only is used to compute total profits but is often of interest in its own right. Business people like to cite statistics on "markups," which are a crude index to per-unit profits. However, ***the profit-maximizing producer never seeks to maximize per-unit profits.*** What counts is *total* profits, not the amount of profit per unit. This is the old $4 ice cream problem again. You might be able to maximize profit per unit if you could sell one cone for $4, but you would probably make a lot more money if you sold 100 cones at a per-unit profit of only 50 cents each.

Similarly, ***the profit-maximizing producer has no desire to produce at that rate of output where*** **ATC** ***is at a minimum.*** Minimum *ATC* does represent least-cost production. But additional units of output, even though they raise average costs, will increase total profits. This is evident in Figure 6.6; *MR* exceeds *MC* for some output to the right of minimum *ATC* (the bottom of the U). Therefore, profits are increasing as we increase the rate of output beyond the point of minimum average costs.

THE SHUTDOWN DECISION

The rule established for short-run profit maximization makes no reference to the costs of building a plant or equipping it with the necessary tools and machines. It speaks only of *marginal* costs and revenues. To determine the most profitable level of doorknob production, for example, we never really worried about the costs of the basic plant and equipment. The fixed costs of production were $10 per day and we accepted them as a fact of life. Yet we surely would have been better off if we could have leased the necessary facilities for only $5 per day. Shouldn't the level of fixed costs have some effect on our output decision?

To understand the influence of fixed costs on supply behavior, we must recall the distinction between the production decision and the investment decision. The *investment decision* requires a potential producer to decide whether he wants to build, buy, or lease a production plant, or to acquire the machinery needed to produce a particular product. That is to say, he must first decide whether he wants to go into business, thereby incurring fixed costs. This is an investment decision. Once in business, the producer must then determine how much to produce in any given day, week, or month. This is a *production decision*. The short-run profit-maximizing rule we have discussed relates only to this second decision; it assumes that a production unit exists.

To producers, of course, the investment decision is of enormous concern. The fixed costs that we have ignored in the production decision represent the producers' (or the stockholders') investment in the business. If they are going to avoid an economic loss, they have to generate at least enough revenue to recoup their investment. Thus it is not enough to generate marginal revenues in excess of marginal costs. To be successful, producers must generate enough income to cover the cost of (fixed) plant and equipment. Failure to do so will result in a net loss, despite allegiance to our profit-maximizing rule.

Even when total revenue does not cover all fixed costs, producers may keep producing. In this case they will be trying to recover as much of their original investment as possible. To do that, they will seek to collect as much revenue from production as they can, even though they know they will never recoup their entire investment. In other words, they must accept the fact that they made one bad decision—the decision to go into business—and seek to minimize the consequences.

variable costs: Costs of production that change when the rate of output is altered; for example, labor and material costs.

They still have the choice of being big losers or small losers, and the rules of profit maximization can guide that choice. Once the plant is built and the tools are acquired, only **variable costs** and revenues count.

The role of costs in investment and production decisions is summarized in Figure 6.7. The curves in Figure 6.7 represent the short-run costs and potential demand curves associated with production of brass doorknobs. As long as the price of brass doorknobs is \$13, the typical firm will produce four doorknobs a day, as determined by the intersection of the *MC* and *MR* (= price) curves (point *X*). In this case, price (\$13) exceeds average total cost (\$11) and doorknob production is profitable; the decision to go into business was a good one.

The investment decision would not look so good, however, if the market price of brass doorknobs fell to \$9. Following the short-run rule for profit maximization, the firm would be led to point *Y*, where *MC* intersects the new demand (*MR*) curve. At this intersection, the firm would produce three doorknobs per day. But total revenues no longer cover total costs, as can be seen from the fact that the *ATC* curve now lies above the demand curve. The *ATC* of producing three knobs is \$10.33 (Figure 6.4); price is \$9. Hence the firm is incurring a loss of \$4 per day (three doorknobs at a loss of \$1.33 each).

FIGURE 6.7 THE FIRMS SHUTDOWN POINT

A firm should cease production only if total revenue is less than total variable cost. The shutdown decision may be based on the *MC*, price, and *AVC* curves. If the price of standard doorknobs were $13, a firm would want to produce at point *X*. At that rate of output, price exceeds average variable cost and production should continue. The same is true when price equals $9 (point *Y*). At point *Y*, the firm is losing money (*p* is less than *ATC*) but more than covering all variable costs (*p* is greater than *AVC*). If the price falls to $4 per doorknob, output should cease.

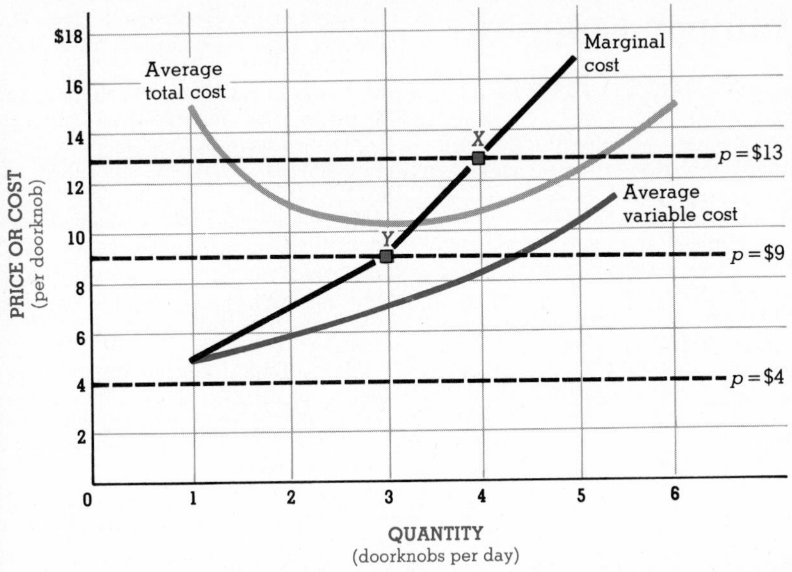

Should the firm stay in business under the circumstances? The answer is yes. Recall that the producer has already leased the plant and equipment required for doorknob production, at a (fixed) cost of $10 per day. The producer will have to pay these fixed costs whether the machinery is used or not. Stopping production of doorknobs would result in a loss amounting to $10 per day. Staying in business, even when doorknob prices fall to $9 each, generates a loss of only $4 a day. In this case, ***where price exceeds average variable costs but not average total costs, the profit-maximization rule minimizes losses.*** The investment decision turns out badly, but at least part of the initial investment is recovered. This was the situation for Ford Motor Company and other auto producers in the early 1980s.

The shutdown point

If the price of doorknobs falls far enough, however, the producer may be better off to cease production altogether. Suppose the price of brass doorknobs fell to $4 each (Figure 6.7). A price this low does

Ford Loses a Record $1.5 Billion in 1980

Ford Motor Co. said its losses for 1980 totaled $1.5 billion after a $316 million loss in the fourth quarter.

Ford's 1980 losses—which were in line with expectations—are, at this point, the largest ever by an American corporation, although it will lose that distinction soon, when Chrysler Corp. reports its 1980 losses—expected to total $1.7 billion. Chrysler lost $1.1 billion in 1979, the previous record.

All three companies were licking their wounds from the impact of high interest rates on their markets. Ford's 1980 after-tax loss of $1.5 billion resulted from declines of 33 percent in domestic sales and 26 percent in worldwide sales from 1979. . . .

Ford Chairman Philip Caldwell said the company had weathered the disastrous year "without basic damage to its operations or a reduction in the scope of its plans for future products."

Ford also was cheered by the showing of its new line of front-wheel-drive subcompacts, the Ford Escort and Mercury Lynx, which thus far has outsold all of the 70 imported car lines in the United States, according to Ford.

But Ford and its chief American competitors, Chrysler and General Motors Co., have had to curtail plant operations to conserve cash and give up hundreds of dollars per car in rebates to stimulate sales.

—Peter Behr

The Washington Post, Washington, D.C., February 20, 1981, p. D1. Copyright © 1981 The Washington Post.

Copper Company Shuts Down

NEW YORK—Phelps Dodge Corp., citing the lowest prices for copper in more than 30 years, said today it will suspend production at all its U.S. copper mines and concentrators and at its three Arizona smelters, effective Saturday, April 17.

The nation's second-largest copper producer said the suspension will last at least until June 1 and will result in the layoff of approximately 3,800 employes. . . .

Phelps Dodge Chairman George B. Munroe said, "the current recession has driven copper prices to their lowest levels in real terms in more than 30 years, and for the past several months we have been selling our copper for less than it costs us to produce it."

Munroe added that "by suspending operations we will conserve our ore reserves, reduce our inventories and cash outflows and thereby serve the long-term best interest of the company."

Phelps Dodge has an annual production of 350,000 short tons of copper, under normal operating conditions, including some 50,000 tons from leaching operations. Since the first of the year, however, operating rates have been curtailed to 80 percent of capacity.

The company said it may continue the cutback beyond June 1 if the copper market remained depressed.

Munroe said the company would resume operations "when conditions warrant."

The Washington Post, Washington, D.C., April 8, 1982. Reprinted by permission of United Press International.

not even cover the marginal cost of producing one doorknob per day ($5). Continued production of even one doorknob per day would imply a total loss of $11 per day ($10 of fixed costs plus $1 of variable costs). Higher rates of output would lead to still greater losses. Hence the firm would be well advised to shut down production, even though that action implies a loss of $10 per day. The initial investment decision was awful. In all cases ***where price does not cover average variable costs at any rate of output, production should cease.*** Thus, the **shutdown point** occurs where price is equal to average variable cost. Any lower price will result in losses that are larger than fixed costs.

shutdown point: That rate of output where *AVC* equals price.

Whether or not fixed costs count, then, depends on the decision being made. For producers trying to decide how best to utilize the resources they have purchased or leased, fixed costs no longer enter the decision-making process. For producers deciding whether to enter business, sign a lease, or replace existing machinery and plant, fixed costs count very much. Business people will proceed with an investment only if the anticipated profits are adequate to compensate for the effort and risk undertaken.

Long-run costs

In contemplating an investment decision, business people confront not one set of cost figures, but many. A plant not yet built can be designed for various rates of production. Producers expecting to sell large quantities of a good may want to build a large plant. In making long-run decisions a given producer is not bound to one size of plant or to a particular mix of tools and machinery. In the long run, one can be flexible. In general, *a producer will want to build, buy, or lease a plant that is most efficient for the anticipated rate of output.*[5] Once such a plant is selected, the producer may proceed with the problem of short-run profit maximization. Once production is started, he can only hope that his choice was a good one and that a shutdown can be avoided.

[5] The choice of long-run plant size (and related cost curves) was illustrated in Chapter 5.

DETERMINANTS OF SUPPLY

Whether the time frame is the short run or the long run, the one central force in production decisions is the quest for profits. Producers will go into production—incur fixed costs—only if they see the potential for economic profits (above-average returns). Once in business, they will continue to expand the rate of output so long as profits are increasing. They will get out of business—cease production—when economic losses exceed the fixed costs of production.

Nearly anyone could make money with these principles if he or she had complete information on costs and revenues. What renders the road to fortune less congested is the general absence of such complete information. In the real world, production decisions involve considerably more risk, since business people often don't know how much profit or loss they will incur until it's too late to alter production decisions. Consequently, business people are compelled to make a reasoned guess about the shape of demand and cost curves and then proceed, trusting to their market researchers, production specialists, and hunches. By way of summary, we can identify the major influences that will shape their short- and long-run decisions on how much output to supply to the market.

Short-run determinants

Since short-run production decisions are dominated by marginal revenues and marginal costs, the quantity of a good supplied will be affected by all forces that alter either *MR* or *MC*. Specifically, ***the quantity of output a producer is able and willing to supply will depend on:***

- The price of factor inputs
- The price of the product
- Technology (the available production function)
- Expectations (for prices, costs, sales, technology)

The costs that count in the short run are marginal costs. The lower they are, the greater the willingness and ability to produce. The price of the good is important because it determines the marginal revenue of the firm—the other half of the profit-maximization equation. Technology is important because it can change production costs (see Chapter 6). And finally, expectations are critical because they express producers' perceptions of what future costs, prices, sales, and profits are likely to be.

ceteris paribus: **The assumption of "everything else being equal," of nothing else changing.**

quantity supplied: The amount of a product offered for sale at a specific price during a given time period (*ceteris paribus*).

THE SHORT-RUN SUPPLY CURVE By using the familiar ***ceteris paribus*** assumption, we can predict quite accurately how the **quantity supplied** in the short run will respond to a change in price. In other words, we can draw a short-run supply curve in the same way that we earlier constructed consumer demand curves. In this case, the forces we assume to be constant are input prices, technology, and expectations. The only thing we allow to change is the price of the product itself. Under these circumstances, how will the quantity supplied change when the price of the product rises or falls?

Figure 6.8 illustrates the response of quantity supplied to a

FIGURE 6.8 THE SHORT-RUN SUPPLY CURVE

A profit-maximizing producer will not supply additional quantities of output unless marginal revenue at least equals marginal cost. For competitive firms, price and marginal revenue are identical. Hence marginal cost defines the lowest price a firm will accept for a given quantity of output. In this sense, the marginal cost curve *is* the supply curve: it tells us how quantity supplied will respond to price. At p = $13, the quantity supplied is four. At p = $9, the quantity supplied is three.

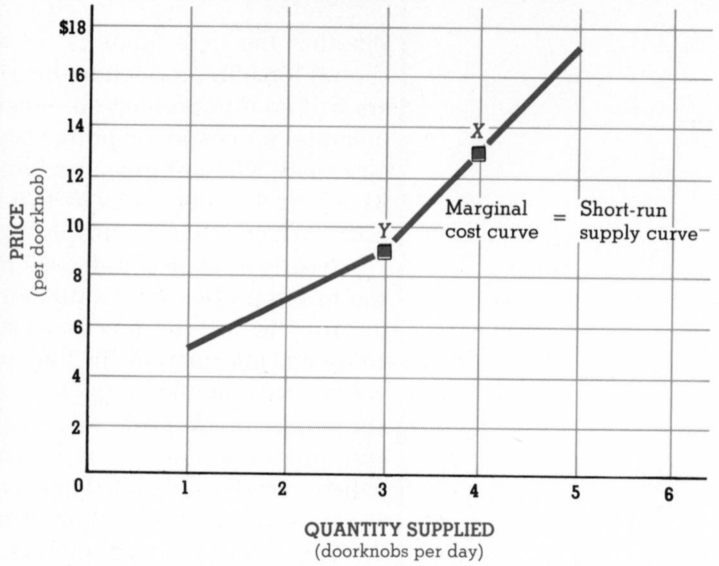

supply curve: A curve describing the quantities of a good a producer is willing and able to sell (produce) at alternative prices in a given time period (*ceteris paribus*).

change in price. Notice the critical role of marginal costs: ***the marginal cost curve is the short-run* supply curve *for a competitive firm.*** Recall our basic profit-maximization rule. A competitive producer wants to supply a good only if its price exceeds its marginal cost. Hence marginal cost defines the lower limit for an "acceptable" price. A producer of doorknobs is willing and able to produce four doorknobs per day only if the price of doorknobs is $13 (point *X*). If the price of doorknobs dropped to $9, the *quantity supplied* would fall to three (point *Y*). The marginal cost curve tells us what the quantity supplied would be at all other prices as well.[6] Hence the *MC* curve summarizes the response of a producer to price changes: it is the short-run supply curve.[7]

Long-run determinants

All of the forces that shape short-run production decisions are relevant in the long run as well. In the long run, however, the other determinants of supply are more likely to change. New technologies, for example, may reduce both the fixed costs of production and the marginal costs of production. Over time, an increase in the number of producers (sellers) may reduce the price of the good or increase the price of required inputs. Hence, even though the list of supply determinants looks the same, it takes on a new dimension in the long run. That dimension includes a greater potential for *change* in the underlying determinants of supply.

[6] There is an exception to this rule: if price is less than *minimum* average variable cost, no output will be supplied. This is the shutdown contingency we just examined.

[7] In noncompetitive situations—where the demand curve facing the firm is downward sloping rather than horizontal—the marginal cost curve does *not* represent the short-run supply curve. Such firms will be discussed in Chapters 8–10.

POLICY IMPLICATIONS: SUPPLY-SIDE TAX INCENTIVES

The motivating force in business supply decisions is the quest for profits. Because the amount of profit a producer can keep depends on taxes, government policy directly affects the incentives for producing goods and services. To the extent that taxes reduce the amount of profit a producer can make or keep, they discourage investment and production. Conversely, policies that reduce net costs or increase after-tax profits encourage additional investment and production. These observations were the basis for the "supply-side" tax reductions implemented by President Reagan in 1981. Some of the major business tax cuts included in the Economic Recovery Tax Act of 1981 are noted below.[8]

Lower corporate profits tax

The profits of U.S. corporations are taxed by the federal government. In 1980 the standard corporate tax rate was 46 percent for profits in excess of $50,000 per year. Forty-six cents out of every profit dollar was turned over to the U.S. Treasury. Firms with less than $50,000 in annual profits paid taxes at lower rates.

The corporate tax does not directly alter either the marginal revenues or marginal costs of a firm.[9] In this sense, ***the corporate profits tax does not affect the short-run production decision.*** Whatever rate of output maximizes short-run profits in the absence of a profits tax will also maximize profits after the tax is levied. The basic difference is that the corporation gets to keep less of the profit it earns.

Although the corporate tax will not alter short-run production decisions, it will affect investment decisions. Decisions to enter or expand a business are based on expected profits. What counts are "after-tax profits," that is, the amount of profit a producer gets to keep. This is the income producers/owners can spend on their own consumption or use for further investment.

To improve the incentives for investment, the Reagan administration proposed a cut in the tax rate for corporate profits. The tax legislation passed by Congress in August 1981 reduced the tax rate on the first $25,000 of annual profit from 17 percent in 1981 to 15 percent in 1983. The tax rate on profits between $25,000 and $50,000 was reduced from 20 percent to 18 percent. But the rate on profits in excess of $50,000 was left unchanged, at 46 percent. Accordingly, the tax reductions were far more significant for smaller corporations than for larger ones.

Faster depreciation

Both large and small corporations received greater tax relief from enlarged tax deductions. A firm pays taxes on its "taxable" income, not its economic profit. In computing taxable income, a firm may

[8] The provisions of the act, and its macroeconomic effects, are discussed in Chapter 15 of *The Macro Economy Today*.

[9] If corporations are able to "pass on" the corporate tax by raising consumer prices, marginal revenues may change. Our short-run analysis ignores this possibility.

depreciation (tax): The tax deduction allowed for the cost of using capital and equipment in production.

deduct the costs of labor and material (variable costs) as well as some portion of its capital (fixed) costs. The critical question in tax accounting is what fraction of fixed costs can be deducted from revenues in any year. The amount of that deduction is referred to as **(tax) depreciation.**

The more depreciation a firm is permitted to deduct from its revenues, the less taxable income it will have. Hence a firm's tax payment can be reduced either by (1) reducing the tax rate on taxable income, as we discussed above, or (2) allowing larger deductions for depreciation, which reduce the amount of income subject to taxation. Faster (larger) depreciation was preferred by the Reagan administration and Congress because depreciation is directly linked to investment. To get a larger tax deduction, a firm must have plant and equipment to depreciate. Hence faster depreciation encourages firms to build new factories and expand or modernize old ones. A reduction in corporate tax rates also encourages investment but is less focused.

The 1981 tax bill severed whatever links existed between depreciation and the actual "wearing out" of capital. Instead of trying to figure out how fast their assets are being "used up" in production, corporations may now depreciate their capital assets according to fixed schedules. According to this new Accelerated Cost Recovery (ACR) system, equipment and machinery may be "written off" in five years. This means that corporations can deduct one-fifth of the cost of machinery and equipment from their annual revenues in any year. Previously the deduction varied from one-fifth to as little as one-fifteenth. Similarly, all buildings can now be depreciated in 15 years, rather than the previous range of 20 to 40 years. These faster depreciation (cost recovery) schedules will reduce the tax bill of U.S. businesses by billions of dollars each year. These tax savings, it is hoped, will encourage still more investment in machinery, equipment, and buildings.

Larger investment tax credits

A third incentive for increased investment was provided by larger investment tax credits. A tax credit directly reduces a firm's tax bill. First a firm calculates its taxable income, based on actual revenues, expenses, and depreciation. Then it applies the corporate tax rate to this taxable income. The result is the firm's tax liability. It need not pay this amount, however. Uncle Sam allows "credits" for various activities, including new investment. The Economic Recovery Tax Act of 1981 permits a tax credit equal to 10 percent of the cost of new investment. Hence a firm that buys $10,000 of new machinery gets a tax credit of $1,000. That credit reduces its tax bill.

Research and development tax credits

Faster depreciation and larger investment tax credits both reduce the dollar cost of plant and equipment. In this sense, they lower the fixed costs of production. They have no direct effect on marginal costs or revenues, however, and so no impact on short-run production decisions. They are designed to increase investment, that is, long-run supply.

Tax credits for research and development expenses are another story. They reduce the dollar cost of using variable inputs. A firm that increases its spending on research and development gets a tax credit equal to 25 percent of that added spending. Suppose a firm hires one new engineer at a salary of $24,000 per year. The firm will get a tax credit of $6,000 (0.25 × $24,000). Hence the *marginal* cost of employing labor is effectively reduced. These reduced marginal costs should encourage the firm to make a new short-run production decision, at a higher rate of output.

The combined incentives

Altogether, these various tax reductions imply a tremendous incentive for increased investment and production. The impact of these tax reductions on a small firm are illustrated in Table 6.6. The figures in the table depict a firm with total revenues of $500,000 per year and operating costs of $350,000. Before the tax cuts, this firm was able to deduct $80,000 in annual depreciation, leaving it with $70,000 in taxable profits. At the old tax rates and without tax credits, the firm paid $14,350 in taxes.

The second column of Table 6.6 shows how the 1981 tax legislation reduced this firm's taxes. Revenues and operating costs are unchanged. But the firm can now deduct $100,000 for depreciation. Its taxable income therefore falls from $70,000 to $50,000. Lower tax rates further reduce its tax liability, to $8,250. It need not pay Uncle Sam this much, however. It gets an investment tax credit of $1,000 for buying $10,000 worth of new machinery. It gets another $6,000 credit for hiring a new engineer. As a result, it pays only $1,250 in taxes, rather than $14,750. This tax reduction directly increases after-tax profits and encourages more production and investment. For the U.S. business community as a whole, the 1981 tax cuts will increase after-tax profits by roughly $160 *billion* during the period 1981–86. Whether these incentives will be sufficient to increase the overall rate of U.S. investment will depend on the condition of the larger economy.[10]

[10] The relationships of aggregate (total) investment to economic activity (GNP) are discussed in Chapters 7–15 of *The Macro Economy Today*.

TABLE 6.6 THE IMPACT OF THE "SUPPLY-SIDE" TAX CUTS ON A FIRM'S TAX BILL

The Economic Recovery Tax Act of 1981 tax cuts reduced business taxes in several ways. Firms are allowed faster depreciation (line 4), pay lower tax rates (line 6), and can get tax credits for new investment (line 7) and expanded research and development (line 8). The "bottom line" is lower taxes. The firm gets to keep more of its net revenues. See text for explanations.

Item	*Before tax reductions*	*After tax reductions*
1. Total revenue	$500,000	$500,000
2. Operating expenses (paid costs)	350,000	350,000
3. Revenue less expense	$150,000	$150,000
4. Depreciation	(80,000)	(100,000)
5. Taxable profit	$ 70,000	$ 50,000
6. Corporate tax	14,750	8,250
7. Investment tax credit	—	1,000
8. R&D credit	—	6,000
9. Taxes due	$14,750	$1,250

SUMMARY

- The public, the business community, and economists all have different ideas about the nature and level of profits. *Economic* profit is the difference between total revenue and total cost. Total economic cost includes the value of *all* inputs used in the production, not just those paid an explicit payment.
- In seeking economic profits (above-average returns), firms make both short-run and long-run decisions. The short-run producton decision concerns the rate of output to produce from existing (fixed) facilities. The long-run investment decision concerns the choice of whether to acquire or expand production facilities.
- Because profits are the difference between total revenues and total costs, a profit-maximizing firm must consider how revenues and costs change as levels of production change. On the cost side, we distinguish three kinds of cost: *fixed, variable,* and *marginal.*
- Only marginal costs (the cost of producing one additional unit of output) influence the short-run production decision. The profit-maximizing producer compares marginal cost to marginal revenue. As long as marginal revenues exceed marginal costs, profits are growing and the producer has an incentive to increase output.
- Output expansion is limited by the tendency of marginal costs to rise and of marginal revenues to remain constant or decline as output increases. Marginal costs will typically catch up to marginal revenues at some point, thereby bringing to a halt profitable output expansion. At the point at which marginal revenue equals marginal cost, total profits are at a maximum.
- A firm will continue to produce in the short run so long as total revenue exceeds variable costs. The firm will shut down when price falls below average variable cost.
- The determinants of supply include all forces that affect costs or revenue. These forces include the price of the product, the price of inputs, technology, and expectations. In the long run all these forces may change significantly.
- Taxes affect the amount of profit a producer can keep. Business tax cuts increase after-tax profits and encourage additional investment and production.

Terms to remember

Define the following terms:

supply
profit
economic cost
economic profit
law of demand
total revenue
price elasticity of demand
marginal cost
total cost
short run
production decision
long run
investment decision
competitive firm
marginal revenue
law of diminishing returns
profit-maximization rule
variable costs
shutdown point
ceteris paribus
quantity supplied
supply curve
depreciation (tax)

Questions for discussion

1. Besides profits, do firms have any other incentive to produce the goods and services we demand?

2. What economic costs is a large corporation likely to overlook when computing its "profits"? How about the owner of a family-run business or farm?

3. If a firm is incurring an economic loss, would society be better off if the firm shut down? Would the firm want to shut down? Explain.

4. Why wouldn't a profit-maximizing firm want to produce at the rate of output that minimizes average total cost? Illustrate your answer with graphs.

5. If new technology or management techniques succeeded in lowering fixed costs but not marginal costs, would production decisions be affected? How about innovations that reduced marginal costs but not fixed costs?

Problem

A firm has leased plant and equipment to produce video-game cartridges, which can be sold in unlimited quantities at $21 each. The figures below describe the associated costs of production:

Rate of output (per day)	**0**	**1**	**2**	**3**	**4**	**5**	**6**	**7**	**8**
Total cost	**$50**	**$55**	**$62**	**$75**	**$96**	**$125**	**$162**	**$203**	**$248**

Using these figures:

(a) Draw total revenue and total cost curves on the same graph. How much are fixed costs?

(b) On a separate graph, draw the average total cost (*ATC*), marginal cost (*MC*), and marginal revenue (*MR*) curves.

(c) What is the profit-maximizing rate of output?

(d) Should the producer stay in business? Why or why not?

CHAPTER 7

COMPETITIVE MARKETS

Millions of individuals and firms participate in product markets daily, buying and selling specific goods and services. Individual consumers enter product markets to purchase goods and services they desire, seeking to get as much utility as they can for the lowest price possible. Producers participate in product markets with the thought of maximizing profits, and so they welcome the chance to sell as many goods as possible for the highest possible price. In view of these disparate interests, what kind of outcome is likely? In particular, how will prices be determined, and how much output will be produced and sold? Are consumer interests likely to prevail in the market, or will all price and production decisions be made by producers?

To answer these kinds of questions, we have to abstract from individual behavior and think in terms of *markets*. As we first observed in Chapter 2, individual consumer demands can be combined to formulate *market* demands for particular goods and services. In the same way, individual firm decisions can be combined to construct *market* supply possibilities. The interaction of these market forces yields the array of goods and services we confront daily and the prices attached to them.

Although the mechanics of supply and demand are fairly simple, we cannot conclude that all markets function alike. Quite the contrary. As we shall discover in this and the following chapters, market outcomes are significantly influenced by the number, the size, and the power of producers. In this chapter we shall observe how markets work when all producers are relatively small and without market power. Chapters 8 and 9 will focus on markets dominated by a small number of powerful firms.

MARKET POWER: A FIRST LOOK

market power: The ability to alter the market price of a good or service.

When asked to identify "powerful" firms, most people respond in terms of corporate size. And it is true that most of the really large corporations—General Motors, IBM, AT&T, and the like—do have market power. But small firms can have power, too, at least according to the concept of market power we are going to use. From an economist's viewpoint, ***market power is gauged by a firm's ability to control the market price of the goods it sells.*** If a firm can alter the market price of its goods, it is said to have **market power.**

Firms without market power

This definition of market power may appear to render all firms powerful, but it doesn't. The important concept here is *market* price, that is, the price at which goods are actually sold. Remember our experience trying to sell ice cream cones at $4 apiece (Chapter 6)? In that episode, we were able to raise the *asking* price for our ice cream. But we didn't *sell* any, because the market price—the price at which other firms' cones were being sold—was much lower. In other words, we had no market power—we could not raise the market price of ice cream cones. To sell our cones, we would have had to lower our prices to the level at which other ice cream vendors were selling them.

The same kind of powerlessness is characteristic of the small wheat farmer. Like any producer, the lone wheat farmer can increase or reduce his rate of output by making alternative production decisions. But his decision will not affect the market price of wheat.

market supply: The total quantities of a good that sellers are willing and able to sell at alternative prices in a given time period (*ceteris paribus*); the combined willingness of all market suppliers to sell.

Even a large farmer who can alter his harvest by as much as 10,000 bushels of wheat per year will not influence the market price of wheat. Why not? Because nearly *2 billion* bushels of wheat are brought to market every year, and another 10,000 bushels simply isn't going to be noticed. In other words, *the output of the lone farmer is so small relative to the* **market supply** *that it has no significant effect on the total quantity or price in the market.*

competitive firm: A firm without market power, with no ability to alter the market price of the goods it produces.

A distinguishing characteristic of *powerless* firms is that, individually, they can sell as much output as they can produce at the prevailing market price. We call all such producers **competitive firms;** they have no independent influence on market prices. In effect, ***a competitive (powerless) producer confronts a horizontal (perfectly elastic) demand curve for his own output,*** as in the case of our doorknob maker (Chapter 6).[1] When an entire market is com-

[1] Notice that a distinction is made between the market demand curve and the demand curve facing a particular firm. Even though the market demand curve for wheat is negatively sloped, the part of market demand satisfied by one farmer is so small that he effectively faces a horizontal demand curve. One can visualize this latter demand as residing in the *width* of the market demand curve. We shall return to this distinction.

perfectly competitive market: A market in which no buyer or seller has market power.

posed of competitive firms (and powerless consumers as well), we call it a **perfectly competitive market.**[2]

Firms with market power

monopoly: A firm that produces the entire market supply of a particular good or service.

A perfectly competitive market can be contrasted with another extreme case, that of monopoly. A **monopoly** exists when one firm is the sole supplier of a particular product. Because such a firm represents the entire supply side of the market, its output decisions are obviously significant for market supply and price; it has market power. Should a monopoly wish to raise the market price of its product, it can simply withhold the product. We might have been successful in our ice cream venture, for example, if we had managed to eliminate all other sellers from the market. As a monopolist, we could have forced people to pay $4 per cone or do without ice cream.

A monopolist's pricing decision is not directly constrained by the behavior of other firms. A monopolist's price decision is limited only by the shape and position of the market demand curve. A monopolist confronts a downward-sloping demand curve and must worry about the impact of its production (output) decision on the market price of its goods.

Degrees of market power

There is, of course, a whole range of market structures between the extremes of perfect competition and monopoly. There are *degrees* of market power. General Motors, for example, does have the power to change the market price of automobiles but is not a monopolist. The amount of power a particular firm has depends on its size, the number of other producers, the number of *potential* producers, the price and availability of similar (substitute) goods, and a number of other factors that we shall discuss in Chapter 10. For the time being, however, we shall focus on the extremes of perfect competition and monopoly, hoping thereby to discover the impact of market power on the behavior of the economy.

THE NATURE OF COMPETITION

Before we look at the behavior of a highly competitive market—the electronic calculator market—it will be useful to preview the primary characteristics of competitive behavior. As we have noted, ***a firm without market power is one whose output is so small in relation to market volume that its output decisions have no perceptible impact on price.*** The complete and sudden demise of such a firm would not be noticed in the market. By contrast, the demise of a large and powerful firm would visibly reduce market supplies and disrupt the previous market equilibrium. One can visualize the difference between these two situations by considering what would happen to U.S. egg supplies and prices if Farmer Kitt's 37 hens were to die, and what would happen to U.S. auto supplies and prices if the Ford Motor Company were to close down suddenly. The one

[2] The potential for power on the demand side of markets is discussed in Chapter 13.

event would go unnoticed; the impact of the other would be dramatic.

The same kind of contrast is evident when an expansion of output is contemplated. Were Farmer Kitt to double his production capacity (breed another 37 hens), the added output would not even show up in commerce statistics, because U.S. egg production is calibrated in the billions. Were Ford, on the other hand, to double its production, the added output not only would be noted, but would tend to depress automobile prices as Ford tried to unload heavy inventories.

The critical distinction between Ford and Farmer Kitt is not in their motivation but in their ability to alter market outcomes. Both are out to make a buck and thus seek to produce the rate of output that maximizes profit. What makes Farmer Kitt's situation different is the fact that his output decisions do not influence egg prices. In this sense, he has one less problem to worry about. Like the doorknob producer of Chapter 6, Farmer Kitt confronts a horizontal demand curve, the level of which is determined by much larger market forces. However much he stimulates his hens to produce, he will have no influence on the price of eggs. In seeking to maximize his profits, Farmer Kitt strives to run an efficient operation, producing up to the point where his marginal cost of production equals the going market price for eggs. In this sense, he is a *price taker,* taking the market price of eggs as a fact of life and doing the best he can within that constraint. Were he to attempt to enlarge his profits by raising his egg prices above market levels, he would find himself without customers, because the consumers would go elsewhere to buy their eggs.

Ford Motor Company, on the other hand, can behave like a *price setter.* Instead of waiting to find out what the market price is and making appropriate output adjustments, Ford has the discretion to "announce" prices at the beginning of every model year. Ford knows that sales will not fall to zero if its car prices are set a little higher than those of other car manufacturers. This, of course, is a consequence of the fact that Ford confronts a downward-sloping rather than a perfectly horizontal demand curve. Accordingly, Ford has some identifiable impact on market prices and seeks to maximize profits by finding the price and output *combination* that equates marginal revenue and marginal cost.

Market demand curves vs. firm demand curves

It is important to distinguish between the market demand curve and the demand curve confronting a particular firm. Farmer Kitt's little operation does not contradict the law of demand. The quantity of eggs purchased in the supermarket still depends on egg prices. That is to say, the *market* demand curve for eggs is still downward-sloping, just as the market demand curve for cars is negatively inclined. Farmer Kitt himself faces a horizontal demand curve only because his share of the market is so infinitesimal that changes in his output do not disturb the market equilibrium.

Were 10,000 competitive farmers to expand their egg production at the same time as Farmer Kitt, the market equilibrium would

FIGURE 7.1 THE COMPETITIVE EGG MARKET

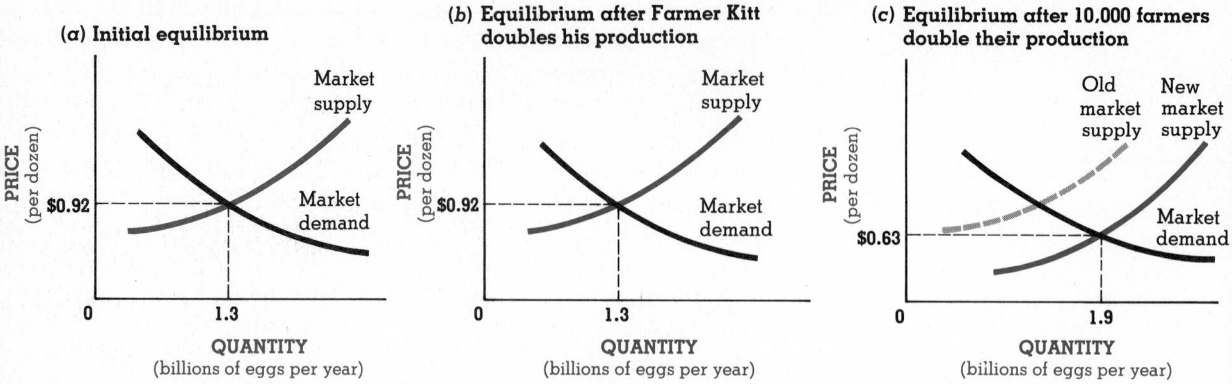

(a) The market price of eggs is determined by the collective behavior of all farmers and consumers. The market demand curve slopes downward; the market supply curve slopes upward. The intersection of these two curves establishes the market equilibrium.

(b) One farmer's decision to double egg output has no significant impact on the market supply or price of eggs. In effect, a single farmer can sell as many eggs as he wishes to at the equilibrium price.

(c) When many competitive egg farmers simultaneously attempt to increase their sales at existing prices, their collective action *shifts* the market supply curve to the right and lowers the equilibrium price.

be disturbed, of course. That is to say, a market composed of 10,000 individually powerless producers still sees a lot of action. The power here resides in the collective action of all the producers, however, and not in the individual action of any one. Were egg production to increase so markedly, the eggs could be sold only at lower prices, in accordance with the downward-sloping nature of the *market* demand curve. The distinction between the actions of a single producer and those of the market are illustrated in Figure 7.1.[3]

The tendency toward zero profits

Whether or not 10,000 farmers will actually double their egg production depends on the profit outlook they perceive. If the price and cost relationship is favorable enough, egg production can be quite profitable. When it is, individual farmers will seek to expand production, and will continue to do so until rising marginal costs catch up with the high price of eggs. If the profit outlook is alluring enough, even city folk will be tempted to get into egg production. This surge of egg production will disturb the market equilibrium, however. As farmers add to market supplies, their collective efforts will begin to depress egg prices. As egg prices slide down the market demand curve (Figure 7.1*c*), the profitability of egg production will begin to decline somewhere along the line. At some point, further expansion of egg production will cease. Farmers and city folk alike will decide that **economic profit** has disappeared. At that point other pursuits may begin to look more attractive. When that happens, egg

economic profit: The difference between total revenues and total economic costs.

[3] Chapter 2 demonstrates how a market's supply curve is derived from the supply curves of individual firms.

New Video-Game Makers Jump into Fight for a Share of the Booming Home Market

The market for home video games is starting to resemble a Space Invaders combat zone.

More than half-a-dozen companies plan to introduce video-game products in 1982, and sales are expected to more than double from last year to $3 billion. Players haven't deserted the arcades. Parents across the country are still battling to outlaw video-game parlors in their towns, and their kids—and others—are still feeding millions of quarters into arcade machines. But the home market is where the rapid growth is expected. . . .

Eighty million households in the U.S. have televisions, but only 8.5% have bought video games. By 1985, some industry analysts predict, 50% of the households with TVs will have video games. And the overseas market has just opened, with a million consoles sold so far in Europe.

Atari's Big Share

Despite the expanding market, the newcomers won't have an easy job. According to industry estimates, Atari controls 75% of the market. Mattel and the Odyssey game marketed by North American Philips Corp.'s Magnavox division dominate the other 25%. All three companies plan new products of their own for 1982. And Atari is expected to double its ad budget to $75 million.

But the newcomers say the risk is worthwhile. One successful cartridge, like Atari's Space Invaders, can generate $100 million to $150 million in sales, with margins of about 20%. And when Atari sells a lot of consoles, the cartridge makers benefit because their market expands.

—Laura Landro

prices will tend to stabilize at a new equilibrium, at least until significant changes occur in technology or market demand.

Egg producers would be happier, or course, if the price of eggs did not decline to the point where profits began to disappear. But how are they going to prevent it? Farmer Kitt knows all about the law of demand and would like to get other farmers to slow production a little before all the profits disappear. But he himself cannot afford to initiate or join such an effort. Were he to reduce his own egg production, nobody would notice the difference in market supplies, and egg prices would continue to slide. The only one affected would be Farmer Kitt, who would be denying himself the opportunity to share in the good fortunes of the egg market while they lasted. As long as others are willing and able to expand production, Farmer Kitt must do likewise or deny himself even a small share of the available profits. Others will be willing to expand egg production so long as eggs breed economic profits—that is, so long as the rate of return in egg production is superior to that available elsewhere. They will be able to do so as long as it is easy to get into egg production.

Farmer Kitt's dilemma goes a long way toward explaining why egg production is not terribly profitable. Every time the profit picture looks good, somebody tries to get in on the action, a phenomenon that keeps egg prices down close to the costs of production. This kind of pressure on prices and profits is a fundamental characteristic of competitive markets. As long as it is easy for existing producers to expand production or for new firms to enter an industry, high profits will attract profit maximizers. Output will expand, market prices will fall, and rates of profit will diminish. Thus the rate of profits in egg production is kept down by the fact that anyone with a good rooster, a couple of hens, and a vacant lot can get into the business fairly easily. People will be tempted to enter the egg business whenever profits are attractive.

We can formulate a few general observations, then, about the structure, behavior, and outcomes of a competitive market:

After Lucrative Run, Atlantic City's Casinos Brace for Profit-Dampening Competition

The long-lived Atlantic City casino boom hasn't gone bust, but the easy-come, easy-go days are fading with the autumn weather.

"The days of just opening your doors and the crowds stampeding in are over," says Stephen Hyde, executive vice president of the Boardwalk Regency, the second casino to open in Atlantic City.

Although the recession spared the casino business, competition and higher costs may not. The opening of a fourth casino in August and the scheduled openings of three more by early 1981 will have created competition that could cut into each casino's revenue. At the same time labor costs are rising as the larger number of casinos compete for pit bosses, croupiers, and other employes. New Jersey's cumbersome regulatory bureaucracy, is also slicing the houses' edge.

September Win Is Off

That's not to say that the house is going broke. With a market of 37 million adults in their territory, the casinos managed to win $193.3 million more than they lost to players in June, July and August. But analysts say the three established casinos won an average of only $17 million each in September, down from $23 million to $25 million each in August. In September 1979, the two then-established outfits, Resorts International and Caesars World Inc.'s Boardwalk Regency, reported gross winnings of $19.6 million and $16.7 million.

If the official September gross win figures to be released today or tomorrow decline as expected, analysts will blame seasonal factors and the effect of an extra weekend in August. Even so, Marvin Roffman, an analyst at Janney Montgomery Scott Inc., calls the September win "horrendous," and he says it spells trouble for casino profits. "There is definitely an erosion of profit margins, and it will continue as more casinos come on stream," he says.

—Ronald Alsop

- A competitive market will include a great many firms, none of which has a significant share of total output.
- All competitive firms will seek to expand output until marginal costs are equal to price, inasmuch as price and marginal revenue are identical for such firms.
- If significant economic profit is available, increasing numbers of producers will enter the industry and participate in the high profit.
- The tendency of production and market supplies to expand when profit is high puts heavy pressure on prices and profits in competitive industries. Economic profit will approach zero as prices are driven down to the level of average production costs.

No barriers to entry

barriers to entry: Obstacles that make it difficult or impossible for would-be producers to enter a particular market; for example, patents.

New producers will be able to enter a profitable industry and help drive down prices and profits as long as there are no significant **barriers to entry.** Such barriers may include patents, control of essential factors of production, long-established consumer acceptance, and various forms of price control. All such barriers make it expensive, risky, or impossible for new firms to enter into production. In the absence of such barriers, new firms can enter an industry more readily and at less risk. Not surprisingly, firms already entrenched in a profitable industry do their best to keep newcomers out, by erecting barriers to entry.

COMPETITION AT WORK: THE POCKET-CALCULATOR MARKET

Although few factor or product markets are completely devoid of market power, many function much like the competitive model we have sketched out. In addition to egg production, most other agricultural product markets are characterized by highly competitive supply conditions, with hundreds of thousands of producers supplying the market.[4] Other highly competitive, and hence not very profitable, businesses are retail food stores, printing, clothing manufacturing and retailing, dry-cleaning establishments, and furniture. Other markets exhibit competitive structures as well, and even more behave as the competitive model suggests. In these markets, prices and profits are always under the threat of expanded supplies brought to market by existing or new producers. Insight into the workings of a particularly interesting competitive market may be gleaned from a look at the electronic calculator market, especially the market for the small pocket calculators.[5]

Electronic calculators consist of a very few components. Their driving force is a set of electronic circuits that are designed to handle specific addition, subtraction, division, and multiplication problems; these circuits are the calculator's "brain." The circuits themselves—referred to as MOS/LSI (or metal oxide semiconductor/large-scale integrated) circuits—take the place of thousands of transistors and are etched onto tiny chips of silicon only one-quarter-inch square and 8/1,000ths-inch thick. The MOS/LSI chips were developed in the course of missile guidance system research and are in common use as the "brains" for Touch-Tone telephones, home computers, video games, and other electronic products.

To signal the electronic brain of a calculator to go to work, all one has to do is press the appropriate keys on the keyboard. Once the problem is entered through the keyboard, the electric impulses go through their programmed motions and flash an answer on the viewing screen. The whole operation is driven by electricity, usually supplied by a rechargeable battery, and takes but a fraction of a second. The only components required other than the chips, keyboard, viewing screen, and battery are a baseboard to hold the pieces together and an exterior shell.

Given the small number and basic simplicity of calculator parts, it is fairly easy to get into the calculator industry. Indeed, quite a few of today's firms got started in their owners' garages. Thus we may characterize the industry as having *minimal barriers to entry*, because anyone with a little capital, a place to work, and a very modest knowledge of electronic circuitry can set up shop.

The initial conditions

The electronic calculator industry really got started in March 1969, when a Japanese electronics corporation, Sharp, introduced the Sharp "Micro-Compet QT-8D," the first commercial calculator to use advanced electronic circuitry. The retail price of the Micro-

[4] In some of these markets, the independent producers may try to exercise market power by forming some form of producer association that can influence market supplies (e.g., the dairy associations); more on this subject in Chapter 10.

[5] The following description of the U.S. calculator market is based on articles in *Barron's*, *Electronic News*, *Business Week*, *Consumer Reports*, and *Popular Science*, on confidential industry reports prepared by investment advisory services, and on annual reports of calculator companies; all figures are approximations. The calculator market was not perfectly competitive in the 1970s, but it did exhibit all of the tendencies described here.

Compet was $395. Within a very brief time, other companies—primarily Japanese firms, such as Ricoh, Canon, and Casio—introduced similar machines, and the price of calculators fell while the size of the market expanded. By the beginning of 1972, the standard pocket calculator was selling for $200 and industry sales were around 17,000 a month (or 200,000 a year).

equilibrium price: The price at which the quantity of a good demanded in a given time period equals the quantity supplied.

Figure 7.2 depicts the initial (1972) equilibrium in the calculator market and the approximate costs of production for the typical calculator manufacturer at that time. Note that the market *demand* curve (Figure 7.2*a*) slopes downward just as the law of demand requires. Note also that the market *supply* curve intersects the demand curve at a price of $200, which thereby becomes the market **equilibrium price.** That same intersection tells us that 17,000 calculators a month will be bought and sold at that price.

Individual producers never see these market curves, of course. All they see are their own cost curves and the price at which calculators are selling. That price ($200) has been determined by market forces.

FIGURE 7.2 INITIAL EQUILIBRIUM IN THE CALCULATOR MARKET

In 1972, the market price of calculators was $200. This price was established by the intersection of the market supply and demand curves as shown in part *a*. Each competitive producer in the market sought to produce calculators at that rate (800 per month) where marginal cost equaled price (point C in part *b*). Profit per calculator was equal to price (point C) minus average total cost (point *D*). Total profits for the typical firm are indicated by the shaded rectangle.

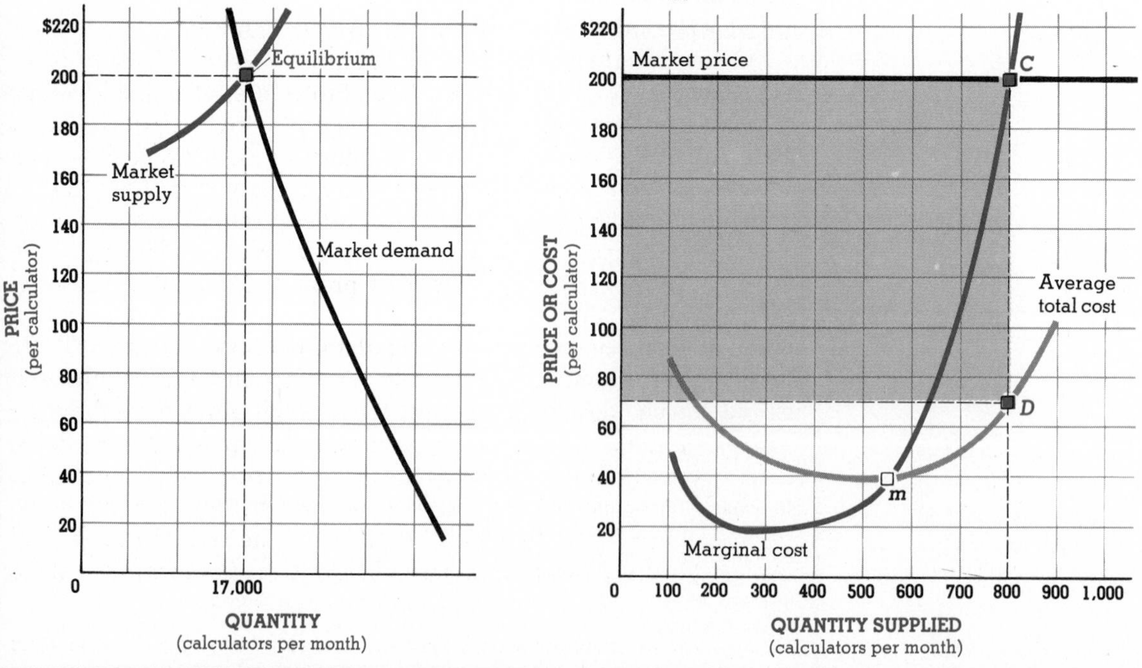

The production decision

production decision: The selection of the short-run rate of output (with existing plant and equipment).

What the individual firm must do in the short run is choose the rate of output that maximizes profits. In the long run, a producer can decide to enter or leave the calculator industry, or alter the firm's scale of operation. In this analysis, however, we shall assume that affirmative investment decisions have been made, and we shall focus on the **production decision.** In this short-run context, each firm seeks the rate of output at which marginal cost equals marginal revenue. For the competitive firm, this means finding the point at which marginal cost equals price.

Figure 7.2*b* illustrates the cost and price (marginal revenue) curves the typical calculator producer confronted in 1972. As in most lines of production, the marginal costs of calculator production tend to rise with the rate of output, as reflected in the rising *MC* curve. Marginal costs rose in part because output could be increased in the short run (with existing plant and equipment) only by crowding additional workers onto the assembly line. As each worker got less capital and land to work with, marginal physical product fell. The law of diminishing returns thus pushed marginal costs up. Moreover, additional labor could be obtained only by paying overtime wages, and even the price of integrated circuits and other materials tended to rise as increased quantities were ordered.

marginal cost: The increase in total cost associated with a one-unit increase in production.

For all of these reasons, marginal costs rose quite sharply, intersecting the price line at an output level of 800 calculators per month (point C in Figure 7.2*b*).[6] That rate of output was the most profitable ($MC = p$), of course, and was chosen by the typical manufacturer. Were the producer to manufacture any more calculators, the excess of **marginal costs** over price beyond the output level of 800 per month would reduce earlier profits. To manufacture less would be to pass up an opportunity to make another buck.

Profit calculations

To figure out how much *profit* a typical calculator manufacturer was making at the output rate of 800 per month, we need to look at something besides marginal cost and price. Profits are, of course, the difference between total revenues and total costs (including the cost of the owner's time and an "average" return on investment). We can calculate those profits quickly (even more quickly if we use a pocket calculator!) by looking at Table 7.1. As the profit column indicates, the calculating calculator manufacturer makes a real killing in the calculator market, reaping a monthly profit of $104,680 by producing and selling 800 calculators.

average total cost: Total cost divided by the quantity produced in a given time period.

We could also calculate the calculator manufacturer's profits by asking how much he makes on *each* calculator and multiplying that figure by his total output. Clearly, the average profit per calculator times the number of calculators sold must be equal to total profits. We can compute these profits by studying the first and last columns of Table 7.1 or by using a little geometry on Figure 7.2*b*. In the figure, average costs (total costs divided by the rate of output) are portrayed by the **average total cost** (*ATC*) curve. At the output rate of

[6] The marginal cost curves depicted here rise more steeply than they did in reality; but the general shape of the curves is our primary concern at this point.

TABLE 7.1 CALCULATOR REVENUES, COSTS, AND PROFITS

The competitive producer seeks to produce at that rate of output where total profit is maximized. This table illustrates the alternatives the typical calculator producer faced in 1972. The profit-maximizing rate of output occurred at 800 calculators per month. At that rate of output, marginal cost was equal to price ($200) and profits were $104,680 per month.

Output per month	*Price*	*Total revenue*	*Total cost*	*Profit*	*Marginal revenue**	*Marginal cost**	*Average cost*	*Profit per unit (price minus average cost)*
0	—	—	$ 2,000	−$ 2,000	—	—	—	—
100	$200	$ 20,000	8,661	11,335	$200	$ 66.65	$86.65	$113.35
200	200	40,000	10,330	29,670	200	16.65	51.65	148.35
300	200	60,000	12,330	47,670	200	20.00	41.10	158.90
400	200	80,000	15,330	64,670	200	30.00	38.33	161.67
500	200	100,000	18,660	81,340	200	33.30	37.32	162.68
600	200	120,000	23,991	96,009	200	53.31	39.99	160.01
700	200	140,000	35,320	104,680	200	113.29	50.46	149.54
800	200	160,000	55,320	104,680	200	200.00	69.15	130.85
900	200	180,000	85,000	95,000	200	296.80	94.44	105.56

*Note that output levels are calibrated in hundreds in this example; therefore, we have divided the *change* in total costs and revenues from one output level to another by 100 to calculate marginal revenue and marginal cost. Very few manufacturers deal in units of one. The additional revenue associated with a multiple-unit increase in sales is often called "incremental revenue" to distinguish it from the *marginal* revenue generated by *one* additional sale; we ignore this distinction here.

profit per unit: Total profit divided by the quantity produced in a given time period; price minus average total cost.

800 (the row in color in Table 7.1), the distance between the price line ($200 at point *C*) and the *ATC* curve ($69.15 at point *D*) is $130.85. This represents the average **profit per unit.** Multiplying this figure by the number of units sold (800 per month) gives us *total* profit per month. Total profits are represented by the shaded rectangle in Figure 7.2*b* and are equal, of course, to our earlier profit figure of $104,680.

While gaping at the calculator manufacturer's enormous profits, we should note two things about the average cost curve. First is its familiar shape. Note that average costs first decline, then bottom out and rise, giving the curve a distinct U shape. The tendency of average costs to fall initially as output is expanded can be attributed to two phenomena: (1) the spreading out of fixed costs over an increasingly large number of calculators,[7] and (2) the tendency for marginal costs to be lower than average costs at low rates of output. At some point, however, marginal costs begin to exceed average costs and exert an upward pull on the *ATC* curve. Thus beyond point *m*, the minimum average cost point, the higher marginal costs begin to raise average costs. There is nothing very tricky about these relationships; they only reflect a little arithmetic.

A more interesting observation about the *ATC* curve depicted in

[7] That is, the tendency for $2,000/x to get smaller as x gets larger. (As Table 7.1 confirms, $2,000 is the *fixed cost* of calculator production, as that much expense is incurred even when output is zero. In this case, fixed costs are the costs of rent, utilities, and equipment leases.

Figure 7.2*b* is the fact that the calculator's maximum profits are not attained at the point where average costs are at a minimum (point *m*). On the contrary, the most profitable rate of output is considerably to the right of point *m*. In general, we may observe that ***a profit-maximizing producer seeks to maximize total profits, and this is not necessarily or even very frequently the same thing as maximizing profits per unit.*** As we observed long ago, it's better to make a nickel on each of 300 ice cream cones than to make 50 cents a cone and sell only four.

The lure of profits

We could discuss the calculator manufacturer's profits at length, but we should not lose sight of the fundamental fact that they are enormous. Indeed, the more quick-witted among us will already have seen and heard enough to know they've discovered a good thing. And in fact, the kind of profits attained by the early calculator manufacturers attracted a lot of entrepreneurial interest. Within a very short time, a whole crowd of profit maximizers entered the calculator industry in hot pursuit of its fabulous profits. As we observed earlier, there were no significant barriers to entry into that industry and thus no mechanism for preventing others from elbowing in to share the spoils.

A SHIFT OF MARKET SUPPLY Figure 7.3 shows what happened to the calculator market and the profits of the typical firm once the word got out. As more and more entrepreneurs heard how profitable calculator manufacturing could be, they grabbed a book on electronic circuitry, rushed to the bank, got a little financing, and set up shop. Before many months had passed, the supply of pocket calculators was much larger, as reflected in a **shift of** the **supply** curve from S_1 to S_2 (Figure 7.3*a*). Almost as fast as a calculator can compute a profit (loss) statement, the willingness to supply increased abruptly.

shift of supply: A change in the quantity supplied at any (every) given price.

The new calculator enthusiasts were in for a bit of disappointment, however, as Figure 7.3*b* suggests. With so many new firms hawking calculators, it became increasingly difficult to make a fast buck. The downward-sloping market demand curve confirms that a greater quantity of calculators could be sold only if the price of calculators dropped. And drop it did. The price slide began as calculator manufacturers found their inventories growing and so offered price discounts to maintain sales volume. The price fell rapidly in 1972 from $200 to $113.

The lower market price changed the profit picture and production decisions for the typical firm. The sliding market price squeezed the profits of each firm, causing the profit rectangle to shrink (compare Figure 7.2*b* to Figure 7.3*b*). Although the typical firm's cost structure hadn't changed, its sales opportunities had been drastically reduced. It now found that marginal cost was equal to marginal revenue (the new price) at an output of 700 calculators per month. As Table 7.1 confirms, the typical firm could produce 700 calculators a month at a marginal cost of $113.29 and an average cost of $50.46. Unfortunately, the prices, revenues, and profits depicted in Table 7.1 no longer applied at the end of 1972, owing to the

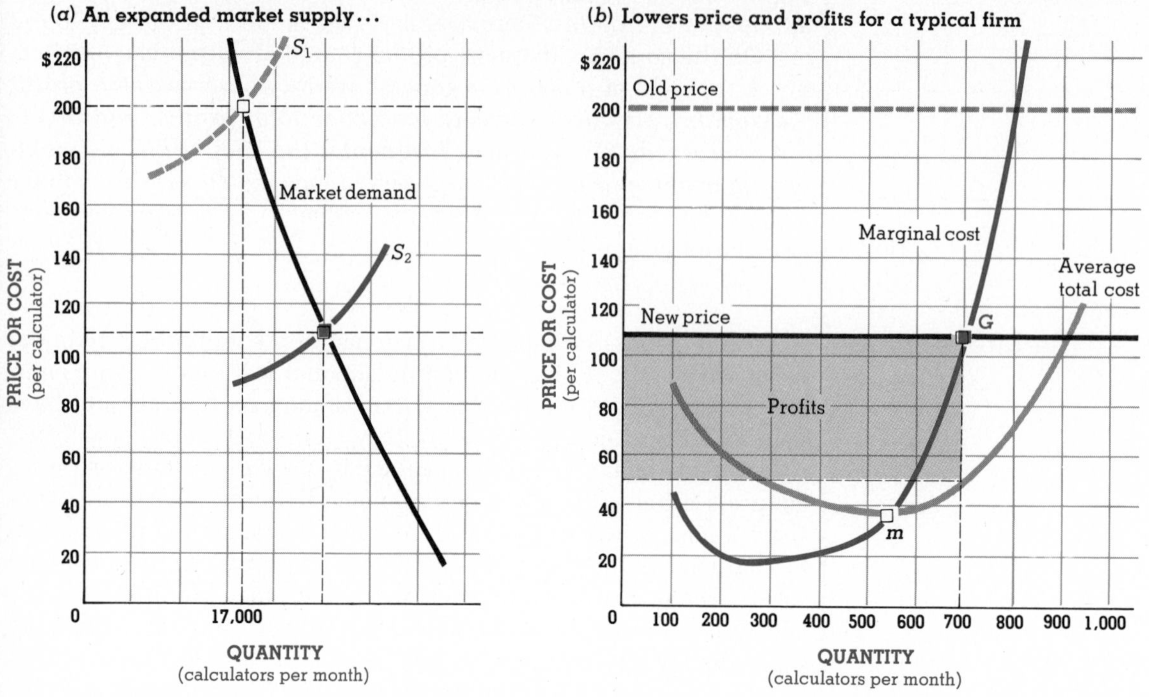

FIGURE 7.3 THE COMPETITIVE PRICE AND PROFIT SQUEEZE UNDER WAY

The availability of substantial economic profits in the calculator industry encouraged new firms to enter the industry. As they did so, the market supply curve in part *a* shifted from S_1 to S_2. This rightward shift of the supply curve lowered the equilibrium price of calculators. The lower price, in turn, forced the typical producer to cut back the rate of output to the point where *MC* and price were equal again (point *G* in part *b*). At this reduced rate of output, the typical firm earned less total profit than it had earned before.

changed market situation. At that time, the typical firm could earn only $43,778 a month (700 × [price of $113 − average total cost of $50.46]); not a paltry sum, to be sure, but nothing like the fantastic fortunes pocketed earlier.

As long as an economic profit is available it will continue to attract would-be suppliers. Those entrepreneurs who were a little slow to digest the implications of Figure 7.2 eventually perceived what was going on and tried to get in on the action, too. Even though they were a little late, they did not wish to bypass the opportunity to make the $43,778 in monthly profits still available to the typical firm. Hence the market supply curve continued to shift and calculator prices slid further, as in Figure 7.4. This process squeezed the profits of the typical firm still more, further shrinking the profit rectangle.

The competitive pressure on market supplies, prices, and profits will continue as long as the rate of profit obtainable in calculator production is higher than that available in other industries. Profit-maximizing entrepreneurs have a special place in their hearts not for

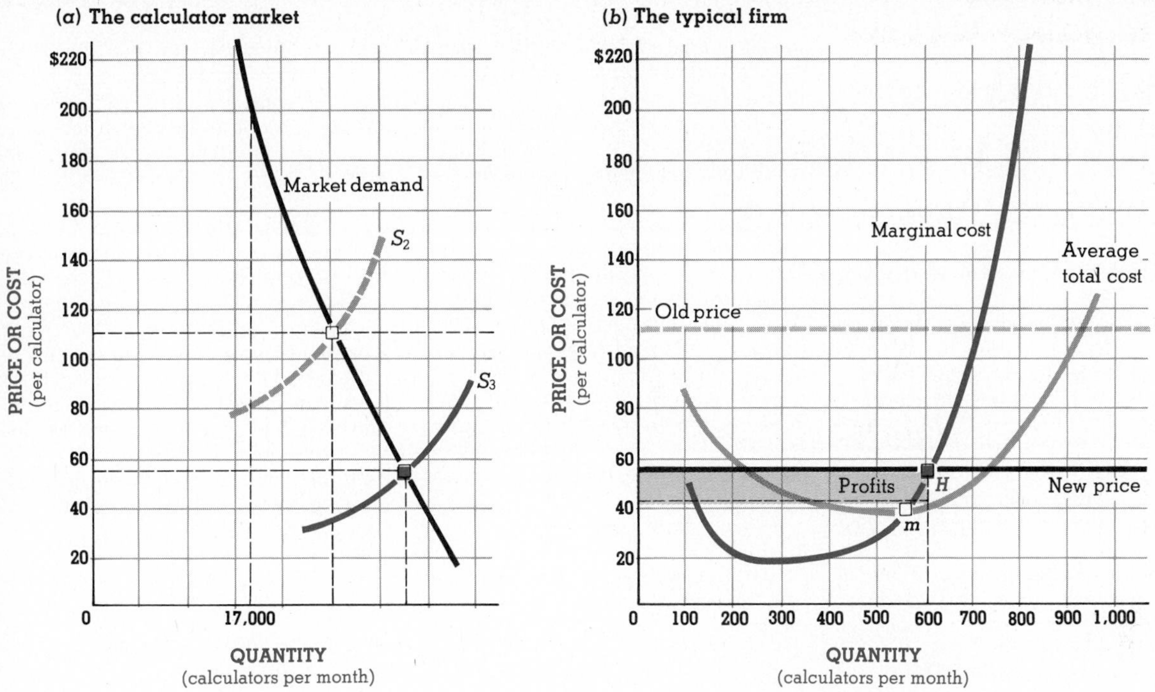

FIGURE 7.4 THE COMPETITIVE SQUEEZE APPROACHING ITS LIMIT

Further shifts of market supply drove down price and profits. Even at a price of $113 per calculator, economic profit was available in the calculator industry. Such profit attracted still more entrepreneurs, shifting the market supply curve further (S_3). The resultant equilibrium occurred at a price of $53 per calculator. At this reduced price, the typical manufacturer wanted to supply only 600 calculators per month (point *H* in part *b*). Total profits were much less than they had been earlier, with fewer producers and higher prices.

calculators but for the economic profit they can produce. When that profit looks no better than the profit obtainable elsewhere, calculator manufacturers may move on to other ventures, and would-be suppliers will lose their fervor. The absolute *limit* to the price and profit decline will occur when the price of calculators is equal to the *minimum* average cost of production (point *m*), at which point there is no longer any economic profit to be squeezed. Further profit (and price competition) will then occur only if market demand shifts outward or technological progress reduces the cost of calculator production. In fact, both of these things happened in the calculator market.

Electric calculators contain very few parts and are easily assembled. Hence, entry into the industry is fairly easy.

Courtesy of Commodore International, Inc.

THE COST BREAKTHROUGH

As profit margins narrowed to the levels shown in Figure 7.4, quick-thinking entrepreneurs realized that future profits would have to come from cost reductions rather than from expanded sales. With

Calculator Makers Add Features and Cut Prices to Find a Niche in a Crowded Market

Casio Inc. sells an electronic pocket calculator that lets its owner conduct boxing matches between calculations. Canon Inc.'s U.S. unit plans to sell a calculator next year for $7.95, its lowest price ever. And today, Hewlett-Packard Co. plans to introduce new products it claims will turn its top calculators into powerful hand-held computers.

These products indicate a few of the ways calculator makers are moving these days to develop niches for their products in a domestic market that is now, or soon will be, saturated. "Everyone owns a calculator," says Bonnie Digruis, an electronics industry analyst for Creative Strategies International, a research concern in San Jose.

At the high-priced end of the market, companies are looking toward—or already producing—products that can compete in the newly formed hand-held computer market, born within the past two years when Tandy Corp., Casio Inc. and others introduced their pocket computers. At the low, or consumer, end, dominated by Japanese producers like Casio, Sharp Corp., and Canon, calculator makers are fighting to produce ever more clever gimmicks and specialties to meet the demands of customers buying replacement calculators. . . .

At the lower end of the calculator market, the big Japanese producers are aiming gimmicks and games at customers who have lost or worn out their old four-function calculators, the so-called replacement market. Casio, for example, is producing and further developing solar calculators that can run by candlelight. It also plans to introduce its MG-777, a calculator with several games including an electronic cube puzzle. "We're probably going to be the Atari of the calculator industry," says Mr. Gordon.

Fit in Shirt Pocket

Canon is trying to get more of the market by driving prices lower still. It was "very successful" at selling one of its calculators for $9.50 in drug stores and other general merchandise outlets, so the company decided to lower the prices once again to $7.95 for its LX-30, says Mitsuru Tamai, vice president, calculator and systems division. It and Casio also are offering low-cost printer calculators that can fit in a shirt pocket. . . .

—Eric Larson and
Brenton R. Schlender

prices continually sliding, the only way to make an extra buck would be to push the cost curve down. A few companies pursued such possibilities and sent costs and calculator prices down to previously unheard-of levels. Indeed, all the way down to $6.95 (which is a long way down from $395 in only a few years' time).

As we noted earlier, an electronic calculator has very few parts, the most important of which are the MOS/LSI chips that function as its brain. The basic determinant of calculator manufacturing costs is the number of chips required to make the calculator work. Fewer chips not only mean a reduction in direct materials costs, but, more important, significantly reduce the amount of labor required for calculator assembly. Indeed, when a lot of chips are required, the labor costs associated with the assembly process dominate cost structures. During the early phases of the calculator boom, it was most economical to buy chips in the United States, send them to Japan for assembly, then reimport them as part of a finished calculator. The method in this madness was the availability of cheap labor in Japan.[8] Thus such firms as Canon, Sharp, Casio, and Commodore were major marketers of pocket calculators in the price range of $80–$160.

What changed the relative position of foreign and domestic manufacturers and brought about another steep decline in calculator prices was the introduction of more sophisticated chips in 1972. Texas Instruments and a few other companies learned how to

[8] Labor is cheaper in Japan than in the United States only if it produces more output per dollar of wages—that is, if it is more cost-*efficient*. Wage comparisons alone convey no information. In the calculator case, the conditions for greater cost efficiency were met. Cost efficiency is discussed in Chapter 12.

miniaturize the chips even further, packaging more functions and circuits in a single chip. This meant that a standard four-function (addition, subtraction, multiplication, and division) calculator could be produced with only one chip, rather than the four or five that had been customary up to that time. This technological breakthrough had dramatic effects on production costs. As the cost of materials for the calculator's "brain" dropped, the amount of labor time required for basic assembly fell from four hours to less than one hour. The size of the calculators shrank, too; some recent models fit into wristwatches.

Further supply shifts

The impact of the miniaturized chips on calculator production costs and profits is illustrated in Figure 7.5, which takes over where Figure 7.4 left off. Recall that the market price of calculators had been driven down to $53 by the beginning of 1972. At this price, the typical firm maximized profits by producing 600 calculators per month, as determined by the intersection of the prevailing *MR* and *MC* curves (point *H* in Figure 7.5).

Technological improvements are illustrated by a downward shift of the ATC and MC curves. Notice, for example, that the new technology permits 600 calculators to be produced for a *lower* marginal cost (about $35) than previously (point *H*).

The lower cost structure increases the profitability of calculator production and stimulates a further increase in production. Note in particular that the *new MC* curve intersects the price ($53) line at an output of 700 calculators per month (point *N*). By contrast, the old, higher *MC* curve dictated a production rate of only 600 calculators per month for the typical firm (point *H*) at that price.

While many Japanese firms saw the desirability of expanding

FIGURE 7.5 A DOWNWARD SHIFT OF COSTS IMPROVES PROFITS AND STIMULATES OUTPUT

The quest for profits encouraged producers to discover cheaper ways to manufacture calculators. The resultant improvements lowered costs and encouraged further increases in the rate of output. The typical calculator producer increased output from point *H* to point *N*.

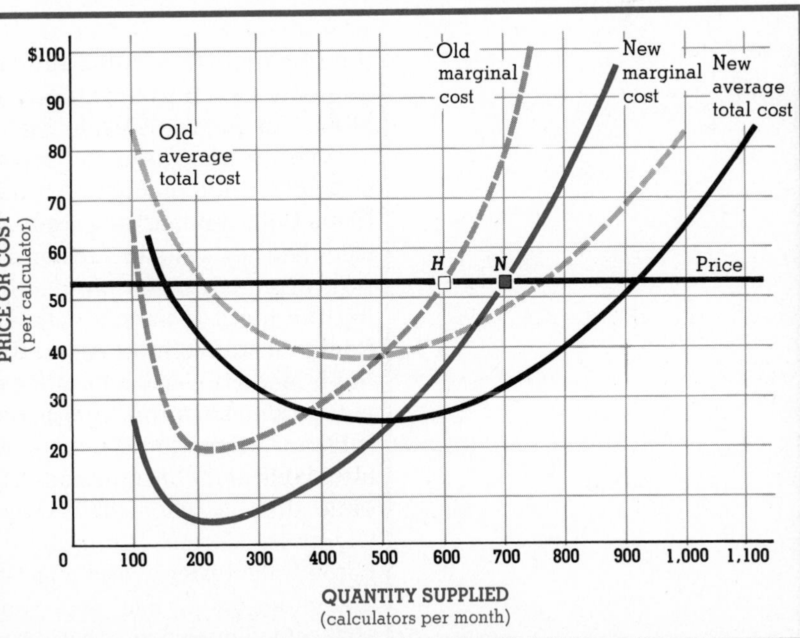

Technology, Competition Cut Price of Electronics Gear as Quality Rises

NEW YORK—Five years ago, a cumbersome Technics tape cassette deck cost about $350. A "needle," now old-fashioned, metered recording levels. The deck required finger pressure to rewind and advance the recording tape. The 50-watt receiver that went with the deck had manual radio control and so-so high fidelity at a cost of $500.

Today, the comparable Technics tape deck is quiet and streamlined with soft-touch controls. A fluorescent light warns of distortions in recording. A dbx device eliminates electronic background "noise." The deck costs just about what it cost five years ago. The receiver costs even less, about $350, although it comes with a new, superaccurate digital tuning mechanism.

Other manufacturers tell the same story: Prices have fallen on just about every product in the world of electronic sound and sight, while quality has increased. "Electronics is the only product group in existence that has undergone reverse inflation," says Richard Ekstract, editor of Consumer Electronics, a monthly trade publication. Says Ray Boggs, head of consumer electronics research at Venture Development Corp.: "If General Motors built cars the way Pioneer builds stereos, you'd have a $200 car and get 1,900 miles to the gallon."

Technological advances have made possible the low-cost production of high-quality electronics gear, but competition has translated those advances into low retail prices. It's fairly easy to get into electronics retailing; manufacturers often help finance newcomers, usually by carrying inventories for retailers who stock only floor samples.

But if the competition makes things nice for shoppers, it's tough on the retailers. Twice as many electronics retailers fold as other retailers, Mr. Boggs says. "Today," he says, "retailers have to compete with the guy who opens on 42nd Street,"—a commercial New York City thoroughfare—"sells for $10 over cost, and then goes bankrupt." Mr. Ekstract says, "There's so much competition to get into the one business where there are a million new products a year that people are willing to sell under the table and steal the sales tax."

Initial High Price Sought

Price-cutting extends to the top of the line in electronics. The manufacturer's "suggested," or retail list, price has become meaningless in most places, even in department stores and at old-line dealerships. . . .

If the product does sell at its initial high prices, the maker recovers some of his research and development costs and can afford to produce in quantity at lower unit costs. Competitors meanwhile also rush to the market. "Whatever we make, once it is on the market, someone can duplicate it at a lower price," Mr. Martin says. "In order to stay ahead, the next time you are able to change models, you have to introduce a more innovative product, or find a way to produce the same thing at a lower price."

The process is expected to occur again next year in the case of digital audio disk players. A number of manufacturers plan to introduce such players, which use a laser to detect audio signals on a palm-size high-fidelity disk, in 1982. The players are expected to go on the market at $2,000 or so. But people in the business think the price could fall to half that in a short time.

—Laura Landro

production, many domestic entrepreneurs perceived that the simplicity of the chips assembly more than offset higher domestic labor costs. The great rush into calculator production was on again.

The market implications of another entrepreneurial stampede should now be obvious. As more and more firms tried to get in on the action, the market supply curve again shifted to the right, and calculator prices slid further down the market demand curve. This shift diminished the profitability of calculator production, squeezing the profit rectangle once again. As prices dropped below $40, foreign manufacturers found that the transportation costs of supplying a market over 6,000 miles away were cutting profits to a minimum. Domestic producers acquired a clear advantage. Indeed, a few, such as Commodore Business Machines, abandoned foreign assembly plants and concentrated production in the United States. At the same time, a whole new crop of companies entered the market: Olympus, Corvus, Columbia, Craig, Bowmar, Eldorado, Master, Rapid Data Systems, and many more. Calculator prices ventured into the under-$30 range, and unit sales reached over 6 million in 1973–74. Those firms that didn't keep up a fast technological pace

SHORT-RUN VS. LONG-RUN EQUILIBRIUM

short-run competitive equilibrium: $p = MC$.

Profit-maximizing competitive firms always strive for the rate of output at which marginal cost (MC) equals price (p). When they achieve that rate of output, they are in **short-run equilibrium,** in the sense that they have no incentive to alter the rate of output produced with existing (fixed) plant and equipment.

But if the short-run equilibrium is profitable (price [p] greater than average total cost [ATC]), existing firms will want to acquire additional plant and equipment, and other firms will want to enter the industry. As they do so, market price will fall until it reaches the level of minimum average total costs, and profits are eliminated. In this **long-run equilibrium,** there is no further incentive to enter the industry or increase the scale of production until technology or market demand improve.

long-run competitive equilibrium: $p = MC =$ minimum ATC.

Hence, in both the short and long run, a competitive industry's marginal cost pricing ($p = MC$) generates reliable signals to consumers about the opportunity cost of producing specific goods and services. In the long run, as profits are driven to a minimum, competitive industries also ensure that goods will be produced for the least opportunity cost (minimum $p = MC =$ minimum ATC).

soon found that their average costs were higher than the market price, and had to cease production. But cost reductions continued, as other profit-hungry firms sought to keep ahead of a rapidly expanding market. By 1982, annual world production of pocket calculators exceeded 20 *million* machines and the price of a basic four-function calculator fell below \$7. Those figures can be compared to the 1972 situation, in which a standard calculator cost close to \$200, and fewer than 200,000 were sold.[9]

REFLECTIONS ON THE COMPETITIVE PROCESS

That consumers reaped substantial benefit from competition in the calculator market is by now evident. A lot of consumers have found that pocket calculators make life a little easier, especially when it comes time to balance the checkbook, do lengthy problem sets, or figure out how much they owe Uncle Sam in income taxes. Perhaps it is true that an abundance of inexpensive calculators would have been produced in other market (or nonmarket) situations as well. But we cannot ignore the fact that competitive market pressures were a driving force in the developments we have reviewed.

The relentless profit squeeze

The unrelenting squeeze on prices and profits which we have observed in the calculator market is a fundamental characteristic of the competitive process. Indeed, the **market mechanism** works best

market mechanism: The use of market prices and sales to signal desired outputs (or resource allocations).

[9] The dramatic drop in calculator prices was due not only to technological breakthroughs, but also to the increased efficiency of calculator companies. As output increased, firms gained experience and learned how to reduce production costs. This phenomenon of "learning by doing" is common in many industries (see Chapter 8).

We've
come
a long
way
Baby

To maintain high profits in the calculator industry, firms must continually lower production costs. A series of technological breakthroughs reduced the size and cost of calculators dramatically in only a few years.

Source: Courtesy of *Washingtonian* and Leon Office Machines.

under such circumstances. The existence of economic profits is an indication that consumers place a high value on a particular product and are willing to pay a comparatively high price to get it. The high price and profits signal this information to profit-hungry entrepreneurs, who eagerly come forward to satisfy consumer demands. Thus ***high profits in a particular industry indicate that consumers want a different mix of output*** (more of that industry's goods). The competitive squeeze on those same profits indicates that resources are being reallocated to produce that desired mix. In a competitive market, consumers get more of the goods they desire, and at a lower price.

When the competitive pressure on prices is carried to the limit, the products in question are also produced at the least possible cost, another dimension of economic efficiency. This was illustrated by the tendency of calculator prices to be driven down to the level of minimum average costs. In this sense, society is getting the most it can from its available (scarce) resources.

Thus society in general benefits from competition in product markets, and the producers who participate in the competitive process come out well, too. At the limit, of course, all economic profit is eliminated. But the limit is rarely if ever reached, because new products are continually being introduced, consumer demands change, and more efficient production processes are discovered. In fact, the competitive process creates strong pressures to pursue product and technological innovation. In a competitive market, the adage about the early bird getting the worm is particularly apt. As we observed in the calculator market, the first ones to perceive and respond to the potential profitability of calculator production were the ones who made the greatest profits. Latecomers did well but never so well as the early entrants. Hence the pressure of competition stimulates a high degree of production responsiveness and a relatively rapid pace of innovation.[10]

[10] The incentives of larger, less competitive firms to pursue or suppress product innovation are discussed in Chapter 8.

Apple's morning after: Lots of competition

Apple Computer Inc.'s $96.8 million initial public offering on Dec. 12 added another chapter to the company's textbook success story. In just four years, the Cupertino (Calif.) concern has evolved from a garage workshop to a leading force in the fast-moving market for personal computers, with annual sales topping $100 million. But as the fanfare of the public offering recedes, Apple faces an onslaught of new high-powered competitors.

Within the next year as many as a dozen large companies are expected to join the battle, offering personal computers costing less than $10,000. International Business Machines, Xerox, and Digital Equipment are all working on personal computers in their laboratories, and each is opening a string of company-owned retail stores as a possible means of distribution. . . . Meanwhile, at least eight Japanese companies—including Nippon Electric, Casio, and Sharp—have introduced personal computers. And some are preparing to come to the U.S. market. "Looking out a few years, the competition will be very rough," notes George P. Elling, industry analyst at Bear, Stearns & Co.

Taking aim

Many of the newcomers are aiming to eat away at Apple's business. At Xerox Corp., in fact, members of the personal computer development team refer to their machine as "the worm." Other manufacturers are elbowing in on Apple's distribution network. Just a week before the Apple offering, Commodore International Ltd., a key Apple competitor, signed a deal with ComputerLand Corp., the independent chain of retail computer stores that sells 15% of all Apple computers.

The sequence of events common to a competitive market situation includes:

- High prices and profits signal consumers' demand for more output.
- Economic profit attracts new suppliers.
- The market supply curve shifts to the right.
- Prices slide down the demand curve.
- A new equilibrium is reached at which increased quantities of the desired product are produced and its price is lower. Average costs of production are at or near a minimum, much more of the product is supplied and consumed, and economic profit approaches zero.
- Throughout the process producers experience great pressure to keep ahead of the profit squeeze by reducing costs, a pressure that frequently results in product and technological innovation.

What is essential to note about the competitive process is that the potential threat of other firms' expanding production or new firms' entering the marketplace keeps existing firms on their toes. In seeking to keep ahead of the game, competitive firms collectively move closer to society's goals, producing the level and mix of output consumers desire with the most efficient combination of resources. In this sense, a market composed of hundreds or even thousands of individually powerless firms is capable of maximizing consumer welfare.

Competitive efficiency

Two specific dimensions of competitive efficiency are worthy of note. First, because competitive pressures continue to squeeze profit margins, the price of a competitively produced good is driven down to its minimum average cost of production. This result can be interpreted in two ways. On the one hand, it means that society is devoting the minimal amount of resources necessary to produce that good. On the other hand, it also means that society is able to get the greatest quantity of goods from a given amount of productive resources. Although these two implications are equivalent, the latter formulation relates directly to the production-possibilities curve we first encountered in Chapter 1. As we observed then, there is a limit to our **production possibilities**—the amount of output we can produce in any time period. That limit is determined by the amount of resources at our disposal and our knowledge of how to use them. This limit is reflected in the production-possibilities curve, which depicts the quantity of various goods and services we are capable of producing.

production possibilities: The alternative combinations of final goods and services that could be produced in a given time period with all available resources and technology.

It is important to emphasize here that competitive pressures tend to stimulate maximum economic **efficiency.** ***Production is pushed to the point of minimum average cost***—thus moving us *closer* to our production possibilities. Moreover, to the extent that competitive forces stimulate new technology, they also serve to *expand* our production possibilities, shifting the production-possibilities curve outward. These phenomena are illustrated in Figure 7.6.

efficiency: Maximum output of a good from the resources used in production.

FIGURE 7.6 THE IMPACT OF COMPETITION ON GNP

Competitive market forces tend to bring us closer to the existing production-possibilities curve and may even shift it outward. In the calculator illustration, competitive forces tended to improve technology and expand output, moving us from point *A* to point *B*. This increased the level of GNP while changing its composition.

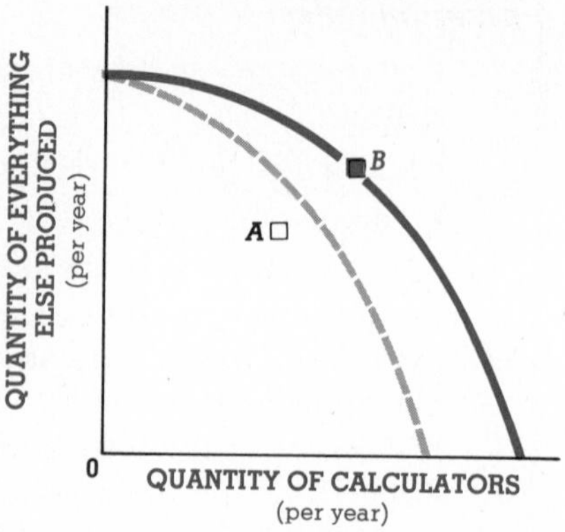

MARGINAL COST PRICING The second dimension of competitive efficiency relates to the *mix* of output we produce rather than the specific level. A basic economic question we must collectively answer is WHAT goods to produce—specifically, how much of one and how much of another. In making such choices, we know that the production of one good must be cut back if we are to get more of another good, at least as long as we are operating on or near the production-possibilities curve. The goods given up are, of course, the **opportunity cost** of getting what we want. We can restate this problem by saying that society must choose some point on the production-possibilities curve. That point represents the desired mix of output.

opportunity cost: The most desired goods or services that are forgone in order to obtain something else.

It would be to our advantage, of course, to know what we have to give up in order to get more of a particular product. Such vital information is a prerequisite to rational choice. In economic terms, what we give up to get more of a particular good is the best alternative use of the resources used in that good's production. The labor and materials used up in the production of calculators cannot be used to produce harmonicas. Accordingly, rational choices about the mix of output require that we know how many resources are required to get one more calculator (or anything else). The amount of resources used to produce one more calculator is its marginal cost. Thus rational decision-making requires that we be able to choose among alternative goods and services on the basis of our desires and each good's marginal cost.

The beautiful thing about a competitive market is that it provides us with the necessary information on which to make such choices. Why? Because competitive firms offer their goods for sale at the level of marginal costs. That is, they always strive to produce at the rate of output at which price equals marginal cost. Hence the price signal the consumer gets in the marketplace is an accurate and reliable basis for making choices about the mix of output and attendant allocation of resources. In this sense, the **marginal cost pricing** characteristic of competitive markets permits society to fulfill its economic goals. The amount consumers are willing to pay for a good (its price) equals its opportunity cost (marginal cost).

marginal cost pricing: The offer (supply) of goods at prices equal to their marginal cost.

POLICY IMPLICATIONS: COMPETITIVE MARKET EFFICIENCY

In Chapter 2 we noted that there is a comparatively strong case to be made for the market mechanism. In particular, we observed that the market mechanism permits individual consumers and producers to express their views about WHAT to produce, HOW to produce, and FOR WHOM to produce by "voting" for particular goods and services by way of market purchases and sales. If a great many people want and are willing to pay for a particular good, the market mechanism will assist in bringing about more of the desired production. If little of a particular good or service is desired, the market mechanism will signal this fact to producers and stimulate a reallocation of the economy's resources in another direction.

We also observed, however, that there are several important qualifications to this laissez faire view of the world. The appropriateness or fairness of consumer "voting" patterns depends on how equitably voting power is distributed. If some consumers have little opportunity to acquire income or wealth, they will be unable to participate fully in the collective decision making in resource and product markets. We also noted that some goods and services cannot be peddled efficiently in the market because their consumption cannot be confined to those who pay for them. These *public goods* are an important exception to laissez faire economics. Finally, we have observed that the concept of public goods applies more generally to externalities—benefits or harm that cannot be communicated efficiently through the marketplace.

In view of these three major qualifications to market efficiency, the argument for a completely laissez faire policy must be met with some skepticism. Nevertheless, we cannot disregard the fact that the market mechanism is an efficient tool for communicating and fulfilling society's wishes when the three qualifications we have noted are compensated for. In this regard, it is particularly important to note that markets tend to be most efficient when competitive forces are at work. As we observed in the calculator illustration, competitive firms and industries tend to respond quickly and efficiently to consumer desires. In this sense, competitive markets do best what markets are supposed to do, and it is in society's interest to maintain competitive market structures. In the following chapters we shall look more closely at our successes and failures in this regard.

SUMMARY

- A firm that has market power can alter the market price of the goods it sells. A monopoly, for example, as the only supplier of a particular good, can raise the market price of that good by reducing the total quantity supplied. In contrast, a competitive firm, one without any market power, has no visible effect on total market supply, and therefore no effect on market price.
- The difference between competitive (powerless) firms and noncompetitive (powerful) firms is reflected in the distinction between

the market demand curve and the demand curve facing an individual firm. If a firm is very small in relation to the size of the market, it can produce up to its capacity without altering the market price of the good it sells. In this sense, the perfectly competitive firm confronts a horizontal demand curve for its own output even though the relevant market demand curve is negatively sloped.

■ The competitive firm translates the basic profit-maximization rule about equating marginal revenue and marginal cost into the simpler rule of equating marginal cost and price. This translation is made possible by the fact that marginal revenue is identical to price for the perfectly competitive (powerless) firm.

■ When economic (above-normal) profit is available in a competitive industry, new firms will enter the market. The resulting shift of supply will drive down market prices in accordance with the downward slope of the market demand curve. As prices fall, the profit of the industry and its constituent firms will be squeezed.

■ The limit to the competitive price and profit squeeze is reached when price is driven down to the level of minimum average cost. At this point (long-run equilibrium) additional output and profit will be attained only if technology is improved (lowering costs) or if demand increases.

■ The most distinctive thing about competitive markets is the persistent pressure they exert on prices and profits. The threat of competition tends to act as a tremendous incentive for producers to respond quickly to consumer demands and to seek more efficient means of production. In this sense, competitive markets do best what markets are supposed to do—efficiently allocate resources.

Terms to remember

Define the following terms:

market power
market supply
competitive firm
perfectly competitive market
monopoly
economic profit
barriers to entry
equilibrium price
production decision
marginal cost
average total cost
profit per unit
shift of supply
short-run competitive equilibrium
long-run competitive equilibrium
market mechanism
production possibilities
efficiency
opportunity cost
marginal cost pricing

Questions for discussion

1. Why would anyone want to enter a profitable industry knowing that profits would eventually be eliminated by competition?

2. Why wouldn't producers necessarily want to produce output at the least average cost? Under what conditions would they end up doing so?

3. If profit-maximizing producers do not generally seek to produce their output at the level where average costs are at a minimum, what sense can be made of the typical plant manager's instructions to "reduce costs to a minimum"?

4. What industries do you regard as being highly competitive? Can you identify any barriers to entry in those industries?

Problem

Suppose that the market demand schedule for frisbees is:

Price	$8	$7	$6	$5	$4	$3	$2	$1
Quantity demanded (per month)	1,000	2,000	4,000	8,000	16,000	32,000	64,000	150,000

Suppose further that the marginal and average costs of frisbee production for every competitive firm are:

Rate of output (per month)	100	200	300	400	500	600
Marginal cost	$2.00	$3.00	$4.00	$5.00	$6.00	$7.00
Average cost	2.00	2.50	3.00	3.50	4.00	4.50

Finally, assume that the equilibrium market price is $6 per frisbee.

(a) Draw the cost curves of the typical firm and identify its profit-maximizing rate of output and its total profits.

(b) Draw the market demand curve and identify market equilibrium.

(c) How many (identical) firms are initially producing frisbees?

(d) In view of the profits being made, more firms will want to get into frisbee production. In the long run, these new firms will shift the market supply curve to the right and price down to average total cost, thereby eliminating profits. At what equilibrium price are all profits eliminated? How many firms will be producing frisbees at this price?

APPENDIX
THE FARM PROBLEM

In 1980, 1981, and again in 1982 the net income of U.S. farmers fell to near-Depression levels. The real income of U.S. farmers in 1982 was only a third of what it had been in 1973—and only a couple of billion dollars higher than the level of 1933. Thousands of farmers were forced to sell their farms and machinery; still more were forced to deplete their savings and go deeply into debt.

This mini-depression in the early 1980s was symptomatic of recurring farm problems. Farmers have to contend with intense competition, abrupt changes in weather, low price elasticity of demand, and sudden shifts in both demand and supply. As a consequence, the agricultural industry is prone to recurring "booms" and "busts." In this appendix, we shall look more closely at these forces that make farm prices, output, and income inherently unstable. We shall also examine the nature and impact of government policies designed to foster greater stability in agricultural markets. As will be seen, those policies have helped stabilize agricultural markets, but at a substantial cost.

DESTABILIZING FORCES

Competition in agriculture

The agricultural industry is one of the most competitive of all U.S. industries. To begin with, there are over 2 million farms in the United States. Although some of these farms are immense in size—with thousands of acres—no single farm has the power to affect the market supply or price of farm products. That is to say, individual farmers have no market power.

Competition in the agricultural industry is also maintained by relatively low barriers to entry. Although farming is becoming increasingly mechanized and scientific, the rudiments of farming are easily mastered. Even most city dwellers learn how to grow vegetables in their backyards or window boxes. Moreover, the investment required to start a farm is relatively modest. A few acres of land, a good plow, and a lot of energy are enough to start a working farm. By contrast, entry into most other industries requires substantial capital investment or technological expertise. This does not imply that it is easy to succeed in farming, but only that it is easy to become a farmer.

Given the competitive structure of U.S. agriculture, ***individual farmers tend to behave like perfect competitors.***[1] Individual farmers seek to expand their rate of output until marginal cost equals price. By following this rule, each farmer makes as much profit as possible from existing resources, prices, and technology.

Like other competitive firms, U.S. farmers can maintain economic profits only if they achieve continuing cost reductions. Above-normal profits obtained from current production techniques and prices are not likely to last. Such profits will entice more people into agriculture and stimulate greater output from existing farmers. This is exactly the kind of dilemma that confronted the early producers of electronic calculators. To stay ahead, individual firms (farms) must continue to improve their productivity.

[1] There are exceptions, including a variety of production and marketing associations. These are discussed in Chapter 10.

Technological advance

The rate of technological advance in agriculture has, in fact, been spectacular. Less land is used for farming today than was used 100 years ago. Yet, farm output today is far larger. Just in the period since 1950 farm output per acre has doubled. Farm output per labor hour has grown even faster, having increased by 700 percent in the same time period. Such high rates of productivity advance rival those of our most "technological" industries. These technological advances have come about in countless ways, including development of higher yielding seeds (the "green revolution"), advanced machinery (e.g., mechanical feeders and milkers), improved animal breeding (e.g., crossbreeding), improved plants (e.g., rust-resistant wheat), better land-use practices (e.g., rotations and fertilizers), and computer-based management systems. These many improvements have been discovered and developed by individual farmers, the companies that sell products to them, and by research supported by the U.S. Department of Agriculture.

Inelastic demand

In most industries, continuous increases in technology and output would be most welcome. The agricultural industry, however, confronts a long-term problem. Simply put, there is a limit to the amount of food people want to eat. Hence, more and more output threatens to satiate our collective hunger.

This constraint on the demand for agricultural output is reflected in the relatively inelastic demand for food. Typically, consumers do not increase their food purchases very much when farm prices fall. The **price elasticity** of food demand is low. As a consequence, abundant harvests (rightward shifts of the supply curve) can lead to sharply lower prices and a *decline* in total revenue.

price elasticity of demand: The percentage change in quantity demanded divided by the percentage change in price.

income elasticity of demand: The percentage change in quantity demanded divided by the percentage change in income.

The **income elasticity** of food demand is also low. As incomes increase, people tend to buy more of many goods and services. But they do not buy much more food. Hence, neither lower prices nor higher incomes significantly increase the quantity of food demanded.

In the long run, then, the increasing ability of U.S. agriculture to produce food must be reconciled with very slow growth of U.S. demand for food. Over time, this implies that farm prices will fall, relative to nonfarm prices. And they have. Between the years 1910–14 and 1980, the ratio of farm prices to nonfarm prices fell by 24 percent. In the absence of government price-support programs and foreign demand for our farm products, farm prices would have fallen still further.

Abrupt shifts of supply

The long-term downtrend in (relative) farm prices is only one of the major problems confronting U.S. agriculture. The second major problem is short run in nature. Prices of farm products are subject to abrupt short-term swings. If the weather is good, harvests are abundant. Abundant harvests imply a severe drop in prices, however, particularly when food demand is relatively inelastic. On the other hand, a late or early freeze, a drought, or an infestation can reduce harvests substantially and push prices sharply higher. So long as agricultural harvests are subject to the whims of nature, farm prices will be highly unstable from year to year. These natural price swings are illustrated in Figure A.1.

FIGURE A.1 SHORT-TERM INSTABILITY

Changes in weather cause abrupt shifts of the food supply curve. When combined with the relatively inelastic demand for food, these supply shifts result in wide price swings. Notice how the price of grain jumps from p_1 to p_2 when bad weather reduces the harvest. If good weather follows, prices may fall to p_3.

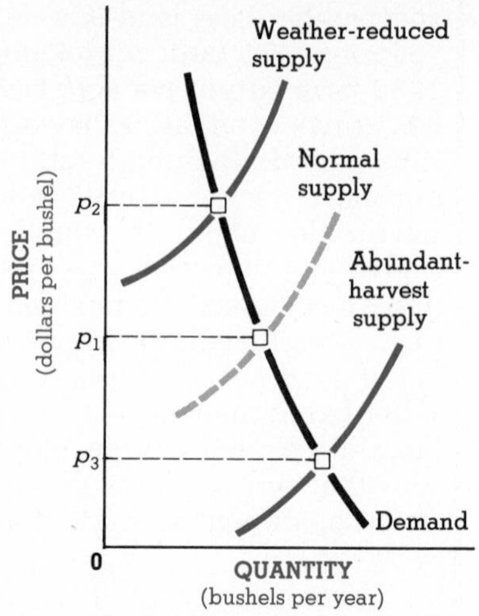

Natural forces are not the only cause of short-term price instability. Time lags between the production decision and the resultant harvest also contribute to price instability. If prices are high one year, farmers have an incentive to increase their rate of output. In this sense, prices serve the same signaling function in agriculture as they do in nonfarm industries. What distinguishes the farmers' response is the lack of inventories and the fixed duration of the production process. In the auto and electronics industries, a larger quantity of output can be supplied to the market fairly quickly. Some additional supplies can be marketed immediately by reducing available inventories. A further increase in the quantity supplied can be obtained by increasing the rate of output, perhaps with periods of overtime. In farming, however, supply cannot respond so quickly. First of all, little inventory is available, because most farm products are highly perishable. Second, overtime efforts won't speed up the growing or breeding cycles. In the very short run, the farmer can only till more land, plant additional seed, or breed more livestock. No additional food supplies will be available until a new crop or herd grows. Hence, the agricultural supply response to a change in prices is always one harvest (or breeding period) later.

The natural lag in responses of agricultural supplies intensifies short-term price swings. Suppose corn prices are exceptionally high at the end of a year, due to a reduced harvest. High prices will make corn farming appear unusually profitable. Hence, farmers will want to expand their rate of output—plant more corn acreage—to share in these high profits. But the corn will not appear on the market until the following year. By that time, there is likely to be an abundance of corn on the market, as a result of both better weather and increased corn acreage. Hence corn prices are likely to plummet (see Figure A.1 again).

No single farmer can avoid the boom-or-bust movement of prices. Even a corn farmer who has mastered the principles of economics has little choice but to plant more corn when prices are high. If he does not plant additional corn, prices will fall anyway, because his own production decisions do not affect market prices. By not planting additional corn, he only denies himself a share of corn market sales. In a highly competitive market, each producer must act independently.

The historical instability of corn prices is illustrated in Figure A.2. Notice how corn prices repeatedly rise, then abruptly fall. This kind of price swing is particularly evident in 1915–20, 1935–37, 1946–48, and 1973–76.

THE CRISIS YEARS

The U.S. agricultural industry operated without substantial government intervention until the 1930s. In earlier decades, an expanding population, recurrent wars, and less advanced technology had helped to maintain a favorable supply-demand relationship for farm products. There were frequent short-term swings in farm prices, but these were absorbed by a generally sound farm sector. The period 1910–19 was particularly prosperous for farmers, largely because of the expanded foreign demand for U.S. farm products by countries engaged in World War I.

The two basic problems of U.S. agriculture grew to crisis proportions after 1920. In 1919, most farm prices were at historical

FIGURE A.2 UNSTABLE CORN PRICES

Most agricultural prices are subject to abrupt short-term changes. Notice how corn prices rose dramatically during World Wars I and II, then fell sharply. Poor harvests in the rest of the world increased demand for U.S. food in 1973–74.

Source: U.S. Department of Agriculture, *Agricultural Statistics*, 1978.

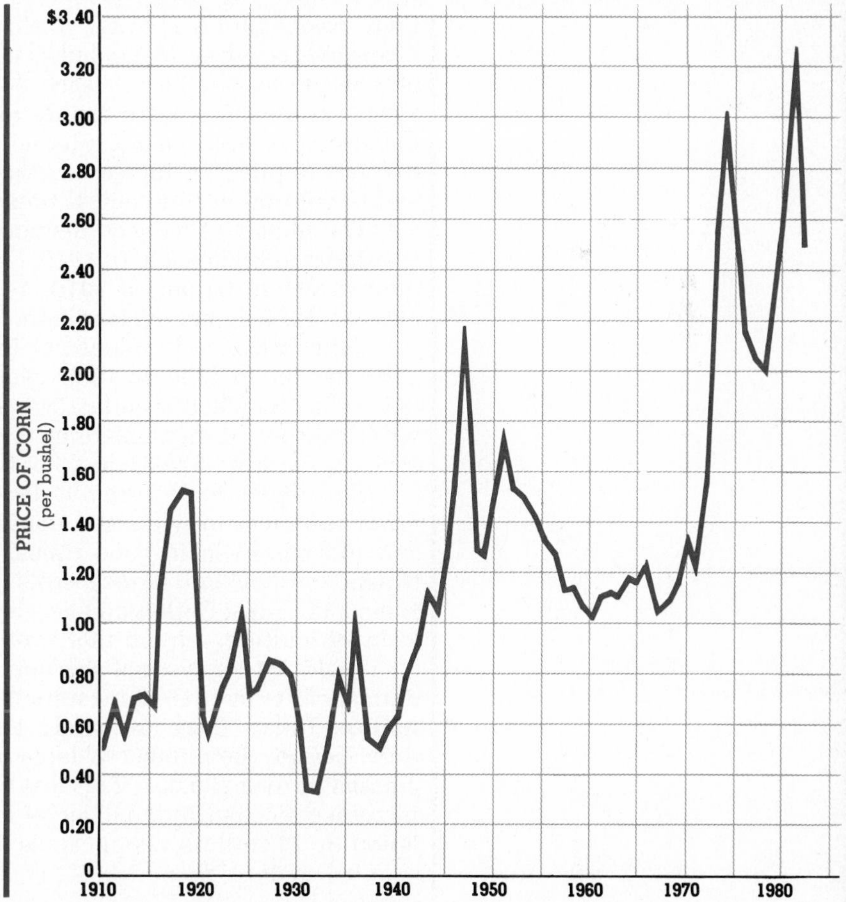

FIGURE A.3 FARM PRICES, 1910–40 (1910–14 = 100)

Farm prices are less stable than nonfarm prices. During the 1930s, relative farm prices fell by 50 percent. This experience was the catalyst for government price supports and other agricultural assistance programs.

Source: U.S. Department of Agriculture, *Agricultural Statistics*, 1950.

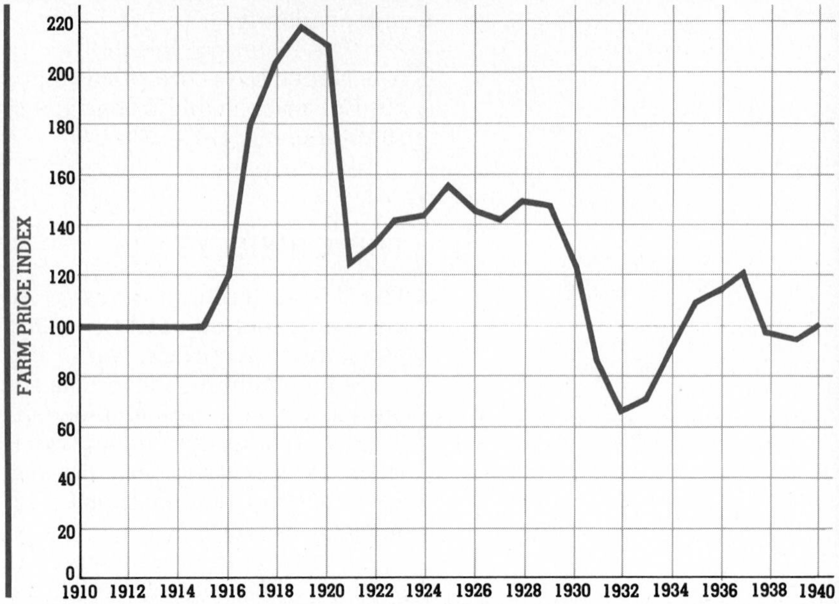

highs (see Figure A.2). After World War I ended, however, European countries no longer demanded as much American food. U.S. exports of farm products fell from nearly $4 billion in 1919 to $1.9 billion in 1921. Farm exports were further reduced in the following years by increasing restrictions on international trade. At home, the end of the war implied an increased availability of factors of production and continuing technological improvement.

The impact of reduced demand and steadily increasing supply is evident in Figure A.3. In 1919, farm prices were more than double their levels of the period 1910–14. Prices then fell abruptly, however. In 1921 alone, average farm prices fell by nearly 40 percent.

Farm prices rose somewhat in the mid-1920s, but resumed a steep decline in 1930. In 1932, average farm prices were 75 percent lower than they had been in 1919, and were only 65 percent of their prewar levels. At the same time, the average income per farmer from farming fell from $2,651 in 1919 to $855 in 1932.

The depression hit smaller farmers particularly hard. They had fewer resources to withstand consecutive years of declining prices and income. Even in good times, small farmers must continually expand output and reduce costs just to maintain their incomes. Hence, the Great Depression accelerated an exodus of small farmers from agriculture, a trend that continues today.

Table A.1 shows that the number of small farms has declined dramatically. In 1910 there were 3.7 million farms under 100 acres in size. Today, there are barely 1 million small farms. During the same period, the number of large farms (500 acres or more) has increased by over 200,000. This loss of small farmers, together with the increased mechanization of larger farms, has reduced the farm population by 23 million people since 1910.[2]

[2] The Census Bureau defines farms as property that produces at least $1,000 worth of agricultural products for the market in a year.

TABLE A.1 SIZE DISTRIBUTION OF U.S. FARMS, 1910 AND 1978

Inelastic food demand, combined with increasing agricultural productivity, implies a declining number of farmers. Small farmers are particularly vulnerable because they do not have the resources to maintain a high rate of technological improvement. As a result, the number of small farms has declined dramatically, while the number of large farms has grown.

Size of farm	*Number, 1910*	*Percent*	*Number, 1978*	*Percent*
Under 100 acres	**3,691,611**	**58.0**	**1,077,000**	**43.4**
100–499 acres	**2,494,461**	**39.2**	**1,024,000**	**41.3**
500–999 acres	**125,295**	**2.0**	**215,000**	**8.7**
1,000 acres and over	**50,135**	**0.8**	**163,000**	**6.6**
Total	**6,361,502**	**100.0**	**2,479,000**	**100.0**

Source: U.S. Department of Commerce, *Statistical Abstract of the United States,* 1933, 1981.

U.S. FARM POLICY

The U.S. Congress has responded to these agricultural problems with a variety of programs. Most seek to raise and stabilize the price of farm products. Other programs seek to reduce the costs of production. More recently, the federal government has also provided direct income support to farmers.

Price supports

market surplus: The amount by which the quantity supplied exceeds the quantity demanded at a given price; excess supply.

Price supports have always been the primary focus of U.S. farm policy. As early as 1926, Congress decreed that farm products should sell at a "fair" price. By "fair," Congress meant a price higher than the market equilibrium. Unfortunately, an above-equilibrium price would create a **market surplus** of food (see Figure A.4). Congress proposed to get rid of this surplus by selling it abroad at world market prices. President Calvin Coolidge vetoed this legislation both times Congress passed it.

The basic notion of "fair" prices resurfaced in the Agricultural Adjustment Act of 1933. The basic objective of the act was to restore the purchasing power of farm products to the 1909–14 level. The farm-nonfarm price relationships of 1909–14 were regarded by Con-

FIGURE A.4 "FAIR" PRICES AND MARKET SURPLUS

The interaction of market supply and demand establish an equilibrium price (p_e) for any product, including food. If a higher price (p_f) is set, the quantity of food supplied (q_s) will be larger than the quantity demanded (q_d). Hence, attempts to establish a "fair" (higher) price for farm products must cope with resultant market surpluses.

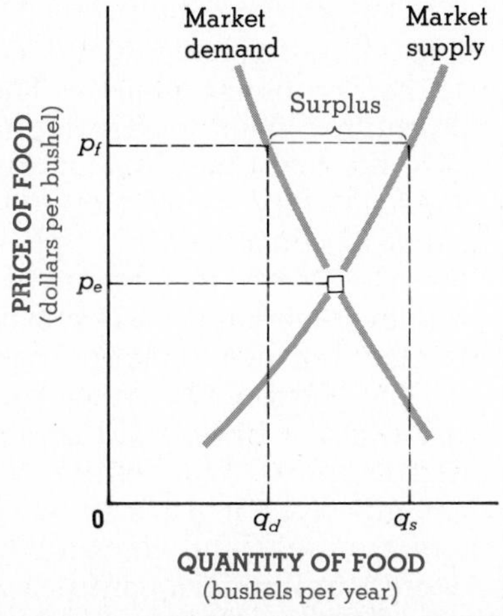

FIGURE A.5 THE IMPACT OF PRICE SUPPORTS

In the absence of price supports, the price of farm products would be determined by the intersection of market supply and demand. In this case, the equilibrium price would be P_1, as shown in part *b*. All individual farmers would confront this price and produce up to the point where $MC = p_1$, as in part *a*.

Government price supports raise the price to p_2. By offering to buy (or "loan") unlimited quantities at this price, the government shifts the demand curve facing each farmer upward. Individual farmers respond by increasing their output to q_2. As farmers increase their output, a market surplus develops (part *b*).

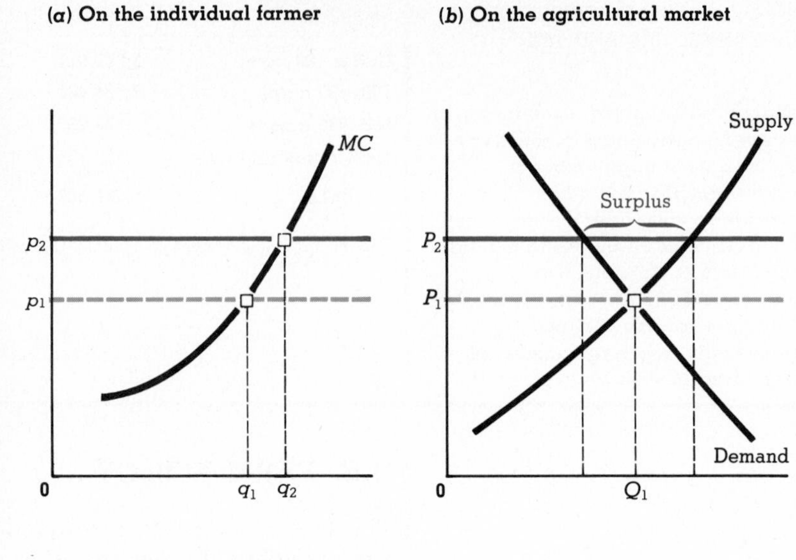

gress as "fair" and came to be known as "parity" prices. The objective of the 1933 act was to restore that parity by raising farm prices. To do so, Congress this time proposed to reduce market supplies (shift the market supply curve to the left), thereby avoiding a market surplus. This reduction in supply would come about by paying farmers for voluntary reductions in crop acreage.

In January 1936 the U.S. Supreme Court ruled that Congress did not have authority to pay farmers not to produce. Congress responded to this decision quickly. In February Congress passed the Soil and Conservation and Domestic Allotment Act. That act authorized payments to farmers for growing soil-conserving legumes and grasses. Hence, farmers were paid for shifting acreage from the production of soil-depleting surplus crops to soil-conserving uses. The effect, of course, was to limit production, thereby increasing market prices. Such acreage "set-asides" are still part of U.S. farm policy.

A second mechanism for reducing market supply was introduced by an executive order of President Franklin Roosevelt. In October 1933 he established the Commodity Credit Corporation (CCC). Its function is ostensibly to lend money to farmers. But farmers may use their crops as collateral. The effect of such loans is to establish a minimum ("floor") price for farm products. If a farmer does not repay the loan, the CCC simply keeps the crops held as collateral. Hence, the farmer effectively "sells" his crops to the CCC whenever he defaults on a loan. The "price" for these crops is equal to the crop loan rate, that is, the amount of money lent for each bushel of grain. Whenever market prices exceed CCC loan rates, the farmer can repay his loan, retrieve his crops, and sell them in the open market.

The effect of CCC price supports on individual farmers and the agricultural market is illustrated in Figure A.5. In the absence of price supports, competitive farmers would confront a horizontal demand curve at price p_1, itself determined by the intersection of market supply and demand (in part *b*). The CCC's offer to buy ("loan") unlimited quantities at a higher price shifts the demand curve facing each farmer upward, to the guaranteed price p_2. This

A mess however it's sliced

One way to unload 30 million lbs. of processed cheddar cheese

Free the cheese! Consumer groups have been beaming that message at the White House in petitions and telegrams for a month, and last week Ronald Reagan agreed to do just that. In an Oval Office ceremony, during which he signed an $11 billion farm price-support bill, the President announced that the Government will give away 30 million lbs. of surplus cheese to states for distribution to the needy. Explained Reagan: "At a time when American families are under increasing financial pressure, their Government cannot sit by and watch millions of pounds of food turn to waste."

As a present to the poor, the free cheese has its drawbacks. Needy recipients will have to scrape mold off some of the cheese, which has been stored in 150 warehouses or limestone caves in 35 states for as long as 18 months. But, insists Merritt Sprague, a commodity supervisor for the Department of Agriculture, "mold does not produce toxin that is harmful." Not much variety in the menu, either: the cheese, stored in 5-lb. loaves, is all processed cheddar, the kind sold in grocery stores as "American cheese." . . .

The giveaway still leaves the Government holding some 530 million lbs. of cheese—more than 2 lbs. for every man, woman and child in the country—plus 848 million lbs. of nonfat dry milk stored in 50-lb. sacks and 212 million lbs. of butter frozen at 0° F in 68-lb. blocks. Annual storage and handling cost: $43 million. As Reagan noted in signing the farm bill last week, "surpluses will continue to pile up" because the Government must keep on buying dairy products at prices ($1.4375 per lb. for processed cheddar) that are currently higher than commercial buyers will pay. Processed cheese presents the biggest storage problem, because it spoils if held too long—beyond a maximum of two years. Secretary of Agriculture John R. Block has taken to waving pieces of moldy cheese during speeches to dramatize the scandal, which has led to the telegrams urging the White House to give cheese to the poor.

Other suggestions for disposing of the surplus range from dumping the cheese in the sea to staging bring-your-own-wine-and-crackers parties at warehouses. Reagan hinted last week that more might be given to the needy, and some of the cheese might be sold abroad, at a loss to the Government. The all-too-obvious solution, of course, would be to lower price-support levels until dairy farmers are no longer tempted to produce more cheese than they can sell commercially. But that would be a lot to ask of politicians. The new farm bill actually increases present price-support levels over four years. Meanwhile, the Government is left with a stockpile that is a mess . . . oh, all right, no matter how you slice it.

higher price induces each farmer to increase his rate of output, from q_1 to q_2.

As all farmers respond to price supports, the agricultural market is pushed out of equilibrium. At the support level p_2, more output is supplied than demanded. The surplus ends up in storage. Since 1977, farmers have been permitted to store their own surplus and bill the federal government for storage costs. Thus farmers get paid to produce output that consumers don't want and are then paid again to store the unsold crops.

The federal government also buys some farm products outright. The most important purchases are for milk products. The Agriculture and Food Act of 1981, like its predecessors, required the U.S. Department of Agriculture to purchase all surplus milk, in the form of butter, cheese, and dry milk. The act also specified what prices were to be paid for this milk. For the years 1982–84, the act set minimum prices of $13.25, $14.00, and $14.60 per hundred weight of milk. The avowed purpose of these prices is to guarantee prices equal to at least 70 percent of parity (the price of milk in 1910–14). Their effect is to raise market prices, reduce consumption, and increase output. The net result is a growing market surplus. In 1981 alone, the federal government purchased nearly $2 *billion* worth of cheese, butter, and nonfat dry milk. Just *storing* this surplus costs over $1 million a day. In fact, inventories of surplus milk products grew so large that in 1981 President Reagan ordered the Agriculture Department to give away 30 million pounds of cheese at Christmas!

FIGURE A.6 THE IMPACT OF COST SUBSIDIES

Cost subsidies lower the marginal cost of producing at any given rate of output, thereby shifting the marginal cost curve downward. The lower marginal costs make higher rates of output more profitable and thus increase output. At price p_2, lower marginal costs increase the desired rate of output from q_2 to q_3.

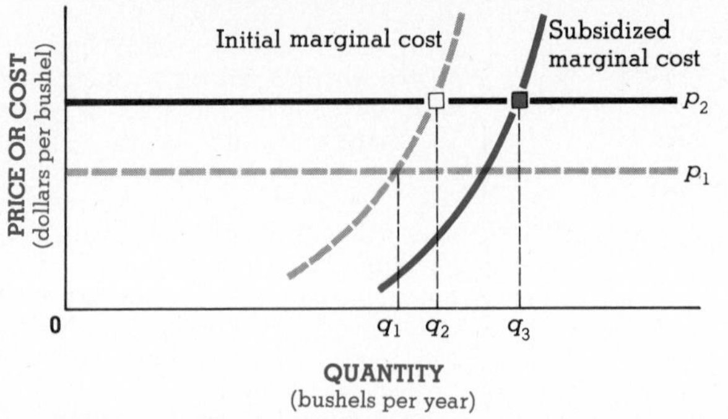

Cost subsidies

To encourage output further, the government also subsidizes various costs of farm production, thereby slowing the rise of marginal costs. Irrigation water, for example, is delivered to many farmers by federally funded reclamation projects. The price paid by farmers for the water is substantially below the cost of delivering it; the difference amounts to a subsidy. Other forms of subsidy have been conveyed by the Department of Agriculture's Rural Environmental Assistance Program (REAP). REAP has distributed something like \$150–\$200 million a year to farmers to help defray the costs of certain production factors (such as fertilizers and drainage).

The federal government has also provided basic research, insurance, marketing, grading, and inspection services to farmers at subsidized prices. All of these subsidies serve to lower fixed or variable costs. Their net impact is to stimulate additional output, as illustrated in Figure A.6.

Direct income support

Price supports and cost subsidies are designed to stabilize agricultural markets and assure farmers an adequate income. As we have seen, however, they entail significant distortions of market outcomes. The Congressional Budget Office estimates that the milk price supports alone have increased retail dairy prices by 3 to 6 percent, reduced consumption by 1 to 5 percent, and encouraged excessive dairy production. Because of such distortions, direct income supports were authorized by the Agriculture and Consumer Protection Act of 1973. The advantage of direct income supports is that they achieve the goal of income security without distortions of market prices and output.

The principal form of direct income support are so-called deficiency payments. Producers of wheat, feed grains, rice, cotton, and other commodities receive direct payments from the federal government when crop prices are low (below stipulated "target prices"). These payments are designed to make up the deficiency in income that results from low prices. Deficiency payments are also made to farmers who agree to reduce their output (acreage) of certain crops.

In principle, direct income payments are a more efficient mechanism for subsidizing farm incomes. But farmers don't like them. In fact, 5,000 angry farmers drove their tractors to Washington, D.C., in February 1979 to protest this policy approach. Their rallying cry was "parity, not charity." They wanted higher price supports (an indirect subsidy) rather than more deficiency payments (a direct subsidy).

CHAPTER 8

MONOPOLY

The price, the quantity, even the quality of the goods and services we buy are determined in product markets by the interaction of supply and demand forces. As we have seen, every potential buyer translates his or her tastes and income into a single denominator—price—and indicates a willingness to buy certain products at various prices. Individual sellers do much the same thing, in their case transforming sales, cost, and profit expectations into a willingness to sell various quantities at particular prices. The interaction of all these individual decisions in the marketplace yields the prices and product flows we observe daily.

The dependence of prices and product flows on the interaction of market supply and demand underscores the importance of market structures and behavior. As we observed in Chapter 7, competitive market structures create a unique kind of pressure on producers. Under the threat of competition, producers are motivated to adapt quickly to changing consumer demands, to improve product quality, and to reduce costs.

market power: The ability to alter the market price of a good or service.

Such pressures are less evident in a market characterized by concentrations of **market power.** A firm with market power has some direct influence over market prices. Its own production decisions have an independent impact on the price at which its product may be sold. A firm with market power may find it more profitable to maintain high prices in a particular market than to increase the rate of output, improve product quality, or experiment with new cost structures. Moreover, a firm with significant market power will be able to keep prices high as a consequence of its control over market supplies. A powerless (or perfectly competitive) firm has no such option, as it is unable to alter market supplies or prices.

The power to influence prices and product flows may have far-reaching consequences for our economic welfare. Changes in prices and product flows directly influence the level and composition of GNP, employment and resource allocation, the level and distribution of income, and, of course, the level and structure of prices. Hence firms that wield significant market power affect all dimensions of economic welfare.

Market power is not the only kind of power wielded in society, of course. Political power, for example, is obviously a different kind of power and important in its own right. Indeed, the power to influence an election or to sway a Senate committee vote may ultimately be more important than the power to increase the price of laundry soap. Nevertheless, market power is a force that influences the way we live, the incomes we earn, and our relationships with other countries. Moreover, market power may provide the basis for other forms of power. The individual or firm with considerable market power is likely to have the necessary resources to influence an election or sway a vote on a congressional committee. Hence market power is a critical dimension of both economic and social welfare.

In light of the potential impact of market power on the way we live and the way the economy functions, we need to determine whether market power exists in the United States. If it does exist, how is it used, and what effects has it had? This chapter begins to answer these questions by examining the way market power may be used to alter market outcomes.

MARKET POWER

The essence of market power is the ability to alter the price of a product. The doorknob producers and calculator manufacturers of Chapters 6 and 7 had no such power. Because many other firms were producing and selling the same good, each doorknob or calculator producer had to act as a *price taker*. Each firm could sell all it wanted at the prevailing price but would lose all of its customers if it tried to charge a higher price. This inability to raise the price of their own output is what we refer to when we say competitive firms have no market power.

The absence of market power is illustrated by a horizontal demand curve. Although the demand for the product itself always slopes downward, the demand curve confronting a single competitive firm is horizontal. ***Horizontal demand curves are the hallmark of perfectly competitive firms.***

The downward-sloping demand curve

Firms that have market power *can* alter the price of their output without losing all their customers. Sales volume may drop when price is increased, but the quantity demanded will not drop to zero.

FIGURE 8.1 FIRM VS. INDUSTRY DEMAND

A competitive firm can sell its entire output at the prevailing market price. In this sense, the firm confronts a horizontal demand curve, as in part *a*. Nevertheless, market demand for the product still slopes downward. The demand curve confronting the industry is illustrated in part *b*. Note the difference in the units of measurement (single doorknobs vs. thousands).

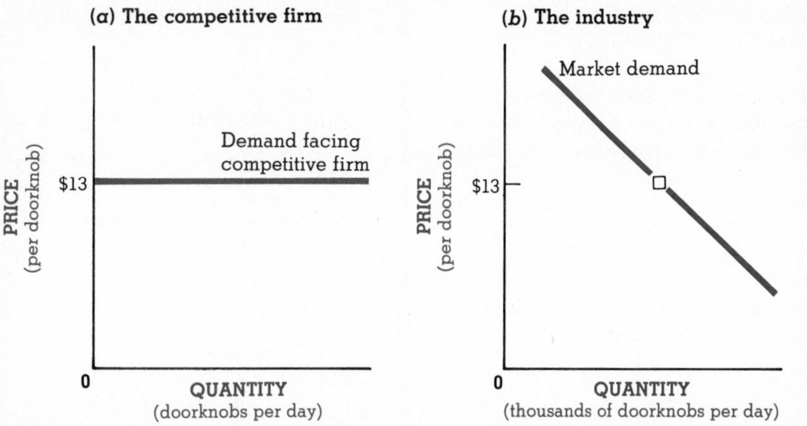

In other words, ***firms with market power confront downward-sloping demand curves.***

The distinction between competitive (powerless) and noncompetitive (powerful) firms is illustrated in Figure 8.1. Figure 8.1*a* recreates the market situation that confronts a single producer of doorknobs. In Chapter 6 we assumed that the prevailing price of brass doorknobs was $13 and that a small, competitive firm could sell its entire output at this price. Hence each individual firm effectively confronted a horizontal demand curve.

We also noted earlier that brass doorknobs are not in violation of the law of demand. As nice as brass doorknobs are, people are not willing to buy unlimited quantities of them at $13 each. The marginal utility of extra doorknobs, in fact, diminishes very rapidly. To induce consumers to buy more doorknobs, the price of doorknobs must be reduced.

This seeming contradiction between the law of demand and the situation of the competitive firm is resolved in Figure 8.1. There are *two* relevant demand curves. The one on the left, which appears to contradict the law of demand, refers to a single competitive producer. The one on the right refers to the entire *industry,* of which the competitive producer is one very tiny part. The industry or market demand curve *does* slope downward, even though individual competitive firms are able to sell their entire output at the going price.

Monopoly

monopoly: A firm that produces the entire market supply of a particular good or service.

An industry need not be composed of many small firms, however. Indeed, the entire output of doorknobs could be produced by a single large producer. Such a firm would be a **monopoly,** that is, a single firm that produces the entire market supply of a good.

The emergence of a monopoly obliterates the distinction between industry demand and the demand curve facing the firm. A monopoly *is* the industry. Hence there is only *one* demand curve to worry about and that is the market (industry) demand curve, as illustrated in Figure 8.1*b*. ***In monopoly situations the demand curve facing the firm is identical to the market demand curve for the product.***

FIGURE 8.2 PRICE EXCEEDS MARGINAL REVENUE

If a firm must lower its price to sell additional output, marginal revenue is less than price. If the firm wants to increase its sales from one to two doorknobs per day, for example, price must be reduced from $13 to $12. The marginal revenue of the second doorknob is therefore only $11. This is indicated in row *B* of the table and by point *b* on the graph.

DOORKNOB SALES AND REVENUES

	(1) Quantity	×	(2) Price	=	(3) Total revenue	(4) Marginal revenue
A	1		$13		$13	
						$11
B	2		12		24	
						9
C	3		11		33	
						7
D	4		10		40	
						5
E	5		9		45	

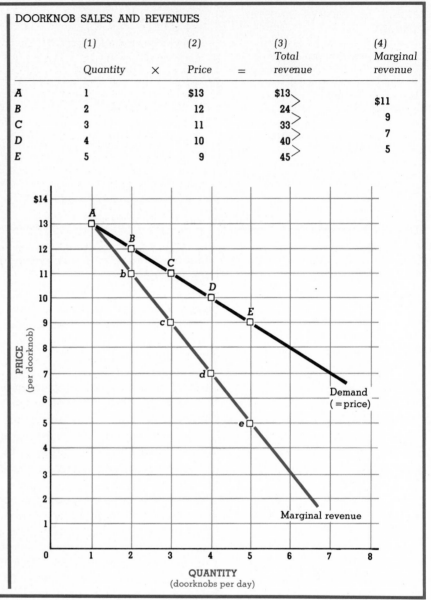

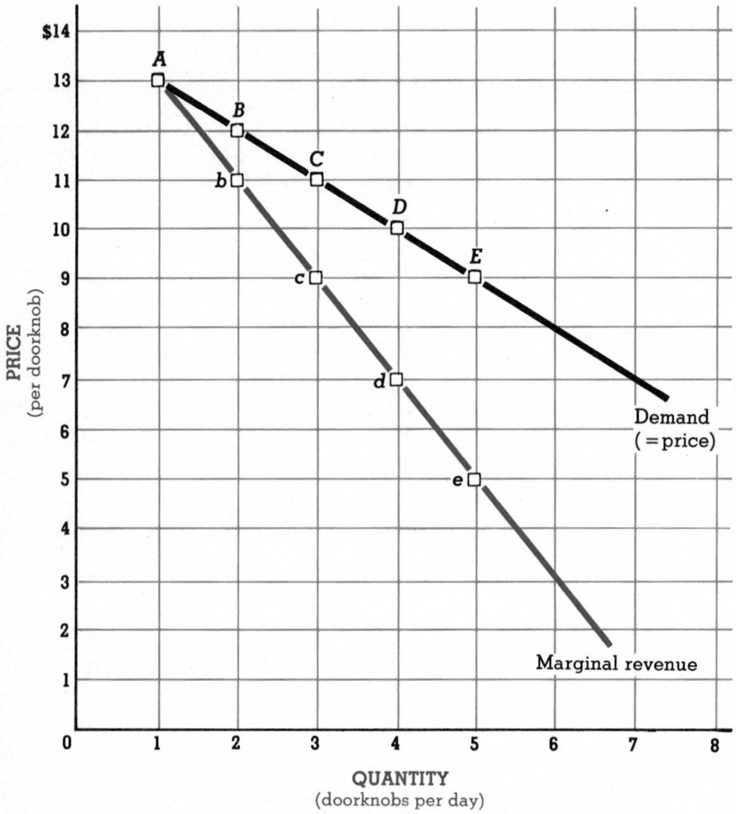

Price and marginal revenue

profit-maximization rule: Produce at that rate of output where marginal revenue equals marginal cost.

Although monopolies simplify the geometry, they complicate the arithmetic of **profit maximization.** The beautiful thing about a horizontal demand curve is that it makes price and marginal revenue equal. Hence a competitive firm can maximize profits by selling that rate of output where price equals marginal cost.

A monopolist also seeks to maximize profits. He, too, seeks that rate of output where marginal revenue equals marginal cost. But that rate of output is not quite so obvious for the monopolist. Because the demand curve slopes downward, price and marginal revenue are not identical. In fact, ***marginal revenue is always less than price for a monopolist.*** This makes it just a bit more difficult to find the profit-maximizing rate of output.

Figure 8.2 provides a simple illustration of the relationship between price and marginal revenue. The monopolist can sell one doorknob per day at a price of $13. If he wants to sell a larger quantity of doorknobs, however, he has to reduce his price. According to the demand curve depicted here, the price must be lowered to $12 to sell two doorknobs per day. This reduction in price is shown by a movement along the demand curve from point *A* to point *B*.

Our primary interest here is marginal revenue. We want to show what happens to total revenue when sales increase by one doorknob per day. To do this, we simply compute the total revenue associated with each rate of output. **Marginal revenue** represents the *change* in total revenue that results from a one-unit increase in the rate of output.

marginal revenue: The change in total revenue that results from a one-unit increase in the quantity sold.

The necessary calculations are summarized in Figure 8.2. Row *A* of the table indicates that the total revenue resulting from one sale per day is $13. To increase sales, price must be reduced. Hence row *B* indicates that total revenues rise to only $24 per day when doorknob sales double. The *increase* in total revenues resulting from the added sales is thus $11. The marginal revenue of the second doorknob is therefore $11. This is illustrated in the last column of the table and by point *b* on the marginal revenue curve. Notice that the *MR* of the second doorknob ($11) is *less* than its price ($12). This is because *both* doorknobs are being sold for $12 apiece. In effect, the firm is giving up the opportunity to sell only one doorknob per day at $13 in order to sell a larger quantity at a lower price. In this sense, the firm is sacrificing $1 of potential revenue on the first doorknob in order to increase *total* revenue. Marginal revenue measures the change in total revenue that results.

So long as the demand curve is downward-sloping, *MR* will be less than price. Compare columns 2 and 4 of the table in Figure 8.2. At each rate of output in excess of one doorknob, marginal revenue is less than price. This is also evident in the graph: ***the* MR *curve lies below the demand (price) curve at every point but the first.***

Profit maximization

The most immediate consequence of market power, then, is an extra curve—one for marginal revenue. The rules of profit maximization remain the same, however. Now instead of looking for an intersection of marginal cost and price, we look for the intersection of marginal cost and marginal revenue. This is illustrated in Figure 8.3 by the intersection of the *MR* and *MC* curves (point *d*). Looking down from that intersection, we see that the associated rate of output is four doorknobs per day. Looking upward from that intersection, we see (point *D*) that consumers are willing to pay $10 each for that many doorknobs.

Also illustrated in Figure 8.3 are the total profits of the doorknob monopoly. To compute total profits we can first calculate profit per unit, that is, price minus *average* total cost. In this case, profit per unit is $2. Multiplying profit per unit by the quantity sold (4) gives us total profits of $8 per day, as illustrated by the shaded rectangle.

FIGURE 8.3 PROFIT MAXIMIZATION

The most profitable rate of output is indicated by the intersection of marginal revenue and marginal cost (point *d*). In this case, marginal revenue and marginal cost intersect at an output of four doorknobs per day. Point *D* indicates that consumers will pay $10 per knob for this much output. Total profits equal price ($10) minus average total cost ($8), multiplied by the quantity sold (4).

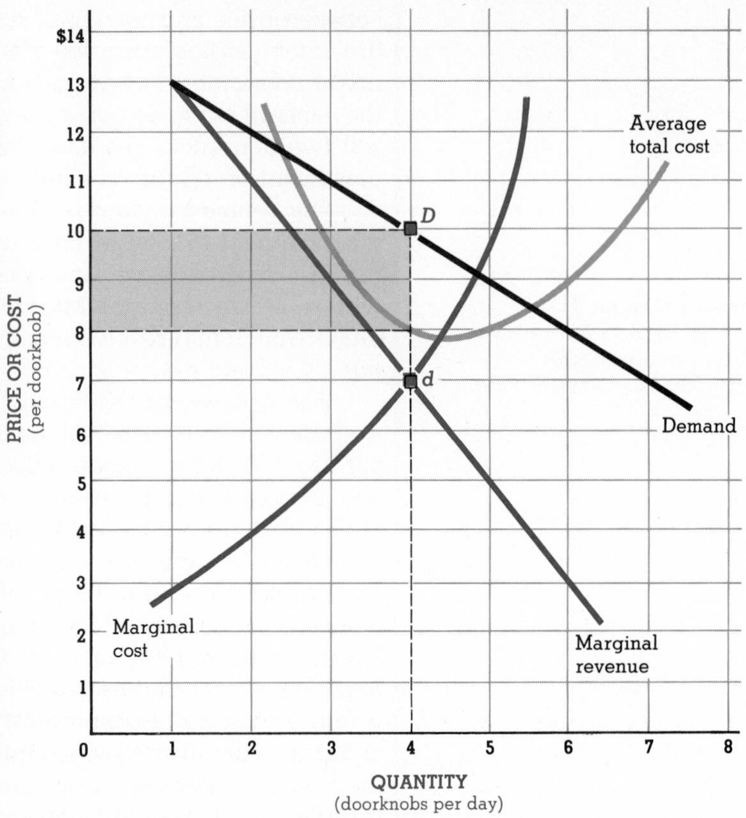

MARKET POWER AT WORK: THE CALCULATOR MARKET REVISITED

barriers to entry: Obstacles that make it difficult or impossible for would-be producers to enter a particular market (e.g., patents).

To develop a keener appreciation for the nature of market power, we can return to the pocket-calculator market of Chapter 7. This time we will make some different assumptions about market structure. In particular, assume that a single firm, Universal Electronics, acquires an exclusive patent on the production of the MOS/LSI chips that run pocket calculators.[1] This one firm is now in a position to deny potential competitors access to the basic ingredient of calculators. The patent thus functions as a significant **barrier to entry,** to be erected or set aside at the will of Universal Electronics.[2]

The management of Universal is familiar enough with the principles of economics (including W. C. Fields's advice about never giving a sucker an even break) to know when it's onto a good thing. It is not about to let every would-be Horatio Alger have a slice of the profit pie. So we shall assume that Universal decides not to sell or give away any rights to its patent or the chips it produces, and thus

[1] In actuality, several firms attempted to obtain such patents, but their applications were rejected by the U.S. Patent Office on the grounds that the chips did not constitute a new technological process.

[2] At least as long as the patent is valid; patents expire at the end of 17 years (although they can usually be extended with product improvements). Other barriers to entry are discussed in Chapter 10.

establishes itself as the sole producer of calculators. That is to say, Universal Electronics sets itself up as a calculator monopoly.

Let us also assume that Universal has a multitude of manufacturing plants, each of which is identical to the typical competitive firm of Chapter 7. This is an unlikely situation, because a monopolist would probably be able to achieve **economies of scale** by closing at least a few plants and consolidating production in larger plants. Universal would maintain a multitude of small plants only if constant returns to scale or actual diseconomies of scale were rampant. This is not likely to be the case. By assuming that multiple plants are maintained, however, we can compare monopoly behavior with competitive behavior on the basis of identical cost structures. In particular, if Universal continues to operate the many plants that once comprised the competitive calculator industry, it will confront the same short-run marginal and average cost curves already encountered in Chapter 7. Later in this chapter we shall relax this assumption of multiplant operations to determine whether, in the long run, a monopolist may actually lower the costs of production below those attained by a competitive industry.

economies of scale: Reductions in average costs that come about through increases in the size (scale) of plant and equipment.

Figure 8.4*a* recreates the marginal costs faced by the typical competitive firm in the early stages of the calculator boom (from Figure 7.2 and Table 7.1). We now assume that this *MC* curve expresses the costs of operating one of Universal's many (identical) plants. Thus the extension of monopoly control is assumed to have no immediate effect on production costs.

The market demand for calculators is also assumed to be unchanged. There is no obvious reason why people should be more or less willing to buy calculators now than they were when the market was competitive. Even if we assumed that consumers were reluctant to purchase the products of a monopolist, Universal could easily camouflage its market position by giving each of its plants a different name. Consumers would then be less likely to know that they were dealing with a monopoly, if that was considered an issue. Thus, Figure 8.4*b* expresses an unchanged demand for calculators.

Our immediate concern is to determine how Universal Electronics, as a monopolist, will respond to these demand and cost curves. Will it produce as many calculators as a competitive industry in the same situation? Can it squeeze out more profits? Will it achieve comparable cost reductions?

The production decision

Like any producer, Universal Electronics will strive to produce its output at the rate that maximizes total profits. But unlike competitive firms, Universal will take explicit account of the fact that an expansion of its output will put pressure on calculator prices and thereby threaten corporate profits.

The implications of Universal's market position for the **production decision** of its many plants can be seen clearly in the new price and marginal revenue curves imposed on each of its manufacturing plants. Universal cannot afford to let each of its plants compete with the others, expanding output and driving down prices. That is the kind of folly reserved for truly competitive firms. Instead,

production decision: The selection of the short-run rate of output (with existing plant and equipment).

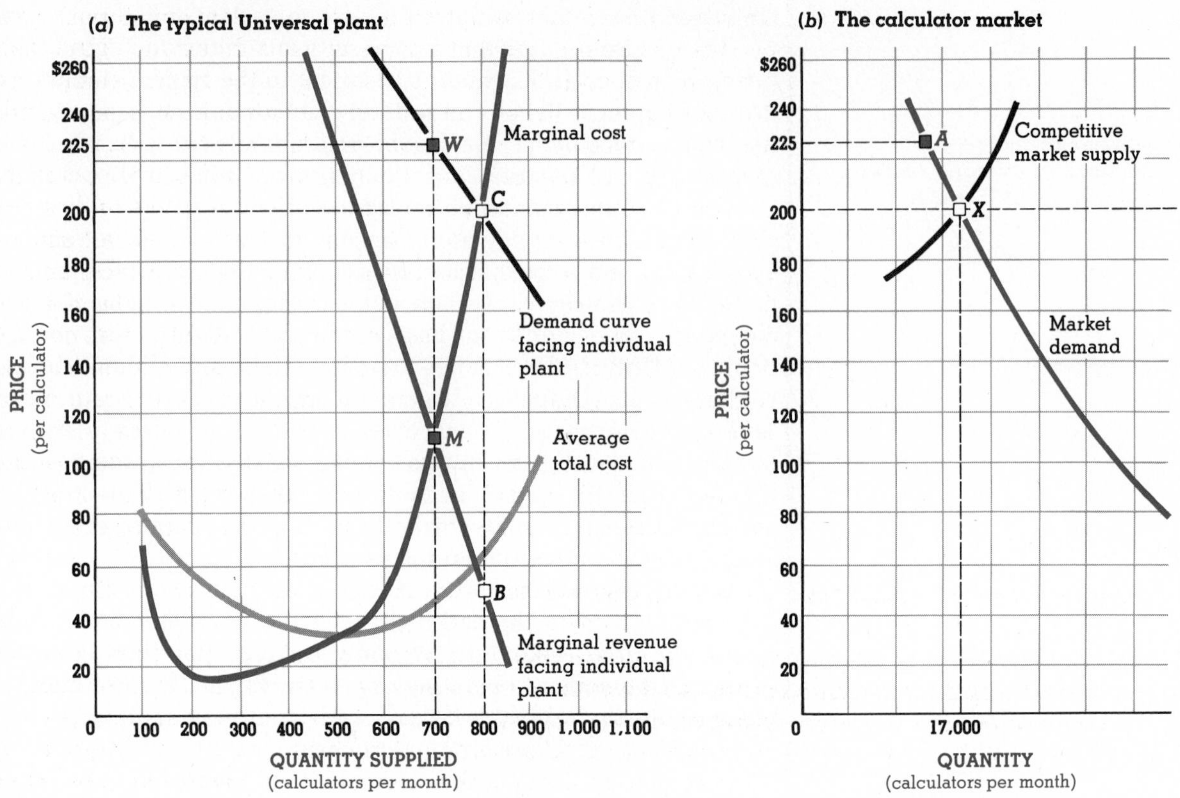

FIGURE 8.4 INITIAL CONDITIONS IN THE MONOPOLIZED CALCULATOR MARKET

We assume that a monopoly firm (Universal Electronics) would confront the same costs (*MC* and *ATC*) and demand as would the competitive industry of Chapter 7. However, the monopolist is not bound by the competitive market price (p_c = $200). Indeed, if each monopoly plant produced where *MC* = $200 (point *C* in part *a*), marginal cost (point *C*) would exceed marginal revenue (point *B*). Instead, the monopolist must contend with downward-sloping demand and marginal revenue curves. He will maximize profits at that rate of output where *MC* = *MR* (point *M* in part *a*). That rate of output can be sold at the monopoly price of $225 (point *W* in part *a*). Part *b* illustrates the market implications of the monopolist's production decision: a reduced quantity is sold at a higher price (point *A*).

Universal will seek to *coordinate* the production decisions of its plants, instructing all plant managers to expand or contract output simultaneously, to achieve the corporate goal of profit maximization.

A simultaneous reduction of output by each Universal plant will lead to a significant reduction in the quantity of calculators supplied to the market. This reduced supply will cause a move up the market demand curve to higher prices. By the same token, an expansion of output by all Universal plants will lead to an increase in the quantity supplied to the market and a slide down the market

FIGURE 8.5 MONOPOLY PROFITS: THE TYPICAL UNIVERSAL PLANT

The profit-maximizing rate of output occurs where the marginal cost and marginal revenue curves intersect (point *M*). The demand curve indicates the price (point *W*) that consumers will pay for this output. Total profit equals price (*W*) minus average total cost (*K*) multiplied by the quantity sold (700). Total profits are represented by the shaded rectangle.

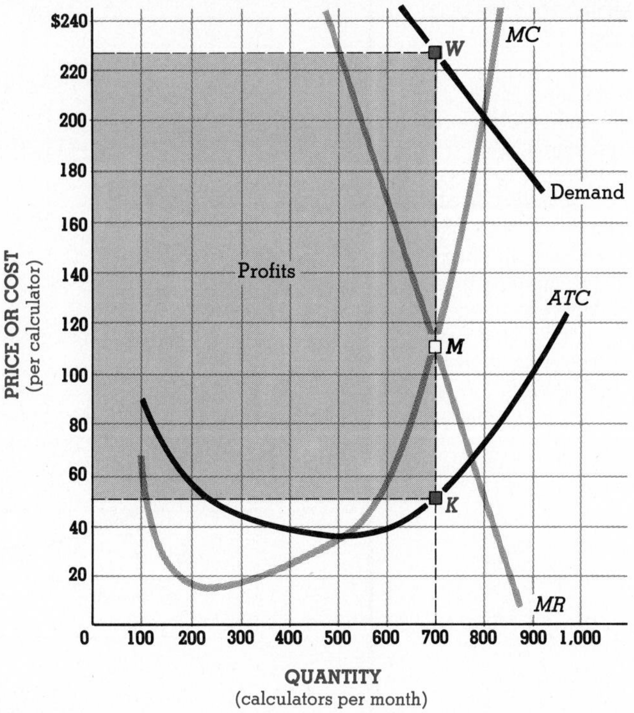

total cost ($50.46) or, in this case, $174.54 per calculator. Multiplying this profit per unit by the number of calculators produced (700 per month), we can see that the typical Universal plant makes a profit of 700 × ($225 − $50.46), or $122,178 a month.[4] This figure may be compared with the monthly profit of $104,680 earned by the typical competitive firm in the early stages of the calculator boom (see Table 7.1.

It is apparent from these profit figures that Universal management has learned its economic principles well. By reducing the output of each plant and raising prices a little, it has managed to enlarge the size of the profit pie, while keeping it all to itself, of course. This can be seen again in Figure 8.6, which is an enlarged illustration of the *market* situations for the calculator industry. The figure translates the economics of our single-plant and competitive-firm comparison into the dimensions of the whole industry. We can see that the competitive industry of Chapter 7 initially produces the quantity q_c and sells it at a price of $200 each. Its profits are denoted by the rectangle formed by the points *R*, *X*, *T*, *U*. The monopolist, on the other hand, produces the smaller quantity q_m and charges a higher price, $225. The monopoly firm's profits are indicated by the larger profit rectangle that is shaded in the figure. We see that ***a monopoly receives larger profits than a comparable competitive industry by reducing the quantity supplied and pushing prices up.*** The larger profits make Universal very happy and make consumers a little sad-

[4] These profit calculations were performed on a pocket calculator.

FIGURE 8.6 MONOPOLY PROFIT: THE ENTIRE COMPANY

Total profits of the monopolist (including all plants) are illustrated by the shaded rectangle. The monopolist's total output (q_m) is determined by the intersection of the (industry) *MR* and *MC* curves. The price of his output is determined by the market demand curve (point *A*). In contrast, a competitive industry would initially produce q_c calculators and sell them at a lower price (*X*) and profit per unit (*X* − *U*).

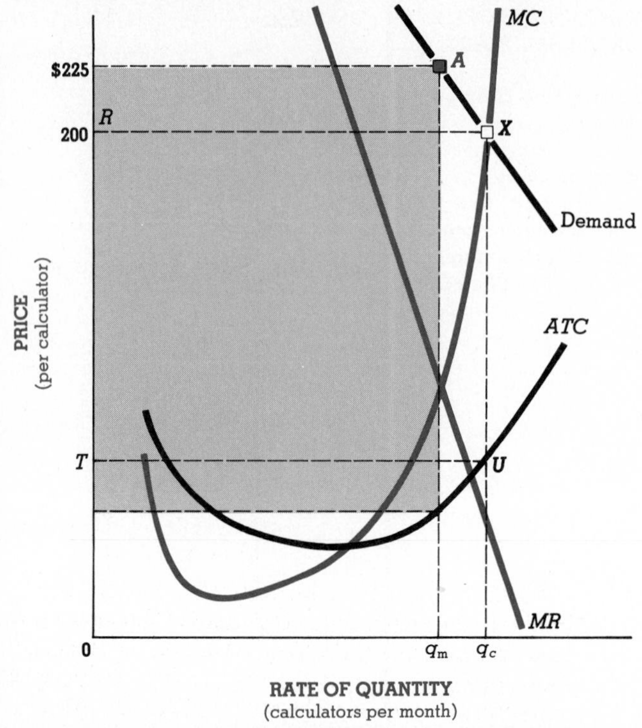

der and wiser. Consumers are now paying more and getting less, in effect, transferring additional income to Universal. Indeed, this kind of income redistribution is the primary objective of those who seek to establish and exploit market power.

Barriers to entry

The higher profits attained by Universal Electronics as a result of its monopoly position are not the end of the story. As we observed earlier, the existence of economic profit tends to bring profit-hungry entrepreneurs swarming like locusts. Indeed, in the competitive calculator industry of Chapter 7, the lure of high profits brought about an enormous expansion of calculator output, a steep decline in calculator prices, and significant technological innovation. What, then, can we expect to happen in the calculator market now that Universal has a monopoly position and is enjoying huge profits?

Remember that Universal is now assumed to have an exclusive patent on MOS/LSI chips and can use this patent as an impassable barrier to entry. Consequently, would-be competitors can swarm around Universal's profits until their wings drop off; Universal is not about to let them in on the spoils. Hence the competitive forces that earlier led to such a dramatic boom in calculator sales are prohibited from going to work. As long as Universal is able to keep the competition out, only the more affluent consumers will be able to use calculators. Universal may discover ways to reduce the costs of production and thus lower prices, but there is no pressure on it to do so, as there was in the competitive situation.

A COMPARATIVE PERSPECTIVE ON MARKET POWER

It may be useful to formulate an interim comparison of the workings of markets under competitive and monopoly conditions. Building on our examination of the electronic calculator market, we may summarize the sequence of events that occurs in each as follows:

Competitive industry	*Monopoly industry*
1. High prices and profits signal consumers' demand for more output.	1. High prices and profits signal consumers' demand for more output.
2. The high profits attract new suppliers.	2. Barriers to entry are erected to exclude potential competition.
3. Production and supplies expand.	3. Production and supplies are cut back.
4. Prices slide down the market demand curve.	4. Prices move up the market demand curve.
5. A new equilibrium is established wherein more of the desired product is produced, its price falls, average costs of production approach their minimum, and economic profits approach zero.	5. A new equilibrium is established wherein less of the desired product is produced, its price rises, average costs are not necessarily at or near a minimum, and economic profits are at a maximum.
6. Price equals marginal cost throughout the process.	6. Price exceeds marginal cost at all times.
7. Throughout the process, there is great pressure to keep ahead of the profit squeeze by reducing costs or improving product quality.	7. There is no squeeze on profits and thus no pressure to reduce costs or improve product quality.

In our discussion, we have assumed that both the competitive industry and the monopolist adjust their production schedules from some given point of departure—a fixed equilibrium in which the price of calculators is $200. In reality, of course, an industry may manifest concentrations of market power *before* such an equilibrium is established. That is to say, the sequence of events we have depicted may be altered (with step 3 occurring first, for example). Nevertheless, the basic distinctions between competitive and monopolistic market behavior are evident.

To the extent that monopolies behave as we have discussed, they alter our output of goods and services in two specific ways. You remember that competitive industries tend, in the long run, to produce at minimum average costs and encourage cost reductions, thereby expanding our production possibilities. No such forces are at work in the monopoly we have discussed here. Hence there is a basic tendency for monopolies to inhibit economic growth.

marginal cost pricing: The offer (supply) of goods at prices equal to their marginal cost.

Another important feature of competitive markets is their tendency toward **marginal cost pricing.** Marginal cost pricing is important to consumers because it permits rational choices among alternative goods and services. In particular, it informs consumers of the true opportunity costs of various goods, thereby allowing them to choose the *mix* of output (GNP) that delivers the most utility with available resources. In our monopoly example, however, consumers end up getting fewer calculators than they would like, while the economy continues to produce other goods that are less desired. Thus the mix of output shifted away from calculators when Universal took over the industry.

In general, we may observe that market power is economically undesirable because it can be used to alter the mix of output, misallocate resources, constrain society's production possibilities, and redistribute income. Not all of these things will necessarily happen, but they may. In addition, the possession of such power can lead to the acquisition of substantial political power, with adverse consequences for other institutions.

The limits to power

Even though market power does permit a producer or supplier to manipulate market outcomes, there is a clear limit to the exercise of power. Even a monopolist cannot get everything he wants. Universal, for example, would really like to sell q_m calculators at a price of $500 each, because that kind of price would bring it even greater profits. Yet, despite its monopoly position, Universal is constrained to sell that quantity of calculators at the much lower price of $225 each. Even monopolists have their little disappointments.

The limitations to a monopolist's exercise of power are evident in Figure 8.6. Universal's attainment of a monopoly position allows it only one prerogative: the ability to alter the quantity of output *supplied* to the market. This is no small prerogative, but it is far from absolute power. Universal, and every other monopolist, must still contend with the market *demand* curve. Note again that the new equilibrium in Figure 8.6 occurs at a point on the *unchanged* demand curve. In effect, a monopolist has the opportunity to pick any point on the market demand curve and designate it as the new market equilibrium. The point it selects will depend on its own perceptions of effort, profit, and risk (in this case point *A*, determined by the intersection of marginal revenue and marginal cost).

The limitation to monopoly power arises from the fact that the monopolist has no direct control over consumer behavior. As a supplier, the monopolist can alter the choices available to consumers, but he cannot force them to pick any combination he desires. Universal could set the price of calculators at $500 each, for example, but it could not compel consumers to purchase the number of calculators it wished to sell at that price. Were the company to set such an exorbitant price, even the more affluent among us would go back to counting on their fingers.

The ultimate constraint on the exercise of market power, then, resides in the market demand curve.[5] The greater the **price elasticity of demand** by consumers, the more a monopolist will be frustrated

price elasticity of demand: The percentage change in quantity demanded divided by the percentage change in price.

[5] Government regulation can also be used to constrain monopolistic behavior, but we are concerned here with market constraints.

PRICE DISCRIMINATION: ANOTHER PREROGATIVE OF POWER

price discrimination: The sale of an identical good at different prices to different consumers by a single seller.

A monopolist has the power not only to raise the market price of a good (by reducing the quantity supplied), but also to charge various prices for the same good. Recall that the market demand curve reflects the combined willingness to buy of many individuals. Some of those individuals are willing to buy the good at prices higher than the market price, just as other individuals will buy only at lower prices. A monopolist may be able to increase total profits by selling each unit of the good separately, at a price each *individual* consumer is willing to pay. This practice is called **price discrimination.**

The airline industry has practiced price discrimination for many years. Basically, there are two distinct groups of travelers, business and nonbusiness travelers. Business executives generally must fly from one city to another on a certain day and at a particular time. They typically must make flight arrangements on short notice and may have no other way to get to their destination. Nonbusiness travelers (for example, people on vacation and students going home during semester break) usually have more flexible schedules. They may plan their trips weeks or months in advance and often have the option of traveling by car, bus, or train.

The different travel needs and opportunities of business and vacation travelers are reflected in their respective demand curves. Business demand for air travel tends to be less price elastic at any given price than the demand of nonbusiness travelers for the same service. Few business executives would stop flying if air fares increased. Higher air fares would, however, discourage air travel by nonbusiness travelers.

What should airlines do in this case? Should they *raise* air fares to take advantage of the relative price inelasticity of business demand, or should they *lower* air fares to attract more nonbusiness travelers?

They should do both. In fact, they have done both. The airlines offer a "full fare" ride, available at any time, and a "discount fare" ride, available only by purchasing one's ticket in advance and agreeing to some restrictions on time of departure. The advance-purchase and other restrictions on discount fares effectively exclude most business travelers, who end up paying full fare. The higher "full" fare does not, however, discourage most nonbusiness travelers, who can fly at a discount. Consequently, the airlines are able to sell essentially identical units of the same good (an airplane ride) at substantially different prices to different customers. Indeed, by experimenting with various discount fares and travel restrictions, airlines can discriminate even more thoroughly among passengers, thereby reaping the highest possible average price for the quantity supplied. The same type of price discrimination is commonly practiced by doctors, lawyers, and new- and used-car dealers. In all of these cases, the seller may "adjust" the price to the income and taste of each individual consumer.

in his attempts to establish both high prices and high volume. Consumers will simply reduce their purchases if price is increased. If, however, consumer demand is highly inelastic—if consumers need or want that product badly and few viable substitutes are available—the monopolist can reap tremendous profit from market power.

PROS AND CONS OF MARKET POWER

Despite the strong and general case to be made against market power, it is conceivable that it could also yield some benefit to society. One of the arguments made for concentrations of market power is that monopolies have greater ability to pursue research and development. Another is that the promise of market power creates a tremendous incentive for invention and innovation and that large companies can produce goods more efficiently than smaller firms. We must pause to reflect, then, on whether and how such benefits flow from market power.

Research and development

The argument that monopolies or other holders of market power are in a position to undertake valuable research and development rests on two facts. First, such firms are sheltered from the constant pressure of competition. Second, they have the resources (monopoly profits) with which to carry out expensive R&D functions. The manager of a perfectly competitive firm, by contrast, has to worry about day-to-day production decisions and profit margins. As a result, he is unable to take the longer view necessary for significant research and development, and could not afford to pursue such a view even if he could see it. Thus, it is contended, market power is desirable because of the research and development opportunities it creates.

The basic problem with the R&D argument is that it says nothing about *incentives*. Although a monopolist has a clear advantage in pursuing research and development activities, he has no clear incentive to do so. He can continue to make substantial profits just by maintaining his market power. Research and development are not necessarily required for profitable survival. In fact, research and development that tend to make his existing plant and equipment technologically obsolete run counter to his vested interest and so may actually be suppressed.[6] In contrast, a perfectly competitive firm cannot continue to make significant profits unless it stays ahead of the competition. This pressure constitutes a significant incentive to discover new products or new and cheaper ways of producing old products.

A very limited but suggestive perspective on the R&D efforts of highly competitive industries can be gained by comparing different industries. The highly competitive semiconductor industry spends less on research and development than the much less competitive automobile industry. But the semiconductor industry is also much

[6] We shall examine this issue further in Chapter 10, especially as it relates to the U.S. auto industry.

smaller. When relative size is considered, the semiconductor industry spends twice as much on R&D as the automobile industry does. In 1981, the semiconductor industry spent 7.1 percent of sales on R&D efforts; the auto industry spent only 3.7 percent.

The commitment of electronics firms to R&D has had dramatic effects on consumer products and prices. Cheap pocket calculators are just one example of the benefits of that competitive R&D. Had technology in the auto industry advanced as rapidly—and had prices fallen as costs were reduced—the 1983 Cadillac would have been priced at less than $100 rather than over $15,000.

It is also important to observe that the R&D efforts that a monopolist does pursue will tend to serve his own interests and probably enhance his market power. The result will be greater redistribution of income and welfare in his direction. Accordingly, if we wish to create research opportunities unattainable by the typical competitive firm, we need not embrace monopolies. A stronger case can be made for directly subsidizing R&D efforts (for instance, through tax credits or research grants) than for indirectly subsidizing them through the mechanism of monopoly profits. In that way, we could achieve our goals of innovation and growth without sacrificing our income-distribution goals.

To some extent, of course, all firms are capable of improving their productive efficiency as they acquire experience. That is to say, firms can develop improved techniques via the process of "learning by doing," a process that may not necessitate any research expenditures. Hence large firms may learn to cut costs as they grow larger. Small firms, too, however, can profit from experience and thus increase their efficiency as well. The critical question is whether experience-based efficiency improvements are intrinsically related to output volume. If so, a case for monopoly can be built on this phenomenon. We shall return to this argument—and potential economies of scale—in a moment.

Entrepreneurial incentives

The second argument proffered in favor of market power is that the potential for monopoly profits acts as a tremendous incentive for entrepreneurial activity. As we observed in Chapter 6, every business is out to make a buck, and it is the quest for profits that keeps industries running. Thus, it is argued, even greater profit prizes will stimulate more entrepreneurial activity. Little Horatio Algers will work harder and longer if they can dream of one day possessing a whole monopoly.

The incentive argument for market power is interesting, but it must be approached cautiously. After all, an innovator can make substantial profits in a competitive market, as it typically takes a considerable amount of time for the competition to catch up. Recall that the early birds still got the worm in the competitive calculator industry of Chapter 7, even though profit margins were later squeezed. Hence it is not evident that the profit incentives available in a competitive industry are at all inadequate.

We must also recall the arguments about research and development efforts. A monopolist has little incentive to pursue R&D and

The new case for monopolists

Monopoly is losing its bad name in court.

For 90 years the antitrust movement has ridden a wave of outrage at the dominance of industries by single companies, a wave that led Congress, in the Sherman Antitrust Act, to make it a federal crime to garner too big a portion of any market. . . . As enunciated by the Supreme Court in 1948, the law was that "monopoly power, whether lawfully or unlawfully acquired, may itself constitute an evil and stand condemned."

But a string of recent court decisions shows that the old outrage at the mere fact of monopoly has cooled, especially if the monopolist champions innovation. . . .

In September, for instance, U.S. District Judge Malcolm M. Lucas in Los Angeles threw out a monopolization charge that a small auto-parts maker brought against W. R. Grace & Co. Even though Grace once had 100% of the market involved—a decorative wheel for sports cars—Lucas ruled that the later entrance of others into the field proved that Grace had no monopoly power.

The most significant indicator of the new attitude toward monopoly came in October, when the Federal Trade Commission dismissed an attempt by its staff to undo Du Pont Co.'s rapid extension of its capacity to produce titanium dioxide, a chemical brightener used in paint and paper. Du Pont's expansion was tied to a cheaper process that the giant chemical manufacturer developed. Explaining the unanimous decision, Commissioner David A. Clanton wrote that "the essence of the competitive process is to induce firms to become more efficient and to pass the benefits of the efficiency along to consumers. That process would be ill-served by using antitrust to block hard, aggressive competition that is solidly based on efficiencies and growth opportunities, even if monopoly is a possible result."

The changed judicial attitude toward monopolies stems from growing concern that innovation is lagging in the U.S. and that clamping down on risk-taking companies will stifle technological experimentation. Du Pont Chairman Irving S. Shapiro made the point repeatedly in lashing out at the FTC titanium dioxide case. In one private suit against IBM, the U.S. Court of Appeals in Denver said that "technical attainments were not intended to be inhibited or penalized" by the Sherman Act. And last year, in overturning much of a monopolization ruling against Eastman Kodak Co., the U.S. Court of Appeals in New York insisted that "innovativeness" is a marketing route open to a monopolist.

Burden of proof

In fact, Boston attorney Thayer Fremont-Smith noted at last month's annual New England Antitrust Conference that so much concern is developing for spurring new products and processes that, he predicts, courts will begin to presume legal any conduct that monopolists could argue would encourage innovation. The burden would then be on plaintiffs to prove that the conduct in question does not benefit the public.

Such a standard would most aid companies in new markets or those in which the technology is changing rapidly. These are the markets where one company is likely to dominate. "The Xerox machine created a short-term monopolist," says Donald I. Baker, former Justice Dept. antitrust chief, "but it has now been caught up with."

Reprinted from the December 15, 1980, issue of *Business Week* by special permission.

may have a vested interest in discouraging such efforts. Furthermore, those who might engage in product innovation or technological improvements for a particular industry may be dissuaded by their inability to penetrate the market. That is to say, the barriers to entry that surround market power may not only keep out potential competitors but also lock out promising ideas. These impediments to entrepreneurship must be balanced against any unique incentives flowing from the promise of market power.

Economies of scale

A third argument for market power is by far the most convincing. The argument is simple. A large firm can produce goods at a lower unit (average) cost than that attainable by a small firm. That is, there are economies of scale. Thus, if we desire to produce goods in the most efficient way—with the least amount of resources per unit of output—we should encourage and maintain large firms. By increasing efficiency through economies of scale, large firms expand society's production possibilities.

Consider once again the comparison we made earlier between Universal Electronics and the competitive calculator industry of

Chapter 7. We explicitly assumed that Universal confronted the same production costs as the competitive industry. We simply converted each typical competitive firm into a separate plant owned and operated by Universal. Thus Universal was not able to produce pocket calculators any more cheaply than the competitive counterpart, and we concerned ourselves only with the different production decisions made by competitive and monopolistic firms.

Over time, however, firms have an opportunity to make different **investment decisions** as well. In this long-run context, there is no compelling reason why we should assume that Universal will construct or maintain a multitude of separate plants. Why wouldn't it instead construct one large plant and centralize its manufacturing operations? One potential advantage to centralization would be an increase in efficiency and an attendant reduction in unit costs.

investment decision: The decision to build, buy, or lease plant and equipment, to start or expand a business.

Even though large firms may be able to achieve greater efficiencies than smaller firms, there is no assurance that they actually will. As we observed in Chapter 5, increasing the size (scale) of a plant may actually reduce operating efficiency (see Figure 5.10). In evaluating the economies of scale for market power, then, we must be careful to recognize that efficiency and size do not necessarily go hand in hand. Some firms and industries may be subject to economies of scale, but others will not be. Therefore, each market-power situation must be examined separately.

NATURAL MONOPOLIES Industries that exhibit economies of scale over the entire range of market output are often referred to as **natural monopolies.** In these cases, one single firm can produce the entire market supply more efficiently than any larger number of (smaller) firms. As the size (scale) of the one firm increases, its minimum average costs continue to fall. These economies of scale give the one large producer a decided advantage over would-be rivals. Hence economies of scale act as a "natural" barrier to entry.

natural monopoly: An industry in which one firm can achieve economies of scale over the entire range of market supply.

Telephone and utility services are classic examples of natural monopoly. A single telephone or utility company can supply the market more efficiently than a large number of competing firms.

Although natural monopolies are economically desirable, they may be abused. We must ask whether and to what extent consumers are reaping some benefit from the efficiency a natural monopoly makes possible. Do consumers end up with lower prices, expanded output, and better service? Or does the monopoly tend to keep much of the benefits for itself, in the form of higher profits, wages, and more comfortable offices? Typically, federal, state, and local governments are responsible for regulating natural monopolies to ensure that the benefits of increased efficiency are shared with consumers.

POLICY IMPLICATIONS: IBM AND AT&T

Monopolies may have adverse effects on prices, output, technological advance, and the distribution of income. For this reason, federal, state, and even local governments have been empowered to prevent or regulate concentrations of market power. The cornerstone of these

Monopoly pays off in the business of sports

When the New York Giants football team opened its 1980 home season against the Washington Redskins on Sept. 13, two sounds were clearly audible at Giants Stadium in New Jersey: the roar of 73,000 fans and the ringing of owner Wellington Mara's cash register. Had the vast stadium been entirely devoid of spectators—who paid roughly $700,000 for the privilege of seeing the Giants lose—Mara's money counter would have slowed somewhat, but the national television contract he shares in equally with other National Football League owners provides about the same amount of revenues as do paid admissions. On that Sunday, for example, the Giants' take for national television rights to the game totaled $620,000.

While football is the blue chip of professional sports, Mara's experiences are not dissimilar from those of many owners of professional baseball, basketball, and hockey teams, for the $700 million-a-year business of professional sports today is a highly charged enterprise capable of producing heavy profits for its owners. . . .

Snowball Effect

Moreover, professional sports is spinning off several times that amount of money to the plethora of businesses that it touches—television, radio, brewing, retailing, and even gambling, where as much as $75 million a year is wagered on sporting events. In fact, given professional sports' monopoly status and self-regulating characteristics, the business can only become bigger. "Americans are affected every day by two cartels—OPEC and professional sports," says one insider. "People just don't realize how powerful the latter one is."

Owning a professional sports franchise is a popular daily double: Huge profits are available both through the ongoing-business side of the venture as well as via the sale of a franchise. Indeed, in becoming America's homegrown cartel, the business of professional sports has undergone a remarkable metamorphosis: Disappearing, for the most part, are the mom-and-pop and family-run operations motivated by civic pride and public relations, replaced instead by savvy broadcasting- and entertainment-sensitive businessmen eager to reap the riches that only a monopoly enterprise can ensure. . . .

Profit is the name of the game. The average National Football League franchise earns a profit of about $1.2 million a year on revenues of $11 million regardless of whether it wins the Super Bowl or winds up the season losing all 16 games. . . .

At the foundation of the boom is an antitrust exemption that has guarded professional sports for many years. Yet the exemption is sketchy at best. Based on a 1922 decision by the Supreme Court, baseball, in fact, is the only sport actually ruled to be exempt. But the same ruling has provided hockey, football, and basketball with de facto exemptions. Sports management bristles at the suggestion that they are getting away with something, however. Baseball Commissioner Bowie Kuhn, for example, has a difficult time admitting that baseball is a business. And Pete Rozelle, commissioner of the NFL, says that football has been scrutinized repeatedly and comes up clean each time. "We've been investigated by the FCC, FTC, Justice Dept., NLRB, and IRS, plus a multitude of state and local bodies," he says. "We are not an unregulated monopoly. We are constantly challenged. What we are is a natural monopoly."

Dividing the Spoils

Natural or not, the monopoly allows baseball to operate with a financial structure under which about 30% of total revenues of about $310 million goes to player salaries, bonuses, and pension costs—which owners constantly cite as the most onerous expense of the business. In football, the figure rises to 40%, and in basketball to some 55%. The remainder, then, is available for other expenses and profits.

"trust-busting" powers is the Sherman Act of 1890, which permits the federal government to penalize and even dismember a corporation that engages in monopoly practices (see the accompanying box). With this act as its principal weapon, the U.S. Department of Justice has blocked attempted mergers and acquisitions, forced changes in price or output behavior, required large companies to sell some of their assets, and even sent corporate executives to jail for "conspiracies in restraint of trade."

Despite all this trust-busting, however, two questions always linger. First, what constitutes a "monopoly" in the real world? Second, what kind of monopoly practices should be prohibited? The

THE LEGAL FOUNDATIONS OF ANTITRUST ACTIONS

The Sherman Act (1890)

The Sherman Act prohibits "conspiracies in restraint of trade," including mergers, contracts, or acquisitions that threaten to monopolize an industry. Firms that violate the Sherman Act are subject to fines of up to $1 million, and their executives may be subject to imprisonment. In addition, consumers who are damaged—for example, via high prices—by a "conspiracy in restraint of trade" may recover treble damages.

The Clayton Act (1914)

The Clayton Act of 1914 was passed to outlaw specific antitrust behavior not covered by the Sherman Act. The principal aim of the act was to prevent the development of monopolies. To this end, the Clayton Act prohibited price discrimination, exclusive dealing agreements, certain types of mergers, and interlocking boards of directors among competing firms.

The Federal Trade Commission Act (1914)

The increased antitrust responsibilities of the federal government created the need for an agency that could study industry structures and behavior so as to identify anticompetitive practices. The Federal Trade Commission was created for this purpose in 1914.

first question relates to the *structure* of markets, the second to their *behavior*. Both questions were the center of attention in two historic cases—against IBM and AT&T. The two cases were ended on the same day (January 8, 1982) but for very different reasons. Together they illustrate the central concerns of public antitrust policy.

AT&T: extending a natural monopoly

The American Telephone and Telegraph (AT&T) Corporation has long held a virtual monopoly on domestic phone service. As recently as 1981, AT&T provided 96 percent of all long-distance phone service and over 80 percent of local phone service. AT&T had total revenues of roughly $60 billion in 1981 (equal to 2 percent of GNP!) and profits of roughly $7 billion.

The dominant position of AT&T in the telephone industry was widely viewed as inevitable. As we noted earlier, telephone service tends to be a *natural monopoly*. One large firm can supply the market more cheaply than a multitude of small, competitive firms. The source of this natural monopoly lies in the economies of scale associated with transmission networks. Once the networks are in place, the marginal costs of increasing output are negligible. In recognition of this situation, the government permitted development of a monopolistic structure in the telephone industry.

While permitting monopoly structure, the government has regulated AT&T's behavior. In particular, state utility commissions and the Federal Communications Commission (FCC) have regulated the price and quantity of phone service while setting a limit on AT&T's

AT&T Divestiture

□ AT&T must divest itself of the local telephone services of its 23 Bell System operating companies.

□ Western Electric, Bell Laboratories and the long-distance division of AT&T will be retained by AT&T. All intrastate long-distance service will be turned over to AT&T by the local companies.

□ AT&T no longer will be barred from offering unregulated nontelephone service, thereby opening the way for the corporation to enter the computer processing and information service business.

□ Local telephone companies divested by AT&T will be required to share their facilities with all long-distance telephone companies on the same terms.

□ Local companies will be barred from discriminating against AT&T competitors in buying equipment and planning new facilities.

□ AT&T shareholders will retain stock in AT&T and will be issued proportionate values of shares in the local exchange companies.

□ The Justice Department will have visiting rights at the local operating companies to interview employes and review the books.

The Washington Post, Washington, D.C., January 8, 1982, p. 1.

monopoly profits. The objective of this regulation was to ensure that consumers reaped the advantages of a natural monopoly.

What got AT&T into trouble was its attempt to extend its monopoly over its "natural" limits. AT&T established a subsidiary, Western Electric, to manufacture phones and other equipment that can be connected to the transmission network. Because it controlled all telephone service, AT&T could effectively dictate whose phones would be used. By establishing Western Electric, AT&T was essentially proclaiming a monopoly in phone manufacturing and sales, as well as in telephone service. Unfortunately, there are no inherent economies of scale in phones themselves, so AT&T's move could not be defended as a "natural" extension of telephone service. Instead, the creation of Western Electric looked like a mechanism for transferring monopoly profits out of a regulated market (phone service) into an unregulated one (phone manufacture).

As the electronics revolution progressed, other firms wanted to produce and sell not only telephones but also more sophisticated services, including satellite transmissions. To do so, however, they had to have access to AT&T transmission networks (including the users' phones). AT&T resisted all such attempts, arguing that the hooking up of non-AT&T equipment would harm the transmission network. When pressed by lawsuits or regulatory actions to permit such hookups, AT&T required costly and cumbersome connection devices.

As a result of such behavior, the U.S. Department of Justice filed suit against AT&T in 1978, arguing that AT&T and "their co-conspirators have used their positions of dominance in long-distance transmission, equipment manufacturing, and local franchise monopolies, and the leverage derived therefrom, to suppress this new competition and to maintain and enhance their monopoly power."[7]

[7] This was the third major antitrust case filed by the Justice Department against AT&T; the second one was settled by consent decree in 1956. That consent decree required AT&T to stay out of all new unregulated markets.

As the federal suit against AT&T made its way through the courts, some of AT&T's competitors filed antitrust suits of their own. Two of these suits, by MCI, Inc., and Litton Industries, ended with huge fines against AT&T. The Federal Trade Commission and the U.S. Congress also increased the pace of their own investigations. By 1982 it was fairly clear that AT&T would not be able to defend itself successfully against the Justice Department's charges. Accordingly, AT&T agreed—without admitting to monopoly practices—to give up its monopoly position in local phone service. Local phone service will be provided instead by new and independent local telephone-service companies ("Baby Bells"), all of which will remain under government regulation. The rest of AT&T ("Ma Bell"), including Western Electric and other subsidiaries (see news clipping), will keep out of local telephone service and thus be free to compete on an equal and unregulated basis in all other segments of the communications industry. In this way, the public can reap the advantages of enhanced competition in markets not subject to natural monopoly while continuing to enjoy the advantages of a natural monopoly in transmission networks. The Justice Department gave AT&T six months to devise a divestiture plan that would satisfy these objectives and another year to implement the plan after court approval.

IBM: big is not necessarily bad

The federal government's antitrust case against IBM was very different. Like AT&T, IBM dominated its industry. At the time the suit was filed in 1969, IBM was producing roughly 70 percent of all computers. The Justice Department argued that there was no "natural" basis for such dominance and thus that the structure of the computer market was anticompetitive.

It was further asserted that IBM's *behavior* stifled increased competition. Three specific practices were cited. First, it was alleged that IBM intimidated customers who wanted to connect non-IBM equipment (e.g., disc drives, add-on memories) to IBM systems (a charge like the one leveled at AT&T). Second, IBM was said to discourage prospective buyers of competing computers by "pre-announcing" new IBM models. By hinting that a newer and better IBM computer was just around the corner, IBM could persuade customers to withhold orders from competitors. Finally, IBM was alleged to engage in aggressive price cutting whenever competition increased.

The IBM suit dragged on for 13 years. During that time, over 66 *million* pages of documents were filed. Both the structure of the industry and IBM's behavior were contested. With respect to structure, IBM claimed the computer market was larger than the government alleged and growing enormously. Although IBM was dominant in one segment of the industry (large main-frame computers), it was a relatively small force in other segments (see Figure 8.7). Furthermore, IBM had to contend with aggressive competitors even in the one market segment it dominated. Hence, IBM argued, the charge of monopoly was baseless.

IBM also denied engaging in monopolistic behavior. IBM

FIGURE 8.7 IBM's SHARE OF THE MARKET
(percentage of dollar value of units installed)

The computer market includes several different kinds of products. IBM has always dominated the market for large, general-purpose computers. In the production of small computers, however, IBM confronts intense competition.

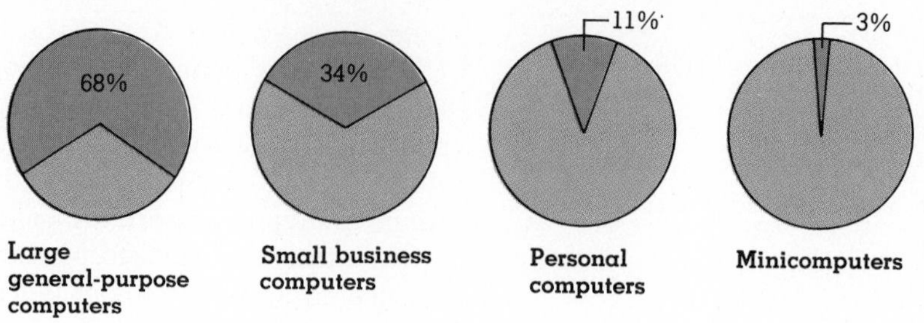

pointed out that it had no barriers to entry (unlike AT&T) and therefore had no power to create or maintain a monopoly. On the contrary, competitors were continually swarming like flies into the computer industry. All IBM was "guilty" of, it argued, was reducing prices, improving its products, and competing aggressively. In the process, consumers had benefited enormously from dramatic technological improvements in computer design and service and markedly lower prices.

On January 8, 1982, the Justice Department accepted these arguments and dropped the antitrust suit against IBM. In explaining his decision, Assistant Attorney General William Baxter said: "What we learned today is that a company that is large and has a large market share should be allowed to compete aggressively. Period." With those remarks, the government acknowledged that monopoly powers can either harm (AT&T) or benefit (IBM) consumers, depending on how that power is obtained and used.

SUMMARY

- Market power is the ability to influence significantly the market price of goods and services. In product markets, such power usually resides on the supply side of the market, as consumers are too numerous and too independent to have any individual influence on the shape of the market demand curve.
- The extreme case of market power is monopoly, a situation in which only one firm produces the entire supply of a particular product, and thus has an immediate impact on the quantity supplied to the market and the market price.
- The distinguishing feature of any firm with market power is the fact that the demand curve it faces is downward-sloping. In the case of monopoly, the demand curve facing the firm and the market demand curve are identical.
- The downward-sloping demand curve facing a monopolist creates a divergence between marginal revenue and price. To sell larger quantities of output, the monopolist must lower product prices. A firm without market power has no such problem.

- Like other producers, a monopolist will produce at the rate of output at which marginal revenue equals marginal cost. Because marginal revenue is always less than price for a noncompetitive firm, the monopolist will produce less output than will a competitive industry confronting the same market demand and cost opportunities. That reduced rate of output will be sold at higher prices, in accordance with the (downward-sloping) market demand curve.
- A monopoly will attain a higher level of profit than a competitive industry because of its ability to equate industry (its own) marginal revenues and costs. By contrast, a competitive industry ends up equating marginal costs and price, because its individual firms have no control over the market supply curve.
- Because the higher profits attained by a monopoly will attract envious entrepreneurs, barriers to entry are needed to prohibit other firms from expanding market supplies. Patents are one such barrier to entry.
- The principal arguments for market power focus on (1) the alleged ability of large firms to pursue long-term research and development, (2) the incentives implicit in the chance to attain market power, and (3) the efficiency that larger firms may attain. The first two arguments are weakened by the fact that competitive firms are under much greater pressure to innovate and can stay ahead of the profit game if they do so.
- A natural monopoly exists when one firm can produce the output of the entire industry more efficiently than can a number of smaller firms. This advantage is attained from economies of scale. Large firms are not necessarily more efficient, however, because either constant returns to scale or diseconomies of scale may prevail.

Terms to remember

Define the following terms:

market power
monopoly
profit-maximization rule
marginal revenue
barriers to entry
economies of scale
production decision
average total cost
marginal cost pricing
price elasticity of demand
price discrimination
investment decision
natural monopoly

Questions for discussion

1. The objective in the game of Monopoly is to get all the property and then raise the rents. Can this power be explained with market supply and demand curves?
2. Is single ownership of a whole industry necessary to exercise monopoly power? How might an industry with many firms achieve the same result? Can you think of any examples?
3. In addition to higher profits, what other benefits accrue to a firm with market power?
4. Why don't monopolists try to establish "the highest price possible," as many people allege? What would happen to sales? to profits?
5. Do consumers have any market power?

Problem

The following table summarizes the sales and cost situation confronting a monopolist:

Price (per unit)	Quantity demanded (per week)	Total revenue (per week)	Marginal revenue	Total cost	Marginal cost	Average total cost
$40.00	20			$510		
40.50	19			466		
41.00	18			424		
41.50	17			384		
42.00	16			346		
42.50	15			310		
43.00	14			276		
43.50	13			244		
44.00	12	$528.00	$38.50	214	$28.00	$17.83
44.50	11			186		
45.00	10			160		

Use the figures provided in the table to:

(*a*) Complete the table (start from the bottom).
(*b*) Graph the demand, *MR*, *MC*, and *ATC* curves.
(*c*) Calculate the maximum total profits obtainable.

CHAPTER 9

IMPERFECT COMPETITION

Although it is convenient to think of the economy as composed of the powerful and the powerless, market realities do not always provide such clear distinctions. There are very few perfectly competitive markets in the world, and few monopolies. But market power is an important phenomenon, nonetheless. It's just that it is typically shared by several firms rather than monopolized by one. In the automobile industry, for example, General Motors, Ford, and Chrysler share tremendous market power, even though none qualifies as a pure monopolist. The same kind of power is shared by Coca-Cola, Pepsi, and Dr Pepper in the soft-drink market, and by Kellogg, General Mills, and General Foods in the breakfast-cereals market.

These kinds of situations, which fall between the extremes of perfect competition and pure monopoly, fall into the category of "imperfect competition." They contain some elements of competitive rivalry, but also exhibit vestiges of monopoly. Indeed, in many cases, imperfect competitors behave much like a monopoly, generally restricting output, charging higher prices, and reaping greater profits than firms in a competitive market. But behavior in imperfectly competitive markets is more complicated than in a monopoly, because it involves a number of decision makers (firms) rather than only one.

In this chapter we shall focus on two major forms of imperfect competition: *oligopoly* and *monopolistic competition*. We shall examine the nature of decision making in each of these market structures and the likely impacts on prices, production, and profits. In Chapter 10 we shall look at the actual behavior of some familiar firms that possess market power.

DEGREES OF POWER

Some individuals and firms have virtually no influence over the prices of the products they buy and sell, and thus no market power. They are constrained to reacting to market prices and are unable to change them by withholding production or purchases. Other individuals and firms do have some influence over prices, and thus some degree of market power. The degree of power they possess, however, varies tremendously. As we saw in Chapter 8, AT&T has been the sole supplier of telephone services in most urban areas of the United States. As a result, it has had tremendous market power. The corner grocery store, on the other hand, must compete with other stores and has less control over prices. But even the corner grocery is not completely powerless. If it is the only grocery within walking distance—or the only one open on Sunday—it, too, may exert *some* influence on prices and product flows. The amount of power it possesses depends on the proximity and convenience of alternative retail outlets.

The same kind of gradations in power can be seen in thousands of products and market situations. Take the case of Coca-Cola. The Coca-Cola Company has an exclusive license to use that particular brand name. As a result, it is the sole supplier of Coca-Cola, and can exert considerable influence on the price of that product. Coca-Cola's market power is diluted considerably, however, by the availability and price of other thirst-quenching alternatives. If Coca-Cola's price rises too far, more and more people will switch to Pepsi, cold beer, or, as a last resort, water. Consequently, the ability of the Coca-Cola Company to alter prices—its market power—is far from absolute.

Market structures

In accordance with the many gradations of market power, each market situation is separately defined. The case of absolute powerlessness is referred to as *perfect competition*. ***Perfect competition is perfect in the sense that no buyer or seller of a particular product has any direct influence on the market price of that good.*** Of course, the interactions of all buyers and sellers together still determine the market price. Each buyer and seller functions independently, however, and with no discernible effect on price determination. Were any single buyer or seller to change his or her behavior, the market price would remain the same. Such a situation, seen in the competitive calculator illustration of Chapter 7, exists when I sell my two shares of IBM stock or when Farmer Evans decides not to harvest his thirty acres of wheat. In each case, the dimensions of individual action are so small in relation to the size of the market that the action has no impact.

At the other extreme of market power is *perfect monopoly*. A perfect monopoly exists when only one individual or firm is the exclusive supplier of a particular product. In such a case, any change in the quantity supplied to the market by the monopolist is immediately reflected in the price and quantity sold of that good. Our illustration of Universal Electronics exemplifies such a firm. The amount of power a "perfect" monopoly can wield still depends on the availability of substitute goods, however. Even as perfect a monopoly as AT&T must take into consideration the prices of alternative communications media: Western Union, communications satellites, and the mail.

Between the two extremes of perfect competition and perfect monopoly lies most of the real world, which is imperfectly competitive. ***In imperfect competition, individual firms have some power in a particular product market.*** Two forms of imperfect competition are particularly noteworthy: oligopoly and monopolistic competition.

oligopoly: A market in which a few firms produce all or most of the market supply of a particular good or service.

monopolistic competition: A market in which many firms produce similar goods or services, but each maintains some independent control of its own price.

Oligopoly is a situation in which only a few firms have a great deal of power in a product market. An oligopoly may exist because only a few firms produce a particular product or because a few firms account for most, though not all, of a product's output. In either case, firms in an oligopoly are highly *interdependent,* because of their very small number. Changes in the price or output of one oligopolist immediately affect the other oligopolists.

A more limited degree of market power is possessed by firms in **monopolistic competition.** In this case, there are many firms supplying the market, not just a few. Because of the larger number of sell-

MARKET STRUCTURES

- PERFECT COMPETITION A market comprised of many powerless firms. The production decisions of any single firm have no effect on other firms or the market price of the product it sells. Individual farmers are classic examples of perfect competitors.
- MONOPOLISTIC COMPETITION A situation in which many firms sell similar products, each of which is perceived by consumers as being in some way unique. Although each firm has some influence over the price at which its own output (brand) is sold, the production decisions of any single firm do not directly affect the sales or selling price of other firms (brands). Examples include fast-food chains (McDonald's, Ponderosa, Burger King), supermarkets, and most apparel manufacturers.
- OLIGOPOLY A market in which a few firms control such a large share of total industry output that they can influence market price. In *pure (perfect) oligopoly,* all firms produce an identical good (for example, cement, steel rods, paper clips). In a *differentiated (imperfect) oligopoly,* each firm's product has a unique identity (for example, cigarettes, breakfast cereals), although all are basically the same. In either kind of oligopoly, the production decisions of any single firm affect all other firms and the market price of the product sold.
- DUOPOLY A market in which two firms produce the entire market supply.
- MONOPOLY A market with only one supplier, who therefore controls the quantity supplied to the market and its price.

ers, the individual firms are less interdependent than oligopolistic firms. An individual firm can alter its own price or output without directly affecting the other firms in the industry. At the same time, each firm has its own identity (brand name and image) in the market, and can therefore increase the price of its own output without losing most of its customers to its rivals.

Determinants of market power

The amount of market power that exists in any given situation depends on several factors, including:

- □ Number of producers
- □ Size of each firm
- □ Barriers to entry
- □ Availability of substitute goods

The most obvious determinant of power is the number of producers or sellers. When only one or a few producers or suppliers exist, market power is automatically conferred. In addition to the number of producers, however, the size of each firm is also important. One large producer competing with 17 small ones may possess more market power than he would if he had to compete with only six relatively large firms. Other firms of comparable size at least have some ability to withstand pressures and threats to change prices or product flows.

A third and critical determinant of market power is the extent of barriers to entry for potential competitors. A highly successful monopoly or oligopoly will tend to arouse the envy of other profit maximizers. They will seek to enter that particular product market in order to share in the spoils. Should they succeed, the power of the former monopolist or oligopolists would be reduced. Accordingly, the ease of entry into an industry is an important dimension of the ability to influence prices and product flow for any substantial period of time. In Chapter 8 we observed how a patent can be used to block entry. In Chapter 10 we shall examine other barriers to entry employed by powerful firms.

Finally, we may note that a fourth factor defining the dimensions of market power is the availability of substitute products. If a monopolist or other power baron sets the price of his product too high, consumers may decide to switch to other products. Thus the price of Coors is kept in check by the price of Coke, and the price of sirloin steak is restrained by the price of chicken and pork. By the same token, a lack of available substitute products may confer very great market power, as reflected in a very low price elasticity of demand for the product in question. Those who possess market power frequently attempt to extend and reinforce it by using advertising to create the impression that their product has no substitutes. If 10 million beer drinkers refuse to quench their thirst with anything but Coors beer, then the Adolph Coors Company will possess considerable market power. For loyal Coors drinkers, it simply doesn't matter how many other beer producers exist or how large they are. The same is true for Tide detergent, Maxwell House coffee, Coca-Cola,

FIGURE 9.1 INITIAL CONDITIONS IN THE CALCULATOR MARKET

As in Chapters 7 and 8, we assume that the initial equilibrium in the calculator market occurs at a price of $200 and a quantity of 17,000 calculators per month. How will an oligopoly alter these outcomes?

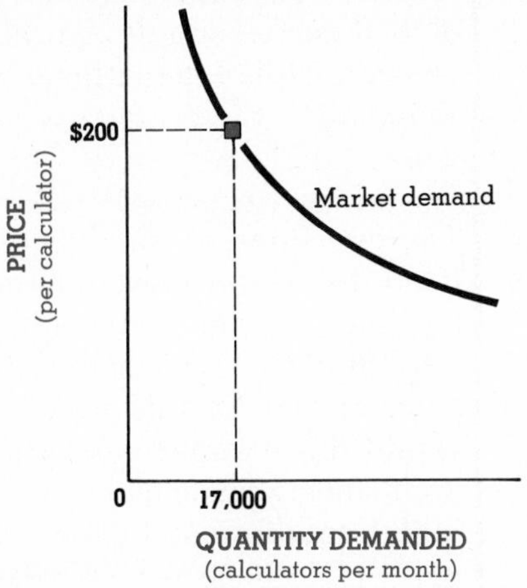

and Zig-Zag cigarette papers. As long as each consumer identifies with and purchases only one brand, it doesn't matter how many other firms produce basically identical products; each consumer will have effectively imposed a monopoly on himself or herself.

OLIGOPOLY BEHAVIOR

We can illustrate the behavior of a typical oligopoly by assuming a different market structure for the electronic calculator market. In Chapter 7 we observed that in the absence of barriers to entry the pocket calculator market was highly competitive. In Chapter 8 we created an impassable barrier to entry (a patent on the electronic brain of the calculator) that transformed the calculator industry into a monopoly of Universal Electronics. Now we shall transform the industry again, this time assuming that three separate firms (Universal, World, and International) all possess patent rights. The patent rights permit each firm to produce and sell all the calculators it desires and to exclude all other would-be producers from the market.

The initial equilibrium

As before, we shall assume that the initial conditions in the calculator market are represented by a market price of $200 and market sales of 17,000 calculators per month, as illustrated in Figure 9.1.

market share: The percentage of total market output produced by a single firm.

We shall also assume that the **market share** of each producer is accurately depicted in Table 9.1. Thus Universal Electronics is as-

TABLE 9.1 INITIAL MARKET SHARES OF CALCULATOR PRODUCERS

The market share of a firm is the percentage of total market output it produces. These are hypothetical market shares of three fictional oligopolists.

Producer	*Output (calculators per month)*	*Market share (percent)*
Universal Electronics	8,000	47.1
World Calculators	5,000	29.4
International Semiconductor	4,000	23.5
Total industry output	17,000	100.0

sumed to be producing 8,000 calculators per month, or 47.1 percent of total market supply. World Calculators has a market share of 29.4 percent, while International Semiconductor has only a 23.5 percent share.

The battle for market shares

The first thing to note about the calculator oligopoly is that it is likely to exhibit great internal tension. Neither World Calculators nor International Semiconductor is really happy playing second or third fiddle to Universal Electronics. Each company would like to be Number One in this market. On the other hand, Universal, too, would like a larger market share, particularly in view of the huge profits being made on calculators. As we observed in Chapter 7, the initial equilibrium in the calculator industry yielded an *average* profit of \$130.85 per calculator, and total *industry* profits of \$2.2 million per month (17,000 × \$130.85). Hence Universal would be very happy to take over the market shares of its fellow oligopolists, thereby increasing its own profits.

The problem here is how to gain a larger market share. In a truly competitive market, a single producer could expand production at will, with no discernible impact on market supply. But ***in an oligopoly, increased sales on the part of one firm will be noticed immediately by the other firms.***

How do we know that increased sales will be noticed so quickly? Because increased sales by one firm will have to take place either at the existing market price (\$200) or at a lower price. Either of these two events will ring an alarm at the corporate headquarters of the other two firms.

INCREASED SALES AT THE PREVAILING MARKET PRICE Consider first the possibility of Universal Electronics' increasing its sales at the going price of \$200 per calculator. We know from the demand curve of Figure 9.1 that consumers are *willing to buy* only 17,000 calculators per month at that price. Hence any increase in calculator sales by Universal must be immediately reflected in *lower* sales by World or International. That is to say, increases in the market share of one oligopolist necessarily reduce the shares of the remaining oligopolists. If Universal were to increase its sales from 8,000 to 10,000 calculators per month, the combined monthly sales of World and International would have to fall from 9,000 to 7,000 (see Table 9.1). The **quantity demanded** at \$200 per calculator remains 17,000 calculators per month (see Figure 9.1).

quantity demanded: The amount of a product a consumer is willing and able to buy at a specific price in a given time period (*ceteris paribus*).

This interaction between the market shares of the three oligopolists assures us that Universal's sales success will be noticed. Moreover, it won't be necessary for World Calculators or International Semiconductor to engage in industrial espionage to acquire the necessary information about Universal. These firms can quickly figure out what Universal is doing simply by looking at their own (declining) sales figures.

INCREASED SALES AT REDUCED PRICES Universal could pursue a different strategy, of course, and attempt to increase its sales by lowering

law of demand: The quantity of a good demanded in a given time period increases as its price falls (*ceteris paribus*).

the price of its calculators. Following the **law of demand,** reduced prices would expand total market sales, as demonstrated by the downward-sloping market demand curve of Figure 9.1. Hence price reductions could enable Universal to increase its sales without directly reducing the sales of either World or International.

But this outcome is most unlikely. If Universal lowered its calculator price from $200 to, say, $190, all consumers would flock to Universal calculators and the sales of World and International would plummet. After all, we have always assumed that consumers are rational enough to want to pay the lowest possible price for any particular good. It is unlikely that consumers would continue to pay $200 for a World or International machine when they could get basically the same calculator from Universal for only $190. If there were no difference, either perceived or real, in the calculators of the three firms, a *pure* oligopoly would exist. In that case, Universal would capture the *entire* market if it lowered its price below that of its rivals. More often, consumers perceive differences in the products of individual oligopolists, creating a *differentiated* oligopoly. In this case, Universal would gain many but not all customers if it reduced its price for its calculators.[1] In either case, there simply isn't any way that Universal can increase its sales at reduced prices without causing all the alarms to go off at World and International.

Retaliation

So what if all the alarms go off at World Calculators and International Semiconductor? As long as Universal Electronics is able to enlarge its share of the market and take in increased profits, why should it care if World and International find out? Indeed, Universal may even get some additional satisfaction out of the fact that World and International are upset by its marketing success.

Universal does have something to worry about, though. World and International may not be content to stand by and watch their market shares and profits diminish. On the contrary, World and International are likely to take some action of their own once they discover what is going on.

There are two things World and International can do once they decide to act. In the first case, where Universal is expanding its market share at prevailing prices ($200), World and International can retaliate by:

- Stepping up their own marketing efforts
- Cutting prices on their calculators

product differentiation: Features that make one product appear different from competing products in the same market.

To step up their marketing efforts, World and International might increase their advertising expenditures, repackage their calculators, put more sales representatives on the street, or sponsor a college homecoming week. All such efforts at **product differentiation** are designed to make World and International calculators appear different and superior to the one produced by Universal Electronics. If successful, such marketing efforts will increase the sales and market shares of World and International, or at least stop Universal from

[1] In this example, we are assuming a differentiated oligopoly.

Marketing: Cold Cures Spread Like Flu as Companies Fight for Sales

Everyone knows the standard prescription for a bad cold: Take two aspirins and go to bed. That's still as good a remedy as most, but it hasn't deterred drug companies from bringing out product after product to stop sniffles, quiet coughs and dry runny noses.

Competition this year is fiercer than ever: More than a dozen new cold cures have hit pharmacy and supermarket shelves, with more on the way. The prize is a piece of the $1.2 billion cold-remedy market, among the largest in the nonprescription drug industry. The problem: Unit sales of cold medicines have been growing only about 3% a year.

"Because the market isn't very dynamic, brands succeed at the expense of others," says Emma W. Hill, a securities analyst with Wertheim & Co. "Companies therefore must maintain a steady flow of new products, enter new segments of the market, do anything to increase their shelf space."

Coming out with new products isn't easy. The ingredients available and levels that can be used are strictly limited by the Food and Drug Administration. A product's success often depends on a company's inventiveness in using these limited ingredients and on its marketing ability. . . .

The company to beat in this business is Richardson-Vicks, which markets 20 different lozenges, syrups, ointments, nasal sprays and other products for the treatment of coughs and colds. It claims to have 30% of the entire market "because we know the cold-remedy consumer and we gear our messages to get a response," according to Ronald A. Ahrens, president of the company's health-care division. "Frankly, our products are no better or worse than anybody else's."

—Michael Waldholz

grabbing a larger share for itself. In either case, Universal's initial sales initiative will fail and may end up requiring increased outlays for advertising or other marketing efforts to combat the efforts of World and International.

An even quicker way to stop Universal from enlarging its market share is for World and International to lower the price of their calculators. Such price reductions will destroy Universal's hopes of increasing its market share. In fact, this is the other side of a story we have already told. If the price of World and International calculators drops to, say, $190, it is preposterous to assume that Universal will be able to expand its market share at a price of $200. Instead, we assume that Universal's market share will drop substantially if it maintains a price of $200 per calculator after World and International drop their prices to $190 per calculator. Hence the threat to Universal's market-share grab is that the other two oligopolists will retaliate by reducing their prices. Should they carry out this threat, Universal would be forced to cut calculator prices, too, or accept a greatly reduced market share.

The same kind of threat exists in the second case, where we assumed that Universal Electronics expands its sales by initiating a price reduction. As we noted earlier, World and International are not going to just sit by and applaud Universal's marketing success. They will have to respond with price cuts of their own. Hence ***an attempt by one oligopolist to increase its market share by cutting prices will lead to a general reduction in the market price*** of calculators. The three oligopolists will end up using price reductions as weapons in the battle for market shares, the kind of behavior normally associated with competitive firms. Should this behavior continue, not only will oligopoly become less fun, but it will also become less profitable as prices slide down the market demand curve (Figure 9.2).

FIGURE 9.2 RIVALRY FOR MARKET SHARES THREATENS AN OLIGOPOLY

If oligopolists start cutting prices to capture larger market shares, they will be behaving much like truly competitive firms. The result will be a slide down the market demand curve to lower prices, increased output, and smaller profits. In this case, the market price and quantity would move from point *F* to point *G* if rival oligopolists cut prices to gain market shares.

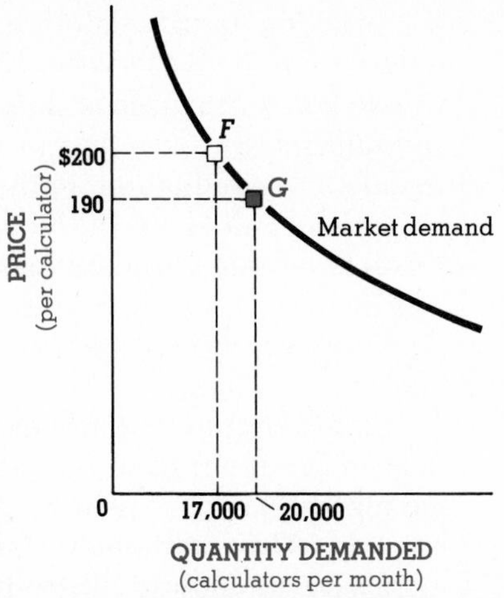

THE KINKED DEMAND CURVE

The close interdependence of oligopolists—and the limitations it imposes on individual price and output decisions—is the principal moral of this story about Universal Electronics, World Calculators, and International Semiconductor. We can summarize this story with the aid of the kinked demand curve in Figure 9.3.

Recall that at the beginning of this oligopoly story Universal Electronics had a market share of 47.1 percent and was selling 8,000 calculators per month at a price of $200 each. This output is represented by point *A* in Figure 9.3. The rest of the demand curve illustrates what would happen to Universal's sales if it changed its selling price. What we have to figure out is why this particular demand curve has such a strange, "kinked" shape.

FIGURE 9.3 THE KINKED DEMAND CURVE CONFRONTING AN OLIGOPOLIST

The shape of the demand curve facing an oligopolist depends on the responses of its rivals to its price and output decisions. If rival oligopolists match price reductions but not price increases, the demand curve will be kinked. Initially, the oligopolist is at point *A*. If he raises his price to $210 and his rivals do not raise their prices, he will be driven to point *B*. If his rivals match a price reduction (to $190), the oligopolist will end up at point *N*.

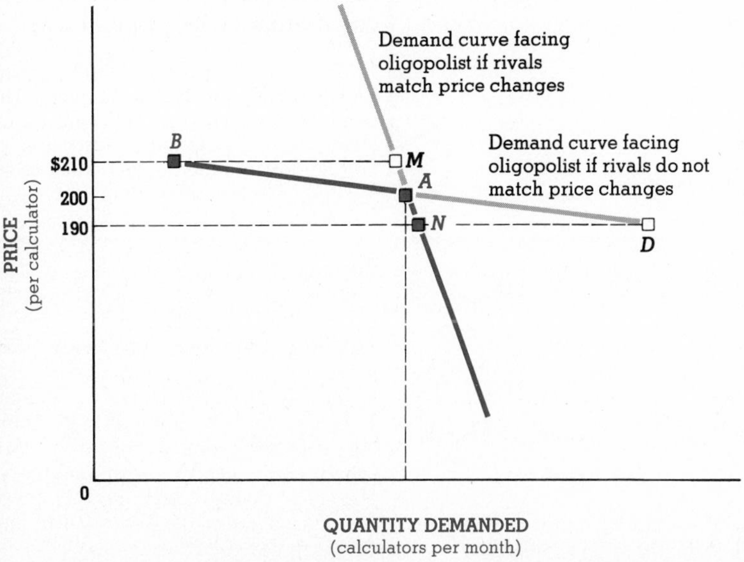

Price reductions

Consider first what would happen to Universal's sales if it lowered the price of its calculators to $190. In general, we expect a price reduction to increase sales. However, ***the degree to which sales increase when the price is reduced depends on the response of rival oligopolists.*** Suppose World and International did not match Universal's price reduction. In this case, Universal would have the only low-priced calculator in the market. Consumers would flock to Universal and sales would increase dramatically, to point *D*. But point *D* is little more than a dream, as we have observed. World and International are sure to cut their prices to $190, too, in order to maintain their market shares. As a consequence, Universal's sales will expand to point *N* (not much), rather than to point *D*. Universal's increased sales at point *N* reflect the fact that the total quantity demanded in the market has risen as the market price has fallen to $190 (see Figure 9.2). Thus, although Universal's *market share* may not have increased, its monthly sales have.

The section of the demand curve that runs from point *A* to point *D* is unlikely to exist in an oligopolistic market. Instead, ***we expect rival oligopolists to match any price reductions*** that Universal initiates, forcing Universal to accept the demand curve that runs from point *A* through point *N*. The accompanying news clipping indicates the consequences of such rivalry.

Price increases

What about price increases? How will World and International respond if Universal raises the price of its calculators to $210?

Recall that the demand for calculators is assumed to be price elastic in the neighborhood of $200 and that all calculators are basically similar. Accordingly, if Universal raises its price and neither World nor International follows suit, Universal will be out there alone with a higher price and reduced sales. Hence ***rival oligopolists may not match price increases.*** In terms of Figure 9.3, a price increase that is not matched by rival oligopolists will drive Universal from point *A* to point *B*. At point *B*, Universal is selling very few calculators at its price of $210 each.[2]

[2] Notice again that we are assuming that Universal is able to sell some calculators at a higher price (point *B*) than its rivals'. The kinked demand curve applies only to differentiated oligopolies. As we shall discuss later, such differentiation may result from slight product variations, advertising, customer habits, location, friendly service, or any number of other factors. Most oligopolies exhibit some differentiation.

Candy War

Snickers Jacks Up Price by 5¢; Hershey Vows to Hold the Line

There's a candy bar war going on between Hershey and Snickers.

The fight is over prices: Snickers, the No. 1-selling candy bar in the country, went to 30 cents last month, up a nickel, while Hershey says it is "holding the line on candy bar prices."

Trouble is, some retailers decided to raise prices for all of their candies—including those of the two other big candy manufacturers, Hershey Foods Corp. and Nabisco Brands, makers of Baby Ruth and Butterfinger. . . .

Hershey was so upset by all this that it launched an advertising campaign to tell consumers that it wasn't responsible for the higher prices that some stores now charge. "We want you to know that Hershey is not raising the price of any of its candy bars," said the ad that appeared in 70 publications around the country in recent days.

—Molly Sinclair

The Washington Post, Washington, D.C., October 17, 1981.

Is this a likely outcome? Suffice it to say that World Calculators and International Semiconductor would not be unhappy about enlarging their own market shares. Therefore they are not likely to come to Universal's rescue with price increases.

Anything is possible, however, and World and International might match Universal's price increase. In this case, the *market* price would rise to $210 and the total quantity of calculators demanded would diminish. Under such circumstances Universal's sales would diminish, too, in accordance with its (constant) share of a smaller market. This would lead us to point *M* in Figure 9.3.

Gamesmanship

We may draw two conclusions from Figure 9.3:

- The shape of the demand curve facing an oligopolist depends on the responses of its rivals to a change in the price of its own output.
- That demand curve will be kinked if rival oligopolists match price reductions but not price increases.

An interesting thing about oligopolies is the potential they create for gamesmanship. The appropriateness of an oligopolist's pricing decision depends on the expected response of one's rivals. But this response is normally not known in advance; it must be guessed. For example, Universal *would* want to lower its prices *if* it thought its rivals would not retaliate with similar price cuts. It probably won't lower its prices, however, since it fears retaliation. Universal might be tempted to experiment a bit, though. It might offer a few large customers a discount, hoping World and International would not notice or would not react to modest reductions of their market shares.

The potential cost of such experimentation is high, however. Selective price cutting may lead to an all-out price war over market shares. In this sense, oligopolistic behavior is not unlike the kind of

United Airlines to Raise Fares on Many Flights

Price War Called 'Ruinous'; American and TWA Plan to Match Most Increases

United Airlines said it will increase transcontinental and midcontinental fares Nov. 1 in an effort to stop a costly fare war with its competitors. Some rivals said they would match at least some of United's increases.

The move comes only nine days after the UAL Inc. subsidiary slashed fares to defend its market share on coast-to-coast routes. United's major transcontinental competition comes from American Airlines, Continental Airlines and Trans World Airlines.

"We didn't start it. We want to stop it," a United spokesman in Chicago said, referring to the fare war that has sent prices tumbling in recent weeks. "It's ruinous for everyone," he said. . . .

In Dallas, a spokesman for American Airlines welcomed the fare increases and said American would match the higher fare on its transcontinental flights, starting Nov. 1.

"United's action is an encouraging sign for the industry," the spokesman said. "It supports the concept of restoring these fares to a more reasonable level." But he said American is still "studying the question" of whether to raise its fares, as United did, for midcontinental flights.

In Los Angeles, Continental Airlines' senior director for pricing, Sandy Rederer, said, "Our reaction is that United's action seems very reasonable.

"What we expect to do is wait to see what TWA and American do," he said, "If they match that, I assume we would adjust our fares as well."

Cold War games that the world's great powers play. Neither side is certain of the enemy's next move but knows it could bring total destruction. As a consequence, the United States and the Soviet Union are continually probing each other's responses but are quick to retreat from the brink whenever all-out retaliation is imminent. Oligopolists play the same kind of game on a much smaller scale, using price discounts and advertising rather than nuclear warheads as their principal weapons. The reward they receive for coexistence is the oligopoly profits that they continue to share. This reward, together with the threat of mutual destruction, leads oligopolists to limit their price rivalry.

Sticky prices

The kinked demand curve confronting the typical oligopolist leads to an even stranger-looking marginal revenue curve. ***The kinked demand curve is really a composite of two separate demand curves*** (Figure 9.4). One curve is predicated on the assumption that rival oligopolists do not respond to price increases (d_1). The other curve is predicated on the assumption that rivals do respond to price cuts (d_2). Each of these curves has its own marginal revenue curve, as illustrated in Figure 9.4. The demand curve d_1, for example, has **marginal revenue** curve mr_1, while demand curve d_2 has marginal revenue curve mr_2.

marginal revenue: The change in total revenue that results from a one-unit increase in the quantity sold.

To the extent that oligopolists behave in accordance with the kinked demand curve, each firm confronts the possibility of starting down the demand curve d_1, and switching to d_2 at point *A*. Hence from point S to point *A* the curve mr_1 depicts the relevant marginal revenues. At point *A* (the quantity of 8,000 calculators per month), however, we suddenly switch demand curves (to d_2). Hence we must seek out a new marginal revenue curve corresponding to d_2. To the right of point *A*, the marginal revenue curve mr_2 is operational.

FIGURE 9.4 AN OLIGOPOLIST'S MARGINAL REVENUE CURVE

A kinked demand curve incorporates portions of two different demand curves (d_1 and d_2). Hence a kinked demand curve also has portions of two distinct marginal revenue curves (mr_1 and mr_2). Below the kink in the demand curve (point *A*) a gap exists between the two marginal revenue curves.

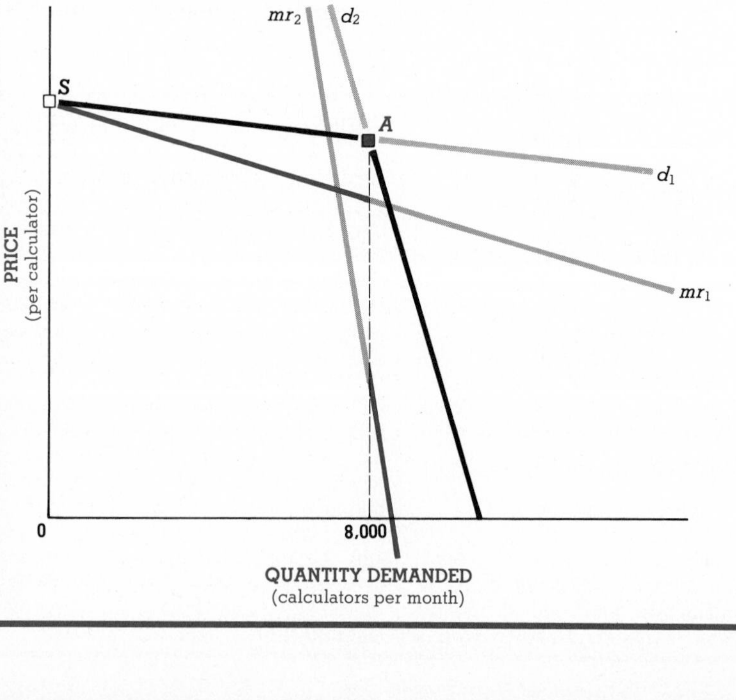

FIGURE 9.5 THE MARGINAL REVENUE GAP

The kinked demand curve confronting an oligopolist creates a gap in his marginal revenue curve. As a consequence, a change in price or cost may not have any impact on the production decision. In this case, higher (MC_2) or lower (MC_3) marginal costs do not change the profit-maximizing rate of output.

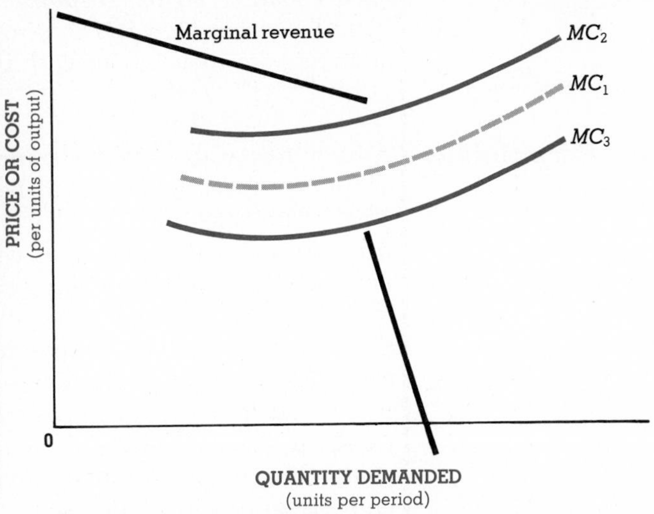

The oligopolist's marginal revenue curve thus contains two distinct segments. Figure 9.4 shows that *there is a gap in an oligopolist's marginal revenue curve, a gap that occurs just below the kink in the demand curve.* This gap turns out to be an important explanation of an oligopolist's behavior.

profit-maximization rule: Produce at that rate of output where marginal revenue equals marginal cost.

Recall that *all* producers **maximize profits** by producing at the rate of output at which marginal revenue equals marginal cost. As a consequence, most producers alter their production decision when the costs of production change. In general, a reduction in production costs (a downward shift of the marginal cost curve) will lead to an increase in the rate of output. An upward shift of the marginal cost curve will lead to a cutback in production.

These expectations are not always fulfilled in an oligopoly, however. Look at the marginal cost curves in Figure 9.5. If the marginal cost curve passes through the gap in the marginal revenue curve, ***modest shifts of the cost curve will have no impact on the production decision of an oligopolist.*** That is to say, an oligopolist need not reduce his rate of output when costs rise somewhat, or increase his rate of output when costs fall. As a consequence, an oligopolist's output does not fluctuate as much as either a competitive firm's or a profit-maximizing monopolist's. An oligopolist has a cost cushion around his production decision. Among other things, this cushion allows him to maintain a given price for longer periods and to incur higher marketing costs (such as advertising) if the need arises. In other words, the kinked demand curve results in "sticky" prices.

OLIGOPOLY VS. COMPETITION

Our examination of the demand and marginal revenue curves confronting an oligopolist reveals the close interdependence of rival oligopolists. Specifically, we have seen that ***an individual oligopolist***

must consider rivals' responses before altering his own rate of output or price. Now it is time to take a broader view of an oligopoly and compare its behavior with that of a competitive market.

Price rigidity

A basic lesson to be learned from the kinked demand curve is that *oligopoly prices will tend to be "sticky"*; they will not fluctuate much. This stickiness arises from the fact that individual oligopolists cannot lower their prices without inviting retaliation and cannot raise them without risking sales losses.

The price behavior of an oligopoly stands in vivid contrast to that of a firm in a competitive market. A competitive market typically has thousands of individual producers. The survival of any individual firm depends on its ability to hold down costs. To increase profits, individual firms must reduce costs. Consequently, competitive firms are under constant pressure to lower their costs (and prices), knowing that some other firm is going to do so eventually. Competitive firms are not restrained by fears of "retaliation"; on the contrary, they are constantly being pushed toward price reductions.

The tendency toward price rigidity in oligopolistic markets is reinforced by the nature of the marginal revenue curves facing individual oligopolists. The gap we saw in oligopoly marginal revenue curves allows oligopolists to withstand modest changes in costs. No such flexibility exists in a competitive industry. Should a competitive firm experience a cost reduction, it will expand production to the point where marginal cost again matches marginal revenue (price). As other firms react in the same way, an increased market supply will drive prices downward. By the same token, a competitive firm cannot afford to absorb cost increases; it will have to cut back output until marginal cost again matches marginal revenue (price). As all firms respond similarly to cost increases, the market supply will diminish and prices will rise. Thus market prices will tend to rise and fall with costs in a competitive market, but may not respond to cost changes in an oligopoly.

The greater size of the typical oligopolist also permits it to withstand changes in costs or demand. An oligopolist with profits in excess of $100 million a year is obviously in a better position to ignore small changes in costs or sales than the competitive firm with typical profits of less than $100,000.

Price and output

Although the kinked demand curve suggests that oligopoly prices will be relatively rigid, it says nothing about the way the market price is established. In our calculator example, we assumed an initial market price of $200, then demonstrated why that price was unlikely to change. But what establishes the (sticky) market price?

The objective of an oligopoly is to establish a price that maximizes total industry profits. A distinguishing feature of oligopolies is that they tend to be more successful in attaining this objective. Clearly, both competitive industries and oligopolies desire to make as much profit as consumer demand and production costs will allow. But competitive industries experience relentless pressure on profits as individual firms expand output, reduce costs, and lower prices. To maximize *industry* profits, competitive firms would have to band together and agree to restrict output and raise prices. If they did, though, the industry would no longer be competitive.

The potential for maximizing *industry* profits is clearly greater in an oligopoly, because very few firms are involved, and each is aware of its dependence on the behavior of the others. In fact, ***an oligopoly will want to behave like a monopoly, choosing a rate of industry output that maximizes total industry profit.*** If successful, the oligopolists will have more total profit to split up among themselves.

Coordination

The problem oligopolists confront is how to coordinate their production decisions. Recall that each firm desires as large a market share as possible, at prevailing prices. But encroachments on the market shares of rival oligopolists threaten to bring retaliation, price reductions, and reduced industry profits. Hence the oligopolists have a mutual interest in coordinating their production decisions so that:

- Industry profits are maximized.
- Each oligopolistic firm is content with its market share.

To bring about this happy outcome, the rival oligopolists could discuss their common interests and attempt to iron out an agreement on both issues. Identifying the profit-maximizing rate of industry output would be comparatively simple, as Figure 9.6 illustrates. The difficult issue would be the division of this output among the oligopolists, that is, the assignment of market shares. The outcome would depend on the relative strength of each firm and its negotiating skills.

Unfortunately for oligopolists, the kind of explicit discussions

FIGURE 9.6 MAXIMIZING OLIGOPOLY PROFITS

An oligopoly strives to behave like a monopoly, maximizing total industry profits. Industry profits are maximized at the rate of output at which the industry's marginal cost equals its marginal revenue (point *J*). In a monopoly, this profit all goes to one firm; in an oligopoly, it must be shared among a few firms.

In an oligopoly, the *MC* and *ATC* curves represent the combined production capabilities of several firms, rather than only one. The industry *MC* curve is derived by horizontally summing the *MC* curves of the individual firms.

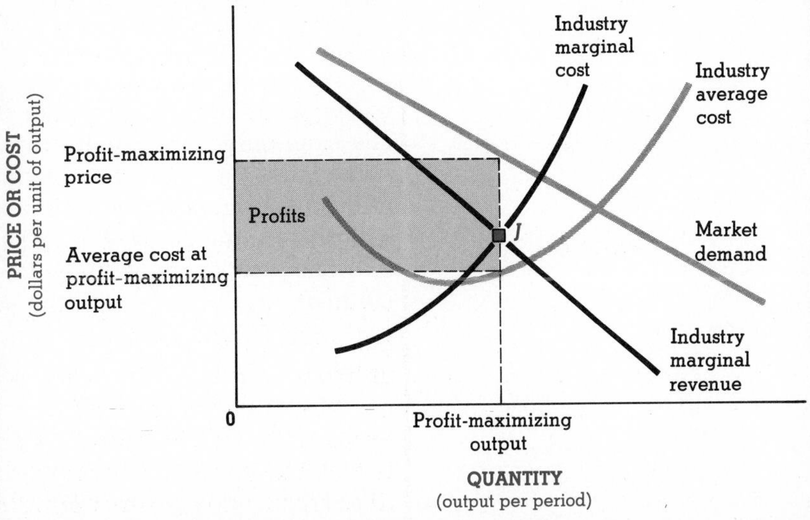

collusion: Explicit agreements among producers to limit competition among them.

price leadership: An oligopolistic pricing pattern that allows one firm to establish the (market) price for all firms in the industry.

or **collusion** we have described are illegal. According to the Sherman Act of 1890, all such discussions are "conspiracies in restraint of trade" and thus illegal. Corporations found to have colluded in this way are subject to stiff financial penalties and their executives may be sent to jail.

Because collusion is illegal (although not extinct, as we shall see in Chapter 10), oligopolistic firms must reach a consensus on total output and market shares in less explicit ways. One firm may "signal" its desire to reduce total output and raise prices by publicly announcing that it is studying the need for a price increase. This announcement gives rival oligopolists the opportunity to assess the implications of a move up the market demand curve. Should they agree that such a move is desirable, they may themselves announce similar "studies" of potential price increases, or simply increase their prices. This process, by which one oligopolistic firm "leads" its rivals to a change in price, is referred to as **price leadership.**

The firm that first expresses concern about potential price increases may be called the *price leader,* although leadership may also be retained by the firm that casts the decisive vote on the size of the ultimate price increase. Typically, the firm with the greatest market share will have the most influence on the oligopoly's final price decision, even if it is not the first one to announce a price increase. Hence price leadership is a matter less of who raises prices first than of whose decision has the greatest influence on the oligopoly.

Some form of industry-wide coordination—be it explicit price fixing, price leadership, or informal experimentation—is required to establish the profit-maximizing price and rate of output for the industry. Once this price is established, the dynamics of the kinked demand curve ensure that it will be maintained—for a while, anyway. When the market demand or the cost curve shifts substantially, or when the rival oligopolists become dissatisfied with their respective market shares, a new price will be established.

MONOPOLISTIC COMPETITION

However harmoniously an oligopoly may function, its existence is always threatened. On the inside, there is always the worry that one of the oligopolists will become dissatisfied with its profits or market share, and take action that ultimately reduces total industry profits. From the outside, there is the persistent threat that high profits will attract new firms into the industry. If the barriers to entry are not formidable enough, sooner or later the oligopoly will be destroyed.

The demise of an oligopoly does not necessarily lead to perfect competition, however. On the contrary, it is at least as likely that each of the many firms that enter the industry will establish its own identity ("brand image"), giving it some modest amount of market power. In this case, the industry will manifest *monopolistic competition.* Note that product differentiation ("brand image") exists in either a differentiated oligopoly or monopolistic competition. The difference here is the number of producers; there are many firms in monopolistic competition, but only a few in oligopoly.

OPEC Agrees to Cut Output

VIENNA, March 20—Fighting to regain control over the world oil market, ministers of the Organization of Petroleum Exporting Countries today agreed to set their first formal production limits, establishing an overall ceiling of 18 million barrels a day while pledging to hold firm on prices.

In a separate action, Saudi Arabia, OPEC's dominant producer, announced an additional unilateral cut in its production of a half-million barrels per day, fixing its daily production for April at 7 million barrels. It was the Arab kingdom's third reduction in five months.

The combined result of today's moves at the conclusion of a two-day emergency conference represents a production drop to 17.5 million barrels a day. That level is about 1.5 million barrels less than what the cartel says it supplied during the first quarter of the year and slightly more than half the 32 million barrels OPEC pumped daily at the peak of its production just three years ago.

OPEC members also called on major oil exporters outside the organization, such as Britain, Norway and Mexico, to reduce their production rather than cut prices further. OPEC's president, United Arab Emirates Oil Minister Mana Said Oteiba, declared the organization's determination to protect prices, saying, "We are ready to go to 10 million barrels a day if necessary." . . .

The oil ministers heralded their decision as a demonstration that OPEC, facing what many regard as the cartel's most serious challenge in its 20-year history, can coordinate production and pricing among its 13 members to save itself from panic and disintegration.

Significantly, today's action marked the first time that organization members formally agreed to honor production quotas. Two previous attempts at drafting OPEC production schedules, in 1978 and 1981, were cast as informal gentlemen's agreements.

To help ensure that OPEC's members hold to their new commitment, the conference decided to establish a special committee, made up of ministers from the United Arab Emirates, Venezuela, Indonesia and Algeria, to monitor compliance. While no sanctions for violators were spelled out, the establishment of a self-policing group was seen as reinforcing the image of OPEC as a traditional cartel actively managing production.

—Bradley Graham

The Washington Post, Washington, D.C., March 21, 1982.

How will a monopolistically competitive industry behave? Will each firm act like an oligopolist? Or will the many firms that comprise the industry behave more competitively?

Independent production decisions

Once many firms enter an industry, each firm's market share will decline. Ultimately, there may be 25 firms in the industry, each with a market share of close to 4 percent. ***In monopolistic competition, modest changes in the output or price of any single firm will have no perceptible influence on the sales of any other firm.*** This relative independence results from the fact that the effects of any one firm's behavior will be spread over 24 other firms (rather than only two or three other firms, as in an oligopoly).

The relative independence of monopolistic competitors means that they don't have to worry about retaliatory responses to every price or output change. As a result, they confront more traditional demand curves, with no kinks. The kink in the oligopolist's curve resulted from the likelihood that rival oligopolists would match any price reduction (to preserve market shares), but not a price increase (to increase their shares). In monopolistic competition, the market shares of rival firms are not perceptibly altered by one firm's price changes.

Product differentiation

A monopolistically competitive firm is distinguished from a purely competitive firm by its downward-sloping demand curve. Individual firms in a perfectly competitive market confront horizontal demand curves because consumers view their respective products as

Those Little Alligators on Clothes Sell Big, Breed Imitators, Impostors and Detractors

What is an inch and a quarter long, three-fourths of an inch high, and oozes snob appeal? Clues: It usually is green or blue; it can be found on practically any piece of apparel except underwear; it is expensive, and it has been imitated endlessly.

The answer, as every proper preppy knows, is the Izod-Lacoste alligator.

In a world smitten by designer emblems, the alligator is everywhere. Mothers send their toddlers to the sandbox, their older children to school and their husbands to the club in alligator wear. President Reagan wore an alligator shirt to a news conference. . . .

Inevitable Reaction

The alligator movement is so advanced that it has spawned an anti-alligator movement. The anti-Izod crown struts around in anti-alligator T-shirts or the Croc O' Shirt, which features an upside-down, dead crocodile. . . .

Going Hog Wild

Then there is the pig shirt, and accessories, offered by Hog Wild!, a Boston retailer. "It's a good way of poking fun at all the fancy designer emblems," says David Mercer, the owner. The original pig shirt has done so well that Hog Wild! introduced another line—the Pork Avenue Collection, featuring designs by Calvin Swine. It is, he adds, the height of hog couture.

Actually, it took quite a while for the alligator to catch on big in the U.S. The emblem dates back to 1926, when French tennis star Rene Lacoste, nicknamed "le Crocodile," wore a polo shirt with a crocodile on it. He began marketing it commercially in 1933 in France.

In 1951, the Izod division of David Crystal Inc. apparel company started importing Lacoste shirts and selling them here, and later it got the license to sell Lacoste-label clothing in the U.S., Canada and the Caribbean. Somewhere along the way, Americans got the idea that the crocodile was really an alligator, and the wrong name stuck. . . .

Then came General Mills Inc., which bought David Crystal in 1969 and began selling alligator wear like breakfast cereal. A boys' line of alligator clothing was added around 1975, a girls' line in 1978 and a line for infants and toddlers in 1979. "We take them from cradle to grave in Izod-Lacoste," says Jane Evans, an executive vice president of General Mills. In 1969, alligator apparel sales were about $15 million; sales now are some $450 million a year. . . .

Still, one shouldn't get carried away with discretion. After all, letting others know that one can afford the alligator is a reason why many people buy it. At $25, the alligator polo shirt sells for $5 to $10 more than most of its rivals (and other alligator apparel is priced accordingly). "It gives you status in the eyes of others. People wouldn't admit it, including myself, but that carries a lot of weight," says Gilbert Perry, a 34-year-old St. Paul, Minn., stockbroker.

"A lot of people aren't confident of their own taste," says William Hull, a Chicago marketing consultant. "With the alligator shirt, you've got some assurance you're not a boob."

Not all alligators are *the* alligator. General Mills attorneys are kept busy fending off impostors. Outright counterfeiters copy Izod-Lacoste clothing stitch for stitch, right down to the label. Other companies have put their own version of the alligator on stationery, wrapping paper, napkins, coasters, shoelaces, checkbook covers, laundry bags, even ice buckets.

Saurian Claims

General Mills, which claims that its license gives it the rights to the trademark of all saurian reptiles (anything resembling a lizard), dashes off nasty notes to infringers. Most back off, and those that don't generally are sued. . . .

—Lawrence Ingrassia

interchangeable ("homogeneous"). As a result, an attempt by one firm to raise its price will drive its customers to other firms. In monopolistic competition, each firm has a distinct identity. Its output is perceived by consumers as being somewhat different from the output of all other firms in the industry. As a consequence, a monopolistically competitive firm can raise its own price without losing all of its customers to rival firms.

In the electronic calculator industry, product differentiation can be (and has been) achieved in a variety of ways. The particular mix of functions performed on any calculator can be varied, as can its appearance ("packaging"). Effective advertising can convince consumers that one calculator is "smarter" than another, even if all calculators have identical "brains." Also, a single firm may differentiate itself by providing faster or more courteous repair service. If

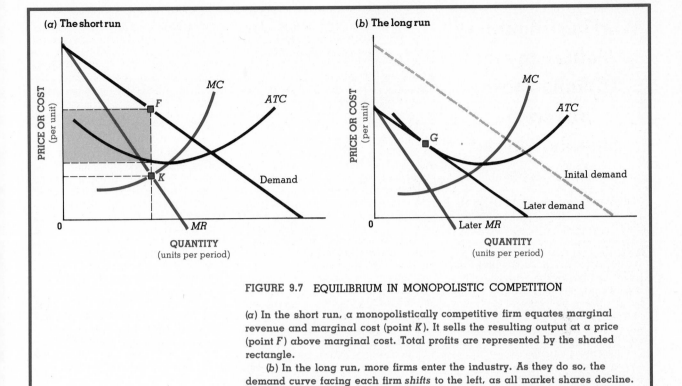

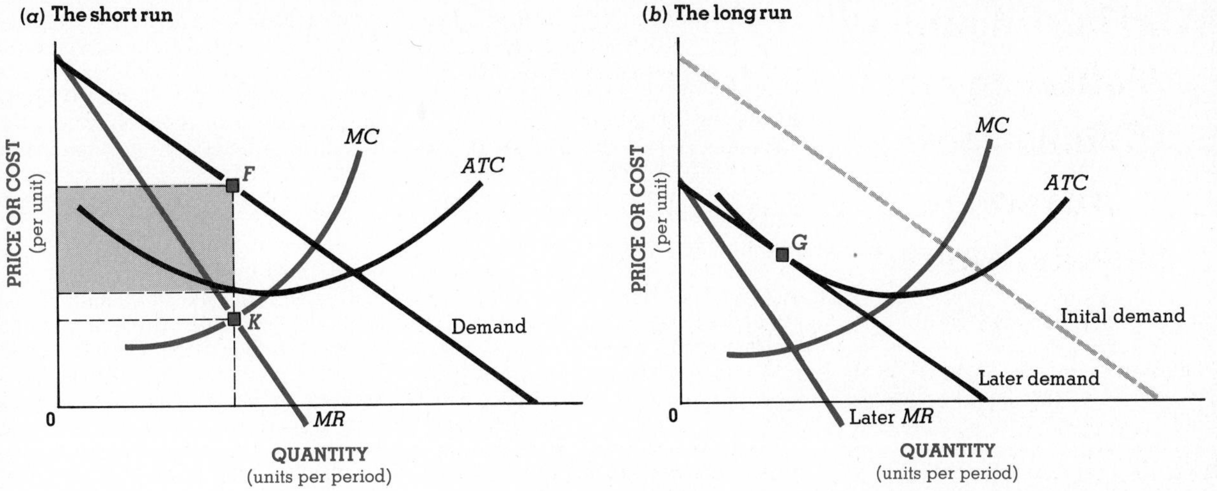

FIGURE 9.7 EQUILIBRIUM IN MONOPOLISTIC COMPETITION

(a) In the short run, a monopolistically competitive firm equates marginal revenue and marginal cost (point *K*). It sells the resulting output at a price (point *F*) above marginal cost. Total profits are represented by the shaded rectangle.

(b) In the long run, more firms enter the industry. As they do so, the demand curve facing each firm *shifts* to the left, as all market shares decline. Ultimately, the demand curve will be tangent to the *ATC* curve (point *G*), at which point price equals average total cost and no economic profits exist.

successful in any of these efforts, ***each monopolistically competitive firm will establish some consumer loyalty.*** Thus it is able to alter its own price somewhat, without fear of great changes in unit sales (quantity demanded). In other words, the demand curve facing each firm will slope downward, as in Figure 9.7*a*.

Inefficiency

marginal cost pricing: The offer (supply) of goods at prices equal to their marginal cost.

Because the demand curve facing a firm in monopolistic competition slopes downward, such a firm will violate the principle of **marginal cost pricing.** Specifically, it will always price its output *above* the level of marginal costs, just like firms in an oligopoly or monopoly (see Figure 9.7*a*). As a consequence, monopolistically competitive industries will tend to restrict output and misallocate society's resources.

In the long run, the profits of a monopolistically competitive industry will be eliminated. In oligopoly or monopoly, an above-normal rate of profit can be maintained indefinitely, because only one or a few firms ever participate in the market. In monopolistic competition, however, new firms can and do enter the market, depressing average prices and profits. In fact, in the absence of significant barriers to entry, new firms will continue to enter a monopolistically competitive industry until its profit potential is no higher than that of alternative pursuits. Point G in Figure 9.7*b* illustrates the absence of **economic profit** in long-run equilibrium.

economic profit: The difference between total revenues and total economic costs.

Warring Toothpaste Makers Spend Millions Luring Buyers to Slightly Altered Products

Proctor & Gamble Co. and Colgate-Palmolive Co. are about to spend $75 million or more touting new toothpastes that are most noteworthy for what they *won't* do.

They won't make teeth whiter than those manufacturers' current offerings. They won't prevent cavities any better. They won't even have new names; P&G's product will wear the Crest banner and Colgate-Palmolive's will be called Colgate.

What the new toothpastes will do is taste different. And they will have a new color; both are translucent blue gels instead of the familiar opaque white and aqua pastes.

New Weaponry

Such are the weapons of war in the $675 million dentifrice industry. The fight is typical of the rivalries becoming increasingly common among manufacturers of everyday personal-care, household-cleaning and food items sold by supermarkets and drug stores. Consumer demand for those products is growing slowly. Most competing brands are pretty much alike, and so is their advertising. Significant technological improvements are hard to come by.

The result is that marketers are pegging their hopes on minor changes in product appearances, packaging, scents or flavors. And the companies are spending tens of million of dollars to advertise those changes and to lure consumers with free samples, price discounts, coupons and other promotions.

"The price of entry into the packaged-goods market has become colossal," says Stanley Canter, a New York marketing consultant. "Companies are attempting to break in by dint of dollars, rather than by the unique features of a product."

Lucrative Margins

Still, rewards often can be great. "In very large categories, small changes in market share are worth a lot of money; that justifies spending a lot to make something happen," says Edward Tauber, chairman of the marketing department at the University of Southern California in Los Angeles. "Whether the consumer reaches to the left or right on the store shelf often depends on very trivial things." . . .

Trade sources indicate that Colgate-Palmolive has budgeted $10 million for the first three months of Colgate gel's introduction and could spend up to $40 million in the first year. Mr. Meade says P&G may well spend $15 to $25 million in Crest gel's first year. Others say the company may spend even more to match Colgate.

Leading National Advertisers Inc., which measures ad spending, estimates that last year $17.9 million was spent on Colgate's television and magazine advertising and $28.6 million was spent on Crest's. Aim was backed by $16 million. Mr. Segalas says an additional 25% or more typically is spent on discounts, coupons and other incentives. . . .

Fluctuating Shares

Since then, Colgate's share has climbed a point or two to 20%. Crest's share, helped by strong shipments in July and August, is near 40%, compared to 36% a year ago. Still, analysts caution, Crest's share may drop back a point or two.

There is no indication what effect the new gels will have on the market. They could take away shares from the other gels or from the regular forms of Crest or Colgate.

—Bill Abrams

The long-run equilibrium of firms in monopolistic competition, as illustrated in Figure 9.7*b*, differs from the perfectly competitive equilibrium. In the long run, a competitive industry produces at the *lowest* point on the average total cost (*ATC*) curve, and thus maximizes efficiency. In monopolistic competition, however, the downward slope of the demand curve facing each firm implies that profits will be eliminated *before* minimum average cost is achieved (see Figure 9.7*b*). As a consequence, an industry characterized by monopolistic competition tends to be less efficient in the long run than a perfectly competitive industry.

POLICY IMPLICATIONS: NONPRICE COMPETITION

A distinguishing feature of competitive markets is that individual firms compete on the basis of price. Through cost and price reductions, competitive firms hope to increase sales and profits. Price competition is not so prevalent in noncompetitive markets. Indeed, in oligopolies, the kink commonly found in the demand curve facing each firm inhibits price reductions, even when cost reductions might otherwise justify a lower price. In monopolistic competition, there is also a tendency toward reduced price competition. Because each firm has its own "captive" market—consumers who prefer its particular brand over competing brands—price reductions by one firm will not induce many consumers to switch brands. Thus ***price reductions are not a very effective way to increase sales or market share in monopolistic competition.***

If imperfectly competitive firms do not compete on the basis of price, do they really compete at all? The answer is evident to anyone who listens to the radio, watches television, reads magazines or newspapers, or drives on the highway. A prominent form of *nonprice competition* is advertising. An imperfectly competitive firm typically uses advertising to enhance its own product's image, thereby increasing the size of its "captive market" (consumers who identify with a particular brand). Through advertising, an imperfectly competitive firm begins to shift its own demand curve to the right, while perhaps making it less price elastic as well (see Figure 4.10). By contrast, competitive firms have no incentive to advertise because they can individually sell their entire output at the current market price.

Advertising is not the only form of nonprice competition. Before the airline industry was deregulated (1978), individual airlines were compelled to charge the same price for any given trip; hence price competition was prohibited. But airlines did compete—not only by advertising, but also by offering "special" meals, movies, more frequent or convenient departures, and "faster" ticketing and baggage services.

Is there anything wrong with nonprice competition? Surely airline passengers enjoyed their "special" meals, "extra" services, and "more convenient" departure times. But these services were not free. As always, there were opportunity costs. From an air traveler's perspective, the "special" services stimulated by nonprice competition substituted for cheaper fares. With more price competition, customers could have chosen to travel more cheaply *or* in greater comfort. From society's perspective, the resources used in advertising (see Table 9.2) and other forms of nonprice competition could be used

TABLE 9.2 ADVERTISING EXPENDITURES

Imperfectly competitive firms tend to engage in nonprice (rather than price) competition. Advertising is a primary form of nonprice competition. In 1980, $54 billion was spent on advertising.

Medium	*Amount (in millions)*
Newspapers	**$15,541**
Radio	**3,827**
Magazines	**3,149**
Direct mail	**7,596**
Business papers	**1,674**
Outdoor	**610**
Television	**11,295**
Miscellaneous	**10,898**
Total	**$54,590**

Source: U.S. Department of Commerce, *Statistical Abstract of the United States,* 1981.

instead to produce larger quantities of desired goods and services (including airplane trips). Unless consumers are given the chance to *choose* between "more" service and lower prices, there is a presumption that nonprice competition leads to an undesirable use of our scarce resources.

SUMMARY

- Imperfect competition refers to markets in which individual suppliers (firms) have some independent influence on the price at which their output is sold. Two prominent forms of imperfect competition are oligopoly and monopolistic competition.
- An oligopoly is a market structure in which a few firms produce all or most of a particular good or service; it is essentially a shared monopoly. Because oligopolies involve several firms rather than only one, each firm must consider the effect of its price and output decisions on the behavior of its rivals. Such firms are highly interdependent.
- A basic conflict exists between the desire of each individual oligopolist to expand its market share and the *mutual* interest of all the oligopolists in restricting total output so as to maximize profits. This conflict must be resolved in some way, via either collusion or some less explicit form of agreement (e.g., price leadership).
- Once a common oligopoly price is established, it tends to be fairly rigid, as illustrated by the kinked demand curve. The kink results from the threat of rival oligopolists to match price reductions but not price increases.
- The basic "stickiness" of oligopoly output and prices is reinforced by the gap that occurs in an oligopolist's marginal revenue curve. The gap itself occurs just below the kink in the demand curve and results from the switch from one marginal revenue (and demand) curve to another. Because marginal cost may not equal marginal revenue in this gap, small changes in cost need not alter the production decision.
- In monopolistic competition, many producers supply the market but each retains some independent control of its own price. The demand curve facing each firm is downward-sloping, but not kinked. Firms in monopolistic competition engage in product differentiation, seeking to maintain and expand "captive" markets.
- In the long run, economic profits are eliminated in monopolistic competition by the entry of additional firms, even though minimum average costs are never attained.
- Oligopoly and monopolistic competition encourage nonprice competition instead of price competition. The resources used in nonprice competition (e.g., advertising, packaging, service) may have more desirable uses, and thus such forms of competition represent a form of resource misallocation.

Terms to remember

Define the following terms:

oligopoly
monopolistic competition
market share
quantity demanded
law of demand
product differentiation
marginal revenue
profit-maximization rule
collusion
price leadership
marginal cost pricing
economic profit

Questions for discussion

1. Can an oligopolist ever increase its market share? How?
2. What is the function of advertising in monopolistic competition? Provide specific examples.
3. What prevents other firms from entering an oligopolistic industry and sharing in the profits? Give some examples.
4. In addition to outright collusion and price leadership, how might oligopolists communicate their desire for a change in price or output?

Problem

Suppose that the following schedule summarizes the sales (demand) situation confronting an oligopolist.

Price (per unit)	**$8**	**$10**	**$12**	**$14**	**$16**	**$17**	**$18**	**$19**	**$20**
Quantity demanded (units per period)	**9**	**8**	**7**	**6**	**5**	**4**	**3**	**2**	**1**

Using the figures provided:

(*a*) Draw the demand and marginal revenue curves facing the firm.

(*b*) Identify the profit-maximizing rate of output in a situation where marginal cost is constant at $10 per unit.

CHAPTER 10

MARKET POWER IN THE U.S. ECONOMY

Chapters 7, 8, and 9 have examined the potential of market power to restrict output, raise prices, and command above-normal profits. But we have not yet demonstrated how much market power actually exists in American product markets or how it is used. In this chapter we shall attempt to measure the extent of market power in U.S. product markets and assess its impact on the economy. In so doing, we will be mindful of the warning given by Adam Smith in 1776: "People of the same trade seldom meet together, but the conversation ends in a conspiracy against the public, or in some diversion to raise prices."

MEASURING MARKET POWER

The degree of market power possessed by any single firm is determined by several factors:

- The number of producers in the market
- Their relative size
- The extent of barriers to entry
- The availability of substitute products

All of these factors are important in both theory and fact. Nevertheless, it is useful—and far simpler—to focus on just one measure of market power to attain some perspective on the structure of U.S. product markets.

Concentration ratio

concentration ratio: The proportion of total industry output produced by the largest firms (usually the four largest).

The standard measure of market power is the **concentration ratio.** This ratio tells the share of output (or combined market share) accounted for by a small number of firms. Using this ratio, one can readily distinguish between an industry composed of hundreds of small, relatively powerless firms and another industry also composed of hundreds of firms but dominated by a few that are large and powerful. Thus ***the concentration ratio is a measure of market power that relates the size of firms to the size of the product market.***

Table 10.1 gives the concentration ratios for selected products in the United States. The standard measure used here depicts the proportion of domestic production accounted for by the largest firms, usually the four largest. In some cases, however, the concentration ratio refers to the combined market share of even fewer firms—for example, the tennis-ball market, which is controlled by only three firms.

oligopoly: A market in which a few firms produce all or most of the market supply of a particular good or service.

As is apparent from the table, the supply of some of the most familiar consumer products is dominated by a very few firms. In most of the examples cited here, producer concentration is so great as to be tantamount to a monopoly shared among a few corporations. Thus the supply side of these product markets can be described as **oligopolies.** Indeed, in some markets, one single firm is so large that an outright monopoly is nearly attained. Eighty percent of all canned soup, for example, is produced by Campbell. IBM supplies 70 percent of all large computers. Western Electric produces 85 percent of all telephone equipment. Eastman Kodak supplies two-thirds of all still cameras and film. Procter & Gamble makes 75 percent of this country's disposable diapers. All of those firms that have a market share of at least 40 percent are printed in boldface type in the table.

Any one of the firms listed in Table 10.1 has considerable potential for influencing the quantity of a particular good supplied to the market and thus its market price. If William Wrigley decides to supply Spearmint gum only at prices higher than those of its competitors, a lot of gum chewers will have to pay more for Spearmint or switch to another brand. If Wrigley, Squibb (Beech-Nut), and Warner-Lambert (Chiclets) all raise their prices at the same time, gum chewers will have to choose between paying higher prices and chewing their nails. This is the essential feature of market power. In

Wm. Wrigley Boosts Gum Prices in U.S. Except Orbit Brand

CHICAGO—Wm. Wrigley Jr. Co. said it increased the wholesale price of all its chewing gum brands in the U.S. except the recently introduced Orbit sugar-free brand. The new schedule brings the price for a regular 20-package box to $2.25, up from $1.72. Wrigley had held the line at $1.72 since December 1974. In that year, the company raised prices three times. . . .

Graham Morgan, Wrigley's vice president, sales, said a factor in the price move was a recent similar increase by American Chicle Co., a Morristown, N.J.-based division of Warner-Lambert Co. He added the effect at the retail level will probably be that a package of seven sticks will sell for 20 cents, up from the current 15 cents.

TABLE 10.1 POWER IN U.S. PRODUCT MARKETS

The domestic production of many familiar products is concentrated among a few firms. These firms have substantial control over the quantity supplied to the market, and thus over market price. The concentration ratio measures the share of total market output produced by the largest producers in a given market.

Product	*Largest firms*	*Concentration ratio (percent)*
Automobiles	**General Motors,** Ford, Chrysler, American Motors	98
Telephone service	**American Telephone & Telegraph,** General Telephone & Electronics, United Telecommunications, Continental Telephone	98
Chewing gum	**Wm. Wrigley,** Warner-Lambert, Squibb, Philip Morris	97
Toothpaste	**Procter & Gamble,** Colgate-Palmolive, Lever Bros., Beecham	85
Tennis balls	**General Tire,** Spalding, Dunlop	100
Breakfast cereals	**Kellogg,** General Mills, General Foods, Quaker Oats	91
Cigarettes	**R. J. Reynolds,** Philip Morris, Brown & Williamson, American Brands	88
Razor blades	**Gillette,** Warner-Lambert (Schick), Procter & Gamble (Wilkinson), Philip Morris (American Safety)	98
Electric razors	**Norelco,** Remington, Warner-Lambert, Sunbeam	96
Sanitary napkins	**Johnson & Johnson** (Modess, etc.), Kimberly-Clark (Kotex)	98
Handguns	**Smith & Wesson,** Sturm, Ruger, Colt, Harrington & Richardson	76

Sources: Data from Federal Trade Commission, *The Wall Street Journal, Advertising Age, Financial World, Standard & Poor's, Fortune,* and industry sources.

a more competitive market, with a large number of small firms, the likelihood of an across-the-board price increase would be much smaller, as we observed in the calculator example of Chapter 7.

Firm size

We noted before that market power is not necessarily associated with firm size—in other words, a small firm could possess a lot of power in a relatively small market. Table 10.1, however, should be convincing testimony that we are not talking about small product markets here. Every one of the products listed enjoys a broad-based market. Annual sales for these products range from approximately $300 million (for men's hair grooming) to over $60 billion (for telephone service). Accordingly, for most of the firms listed in the table, market power and firm size go hand in hand. Indeed, the largest of

Product	*Largest firms*	*Concentration ratio (percent)*
Canned soup	**Campbell,** Heinz	90
Cameras and film	**Eastman Kodak,** Polaroid, Bell & Howell, Berkey Photo	98
Disposable diapers	**Procter & Gamble** (Pampers), Kimberly-Clark, Curity, Romar Tissue Mills	99
Detergents	**Procter & Gamble,** Lever Bros., Colgate-Palmolive	86
Soft drinks	**Coca-Cola,** PepsiCo, Philip Morris (Seven-Up), Dr Pepper	65
Office typewriters	**IBM,** Royal, SCM, Olivetti	85
Portable typewriters	**SCM,** Royal, Brother, Olivetti	86
Records and tapes	Warner Bros., CBS, Capitol, RCA	54
Tires and tubes	Goodyear, Firestone, Uniroyal, B. F. Goodrich	85
Coffee	General Foods, Procter & Gamble, Hills Bros., Standard Brands	64
Chocolate candy	**Hershey,** Peter Paul, Russell Stover, Fanny Farmer	79
Beer	Anheuser-Busch, Miller, Stroh (Schlitz), Pabst	72
Large computers	**IBM,** Honeywell, Sperry-Rand, Burroughs	89
Personal computers	**Apple,** Tandy, Commodore, IBM	60
Photocopiers	**Xerox,** Minnesota Mining & Mfg., SCM, Addresso-Multigraph	90
Telephones	**Western Electric,** General Telephone, United Telecommunications, Continental Telephone	95
Men's hair grooming	Bristol-Myers, Gillette, Beecham, Mennen	62
Air travel	United Air Lines, TWA, American, Delta	61
Bicycles	**Huffy,** Murray Ohio, Schwinn, AMF	67

Note: Individual corporations with a market share of at least 40 percent are designated in boldface type. Market shares based on sales for selected years, 1970–82.

the firms listed here (AT&T and General Motors) enjoy sales volumes that exceed the entire output of most of the *countries* in the world (see Table 10.2). That kind of size and market concentration constitutes undeniable power.

Although concentration ratios are a neat summary of power in a particular product market, they do not fully convey the extent to which particular firms can influence the production and consumption of goods and services. The vast size of the corporations listed in Tables 10.1 and 10.2 creates the potential for extending market power beyond the confines of a particular product market. Firms with sales and assets measured in billions of dollars have the power to extend their influence into other production areas. The most striking example of such an extension is AT&T, which until recently not only supplied nearly all telephone services, but also owned the firm

TABLE 10.2 CORPORATE SALES AND WORLD GNP, BY RANK, 1980 **(in billions of dollars)**

The dominant firms in U.S. product markets sell as much output each year as most countries produce.

Rank	Country or corporation	Sales or GNP	Rank	Country or corporation	Sales or GNP
1	United States	$2,582	26	**Mobil**	$69
2	USSR	1,212	27	South Africa	67
3	Japan	1,153	28	Argentina	66
4	West Germany	828	29	Denmark	66
5	France	628	30	Turkey	66
6	United Kingdom	443	31	**General Motors**	63
7	Italy	369	32	Indonesia	62
8	China	283	33	**Texaco**	59
9	Brazil	243	34	Yugoslavia	59
10	Canada	223	35	**AT&T**	57
11	Spain	200	36	Venezuela	54
12	The Netherlands	161	37	Romania	52
13	Iran	159	38	Norway	52
14	Australia	142	39	Finland	47
15	Poland	140	40	**Standard Oil (Calif.)**	47
16	Mexico	123	41	Hungary	45
17	East Germany	121	42	Greece	42
18	Belgium	120	43	Iraq	40
19	**Exxon**	115	44	**Ford Motor Co.**	38
20	Sweden	112	45	Bulgaria	37
21	Switzerland	106	46	Algeria	36
22	Saudi Arabia	101	47	Philippines	34
23	Czechoslovakia	89	48	**Standard Oil (Indiana)**	32
24	Nigeria	86	49	Colombia	32
25	Austria	77	50	Thailand	31

Source: *World Bank Atlas,* 1981, and *Fortune,* March 1982.

(Western Electric) that manufactures most telephone hardware. Thus the sixth largest corporation in the country owned the tenth largest manufacturing corporation.[1]

Other corporations, too, have considerable power in more than one product market. Procter & Gamble, for example, shows up in 5 of the 29 markets listed in Table 10.1, producing not only 75 percent of all disposable diapers, but also 50 percent of all detergents, 40 percent of all toothpaste, 10 percent of all razor blades, and 20 percent of all coffee. Warner-Lambert, IBM, and Philip Morris also appear in many of the product markets listed here.

Table 10.1 indicates the market power possessed by corporations in specific product markets. But because concentration ratios refer to only one product or industry, they tend to understate the power of many corporations to influence economic outcomes. Obviously, a firm that can affect the supplies (and prices) of many products may have at least as much power as those that wield control

[1] As noted in Chapter 8, the U.S. Department of Justice ordered AT&T to divest its local phone service by the end of 1983.

over a single product. Procter & Gamble, Warner-Lambert, and Philip Morris are clear examples. In fact, many other corporations control some of the action in many product markets, although not necessarily a large share of the action in any single market. Such heterogeneous firms even have a special name: **conglomerates.**

conglomerate: A firm that produces significant quantities of output in several industries.

Although rarely observed in concentration ratio lists, conglomerates (such as ITT, LTV, Litton Industries, Tenneco, Textron, Rockwell International) are among the largest corporations in the country. International Telephone & Telegraph, for example, with annual sales in excess of $23 billion, has supplied such familiar products as Avis Rent-A-Cars, Levitt housing, Sheraton hotels, Hartford Life Insurance, and Hostess Twinkies.[2] Litton Industries, with sales in the $5 billion range, has supplied S&H Green Stamps, Stouffer foods, missile guidance systems, and nuclear attack submarines. At the same time, Litton has participated in domestic social programs and foreign economic development planning. Such conglomerate firms enjoy many of the prerogatives otherwise reserved for those with extensive power in a single market.

Other measures of market power

It is also important to note that a high concentration ratio is not the only way to achieve market power. The supply and price of a product can be altered by the actions of many firms acting in unison. Even if a thousand producers supply one product and none of them has a strikingly large share of total output, they may still band together to change the quantity supplied to the market, thus exercising market power. Recall how Universal Electronics exercised market power by coordinating the production decisions of its many separate plants. Clearly those plants could have attempted such coordination on their own even if they had not all been owned by the same corporation. Lawyers and doctors possess and exercise this kind of power by maintaining uniform fee schedules for members of the American Bar Association (ABA) and the American Medical Association (AMA).[3] Dairy farmers exercise the same kind of power by acting jointly through three large cooperatives (the American Milk Producers, Mid-America Dairies, and Dairymen, Inc.), which together control 50 percent of all milk production.

Finally, all the figures and corporations cited here refer to *national* markets. They do not convey the extent to which market power may be concentrated in a *local* market. Yet local concentrations of market power are of immediate concern to every consumer, even if the firms and stores that possess such power have little national impact. In fact, many industries with low concentration ratios nationally tend to be represented by just one or a few firms locally. Prime examples include milk, newspapers, and transportation companies (both public and private). For example, of the 35,000 cities in the United States, fewer than 60 have two or more independently

[2] ITT was forced to sell Avis and Levitt after threat of antitrust action.

[3] In recent years, the courts have ruled that uniform fee schedules are illegal and that individual lawyers and doctors have the right to advertise their prices (fees). Nevertheless, a combination of inertia and self-interest has effectively maintained high fee schedules and inhibited advertising.

owned daily newspapers, and nearly all rely on only two news services (Associated Press and United Press International).

We may conclude, then, that market power is real and pervasive in the U.S. economy. The corporations listed in Table 10.1 only suggest the dimensions of that power. Other elements of power are discussed in later chapters, but note here that these firms have combined sales of well over $300 billion and employ nearly 7 million people. The 200 largest manufacturing companies—only 0.06 percent of the total—account for almost one-half of all manufacturing output, assets, and employment. Accordingly, although many product markets can also be characterized as highly competitive (furniture, fashions, computer software, printing, motels, produce), concentration and market power characterize a broad spectrum of American industry. As Professors Carl Kaysen and Donald Turner concluded in 1959, "There are more concentrated than unconcentrated industries in manufacturing and mining, they are larger in aggregate size, and they tend to occupy a more important position in the economy."[4] More recent studies have estimated that market power pervades something like two-thirds of American industry; in most instances, product markets are dominated by oligopolies.

POWER AT WORK

With so much market power concentrated in so few hands, evidence of power at work should be easy to find. Indeed, it would be surprising to find many product markets unaffected by the concentration ratios we have surveyed. As we review examples of market power at work in some of these markets, the ultimate objective of those who wield the power must be kept in view. Power in product markets is sought and exercised for the primary purpose of increasing the profits of those who wield the power.[5] In pursuit of higher profits, monopolies and oligopolies may seek to restrict market supplies, raise product prices, lower product quality, or reduce direct costs. In all of these cases, they rely on their ability to control market supply. Where possible, they attempt to extend such power by influencing market demand as well.

Successful use of market power will, of course, attract the interest and envy of other profit maximizers and can thus lead to its own destruction. Hence a monopoly or oligopoly with extensive control of a particular market must take steps to protect its position by erecting **barriers to entry.** ***Above-normal profits cannot be maintained over the long run unless barriers to entry exist.*** In the following pages we will focus on both the exercise of market power and the kinds of barriers to entry that establish and preserve such power.

barriers to entry: Obstacles that make it difficult or impossible for would-be producers to enter a particular market; for example, patents.

[4] Carl Kaysen and Donald Turner, *Antitrust Policy* (Cambridge: Harvard University Press, 1959).

[5] The profits accrue not just to the faceless corporations, of course, but also to the stockholders who own them. In this regard, it is well to remember that 5 percent of the population owns 83 percent of all corporate stock. See Frank Ackerman et al., "Income Distribution in the United States," *Review of Radical Political Economics*, Summer 1971, p. 23. In addition, the executives and employees of powerful corporations are themselves paid above-average wages.

Control of prices

A basic focus of market power is the price at which particular goods and services are sold. In general, we expect firms with market power to raise prices whenever it is profitable to do so and to maintain prices at levels higher than a more competitive market would sustain.

price fixing: Explicit agreements among producers regarding the price(s) at which a good is to be sold.

PRICE FIXING In oligopolies, the establishment and maintenance of a high market price requires some form of coordination among the rival firms. The most explicit form of coordination among oligopolists involves **price fixing:** the oligopolists explicitly agree to charge a uniformly high price. Consumers are compelled to pay that high price or do without.

Price-fixing agreements are particularly successful when market demand for the product is highly inelastic, as high prices will not significantly reduce the quantity demanded. Although price fixing is outlawed by the Sherman Antitrust Act—and therefore often difficult to document—a few examples may serve to convey the nature of such agreements:

□ In 1961, General Electric, Westinghouse, and a group of other producers in the electrical-products industry were convicted of criminally conspiring to fix prices on turbine generators, transformers, and several other kinds of electrical equipment that they had been selling to the Tennessee Valley Authority and commercial customers. Available evidence suggested that the price-fixing conspiracy had significantly raised product prices on sales totaling nearly $2 billion per year. As a result of their participation in the conspiracy, seven corporate executives went to jail and twenty-three others were put on probation. In addition, the companies were fined a total of $1.8 million and compelled to pay triple damages in excess of $500 million to their victimized customers. Nevertheless, another suit was filed against General Electric and Westinghouse in 1972, charging these same companies—still the only two U.S. manufacturers of turbine generators—with continued price fixing.

□ In January 1982, three major dairies in Arkansas pleaded no contest to federal charges of price fixing. State officials had discovered that the three firms (Borden, Inc.; Coleman Dairy, Inc.; and Dean Foods) had been submitting identical bids to provide milk for schools in Little Rock and other cities in central Arkansas. They were also said to be fixing the price of milk sold to the public. The state attorney general estimated that the price fixing, which had begun as far back as 1963, had boosted prices by $3 million per year. Two salesmen were sent to jail and the companies were fined $2.4 million.

□ In 1981 the three largest supermarket operators in Cleveland agreed to give consumers $21.5 million worth of free groceries to settle price-fixing charges. Suits against the companies (Fisher Foods, First National Supermarkets, and Association of Stop-N-Shop Supermarkets) asserted that officers of the three supermarkets had secretly met in parking lots, hotels, and an apartment to fix meat and grocery prices.

□ Control of the supply of quinine was achieved by a group of international firms in the early 1960s. The firms then raised the price of quinine from $0.37 an ounce to $2.13. The demand for quinine (in the form of the drug quinidine), it may be noted, is highly inelastic; the drug is taken primarily by the elderly to restore natural heart rhythm. Profits of the quinine suppliers and their distributors skyrocketed, the profits of one company quintupling in a period of six months.

□ The price of tetracycline (a common antibiotic) was allegedly inflated by an illegal conspiracy involving five leading drug companies (American Cyanamid, Pfizer, Bristol-Myers, Upjohn, and Squibb Beech-Nut). Although the drug cost only $1.52 (per 100 capsules) to manufacture, the companies sold it to druggists at a price of $30.60. The druggists, in turn, sold it to the public at $51. After the government began to prosecute the companies for a price-fixing conspiracy, the retail price fell to $6. The five companies agreed to pay over $120 million to settle claims resulting from their pricing behavior.

□ The price of bread in the state of Washington was raised to artificially high levels as a result of price fixing among major bakers (including ITT's Wonder Bread and Safeway's Mrs. Wright's). The price-fixing conspiracy lasted over ten years (1954–64) and ended up costing Washington residents over $35 million in excessive bread prices. After the conspiracy was uncovered, bread prices in the state fell by nearly 6 cents a loaf.

Similar price-fixing agreements have been discovered in a variety of product markets, including plumbing fixtures, cigarettes, drugs, and newspaper advertising. Even the pocket-calculator industry, discussed in Chapters 7–9, was the target of price fixing. According to *Electronic News* (August 7, 1972), leading Japanese firms were able to fix calculator prices until technological innovations facilitated competition by American producers.

PRICE LEADERSHIP Although price-fixing agreements are undoubtedly still a reality in many product markets, oligopolies have discovered that they do not necessarily need *explicit* agreements to arrive at uniform prices. If all oligopolists in a particular product market

Levi Strauss Agrees to Pay $3.5 Million to Settle Price Case

SAN FRANCISCO—Levi Strauss & Co. said it agreed to a $3.5 million settlement of a court action by the California Attorney General.

The action, filed in superior court here, charged illegal price maintenance between 1972 and 1975. It alleged that jeans purchasers had been overcharged by retailers as a result of Levi's alleged efforts to maintain suggested retail prices.

A company spokesman said the company agreed to the settlement to avoid costly and time-consuming litigation. The spokesman also said the company stopped suggesting retail prices a year and a half ago. The settlement doesn't involve any admission by the company that it violated any law or that consumers were overcharged, he said.

Adolph Coors Co. Gets FTC Order to Stop Fixing Its Beer Prices

Agency Says Charges Controlled at Wholesale, Retail Levels, Selling Restrictions Imposed

WASHINGTON—The Federal Trade Commission ordered Adolph Coors Co. to stop fixing prices of its Coors beer.

The FTC ruled that Coors "has pursued a policy of fixing, controlling and maintaining prices" at both the wholesale and retail levels. The commission said Coors specifically threatened to refuse to deal with some concerns that sold Coors beer at prices below those suggested by the company.

The FTC also found that Coors imposed illegal territorial and other selling restrictions on distributors or retailers. The commission's order also prohibits such restrictions.

Coors, a privately owned brewery based in Golden, Colo., sells beer in 11 states, the FTC said. Coors is the top-selling beer in 10 of those states, according to the agency. The company is the nation's fourth largest beer producer, and had sales of about $350 million in 1971. All the company's beer is produced from a single plant in Golden, the FTC said.

In Golden, an Adolph Coors spokesman said it wouldn't have comment at this time on the FTC action.

follow the lead of one firm in raising prices, the result is the same as if they had all agreed to raise prices simultaneously. Instead of conspiring in motel rooms (as in the electrical-products case), the firms can achieve their objective simply by reading *The Wall Street Journal* or other industry publications and responding appropriately. Such **price leadership** is exercised annually in the automobile industry and frequently characterizes other product markets (television, cigarettes, detergents).

price leadership: An oligopolistic pricing pattern that allows one firm to establish the (market) price for all firms in the industry.

What happens in these cases is that one firm announces a price increase of x percent. In a highly competitive market, other companies would exploit this price differential by continuing to sell their products at lower prices. The more expensive firm would thus be driven out of business or forced to rescind its price increases. In a highly concentrated industry, however, the remaining oligopolists may raise their prices in accordance with the price increases initiated by the price leader. Often the price followers raise their prices a bit less than x percent, compelling the price leader to reduce its price increases and giving the impression of intense competition. These little "adjustments," however, do not alter the fact that in highly concentrated industries a price increase by one firm usually signals price increases by all firms.[6]

Allocation of market shares

Whenever oligopolists successfully raise the price of a product, the quantity of that good sold in a particular period decreases, in accordance with the law of demand. Even in markets with highy inelastic demand curves (such as those for tetracycline and quinine), *some* decrease in sales always accompanies an increase in price. When this happens in a monopolistic industry, the monopolist simply cuts back his rate of output to adjust to the reduced sales. In an oligopolistic industry, however, it is not obvious which of the oligopoly firms will confront diminished sales. A reduction in sales and output will occur; how will that reduction be spread around? Clearly, no single firm will wish to incur the whole weight of that cutback while the other oligopolists maintain their previous output; some form of accommodation is required.

The adjustment to the reduced sales volume can take many forms. Once again, the firms may engage in an explicit agreement on dividing up the sales reduction. If market sales drop by 10 percent, each firm may agree to reduce its rate of output by that same proportion. Such an agreement would preserve the **market share** previously enjoyed by the separate companies.

market share: The percentage of total market output produced by a single firm.

A particularly novel and ingenious method of allocating market shares occurred in the price-fixing case involving General Electric and Westinghouse. Agreeing to establish high prices on electrical equipment was not particularly difficult; but how would the companies decide who was to get the sales? In a competitive market, sales would be distributed according to prices, with the firm charging the

[6] As the kinked demand curve of Chapter 9 illustrated, no single oligopolistic firm will raise its price unless it is convinced that rivals will follow suit. When they do, a new market price is established from which the rival firms are not expected to deviate.

Toilet Seat Makers Said to Fix Prices

A federal grand jury yesterday charged four leading makers of toilet seats with a decade-long conspiracy to fix prices.

The indictment was handed down in Detroit at the same time the Justice Department filed a civil suit against the companies asking for an injunction to bar such collaboration in the future.

The indictment and civil action named the Beatrice Foods Co. of Chicago, which markets seats through its Beneke Division; the Olsonite Corp. of Detroit; the Bemis Manufacturing Co. of Sheboygan Falls, Wis., and the Standard Tank and Seat Co. of Camden, N.J.

Reuters dispatch reprinted from *The Washington Post*, Washington, D.C., June 20, 1974.

predatory price cutting: Temporary price reductions designed to alter market shares or drive out competition.

lowest price getting most of the business. But in this case, General Electric, Westinghouse, Allis-Chalmers, and a few other companies had agreed that low prices would be unseemly (and less profitable). Accordingly, they needed another mechanism for allocating sales. They agreed that each firm would be designated as the "low" bidder for a particular phase of the moon. The "low" bidder would charge the previously agreed-upon (high) price, with the other firms offering their products for sale at a higher price. The "low" bidder would naturally get the sale. Each time the moon entered a new phase, the order of "low" and "high" bidders would change. Hence each firm got a share of the business, and the price-fixing scheme was hidden behind a facade of "competitive" bidding.[7]

Such intricate plans for allocating market shares are probably more the exception than the rule. More often the oligopolists let the sales and output reduction be divided up according to consumer demands, intervening only when market shares are thrown markedly out of balance. At such times an oligopolist may take drastic action. A popular mode of action is **predatory price cutting.** Predatory price cuts are temporary price reductions that are intended to drive out new competition or reestablish market shares. The sophisticated use of price cutting can function as a significant barrier to entry, inhibiting potential competitors from trying to gain a foothold in the price cutter's market.

Gasoline station "price wars" were once a familiar manifestation of the price-cutting technique, although other examples abound. In the 1930s, for example, the cigarette oligopoly successfully raised cigarette prices (in the middle of the depression!). It was soon threatened, however, by new competitors, who managed to achieve 23 percent of total market sales. In early 1933 the oligopolists decided to reestablish their previous market shares and dropped cigarette prices from $6.04 per thousand to $4.85. Some brands were actually sold below cost, a practice the small competitors could not afford. The effect was to reduce the market share of the new competitors to less than 10 percent. Their objective attained, the oligopolists increased the price of cigarettes again in January 1934.

A more recent example of price cutting occurred in the supermarket (retail food) industry. Although the industry is a comparatively competitive one, a few giant chains (A&P, Safeway, Kroger,

[7] For a detailed description of this price-fixing arrangement, see Richard Austin Smith, "The Incredible Electrical Conspiracy," *Fortune*, May 1961.

Predatory bread prices

ITT Continental Baking Co., one of the world's largest bakers, has for decades been illegally snuffing out competition, often by charging too little for its Wonder, Home Pride, and other brands of white bread, a Federal Trade Commission administrative law judge ruled. The decision, which can be reviewed by the entire commission, handed a major victory to the FTC's antitrust staff, which brought the case in 1974 against Continental and its parent, International Telephone & Telegraph Corp. Judge Miles J. Brown told Continental it cannot win new business by offering prices below fully allocated costs or attack competition by lowering prices in selective markets. Brown also suggested that the commission consider forcing ITT to sell off Continental.

Reprinted from the May 25, 1981, issue of *Business Week* by special permission.

Food Fair) still possess significant market power. Unhappily, the largest chain grocer, A&P, found its market share declining in the late 1960s. It decided to stop that erosion of power with price cuts so drastic that smaller competitors would be driven out of business. According to *Fortune* magazine and the Federal Trade Commission, A&P initiated price cuts in 1972 that brought some prices below costs and led to huge losses in the industry. A&P was able to increase its market share, however, and later raise prices to their "normal" level.

One last example of price cutting to enforce market power suggests elements of both collusion and price fixing. The automobile manufacturers sell a substantial number of cars to fleet owners—firms or agencies that purchase at least ten vehicles. General Motors and Ford had always dominated fleet sales. Chrysler's share of the market, however, grew from 4 to 25 percent after it refused to maintain high prices and introduced price reductions. As a result, Ford and GM were compelled to lower their prices in order to maintain sales. The price reductions, however, lowered profits, a most unwelcome result. According to government complaints, GM and Ford then conspired to cut prices so low that they actually fell below cost, thus forcing losses and a change of attitude on Chrysler. Chrysler apparently took the hint. When GM and Ford eliminated all price concessions on 1971 models, Chrysler followed suit the following week. As *Business Week* reported, "GM let it be known that it planned to retaliate, presumably by further price cutting, if Chrysler did not go along."[8]

Control of supply

Price cutting, either real or threatened, can be an effective weapon for excluding competition. It is by no means the only available weapon, however. Patents, control of distribution outlets, acquisitions, and product differentiation can also be used to limit competition.

PATENTS Patents prohibit potential competitors from using developed technology, since a patent endows the holder with exclusive use of his technology for seventeen years. A potential competitor cannot set up shop until he either develops an alternative method for producing a product or receives permission from the patent holder to use the patented process. Such permission, when given, will cost something, of course. Moreover, the larger, more powerful firm will always have more resources available to pursue further research and development, thus increasing the comparative disadvantage of the would-be rival. Patents were the primary source of market power for the hypothetical Universal Electronics case of Chapter 7. In the real world, they also provide a substantial explanation for the market power of such firms as Xerox and Polaroid.

Even tennis rackets are now patented. In 1976 the Prince Manufacturing Company convinced the U.S. Patent Office that its over-

[8] *Business Week*, January 27, 1973, p. 24. In December 1973 GM and Ford were acquitted of criminal charges by a federal district court in Detroit; civil suits against these companies were dismissed in 1977 on the basis of inadequate evidence of collusion.

sized rackets were a unique product. The racket's design, it was claimed, provided more power and stability than conventionally sized (70-square-inch) rackets. The Patent Office agreed and gave Prince the exclusive right to produce rackets with surface areas of 85 to 130 square inches. With that patent, Prince has been able to monopolize sales of oversized rackets and reap extraordinary economic profits.[9]

DISTRIBUTION CONTROL Another way to control the supply of a product is to take control of distribution outlets. A firm will usually sell wares in a variety of retail outlets. If it can persuade those outlets not to peddle anyone else's competitive wares, it will have further solidified its market position. This control of distribution outlets can be accomplished through many means, including price concessions, long-term supply contracts, and expensive gifts at Christmas. The automobile industry provides an even more effective option.

Nearly all new cars in the United States are sold through dealerships franchised by car manufacturers. The individual dealers are beholden to the manufacturer for the "right" to buy and sell cars. As a condition of their franchises, dealers are prohibited from selling cars produced by a competitor. Although the clause detailing this prohibition was ruled illegal by the Supreme Court in 1949, few dealers have taken it upon themselves to defy the wishes of GM, Ford, and Chrysler. As a result, the supply of new cars sold to the public is effectively governed by a few manufacturers who exercise control over approximately 26,000 dealerships (GM alone has over 12,000).

To tighten their control over distribution networks, auto manufacturers have also entered the financing and parts-replacement industries. Nearly all new cars purchased are "financed" (paid for in part by a loan). Thus a firm that can gain control of the financing mechanisms can tighten its control over sales. As early as 1919—and shortly after buying out Buick, Cadillac, Oldsmobile, and a score of other producers—General Motors organized the General Motors Acceptance Corporation (GMAC) for that very purpose. Ob-

[9] Prince sold Wilson a license to manufacture oversized rackets through 1983; such licenses do not alter Prince's primary monopoly.

Transamerica Unit, 3 Car-Rental Firms Agree to Settle Suit

NEW YORK—The nation's three largest rent-a-car companies—Hertz Corp., Avis Inc. and National Car Rental System Inc.—have privately agreed to settle a lawsuit filed against them by Budget Rent-A-Car Systems Inc. in 1977.

It's understood that the three larger companies have agreed to pay Budget more than $9 million under terms of the tentative agreement. . . .

Budget filed suit against the three larger companies after they consented in 1976 to Federal Trade Commission orders barring them from conspiring to monopolize the car-rental industry and from participating in other anticompetitive practices including monopolizing car-rental concessions at airports. The three big companies consented to the FTC order without admitting to the practices.

Since 1976 the number of airport counters operated by Budget and smaller companies has increased significantly, with Budget increasing its total to 159 from 94 just three years ago.

—Priscilla S. Meyer

viously, the consumer who wishes to purchase a competitor's car would have difficulty obtaining financing from GMAC. Accordingly, the convenience and financial resources of GMAC serve to reduce potential competition.

The control that the auto manufacturers exert over parts and services is as familiar as your car warranty or neighborhood dealership. Although most auto parts could easily be designed to be interchangeable, only "authorized" parts and services, provided by franchised dealers, may be used to maintain the warranty. Hence the Big Three effectively fragment the independent parts and service market. They force auto purchasers to pay higher prices for such services, and compel would-be entrants to the auto industry to establish their own parts and service networks. As a result of these many barriers to entry, it has been estimated that a potential competitor would need at least $1 *billion* to establish a foothold in the automobile industry. Few entrepreneurs are prepared for that kind of investment.

Similar control of distribution outlets can be found in many industries—photocopying, beer, telephones, computers, and cameras, for example. One particular industry, breakfast cereals, is especially noteworthy in this regard for its direct and simple approach to control of sales. Sales of breakfast cereals are heavily influenced not only by product advertising but also by shelf displays at the local supermarket. The package with the most prominent display (shelf height, space, and position) is most likely to catch the attention of the shopper (or child-in-tow). One might think that the grocer took responsibility for such displays, but the Federal Trade Commission claimed that is often not the case. In particular, the FTC discovered that

> Kellogg is the principal supplier of shelf space services for the RTE [ready-to-eat] cereal sections of retail grocery outlets. Such services include the selection, placement and removal of RTE cereals to each respondent and to other RTE cereal producers.
>
> Through such services respondents have interfered with and now interfere with the marketing efforts of other producers of RTE and other breakfast cereals and producers of other breakfast foods. Through such services respondents restrict the shelf positions and the number of facings for Nabisco and Ralston RTE cereals, and remove the RTE cereals of small regional producers.
>
> All respondents [Kellogg, General Mills, General Food, Quaker Oats] acquiesce in and benefit from the Kellogg shelf space program which protects and perpetuates their respective market shares through the removal or controlled exposure of other breakfast food products including, but not limited to, RTE cereal products.[10]

According to the FTC complaint, this control over shelf space gave the cereal makers control of the market supply curve, and cost consumers $1.2 billion in higher grocery prices between 1958 and 1972.

ACQUISITION Large and powerful firms can restrain competition and attain control of product supply by a number of means, but none

[10] Complaint, *Kellogg Company et al.*, FTC Dkt. 8883 (1972). The FTC dropped the case in 1982 after ten years of litigation.

"With our latest merger, gentlemen, we've passed from a conglomerate to a world power!"

GRIN AND BEAR IT by Lichty and Wagner. Copyright Field Enterprises, Inc., 1978. Courtesy Field Newspaper Syndicate.

quite so direct as outright *acquisition*. When one firm buys another, the effect on its market share, and thus its market power, is fairly obvious. A *merger* between two firms amounts to the same thing, although mergers often entail the creation of new corporate identities. The new identity, however, does not alter the fact that a single firm has attained increased market power.

Perhaps the single most dramatic case of acquisition for this purpose occurred in the breakfast cereal industry. In 1946 General Foods acquired the cereal manufacturing facilities of Campbell Cereal Company, a substantial competitor. Following this acquisition, General Foods dismantled the production facilities of Campbell Cereal and shipped them off to South Africa!

Although the General Foods acquisition was more dramatic than most, acquisitions have been the most popular route to increased market power. General Motors, for example, attained a dominant share of the auto market largely by its success in merging with and acquiring two dozen independent manufacturers. In the cigarette industry, the American Tobacco Company attained monopoly powers by absorbing some 250 independent companies. Each acquisition increased the company's market control and ability to acquire additional companies. Later antitrust action (1911) split up the resultant tobacco monopoly into an oligopoly consisting of four companies (R. J. Reynolds, Liggett & Myers, Lorillard, and American Tobacco), which continued to dominate the cigarette market. Other companies that came to dominate their product markets through mergers and acquisitions include U.S. Steel, U.S. Rubber, General Electric, United Fruit, National Biscuit Company, and International Salt. In addition, all the conglomerates discussed earlier attained their size and power via the acquisition route. ITT alone purchased an average of ten companies per year in the period 1964–69.

Nonprice competition

Producers who have control over market supply, as we have seen, are in a position to alter prices and thereby increase their share of economic welfare. They can expand their power and share of income even further by establishing some influence over market demand.

The means for acquiring some degree of control over the market demand curve are familiar from Chapters 4 and 9. The primary mechanism of control is *advertising*. To the extent that a firm can

Christmas Tree Makers Sued by Justice

The government asked a federal court yesterday to hold the nation's two largest producers of artificial Christmas trees in contempt for violating a 1975 agreement prohibiting anticompetitive mergers in the industry.

Named in a petition filed by the Justice Department in U.S. District Court in Harrisburg, Pa., were American Technical Industries Inc. (ATI) of Pittsburgh and Marathon Manufacturing Co. of Houston.

ATI is the country's No. 1 producer of artificial Christmas trees and Marathon Manufacturing ranks second.

The 1975 agreement had settled a 1973 civil suit against ATI and had prohibited the firm from acquiring the assets of any company engaged in the manufacture or sale of artificial Christmas trees in the United States.

—Ranjit de Silva

Reuters dispatch reprinted from *The Washington Post*, Washington, D.C., March 23, 1982.

convince you that its product is essential to your well-being and happiness, it has effectively shifted your demand curve. If the firm can convince millions of other consumers in the same way, it will have acquired some degree of direct control over the *market* demand curve. With such control, the producer can attain a still more profitable price-quantity equilibrium. Accordingly, we may anticipate that firms with large amounts of market power will tend to advertise most heavily.[11]

Advertising deepens the attachment of consumers to particular brands (thus rendering their demand curves less elastic). It also makes it expensive for new producers to enter the market, because a new entrant must buy not only production facilities but advertising outlets as well. In addition, the proliferation of brand names—all produced by a few companies—tends to mask the concentration of power that exists. Thus **product differentiation** both increases profits (and prices) and camouflages the true extent of market power.

product differentiation: Features that make one product appear different from competing products in the same market.

The cigarette industry is a classic case of high concentration and product differentiation. As Table 10.1 shows, the top four cigarette companies produce 88 percent of all domestic output; two more firms (Lorillard and Liggett & Myers) produce the rest. Yet you would never guess that such high concentration exists in the industry if you were merely to survey the cigarette shelves at the local supermarket. Together, the six cigarette companies produced well over a 100 brands in 1982. Confronted with such a diversity of choices, how many consumers would even imagine that Marlboro, Benson & Hedges, Parliament, Virginia Slims, Philip Morris, Alpine, Galaxy, English Ovals, Merit, Saratoga, Players', and Cambridge are all produced by a single company (Philip Morris)? To maintain the

[11] Next time you watch television, note who sponsors the commercials. Then check to see if they, or their parent corporations, are included in our list of powerful firms (Table 10.1).

DESIGNER JEANS: PRODUCT DIFFERENTIATION IS EVERYTHING

The Levi Strauss Company first produced jeans in the 1850s and has dominated the industry ever since. In the late 1970s, however, a whole new mini-industry evolved: the "designer jeans" market. It all started when Puritan Corporation came up with the idea of selling jeans emblazoned with the label of fashion designer Calvin Klein. Calvin Klein jeans sold like hot cakes, at about twice the price of traditional jeans. Within only a few years' time, Puritan was selling over $30 million worth of Calvin Klein jeans.

Other companies were quick to follow Puritan's lead. Murjani Industries was the next big success story. In 1978 Murjani put the Gloria Vanderbilt label on its jeans and started advertising heavily. Sales in 1979 reached $150 million. Jordache came next, also in 1978. In its second year sales of Jordache jeans reached $75 million.

By 1981 the status jeans industry looked like a classic case of monopolistic competition. There were over 200 different labels available. Yet all of the jeans were basically identical, their only difference residing in the designer's name and the color or pattern of the stitching. To make their own jeans seem different, the designer-jeans makers advertise extensively.

appearance of competition in the industry and to intensify consumer loyalties, the cigarette industry spent over $700 million in 1982 for advertisements in newspapers, magazines, and on radio (television ads were banned after 1971).

Another highly concentrated industry that spends great amounts of money on advertising is the breakfast cereal industry. Although the Federal Trade Commission has suggested that "a corn flake is a corn flake no matter who makes it," the four firms (Kellogg, General Foods, General Mills, Quaker Oats) that supply more than 90 percent of all ready-to-eat breakfast cereals spend over $200 million a year to convince consumers otherwise. During the last 20 years, more than 150 brands of cereals have been marketed by these companies. As the FTC has documented, the four companies "produce basically similar RTE [ready-to-eat] cereals, and then emphasize and exaggerate trivial variations such as color and shape. . . . [They] employ trademarks to conceal such basic similarities and to differentiate cereal brands."[12] Most cereal advertising, the commission noted, is aimed at children. Here again the diversity of brands creates the impression of intense competition, and the attendant advertising leads consumers (especially children) to purchase a particular brand with which they can identify (as athletes, outer-space heros, or cowboys).

One final example of market power manifested in product differentiation is the detergent industry. Only three firms (Procter & Gamble, Lever Brothers, and Colgate-Palmolive) account for 86 percent of all detergent output. These firms, however, package detergents under 20 trademarked brands and a host of private labels for supermarket chains. Procter & Gamble alone, with over 50 percent of the market, produces nine trademarked brands (including Tide, which accounts for nearly one-fourth of all detergent sales). It is not completely coincidental that Procter & Gamble spends more on advertising than any other company in the world (see Table 10.3).

[12] Complaint, *Kellogg Company et al.*, FTC Dkt. 8883 (1972).

Sears' Dishwasher Claims Ruled False

Sears, Roebuck and Co. falsely claimed its dishwashers make prior rinsing or scraping of dishes unnecessary, the Federal Trade Commission ruled yesterday.

Sears, the nation's largest retailer and biggest marketer of household dishwashers, sells them under its Kenmore and Lady Kenmore brands.

The $8 million broadcast and print ad campaign made such claims as "now's the time to really clean up during Sears' gigantic dishwasher sale. With a Kenmore you'll never have to scrape or rinse again" and "Sears Lady Kenmore. The do-it-yourself dishwasher. No scraping. No prerinsing."

The opinion by Commissioner Paul Rand Dixon said the campaign lasted three to four years and that "even at the time that the no-scrape, prerinse claim was first disseminated, Sears lacked substantiation or a reasonable basis for making it.

"Indeed, if anything, the tests purportedly relied upon by Sears at the time that it made its claim demonstrated precisely the reverse—that the Lady Kenmore could not ensure the consumer 'would never have to scrape or rinse again,' the commission said.

In Chicago, Sears said it will appeal the decision to a federal appeals court.

—Jeffrey Mills

The Washington Post, Washington, D.C., May 17, 1980. Reprinted by permission of the Associated Press.

TABLE 10.3 ADVERTISING EXPENDITURES OF THE TOP TEN ADVERTISERS

Firms with market power attempt to preserve and extend that power through advertising. A successful advertising campaign alters the demand curve facing the firm, thus increasing potential profits.

Company	*Advertising expenditure (millions of dollars)*
Procter & Gamble	$650
Sears Roebuck	600
General Foods	410
Philip Morris	365
K-Mart	319
General Motors	316
R. J. Reynolds Industries	299
Ford Motor	280
AT&T	259
Warner-Lambert	235
Total	$3,733

Source: *Advertising Age*, September 10, 1981.

Other barriers to entry

Predatory price cutting, patents, control of distribution outlets, acquisitions, and product differentiation are all effective barriers to entry. Individually and collectively, they enable powerful producers to maintain high prices and profits without fear of attracting too much competition. As important as these barriers are, however, they do not exhaust the supply of weapons available to a successful oligopoly. Market power may be solidified in other ways as well.

The very size of a powerful oligopoly may preclude effective competition. Once a firm or group of firms attains tremendous size, potential competitors may be kept at bay by the capital-investment requirements necessary to attain competitive status. In the pocket-calculator market, at which we looked earlier, initial capital-investment requirements were minimal. In heavy manufacturing industries, however, the initial outlay for plant and equipment may be colossal. Even in disposable diapers, initial capital investment and advertising expenses were so high that only one new entrant—Johnson & Johnson, already a large corporation—joined this highly concentrated industry in the 1970s, despite the rash of profits available. Smaller firms were reluctant to enter, for fear that the existing firms could use their control over prices, supply, and demand to destroy competitive possibilities. Johnson & Johnson itself pulled out of the industry after only a few years.

A single firm or group of firms with considerable market power can also extend and solidify that power by exacting concessions from resource suppliers. Powerful firms can erect protective entry barriers by winning price concessions or distribution guarantees from those who supply them with labor, capital, or other productive inputs.

Finally, we must confront the potential that oligopolists possess to influence government regulation. As we saw in Chapter 3, government activities reach into all sectors of the economy. What is of particular interest here is the role of government in restricting competition. Government restricts competition through various

Topps Gum Strikes Out on Baseball Card Game

PHILADELPHIA (UPI)—Topps Chewing Gum Inc. lost its 14-year monopoly of the bubblegum baseball card industry this week and was ordered to pay triple damages of $3 to a Philadelphia competitor.

Fleer Corp. of Philadelphia filed a lawsuit in 1975 against Topps of Brooklyn, which since 1966 signed exclusive contracts with virtually every major and minor league baseball player to appear on 2½-by-3½ cards tucked in with a sheet of pink bubble gum.

U.S. District Judge Clarence Newcomer ruled that Topps and the Major League Baseball Players' Association unfairly edged Fleer out of the market.

But he balked at what he called "guesswork" at determining the extent of Fleer's loses. Newcomer awarded Fleer a nominal $1 damage award, which under antitrust laws is tripled to $3. . . .

Topps is the nation's largest manufacturer and seller of baseball cards, selling $6.6 million worth in 1978.

The Washington Post, Washington, D.C., July 5, 1980. Reprinted by permission of United Press International.

proscriptions, licensing arrangements, differential taxes, import quotas and tariffs, and an all-too-frequent tendency to award contracts to the largest firms. Patents, too, could be included in this category, because they are issued and enforced by the federal government. What makes government regulation particularly hazardous for would-be rivals is the potential for influence possessed by large and powerful firms. It is worthwhile to recall the words of Senator Russell Long, chairman of the powerful Senate Finance Committee:

> Most campaign money comes from businessmen. Labor contributions have been greatly exaggerated. It would be my guess that about 95 percent of campaign funds at the congressional level are derived from businessmen. At least 80 percent of this comes from men who could sign a net worth statement exceeding a quarter of a million dollars. Businessmen contribute because the Federal Corrupt Practices Act prohibits businesses from contributing. . . .
>
> A great number of businessmen contribute to legislators who have voted for laws to reduce the power of labor unions. . . .
>
> Many businessmen contribute to legislators who have fought against taxes that would have been burdensome to their businesses, whether the tax increase was proposed as a so-called reform, a loophole closer, or just an effort to balance the Federal budget.
>
> Power company officials contribute to legislators who vote against public power. . . .
>
> Bankers, insurance company executives, big moneylenders generally contribute to legislators who vote for policies that lead to high interest rates.
>
> Many large companies benefit from research and development contracts which carry a guaranteed profit, a so-called fixed fee of about 7 percent of the amount of the contract. Executives of such companies contribute to those who help them get the contracts or who help make the money available. . . . Research contractors contribute to legislators who vote to permit them to have private patent rights on government research expenditures.
>
> Drug companies are often able to sell brand-name drug products at anywhere from twice to 50 times the price of identical nonbranded products for welfare and Medicare patients if the companies can prevail upon government to permit their drugs to be prescribed and dispensed by their private brand names rather than by the official or generic name of the product. Executives of drug companies will contribute to legislators who vote to permit or bring about such a result.
>
> Many industries are regulated. This includes the railroads, the truckers, the airlines, the power companies, the pipelines, to name but a few. Executives of regulated companies contribute to legislators who vote to go easy on

the regulation, and ask no more questions than are necessary about their rates.

Companies facing threat of ruinous competition from foreign sources have executives who contribute to those who help protect them from competition by means of tariffs and quotas.

Many industries are subsidized . . . the merchant marine, the shipbuilders, the sugar producers, the copper producers and a host of others. Executives in such industries contribute to those who help keep them in business.

This list is merely illustrative. . . . Merely by assiduously tending to the problems of business interests located in one's own state, a legislator can generally assure himself of enough financial support to campaign effectively for re-election.[13]

POLICY IMPLICATIONS: ANTITRUST LIMITATIONS

Examples of market power at work in U.S. product markets could be extended to the closing pages of this book. The few cases cited here, however, are testimony enough to the fact that market power has some influence on our lives. Market power *does* exist; market power *is* used. It is not possible to summarize briefly all the ways in which seller concentrations influence market outcomes. In general, power in U.S. product markets has contributed to resource misallocations, higher prices, restricted output, higher levels of unemployment, and greater inequality of income and wealth. A staff study by the Federal Trade Commission has suggested that product prices in oligopolistic industries are at least 25 percent higher than they would be in the absence of such market power. Economists have estimated that oligopolies have constrained GNP—that is, restricted output—by approximately 6 percent. Neither of these estimates is beyond dispute (indeed, they are often disputed), but they are suggestive.

The demonstrated potential and use of market power to transform the dimensions of our economic welfare make the subject of power in product markets a basic issue for economic policy. Do we want to delegate so much authority to determine prices, incomes, employment, and output to a relatively small number of corporations with extensive market power? As we have seen, that authority has often been used to the marked disadvantage of consumers and society as a whole. If we choose to regain authority over economic outcomes, we must decide the appropriate focus of public policy and the most appropriate kinds of policy intervention.

Industry behavior

Our primary concern in product markets is the *behavior* of those who buy and sell goods and services. We have an interest in the way goods and services are priced, in collusion (explicit or otherwise) among producers, and in the erection of barriers to new competition.

[13] *Congressional Record*, April 4, 1967, cited in Morton Mintz and Jerry S. Cohen, *America, Inc.: Who Owns and Operates the United States* (New York: Dial Press, 1971), pp. 203–205.

All of these elements of industry behavior will directly affect economic outcomes.

A variety of policy options are available to influence the behavior of oligopolists and thereby assure a more desirable set of economic outcomes. We could, for example, explicitly outlaw collusive agreements and cast a jaundiced eye on industries that regularly exhibit price leadership. We could also prohibit oligopolists from extending their market power via such mechanisms as acquisitions, excessive or deceptive advertising, and, alas, the financing of political campaigns. In fact, we have established mechanisms for each of these kinds of control. Such agencies as the Justice Department, the Federal Trade Commission, and the Food and Drug Administration have authority to assess and control market behavior.

Two limitations to the behavioral orientation of public policy should be noted, however. First, public resources to control market behavior have always been and continue to be extremely limited. Indeed, the advertising expenditures of just one oligopolist, Procter & Gamble, are more than ten times as large as the *combined* budgets of both the Justice Department's Antitrust Division and the Federal Trade Commission. As Ralph Nader has suggested, "The posture of two agencies with a combined budget of $20 million and 550 lawyers and economists trying to deal with anticompetitive abuses in a trillion-dollar economy, not to mention an economy where the 200 largest corporations control two-thirds of all manufacturing assets, is truly a charade."[14] The dimensions of this charade were poignantly demonstrated in 1969, when the Justice Department filed suit against IBM for monopoly practices. In the subsequent 13 years, IBM submitted 66 million pages of documents in its own defense, effectively stymieing the prosecution. By the time the case was dropped (see Chapter 8), all of the Antitrust Division lawyers who had originally prepared the IBM case had left the Justice Department.

There are many reasons why efforts to control market behavior are so limited. For one thing, consumers are generally insensitive to the relationship between market structure and their own economic welfare. They (and you) rarely think about the connection between market power and the price of the goods they buy, the wages they receive, or the way they live. Furthermore, as Ralph Nader sadly discovered, "Antitrust violations are part of a phenomenon which, to the public, is too complex, too abstract, and supremely dull."[15] As a result, there is little public pressure for a more concerted effort to regulate market behavior. Moreover, the direct and vested interest of oligopolists in behavioral freedom creates an active lobby to constrain regulation efforts. Accordingly, the first requirement of effective antitrust efforts is public knowledge and concern. The second is the mobilization of that concern in the form of pressure for antitrust resources.

Industry structure

Another reason why regulatory efforts have not yielded greater success is their focus on market behavior. Such exclusive focus on behavior ignores the relationship between market structure and behav-

[14] Mark J. Green et al., *The Closed Enterprise System: The Report on Antitrust Enforcement* (New York: Grossman, 1972), p. x.
[15] Ibid., p. ix.

ior. As former Supreme Court Chief Justice Earl Warren observed, "An industry which does not have a competitive structure will not have competitive behavior."[16] To expect an oligopolist to disavow profit opportunities or to ignore the potential effect of its actions on its fellow oligopolists (and vice versa) is naive. It also violates the basic motivations imputed to a market economy. As long as markets are highly concentrated, we must expect to observe oligopolistic behavior.

Public efforts to alter market structure have been even less frequent than efforts to alter market behavior. With the exception of the AT&T case (Chapter 8), the few really concerted efforts to break up market concentration occurred at the beginning of the century, when Standard Oil and the Tobacco Trust were partially dismantled. The prevalent feeling today, even among antitrust practitioners, is that the oligopolies are too big and too powerful to make deconcentration a viable policy alternative. There is also a feeling that big firms are needed to maintain America's competitive position in international markets (which are themselves often dominated by foreign monopolies and oligopolies).

In addition to explicit antitrust efforts, two other mechanisms are available to alter market structure and behavior. First, there is the force of market demand. Consumers do have the power to reject shoddy products, exaggerated advertising claims, and high prices. The exercise of such power depends on consumer willpower, the extent of market and product information, and the availability of substitute products. Consumers' persistent demands for smaller, cheaper cars, for example, coupled with the availability of foreign substitutes, finally prodded the U.S. auto industry in that direction. Typically, however, determined consumer action can only moderate prices, profits, and power enjoyed by oligopolists. Movements of the market demand curve will not by themselves significantly alter the concentration of supply.

Another mechanism to influence market behavior and structure is international trade. To the extent that foreign producers are allowed to sell their products in the American market, the impact of domestic concentration can be contained. When foreign producers are permitted to compete in domestic markets, oligopolists must contend with their reactions when formulating price and output decisions. Thus international trade may serve to broaden market structure and render market behavior more competitive.[17] Indeed, the increased competition that international trade promises has led many oligopolies to seek strengthened barriers to trade (in the form of tariffs and quotas) and increased control of foreign supplies (through mergers, acquisitions, and supply agreements).

SUMMARY

- The concentration ratio is a measure of the extent of market power in a particular product market. It equals the share of total industry output accounted for by the largest firms, usually the top four.

[16] Ibid., p. 7.
[17] International economic relations are discussed in Chapters 19 and 20.

- Market power, particularly *oligopoly,* characterizes many of the product markets in the United States. As much as two-thirds of all manufacturing output is produced by firms with market power.
- In addition to those firms with a large *market share* in one product market, many others have large market shares in several markets. Also, *conglomerates* have a little power in each of many markets. Finally, regional and local markets create still further opportunities for market power.
- The primary mechanism for the exercise of market power is control over prices, particularly price fixing and price leadership.
- In order to maintain and exercise market power, firms must be sheltered from potential competition by barriers to entry. Patents are one form of barrier, but others abound as well. Occasional predatory price cutting ("price wars"), control of distribution outlets, high capital-investment requirements, advertising and product differentiation, and resource control constitute important and frequent barriers to entry. Outright acquisition or merger offer additional means to eliminate competition.
- The effects of market power include increased prices, reduced output, and a transfer of income from the consuming public to a relatively few powerful corporations and the people who own them.
- Among the policy álternatives available to combat oligopolistic structure or behavior are antitrust action, government regulation, consumer action, and international trade.

Terms to remember

Define the following terms:

concentration ratio
oligopoly
conglomerate
barriers to entry
price fixing
price leadership
market share
predatory price cutting
product differentiation

Questions for discussion

1. Market power usually results in high profits. Why, then, don't more firms enter an oligopolistic industry to share in the high profits, and thereby increase competition? Why don't more firms enter the auto industry? the photocopying industry?

2. In 1977 Laker Airways, then a three-plane airline, introduced a "Skytrain" air fare between New York and London that was less than half the fare previously charged by TWA, Pan Am, and other large airlines. Why didn't some other firm lower the fare sooner? Why did Laker eventually go bankrupt (in 1982)?

3. On what grounds is price fixing distinguished from price leadership?

4. What would be the advantages of breaking up the market power depicted in Table 10.1? What problems would such "trust busting" create?

PART B

FACTOR MARKETS AND INCOME DISTRIBUTION

CHAPTER 11

THE SUPPLY OF LABOR

The following two ads recently appeared in the campus newspaper of a well-known university:

Will do ANYTHING for money: able-bodied liberal-minded male needs money, will work to get it. Have car. Call Tom 765-3210.

Computer Programmer: Computer sciences graduate, fluent in FORTRAN, COBOL, APL; experience with UNIVAC, IBM and CDC systems. Looking for part-time position on or off campus. Please call Judy, ext. 4120, 9–5.

Although placed by individuals of very different talents, the ads clearly expressed Tom's and Judy's willingness to work. While we don't know how much money they were asking for their respective talents, or whether they ever found jobs, we can be sure that they were prepared to take a job at some wage rate. Otherwise, they never would have paid for the ads in the "Jobs Wanted" column of the campus newspaper.

LABOR SUPPLY: A FIRST LOOK

labor supply: The willingness and ability to work specific amounts of time at alternative wage rates in a given time period; the quantities of labor that would be supplied at specific wage rates (*ceteris paribus*).

The advertised willingness to work expressed by Tom and Judy represents a **supply of labor.** They are offering to sell their time and talents to anyone who is willing to pay the right price.

The explicit offers of Tom and Judy are similar to that of anyone who looks for a job. Job seekers who check the current job openings at the student employment office or send résumés to potential em-

FIGURE 11.1 THE SUPPLY OF LABOR

The quantity of any good or service offered for sale typically increases as its price rises. Labor supply responds in the same way. At the wage rate w_1, the quantity of labor supplied is q_1 (point A). At the higher wage w_2, workers are willing to work more hours per week, that is, to supply a larger quantity of labor (q_2).

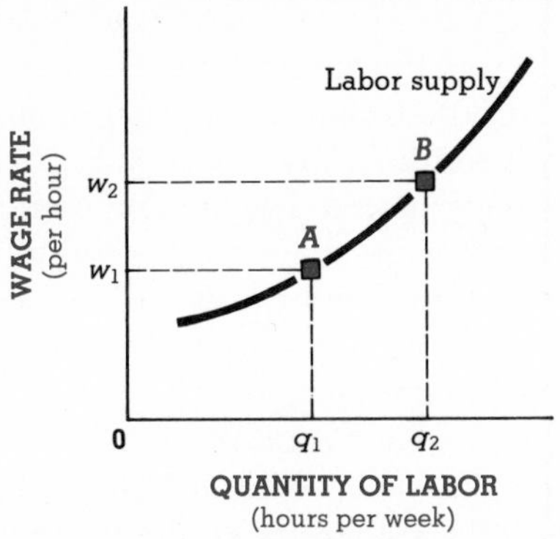

ployers are demonstrating a *willingness* to accept employment, that is, to supply labor. Whether they accept an available job or not will depend on the nature of the job and the wage it pays. Thus we can say that the decision to work will depend at least in part on the pay that is offered. ***The quantity of labor supplied depends on the wage rate.*** In general, we anticipate that the quantity of labor supplied—the number of hours people are willing to work—will increase as wage rates rise (see Figure 11.1).

Labor supply is analogous to the supply of any other good or service. As we observed in our discussion of product markets, would-be sellers of calculators participate in the calculator market by offering to sell calculators at specific prices. We also observed that the quantity of calculators supplied tends to increase as prices rise.

People and calculators obviously differ considerably, however, and some of their differences are important in explaining the particular shape of the labor-supply curve. The motivation for supplying calculators is the maximization of profits. But why do people supply labor? And how do these motivations affect the quantity of labor supplied at various wage rates? Our primary concern in this chapter is to answer these questions. We begin by looking at the motivations for working, then examine the actual labor-supply decisions that result.

150,000 Line Up for Postal Jobs

MIAMI—Approximately 150,000 job-seekers rushed to south Florida post offices this week to fill out applications for 700 letter carrier and postal clerk positions that will become available in south Florida over the next few years.

"We're still trying to absorb it all," said Steve Korker, postal public information officer. "We've had it going on all week, but it's still unbelievable."

The jobs are for postal workers in 60 outlets in Dade and Broward counties.

About 90,000 applicants waited hours in line Monday, Tuesday and Wednesday to get applications for the 700 positions expected to open up through attrition in the next two to three years. Another 25,000 grabbed applications Thursday and yesterday's total was estimated at 35,000.

"I guess given the economy today, that's what's happening," Korker said.

"You can see how serious people are about this by looking at who is waiting in line. We've had a lawyer, an accountant. These are very insecure times and people are looking for a little more security. The Postal Service is historically secure."

The last time the Postal Service advertised in Miami for letter carrier and clerk positions was in 1978. "Then, we gave out only 17,000 applications," Korker said. "Some difference, huh? It's the times."

San Francisco Chronicle, February 27, 1982. Reprinted by permission.

THE MOTIVATION TO WORK

From the comfortable perspective of an overstuffed chair or a blanket on the beach, the notion of supplying labor often seems quite alien. It reminds one of the bees, whose only function in life is to work, work, work. They spend every available moment of their short lives gathering pollen and producing honey. They rarely, if ever, get or take the opportunity to enjoy the fruits of their labor. Yet one imagines the bees might be a whole lot happier by producing less and consuming more.

The lesson of the bees has not been lost on all of nature's creatures. The bears, for example, have adopted a very different life-style. Generally contemptuous of hard labor, the bears prefer to let the bees do all the work. The bears themselves choose to hibernate half the year, later stealing and consuming the honey produced by the bees. This particular life-style seems most compatible to the bears, who have a life expectancy 600 times as long as that of the bees.[1]

Two distinctive elements in the bear's life-style are worthy of note. Its preference for leisure over material consumption frees the bear from most of the agonies associated with production. By hibernating half the year, it drastically reduces its needs and demands. Thus it attains substantial contentment with very little effort, by substituting leisure for other forms of satisfaction that require material support.

The second distinctive element in the bear's life-style is its tendency to satisfy its remaining few needs through plunder. This particular habit is easier to admire than to replicate in a civilized world, yet it unquestionably increases the bear's total satisfaction. It satisfies its consumption needs without great expenditure of time and effort. Were the bee's sting mightier or the honey yield smaller, the bear would not be so well off.

The distinctive life-styles of the bees and bears have not escaped human notice. The ancient Greeks, for example, were quick to perceive the relative desirability of the bear's status. They put great emphasis on leisure and eschewed both excessive consumption and manual labor. As Aristotle put it, "All paid employments absorb and degrade the mind." Like the bears, the Greeks took long naps and relied on others (primarily slaves) to produce their modest consumption needs.

The commitment to work

Given the apparent satisfaction of the bears and the ancient Greeks, how can we explain our own demonstrated willingness to work? Most people confront the prospect of eight hours of work per day, five days a week, for most of their adult lives. Yet most of us could enjoy standards of living unimagined by the ancient Greeks by working only a few hours a day. Why do we choose to work more? Have our material needs and wants expanded? Have we discovered new virtues and satisfactions in the act of producing?

[1] Lest the bees feel unfairly ridiculed here, let it stand as a matter of record that the male members of the bee colony, the drones, behave very much like bears, although they are later severely penalized.

To some extent, the present commitment to work can be explained by various forms of sanctions. In the first place, plundering and slavery have come to be regarded as antisocial activities. As a result, we are largely dependent on our own productive resources for the staples and frills of consumption. St. Paul, an early convert to the work ethic, put it succinctly: "If any one will not work, let him not eat."

Although the proscription of slavery and theft helps explain our commitment to work, it is hardly a complete explanation. Recall that there are two distinctive features in the life-styles of the bears and Greeks, and that only one of these has been denied us. The bears and Greeks also learned how to get by on relatively little. Surely we, too, could reduce our consumption, and thereby eliminate the necessity for so much work.

Sociopsychological forces

Our commitment to work beyond the provision of basic necessities can be explained by two complementary forces. On the one side, we have been persuaded to regard work as an end in itself. With the advent of Christianity, work came to be regarded as a form of worship. The Benedictine monks set the tone for many of us with their maxim, "Laborare est orare"—to work is to pray. Later sects, especially the Calvinists, carried forth this message, equating work with righteousness, worthiness, and chastity. Building on this tradition, the Puritans enshrined work as a form of salvation, and proclaimed that the devil would find work for idle hands. Much of the satisfaction derived from leisure became tarnished.

Sociological factors have also enhanced our attachment to work. Just as some people find their identity in conspicuous consumption, so do others find their identity in work. To be a banker, a salesperson, or a plumber is to have a distinct identity, to *belong*. Many people look to jobs for self-identification and a definition of their role in society. As Elliot Liebow has observed, "no man can live with the terrible knowledge that he is not needed," and work may make a person feel needed.[2] Co-workers also provide a small community of friends and acquaintances. These sociological aspects of working help explain why the vast majority of working Americans report that they like their jobs (see box). It also may explain why millions of people do volunteer work or continue working even when they don't need the income.

Economic forces

Reinforcing these religious and sociopsychological pushes toward work effort is the pull of materialist appetites. As we saw in Chapter 18, producers, their advertising agents, and our next-door neighbors are continually urging us to buy, buy, buy. As we seek to increase our consumption, we find ourselves needing more income. Even our leisure time often ends up being expensive. We currently spend nearly $244 billion on "leisure time" pursuits each year (see Table 11.1). To pay for all this activity, we often find ourselves in need of a job.

[2] Elliot Liebow, "No Man Can Live with the Terrible Knowledge That He Is Not Needed," *New York Times Magazine*, April 5, 1970.

DO AMERICANS LIKE THEIR JOBS?

Question or statement	*Response category*	*Percent*
All in all, how satisfied would you say you are with your job—very satisfied, somewhat satisfied, not too satisfied, or not at all satisfied?	**Very satisfied**	**46.7**
	Somewhat satisfied	**41.7**
	Not too satisfied	**8.9**
	Not at all satisfied	**2.7**
The work is interesting	**Very true**	**57.2**
	Somewhat true	**28.3**
	Not too true	**12.1**
	Not at all true	**6.9**
The pay is good	**Very true**	**27.2**
	Somewhat true	**38.0**
	Not too true	**20.2**
	Not at all true	**14.6**

Source: *The 1977 Quality of Employment Survey*, University of Michigan Institute for Social Research, Ann Arbor, Michigan, 1979.

THE LABOR VS. LEISURE TRADE-OFF

The psychological and economic forces that motivate us to work are only part of the story, of course. We do not work *all* of the time, but instead choose to devote some of our time to nonwork activities (leisure). That is to say, *not* working obviously has some value, too. In part, we need some nonwork time just to recuperate from working. But we also want some time to watch TV, go to a soccer game, or otherwise enjoy the goods and services we have purchased.

The more time we spend working, the less time we have to enjoy our incomes, or simply to relax. Accordingly, we recognize that working, like all activities, involves an opportunity cost. Generally, we say that ***the opportunity cost of working is the amount of leisure time that must be given up in the process.***

The conflicting desires for work and leisure create an obvious dilemma: we can't increase one without decreasing the other. The

TABLE 11.1 LEISURE EXPENDITURES, 1980

The demise of philosophical contemplation as a form of leisure has been accompanied by a rise in more expensive pursuits. It now costs a lot more to relax, as these figures confirm. Can we afford not to work?

Item	*Amount (in billions of dollars)*
Vacation travel	**$130.0**
Recreation/sports equipment	**33.0**
TV sets, records, etc.	**21.6**
Admission tickets	**6.4**
Books, magazines, etc.	**14.8**
Gardens	**4.5**
Miscellaneous	**33.7**
Total	**$244.0**

Source: *U.S. News & World Report*, August 1981.

FIGURE 11.2 THE LEISURE VS. WORK CHOICE

There are only 24 hours in a day and we must allocate them between work and nonwork (leisure). The choices available are represented by the line stretching from point *A* (all leisure) to point *W* (all work). The actual choice of a particular labor-leisure combination (e.g., point *B*) is based on the satisfaction one obtains from either activity.

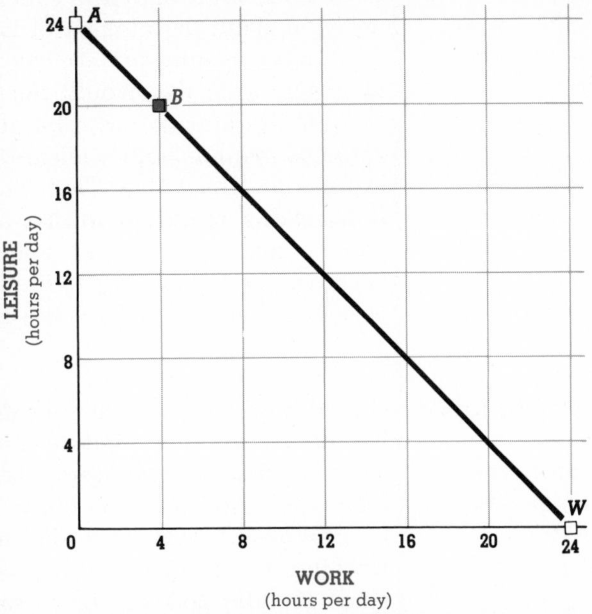

question we must decide is how to allocate our available time between these two competing activities. To see how this conflict is resolved—and the kind of labor-supply curve that emerges—we may examine the labor-supply decision of a single worker. For this purpose, we may study the behavior of Freddie, a fictional freshman economics major whose great ambition is to spend the rest of his life sleeping, listening to his stereo, and playing video games.

Unfortunately for Freddie, at least two of his life's goals require payment of money, and his parents cut off his allowance when he got three F's in his first semester. Even his continued sleeping in a warm bed is contingent upon payment of rent. As a consequence, Freddie, who has never felt a strong religious or sociopsychological attachment to work, now confronts the awful prospect of getting a job. The question becomes: How much is he willing to work?

The time constraint

Like everyone else, Freddie has only 24 hours in a day, so his work decision can be formulated in terms of the number of hours per day he is willing to give up for a job. Figure 11.2 illustrates the choices he confronts. At present, Freddie is not working at all, but is devoting all 24 hours per day to leisure (nonwork). This choice is represented by point *A* in Figure 11.2. Now that Freddie's allowance has been cut off, the question becomes: How much leisure will he give up? That is, how far will he proceed down the curve toward point *W*, which represents the extreme case of "all work and no play"?

Marginal utility of leisure

In order to make a rational work vs. leisure decision, Freddie must compare the relative values of labor and leisure. What is an hour of leisure worth to him? What is an hour of labor worth? By comparing these two values, Freddie can make a rational, utility-maximizing decision about the number of hours he will work.

On the leisure side, we can presume that giving up a few hours of leisure each day would not represent a great loss of **utility** to Freddie. He already has a lot of free time. And we expect that the value of another hour's leisure depends in part on the amount of leisure one already has. That is to say, leisure is subject to the **law of diminishing marginal utility:** additional hours of leisure tend to yield increasingly smaller amounts of satisfaction. From this perspective, the relative loss to Freddie would not be great if he were to get out of bed and work a few hours a day.

utility: The pleasure or satisfaction obtained from a good or service.

law of diminishing marginal utility: The *marginal* utility of a good declines as more of it is consumed in a given time period.

Marginal utility of labor

marginal utility of labor: The change in total utility derived from another hour's work.

On the work side, similar considerations apply. Work has some utility, too. By working, Freddie can earn income to pay rent, buy food, and play video games. From this perspective, ***the* marginal utility of labor *is measured by the utility of the goods and services that can be purchased with an additional hour's wages.*** If Freddie *liked* working, the marginal utility of labor would be higher still. But since Freddie gets no *direct* satisfaction from working, only the wages are of value to him.

Since working is now Freddie's only source of income, the marginal utility of labor is presumably very high. The first few hours of work represent the difference between sleeping in a warm bed (paying rent) and getting thrown out in the cold. Under the circumstances, the *MU* of labor at point *A* in Figure 11.2 is sure to exceed the *MU* of leisure. As an economics major, Freddie realizes that he will be better off giving up some hours of leisure for paid employment. Accordingly, he goes to work, thereupon beginning the long descent from point *A*.

Changes in marginal utility

The calculation of marginal utility that drove Freddie from the idle comforts of point *A* will also determine the number of hours per day he works. The decisive factor will again be the law of diminishing marginal utility. On the leisure side, the law of diminishing marginal utility begins to work in reverse. As Freddie spends more time working each day, his leisure hours become increasingly precious. That is to say, the marginal utility of an hour's leisure is high when one has few such hours.

The law of diminishing marginal utility is illustrated in Figure 11.3. At point *A*, where Freddie is not working at all, the marginal utility of leisure is very small. In other words, that twenty-fourth hour of leisure is of relatively little value to Freddie, inasmuch as he has spent the last 23 hours relaxing. As Freddie begins working—substituting labor for leisure—he moves up the marginal-utility-of-leisure curve. In the process, each hour of leisure given up becomes increasingly valuable.

Suppose that Freddie's initial job involves four hours of work per day. This amount of work is represented by a move from point *A* to point *B* in Figures 11.2 and 11.3. From Figure 11.2 all we learn is that Freddie has gone to work. From Figure 11.3 we learn that

FIGURE 11.3 DIMINISHING MARGINAL UTILITY OF LEISURE

The amount of utility derived from an additional hour's leisure depends on the amount of leisure a person already has. If a person worked all of the time (point *W*), leisure would have a high marginal utility. However, the last four hours of leisure (point *B* to *A*) are not as satisfying as the first four hours. In general, the marginal utility of leisure diminishes as leisure time is increased. Would you agree?

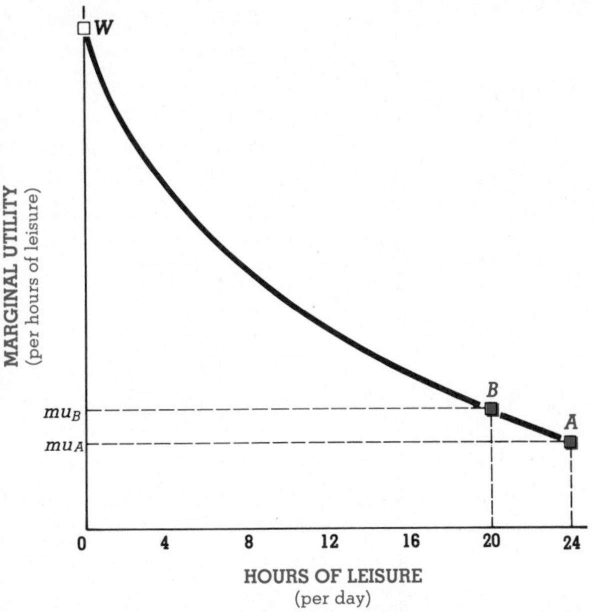

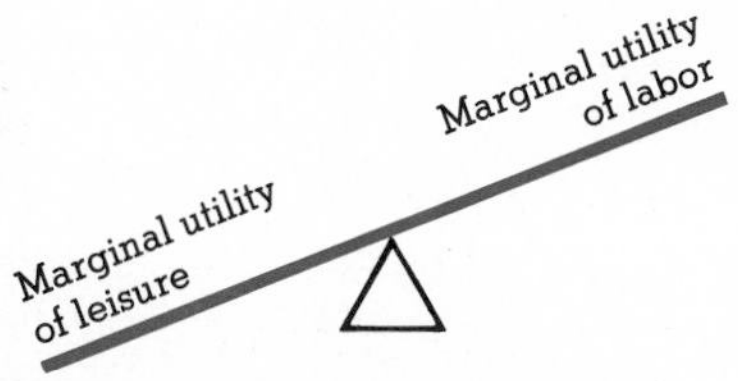

FIGURE 11.4 BALANCING THE MARGINAL UTILITIES OF WORK AND LEISURE

The marginal utility of labor is very high when one is not working at all and needs some income, while the marginal utility of leisure is quite low. As we substitute labor for leisure (go to work), however, the marginal utility of labor starts to fall while the marginal utility of leisure rises. Our objective is to balance the marginal utilities of labor and leisure. At that point, our work effort is optimal.

optimal work effort: The amount of work at which the marginal utility of an hour's labor is just equal to the marginal utility of another hour's leisure.

Freddie's marginal utility of leisure has *risen* as a consequence. We don't know how marginal utility is measured, but we do know that Freddie's perceived value of leisure has gone up.

When labor is substituted for leisure, the marginal value of leisure increases and the marginal utility of work declines. Recall that the value of work to Freddie is simply the goods and services he can buy with his paycheck (he gets no intrinsic satisfaction from work). Those first few dollars were precious to him, as they enabled him to pay the rent, eat, and even play a few video games. But the marginal utility of additional dollars quickly diminishes. Because Freddie is a person of simple tastes, the pleasures he can buy with an additional hour's wages are of relatively little value to him.

Freddie was driven from complete idleness (point *A* in Figure 25.2) to four hours of work per day (point *B*). The marginal utility of an hour's work exceeded the marginal utility of another hour's leisure at that point. But as Freddie descends from point *A*, the marginal utility of an hour's work falls, while the marginal utility of leisure rises. Sooner or later the marginal utility of an hour's work will no longer exceed the marginal utility of an hour's leisure. At that point, Freddie will no longer be willing to substitute labor for leisure. His descent toward point *W* in Figure 11.2 will come to a screeching halt. At that point, where the marginal utility of an hour's work is equal to the marginal utility of an hour's leisure, Freddie will have no further incentive to alter his life-style. He will be getting as much satisfaction as his talents, wages, and tastes allow. At this point, we say that Freddie has achieved an **optimal work effort** (see Figure 11.4). ***Optimal work effort is the combination of work and leisure that yields the greatest total utility available from given tastes and wages.***

We can assure ourselves that a balance of the marginal utilities

TABLE 11.2 THE MARGINAL UTILITY OF LEISURE AND LABOR

The table depicts the marginal utility of each hour of labor or leisure, as perceived by Freddie. Initially (point *A*), Freddie isn't working at all. Yet the table confirms that he would be better off (happier) if he *substituted* one hour of labor (*MU* = 432) for the twenty-fourth hour of leisure (*MU* = 2). He should continue to substitute labor for leisure until he is working six hours a day. The *MU* of a seventh hour of labor (*MU* = 196) does not exceed the *MU* of the additional (eighteenth) leisure hour that would be given up (*MU* = 196).

	Total hours		*Marginal utility (in utils)*	
	Leisure	*Labor*	*Leisure*	*Labor*
Point *A*	24	0	2	—
	23	1	11	432
	22	2	39	421
	21	3	68	408
Point *B*	20	4	104	386
	19	5	153	360
	18	6	196	329
	17	7	213	196
	16	8	232	172
	15	9	247	140
	14	10	291	113
	13	11	339	96
	12	12	367	88
	11	13	392	73
	10	14	450	61
	9	15	473	50
	8	16	499	42
	7	17	531	25
	6	18	586	3
	5	19	644	−2
	4	20	721	−29
	3	21	805	−61
	2	22	911	−105
	1	23	962	−167
Point *W*	0	24	—	−349

represents an optimal situation by considering the implications of an imbalance. Suppose that the marginal utility (*MU*) of labor is greater than the marginal utility of leisure, that is,

$$MU_{\text{labor}} > MU_{\text{leisure}}$$

when Freddie is working five hours a day. Could Freddie be better off with another mix of work and play? Clearly, yes. If another hour's labor is worth more than another hour's leisure, a person should trade in one hour of leisure for one hour of labor. That is to say, Freddie should work another hour each day. By so doing, he will increase his *total* utility, that is, the satisfaction he gets out of life. Optimal work effort occurs when the marginal utilities of labor and leisure are equal.

Once the *MU* of labor equals the *MU* of leisure, there is no incentive to substitute one activity for the other. Further changes in the leisure vs. labor decision will not increase total utility (see Table 11.2).

ALTERNATIVE WAGE RATES

wage rate: The amount of money paid for an hour's work; the price of labor.

So far we have said nothing about the **wage rate** Freddie is receiving, because the hourly wage was not really relevant to our analysis.

FIGURE 11.5 THE EFFECT OF WAGE RATES ON THE MARGINAL UTILITY OF LABOR

Higher wage rates imply more goods and services for every hour worked. Hence the marginal utility of labor increases when wage rates rise. The marginal utility of the fourth work hour increases from mu_1 (point *B*) to mu_2 (point C) when the wage rate increases from \$2 to \$10 per hour.

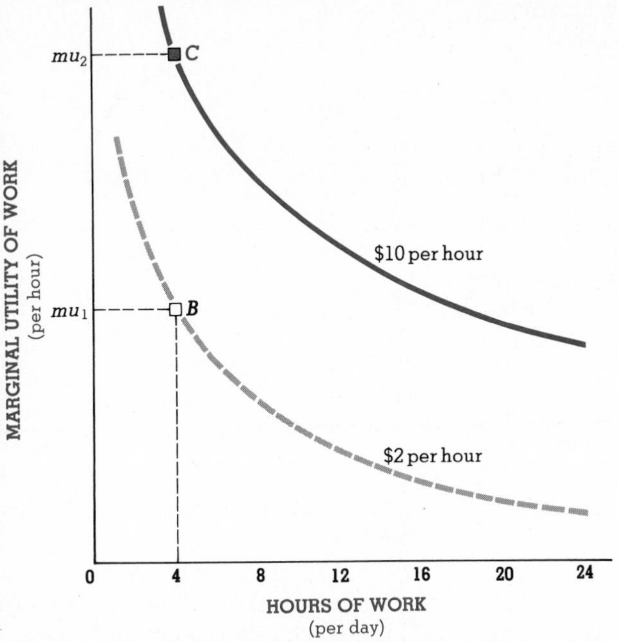

Whether Freddie is paid \$2 an hour or \$10 an hour, the law of diminishing marginal utility still applies. That is to say, the *marginal* utility of an hour's work will decline as Freddie works longer hours. Thus no matter how great the initial imbalance between the marginal utilities of labor and leisure, we still expect them to balance before Freddie is working 24 hours a day.

The wage rate will help Freddie to decide how much he will work, however. A wage of \$10 an hour is clearly superior to a wage of \$2 an hour, because it enables Freddie to buy more goods and services for any given amount of work. Thus ***as wage rates rise, the marginal utility of work tends to increase.*** We can see this effect in Figure 11.5. The lower curve represents the marginal utility associated with work when the wage rate is \$2 an hour. Were Freddie to work four hours a day at this wage rate, the marginal utility of another hour's labor would be equal to the value mu_1 (point *B* in Figure 11.5).

If by some miracle Freddie's wage rate were suddenly increased to \$10 an hour, a new and higher marginal utility curve would apply. Each hour of work would provide more income and thus greater utility. Note that the entire marginal utility curve in Figure 11.5 shifts upward. At the wage of \$10 an hour, Freddie would enjoy a marginal utility of mu_2 by working four hours a day (point *C*) rather than only mu_1.

Suppose for the moment that point *B* initially represented Freddie's *optimal work effort*. That is, at point *B* the marginal utility of an hour's labor equaled the marginal utility of an hour's leisure. Were Freddie's wage rate really to increase, this equality would be thrown out of balance. The higher wage rate would not affect the value of leisure, but it would increase the value (marginal utility) of

FIGURE 11.6 THE BACKWARD-BENDING SUPPLY CURVE

Increases in wage rates make additional hours of work more valuable, but also less necessary. Higher wage rates increase the quantity of labor supplied as long as substitution effects outweigh income effects. At the point where income effects begin to outweigh substitution effects, the labor-supply curve starts to bend backward.

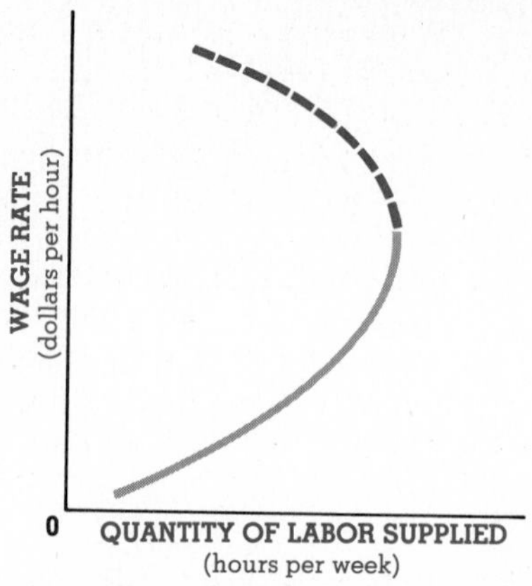

labor. Thus an increase in the wage rate raises the marginal utility of labor.

We can induce Freddie to work more, then, by raising his hourly wage rate. Thus the quantity of labor supplied tends to increase as the wage rate rises. This kind of labor-supply response is illustrated by the solid portion of the **labor-supply curve** in Figure 11.6.

labor-supply curve: A curve depicting the quantities of labor supplied (offered) in a given time period at alternative wage rates (*ceteris paribus*).

The solid portion of the labor-supply curve illustrated in Figure 11.6 should look familiar. In fact, it looks very much like the supply curve for *any* product or resource, with the quantity supplied increasing as prices rise. What we have demonstrated here is that this kind of supply curve applies to labor as well.

The backward bend

The supply curve in Figure 11.6 does not look exactly like other supply curves we have studied. As wage rates continue to rise, the supply curve appears to *bend backward,* as indicated by the dashed portion of the curve. How does this strange result come about?

The force that drives people up the labor-supply curve is the marginal utility of labor, as represented by the goods and services that wages can buy. Higher wages represent more goods and services and thus induce people to **substitute** labor for leisure.

substitution effect of wages: An increased wage rate raises the marginal utility of an hour's labor, thereby encouraging people to work more hours (to substitute labor for leisure).

At some point, however, additional goods and services will be of little value. Individuals whose incomes are already extremely high have a multitude of goods and services to enjoy. More income is of relatively little value to them. If they are offered a wage rate higher still, they are likely to respond by *reducing* the number of hours they work, thereby maintaining a high income *and* increasing their leisure. While you might do cartwheels for $4 an hour, a Rockefeller or Du Pont might not lift an eyelash for such a paltry sum. Muhammad Ali once announced that he would not spend an hour in the ring for less than $1 million, and would box *less,* not more, as the pay for his fights exceeded $3 million. For him, the added income obtainable from one championship fight was so great that he felt he did not have to fight more to satisfy his income and consumption desires. Many entertainers and other high-income earners respond in the same way to high wage offers. In such cases, we may say that

THE SHRINKING WORK WEEK

In 1890 the average worker was employed 60 hours a week at a wage rate of $0.20 an hour. In 1982, the average worker worked only 35 hours per week, at a wage rate of close to $7 an hour.

How can we explain this marked reduction in the quantity of labor supplied? The answer seems to reside in our affluence. As our material possessions have proliferated and our standards of living have risen, the marginal utility of further increments of income has diminished. Leisure has become relatively more valuable. As a result, the income effect of higher wages has begun to outweigh the substitution effect, and society's labor-supply curve has been bending backward.

income effect of wages: An increased wage rate allows a person to reduce hours worked without losing income.

the higher income made possible by increased wage rates induces a *negative* supply reaction, a reduced willingness to work. This negative response to increased wage rates is referred to as the **income effect** of a rise in wages. This kind of reaction is illustrated by the backward-bending portion of the supply curve in Figure 11.6.[3]

A worker's decision to work more or less at higher wages depends on the way the conflict between income effects and substitution effects is resolved. As long as substitution effects outweigh income effects—that is, as long as the lure of increased income outweighs the sense of sufficiency—the labor-supply curve will have its more conventional upward slope.

NONMONETARY INCENTIVES

Some people work for reasons other than money alone, of course. As we observed earlier, millions of individuals find some status or salvation in their jobs. As a consequence, each hour of labor yields more satisfaction than just a paycheck.

Were Freddie to start enjoying his job, his marginal utility calculations would change, too. In Figure 11.7*a*, the curve MU^1 represents Freddie's marginal-utility-of-labor curve before he found salvation in work. After he finds out that people like him more when he has a job, the marginal utility of each hour's labor increases. This change is represented by an upward *shift* of Freddie's marginal utility curve to MU_2. The resultant increase in marginal utilities will also shift Freddie's labor-supply curve to the right, as in Figure 11.7*b*. All we are saying here is that if Freddie likes his job, he will be willing to work more hours per day for any given wage rate.

Like Freddie, workers on the assembly line or in offices are also influenced by nonmonetary incentives. Pleasant surroundings, piped-in music, and colorful walls are often used to make employees

[3] Income effects are relevant at low incomes also. A person paid very low wage rates (e.g., migrant workers, baby sitters, household workers) may end up working more hours at low wages in order to maintain some minimum level of income. The higher income made possible by higher wage rates may induce some cutback in hours of work. These are the kinds of situations Karl Marx had in mind when he said that capitalists would strive to keep wage rates low to induce people to work. The modern version of this problem is discussed in Chapter 17, where the welfare system is considered.

FIGURE 11.7 THE EFFECT OF INCREASED JOB SATISFACTION

A given labor-supply curve is based on the assumption that the "taste" for work is constant. If work becomes more enjoyable, however, its marginal utility increases and the assumption is no longer valid. An increase in job satisfaction is illustrated in part *a* by an upward shift of the marginal utility curve. When job satisfaction increases, the labor-supply curve shifts to the right, as in part *b*. People are willing to work more hours at any given wage rate when they enjoy their work.

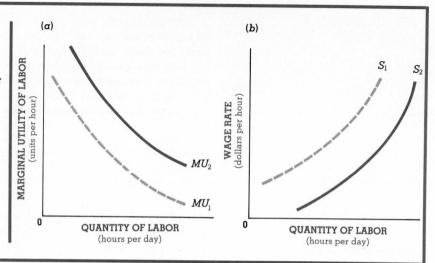

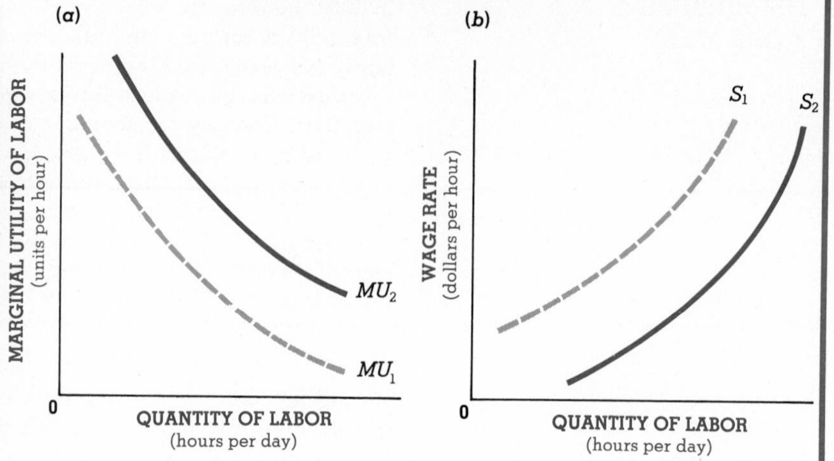

"Leave it to good old G.M. to break the monotony of the assembly line!"

Drawing by Alan Dunn: © 1972 The New Yorker Magazine, Inc.

feel they are on some tropical beach, and help make the trade-off between work and leisure less apparent.

High wages and superficial changes in the work environment are not the only relevant incentives, of course. Worker behavior is also affected by the nature of the work to be performed and the sense of attachment the worker associates with the job. If people can identify with their work and feel their efforts are important, they are likely to perform not only more work but better work for a given rate of pay. When they perceive little interest or significance in their efforts, the willingness to work declines. Industrial research has suggested that the problem of worker alienation is particularly acute in jobs that are exceedingly specialized and routine. It is difficult to sustain interest in a job that requires one to tighten bolts on the left rear wheel of every car moving down the assembly line or punch holes in IBM computer cards. Wage increases may not be sufficient to improve worker motivation in such cases.

Finally, willingness to work may be affected by more general perceptions of the significance of work. The women's liberation movement, for example, has allayed the guilt feelings formerly associated by many wives and mothers with work performed outside the home. As a consequence, more women are willing to work at existing wage rates (that is, their supply curves have shifted to the right). Other forms of persuasion have been used to motivate entire countries, such as patriotic appeals in Cuba and China during the 1960s and 1970s to produce more sugar and wheat.[4] In each case, the objective of policy was to raise workers' perception of the value of work, to make them feel that they gave up less than they got when they sacrificed leisure for work.

[4] The extensive use of nonmonetary incentives in the People's Republic of China is discussed in Chapter 21 in *The Macro Economy Today*. Of particular interest in this regard is the way socialist countries rely on various combinations of monetary and nonmonetary incentives.

INSTITUTIONAL CONSTRAINTS

Both the monetary and the nonmonetary incentives offered to workers are intended to alter their work patterns, the amount of labor they supply. We must recognize, however, that people seldom have the opportunity to adjust their hours of employment in accordance with their desired trade-off between work and leisure. True, Sugar Ray Leonard, Devo, Richard Pryor, Chris Evert Lloyd, the Rolling Stones, and many others may alter their labor supply almost at will. Most workers, however, face more rigid choices. They must usually choose to work at a regular eight-hour-day, five-day-week job or not to work at all. Very few firms are flexible or interested enough to accommodate a desire to work only between the hours of 11 A.M. and 3 P.M. on alternate Thursdays. As a consequence, relatively few people are able to achieve the optimum balance between work and leisure suggested by their labor-supply curves (see box). Adjustments in work hours are more commonly confined to choices about overtime work or secondary jobs ("moonlighting") and vacation and retirement decisions. Insofar as families make collective decisions about the labor they supply, adjustments in work effort may also be reflected in decisions about the number of family members to send into the labor force at any given time.

POLICY IMPLICATIONS: A VOLUNTEER ARMY

The desire of consumers for income and status creates the conditions for altered patterns of work effort. As we have seen, people can be induced to increase or reduce their work effort simply by changes in the monetary or nonmonetary incentives they confront. If workers

MISSING THE OPTIMUM: INFLEXIBLE WORK SCHEDULES

The U.S. Department of Labor recently surveyed American workers to determine whether they were satisfied with their present mix of labor and leisure. Specifically, workers were asked if they would prefer a bit more leisure in exchange for a bit less income. Would they, in other words, substitute more leisure for a few hours of work if they had the opportunity? The added leisure could take the form of fewer hours per day or week, longer vacations, occasional sabbaticals, or earlier retirement. The "cost" of the added leisure would be a reduction in income.

The responses were overwhelming. Eighty-five percent of all workers said they would gladly give up a raise (marginal income) for added leisure. Sixty percent said they would give up some of their *current* income for added leisure. In other words, the vast majority of American workers feel they have not achieved their optimal work effort. Inflexible work schedules prevent them from achieving the most satisfying combination of labor and leisure.

can be persuaded to work long or little, they may also be induced to move from one occupation to another with appropriate encouragement. Suppose that prospective wage earners would rather be social workers than accountants but that we need more accountants. Are we helpless to change people's occupational choices? Certainly not. Recognizing the various incentives that shape occupational choices, we can offer higher pay for accountants than for social workers. As the relative pay of accountants rises, more and more people will choose that occupation. As a result, we will have more accountants and fewer social workers. In general, we can alter people's occupational choices by changing the structure of employment rewards.

market mechanism: The use of market prices and sales to signal desired outputs (or resource allocations).

In a completely totalitarian regime, we could impose the same kind of results by fiat. The theory of labor supply explains how various work patterns can be induced by the **market mechanism.** A classic example of labor-supply theory at work was the conversion from a draft army to an all-volunteer army.

The hope has long existed that we could fill our armies with dedicated volunteers serving at low pay, but those expectations have usually remained unfulfilled. We have found that the willingness to do battle with the enemy varies considerably from one person to another and from one war to the next. Generally, however, the total number of people volunteering to serve in the armed forces has been below the number required. As a result, we have had to go to war without a sufficient army, increase the willingness to serve, or compel people to serve against their will. Each solution has been tried at one time or another.

In the early years of the Republic, there was widespread hostility to the notion of military conscription. Although local conscription laws did exist, they were rarely enforced. For the most part, local defenses consisted of militia volunteers who rallied to repel outside attacks. Even the Revolutionary War was fought almost entirely by volunteers, who were encouraged by patriotism and financial bounties to join the state militias or the Continental Army. In effect, the supply of labor shifted to the right when independence was declared (see Figure 11.8), and military service was encouraged by higher wages.

Soon after the Revolutionary War, both the need for armed forces and the willingness to serve declined. The standing army of the United States was reduced to a mere 80 men. To enlarge our defenses, Secretary of War Henry Knox proposed in 1790 to create a universal draft, compelling military service. Congress, however, rejected his proposal. As a result, when the United States entered the less popular War of 1812, we found ourselves seriously short of military manpower. This shortage led to an almost unbroken series of defeats, including the humiliating burning of the nation's capital in 1814.

The Civil War, too, was fought primarily by volunteers on both sides. When war was declared, the Union Army had fewer than 16,000 officers and men. Within the first two years, however, more than 1 million men voluntarily answered the call to arms, reflecting another shift in the supply curve. Nevertheless, at the outset of the war, President Abraham Lincoln had proposed a national draft to

FIGURE 11.8 THE WILLINGNESS TO SERVE

A person's willingness to serve in the military depends on both attitudes and pay scales. Suppose an individual's perceptions of national defense are expressed by supply curve *A*. Clearly, this person is more likely to serve, or voluntarily to serve more time, if military wage rates are increased (say, from w_1 to w_2). If the army's image improves or a particularly righteous war commences, however, the general commitment to national defense will increase, as reflected by supply curve *B*. If the popularity of war falls, the commitment to defense will decline, as expressed by supply curve *C*.

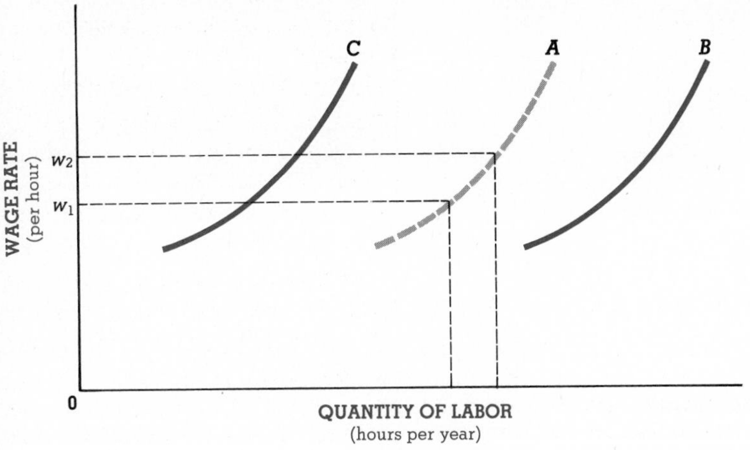

ensure an adequate supply of manpower. When the draft was enacted in March 1863, widespread resistance erupted, reaching a bloody climax in the New York draft riots, in which more than 1,000 people were killed. During the course of the war, the new powers of conscription were used sparingly, with draftees accounting for only 2.3 percent of the North's military manpower and about 14 percent of the South's.

In 1917 a comprehensive draft law was passed immediately after the United States entered World War I. Because of extensive opposition to the war, Congress felt compelled to forgo reliance on voluntary enlistments. Congress felt that compulsory service was cheaper than the pay increases and enlistment bonuses that had been used to recruit volunteers in earlier crises. Evasion of the draft replaced open resistance during World War I, with more than 250,000 draftees failing to appear for induction. The draft law expired after the end of the war.

With the onset of World War II, we were again faced with the problem of recruiting additional manpower. The Selective Service Act of 1940 created the authority by which the government could compel men to join the army, regardless of their willingness to serve. The act not only gave the government new authority, but also permitted it to keep military pay at levels significantly lower than comparable civilian pay. More than 10 million men were drafted for service in World War II.

The unpopularity of the Vietnam War aroused resistance to the draft once again. As a result, Congress debated the possibility of returning to the concept of an all-volunteer army. In accordance with the theory of labor supply, Congress concluded that such an army was possible only if a war were particularly popular or if military pay and status were considerably increased. The first condition was clearly not met. The President's Commission on an All-Volunteer Armed Force estimated in 1970 that basic military pay would

Reagan on draft—why he changed

Ronald Reagan's decision to continue Jimmy Carter's draft-registration system demonstrated that issues can look different when seen from the White House instead of the campaign trail.

The crackdown in Poland, tensions in the Mideast, uprisings by Soviet surrogates in Central America—all prompted Reagan on January 7 to abandon his 1980 campaign claim that registration is a meaningless gesture that "destroys the very values that our society is committed to defending."

Carter reinstated registration for a possible draft in July, 1980, in response to the Soviet invasion of Afghanistan. Reagan now believes, aides said, that dropping registration would send a wrong signal to Moscow. "We live in a dangerous world," he said.

Advisers hoped Reagan's action will reverse a falloff in draft registrations, a slump that accelerated after Reagan took office. At last check, 1 of every 4 youths had declined to sign up within 30 days of his 18th birthday as required by law. During the Vietnam War, the level of noncompliance did not exceed 2 percent.

The Justice Department moved to establish a grace period of 30 to 60 days for late registrations. After that, officials warned, laggards may be hit by penalties ranging up to five years in prison and a $10,000 fine.

Reagan changed his mind on registration, aides said, after a military task force concluded that the system would save up to six weeks in mobilization time—virtually the same conclusion as in a study done for Carter two years ago.

have to rise from $180 to $315 a month to attract an additional 100,000 men per year. In the light of these facts, Congress opted to study and debate the subject for two years. Congress finally allowed the authority for conscription to expire only at the war's end in 1973.

Our experiences with an all-volunteer army have demonstrated the principles of labor-supply theory. Willingness to serve is directly affected not only by one's perception of patriotism and danger, but also by military wage rates and status. Since 1973 we have placed increased reliance on higher pay scales, early retirement benefits, and advertising to induce a steady flow of volunteers. While military wages have skyrocketed, the old, drab army has become "Today's Army," with spruced-up and tailor-fitted uniforms and more amenities. In addition, the Army, Navy, and Air Force have vastly enlarged the pool of potential volunteers by actively recruiting women and providing them with more equal status and benefits.

Although we have generally succeeded in "buying" an all-volunteer armed force, several problems remain. Critics claim that the all-volunteer army is most attractive to low-income and minority people, who have fewer civilian job opportunities (and thus lower opportunity costs). Also, the armed forces have not been very successful in retaining experienced personnel or in maintaining a pool of reservists. The armed services have tried to remedy the first problem by substantial reenlistment bonuses (up to $15,000), but even this "wage" has not been adequate. To help overcome the lack of reservists, Congress reinstated Selective Service registration in July 1980. All men must register at the age of 18 and provide their permanent address. Registration will enable the Selective Service to find and recruit military personnel more quickly in the event of a war. In the meantime, however, the armed forces must recruit more than one out of every five 18-year olds (roughly 2 million personnel) just to keep our peacetime forces at full strength.

SUMMARY

▪ The motivation to work arises from a variety of social, psychological, and economic forces. People need income to pay their bills, but they also need to feel they have a role in society's efforts, and to attain a sense of achievement. As a consequence, people are *willing to work—to supply labor.*

▪ There is an opportunity cost involved in working; namely, the amount of leisure one sacrifices. By the same token, the opportunity cost of not working (leisure) is the income and related consumption possibilities thereby forgone. Thus each person confronts a trade-off between leisure and income.

▪ People choose between labor and leisure according to the perceived rewards of each. The marginal utility of labor reflects the satisfaction to be gained from added income, as well as any direct pleasure a job may provide. A worker compares these satisfactions with those of leisure and chooses the one that yields greater marginal utility.

▪ An individual's work effort is optimal when the marginal utility of labor equals the marginal utility of leisure. This particular combination of labor and leisure yields the greatest utility for available time and wage rates.

▪ Increases in wage rates raise the marginal utility of labor and tend to induce people to increase their hours of work, that is, to substitute labor for leisure. But this substitution effect may be offset by an income effect. That is, increased wage rates also enable a person to work fewer hours with no loss of income. When income effects outweigh substitution effects, the labor-supply curve begins to bend backward.

▪ The choice between labor and leisure is also affected by nonmonetary incentives and institutional constraints. Inflexibility of working hours may preclude the attainment of an optimal labor-leisure combination.

Terms to remember

Define the following terms:

labor supply
utility
law of diminishing marginal utility
marginal utility of labor
optimal work effort
wage rate
labor-supply curve
substitution effect of wages
income effect of wages
market mechanism

Questions for discussion

1. Would you continue to work after winning a lottery prize of $50,000 a year for life? Would you change schools, jobs, or career objectives? What factors besides income influence work decisions?

2. If garbagemen were paid twice as much as doctors, how would this reversal affect people's occupational or educational plans?

3. Will a doubling of wage rates stimulate people to work twice as long? Why, or why not?

4. If daytime television were to improve dramatically, would labor supplies be affected?

Problem

Use the following schedules of individual labor supply to construct a *market* labor-supply curve.

Hourly wage rate	Number of hours supplied per week			
	Adam	*Susan*	*Linda*	*David*
$ 1	6	0	28	0
2	14	0	25	0
3	18	5	20	0
4	22	8	16	10
5	27	18	12	15
6	35	27	10	20
7	40	35	8	25
8	46	35	7	30
9	40	35	6	30
10	28	35	6	40

What wage rate is required to enlist at least 100 hours of help per week?

CHAPTER 12

THE DEMAND FOR LABOR

In 1982 the president of General Motors was paid over half a million dollars for his services. The president of the United States was paid $200,000. And the secretary who typed the manuscript of this book was paid $8,000. What accounts for these tremendous disparities in earnings?

And why is it that the average college graduate was earning over $20,000 in 1982 while the average high school graduate earned only $12,000 ? Do such disparities simply reflect a reward earned by those who endured the rigors of four years of college, or do they reflect real differences in talent? Are you really learning anything that makes you that much more valuable than a high school graduate?

Surely we cannot hope to explain these earnings disparities on the basis of the willingness to work. After all, my secretary would be more than willing to work day and night for $500,000 per year. For that matter, so would I. Accordingly, the earnings disparities cannot be attributed to differences in the quantity of labor supplied. If we are to explain why some people earn a great deal of income while others earn very little, we will have to consider also the *demand* for labor. What determines the wage rate employers are *willing to pay*, and why do they pay individual workers such disparate wage rates? These are the primary concerns of this chapter.

DERIVED DEMAND

Employers tend to be profit maximizers. That is to say, their primary motivation in going into business is to make as much income as possible. In their quest for maximum profits, firms attempt to identify the rate of output at which marginal revenue equals marginal cost. Once they have identified the profit-maximizing rate of output, firms enter factor markets to purchase the required amounts of labor, equipment, and other resources. The quantity of resources purchased by business firms depends, then, on the firm's expected sales and output. In this sense, we say that the demand for factors of production, including labor, is a **derived demand;** it is derived from the demand for goods and services.

derived demand: The demand for labor and other factors of production results from (depends on) the demand for final goods and services produced by these factors.

Consider the plight of strawberry pickers. Strawberry pickers are paid very low wages and are employed only part of the year. But their plight cannot be blamed on the greed of the strawberry growers. Strawberry growers, like most producers, would love to sell more strawberries at higher prices. If they did, there is a strong possibility that the growers would hire more pickers and even pay them at a higher wage rate. But the growers must contend with the market demand for strawberries. Growers have discovered that consumers are not willing to buy more strawberries at higher prices. As a consequence, the growers cannot afford to hire more pickers or pay them higher wages. In contrast, producers of computers are always looking for more workers and offer very high wages to get them (see news clipping).

The principle of derived demand suggests that if consumers

SHIFTING DEMANDS FOR LABOR

Wages and job prospects in future years will depend on changes in the demand for labor. The U.S. Department of Labor foresees major increases in the demand for computer technicians and paralegals as consumer demands for computer and legal services continue to increase. Conversely, an actual decline in the demand for college professors is anticipated as college enrollments decline. Things look even worse for shoemakers and farm workers. These figures show projected growth in employment for the fastest- and slowest-growing occupations.

Occupations in high demand	*Projected growth of jobs, 1978–1990*
Computer technicians	148%
Paralegal aides	132
Office machine technicians	81
Computer programmers	74
Food-service workers (including fast-food outlets)	69
Tax preparers	65
Correction officials and jailers	60
Architects	60
Dental assistants	57
Veterinarians	56
Travel agents	56
Nurse's aides	55
Occupations in low demand	
College and university teachers	−10%
Textile weavers	−11
Secondary school teachers	−13
Taxi drivers	−13
Private household workers	−15
Railroad car repairers	−19
Shoemaking machine operators	−20
Farm laborers	−25

FIGURE 12.1 THE DEMAND FOR LABOR

The higher the wage rate, the smaller the quantity of labor demanded *(ceteris paribus)*. At the wage rate W_1, only L_1 of labor is demanded. If the wage rate falls to W_2, a larger quantity of labor (L_2) will be demanded. The labor-demand curve obeys the law of demand.

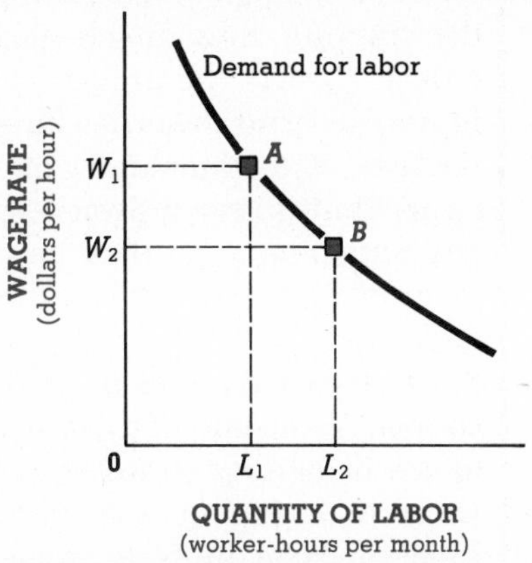

really want to improve the lot of strawberry pickers, they should eat more strawberries. An increase in the demand for strawberries will motivate growers to plant more berries and hire more labor to pick them. Until then, the plight of the pickers is not likely to improve.

THE DEMAND FOR LABOR

demand for labor: The quantities of labor employers are willing and able to hire at alternative wage rates in a given time period *(ceteris paribus)*.

The number of strawberry pickers hired by the growers is not completely determined by the demand for strawberries, of course. On the contrary, the number of pickers will also depend on the wage rate of pickers. That is to say, ***the quantity of labor demanded will depend on its price (the wage rate).*** In general, we expect that strawberry growers will be *willing to hire* more pickers at low wages than at high wages. Hence the **demand for labor** looks very much like the demand for any good or service (see Figure 12.1).

Marginal physical product

The fact that the demand curve for labor slopes downward does not tell us very much about the quantity of labor that will be hired, of course. Nor does it tell us the wage rate that will be paid. To answer such questions, we need to know what determines the particular shape and position of the labor-demand curve.

A strawberry grower will be willing to hire another picker only if that picker contributes more to output than he costs. Growers, as rational business people, recognize that *every* sale, *every* expenditure has some impact on total profits. Hence the truly profit-maximizing grower will want to evaluate each picker's job application in terms of the applicant's potential contribution to profits.

marginal physical product *(MPP)*: The change in total output associated with one additional unit of input.

Fortunately, a strawberry picker's contribution to output is easy to measure; it is the number of boxes of strawberries he or she picks. Suppose for the moment that Sunshine, a college dropout with three summers of experience as a canoe instructor, can pick five boxes per hour. These five boxes represent Sunshine's **marginal physical product *(MPP)*,** that is, the *addition* to total output that will occur if the grower hires Sunshine for an hour.

The concept of marginal physical product is extremely useful in determining how much Sunshine might make as a strawberry picker. Clearly the grower can't afford to pay Sunshine more than five boxes of strawberries for an hour's work; to do so would imply a net loss. Thus Sunshine's marginal physical product establishes an *upper limit* to the grower's willingness to pay. The grower will not pay Sunshine more than he produces.

Marginal revenue product

marginal revenue product *(MRP):* **The change in total revenue associated with one additional unit of input.**

Most strawberry pickers don't want to be paid in strawberries, of course. At the end of a day in the fields, the last thing a picker wants to see is another strawberry. Sunshine, like the rest of the pickers, wants to be paid in cash. Fortunately, the conversion of productivity from physical units to monetary units is straightforward. All we need to know is what a box of strawberries is worth. The market value of a box of strawberries is simply the price at which the grower can sell it. Thus Sunshine's contribution to output can be measured in either marginal physical product (five boxes per hour) or the dollar value of that product. The latter is called Sunshine's **marginal revenue product.** If the grower can sell strawberries for \$2 a box, Sunshine's marginal revenue product is easily calculated; it is simply 5 boxes per hour × \$2 per box, or \$10 per hour. In compliance with the rule about not paying anybody more than he or she contributes, the profit-maximizing grower should be willing to pay Sunshine up to \$10 an hour. Thus ***marginal revenue product sets an upper limit to the wage rate an employer will pay.***

But what about a lower limit? Suppose that the pickers aren't organized and are desperate for money. Under such circumstances, they might be willing to work—to supply labor—for only \$3 an hour.

Should the grower hire Sunshine for such a low wage? The profit-maximizing answer is obvious. If Sunshine's marginal revenue product is \$10 an hour and his wages are only \$3 an hour, the grower will be eager to hire him. Obviously Sunshine promises to contribute to profits at the rate of \$7 an hour. In fact, the grower will be so elated by the economics of this situation that he will want to hire everybody he can find who is willing to work for \$3 an hour. After all, if the grower can make \$7 an hour by hiring Sunshine, why not hire 1,000 pickers and accumulate profits at an even faster rate?

THE LAW OF DIMINISHING RETURNS

The exploitive possibilities suggested by Sunshine's picking are clearly attractive; however, they merit some careful consideration. It isn't at all clear, for example, how the grower could squeeze 1,000 workers onto one acre of land and have any room left over for strawberry plants. There must be some limit to the profit-making potential of this situation.

A few moments' reflection on the absurdity of trying to employ 1,000 people to pick one acre of strawberries should be convincing evidence of the limits to profits here. You don't need two years of business school to recognize this. But some economics may help explain exactly why the grower's eagerness to hire additional pickers will begin to fade long before 1,000 are hired. The magic concept here is *marginal productivity.*

Diminishing marginal physical product

The decision to hire Sunshine originated in his marginal physical product, that is, the five boxes of strawberries he can pick in an hour's time. To assess the profitability of hiring additional pickers, we again have to consider what will happen to total output as additional labor is employed. To do so we will need to keep track of marginal physical product.

Table 12.1 provides a summary of the increases in strawberry output as additional pickers are hired. We start with Sunshine, who picks five boxes of strawberries per hour. Total output and his marginal physical product are identical, because he is initially the only picker employed. When the grower hires Moon, Sunshine's old college roommate, we observe that total output increases to ten boxes per hour. This figure represents another increase of five boxes per hour. Accordingly, we may conclude that Moon's *marginal physical product* is five boxes per hour, the same as Sunshine's. Naturally, the grower will want to hire Moon and continue looking for more pickers.

Sara is also willing to work for $3 an hour, so the grower agrees to employ her as well. But the output statistics don't look quite so good this time. Total output rises from ten boxes an hour to fourteen, indicating that Sara's marginal physical product is only four boxes per hour. But Sara is working just as hard as Sunshine and Moon and is at least as capable. What accounts for this decline in marginal physical product?

If the observed decline in *MPP* can't be blamed on Sara herself, then it must be attributable to the production process. After careful investigation, the grower discovers that Sunshine and Moon have been picking the largest strawberries first, leaving the smaller ones for someone else. As a consequence, further picking yields smaller strawberries and thus fewer boxes. The decline in *MPP* therefore has nothing to do with Sara's abilities; any other picker would have ex-

TABLE 12.1 MARGINAL PHYSICAL PRODUCT

Marginal physical product *(MPP)* measures the change in total output that occurs when one additional worker is hired. When the second worker (Moon) is hired, total output increases from five to ten boxes per hour. Hence the second worker's *MPP* equals five boxes per hour.

Number of pickers (per hour)	*Total strawberry output (boxes per hour)*	*Marginal physical product (boxes per hour)*
1 (Sunshine)	5	5
2 (Moon)	10	5
3 (Sara)	14	4
4 (Eddy)	17	3
5	19	2
6	20	1
7	20	0
8	18	−2
9	15	−3

FIGURE 12.2 DIMINISHING MARGINAL PHYSICAL PRODUCT

The marginal physical product of labor is the increase in total production that results when one additional worker is hired. Marginal physical product tends to fall as additional workers are hired in any given production process. This decline occurs because each worker has increasingly less of other factors (e.g., land) with which to work. (Note that these curves correspond to the last two columns in Table 12.1.)

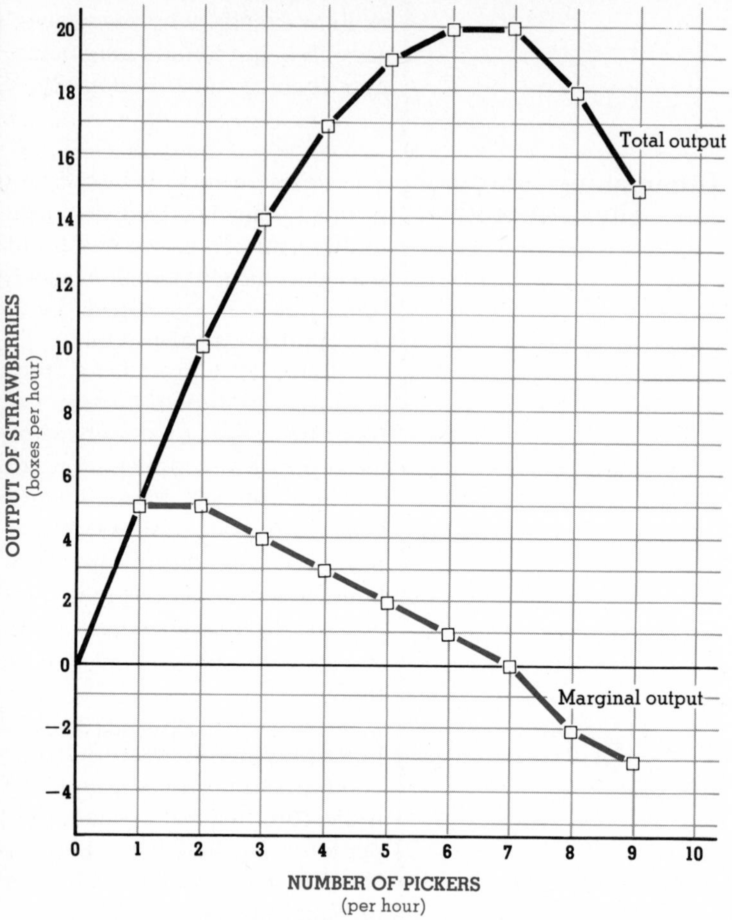

perienced the same problem. There simply aren't that many large berries.

When the grower hires Eddy, still another decline in marginal physical product occurs. Total output rises from fourteen boxes an hour to only seventeen, yielding an *MPP* of three boxes per hour. Again the problem appears to have nothing to do with Eddy personally, because he has been picking strawberries over eight years. The problem, it appears, is the number of boxes. There are only a dozen boxes, and the four pickers often have to wait for an empty box. The time spent waiting lowers output and thus drives down marginal physical product.

As the grower continues to hire pickers, still more problems arise. The worst problem is space: as additional workers are crowded onto the one-acre patch, they begin to get in each other's way. The picking process is slowed and marginal physical product is further depressed. Note that the *MPP* of the fifth picker is two boxes per hour, while the *MPP* of the sixth picker is only one box per hour. By the time we get to the seventh picker, marginal physical product actually falls to zero, as no further increases in total strawberry output take place.

Things get even worse if the grower tries to hire still more pickers. If eight pickers are employed, total output actually *declines*, because the pickers can no longer work efficiently under such crowded conditions. Hence the *MPP* of the eighth worker is *negative*, no matter how ambitious or hard-working this person may be. Figure 12.2 illustrates this decline in marginal physical product.

law of diminishing returns: The marginal physical product of a variable factor declines as more of it is employed with a given quantity of other (fixed) inputs.

Our observations on strawberry production are similar to those made in most industries. In general, ***the marginal physical product of labor declines as the quantity of labor employed increases.*** This is the **law of diminishing returns** we first encountered in Chapter 5. It is based on the simple observation that an increasing number of workers leaves each worker with less land and capital to work with.

Diminishing marginal revenue product

As marginal *physical* product diminishes, so does marginal revenue product *(MRP)*. As we noted earlier, marginal revenue product is the increase in the *value* of total output associated with an added unit of labor (or other input). In our example, it refers to the increase in strawberry revenues associated with one additional picker.

The decline in marginal revenue product mirrors the drop in marginal physical product. Recall that a box of strawberries sells for $2. With this price and the output statistics of Table 12.1, we can readily calculate marginal revenue product, as summarized in Table 12.2. As the growth of output diminishes, so does marginal revenue product. Sunshine's marginal revenue product of $10 an hour has fallen to $4 by the time four pickers are employed and reaches zero when seven pickers are employed.[1]

[1] Marginal revenue product would fall even faster if the price of strawberries declined as increasing quantities were supplied. We are assuming that the grower's output does not influence the market price of strawberries, and hence that the grower is a competitive producer.

TABLE 12.2 DIMINISHING MARGINAL REVENUE PRODUCT

Marginal revenue product (*MRP*) measures the change in total revenue that occurs when one additional worker is hired. At constant product prices, *MRP* equals *MPP* × price. Hence, *MRP* declines along with *MPP*.

Numbers of pickers (per hour)	Total strawberry output (in boxes per hour)	×	Price of strawberries (per box)	=	Total strawberry revenue (per hour)	Marginal revenue product
0	0		$2		0	—
1 (Sunshine)	5		2		$10	$10
2 (Moon)	10		2		20	10
3 (Sara)	14		2		28	8
4 (Eddy)	17		2		34	6
5	19		2		38	4
6	20		2		40	2
7	20		2		40	0
8	18		2		36	−4
9	15		2		30	−6

FIGURE 12.3 THE MARGINAL REVENUE PRODUCT CURVE IS THE LABOR-DEMAND CURVE

The *MRP* curve tells us how many workers an employer would want to hire at various wage rates. An employer is willing to pay a worker no more than his or her marginal revenue product. In this case, a grower would gladly hire a second worker, because that worker's *MRP* (point *B*) exceeds the wage rate ($3). The sixth worker will not be hired at that wage rate, however, since his *MRP* (at point *D*) is less than $3. The *MRP* curve is the labor-demand curve.

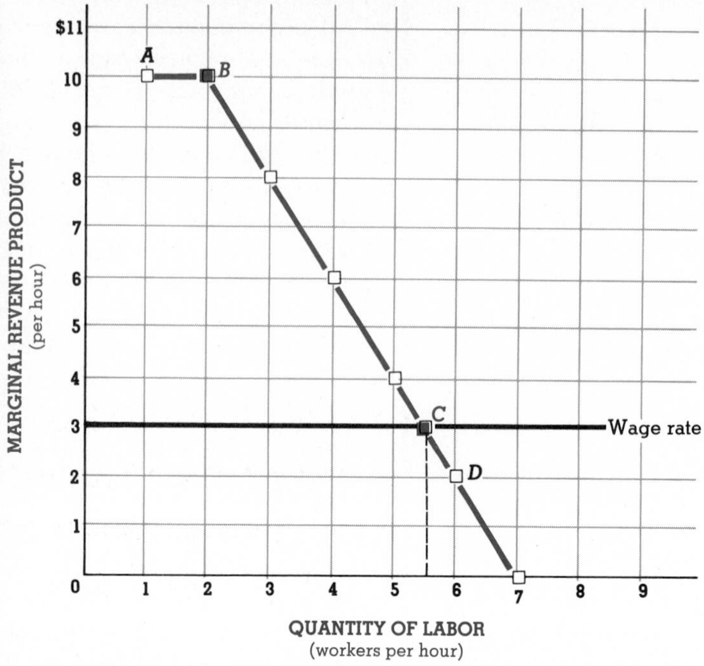

THE HIRING DECISION

The tendency of marginal revenue product to diminish will clearly cool the grower's eagerness to hire 1,000 more pickers like Sunshine. As we observed earlier, marginal revenue product establishes a *limit* to the wage rate an employer is willing to pay for hired labor.

The labor-demand curve

Consider Figure 12.3, which provides a graphic illustration of the decline in marginal revenue product indicated in Table 12.2. With this curve, we can quickly determine the quantity of labor that the grower will be *willing* to hire at any particular wage rate. That is to say, we can readily determine his *demand for labor*.

Let us continue to assume that an unlimited number of strawberry pickers are willing to work for $3 an hour. The grower must then decide how many pickers to hire at this wage. Figure 12.3 provides the answer. We already know that the grower is eager to hire at least one worker at that wage, because the *MRP* of the first picker is $10 an hour (point *A* in Figure 12.3). A second worker will be hired as well, because the picker's *MRP* (point *B* in Figure 12.3) also exceeds the going wage rate. In fact, ***the grower will continue hiring pickers until the* MRP *has declined to the level of the market wage rate.*** Figure 12.3 indicates that this intersection (point *C*) occurs after five pickers are employed. Hence we can conclude that the grower will be willing to hire—will *demand*—five pickers if wages are $3 an hour.

The folly of hiring more than five pickers is also apparent in

Figure 12.3. The marginal revenue product of the sixth worker is only \$2 an hour (point *D*). Hiring a sixth picker will cost more in wages than the picker brings in as revenue. The *maximum* number of pickers the grower will employ at prevailing wages is five and one-half (point *C*).

The law of diminishing returns also implies that all of the five pickers will be paid the same wage. Once five pickers are employed, we cannot say that any single picker is responsible for the observed decline in marginal revenue product. Marginal revenue product of labor diminishes because each worker has less capital and land to work with, not because the last worker hired is less able than the others. Accordingly, the "fifth" picker cannot be identified as any particular individual. Once five pickers are hired, Sunshine's *MRP* is no higher than Eddy's or any other picker's. Thus each (identical) worker is worth no more than the marginal revenue product of the last worker hired, and all workers are paid the same wage rate.

Changes in wage rates

law of demand: The quantity of a good demanded in a given time period increases as its price falls *(ceteris paribus)*.

The grower's decision to hire only five pickers is not unalterable. If the wage rate were to drop, more pickers would be hired. Suppose for the moment that the pickers agree to work for only \$2 an hour. The grower will now be able to hire a sixth worker without sacrificing any profits. Figure 12.4 illustrates the effect of a reduction in wage rates. When wages drop, the employer moves down the labor-demand curve to a larger quantity of labor. Hence the labor-demand curve obeys the ancient **law of demand.**

FIGURE 12.4 LOWER WAGE RATES INCREASE THE QUANTITY OF LABOR DEMANDED

If the wage rate drops, an employer will be willing to hire additional workers *(ceteris paribus)*. At \$3 an hour, only 5½ pickers per hour would be demanded (point *C*). If the wage rate dropped to \$2 an hour, 6 pickers per hour would be demanded (point *D*).

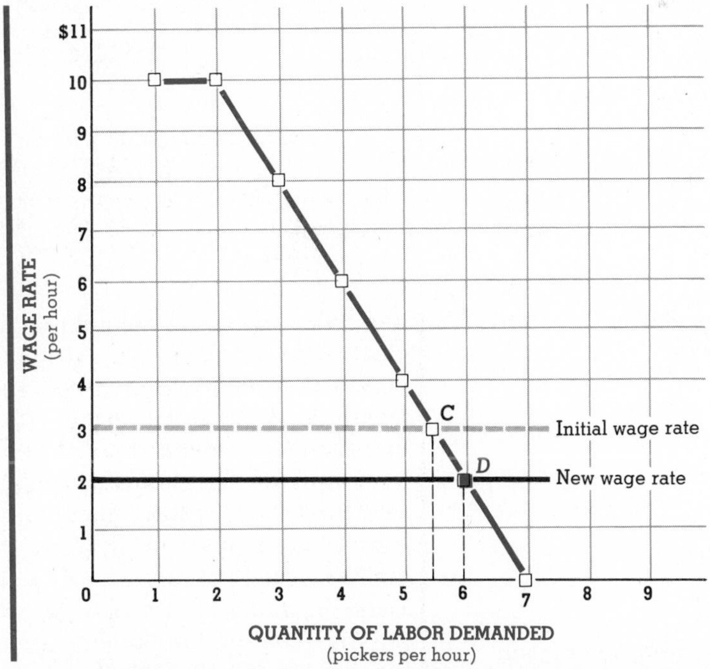

THE MINIMUM WAGE AND EMPLOYMENT

The Fair Labor Standards Act of 1938 decreed that workers had to be paid a wage of at least 25 cents per hour. Since that time, Congress has repeatedly raised the minimum wage, up to its current level of $3.35 per hour. The objective of the minimum wage law is to ensure workers a decent standard of living. But the rules for profit maximization create a problem. An employer will not hire a worker unless marginal revenue product exceeds the wage rate. Accordingly, higher minimum wages tend to reduce the quantity of labor demanded. This is illustrated on the graph below; note the drop in quantity demanded, from q_1 to q_2, when the minimum wage is introduced.

When the minimum wage was increased to $3.35 in 1981, over 5 million workers were earning less than that amount. Most of them probably got a raise, but others may have lost their jobs. Still others, particularly teenagers looking for their first jobs, found employers less willing to hire them. In other words, some workers gain but others lose when the minimum wage is increased. The actual distribution of gains and losses is hotly debated. The negative impact of a higher minimum wage will be smaller if (1) the minimum wage is close to the equilibrium wage; (2) the demand for labor is relatively inelastic; and (3) wage rates are not directly related to marginal revenue product.

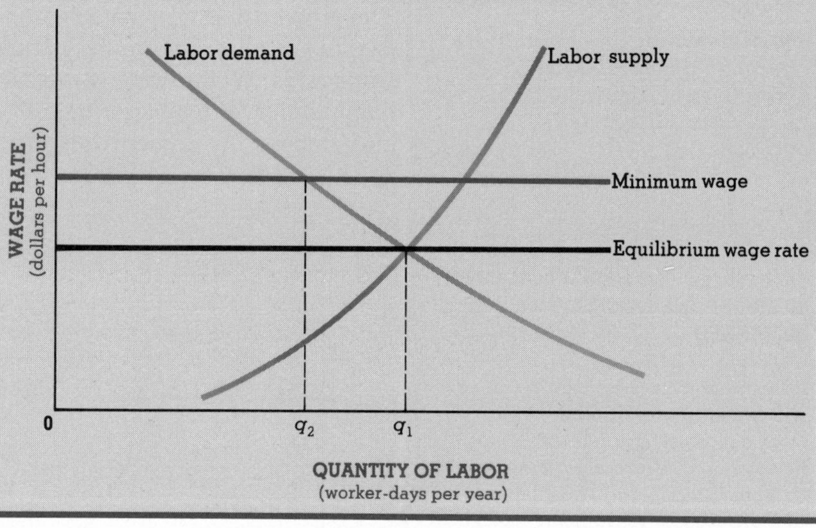

Changes in productivity

Reductions in wages are not the only path to increased employment of strawberry pickers. The hiring decision involves a comparison of marginal revenue product and the wage rate. Accordingly, an increase in *MRP* can be just as effective as a wage (*W*) reduction in increasing employment.

Suppose that Sunshine and his friends all enroll in the local agricultural extension course on strawberry-picking techniques and learn new methods of picking. With these new methods, the marginal physical product of each picker increases by one box per hour. With the price of strawberries still at $2 a box, this productivity improvement implies an increase in marginal *revenue* product of $2 per worker. This change causes a rightward **shift** of the labor-demand (*MRP*) curve, as in Figure 12.5.

shift in demand: A change in the quantity demanded at any (every) given price.

FIGURE 12.5 A SHIFT IN LABOR DEMAND

The willingness of an employer to hire labor at any specific wage rate is based on labor's marginal revenue product. If the marginal revenue product of labor improves, the employer will be willing to hire a greater quantity of labor at any given wage rate. The labor-demand curve will shift to the right (e.g., from D_1 to D_2). In this case, an increase in *MRP* leads the employer to hire 6 workers (point *E*) rather than only 5½ workers (point *C*) at \$3 per hour.

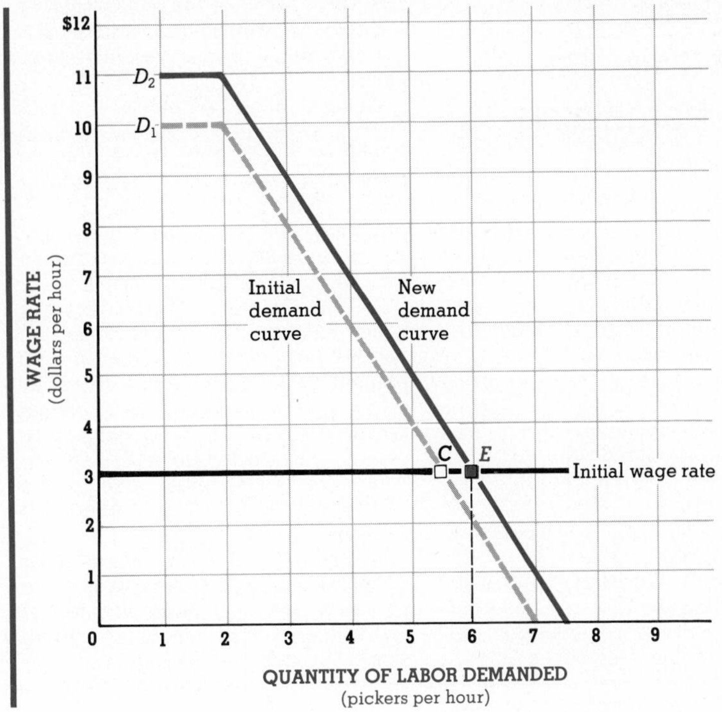

Notice that the old wage rate of \$3 an hour, when combined with the new labor-demand curve, leads to the employment of a sixth picker. Hence ***either an increase in productivity or a fall in wage rates can bring about an increase in the quantity of labor demanded.*** Naturally, the pickers are happier when the additional employment comes about through increased productivity, because in that case they don't suffer a wage reduction.

CHOOSING AMONG INPUTS

The principles determining the shape and position of the demand curve for labor can be extended to rationalize the choice among various factors of production. Suppose that someone invents a mechanical strawberry picker that can pick berries twice as fast as Sunshine. Who will the grower hire, Sunshine or the mechanical picker?

At first it would seem that the grower would choose the mechanical picker. But the choice isn't so obvious. So far, all we know is that the mechanical picker's *MPP* is twice as large as Sunshine's. But we haven't said anything about the *cost* of the mechanical picker.

Cost efficiency

Suppose that a mechanical picker can be rented for \$10 an hour, while Sunshine is still willing to work for \$3 an hour. Will this difference in hourly cost change the grower's input choice?

Givebacks: Latest twist in union bargaining

For a growing number of workers in troubled industries, dickering over wages is becoming a two-way street.

Faced with the prospect of long-term layoffs or permanent job losses, unionized employes in one ailing firm after another are choosing to give back hard-won pay hikes or other benefits.

Latest to forgo or agree to at least reconsider negotiated gains are workers in airline, auto, rubber and trucking companies.

"It's an enormous sacrifice," says Douglas Fraser, president of the United Auto Workers. "But when you're talking about saving thousands of jobs, you do what you have to do."

Whatever the long-range impact, the trend toward unions accepting less pay to prevent a loss of jobs is unmistakable. Some recent examples—

□ General Motors employes at a ball-bearing plant in Clark, N.J., tentatively agreed to buy the facility to prevent it from closing. GM says it will continue to purchase the plant's products, but at market prices. The net result: a 30 percent pay reduction for the facility's 2,000 workers.

□ At Pan American World Airways, which has lost 218 million dollars so far this year, employes agreed to a 10 percent cut in wages and a freeze at those levels through 1982. Trans World Airlines also is seeking a 10 percent pay reduction and Eastern, American and Republic airlines are asking employes to make other concessions.

□ A majority of Consolidated Rail Corporation's 66,000 employes have agreed to give up negotiated raises of as much as 12 percent. This concession will save the beleaguered railroad some 200 million dollars in the next three years and prevent it from being sold piecemeal to its competitors.

□ Workers at a Firestone Tire & Rubber Company rubber-mixing plant in Akron, Ohio, agreed to a $1-an-hour pay cut and other concessions to keep the plant operating. The company says that, even with the givebacks, it is not certain that the plant will remain open. Employes at a Goodyear Tire & Rubber Company plant in Akron recently made similar concessions.

□ In Detroit, Wayne County employes, members of the American Federation of State, County and Municipal Employes, opted to defer cost-of-living raises totaling more than 5 million dollars to avert the layoff of 665 workers. The agreement affects some 3,000 county employes.

To determine the relative desirability of hiring Sunshine or renting the mechanical picker, the grower must compare the ratio of their marginal physical products to their cost.[2] Sunshine's *MPP* is five boxes of strawberries per hour and his cost (wage) is $3. Thus the return on each dollar of wages paid to Sunshine is:

$$\text{Cost efficiency of labor} = \frac{MPP_{\text{labor}}}{\text{cost}_{\text{labor}}} = \frac{5 \text{ boxes}}{\$3} = 1.67 \text{ boxes per } \$1 \text{ of cost}$$

By contrast, the mechanical picker has an *MPP* of ten boxes per hour and costs $10 an hour, yielding a return per dollar of:

$$\text{Cost efficiency of mechanical picker} = \frac{MPP \text{ of mechanical picker}}{\text{cost of mechanical picker}} = \frac{10 \text{ boxes}}{\$10} = \text{1 box per dollar of cost}$$

These calculations indicate that Sunshine is more cost-effective than the mechanical picker. From this perspective, the grower's money will be put to best use by the hiring of Sunshine rather than by the rental of a mechanical picker.

cost efficiency: The amount of output associated with an additional dollar spent on input; the *MPP* of an input divided by its price (cost).

From the perspective of **cost efficiency**, the "cheapness" of a productive input is measured not by its price but by the amount of

[2] Note that it doesn't matter whether we are dealing with marginal physical product or marginal revenue product, because we are only comparing the productivity of two inputs used to produce the same good.

output it delivers for that price. Thus ***the most cost-efficient factor of production is the one that produces the most output per dollar.***

The concept of cost efficiency helps to explain why American firms don't move en masse to Haiti, where peasants are willing to work for as little as 10 cents an hour. Although this wage rate is far below the minimum wage in the United States, the marginal physical product of Haitian peasants is even further below American standards. Hence American workers remain more cost-efficient than the "cheap" labor available in Haiti and other less developed countries.

ALTERNATIVE PRODUCTION PROCESSES

production process: A specific combination of resources used to produce a good or service.

Typically a producer does not choose between individual inputs, but rather between alternative production processes. General Motors, for example, cannot afford to compare the cost efficiency of each job applicant with the cost efficiency of mechanical tire mounters. Instead, GM compares the relative desirability of a **production process** that is labor-intensive (uses a lot of labor) with others that are less labor-intensive. GM ignores individual differences in marginal revenue product. Nevertheless, the same principles of cost efficiency guide the decision.

The efficiency decision

Let us return to the strawberry patch to see how the choice of an entire production process is made. We shall again assume that strawberries can be picked by either human or mechanical hands. Now, however, we shall assume that one ton of strawberries can be produced by only one of the three production processes described in Table 12.3. Process *A* uses the most labor and thus keeps more human pickers employed. By contrast, process C uses many mechanical pickers and provides less employment to human pickers. Process *B* falls in between these two extremes.

Which of these three production processes should the grower use? If he used process *A*, he would demand the largest quantity of labor, and in this sense do the pickers a real favor. But his goal is to maximize profits, so we assume he will choose the production process that best serves this objective. That is to say, he will choose the *least-cost* process to produce one ton of strawberries.

TABLE 12.3 ALTERNATIVE PRODUCTION PROCESSES

One ton of strawberries can be produced with varying input combinations. Which process is most efficient? What information is missing?

	Alternative processes for producing one ton of strawberries		
Input	*Process A*	*Process B*	*Process C*
Labor (hours)	**400**	**270**	**220**
Machinery (hours)	**13**	**15**	**18**
Land (acres)	**1**	**1**	**1**

But which of the production processes in Table 12.3 is least expensive? We really can't tell on the basis of the information provided. To determine the relative cost of each process—and thus to understand the producer's choice—we have to know something more about costs. In particular, we have to know how much an hour of mechanical picking costs and how much an hour of human picking (labor) costs. Then we can determine which combination of inputs is least expensive in producing one ton of strawberries, that is, which is most *cost-efficient*. Note that we don't have to know how much the land costs, because the same amount of land is used in all three production processes. Thus land costs will not affect our efficiency decision.

Suppose that strawberry pickers are still paid $3 an hour and that mechanical pickers can be rented for $10 an hour. The acre of land rents for $500 per year. With this information we can now calculate the total dollar cost of each production process and quickly determine the most cost-efficient. Table 12.4 summarizes the required calculations.

The calculations performed in Table 12.4 clearly identify production process *C* as the least expensive way of producing one ton of strawberries. Process *A* entails a total cost of $1,830 while process *C* costs only $1,340 to produce the same quantity of output. As a profit-maximizer, the grower will choose process *C*, even though it implies less employment for strawberry pickers.

efficiency decision: The choice of a production process for any given rate of output.

The choice of an appropriate production process is called the **efficiency decision.** As we have suggested, a producer seeks to employ the combination of resources that produces a given rate of output for the least cost. The efficiency decision requires the producer to find that particular least-cost combination.

The three profit-maximizing decisions

Given the input choices faced by a producer, can we still make sense of our earlier ground rules for profit maximization, especially the one about equating marginal revenues and marginal costs? If many

TABLE 12.4 THE LEAST-COST COMBINATION

A producer wants to produce a given rate of output for the least cost. Choosing the least expensive production process is the efficiency decision. In this case, process C represents the most cost-efficient production process for producing one ton of strawberries.

Input	*Cost calculation*		
PROCESS *A*			
Labor	400 hours at $3 per hour	=	$1,200
Machinery	13 hours at $10 per hour	=	130
Land	1 acre at $500	=	500
	Total cost		$1,830
PROCESS *B*			
Labor	270 hours at $3 per hour	=	$ 810
Machinery	15 hours at $10 per hour	=	150
Land	1 acre at $500	=	500
	Total cost		$1,460
PROCESS C			
Labor	220 hours at $3 per hour	=	660
Machinery	18 hours at $10 per hour	=	180
Land	1 acre at $500	=	500
	Total cost		$1,340

ROBOTICS: THE ROLE OF TECHNOLOGY

In 1982, 4,000 robots were at work in U.S. factories. According to a Carnegie-Mellon study, over 4 million factory jobs may be performed by robots in the year 2000. Robots, which have arms, hands, and independent "brains," are going to become increasingly important in production processes. Is this robotics revolution a threat to American workers?

Mechanical strawberry pickers illustrate the kind of dilemma robotics poses. Strawberry-picking robots are a direct threat to the livelihood of human pickers and will actually replace them as either the price of robots falls or their marginal productivity rises. That is to say, the demand for human pickers will fall when robot pickers become more cost-efficient.

Although the mechanization of strawberry patches will reduce the employment and income of human pickers, it will benefit many other groups in society. The people who manufacture robots will obviously benefit from increasing automation; their employment and earnings will rise. Strawberry consumers will also benefit as the price of strawberries is reduced by the greater cost efficiency of the robots.

The fact that many individuals benefit from robotics while a few are harmed raises difficult questions for society. In essence, we have an income-distribution problem. How can the benefits of robotics (of increased cost efficiency) be shared by those who, like the strawberry pickers, are threatened by advancing technology? Our answers to date have taken the form of unemployment benefits, retraining programs, and relocation assistance. All of these programs are intended to help workers who are displaced by robots to find new jobs and maintain their incomes.

possible input combinations are available for the production of every product—and thus a number of cost alternatives—how can we determine when marginal revenue exceeds marginal cost?

Recall that we used only one set of cost estimates in our earlier analysis of short-run production decisions (Chapters 5–9). This simplification was possible because we assumed that the producer based his output decision on a comparison of revenues and the *least expensive* set of production costs. Thus we assumed he was contemplating producing only in the most economical or *cost-efficient* way. The focus of attention then settled on the question of how much output to produce with existing plant and equipment.

Hard-nosed, calculated, profit-maximizing behavior thus involves three distinct steps. The first step, the *efficiency decision*, requires the producer to determine the most efficient way of organizing the production process for some particular rate of output. This determination is based on the technical requirements of production and the costs of various factors of production. As a result of this inquiry, the producer will have a single set of production costs (or cost curves, if graphs are preferred). These costs will represent a particular plant size and related equipment.

The second step involves the comparison of potential sales revenues with the set of costs already identified as most efficient and the selection of the optimal rate of output. We have already identified this step as the **production decision**.

production decision: The selection of the short-run rate of output (with existing plant and equipment).

After completing the first two steps, the producer can decide

investment decision: The decision to build, buy, or lease plant and equipment to start or expand a business.

whether to go into business or, if he is already in business, whether to expand. This is the **investment decision.**

POLICY IMPLICATIONS: UNEQUAL WAGES

The concepts of marginal productivity and cost efficiency can be used to help explain the very disparate wages paid to individuals in our economy. The theory of labor demand suggests that workers are evaluated in terms of their *marginal revenue product*. Individuals who contribute the most to the revenues of a firm will be paid the highest wage rates, those whose *MRP* is low will be paid little. As we observed at the beginning of this chapter, the president of General Motors is paid over half a million a year. Why are GM's stockholders willing to pay him so much? The only rational explanation is that his marginal revenue product exceeds $500,000. Presumably his managerial skills and knowledge of the automobile market are considered to be so vast that GM's total revenues might fall by at least $500,000 a year if he departed. While this might sound extraordinary, it is certainly not impossible in the case of a firm with over $60 *billion* in annual revenues.

GM does not pay all its employees so handsomely, of course. The worker who tightens the bolts on the left rear wheel of every Chevette rolling down the assembly line earns only $11.67 an hour, a far cry from the $250 an hour GM's president is paid. This difference in wage rates is explained in part by their respective marginal revenue products. GM has discovered that tight rear wheel bolts aren't an essential determinant of car sales and represent a very small proportion of total cost. No matter how hard the bolt tighteners work, they have very little influence on GM's total revenues. Thus both the marginal revenue product and the wage rate of bolt tighteners are comparatively low.

The fantastic incomes of top entertainers and athletes can also be explained in terms of marginal revenue product. Muhammad Ali was paid $3.5 million in 1978 for one boxing match (one he lost, no less!). This wage reflected the fact that fight fans were *willing to pay* relatively high prices to see Ali fight. In fact, the fight promoters (the people who paid Ali) figured that thousands of people would buy high-priced tickets to see the fight at ringside. Millions of others would watch the fight on television. The total revenues generated by the fight included the ticket sales and the sale of TV advertising time. If a pair of nobodies were fighting, total revenue might equal only a few hundred dollars, but with Ali in the ring total revenues might soar into the millions. This increased revenue represented Ali's *MRP* and thus set the limit to the amount of money the fight promoters were *willing to pay* for Ali's labor.

The same considerations induced Texas A&M to pay its new football coach $287,000 per year (see news clipping). Texas A&M has a football stadium that will seat 70,016 fans. But attendance in 1980–81 averaged only 63,833 persons. If a new coach could create a winning team, the stadium might fill up. An additional 6,183 paying fans would bring in more than enough (marginal) revenue to pay the coach's salary.

Campus millionaire — the football coach

Educators across the country looked on in anger and dismay in late January at a bidding war that produced some 1.7 million dollars in pay and benefits for a collegiate-football coach.

Jackie Sherrill, coach at the University of Pittsburgh for the last five seasons, agreed to become coach and athletic director at Texas A&M for six years at $287,000 a year—$95,000 in base salary and the rest in fringe benefits and television earnings.

Robert Atwell, vice president of the American Council on Education, called it a "terrible distortion of values when the compensation of coaches exceeds that of Nobel laureates."

Sherill's $95,000 base salary will be more than triple the $31,649 average pay of university professors in the U.S. and double the $47,610 median salary of university presidents.

Texas A&M officials quickly pointed out that Sherrill will be paid not by the university but by donations to the athletic department. This, too, worried some critics, who said it gave A&M's "boosters" a strong voice in the running of a university program.

Sherrill is not the only college coach with six-figure pay. The University of Kentucky in December hired Jerry Claiborne from the University of Maryland for a package estimated at $200,000 a year. Frank Broyles, athletic director at the University of Arkansas, said he was offered 1.2 million dollars over several years to coach Georgia Tech.

Some defended high pay for coaches. Said Dick Dull, athletic director at the University of Maryland: "A winning football program gives institutions exposure on radio, television and print that they couldn't afford to buy."

Others agreed with Howard Swearer, president of Brown University, who contended: "When schools are paying these kinds of salaries to coaches, you begin to wonder whether there is a clear demarcation between college and professional sports."

The value of a college education

The higher earnings of college graduates also reflect differences in marginal revenue product. Recent estimates by the Census Bureau suggest that the average male college graduate will earn $1.4 million during his lifetime, while the average high school graduate will earn only $960,000 (see Table 12.5). This difference of $440,000 presumably reflects the higher marginal productivity of college-educated labor. Apparently people do learn some skills in four years of college.

Unmeasurable *MRP*

We cannot hope to explain all wages on the basis of marginal revenue product, however. We noted earlier that the president of the United States is paid $200,000. Can we argue that this salary represents his marginal revenue product? For that matter, how would one begin to measure the *MRP* of the president? The wage we pay the president of the United States is less a reflection of his contribution to total output than a matter of custom. His salary also reflects the

TABLE 12.5 INDIVIDUAL LIFETIME EARNINGS, BY YEARS OF EDUCATION

Additional years of schooling translate into increased earnings in the labor market. Over a lifetime, these differences in earnings accumulate into tremendous disparities. College graduation, for example, increases average lifetime earnings by $300,000 over those of college dropouts.

Years of school completed	*Lifetime earnings*
8 or less	**$ 600,000**
9–11 (high school dropout)	**780,000**
12 (high school graduate)	**960,000**
13–15 (college dropout)	**1,100,000**
16 (college graduate)	**1,400,000**
17 or more (some graduate school)	**1,600,000**

Source: U.S. Department of Commerce, Bureau of the Census, *Consumer Income*, March 1974; updated to 1982 wages by author.

opportunity wage: The highest wage an individual would earn in his or her best alternative job.

price voters believe is required to induce competent individuals to forsake private-sector jobs and assume the responsibilities of the presidency. In this sense, the wage paid to the president and other public officials is determined by their **opportunity wage,** that is, the wage they could earn in private industry.

The same kinds of considerations influence the wages of college professors. The marginal revenue product of a college professor is not easy to measure. Is it the number of students he or she teaches, the amount of knowledge conveyed, or something else? Confronted with such problems, most universities tend to pay college professors according to their opportunity wage, that is, the amount they could earn elsewhere.

Opportunity wages also help explain the difference between the wage rate paid to GM's president and that paid to its rear-wheel bolt tighteners. The low wage of bolt tighteners reflects not only their marginal revenue product at General Motors, but also the fact that they are not trained for many other jobs. That is to say, their opportunity wages are low. By contrast, GM's president has impressive managerial skills that are in demand by many corporations; his opportunity wages are high.

Market power and segmentation

Although marginal productivity theory and opportunity costs explain much inequality, they do not fully account for all wage differentials. Two individuals of equal productivity may command very different wages simply because of race or sex, or because of membership in a powerful labor union. That is to say, not all workers engage in perfect wage competition. Some workers are sheltered from wage competition by market power (e.g., labor unions) or discriminatory employment practices. Indeed, many economists argue that the U.S. labor market is highly segmented, with each segment defined by race, sex, or institutional barriers. Once assigned to a particular segment of the labor market, workers have little or no chance to acquire the skills or wage rates available in other segments. These arguments, which represent major qualifications to marginal productivity theory, are discussed at length in Chapters 13 and 18.

SUMMARY

- The rate of output a firm produces, and therefore the amount of resources it uses, depends on the extent of consumer demand. The demand for labor and other resources is a derived demand.
- The demand for labor is a direct reflection of labor's marginal revenue product. The greater the marginal revenue product of labor, the larger the quantity of labor a firm is willing to hire at any given wage.
- The marginal revenue product of labor also establishes a limit to the wage rate that firms willingly pay. A profit-maximizing employer will not pay a worker more than the worker produces.
- The marginal revenue product of labor tends to diminish as additional workers are employed on a particular job (the law of diminishing returns). This decline occurs because additional workers have to

share existing land and capital, leaving each worker with less land and capital to work with.

- A producer seeks to get the most output for every dollar spent on inputs. This means getting the highest ratio of marginal product to input price. Accordingly, a profit-maximizing producer will always choose the most cost-efficient input (not necessarily the one with the cheapest price).
- The efficiency decision involves the choice of the least-cost production process and is also made on the basis of cost efficiency. A producer seeks the least expensive process to produce a given rate of output.
- Differences in marginal revenue product offer an important explanation for existing wage inequalities. But the difficulty of measuring *MRP* in many instances leaves many wage rates to be determined by custom, power, discrimination, or opportunity wages.

Terms to remember

Define the following terms:

derived demand
demand for labor
marginal physical product *(MPP)*
marginal revenue product *(MRP)*
law of diminishing returns
law of demand
shift in demand
cost efficiency
production process
efficiency decision
production decision
investment decision
opportunity wage

Questions for discussion

1. Is this course increasing your marginal productivity? If so, in what way?
2. Suppose George is making $13 an hour installing transistorized digital chips in electronic calculators. Would your offer to work for $8 an hour get you the job? Why might a profit-maximizing employer turn down your generous offer?
3. What do you think happened to the marginal productivity of painters when the paint roller was invented? Did it improve their wages?
4. Explain why marginal physical product would diminish as
(a) More secretaries are hired in an office
(b) More professors are hired in the economics department
(c) More construction workers are hired to build a school
5. How is the wage of a judge determined?

Problem

The following table depicts the number of grapes that can be picked in an hour with varying amounts of labor.

Number of pickers (per hour)	**1**	**2**	**3**	**4**	**5**	**6**	**7**	**8**
Output of grapes (in flats)	**20**	**38**	**53**	**64**	**71**	**74**	**74**	**70**

Using these data, determine how many pickers will be hired if the wage rate is $10.00 per hour and a flat of grapes sells for $1.25. Illustrate graphically.

CHAPTER 13

POWER IN LABOR MARKETS

Labor markets are no different in concept from other markets. Market supply and market demand interact to determine the quantity of labor hired and its price (the wage rate). Like all markets, also, labor markets can be distorted by market power. Power may reside on the supply side of the market (labor unions) or on the demand side (large employers). In either case, the objective of those who hold market power is to alter wages and employment conditions. This chapter focuses on the extent of **market power** in the U.S. labor market, the kinds of confrontations that occur, and the impact of labor-market power on our economic welfare.

market power: The ability to alter the market price of a good or service.

THE LABOR MARKET

To gauge the impact of labor-market power on wages and employment, we can review the nature of a competitive labor market. On the supply side, we have all those individuals who are willing to work—to supply labor—at various wage rates. By counting the number of individuals who are willing to work at each and every wage rate, we can construct a *market* **labor-supply** curve, as in Figure 13.1.[1]

labor supply: The willingness and ability to work specific amounts of time at alternative wage rates in a given time period; the quantities of labor that would be supplied at alternative wage rates (*ceteris paribus*).

The willingness of producers (firms) to hire labor is reflected in

[1] The *market* supply curve may slope upward even if individual workers have backward-bending supply curves (Chapter 11) as long as additional workers are attracted into the labor force by high wages.

FIGURE 13.1 COMPETITIVE EQUILIBRIUM IN THE LABOR MARKET

In a competitive market, the intersection of the labor-supply and labor-demand curves (point C) determines the equilibrium wage rate (w_e) and the amount of employment (q_e).

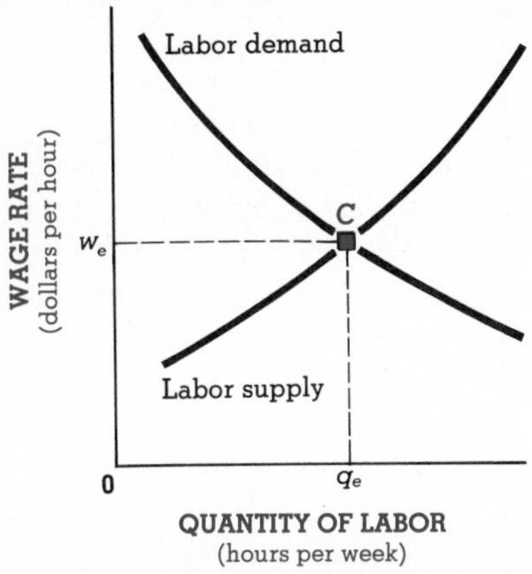

demand for labor: The quantities of labor employers are willing and able to hire at alternative wage rates in a given time period (*ceteris paribus*).

the market labor-demand curve. The curve itself is constructed by simply counting the number of workers each firm says it is willing and able to hire at each and every wage rate. The curve illustrates the market **demand for labor.**

Competitive equilibrium

equilibrium wage: The wage rate at which the quantity of labor supplied in a given time period equals the quantity of labor demanded.

The intersection of the market supply and demand curves (point C in Figure 13.1) reveals the **equilibrium wage** rate (w_e): the wage rate at which the quantity of labor supplied equals the quantity demanded. At this wage rate, every job seeker who is willing and able to work for the wage w_e is employed. In addition, firms are able to acquire all the labor they are willing and able to hire at that wage. Not everyone is employed, of course; workers who demand wages in excess of w_e are unable to find jobs. By the same token, employers who refuse to pay a wage as high as w_e are unable to attract workers.

Local labor markets

Figure 13.1 appears to suggest that there is only *one* labor market, and thus only one equilibrium wage. But we already know this is a gross simplification. Although the concept of a national labor market is important and useful, it is more appropriate to think in terms of localized labor markets. If you were looking for a job in Tulsa, Oklahoma, you would have little interest in employment prospects or power configurations in New York City. You would be more likely to be concerned about the number of job openings and job seekers in Tulsa—that is, the condition of the *local* labor market.

Even within the confines of a particular geographical area, interest usually focuses on particular classes of jobs and workers rather than on all the people supplying labor. If you were looking for work as a disco dancer, you would have little interest in the employment situation for carpenters or dentists. Rather, you would want to know how many discos or nightclubs had job vacancies and what wages and working conditions they offered. By the same token, people in the construction industry or in dentistry would probably have no more than a passing interest in the job market for disco dancers. Accordingly, we can focus not only on geographically defined labor markets, but also on labor markets for particular industries or occupations.

The distinction among various geographical, occupational, and industrial labor markets provides a more meaningful basis for analyzing labor-market power. The tremendous size of the national labor market, with over 100 million workers, precludes anyone from acquiring control of the entire market. The largest private employer in the United States (General Motors) employs less than 1 percent of the labor force. The top 500 industrial corporations employ only 20 percent of all workers. The situation on the supply side is similar. The largest labor union (the Teamsters) represents just slightly more than 2 percent of all workers in the country. *All* unions together represent only one-fifth of the labor force. This does not mean that the actions of particular employers or unions have no important effects on our general economic welfare. It does, however, show that power in labor markets is likely to be more apparent and effective in particular areas, occupations, and industries than in others.

LABOR UNIONS

Types of unions

The immediate objective of labor unions is to alter the equilibrium wage and employment conditions in specific labor markets. To be successful, unions must be able to exert control over the market-supply curve. For this purpose, workers have organized themselves along either industry or occupational craft lines. *Industrial unions* include workers in a particular industry (the United Auto Workers, for example). *Craft unions* represent workers with a particular skill (e.g., the International Brotherhood of Electrical Workers), regardless of the industry in which they work.

The purpose of both types of labor union is to coordinate the actions of thousands of individual workers, thereby achieving control of market supply. If a union is able to control the supply of workers in a particular industry or occupation, the union acquires a monopoly in that market. Like most monopolies, unions attempt to use their market power to increase their incomes.

Union objectives

A primary objective of unions is to raise the wages of union members. But union objectives also include improved working conditions, job security, and other forms of compensation, such as retirement (pension) benefits, vacation time, and health insurance. The Players' Association and the National Football League have bargained about the use of artificial turf, early retirement, player fines, and the revenues derived from closed-circuit television broadcasts. In 1981 the Major League Baseball Players Association stopped all games for 49 days while the players and team owners bargained over the rules for "free agents." In that same year the Professional Air Traffic Controllers Organization (PATCO) struck for shorter workweeks and earlier retirement. A few years earlier the Air Line Pilots Association had worried about weight restrictions for flight attendants (United Airlines required that a female flight attendant five feet,

Auto workers take a wage cut

American auto companies and their employees have been caught for months in a quandary. As car sales dragged along at their lowest level in 21 years, more and more workers lost their jobs. Some 240,000 United Auto Workers members are on indefinite layoff. Auto companies claimed that high salaries and benefits helped push up the price of American cars and made it hard to compete against Japanese imports. Although worried about further layoffs, workers were reluctant to accept substantial wage reductions. But last week Ford and the U.A.W. agreed to a new 2½-year contract that cuts workers' benefits in return for guarantees of job security. . . .

Indeed, the union won a surprising two-year moratorium on closing plants because of outside suppliers and an agreement in principle that future labor reductions would come only as a result of attrition. In addition, Ford promised to replace all union jobs lost because of out-sourcing. In exchange, the union will give up its 3% pay increase this year and in 1983, ten paid personal holidays and cost of living increases for the next nine months.

four inches tall weigh no more than 125 pounds). In the United Farm Workers' grape strike of 1965–70, the primary issue was the growers' recognition of the UFW as the legitimate spokesman for the grape pickers. The UFW was striking to force the growers into bilateral negotiations—to discuss employment issues with the workers' representatives.

Although union objectives tend to be as broad as the concerns of union members, we shall focus here on just one objective, wage rates. This is not too great a simplification, because most nonwage issues can be translated into their effective impact on wage rates. In 1979, for example, the Teamsters secured a wage increase of 80 cents per hour. Additional benefits (cost-of-living allowance, increased pension and health benefits, additional days off, etc.) cost employers another 70 cents an hour. Hence the increase in total wage costs was

WHAT MINE WORKERS WON IN THE 1981 COAL STRIKE

In 1981 a 71-day coal strike cost the industry an estimated $1 billion in lost sales and over $100 million in vanished profits. The miners lost over $50 million in wages while on strike. When the United Mine Workers (UMW) and the Bituminous Coal Operators Association finally signed a new 40-month contract, it included:

WAGES **An increase in average wages from $10.10 an hour in 1981 to $13.70 an hour in 1984.**

ROYALTY PAYMENTS **An increase in the royalty paid by producers to the UMW for coal mined from non-UMW mines from $1.90 to $2.23 per ton.**

SUNDAYS OFF **Continuation of a ban on Sunday work.**

NONUNION LABOR **Agreement by the producers to use nonunion subcontractors only when UMW members are unavailable.**

ARBITRATION **Abolition of the arbitration review board, which had previously acted as the judge of grievances.**

WORKING VACATIONS **Authorization for UMW members to work through their scheduled 1981 vacations, thereby drawing double pay.**

CLOTHING ALLOWANCE **An increase from $125 to $150.**

HEALTH BENEFITS **An increase in payments for sickness and injury from $150 to $185 per week.**

HOLIDAYS **One additional paid holiday per year.**

BACK-TO-WORK BONUS **A $150 bonus for miners who reported for work on the first poststrike shift.**

$1.50 per hour. Accordingly, our simple two-dimensional illustration of union objectives can be used to convey the nature and substance of most collective-bargaining situations. What we seek to determine is whether and how unions can raise wage rates in a specific labor market by altering the competitive equilibrium depicted in Figure 13.1.

THE POTENTIAL USE OF POWER

In a competitive labor market, each worker makes a labor-supply decision on the basis of his or her own perceptions of the relative values of labor and leisure (Chapter 11). Whatever decision is made, it will not alter the market wage. One worker simply isn't that significant in a market composed of thousands of workers. Once a market is unionized, however, these conditions no longer hold. A union must evaluate job offers on the basis of the *collective* interests of its members. In particular, it must be concerned with the effects of increased employment on the wage rate paid to its members. ***Like all monopolists, unions have to worry about the downward slope of the demand curve.*** In the case of labor markets, a larger quantity of labor can be "sold" only at lower wage rates.

The marginal wage

Suppose that the workers in a particular labor market confront the market labor-demand schedule depicted in Table 13.1. This schedule tells us that employers are not willing to hire any workers at a wage rate of $6 per hour (row *S*) but will hire one worker per hour if the wage rate is $5 (row *T*). At still lower wage rates, the quantity of labor demanded increases; five workers per hour are demanded at a wage of $1 per hour.

An individual worker offered a wage of $1 an hour would have to decide whether such wages merited the sacrifice of an hour's leisure. But a union would evaluate the offer differently. Notice that when four workers are hired at a wage rate of $2 an hour (row *W*), total wages are $8 per hour. In order for a fifth worker to be employed, however, the wage rate must drop to $1 an hour (row *X*), whereupon *total* wages paid amount to only $5 per hour. Thus total

TABLE 13.1 THE MARGINAL WAGE

The *marginal wage* is the change in *total* wages (paid to all workers) associated with the employment of an additional worker. If the wage rate is $4 per hour, only two workers are hired. The wage rate must fall to $3 per hour if three workers are to be hired. In the process, *total* wages paid rise from $8 ($4 × 2 workers) to $9 ($3 × 3 workers). The *marginal* wage of the third worker is only $1.

	Wage rate (per hour)	×	*Number of workers demanded (per hour)*	=	*Total wages paid (per hour)*	*Marginal wage (per labor-hour)*
S	$6		0		$0	$0
T	5		1		5	5
U	4		2		8	3
V	3		3		9	1
W	2		4		8	−1
X	1		5		5	−3

FIGURE 13.2 THE MARGINAL WAGE

Additional workers will be hired only if the wage rate drops (*ceteris paribus*). Hence the wages of an additional worker are offset by reduced wage rates for all other workers already employed. In this case, a second worker will be employed only if the wage rate drops from $5 (point *T*) to $4 (point *U*). Total wages increase from $5 ($5 × 1 worker) to $8 ($4 × 2 workers). The *marginal* wage is therefore $3 (point *u*).

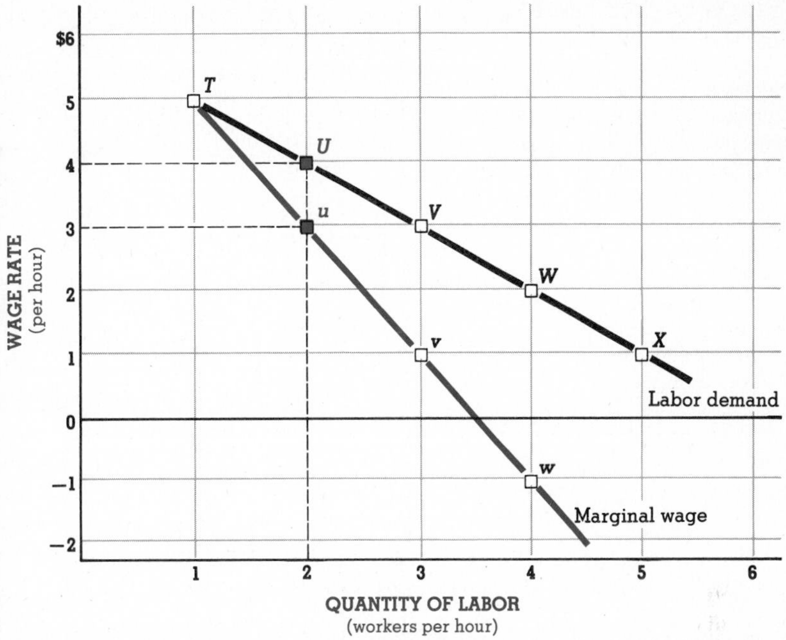

marginal wage: The change in total wages paid associated with a one-unit increase in the quantity of labor employed.

wages paid to the workers actually *fall* when a fifth worker is employed. Collectively, then, the workers would be better off sending only four workers to work at the higher wage of $2 an hour and paying the fifth worker $1 an hour to stay home!

The basic mandate of a labor union is to evaluate wage and employment offers from this collective perspective. To do so, ***a union must distinguish the marginal wage from the market wage.*** The market wage is simply the current wage rate paid by the employer; it is the wage received by individual workers. The **marginal wage,** on the other hand, is the change in *total* wages paid (to all workers) when an additional worker is hired.

The distinction between marginal wages and market wages arises from the downward slope of the labor-demand curve. It is analogous to the distinction we made between marginal revenue and price for monopolists in product markets. The distinction simply reflects the law of demand: as wages fall, the number of workers hired increases.

The impact of increased employment on marginal wages is also illustrated in Figure 13.2. According to the labor-demand curve, one worker will be hired at a wage rate of $5 an hour (point *T*). Two workers will be hired only if the market wage falls to $4 an hour (point *U*). At this point, the first and second workers are each getting $4 an hour.[2] Thus the increased wages of the second worker (from zero to $4) are partially offset by the reduction in the wage rate paid to the first worker (from $5 to $4). *Total* wages paid increase by only $3; this is the *marginal* wage (point *u*). The marginal wage actually

[2] Recall that the decline in wage rates reflects the law of diminishing marginal productivity and is not caused by any particular worker (see Chapter 12).

FIGURE 13.3 THE UNION WAGE OBJECTIVE

The intersection of the marginal wage and labor-supply curves (point *u*) determines the union's desired employment. Employers are willing to pay a wage rate of $4 per hour for that many workers, as revealed by point *U*.

More workers (*N*) are willing to work at $4 per hour than employers demand (*U*). To maintain that wage rate, the union must exclude some workers from the market. In the absence of such power, wages would fall to the competitive equilibrium (point *C*).

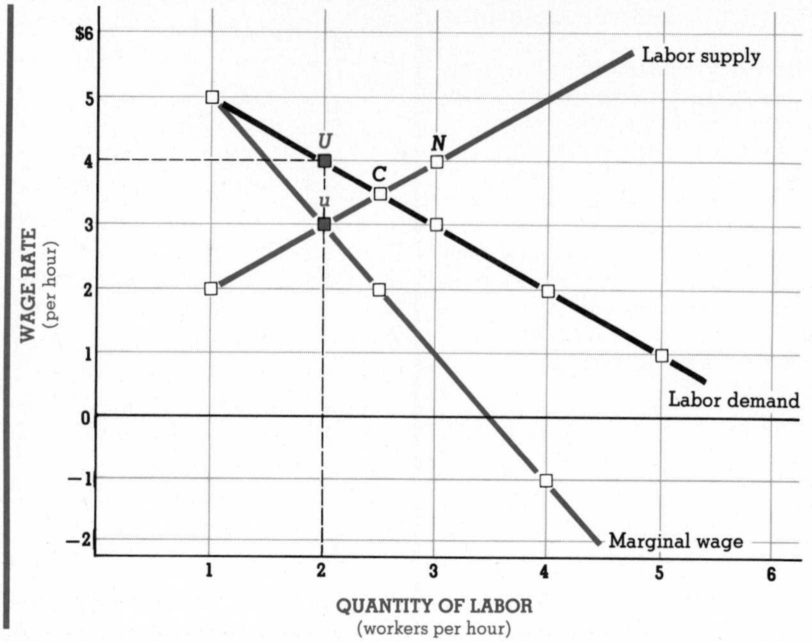

becomes negative at some point, when the implied wage loss to workers already on the job begins to exceed the wages of a newly hired worker.

Monopolistic equilibrium

A union never wants to accept a negative marginal wage, of course. At such a point, union members would be better off paying someone to stay home. The question, then, is what level of (positive) marginal wage the union should accept.

We can answer this question by looking at the labor-supply curve. The labor-supply curve tells us how much labor workers are *willing to supply* at various wage rates. In Figure 13.3, ***the intersection of the marginal wage curve with the labor-supply curve identifies the optimal level of employment for the union.*** In Figure 13.3 this intersection occurs at point u, yielding total employment of two workers per hour.

Notice that the union-imposed wage rate is $4 per hour. Graphically, we locate this wage rate by moving straight upward from point u to the labor-demand curve. Point *U* on the demand curve tells us that employers are *willing to pay* a wage rate of $4 an hour to employ two workers per hour. Hence $4 becomes the union wage.

What the union is doing here is choosing a point on the labor-demand curve that the union regards as the optimal combination of wages and employment. In a competitive market, point C would represent the equilibrium combination of wages and employment. But the union forces employers to point *U*, thereby attaining a higher wage rate and reducing employment. The union's motivation for moving to point U arises from its recognition of the *marginal wage*, that is, the impact of increased employment on the total wages of its members.

Exclusion

The union's ability to maintain a wage rate of $4 an hour depends on its ability to exclude some workers from the market. Figure 13.3 suggests that three workers are willing and able to work at the union wage of $4 an hour (point N), whereas only two are hired (point U). If the additional worker were to offer his or her services, the wage rate would be pushed down the labor-demand curve (to $3 per hour). Hence ***to maintain a noncompetitive wage, the union must be able to exercise some control over the labor-supply decisions of individual workers.*** The essential force here is union solidarity. Once unionized, the individual workers in an industry or occupation must agree not to compete among themselves by offering their labor at nonunion wage rates. Instead, the workers must agree to withhold labor—to strike, if necessary—if wage rates are too low, and to supply labor only if a specified wage rate is offered.

union shop: An employment setting in which all workers must join the union within 30 days after being employed.

Unions attempt to solidify their control of the labor supply by establishing **union shops,** workplaces where workers must join the union within 30 days after being employed. In this way, the unions gain control of all the workers employed in a particular company or industry and thereby reduce the number of workers available for employment during a strike. Stiff penalties (such as loss of seniority or pension rights) and general union solidarity ensure that only nonunion workers will "fink" or "scab"—take the job of a worker on strike. When the United Auto Workers (UAW) threatens a strike, the Big Three auto makers know that nonunion automotive workers will be hard to find and thus take the UAW threat seriously. But the grape growers in California ignored the UFW strike for five years because unionization among farm workers was minimal and substitute labor (including Mexican *braceros*) was readily available.

Union shops help to increase the degree of unionization within an industry, but they are not so effective as the closed shop. A closed shop permits only union members to be hired by an employer. Under a closed-shop arrangement, a worker must first be accepted by the union, whereas in a union shop, the employer makes the initial employment decision. Although closed shops are illegal under the provisions of the Taft-Hartley Act, they still operate under the guise of union shops coupled with union hiring halls (union-run employment referrals). In many states, however, even union shops may be prohibited by the provisions of "right-to-work" laws that make union membership completely voluntary.

Another mechanism for restricting the use of substitute labor is union control of training facilities. Union-controlled apprenticeship programs offer skill training for persons found acceptable for union membership. Thus nonunion workers will have less chance of acquiring the necessary skills and hence will be less available to substitute in case of a strike. Apprenticeship programs are particularly effective when linked to certification programs, which grant people the right to practice a particular craft or trade or to affirm their vocational skills. For example, individuals are required to undertake a four-year apprenticeship program before they can be certified as union plumbers.

THE EXTENT OF UNION POWER

Early growth

The first labor unions in America were organized as early as the 1780s and the first worker protests as early as 1636. Union power was not a significant force in labor markets, however, until the 1900s, when heavily populated commercial centers and large-scale manufacturing became common. Only then did large numbers of workers begin to view their employment situations from a common perspective.

The period 1916–20 was one of particularly fast growth for labor unions, largely because of the high demand for labor resulting from World War I. All of these membership gains were lost, however, when the Great Depression threw millions of people out of work. By 1933, union membership had dwindled to the levels of 1915.

As the depression lingered on, public attitudes and government policy toward the relationship between labor and business began to reflect a new perspective. No longer was the public willing to let the business community render all economic decisions. Too many people had learned the meaning of layoffs, wage cuts, and prolonged unemployment. Moreover, the notion was growing that layoffs and wage cuts were not appropriate solutions to economic recessions. Accordingly, as the country began to work its way out of the depression, the labor union movement was infused with renewed vigor. In 1933 the National Industrial Recovery Act (NIRA) was passed, including provisions that established the right of employees to bargain collectively with their employers. When the NIRA was declared unconstitutional by the Supreme Court in 1935, its labor provisions were incorporated into a new law, the Wagner Act. With the encouragement of these legislative developments, union membership doubled between 1933 and 1937. It continued to grow markedly during the subsequent eight years, as the production needs of World War II enhanced the marginal revenue product and bargaining strength of labor. The tremendous spurt of union activity between the depths of the depression and the height of World War II is reflected in Figure 13.4.

Union power today

Since World War II, union membership has continued to grow, but not as fast as the labor force. As a consequence, union power, expressed as the percentage of workers belonging to labor unions, has fallen. Today roughly 21 percent of the labor force is enrolled in labor unions for a combined membership of over 22 million workers.[3]

[3] These and the following figures include membership in the professional associations (such as the National Educational Association), which function much like unions.

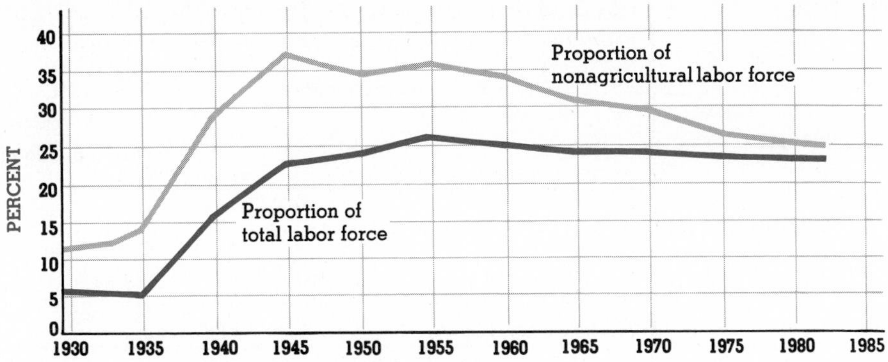

FIGURE 13.4 UNIONIZATION OF THE LABOR FORCE

Unions grew most rapidly during the decade 1935–45. Since that time, the growth of unions has not kept pace with the growth of the U.S. labor force.

Source: U.S. Department of Labor, Bureau of Labor Statistics.

unionization ratio: The percentage of the labor force belonging to a union.

Although a **unionization ratio** of 21 percent is an impressive basis for market (and political) power, union strength varies greatly from labor market to labor market. As we noted before, the national labor market is really a mix of thousands of distinguishable labor markets, each defined by geographical, industrial, or occupational characteristics. Concentrations of union power in any of these localized labor markets can be far greater than the national average. Moreover, these local concentrations can have tremendous influence on related economic outcomes. This situation is analogous to concentration among producers. As we noted in Chapter 10, concentration in particular product markets is much higher and of more immediate consequence than national averages sometimes suggest.

Table 13.2 provides an overview of union power in various industries. As is apparent, there is tremendous variation in labor-supply concentration among industries. In group *A*, labor-supply concentration is so high (75–100 percent) as to confer monopoly powers on particular unions. The Teamsters, Longshoremen, and United Mine Workers stand out in this regard. The unions in group *B* also have great market power, because they represent over half the workers in each industry. Many of the unions are familiar from their many confrontations with business over the exercise of market power (the United Auto Workers, the garment unions, the communications unions, and the printers stand out).

Although Table 13.2 provides a convenient index to who's who on the supply side of the labor market, some additional observations are in order. Each industry classification depicted in the table represents a broad assortment of firms and products. Accordingly, a low degree of unionization for an industry may mask very high levels of supply concentration in particular labor markets. The "service industry" (group *D*), for example, has a relatively low level of unionization but includes such disparate workers as professional football players, laundry workers, barbers, and broadcasters. Obviously, the

TABLE 13.2 UNION POWER

A union's power may be measured by the percentage of the related work force that it controls. The Teamsters, for example, have substantial market power because most truck drivers belong to that union.

Degree of unionization	*Industry*	*Principal unions*
A: 75–100 percent	Transportation	Teamsters
		Longshoremen
		Maintenance of Way
		Maritime
		Railway unions
	Contract construction	Carpenters
		Painters
		Plumbers
		Laborers
	Mining	United Mine Workers
B: 50–75 percent	Transportation equipment	United Auto Workers
		Marine and Shipbuilding
	Primary metals	Steelworkers
	Apparel	Amalgamated Clothing Workers
		Garment Workers
		Ladies' Garment Workers
	Tobacco manufactures	Cigar
		Tobacco Workers
	Electrical machinery	International Brotherhood of Electrical Workers (IBEW)
		International Union of Electrical Workers
	Federal government	Government Employees (AFGE)
		Letter Carriers
		Post Office Clerks
	Paper	Papermakers
		Pulp, Sulphite
C: 25–50 percent	Rubber	Rubber Workers
	Machinery	Automobile
		United Electrical Workers
	Lumber	Coopers
		Woodworkers
	Leather	Shoe Workers

low level of unionization reflected in the industry average is of little relevance to you when you go to get a haircut. It certainly offers no comfort to the owners of NFL football teams when they have to negotiate playing conditions or retirement benefits. Even relatively small unions may have great market power if they control labor supply for a particular area, company, product, or occupation.

One union noticeably missing from the table is the AFL-CIO (the American Federation of Labor–Congress of Industrial Organizations). To comprehend this omission, we must refer back to the structure of labor organizations, especially the need for intercompany and interindustry affiliations. The AFL-CIO is not a separate union, but a representational body of 120 national unions. It does not represent or negotiate for any particular group of workers, but instead focuses on issues of general labor interest. Thus to a large

Degree of unionization	Industry	Principal unions
C: 25–50 percent	Electric, gas, utilities	Electrical (IBEW)
	Furniture	Furniture Workers
	Government (state and local)	Teachers Fire Fighters
	Telephone and telegraph	Communications Workers Electrical (IBEW)
	Petroleum	Oil, Chemical Operating Engineers
	Food and kindred products	Bakery Workers Brewery Meat Cutters
	Stone, clay, and glass products	Glass Cutters
	Fabricated metals	Boilermakers Steelworkers Iron Workers
D: Less than 25 percent	Chemicals	Chemical District 50
	Textiles	Textile Workers
	Instruments	Machinists
	Service	Hotel Laundry Workers Watchmen
	Finance	Insurance Agents
	Agriculture and fishing	Teamsters United Farm Workers
	Trade	Retail Clerks
	Printing, publishing	Newspaper Guild Printing Pressmen Typographers

Source: U.S. Department of Labor, Bureau of Labor Statistics, *Directory of National Unions and Employee Associations,* 1979.

extent its role is to act as a spokesman for the labor movement and represent labor's interest in legislative areas. It is the primary vehicle for political action. In addition, the AFL-CIO may render economic assistance to member unions or to groups of workers who wish to organize into an AFL-CIO affiliate. Not all national or local unions belong to the AFL-CIO—the Teamsters, United Mine Workers, and United Auto Workers being notable (and powerful) exceptions—but three out of four union members are affiliated with it.

EMPLOYER POWER

The impressive power possessed by labor unions in various areas and industries seldom exists in a power vacuum. On the contrary, tremendous power exists on the demand side of labor markets, too. The United Auto Workers confront GM, Ford, and Chrysler; the Steelworkers confront U.S. Steel, Bethlehem, Republic, and Armco; the Teamsters confront the Truckers' Association; the Communications Workers confront AT&T; and so on. An imbalance of power often exists on one side of the market or the other (as with, say, the Carpenters versus individual construction contractors). Labor markets with significant power on both sides, however, are common. To understand how wage rates and employment are determined in such markets, we have to consider the nature and potential of market power possessed by employers.

Monopsony

Power on the demand side of a market is analogous to power on the supply side. Such power belongs to a *buyer* who is able to influence the market price of a good. With respect to labor markets, market power on the demand side implies the ability of a single employer to alter the market wage rate. The extreme case of such power is called a **monopsony**, a situation in which one employer is the only buyer in a particular market. The classic example of a monopsony is a company town, that is, a town that depends for its livelihood on the decisions of a single large employer.

monopsony: A market in which there is only one buyer.

There are many degrees of market power, of course, and they can be defined in terms of *buyer concentration*, the converse of the seller concentration we have discussed. When buyers are many and of limited market power, the demand for resources is likely to be competitive. When only one buyer has access to a particular resource market, a monopsony exists. In between the two extremes lie the various degrees of imperfect competition, including the awkward-sounding but empirically important case of oligopsony. In an oligopsony only a few buyers account for most of the purchases of a particular resource. The similarity of these definitions to those used to characterize power on the supply side of markets should be obvious.

The potential use of power

Firms with power in labor markets generally have the same objective as all other firms; to maximize profits. What distinguishes them from competitive (powerless) firms is their ability to attain great profits. Firms with monopsony power can exploit the market supply curve, and end up using fewer resources and paying less for them than competitive firms would. In labor markets, this means using fewer workers and paying them lower wages than a firm in a competitive market would have to do.

The distinguishing characteristic of labor-market monopsonies is the fact that their hiring decisions influence the market wage rate. In a competitive labor market, no single employer has any direct influence on the market wage rate. Each firm can hire as much labor as it needs at the prevailing wage. But a monopsonist recognizes that an increase in the quantity of labor demanded will force him to climb up the labor-supply curve in search of additional workers. In

TABLE 13.3 MARGINAL COST OF LABOR

An additional worker can be attracted only if the wage rate increases. As it rises, all workers must be paid the higher wage. Consequently, the change in *total* wage costs exceeds the actual wage paid to the last worker. Notice that in row *I*, for example, the marginal wage of the fourth worker ($8) exceeds the wage actually paid to that worker ($5).

	Wage rate (per hour)	×	*Quantity of labor supplied (workers per hour)*	=	*Total wage cost (per hour)*	*Marginal cost of labor (per labor-hour)*
D	$0		0		$ 0	$0
E	1		0		0	0
F	2		1		2	2
G	3		2		6	4
H	4		3		12	6
I	5		4		20	8
J	6		5		30	10

other words, ***a monopsonist can hire additional workers only if he offers a higher wage rate.***

MARGINAL COST OF LABOR Any time the price of a resource (or product) changes as a result of a firm's purchases, a distinction between marginal cost and price (average cost) must be made. Making this distinction is one of the little headaches—and potential sources of profit—of a monopsonist. In the case of labor, the distinction to be made is between the **marginal cost of labor** and its wage rate.

marginal cost of labor: The change in total wage costs that results from a one-unit increase in the quantity of labor employed.

Suppose for the moment that Table 13.3 accurately describes the labor-supply schedule confronting a monopsonist. It is evident that the monopsonist will have to pay a wage of at least $2 an hour if he wants any labor. But even at that wage rate only one worker is willing to work. If the firm wants more labor, it will have to pay higher wages.

Two things happen when the firm raises its wage offer to $3 an hour (row G). First, the quantity of labor supplied increases (to two workers per hour). Second, the total wages paid rise by $4. This high *marginal* cost of labor is attributable to the fact that the first worker's wages rise when the wage rate is increased to attract additional workers. If all the workers perform the same job, the first worker will demand to be paid the new (higher) wage rate. Thus the marginal cost of labor exceeds the wage rate because additional workers can be hired only if the wage rate for all workers is increased.

MONOPSONISTIC EQUILIBRIUM The marginal-cost-of-labor curve confronting this monopsonist is shown in Figure 13.5. It starts at the bottom of the labor-supply curve and rises above it. The monopsonist must now decide how many workers to hire, given the impact of his hiring decisions on the market wage rate.

Recall from Chapter 12 that the labor-demand curve reflects labor's **marginal revenue product,** that is, the increase in total revenue attributable to the employment of one additional worker.

marginal revenue product (*MRP*): The change in total revenue associated with one additional unit of input.

As we have seen before, the profit-maximizing producer always seeks to equalize marginal revenue and marginal cost. Accordingly, the monopsonistic employer will seek to hire the amount of labor at which the marginal revenue product of labor equals its marginal

FIGURE 13.5 THE MONOPSONIST'S DESIRED EQUILIBRIUM

The intersection of the marginal cost of labor and labor-demand curves (point *U*) indicates the quantity of labor a monopsonist will want to hire. The labor-supply curve (at point *G*) indicates the wage rate that must be paid to attract the desired number of workers. This is the monopsonist's desired wage ($3). In the absence of market power, an employer would end up at point *C* (the competitive equilibrium), paying a higher wage and employing more workers.

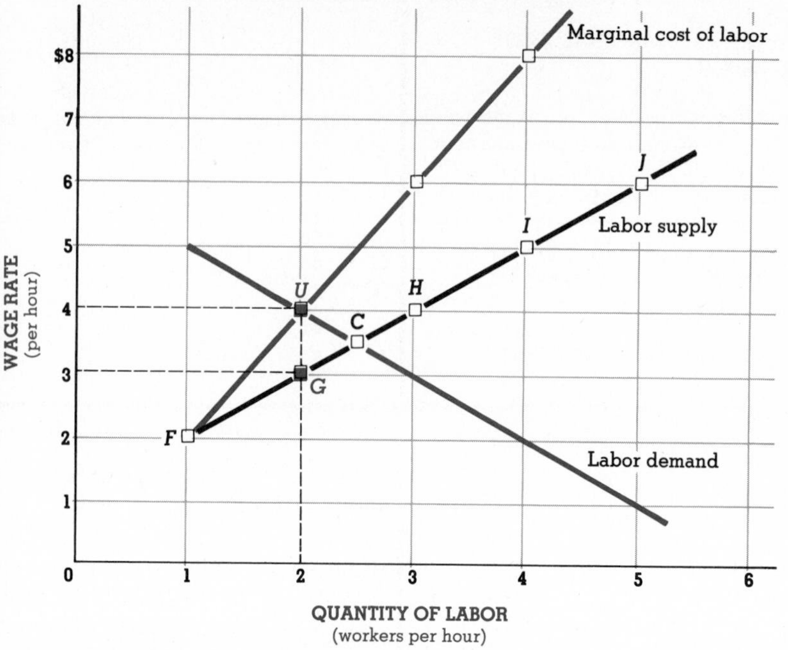

bilateral monopoly: A market with only one buyer (a monopsonist) and one seller (a monopolist).

collective bargaining: Direct negotiations between employers and unions to determine labor-market outcomes.

cost. In Figure 13.5, this objective is illustrated by the intersection of the marginal cost and labor-demand curves, at point *U*.

At point *U* the monopsonist is *willing to hire* two workers per hour at a wage rate of $4. But he doesn't have to pay this much. The labor-supply curve informs us that two workers are *willing to work* for only $3 an hour. Hence the firm first decides how many workers it wants to hire (at point *U*), then looks at the labor-supply curve (point G) to see what it has to pay them. As we suspected, a monopsonistic employer ends up hiring fewer workers at a lower wage rate than would prevail in a competitive market (point C).

COLLECTIVE BARGAINING: A CLASH OF POWER

The potential for conflict between a powerful employer and a labor union should be evident. The objective of a labor union (Figure 13.3) is to establish a wage rate that is *higher* than the competitive wage. A monopsonistic employer, on the other hand, seeks to establish a wage rate that is *lower* than competitive standards (Figure 13.5). The resultant clash is often exciting.

The confrontation of power on both sides of the labor market is referred to as **bilateral monopoly.** In such a market, wages and employment are not determined simply by supply and demand. Rather, economic outcomes must be determined by deliberate negotiations between buyers and sellers. Such negotiations in the labor market have acquired a unique name and status: collective bargaining. **Collective bargaining** consists of negotiations between employers and labor unions for the purpose of determining wages, employment, working conditions, and related issues.

Possible agreements

In a typical labor-business confrontation, the two sides begin by stating their preferences for equilibrium wages and employment. The *demands* laid down by the union are likely to revolve around point *U* in Figure 13.6; the *offer* enunciated by management is likely to be at point G.[4] Thus the boundaries of a potential settlement—a negotiated final equilibrium—are usually established at the outset of collective bargaining.

The interesting part of collective bargaining is not the initial bargaining positions but the negotiation of the final settlement. The speed with which a settlement is reached and the nature of the compromise it embodies depend on the patience, tactics, and resources of the negotiating parties. The fundamental source of negotiating power for either side is its ability to withhold employment or jobs. The union can threaten to strike, thereby cutting off the flow of union labor to the employer. In a strike, union members simply refuse to work under existing conditions and force a cutback or cessation of production activities. The employer can impose a lockout, thereby cutting off jobs and paychecks previously available to union members. In practice, each weapon constitutes an ultimate threat to the other side of the collective-bargaining negotiations. The effectiveness of those threats depends on the availability of alternative workers or jobs and the credibility of the strike or lockout threat.

The pressure to settle

The essential strength of both labor and management in collective bargaining emanates from their ability to cut off the flow of revenues (in the form of sales or wages). But both sides suffer from either a strike or a lockout, no matter who initiates the work stoppage. The strike benefits paid to workers are rarely comparable to wages they would otherwise have received, and the payment of those benefits

[4] Even though points *U* and G may not be identical to the initial bargaining positions, they represent the positions of maximum attainable benefit for both sides. Points outside the demand or supply curve will be rejected out of hand by one side or the other.

FIGURE 13.6 THE BOUNDARIES OF COLLECTIVE BARGAINING

Firms with power in the labor market seek to establish wages and employment levels corresponding to point G. Unions, on the other hand, seek to establish an equilibrium at point *U*. The competitive equilibrium is at point C. The function of collective bargaining is to identify a compromise between these points, that is, to locate an equilibrium somewhere in the shaded area.

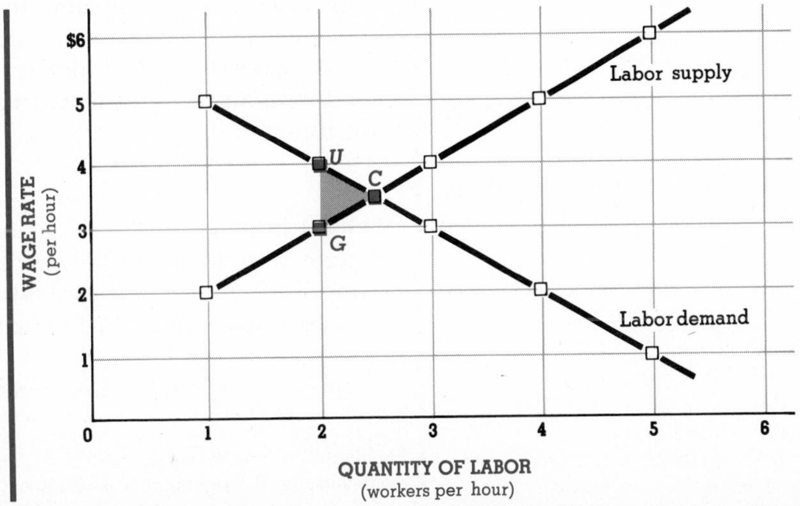

The Baseball Strike Is a Monopolists' Slugfest

So you think the baseball strike is a classic struggle between greedy owners and embattled players. Or perhaps you see greedy players preying on sports-loving owners.

Before you cast Tom Seaver as Luke Skywalker and George Steinbrenner as Darth Vader, consider another view: This strike is just a tiresome squabble between greedy owners and greedy players for slices of a pie baked by embattled, sports-loving fans. Baseball is, as an economist would put it, a textbook illustration of a bilateral monopoly. And the strike is no more than the owners' monopsony power (that means a monopoly-buyer-of-labor, and I promise not to use the word again) pitted against the monopoly power of the players for the possession of the "scarcity rents" accruing from the teams themselves. To explain:

As a group, the owners are the sole employers of major-league baseball players; they could, and did, collude to limit the salaries and job mobility of those players. What were the hired hands to do? If they wanted to hit homers and be memorialized in candy bars (i.e., keep their jobs), they had to settle for a less-than-competitive wage. The hapless sluggers were faced with a take-it-or-leave-it wage, and from the days of Abner Doubleday till a few years ago, they took it.

But the players have a monopoly, too: Their organization, the Players Association, is a genteel name for a labor union that is the sole supplier of major-league-quality baseball players. And now that monopoly is refusing to supply the owners with sluggers or hurlers or fielders until the owners come to terms. In short, the players want the owners' monopoly to compete within itself for the players' services.

Back in 1976, the owners took the players' terms—sort of—and free-agent status got underway. Players whose contracts expired were free to sell their hitting or hurling to the highest bidder. Star players started shining in different cities in different uniforms—and salaries shot up. Indeed, average salaries zoomed 175% over the past five years, from the low $50 Ks in 1976 to the high $140 Ks last year.

The owners, feeling the squeeze from a monopoly other than their own, squawked about restoring "competitive balance." The players, enjoying the fruits of their own monopoly power, jawed about finally being paid a "just and reasonable wage." . . .

Until 1976, the monopolistic owners ate the full share of those big, juicy pies made from fans' ticket receipts, broadcasting rights and so forth. After 1976 and free agency, however, the players' monopoly started grabbing slices of the money pie. This strike, then, is just a tug-of-war between monopolists—and it is every bit as unseemly as these fights are.

—Susan Lee

depletes the union treasury.[5] By the same token, the reduction in labor costs and other expenses rarely compensates the employer for lost profits. In the 67-day auto strike of 1970, General Motors lost $90 million a day in sales, while the United Auto Workers spent $160 million in strike benefits. The 49-day baseball strike of 1981 cost the players $600,000 in salaries for every game canceled and the owners an estimated $1.25 million. These kinds of losses create pressure to reach a settlement.[6]

Because potential income losses are usually high, both labor and management try to avoid a strike or lockout if they can. In fact, over 90 percent of all collective-bargaining agreements are concluded without recourse to a strike, and often without even the explicit threat of one.

The final settlement

The built-in pressures for avoidance or quick termination of a work stoppage help to ensure the successful resolution of collective bargaining. They do not tell us, however, what the dimensions of that final settlement will be. All we know is that the settlement will be

[5] A wage increase of 5 cents an hour works out to only $100 per year for the average worker. A one-month strike over such an increase would cost union members more than they would recoup in six to eight years.

[6] Interestingly, the baseball owners had insurance to cover $50 million of strike-related losses. A settlement was reached shortly after losses exceeded this amount.

located within the boundaries established in Figure 13.6, and that the relative pressures on each side will determine whether the final equilibrium is closer to the union or the management position.

The final settlement reached will almost always necessitate hard choices on both sides. The union will usually have to choose between a slight increase in job security or slightly higher pay. In other words, higher wage rates may be acceptable to management only if the labor force is reduced somewhat. For the union, this would mean a cutback in employment and possibly even union membership, a potentially stiff price to pay. A union must also consider how management will react in the long run to higher wages. That is, the union must consider the likelihood that management will introduce new technology that reduces its dependence on labor.

POLICY IMPLICATIONS: THE IMPACT OF UNIONS

Stepping back from the negotiations that take place between individual unions and companies, we may ask whether the presence of unions has altered economic outcomes in general. We do know that unions tend to raise wage rates in individual companies, industries, and occupations. That, after all, is one of their basic objectives. But can we be equally sure that unions have raised wages in general? If the UAW is successful in raising wages in the automobile industry, what, if anything, happens to wages in the breakfast cereal industry? Or what, for that matter, happens to the price of automobiles when auto workers' wages go up? If car prices rise in step with UAW wage rates, labor and management in the auto industry will get proportionally larger slices of the economic pie. At the same time, workers in other industries are burdened with higher car prices.

Relative wages

One measure of union impact is *relative* wages, the wages of union members in comparison with those of nonunion workers. As we have noted, unions seek to control the supply of labor in a particular industry or occupation and thereby increase union wages. In their efforts to control labor supply, they restrict the number of people who can compete for available jobs, forcing those workers who are excluded to seek work elsewhere. Accordingly, unions reduce the supply of labor available to unionized industries and increase the supply of labor available to nonunion industries. As a result of this imbalance, wages tend to be higher in union industries than in nonunion industries. Figure 13.7 illustrates this effect.

Although the theoretical impact of union exclusionism on relative wages is clear, empirical estimates of the extent of that impact are fairly rare. We do know that union wages in general are significantly higher than nonunion wages ($3.20 versus $2.78 per week in 1980). But part of this differential is due to the fact that unions are more common in industries that have always been more capital-intensive and paid relatively high wages. When comparisons are made within particular industries or sectors, the differential narrows considerably. Nevertheless, there is a general consensus, based on

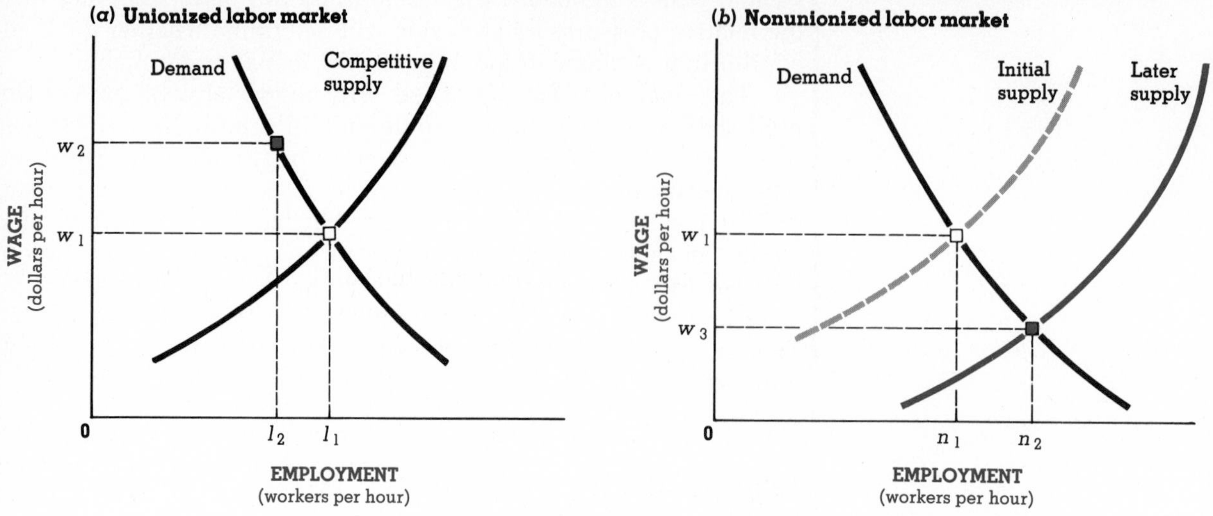

FIGURE 13.7 THE EFFECT OF UNIONS ON RELATIVE WAGES

In the absence of unions, the average wage rate would be equal to w_1. As unions take control of the market, however, they seek to raise wage rates to w_2, in the process reducing the amount of employment in that market from l_1 to l_2. The workers displaced from the unionized market will seek work in the nonunionized market, thereby shifting the nonunion supply curve to the right. The result will be a reduction of wage rates (to w_3) in the nonunionized market. Thus union wages end up higher than nonunion wages.

limited studies, that unions have managed to increase their relative wages by anywhere from 15 to 20 percent. Some unions, of course, have been markedly more successful than others, as a comparison of the wages received by Teamsters and United Farm Workers attests.

Labor's share of total income

Even though unions have been successful in redistributing some income from nonunion to union workers, the question still remains as to whether they have increased labor's share of *total* income. The labor share of total income is the proportion of income received by all workers, in contrast to the share of income received by owners of capital (the capital share). If unions are effective in excluding nonunion workers from highly productive industries and also in increasing their share of income in those industries, the total labor share will grow. In this case, unions redistribute from capital owners to workers. Thus the increase in relative union wages is the result of two factors: redistribution from capital to labor and union exclusion of nonunion workers.

Evidence of unions' impact on labor's share is almost as difficult to assemble as evidence on relative wages, and for much the same reasons. Labor's share has risen dramatically, from only 56 percent in 1919 to over 76 percent in 1982.[7] But there have been tremendous changes in the mix of output during that same period. The proportion of output composed of personal services (accountants, teachers,

[7] The functional distribution of income is discussed in Chapter 15.

electricians) is much larger now than it was in 1919. The labor share of income derived from personal services is and always was close to 100 percent. Accordingly, most of the rise in labor's share of total income is due to changes in the structure of the economy rather than to unionization.

Prices

Closely related to the issue of the labor share is the question of union impact on product prices. If all union wage increases were reflected in the prices of related products, the ability of unions to increase the labor share of income would be limited severely. In such a case, the additional money firms needed to pay their workers would come out of increased prices, not out of profits. Accordingly, the ability of firms to "pass on" wage increases to consumers is a major determinant of their ability to maintain their capital share. If they are successful, they may contribute to cost-push inflation, a subject of Chapters 6 and 13 in *The Macro Economy Today*. At this juncture, we may note that the cause of price increases, especially in oligopolistic market situations, is usually very difficult to identify. Undoubtedly, however, unions have provided an incentive for firms to increase product prices faster than they otherwise would have done.

Political impact

Perhaps more important than any of these specific union effects is the general impact the union movement has had on our economic, social, and political institutions. Unions are a major political force in the United States. They not only have provided critical electoral and financial support for selected political candidates (mostly Democrats), but have also fought hard for important legislation. Unions have succeeded in establishing minimum-wage laws, work and safety rules, and retirement benefits. They have also actively lobbied for such things as civil rights legislation and health and education programs. Whatever one thinks of any particular union or specific union action, it is clear that our institutions and welfare would be very different in their absence.

SUMMARY

- Power in labor markets is the ability to alter market wage rates. Most often, such power is evident in local labor markets defined by geographical, occupational, or industrial boundaries.
- Power on the supply side of labor markets is typically manifested by labor unions, organized along either industry or craft lines. The basic function of a union is to evaluate employment offers in the light of the *collective* interest of its members.
- The downward slope of the labor-demand curve creates a distinction between the marginal wage and the market wage. The marginal wage is the change in *total* wages occasioned by employment of one additional worker and is less than the market wage.
- Unions seek to establish that rate of employment at which the mar-

ginal wage curve intersects the labor-supply curve. The desired union wage is then found by following the labor-*demand* curve to the wage that employers are willing to pay for that number of workers.

- Power on the demand side of labor markets is manifested in buyer concentrations such as monopsony and oligopsony. Such power is usually found among the same firms that exercise market power in product markets.
- Be definition, power on the demand side implies some direct influence on market wage rates: additional hiring by a monopsonist will force up the market wage rate. Hence a monopsonist must recognize a distinction between the marginal cost of labor and its (lower) market wage rate.
- The goal of a monopsonistic employer is to hire the number of workers indicated by the point at which the marginal cost of labor equals its marginal revenue product. The employer then looks at the labor-supply curve to determine the wage rate that must be paid for that number of workers.
- The desire of unions to establish a wage rate that is *higher* than competitive wages directly opposes the desire of powerful employers to establish *lower* wage rates. In bilateral monopolies, in which power exists on both sides of the labor market, unions and employers engage in collective bargaining to negotiate a final settlement.
- The impact of unions on the economy is difficult to measure. It appears, however, that they have increased their own relative wages and contributed to rising prices. They have also had substantial political impact.

Terms to remember

Define the following terms:

market power
labor supply
demand for labor
equilibrium wage
marginal wage
union shop
unionization ratio
monopsony
marginal cost of labor
marginal revenue product
bilateral monopoly
collective bargaining

Questions for discussion

1. Collective-bargaining sessions often start out with "unreasonable" demands and "categorical" rejections. Why do unions and employers tend to begin bargaining from extreme positions?

2. Does a strike for a 5-cent-an-hour raise make any sense? What kinds of long-term benefits might a union gain from such a strike?

3. Are large and powerful firms easier targets for union organization than small firms? Why, or why not?

4. Nonunion firms tend to offer wage rates that are close to rates paid by unionized firms in the same industry. How do you explain this?

5. In 1973 a group of priests in Milwaukee sought to establish a union to bargain over wages and retirement benefits. Whom would the priests negotiate with, and what kinds of tactics could they use to achieve their demands?

Problem

Suppose that the following supply and demand schedules apply in a particular labor market.

Wage rate (per hour)	**$4**	**$5**	**$6**	**$7**	**$8**	**$9**	**$10**
Quantity of labor supplied (workers per hour)	**2**	**3**	**4**	**5**	**6**	**7**	**8**
Quantity of labor demanded (workers per hour)	**6**	**5**	**4**	**3**	**2**	**1**	**0**

Graph the relevant curves and identify:

(*a*) The competitive wage rate
(*b*) The union wage rate
(*c*) The monopsonist's wage rate

CHAPTER 14

RENT, INTEREST, AND PROFIT

Chapters 11–13 have focused on only one factor of production—labor. The emphasis on labor reflects the fact that wages and salaries account for three-fourths of total national income. Hence any forces that influence the level and distribution of wages and salaries largely determine FOR WHOM our output is produced. Nevertheless, the share of income received by capital (25 percent) is not negligible, and its distribution significantly affects our collective answer to the basic question of FOR WHOM to produce.

The basic purpose of this chapter is to examine the nature of the income commonly included in the capital share of total income. What is the nature of rent, interest, and profit, and what forces determine their market value? How are **factor shares** determined?

factor share: The proportion of total income received by a factor of production.

RENT

In macroeconomics "rent" is one of the payments included in the capital share (see Table 14.1). Yet the term "rent," as used by economists, does not necessarily refer to returns to "capital." Nor does it even refer to the monthly payments made by tenants to landlords. In other words, ***economists use the term "rent" differently from the way it is used by almost everyone else in the world.***

The origins of this confusion go back to nineteenth-century England. At that time, there was great concern about the rapidly increasing price of "corn" (actually all grains), the staple of English diets. In

TABLE 14.1 THE FUNCTIONAL DISTRIBUTION OF INCOME

Wages and salaries account for 75 percent of all income; this is the labor share. The capital share is divided among farmers, small businesses, landlords, corporations, and lenders.

Source of income	*Capital share (percent)*	*Labor share (percent)*
Agriculture	**1.1**	
Nonfarm business	**4.7**	
Rents	**1.4**	
Corporate profits	**8.2**	
Interest	**9.3**	
Wages and salaries		**75.3**
Total	**24.7**	**75.3**

Source: *Economic Report of the President,* 1982.

looking for an explanation for the rising price of corn, many Englishmen (including quite a few economists) pointed to the escalating prices being demanded and paid for agricultural land. The landlords, it appeared to them, were the villains responsible for the plight of the working masses. By raising land rents, they were driving up the price of corn and driving the population of England into poverty.[1]

Not so, argued David Ricardo, one of the great classical economists: "Corn is not high because a rent is paid, but a rent is paid because corn is high." Were landlords to reduce their rents, Ricardo noted, this action would only increase the incomes of tenant farmers: the price of corn itself would not drop.

Ricardo's view of land rents as *price-determined* rather than *price-determining* can be explained in terms of either the corn market or the land market.

The price of corn

The market price of corn, like that of any other product, is determined by the intersection of market supply and demand curves. In Figure 14.1, the price p_1 prevails as long as D_1 and S_1 represent the market demand and supply curves.

[1] Chapter 17 in *The Macro Economy Today* provides more detail on nineteenth-century agricultural output and living standards.

FIGURE 14.1 THE PRICE OF CORN

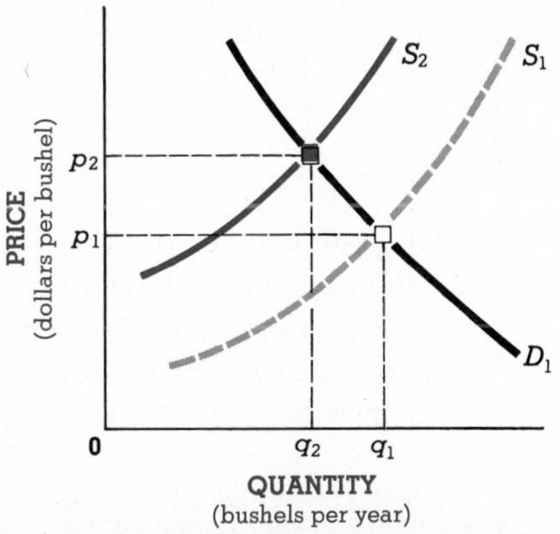

The market price of corn is established by the intersection of market supply and demand. The corn controversy in nineteenth-century England was based on the assumption that rising land rents shifted the corn supply curve upward (to S_2). They did not. Rising corn prices led to rising land prices, not vice versa.

In essence, the nineteenth-century debate over corn prices focused on the effect of rising land prices on the market supply of corn. Those who blamed landlords for rising corn prices were implicitly arguing that increases in land rents would cause an upward *shift* of the corn supply curve, to S_2. The increased costs associated with S_2, they argued, led to a reduction in the quantity of corn supplied (q_2) and a higher corn price (p_2).

marginal cost: The increase in total cost associated with a one-unit increase in production.

But Ricardo argued that rising land rents would *not* shift the corn supply curve. His argument was based on the concept of marginal cost. In his own words, "The reason why raw produce rises in comparative value (price) is because more labor is employed in the production of the last portion obtained, and not because a rent is paid to the landlord." In other words, **marginal costs** determine the supply price of competitively produced goods.

fixed costs: Costs of production that do not change when the rate of output is altered; for example, the cost of basic plant and equipment.

We saw in Chapter 6 that producers will be willing to produce and sell goods in competitive markets as long as price exceeds marginal cost. In fact, the short-run supply curve of a competitive firm is identical to its marginal cost curve. Hence the market supply curve for corn (a competitively produced good) will shift upward only if the marginal cost of producing a given quantity of output changes. Thus an increase in land rent will not alter the market supply or price of corn, because land rent is a **fixed cost** for farmers.

As Ricardo himself concluded, an increase in land rent only served to redistribute income from farmers to landlords. In his own words again, "No reduction would take place in the price of corn, although [even if] landlords should forgo the whole of their rent. Such a measure would only enable some farmers to live like gentlemen, but would not diminish the quantity of labor necessary to raise raw produce on the least productive land in cultivation."[2]

The price of land

Landlords do not have the power to raise rents indiscriminately. Land rents, too, are determined by market supply and demand. As Figure 14.2 reveals, however, the supply curve of land has an unconventional shape: it is vertical.

price elasticity of supply: The percentage change in quantity supplied divided by the percentage change in price.

Typically, we expect producers to respond positively to increased prices. That is, we expect the **price elasticity of supply** to be greater than zero; the quantity supplied increases as prices rise, as in Figure 14.1. In the case of land, however, few such possibilities exist. Although some possibilities exist for increasing the amount of cultivable land through swamp drainage or filling in tidal areas, the quantity of land available is basically fixed. As a consequence, the quantity of land supplied *cannot* increase in response to rising prices. The supply of land is perfectly price inelastic, as illustrated by the vertical supply curve of Figure 14.2.

Because the supply of land is price inelastic—does not change as prices rise and fall—changes in the price of land must be completely determined by market demand. Notice that the initial price of land in Figure 14.2 is R_1, as determined by the intersection of D_1

[2] Ricardo blamed the high price of English corn on the Corn Laws of 1815, which placed high tariffs (taxes) on imported corn (grains), forcing domestic farmers to expand output into the range of substantially higher marginal cost. The impact of international trade restrictions on domestic prices is discussed in Chapter 19.

FIGURE 14.2 THE PRICE OF LAND

The quantity of land available to the market is essentially fixed (Q_1). Hence changes in the price of land will be determined by market demand. In this case, land rents increase from R_1 to R_2 as a result of an upward shift of the demand curve from D_1 to D_2.

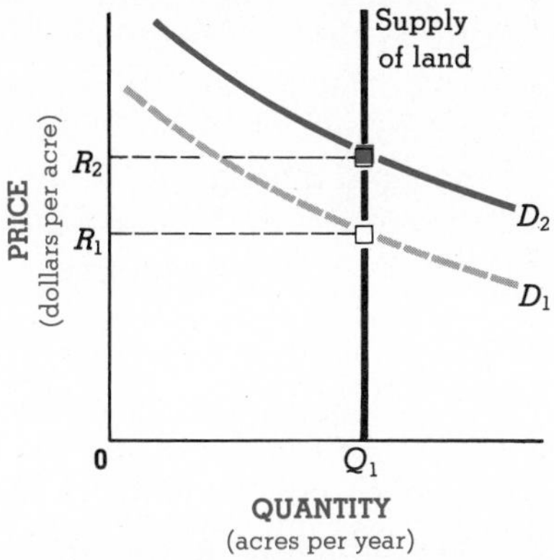

and the land supply curve. If the demand for land were to shift upward, to D_2, the price of land would rise to R_2. But no additional land would be supplied, and no less. This is exactly the kind of situation that occurred in Ricardo's time, when the demand for corn rose, increasing the (derived) demand for agricultural land.

Economic rent

Normally the function of price increases is to signal consumers' desire for more of a particular good or service. Indeed, price signals are the basic characteristic of the market mechanism. In the case of land, however, the price signals have no effect: the quantity of land is unchanged. In this sense, rising prices for land exceed the amount required to call forth the available quantity of land. In fact, the land would be available even if no price were paid for it! Hence any rent paid for the use of land exceeds the price required to call forth the available supply; in this sense, all rent is "surplus" payment.

The term "economic rent" is used to refer to such surplus payments, whether they are paid for land or for any other factor of production. Specifically, ***economic* rent *is a factor payment above the minimum necessary to attract a given quantity of an input.*** In the case of "pure," unimproved land, all payments made are regarded as economic rent.

rent: Payments to a factor of production in excess of the amount required to call forth a given quantity of the factor.

U.S. FARM INCOMES AND LAND PRICES

In 1972–73 the demand for U.S. farm output increased substantially as a consequence of poor harvests elsewhere in the world. U.S. farm output could not expand fast enough to keep pace with demand. As a result, the price of farm products increased dramatically; the average price of farm output rose by nearly 40 percent in one year.

The rising prices of farm goods sharply increased farm incomes. They also made farmland more valuable. The resultant competition for farmland pushed land prices up by more than 25 percent in 1973–74. The rest of the 1970s continued to be good for farmland. Crop prices generally increased faster than inflation, and the value of farmland more than tripled.

The 1980s have not been so good for farm prices. The prices of major agricultural products started falling in 1980, as a consequence of huge harvests and generally weak demand. The price of farmland started falling as well. In 1981–82 farmland prices fell sharply, along with the price of farm products.

Clearly, "pure" rent, as defined by economists, is not the same thing as the rent people pay for their homes or apartments. Rental payments made to landlords typically include compensation for the use of capital (the building structure) and labor (building maintenance and management), and for the use of utility services (water, electricity, gas). In most cases, a very small fraction of the rental payment represents pure economic rent, as defined here.

Even in Ricardo's time, a distinction was drawn between "pure," "natural" land and land that had been improved through cultivation, irrigation, or fencing. Land improvements entail resource costs and will not be made unless a sufficient compensation (price) is offered. Only the land itself will be there at any price. Hence the rental payments made by nineteenth-century farmers included economic rent as well as compensation for the use of labor and capital in improving the land.

The concept of pure rent applies to other factors of production besides land. The demand for the services of Devo, The Police, the Rolling Stones, and Dave Winfield is very high, because these performers can generate substantial revenues for an athletic or musical event. In other words, their **marginal revenue product** is high in certain situations. As a result, sports and music promoters are willing to pay very high prices for performances by such individuals.

marginal revenue product (*MRP*): The change in total revenue associated with one additional unit of input.

Marginal revenue product only establishes a *limit* to a factor's price, however. To determine the market price of the factor, we have to examine the supply curve as well. We find that the supply curves of individual performers are relatively vertical, much like that in Figure 14.2. They can perform only a limited number of times in a given time period. Consequently, these performers are getting eco-

The man with the golden bat

Just as you knew there would be, there are two points of view about the latest big deal in baseball. First, there is the view that it is ridiculous for Yankee owner George Steinbrenner to give a reported $25-million contract to outfielder Dave Winfield. Among those in the ridiculosity camp is Edward Bennett Williams, the well-known mouthpiece and sports investor—he has interests in both the Washington Redskins and Baltimore Orioles. Said Williams of the Winfield deal: "It's just another example of economic madness. If this irrational spending continues, it's going to destroy the industry."

The other point of view, expressed by Winfield himself, derives from classical economics. "There's a market value for everything," Dave observed genially.

Our own instinct is, of course, to side with Dave here and to maintain that the only ridiculous prices in this world are the ones that don't get paid. We will go further: multiyear contracts with star athletes can be viewed as another of those "collectibles" that give wealthy investors like Steinbrenner some protection against galloping inflation. Winfield will look cheap if inflation is bad enough. His deal actually provides $1 million for signing and then $1.5 million annually for ten years, plus cost-of-living increases capped at 10%. (Those who are putting a $25 million total on the payment assume that there will in fact be a 10% increase each year.) If the inflation rate started galloping again, and averaged, say, 25% over the decade, then by 1990 Winfield would be earning a mere $380,000 in today's prices.

It's true that, like many other collectibles, Dave could begin to look rather expensive if inflation does not accelerate. If the rate stays below 10%, he really would be collecting 1.5 million 1980 dollars every year between now and 1990. Even on the optimistic assumption that he will average 150 hits a year during this decade, which ends when he's 39—150 being roughly his average for the seven full years he has been in the major leagues thus far—the deal would leave him collecting 10,000 1980 dollars per hit, which does seem on the high side.

There was a time, within the memory of persons still breathing, when baseball's best hitters got $10,000 for a whole season's work. That is, in fact, what Napoleon Lajoie boasted of collecting in 1906, a year in which he generated 214 hits. But, of course, prices were lower then, players' earnings were depressed by the reserve clause, and Lajoie knew little about classical economics.

nomic rent, that is, payments in excess of the amount required to call forth their services. If all performers' wages were cut in half, Rick Springfield, for example, would probably continue to sing just as well and just as often. Whatever he is being paid in excess of the amount required to get him to sing is economic rent.

RENTS AS AN ALLOCATION MECHANISM Although rising economic rents do not increase the quantity of a factor supplied, they do serve an economic function. Why have all the farmers left Manhattan, where much of the land was once used for pasture and crops? The answer is simple. The rising price of land drove the fixed costs of farming so high that farmers could no longer earn a profit in New York City. Hence, in the long run, as they made new investment decisions, the farmers migrated to less expensive land in the Midwest.

The farmers were initially replaced by modest homes, rooming houses, and factories, and ultimately by skyscraping office buildings. Each step in the evolutionary process was propelled in part by increasing rents. Firms and individuals with more valuable uses for the scarce land offered increasingly high prices for its use. In turn, the high rents forced others to move their firms or households to other locations. Accordingly, ***rents serve to allocate a scarce factor among competing uses. The most valuable use will determine the market rent.*** People seeking to make less valuable use of the scarce factor will not be able to pay the price and will therefore not acquire it. In this way, the market mechanism determines who will use society's scarce resources.

Rent control

In many cities apartment rents are "controlled" by the city government. Rent control generally places a limit on the amount of rent or annual rent increases a landlord can charge. Although apartment rents and economic rents are not the same thing, the theory behind rent control is related to the concept of economic rent.

In cities such as New York there isn't much room for new apartment buildings. Yet the city's population keeps growing. This implies that apartment rents will keep escalating in the manner of Figure 14.2. Upward shifts of demand, together with an inelastic supply of apartments, will drive apartment prices up. In the process, landlords will reap extraordinary gains (economic rents).

Rent control is imposed to prevent apartment rents from becoming economic rents. They are based on the assumption that the supply of apartments is highly inelastic. This is not a valid assumption. The supply of apartments *can* change over time, as new and larger buildings replace old, smaller ones. In the short run, the supply of habitable apartments also depends on continued maintenance. If landlords earn below-average incomes as a consequence of rent control, they will not build new apartments or maintain old ones. (Landlords will also want to convert rent-controlled apartments into uncontrolled condominiums.) Over time, the quantity of apartments will fall, thereby aggravating the market shortage.

Rent control also implies a windfall gain for people who already occupy rent-controlled apartments. If rents are kept below their

Panel's Plan Would End Rent Control

Local rent controls such as those in the District [of Columbia] would effectively be prohibited by federal law under a recommendation approved last night by the President's Commission on Housing. . . .

The commission's regulations panel said that rent controls in some 200 cities throughout the country prevent landlords from getting a fair return on their investment and therefore prevent new construction of rental housing. This is one of the main arguments used by developers and lenders in the District in opposing the controls that affect around 120,000 apartments in Washington.

New York City has had an "emergency" rent control law in effect since 1943.

In calling for a prohibition, and in justifying it in the face of the Reagan administration's dedication to federalism, the commission took circuitous routes.

The mechanism recommended for ending controls was denial of federal assistance, direct or indirect, for housing for any state that did not agree to remove controls in its jurisdiction. This would force a ban throughout the country, as it would include such widespread housing programs as FHA- and VA-insured loans or mortgages from any federally insured lending institution. The states would have five years to end rent controls or lose all such assistance.

—Sandra Evans Teeley

equilibrium price, the quantity demanded will exceed the quantity available. People who are lucky enough to live in rent-controlled apartments will be able to "sell" their leases to others. The "price" of occupancy rights will be determined by market forces. Those consumers most able and willing to "buy" occupancy will get the scarce apartments. In this case, the initial occupants, rather than the landlord, get the *economic* rent. New occupants still pay higher (equilibrium) rents; only the form and direction of the payments are changed.

INTEREST

interest rate: The price paid for the use of money.

Interest payments are a second major form of property income and are also included in the capital share of income. In its purest form, interest is simply the amount of money paid for using someone else's money; typically, it is expressed in percentage terms, as the **interest rate.** An interest rate of 9 percent means that the borrower must pay $9 yearly for every $100 borrowed until the loan is repaid.

The loanable funds market

opportunity cost: The most desired goods or services that are forgone in order to obtain something else.

The rate of interest may be determined through a study of supply and demand forces in the loanable funds market. Some people and firms (particularly banks) are willing and able to lend money at alternative interest rates. From a consumer's point of view, lending money entails the sacrifice of some immediate consumption possibilities and thus real **opportunity costs.** As interest rates climb, however, the trade-off between future consumption and present consumption tilts in the direction of future consumption. In other words, high interest rates make it appealing to sacrifice some consumption now for more consumption later. As a consequence, the quantity of loanable funds *supplied* increases as interest rates rise, as indicated by the upward slope of the supply curve in Figure 14.3. (This situation contrasts with that of land, which entailed a vertical supply curve. Higher interest rates *do* call forth larger quantities of loanable funds.)

The quantity of loanable funds *demanded* has the familiar downward slope, as Figure 14.3 illustrates. From an individual consumer's perspective, borrowing money at high interest rates implies sacrificing a relatively large amount of future consumption possibilities (when the loan must be paid back) for a smaller increase in present consumption. As the implied cost of borrowing diminishes, the quantity of loanable funds demanded increases.

From a potential investor's point of view, increases in interest rates represent an increase in investment costs. Hence high interest rates reduce the net revenues of any potential investment. Here again we anticipate an increase in the quantity of loanable funds demanded as interest rates decline (*ceteris paribus*).

The rate of return to capital

Although we can readily determine the equilibrium rate of interest by studying the supply and demand for loanable funds, the significance of the interest rate for factor prices is not always apparent. After all, money is not a factor of production; it cannot produce anything. Instead, money is a medium of exchange that can be used to acquire both goods and services. When people lend or borrow money, they are really lending or borrowing access to goods and services.

People who use their own or someone else's money to build an apartment house or factory are making the same kind of sacrifice a lender makes. They are giving up the opportunity to spend their money on consumer goods, choosing instead to build, buy, or lease plant and equipment. As compensation for this use of funds, an investor expects increased consumption opportunities in the future. Essentially, the investor expects to be paid interest on his investment. In this case, however, the resultant payments represent *returns to capital*, that is, payments for the use of real plant and equipment.

Typically, an investment is made for many years. A person who builds a factory does not begin to receive any income back until the factory is constructed and in use. The same is true of an apartment

FIGURE 14.3 THE LOANABLE FUNDS MARKET

The market rate of interest (r_e) is determined by the intersection of the curves representing supply of and demand for loanable funds. The rate of interest represents the price paid for the use of money.

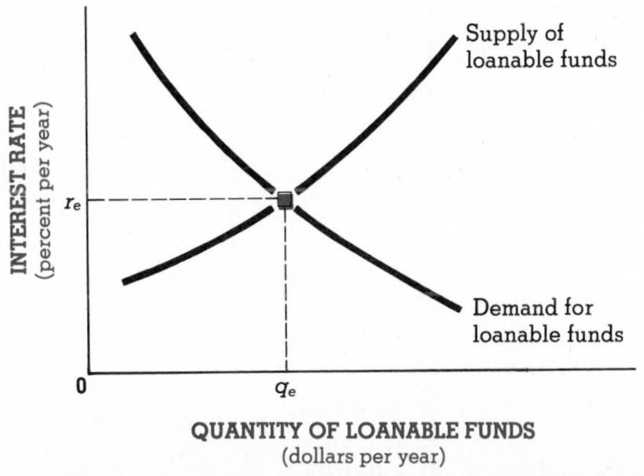

building. It may take a year to construct an apartment building and years more before rent payments equal the owner's original investment. Such investments return a *flow* of income over time. To compute the rate of return to capital in these situations, that future flow of income must be summarized in a meaningful way.

Suppose that the cost of constructing an apartment building is $1 million. After completion, the apartments will generate net rent payments (after expenses) of $100,000 per year, forever. Is this a good investment?

One way to answer this question is to calculate the implicit rate of return. Rent payments of $100,000 per year represent a 10 percent return on a million-dollar investment. This is a "good" investment so long as money can be borrowed for less than 10 percent. If, for example, $1 million could be borrowed at 9 percent, the landlord would have to make annual interest payments of $90,000. But he would get back $100,000 in annual rent payments. He could pocket the difference of $10,000 per year. Hence ***it pays to invest so long as the return on capital exceeds the cost of money.***

Present discounted value

Another way of evaluating the attractiveness of an investment is to *discount* the future stream of rental income to a lump-sum figure. If the rate of interest is 9 percent, $100,000 received one year from today is worth only $91,743 today. This is because money earns interest. If we had $91,743 today, we could deposit it and earn interest. If the interest rate were 9 percent, our $91,743 deposit would be worth $100,000 at year's end. Hence "discounting" involves adjusting future income receipts for forgone interest. By discounting, we translate future receipts into *present* values.

Our apartment building generates $100,000 in income every year, not just the first. Hence we need to discount the *entire* future stream of rent payments, not just the first year's. This is done with the formula:

$$\text{Present discounted value} = \frac{\$100{,}000}{1.09} + \frac{\$100{,}000}{(1.09)^2} + \frac{\$100{,}000}{(1.09)^3} + \cdots \frac{\$100{,}000}{(1.09)^n}$$
$$= \$91{,}743 + \$84{,}168 + \$77{,}218 + \ldots$$

All this formula does is discount each future year's rent back to today's value, then add the values up. The second year's income of $100,000 must be discounted back two years; therefore, the interest rate in the denominator is squared. If the investment income stretches far into the future (n is large), this sum equals $1,111,111.

Fortunately, the formula for computing present discounted values can be simplified to a much shorter expression. If the same income is received every year into the indefinite future, the formula becomes

$$\text{Present discounted value} = \frac{\text{annual income}}{\text{interest rate}} = \frac{\$100{,}000}{0.09} = \$1{,}111{,}111$$

This is the same answer we got above. What it means is that the future stream of rental payments is worth $1.11 million when it is discounted at 9 percent. Since the cost of the investment is only $1 million, the investment is attractive.

In equilibrium, the rate of return to capital will be equal to the rate of interest. Likewise, the present discounted value of future income will be equal to the cost of the investment. This is evident when you think what would happen if an inequality existed. So long as the rate of interest is less than the rate of return to capital, people will continue to borrow and invest. This will drive up interest rates and lower the rate of return to capital. On the other hand, if the rate of interest were higher than the rate of return to capital, investors would simply lend out funds rather than purchase plant and equipment. By doing so, they would increase their future incomes. As the quantity of loanable funds increased, the market rate of interest would fall. At the same time, the rate of investment would slow, because investors were lending their funds rather than buying plant and equipment. With less new investment, marginal revenue product and thus the returns to capital would increase. Ultimately the rate of interest and the rate of return to capital would converge, eliminating motives for any further changes in investor behavior.

PROFIT

economic profit: The difference between total revenues and total economic costs.

economic cost: The value of all resources used to produce a good or service; opportunity cost.

The last major form of income is profit. Like rent, its economic definition differs from common perceptions of the term. As we saw in Chapter 6, **economic profit** is the difference between total revenues and all factor payments, whether explicitly made or not. It is the residual that remains after all **economic costs** have been subtracted.

Entrepreneurship

In view of the fact that profit is a residual that remains after all factors of production have been paid, the question arises as to what profit "buys" in the market. Wages, for example, buy the use of labor, interest rates buy the use of money and capital, and rent buys the use of land. But what does society get in return for profits paid to business?

One of the most prevalent theories of profit regards profit as the reward for entrepreneurship, the ability and willingness to take risks, to organize factors of production, and to produce something society desires. From this perspective, profit represents a return to an intangible but vitally important "fourth factor of production." Profit represents the payoff for making an "extra" effort, over and above "normal" factor payments. In the absence of such additional compensation, few people would want to make the extra effort required.

Risk

It is also important to observe that the *potential* for profit is not a *guarantee* of profit. Quite the contrary. Substantial risks are attached to starting and operating a business. In fact, thousands of businesses

The Top 10 New Products

The top 10 new products of all time, according to 350 research and development executives polled by New Product Development newsletter, are, in order: the wheel, bow and arrow, telegraph, electric light, plow, steam engine, vaccine, telephone, paper, flush toilet.

fail every year, and still more suffer economic losses. From this perspective, profit represents compensation for risks incurred.

The risks associated with a new business are particularly high when new products or processes are being developed. The electronic calculator industry, discussed in Chapters 7–9, for example, was developed on the basis of repeated technological improvements, each of which required substantial investments of labor and capital. Who would have risked such investments without some potential for high profits?

Monopoly profits

Although profits serve an important function in stimulating economic activity, not all profits can be justified on that basis. In many situations, profits may result from the exercise of market power that inhibits rather than encourages economic progress. Monopolies provide a classic example. As we observed in Chapter 8, a monopoly can maintain economic profits by limiting the market output of a good or service. Such profits take on the appearance of economic rent, as high prices and profit do not necessarily call forth a greater quantity supplied. The same kind of quasi-rent is obtained by other firms and unions that possess market power.

POLICY IMPLICATIONS: EXCESS-PROFITS TAX

In a market economy, profits do perform an important economic function. In particular, the potential for profits creates an incentive for entrepreneurs to mobilize society's resources to satisfy consumer demands. The question remains, however, as to how much profit is required to bring about the desired response. As we have observed, any profits in excess of the amount required to elicit desired entrepreneurial responses represent economic rent and do not contribute to increased output. Hence such ***"excess" profits could be taxed away with no impairment of economic goals.*** In fact, taxation of excess profits might improve the distribution of income without impairing economic efficiency, thereby improving total social welfare.

Unfortunately, it is far easier to state the general case for excess-profits taxes than it is to identify excess profits in the real world. We may, however, point to monopolies or other concentrations of economic power as likely sources of excess profit.[3] Excess profits may also emerge when external events abruptly alter market supply or demand forces. When World War II broke out, for example, there was

[3] Public regulation of monopoly behavior (e.g., utility rates) is designed to minimize economic rent.

THE CRUDE OIL WINDFALL PROFIT TAX ACT OF 1980

Tier	*Oil covered*	*Maximum tax rate on windfall profit**
1	**Lower- and upper-tier oil under previous price controls**	**70%**
2	**Stripper well oil**	**60**
3	**Newly discovered (since 1978) oil, certain "heavy" oil, and incremental tertiary oil**	**30**

*"Windfall profit" is the difference between the selling price and an "adjusted base price." Average adjusted base prices per barrel are $13.06 for Tier 1, $15.50 for Tier 2, and $16.96 for Tier 3. This windfall profit is limited to 90 percent of net income per barrel.

a dramatic increase in the demand for U.S. armaments but little change in our production possibilities. Hence armaments producers suddenly found themselves confronting a market shortage that they could not satisfy. Under such circumstances, the potential for reaping high economic rents was enormous. To prevent U.S. producers from profiting excessively from the war, Congress enacted an excess-profits tax.

The same kind of dilemma has inhibited U.S. energy policies. If we truly want to curb U.S. consumption of energy (particularly imported oil), we have to raise domestic energy prices. As prices rise, the quantity of energy demanded will fall, and U.S. producers will increase their domestic exploration and production activities. Higher energy prices, however, will also bestow a "windfall" profit on the owners of existing oil and gas wells. Wells already in production require no further incentives. Higher energy prices represent a "surplus" over the amount required to attract the quantity of oil or gas supplied from "old" wells. Unless this redistribution of income is desired on grounds of equity, the windfall profits serve no function.

To achieve our energy goals without generating windfall profits, Congress tried to distinguish between "old" oil (from established wells) and "new" oil (from new wells) and established separate prices for each.[4] Unfortunately, old oil looks exactly like new oil, and this policy generated high administrative costs and reduced production efficiency. By contrast, a direct excess-profits tax looks more appealing. In 1979 President Carter moved to dismantle the distinction between "old" and "new" oil prices by partially decontrolling the price of domestic oil and establishing a timetable for complete decontrol. President Reagan speeded up the process by eliminating all controls on crude oil prices in February 1981. To limit the economic rent producers might receive, Congress enacted the Crude Oil Windfall Profit Tax Act of 1980. The act established tax rates of 30 percent (on "new oil") to 70 percent (on "old" oil) on the windfall profits producers would reap from higher oil prices.

[4] The actual definitions of "old" and "new" oil were more complex; in 1978 the Carter administration also proposed a third category of oil, called "new new oil." New new oil consists of "oil which is located more than 2½ miles from any onshore domestic well in existence on April 20, 1977, or more than 1,000 feet deeper than any well within the 2½ mile radius, or from an offshore lease entered into after April 20, 1977."

SUMMARY

■ Total income in the economy includes payments for labor, capital, land, and entrepreneurship. Each form of compensation has some unique characteristics.

■ Economic rent is defined as payments for a factor of production in excess of the amount required to call forth the desired supply. Because the quantity of "pure," unimproved land is fixed—cannot respond to increases in prices—all payments for the use of unimproved land represent economic rent. Rents are also paid for the use of other factors whose supply is essentially fixed.

■ Economic rent does not attract a larger quantity of the fixed factor for which it is paid. The "surplus" factor payments, however, do serve to allocate the fixed resource among competing uses.

■ Interest payments are the price paid for the use of money. Interest rates measure the opportunity cost of investing one's funds in plant and equipment. The payments made for the use of such capital are the returns to capital. In equilibrium, the returns to capital will equal the market rate of interest.

■ Economic profits are the income that remains after all economic costs have been accounted for. These above-normal profits represent a reward for entrepreneurship and compensation for its risks. When market power or other institutional barriers inhibit economic activity, however, profits may take on the appearance of economic rent.

■ Profits in excess of those needed to call forth increased supply represent a "windfall" that can be taxed away without reducing market supplies.

Terms to remember

Define the following terms:

factor share
marginal cost
fixed costs
price elasticity of supply
rent
marginal revenue product
interest rate
opportunity cost
economic profit
economic cost

Questions for discussion

1. Dave Winfield, the former San Diego outfielder, was hired by the New York Yankees in 1981 for a contract worth over $25 million. How much of this payment represents economic rent?

2. A 1981 Rand Corporation study of rent control in Los Angeles concluded that "rent control confers its benefits early and exacts its costs late." What is meant by this statement?

3. What functions, if any, do economic profits perform? Do they help allocate any scarce resources?

4. Henry George, a nineteenth-century printer, author, and politician, advocated adoption of a single property tax that would replace all other taxes. What economic arguments might be used to defend or reject such a tax?

5. Why do lenders charge interest on loans? Why are borrowers willing to pay it?

Problem

Suppose that the following figures summarize the annual revenues and costs of operating a Baskin-Robbins ice cream store.

(*a*) Investment in store equipment and franchise	$100,000
(*b*) Annual sales	
Ice creams	180,000
Other confections	32,000
(*c*) Cost of goods	134,000
(*d*) Lease expenses ($600 per month)	________
(*e*) Employee wages (4 workers @ $8,000 per year each)	________
(*f*) The owner-manager works in the store 50 hours per week except for a two-week vacation; his opportunity wage ($8 per hour)	________
(*g*) Interest (9 percent)	________

Using these figures, determine the net revenue and economic profit of the store's owner-operator. Assume that half of the initial investment is borrowed.

CHAPTER 15

THE DISTRIBUTION OF INCOME

The outcomes of individual factor markets consist of wage levels, profit rates, interest rates, and rents. Taken together, they add up to the distribution of income. The distribution of income, in turn, represents our collective response to the basic FOR WHOM question, that is, who gets to consume the goods and services that are produced. People who participate more extensively in factor markets, or whose efforts are rewarded more generously, get more income. With that income, they have a greater claim on the goods and services produced.

The issue of FOR WHOM we produce is not entirely resolved by market forces, of course. The government plays a major role in redistributing incomes. The government takes income from some people (via taxes) and gives it to others (via income transfers). In the process, it reshapes the distribution of income and changes our answer to the FOR WHOM question.

In this chapter we shall examine the actual distribution of income. Who gets the most income from factor markets? How much do taxes and transfers alter the income distribution?

WHAT IS "INCOME"?

Before examining the distribution of income in the United States, we have to decide what to include in our concept of "income" and what to leave out. There are several possibilities. In the national-income

personal income *(PI)*: Income received by households before payment of personal taxes.

accounts (Chapter 4 in *The Macro Economy Today*) we typically focus on **personal income**—the flow of annual income received by households before payment of personal income taxes. Personal income includes wages and salaries, corporate dividends, rent, interest, social security benefits, welfare payments, and any other form of money income.

Personal income is not a completely satisfactory basis for measuring the distribution of income, however. Measures of the distribution of income should tell us FOR WHOM our output is produced. The distribution of personal income does not fully answer this question. Many goods and services are distributed directly ("in kind"), rather than through market purchases. Many poor people, for example, live in public housing and pay no (or little) rent. As a consequence, they receive a larger share of total output than their money incomes imply. Low-income people also receive food stamps with which to purchase more food than their money incomes would allow. In this sense, food-stamp recipients are better off than the distribution of personal income (which does not include food stamps) implies.

The distinction between the distribution of money incomes and the distribution of real output is not confined to welfare recipients. Students who attend public schools and colleges consume more goods and services than they directly pay for; public education is subsidized by all taxpayers. As a consequence, the distribution of money income understates the share of output received by students in public schools.

So long as some goods and services need not be purchased in the market, ***the distribution of money income is not synonymous with the distribution of goods and services.*** Accordingly, the distribution of money receipts is not a complete answer to the question of FOR WHOM we produce. This measurement problem is particularly important when comparisons are made over time. For example, the federal government officially classifies people as "poor" if their money income is below a certain threshold. By this standard, the number of poor people in America has been roughly constant for more than 15 years. In that time, however, we have provided a vastly increased amount of in-kind benefits to low-income people. Hence their *real* incomes have risen much more than the *money* statistics indicate. In this case, money statistics give a misleading picture of the changing income distribution.[1]

The distinction between money incomes and real incomes also affects international comparisons. Many people in less-developed countries rely more on home production than on market participation for essential goods and services. As a consequence, the measured distribution of money income may look more unequal than it really is. This overstatement affects comparisons between the United States and such countries as Sweden and Great Britain, although for different reasons. In those countries, the governments provide more direct goods and services (e.g., housing, medical care) than the U.S. government does. Hence *real* income is more evenly distributed in those countries than money incomes imply.

[1] The poverty problem is discussed in more detail in Chapter 17.

Wealth and happiness

Concentration on money incomes raises still other problems. If our real concern is access to goods and services, the distribution of wealth is also important. "Wealth" refers to the market value of the assets (e.g., houses, bank accounts) people own. Hence wealth represents a stock of potential purchasing power. Income statistics tell us only how *this* year's flow of purchasing power (income) is being distributed. Yet goods and services can be purchased with income saved in previous years (or generations, through inheritance). That is to say, ownership of wealth implies greater access to goods and services than income alone permits. Accordingly, to provide a complete answer to the FOR WHOM question, we have to know how wealth, as well as income, is distributed. In general, wealth tends to be distributed much less equally than income.[2]

Finally, we have to confront a very basic question about the importance of income and wealth. By focusing on access to goods and services, we are implicitly asserting that material things are primary determinants of individual well-being. Does money really buy happiness? Apparently so. In a study of attitudes and income in 19 countries, Richard Easterlin of the University of Pennsylvania came to the following conclusion:

> Does greater happiness go with higher income? The answer is, quite clearly, yes. This does not mean there are no unhappy people among the rich and no happy people among the poor. On the average, however, higher-income people are happier than the poor.[3]

Professor Easterlin also noted, however, that entire societies don't become happier as their abundance grows. What matters to people is their *relative* position in society, not the absolute quantity of goods and services they consume. Hence a "rich" fisherman in Sri Lanka might feel better off than a "poor" American, even though the American has access to far more goods and services.

THE FUNCTIONAL DISTRIBUTION OF INCOME

There are a variety of ways to measure the distribution of money income, and thus to gauge relative economic position. Karl Marx believed that the most meaningful way was to focus on the shares of total income received by the two primary factors of production, labor and capital. He recognized that incomes varied *within* the capitalist and proletariat (laboring) classes. He believed, however, that the distinction between those who owned the means of production (the capitalists) and those whose labor was exploited (the proletariat) overwhelmed all other differences. He predicted that the capitalists would continue to accumulate wealth, power, and income, steadily increasing their share of total output. Ultimately, those who had little would vastly outnumber those who had much and would come to resent them. This resentment at inequality would lead to a proletarian revolution.

[2] Recent estimates indicate that 1 percent of the U.S. population owns more than one-fifth of all wealth in the United States (see Anthony Atkinson, "The Concentration of Wealth in Britain," *Challenge*, July–August 1978).
[3] Richard A. Easterlin, "Does Money Buy Happiness?" *Public Interest*, Winter 1973.

TABLE 15.1 THE FUNCTIONAL DISTRIBUTION OF INCOME, 1929–1981

Labor's share of total income has risen substantially in the last fifty years. Much of this increase is due to the shift away from manufacturing to more labor-intensive service industries. Increased capital investment, education, skill training, and labor organization have also contributed to a rising labor share of income.

Year	Total labor share (percent)	Capital share (percent)*					
		Total	Farmers	Nonfarm proprietors	Rental income	Corporate profits	Interest income
1929	60.3	39.7	7.3	10.4	5.8	10.8	5.5
1933	73.9	26.1	6.5	8.0	5.5	– 4.3†	10.3
1943	64.8	35.2	6.9	10.2	2.6	13.9	1.6
1953	69.9	30.1	4.3	9.5	3.3	11.8	1.1
1963	71.0	29.9	2.4	8.0	3.3	12.3	3.0
1973	75.1	24.9	3.0	5.7	2.0	9.3	4.9
1981	75.6	24.4	1.0	4.8	1.4	8.1	9.1

*Includes income of farmers, landowners, and landlords, as well as those who own plant and equipment.
†In 1933, corporate profits were negative, as was net investment.
Source: *Economic Report of the President*, 1982.

functional distribution of income: The division of income among factors of production, especially between capital and labor.

factor share: The proportion of total income received by a factor of production.

The division of income between labor and capital is now called the **functional distribution of income.** No one is quite sure what the functional distribution looked like in the mid-nineteenth century (when Marx was writing). Recent estimates suggest, however, that wage and salary workers were getting less than 40 percent of total output. This low labor share was explained largely by the prevalence of small farmers, whose income was derived primarily from their own labor, and was not paid in wages and salaries. More recent statistics, as provided in Table 15.1, may be more representative of basic trends in the functional distribution of income.

Since 1929, labor's share of total income has increased substantially and now accounts for three-fourths of total income. In part, this trend is explained by the substantial shift in our GNP away from heavy manufacturing (which is capital-intensive) to labor-intensive services (including government services and education). As the mix of output continues to shift toward goods and services that use little capital and much labor, labor's share of total income—its **factor share**—may be expected to rise.

Another force that has helped to boost labor's share of total income is labor unionism. Unions have reduced the size of the labor force (by demanding earlier retirements, longer school attendance, and tougher immigration restrictions) and have shortened the working day. These actions have served to make labor a scarcer commodity and thus more valuable.

Finally, we may note that the supply of capital has expanded much more quickly than the supply of labor. While the labor force has grown at a rate of something like 1 percent a year, the stock of capital has grown by 3 to 4 percent a year. This disparity has the effect of making capital relatively abundant and thus cheaper, while making labor relatively scarce and thus expensive.[4]

[4] Also, by making more capital available to the average worker, this trend raises the productivity of labor. The concept of marginal productivity and its determinants are discussed in Chapter 12.

THE SIZE DISTRIBUTION OF INCOME

In view of the fact that labor's share of income is already so large, the functional distribution of income no longer arouses much interest. People are now more concerned about the distribution of income among *individuals* than about its distribution among anonymous factors of production. To address this concern, we need to know what the distribution of personal income looks like *within* functional classes (labor and capital), as well as between them.

size distribution of income: The way total personal income is divided up among households or income classes.

The most common measure of the income shares received by individuals is the **size distribution of income.** This measure tells us how large a share of total personal income is received by various households, grouped by income class. Imagine for the moment that the entire population is lined up in order of income, with lowest-income recipients in front and highest-income recipients at the end of the line. What we want to know is how much income the people in front get, in comparison with those at the back. Table 15.2 provides the answer.

income share: The proportion of total income received by a particular group.

The figures in Table 15.2 indicate that no household in the first (lowest) fifth of the line received more than $10,286 in 1980; thus $10,286 was the upper boundary for the lowest income class. Note also that this class received only 5.1 percent of total income, despite the fact that it included 20 percent of the population (the lowest *fifth*). Thus the **income share** of the people in the lowest group was much smaller than their proportion in the total population.

Moving back to the end of the line, we observe that a family needed only $35,000 in annual income to make it into the highest income class in 1980. Naturally, many families in that class made much more than $35,000, some even millions of dollars. But $35,000 was at least enough to get into the top fifth (or quintile).

The top fifth of all families obviously fared much better than everyone else. The extent of their prosperity is indicated by their relative income share. They got 41.5 percent of total income and, by implication, that much of total output. This was eight times as much income as the lowest class received.

The Lorenz curve

The size distribution of income provides the kind of information we need to determine how total personal income is distributed. A more convenient summary of that same information is often desired, how-

TABLE 15.2 SIZE DISTRIBUTION OF PERSONAL INCOME, 1980

The size distribution of income indicates how total income is distributed among income classes. That fifth of our population with the lowest incomes received only 5.1 percent of total income. The highest-income class (fifth) received over 41 percent of total income.

Household income group	*1980 income*	*Aggregate income (billions of dollars)*	*Share of total income (percent)*
Lowest fifth	**$ 0–10,286**	**$ 73.7**	**5.1**
Second fifth	**10,287–17,390**	**167.7**	**11.6**
Third fifth	**17,391–24,630**	**253.0**	**17.5**
Fourth fifth	**24,631–34,534**	**351.3**	**24.3**
Highest fifth	**above 34,534**	**601.4**	**41.5**

Source: U.S. Department of Commerce, Bureau of the Census.

Reprinted by permission of the *San Francisco Chronicle*. Artist: Robert Graysmith.

ever. For this purpose we can draw a Lorenz curve, first suggested by an American statistician, Max Otto Lorenz, in 1905.

A Lorenz curve for the United States is illustrated in Figure 15.1. Our line-up of individuals is on the horizontal axis, with the lowest income earners on the left. On the vertical axis we depict the cumulative share of income received by people in our income line. Consider the lowest fifth of the distribution again, that is, the people in front of our income line. They are represented on the horizontal axis at 20 percent. What we want to know is how large a share of income they receive. If their share of income was identical to their share of population, they would get 20 percent of total income. This

FIGURE 15.1 THE LORENZ CURVE

The Lorenz curve illustrates the extent of income inequality. If all incomes were equal, each fifth of the population would receive one-fifth of total income. In this case, the diagonal line through point C would represent the cumulative size distribution of income. In reality, incomes are not distributed equally. Lower-income groups receive smaller income shares. Point *A*, for example, indicates that 20 percent of the population with the lowest income receives only 5.1 percent of total income.

Source: Table 29.2.

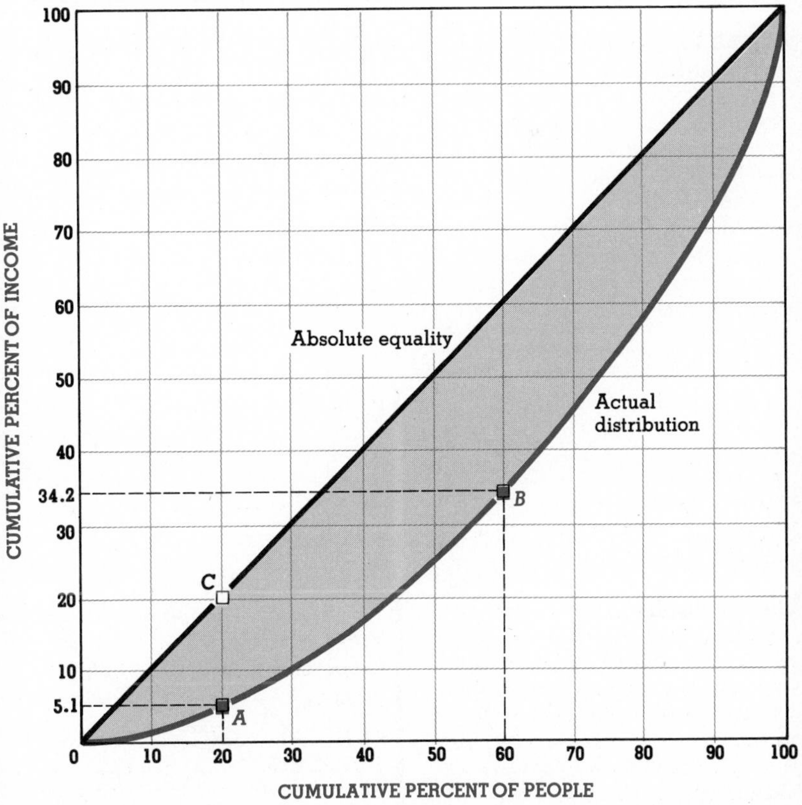

would be represented by point C in the figure. In fact, the lowest quintile gets much less than 20 percent of total income. They get only 5.1 percent, as indicated by point *A*. We already knew this from Table 15.2, of course.

Lorenz curve: A graphic illustration of the cumulative size distribution of income; contrasts complete equality with the actual distribution of income.

Past point *A*, the **Lorenz curve** starts to provide a bit more information. Point *B*, for example, tells us that the *cumulative* share of income received by the lowest three-fifths of the population was 34.2 percent. We could have gotten this information from Table 15.2 as well, but it would have required a little addition.

The really handy feature of the Lorenz curve is the way it contrasts the actual distribution of income with an absolutely equal one. If incomes were distributed equally, all income shares would be identical. In that case, the first 20 percent of the people in line would be getting exactly 20 percent of all income and the Lorenz curve would run through point C. Indeed, the Lorenz "curve" would be a straight line along the diagonal. The fact that the actual Lorenz curve lies below the diagonal indicates that our national income is not distributed equally. In fact, the area between the diagonal and the actual Lorenz curve (the shaded area in Figure 15.1) is a convenient measure of the degree of inequality. ***The greater the area between the Lorenz curve and the diagonal, the more inequality exists.***[5]

[5] The ratio of the shaded area to the area of the triangle formed by the diagonal and the axes is often used as a numerical summary of the Lorenz curve. This ratio, called the "Gini coefficient," was 0.359 in 1972.

FIGURE 15.2 INCOME INEQUALITY IN THE UNITED STATES AND SWEDEN

These Lorenz curves illustrate the distribution of *after-tax* money incomes in the United States and Sweden for standardized household size. The greater equality of Swedish incomes is apparent from the fact that the Swedish Lorenz curve is closer to the diagonal.

Source: Organization for Economic Cooperation and Development, 1976.

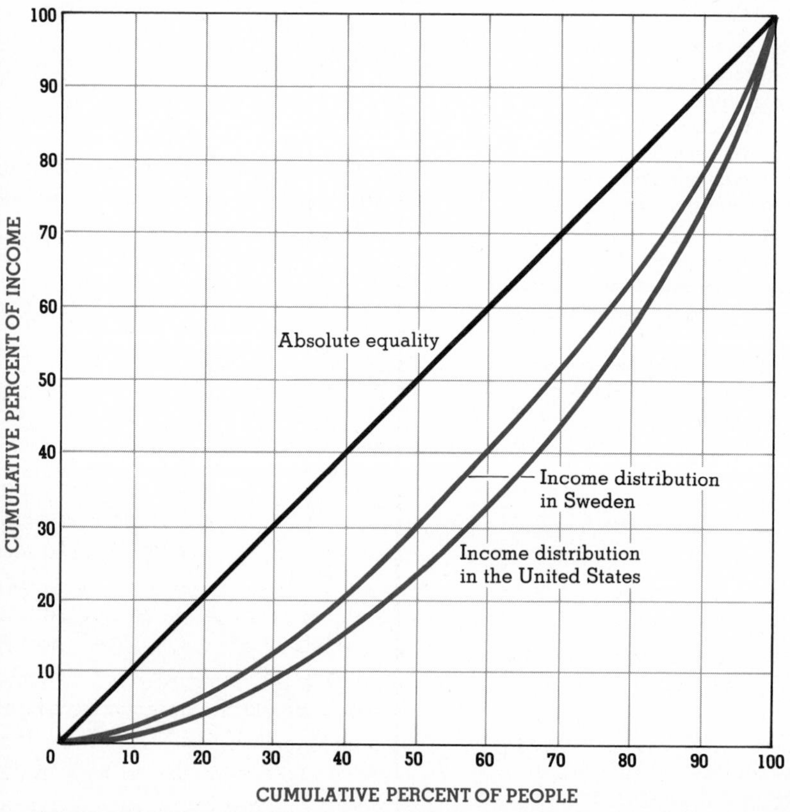

FIGURE 15.3 THE IMPACT OF TAXES ON INEQUALITY

These Lorenz curves depict distributions of adjusted family income before and after federal, state, and local taxes. The tax system does not substantially reduce income inequality.

Source: Joseph A. Pechman and Benjamin A. Okner, *Who Bears the Tax Burden?* Fig. 1-3, p. 7. Copyright © 1974 by the Brookings Institution, Washington, D.C.

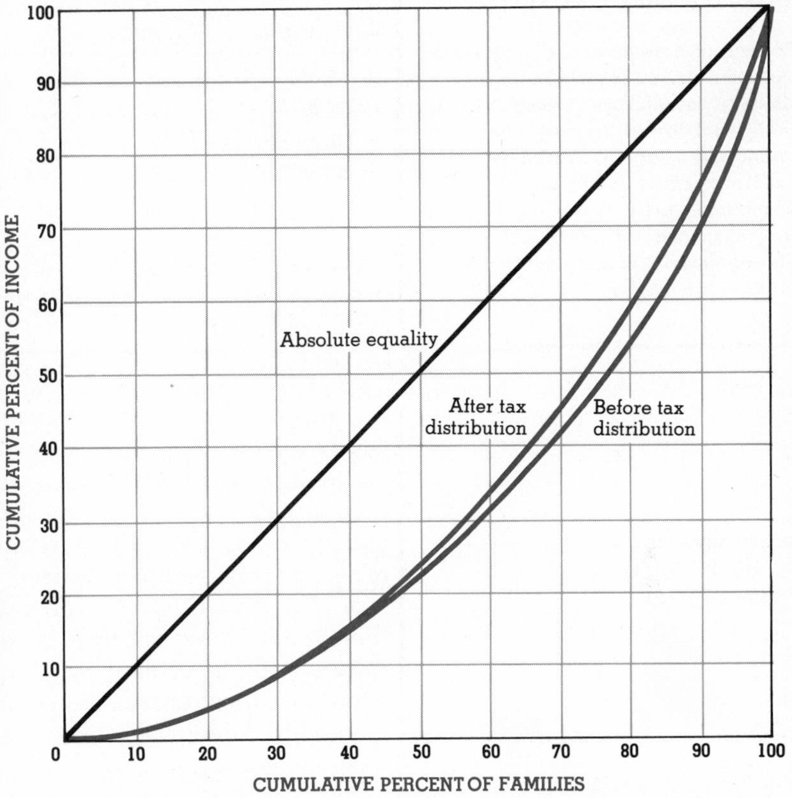

The Lorenz curve is a particularly useful tool for comparing the income distributions of countries or of the same country at two or more points in time. Figure 15.2, for example, provides a quick comparison of income inequalities in the United States and Sweden. The Lorenz curve for Sweden lies closer to the diagonal, indicating that money incomes are distributed more equally in Sweden than in the United States. Other countries, including West Germany, France, and most less developed nations, exhibit less equality than the United States.

The impact of taxes

progressive tax: A tax system in which tax rates rise as incomes rise.

marginal tax rate: The tax rate imposed on the last (marginal) dollar of income.

A particularly interesting Lorenz curve comparison is illustrated in Figure 15.3. It shows the reduction in inequality brought about by federal, state, and local taxes. Many people regard the tax system as a major tool for equalizing incomes, particularly for reducing the very high incomes of the wealthiest classes. In fact, the federal income tax is designed to be **progressive,** that is, to impose higher tax *rates* on high incomes than on low ones. As Table 15.3 illustrates, the **marginal tax rate** for single taxpayers increases from zero on incomes under $3,400 to 26 percent on incomes over $30,000. For extremely high incomes—those above $150,000—the marginal tax rate is 50 percent.

TABLE 15.3 FEDERAL INCOME TAX RATES FOR SINGLE TAXPAYERS, 1983

Federal income taxes are progressive: tax rates rise as income increases. However, many high-income individuals avoid high tax rates by taking advantage of available exemptions and deductions ("loopholes"). The progressivity of the federal tax system is further offset by the regressivity of state and local taxes.

Total income	*Marginal tax rate (percent)*	*Total income*	*Marginal tax rate (percent)*
$0– 3,400	0	$ 30,000	26
5,000	11	60,000	40
10,000	15	100,000	48
20,000	19	150,000 or more	50

Note: The tax rates given here assume all income is fully taxable (as it would be if it were derived solely from wages and salaries) and that the standard deduction is used at incomes below $20,000. Actual tax rates very with the sources of income, the number of dependents, and the availability of additional deductions and credits.
Source: Internal Revenue Service.

regressive tax: A tax system in which tax rates fall as incomes rise.

But the progressive nature of our federal income tax is significantly reduced by a variety of special provisions, including various tax deductions, exemptions, and credits, that benefit higher income groups. Moreover, most state and local taxes—on income, property, and sales—are actually **regressive.** That is, they impose higher tax rates on *lower* incomes. Indeed, state and local taxes are so regressive that they offset the progressivity of the federal income tax, thereby rendering our total tax system ineffective as a leveler of incomes. This is evident in Figure 15.3, where the before-tax and after-tax Lorenz curves are compared. The tax system does reduce inequality somewhat—the after-tax Lorenz curve is closer to the diagonal—but the reduction is slight.

The impact of transfers

The tax system tells only half the redistribution story. It tells whose income was taken away. Equally important is who gets the income the government collects. The government completes the redistribution process by *transferring* income to consumers. The transfers may be explicit, as in the case of welfare benefits, social security payments, and unemployment insurance. Or the transfers may be indirect, as in the case of public schools, farm subsidies, and student loans. The direct transfers are more likely to be progressive, that is, to increase the income share of lower-income households. This

Reagans Made $418,826 in '81, Paid U.S. 40%

President Reagan and his wife, Nancy, made $418,826 in 1981 and paid nearly 40 percent of it in federal income taxes, according to returns made public at the White House without comment yesterday.

The Reagans' joint return shows that they paid income taxes of $165,305 and claimed charitable deductions of $11,895. Nearly half of this ($5,930) was in clothes donated by Mrs. Reagan to two museums two weeks before her husband was inaugurated president. . . .

Reagan earns $200,000 a year as president. His presidential salary in 1981, however, was $189,167, because he did not take office until Jan. 20.

The president's other income included $42,635 in royalties and payments for past writings, radio or acting performances, $66,558 from investments made by his blind trust and $51,482 for a past property sale.

Reagan also receives a pension of $22,197 from the state of California, where he was governor for eight years.

—Lou Cannon

The Washington Post, Washington, D.C., April 17, 1982.

CBO Says Benefit Cuts, Tax Rises Hit Hardest at Under-$10,000 Households

More than half of all the benefit cuts and individual tax increases proposed by President Reagan for fiscal 1983 would fall on households with less than $10,000 annual income, according to a Congressional Budget Office study sent to Congress yesterday.

The CBO said the average loss as a result of Reagan's proposals would be about $320 for households with income less than $10,000, about triple the figure for families earning more than $10,000.

The study, requested by Sen. Ernest F. Hollings (D-S.C.) and other members of Congress, estimated that Reagan's request for cash and in-kind benefit program cuts directly affecting individuals would total $10.8 billion in fiscal 1983 if enacted. The cuts would come largely from reductions in food stamps and Medicare, but also include housing, Medicaid, welfare, education benefits, civil service, veterans' and military benefits.

The individual tax increases, totaling $830 million, would result from Reagan's request for imposition of the federal Medicare tax on civil servants.

Of the $11.6 billion total from the cuts and tax increases, the CBO said $6.2 billion would come from households with less than $10,000 income a year; about $2.3 billion from those in the $10,000 to $20,000 category; about $2.1 billion from the $20,000 to $40,000 group, and about $950 million from those with incomes of more than $40,000.

The CBO figures show that the same general pattern would hold for 1984 and 1985 as well.

—Spencer Rich

The Washington Post, Washington, D.C., April 15, 1982.

progressiveness results from the fact that low-income status is often a requirement for a direct income transfer. By contrast, most indirect transfers are ostensibly designed to fulfill other purposes (e.g., education, agricultural stability). As a consequence, they are less likely to be progressive, and may even be regressive in some cases. A recent study of "social welfare" expenditures (including all direct transfers, housing, and education) attempted to assess the share of such transfers going to the poor. It found that only half of federal transfers and even a smaller proportion (30 percent) of state and local transfers go to the poor.[6] Were indirect transfers included, the proportions would be smaller yet.

WHAT IS "FAIR"?

It is evident that incomes are distributed unequally in the United States, even after all taxes and transfers are considered. It is not at all clear, however, in which direction we should go from here. Should we make the tax system more progressive? Do we really want greater equality? Or are the existing inequalities sufficiently justified to preclude further efforts at redistribution?

Nearly everyone has an answer to these questions, but the answers vary widely. "Fairness" is a subjective concept that is often indistinguishable from self-interest. Rich people, for example, can rattle off as many good reasons for preserving income inequalities as poor people can recite for eliminating them. People in the middle income brackets tend to be ambivalent.

Economists are not uniquely qualified to overcome self-interest, much less to divine what a fair distribution of income might look

[6] Robert Plotnick and Felicity Skidmore, *Progress against Poverty* (New York: Academic Press, 1975).

like. But economists are in a position to assess some of the costs and benefits of altering the distribution of income, and such assessments can facilitate policy decisions.

The costs of greater equality

The greatest potential cost of a move toward greater equality is the reduced incentives it might leave in its wake. People *are* motivated by income. In factor markets, higher wages call forth more workers and may induce them to work longer hours. Indeed, in fields where earnings are exceptionally high, as in the medical and legal professions, people are willing to spend years of their lives and many thousands of dollars acquiring the skills such earnings require. Could we really expect people to make such sacrifices in a market that paid everyone the same wage?

The same problem exists in product markets. The willingness of producers to supply us with goods and services depends on their expectation of profits. Why should they work hard and take risks to produce goods and services if their efforts will not make them any better off? If incomes were in fact distributed equally, producers might just as well sit back and enjoy the fruits of someone else's labor.

The essential economic problem that absolute income equality poses is that it breaks the market link between effort and reward. If all incomes were equal, it would no longer pay to make an above-average effort. If people stopped making such efforts, total output would decline and we would have less income to share. Not that all high incomes are attributable to great skill or effort. Such factors as luck, market power, and family connections also influence incomes. It remains true, however, that the promise of higher income encourages work effort. Moreover, we can reach our production-possibilities curve only if we are efficient, highly motivated producers. Absolute income equality threatens those conditions.

The argument for preserving income inequalities is thus anchored in a concern for productivity. From this perspective, income inequalities are the driving force behind much of our production. By preserving such inequalities, we not only enrich the fortunate few but also, by providing incentives to increase total output, make more goods and services available to lower income groups. Thus everyone is potentially better off, even if only a few end up "rich."

The benefits of greater equality

Although the potential benefits of inequality are impressive, ***there is a trade-off between efficiency and equality.*** Moreover, many people are convinced that the terms of the trade-off are exaggerated and the benefits of greater equality are ignored. These rebuttals are both economic and noneconomic.

The economic arguments for greater equality also focus on incentives. The first argument is that the present degree of inequality is more than necessary to maintain work incentives. Upper-class incomes need not be eight times as large as those of the lowest income classes; perhaps *five* times as large would do as well.

The second argument is that low-income earners might actually

Fame drain

Over the years Great Britain has produced countless men of fame—scientists, artists, entertainers of every stripe.

Now it is in danger of losing its current crop of star achievers.

The income tax rates are largely to blame. They range up to 83 percent on earned income and up to 98 percent on investment income. After a certain point such rates become confiscatory.

As a result the Bay City Rollers, the No. 1 pop group, will probably leave Britain and join the growing number of tax exiles seeking refuge in the United States, France, Switzerland, and other countries.

Mick Jagger and the Rolling Stones left England in 1971. "If the maximum tax was reduced to 50 percent," says Jagger, "which is what it is in America, it's more than likely that the Rolling Stones would return to England."

Former Beatle Ringo Starr, living in California, says, "I'd love to live in Britain again. But it seems terribly unfair that so much of what we earn should be taken away from us in taxes."

Another recent tax exile, singer Rod Stewart, also living in California, joins in with, "Let the government reduce that awful tax rate, and I'll be back in London in the morning."

Richard Burton, David Niven, Rex Harrison, Elizabeth Taylor, Charlotte Rampling—the cream of the British entertainment world—have all escaped from the oppression of British taxes by living abroad. Nor are tax exiles limited to entertainers. The loss of eminent scientists and highly qualified doctors is now arousing governmental concern. An estimated 1500 physicians are reportedly leaving Great Britain each year, largely because no senior doctor or surgeon on the National Health Service earning $20,000 or more a year is allowed an increase in salary.

—Lloyd Shearer

Parade, 1977. Reprinted by permission.

work harder if incomes were distributed more fairly. As matters now stand, the low-income worker sees little chance of making it big. Extremely low income can also inhibit workers' ability to work, by subjecting them to poor health, malnourishment, or inadequate educational opportunities. Accordingly, some redistribution of income to the poor might improve the productivity of low-income workers and compensate for reduced productivity among the rich. Together, these two arguments suggest that greater equality could be attained with little loss of total output.

There are noneconomic arguments for greater equality as well. To the extent that high incomes go hand in hand with political power, an unequal distribution of income weakens the democratic process. Inequalities may also tend to distort our values by their very emphasis on material reward. By the same token, the anxieties and frustrations created by the quest for upper-income positions may actually make us less happy as a society, even if somewhat richer.

The compromises

There are strong arguments both for and against greater income equality. In the absence of hard facts about the effect of income inequalities on work incentives, it is difficult to tell who is right. By how much would output drop if we actually raised taxes on the rich and distributed incomes more equally? By how much, if at all, would the productivity of low-income workers increase? Without such answers, we cannot claim that any income-redistribution plan represents the "right" compromise of equality and efficiency. Instead, we are virtually compelled to proceed in piecemeal fashion, altering our tax and transfer systems slightly and observing the impact of such changes. The alternative approach—a wholesale restructuring of the tax and transfer system—risks a severe reduction in total output and income.[7]

[7] "Radical" economists are quick to point out that this approach amounts to a defense of the status quo and existing income and wealth distributions, whether so intended or not. They are right.

SUMMARY

- The distribution of income is a vital economic issue because money incomes largely determine access to the goods and services we produce. Wealth distributions are also important, for the same reason.
- The functional distribution of income tells us how incomes are divided up between capital and labor. Over time, labor has received an increasing income share.
- The size distribution of income tells us how incomes are divided up among individuals. The Lorenz curve provides a graphic summary of the cumulative size distribution of income.
- Personal incomes are distributed quite unevenly in the United States. At present, the highest income group (the top 20 percent) gets eight times as much income as the lowest income group.
- Our tax system has had little impact on the distribution of personal income. Mildly progressive federal income taxes are offset by regressive state and local taxes. Income transfers may be more progressive, but their net effect is not certain.
- There is a trade-off between efficiency and equality. If all incomes are equal, there is no economic reward for superior productivity. On the other hand, a more equal distribution of incomes might increase the productivity of lower income groups and serve important noneconomic goals as well. The actual terms of this trade-off between equality and efficiency are not known, however, and the debate on the appropriate distribution of our income continues.

Terms to remember

Define the following terms:

personal income
functional distribution of income
factor share
size distribution of income
income share
Lorenz curve
progressive tax
marginal tax rate
regressive tax

Questions for discussion

1. What goods or services does the average American receive without directly paying for them? How do these goods affect the distribution of economic welfare?
2. Why are incomes distributed so unevenly? Identify and explain three major causes of inequality.
3. Do inequalities stimulate productivity? In what ways? Provide two specific examples.
4. Should parents have the right to bequeath their assets to their children, without inheritance taxes? Is productivity a relevant concern here? Explain.

Problem

Using the numbers in Table 15.2 as a base, calculate the average tax rates that would have to be imposed on each income class to bring about absolute equality across income classes.

PART C

MICROECONOMIC ISSUES

CHAPTER 16

POLLUTION

Progress in environmental problems is impossible without a clear understanding of how the economic system works in the environment and what alternatives are available to take away the many roadblocks to environmental quality.

—COUNCIL ON ENVIRONMENTAL QUALITY, FIRST ANNUAL REPORT

What good is a clean river if you've got no jobs?

—STEELWORKER UNION OFFICIAL IN YOUNGSTOWN, OHIO (1977)

According to the President's Council on Environmental Quality, 1970 marked "a turning point, a year when the quality of life [became] more than a phrase; environment and pollution [became] everyday words; and ecology [became] almost a religion to some of the young." That is not to say that pollution was never a problem before 1970. As early as A.D. 61, the statesman and philosopher Seneca was complaining about the smoky air emitted from household chimneys in Rome. And historians are quick to remind us that open sewers running down the street were once the principal mode of urban waste disposal and that typhoid epidemics were a recurrent penalty for water pollution. So we cannot say that pollution is a new phenomenon, or that it is now worse than ever before.

But we do know more about the sources of pollution than our ancestors and can better afford to do something about them. After all, it was centuries before people discovered the scientific relationship between open sewers and periodic epidemics. And it took just about as long for us to discern the chemical link between auto exhaust and air pollution.

Our understanding of the economics of pollution has increased as well. On the one hand, we have come to recognize that pollution imposes direct costs on the economy. Pollution impairs health and thus reduces labor-force activity and output. Pollution also destroys capital (e.g., the effects of air pollution on steel structures) and diverts resources to undesired activities (e.g., car washes, laundry, and cleaning). Not least of all, pollution directly reduces our social welfare by denying us access to clean air, water, and beaches.

On the other hand, we have also learned that *controlling* pollution is costly, too. To clean up sewage, car exhausts, and smoke stains, we have to employ scarce factors of production to build, install, and maintain antipollution equipment. These factors of production could be used elsewhere. Hence there is an *opportunity cost* associated with pollution control. Much of the recent debate over pollution policy has focused on balancing these costs against the benefits of a cleaner environment.

Finally, we now recognize that much pollution is actually *encouraged* by the market system. People and industries typically pollute because they have no financial incentive to do otherwise. Accordingly, public antipollution policy has placed increasing emphasis on the profitability of not polluting. In this chapter we shall first review the nature and origins of pollution, then examine the market incentives for polluting. We conclude with a look at recent attempts to balance the costs and benefits of pollution control.

WHO POLLUTES WHAT?

Everyone seems to have his or her own idea of what pollution is and who causes it. Typically one particular pollutant comes to mind most quickly or is regarded as most annoying. Usually associated with that pollutant is an image—say, of an automobile—identified as the culprit. Such personal perspectives, however, tend to be incomplete. Accordingly, before we consider the alternatives available to eliminate pollution, we shall review the nature and sources of three major forms of pollution: air, water, and solid waste.

Air pollution

Air pollution is as familiar as a smoggy horizon. But smog is only one form of air pollution, as Table 16.1 indicates. There are five major air pollutants: carbon monoxide (CO), total suspended particulates (TSP), sulfur dioxide (SO_2), hydrocarbons (HC), and nitrogen oxides (NO_X). Each comes from a variety of sources.

Carbon monoxide (CO) is the colorless, odorless, and poisonous gas that is produced by incomplete burning of the carbon in fuels. In general, carbon monoxide slows reaction speeds and contributes to a wide variety of heart and lung problems. As is apparent from Table 16.1, the primary source of CO pollution is the automobile. Automobiles accounted for two-thirds of all CO emissions in 1977 (nine years after federal auto-emission controls were initiated). Another familiar source of carbon monoxide is cigarette smoking, which ac-

TABLE 16.1 ESTIMATED EMISSIONS OF AIR POLLUTANTS BY WEIGHT
(in millions tons per year)

There are five major air pollutants. Automobiles account for most carbon monoxide (CO) emissions, but utilities and industrial plants are prime sources of other air pollutants.

Source	*CO*	*TSP*	SO_2	*HC*	NO_x
Transportation	85.7	1.1	0.8	11.5	9.2
Fuel combustion in stationary sources	1.2	4.8	22.4	1.5	13.0
Industrial processes	8.3	5.4	4.2	10.1	0.7
Solid-waste disposal	2.6	0.4	0	0.7	0.1
Miscellaneous	4.9	0.7	0	4.5	0.1
Total	102.7	12.4	27.4	28.3	23.1

Source: Environmental Protection Agency (1977 data).

counts for a tiny fraction of total air pollution but for most of the CO in the lungs of smokers.

The second major air pollutant depicted in Table 16.1, particulates (TSP), includes such visible annoyances as soot and smoke. These, too, are products of combustion, especially from industrial plants and power-generating plants. Particulates contribute to respiratory problems and are a major factor in the reduction of visibility. Some specific particulates, such as asbestos (from construction materials and brake linings) and lead (from car exhausts), have been identified as particularly dangerous to health.

Sulfur dioxide (SO_2), an acrid, corrosive, and poisonous gas, also comes from combustion, whenever fuels containing high levels of sulfur are burned. Electric utilities and industrial plants that burn high-sulfur coal or fuel oil are the prime sources of SO_2. Coal burning alone accounts for about 60 percent of all emissions of sulfur oxides. Sulfur oxides have been identified as the primary cause of the deaths and respiratory ailments accompanying air-pollution disasters. During one such disaster, in Donora, Pennsylvania, in 1948, half of the town's 14,000 inhabitants fell ill and twenty died. In 1952 a "killer smog" in London accounted for 1,600 deaths. Sulfur dioxide emissions also play a major role in the creation of acid rain.

Hydrocarbons (HC), like carbon monoxide, represent unburned and wasted fuel. Hydrocarbons are not normally toxic, but they are still regarded as a major pollutant because they contribute to the chemical formation of smog. Most HC emissions come from automobiles.

The other principal source of smog is nitrogen oxides (NO_X), which are produced when fuel is burned at very high temperatures, especially when the exhaust gases are cooled too quickly. Automobiles again are among the prime polluters, but electric power plants and industrial boilers account for most NO_X pollution.

The seriousness of a pollution problem is not adequately conveyed by emission measures alone. In particular, one should not use Table 16.1 to compare the significance of various pollutants. Some pollutants (such as CO) are considerably more dangerous than others, pound for pound. Weight measures are simply a convenient and common frame of reference. More important, national emissions data combine the very distinct environments of all cities, states, and regions. Thus the data tell us nothing about how the air around Chi-

TABLE 16.2 THE POLLUTED CITIES

Most large cities suffer from air pollution. Cars are the principal source of most urban air pollution, but industrial plants and utilities also pollute the air.

City	*Number of "unhealthful" days in 1980*[a]	*City*	*Number of "unhealthful" days in 1980*[a]
Los Angeles	**243**	**Salt Lake City**	**81**
New York	**224**	**Birmingham**	**75**
Pittsburgh	**168**	**Portland**	**75**
San Bernardino	**167**	**Houston**	**69**
Cleveland	**145**	**Detroit**	**65**
St. Louis	**136**	**Jersey City**	**65**
Chicago	**124**	**Baltimore**	**60**
Washington, D.C.	**97**	**San Diego**	**50**
Phoenix	**84**	**Cincinnati**	**45**
Philadelphia	**82**	**Dayton**	**45**
Seattle	**82**	**San Francisco**	**30**

Source: Council on Environmental Quality.

[a] Number of days the Pollutant Standards Index (PSI) exceeded 100. The PSI measures exposure to sulfur oxides, particulates, carbon monoxide, photochemical oxidants, and nitrogen dioxide.

cago compares to the air around Fossil, Oregon.[1] Table 16.2 indicates the extent of air pollution in some of our largest cities.

Water pollution

Water pollution is the second major category of pollution. Its effects are apparent in the contamination of drinking water, restrictions on swimming and boating, foul-smelling waterways, and swarms of dead fish and floating debris. Statistics on water pollution, like those on air pollution, are still fragmentary. The Environmental Protection Agency (EPA) estimates, however, that one-third of U.S. water characteristically is polluted, in the sense that it violates federal water-quality standards. Nearly 80 percent of all water basins suffer measurable pollution, though not necessarily enough to make the water unsafe. Table 16.3 provides a rough impression of annual discharges into U.S. waterways.

[1] You've probably never heard of Fossil, Oregon, which is one reason the air is so clean there.

TABLE 16.3 WATER POLLUTANTS

Enormous volumes of material are discharged into U.S. waterways each year. Most discharges come from so-called nonpoint sources—namely, agricultural runoff, urban runoff, and solid-waste-disposal sites. The rest come from point sources, particularly industrial and municipal discharge pipes.

Pollutant	*Annual discharge (millions of pounds)*
Suspended solids	**3,436,596**
Dissolved solids	**1,707,594**
Biochemical oxygen demand	**25,722**
Nitrogen	**13,743**
Phosphorus	**3,181**
Dissolved heavy metals	**98**

Source: Council on Environmental Quality, *Environmental Trends* (Washington, D.C.: Government Printing Office, 1981).

ORGANIC POLLUTION The most common form of water pollution occurs in the disposal of organic wastes. They not only are unsightly and foul-smelling, but also strain the biological capacity of water to sustain life. Organic wastes are decomposed in water by natural processes, but the decomposition process reduces the amount of oxygen available in the water to support aquatic life.[2]

The most familiar sources of organic waste are the bathroom toilet and the kitchen garbage disposal. The wastes that originate there are collected in sewer systems and ultimately discharged into the nearest waterway. The key question is whether the wastes are treated (separated and decomposed) before ultimate discharge. Sophisticated waste-treatment plants can reduce organic pollution by up to 99 percent.[3] Unfortunately, as recently as 1978 only one-half of the U.S. population was served by a system of sewers and adequate (secondary) treatment plants.

In addition to household wastes, our waterways must also contend with industrial wastes. Over half the volume of industrial discharge comes from just a few industries—principally paper, organic chemicals, petroleum, and steel. And within these industries, a relatively small number of very large firms account for most of the discharge. In a study of industrial pollution in the Southeast, the EPA found that only 1 percent of the 1,920 operating plants were responsible for more than 50 percent of the total untreated waste discharged.

Finally, there are all those herds of cattle and other farm animals that are being raised to provide us with food. Naturally, livestock contribute a little organic waste, too. Much of this waste enters waterways directly, particularly after heavy rains. Animal wastes don't cause too great a problem in such places as Boston and New York, but they can work havoc on the water supplies of towns in California, Texas, and Kansas.

THERMAL POLLUTION *Thermal pollution* is an increase in the temperature of waterways brought about by the discharge of steam or heated water. Among other consequences, heat discharges can kill fish, upset marine reproductive cycles, and accelerate biological and chemical processes in water, thereby reducing its ability to retain oxygen.

The sources of thermal pollution are very few and quite specific. In general, the heat discharge is the result of using water to cool an industrial process, just as radiator water is used to cool a car's engine. In the United States, electric power plants account for over 80 percent of all such discharges, with primary metal, chemical, and petroleum-refining plants accounting for nearly all the rest.

[2] The standard measure of such pollution is *biochemical oxygen demand* (BOD), the amount of oxygen used in five days to decompose organic wastes. Waste-treatment plants help reduce BOD by separating out and decomposing some of the waste before it is discharged into the water.

[3] But that doesn't mean that all our pollution problems will be solved. On the contrary, the treatment of sewage creates new disposal problems, as we shall discuss shortly.

EUTROPHICATION Another common form of water pollution results from the discharge of sediments and nutrients into waterways. The sediments tend to make the water shallower while the nutrients increase algae growth. During the process, called "eutrophication," the character of the waterway is altered, with fish populations changing and eventually disappearing. If eutrophication continues long enough, a lake will "die," ultimately turning into marshland and swamp. The Great Lakes, particularly Lake Erie, are typical examples of bodies of water undergoing the eutrophication process.

Although the causes of eutrophication are not completely known, phosphates and nitrogens have been identified as major factors in the process. Phosphates in household detergents, which reach waterways via municipal sewage systems, account for approximately half the phosphate volume. Chemical fertilizers, which are used to increase agricultural output, reach waterways via the runoff from rain and natural drainage and are another major source of eutrophication.

Litter: solid-waste pollution

The third major form of pollution is solid waste. Solid-waste pollution is apparent everywhere, from the garbage can to litter on the streets and beaches, to debris in the water, to open dumps. Although we tend to think of consumption as the end of the line for economic activity, a great deal of solid waste is generated in the process of consumption. Indeed, from a physical point of view, all we do in production and consumption is change the form of the earth's fixed stock of resources. Our world environment contains as many atoms now as it did ten thousand years ago. During those years, however, we (and nature) have continually changed the physical form of our resources. Virgin timber is converted into pulp, the pulp into newsprint, the newsprint into a newspaper; the newspaper is read (thereby "consumed") and discarded; the discarded newspaper ends up at the dump. No material is lost, it just takes on several different forms. This is what environmentalists refer to as the "materials-balance problem." Resources will not disappear once we have used them but must instead be shuffled around into a new use or hidden from view.[4]

Empty cans and bottles, discarded packaging, paper bags, old tires, and steak bones are sufficient reminders of the materials-balance problem. According to EPA estimates, we generate over 5 billion tons of solid waste each year (see Table 16.4). This figure includes more than 30 billion bottles (!), 60 billion cans, 100 million tires, and millions of discarded automobiles and major appliances. Where do you think all this refuse goes?

As Table 16.4 indicates, most solid wastes originate in agriculture (slaughter wastes, orchard prunings, harvest residues) and mining (slag heaps, mill tailings). The much smaller amount of solid waste originating in residential and commercial use is considered

[4] This is true even of wastes that are treated in an attempt to eliminate water pollution. The treated (removed) wastes are referred to as "sludge," which, alas, transforms the water-pollution problem into a waste-disposal problem. If we choose to burn the solid waste, we create an air-pollution problem.

TABLE 16.4 WHAT MAKES SOLID WASTES

Over 5 billion tons of solid waste (paper, glass, scraps, etc.) are generated each year. Where does it all go?

Source	Tonnage (millions)
Municipal trash and garbage	**173**
Sewage sludge	**5**
Industrial wastes	**340**
Mineral wastes	**2,100**
Agricultural wastes	**2,600**
Total	**5,218**

Source: Environmental Protection Agency.

more dangerous, however, simply because it accumulates where people live. Refuse collected in urban areas, for example, increased from 2.75 pounds per person per day in 1920 to nearly 4 pounds in 1980.

THE COST OF POLLUTION

Enough has been said at this point to convey the seriousness of our pollution problems. Pollution of the air, the water, and the landscape is pervasive, originates from a variety of specific sources, and is damaging our social welfare. The EPA estimates that air pollution costs us over $30 billion a year in health, property, and vegetation damage, not to mention aesthetic costs. Total damages inflicted by water pollution, particularly in the form of foreclosed recreational opportunities, may be greater still. As one indication of water-pollution damages, the EPA says 482 million fish were *reported* killed between 1961 and 1976 as a direct result of pollution. These reports account for only a fraction of the total kill. More than one-fifth of the nation's shellfish beds have been closed for the same reason. Although all estimates of pollution damages are necessarily inexact, it is clearly in the public interest to avoid such damages and to improve our enviroment.

Cleanup possibilities

Not only is the reduction of pollution in the public interest, but the means for reducing it are readily at hand. The EPA estimates that 95 percent of current air and water pollution could be eliminated by known and available technology. Nothing very exotic; just simple things like auto-emission controls, smokestack cleaners, improved sewage and waste-treatment facilities, and cooling towers for electric power plants. Even solid-waste pollution could be reduced by comparable proportions if we made the necessary effort. Approximately half of our municipal and commercial wastes represent salvageable materials (paper, glass, metal) that can readily be recycled for further use. Or we could compact and burn the whole mess under controlled conditions, thereby transforming our garbage into a useful (relatively low-polluting) energy source. That would still leave us with some noncombustible residuals and hydrocarbons to con-

New York City Is Looking to Its Garbage As Source of Methane Gas, Steam Power

NEW YORK —This city has decided to prospect for energy in its mountains of garbage. And it hopes to mine a few royalties along the way.

Plans call for tapping the decayed debris in landfills for methane gas, and for burning fresh garbage to make steam. The developers of the projects will pay royalties to the city while helping it reduce its dependence on oil.

UOP Inc., a Des Plaines, Ill., subsidiary of Signal Cos., will build and operate a plant designed to burn 3,000 tons of fresh garbage a day—or about 15% of the 20,000 tons of refuse the city produces daily. The steam generated at the plant, to be built at the Brooklyn Navy Yard and operating in 1986, will be used by Consolidated Edison Co., the city's electricity supplier.

And on the other front, the city has moved to utilize the hidden energy in Fresh Kills, the sprawling, 3,000-acre Staten Island landfill reputed to be the world's largest. In a joint venture, Getty Oil Co. and Brooklyn Union Gas Co. are building a $20 million plant capable of producing four million cubic feet of methane gas a day for 15 years. The city hopes the plant will be producing enough gas this summer to meet the needs of about 10,000 homes in the borough.

—Raymond A. Joseph

tend with, but we would at least be getting some cheap energy in the form of heat. The EPA estimates that if we converted all our solid wastes into energy, we could save over 200 million barrels of oil per year.

During the last decade, public policy has been increasingly forceful in combating pollution. In many cases (as in that of auto emissions), the results have been dramatic. The question remains, however, why we continue to pollute so much. Why do individual consumers and business firms pollute the air, water, and land?

THE ROLE OF MARKET INCENTIVES

Previous chapters have laid great stress on the market forces that influence the economic behavior of individual consumers, firms, and even government agencies. A persistent theme running through those discussions was the role that various kinds of incentives can play in altering behavior. As we have noted, incentives in the form of price reductions can be used to change consumer buying habits. Incentives in the form of high profit margins serve to encourage production of desired consumer goods and services. And market incentives in the form of cost differentials help to allocate resources efficiently. Accordingly, we should not be too surprised to learn that market incentives play a major role in pollution behavior and can be used as a tool of abatement policies.

The production decision

Imagine that you are the majority stockholder and manager of an electric power plant. As we have observed, such plants are responsible for a significant amount of air pollution (especially sulfur dioxide and particulates) and nearly all thermal water pollution. Hence your position immediately puts you on the most-wanted list of pollution offenders. But suppose you bear society no grudges and would truly like to help to eliminate pollution. Let's consider the alternatives.

production decision: The selection of the short-run rate of output (with existing plant and equipment).

As the owner-manager of an electric power plant, you will strive to make a profit-maximizing **production decision.** That is to say, you will seek the rate of output at which marginal revenue equals marginal cost. We shall assume that the electric power industry is regulated by the state power commission so that the price of electricity is fixed, at least in the short run. The effect of this assumption is to render marginal revenue equal to price, thus giving us a horizontal price line, as in Figure 16.1*a*.

Figure 16.1*a* also depicts the marginal and average total costs (*MC* and *ATC*) associated with the production of electricity. By equating marginal cost (*MC*) to price (marginal revenue, *MR*), we observe (point *A*) that profit maximization occurs at an output of 1,000 kilowatt hours per day. Total profits are illustrated by the shaded rectangle between the price line and the average total cost (*ATC*) curve.

The efficiency decision

efficiency decision: The choice of a production process for any given rate of output.

The profits illustrated in Figure 16.1*a* are achieved in part by use of the cheapest available fuel under the boilers (which create the steam that rotates the generators). Recall that the construction of a marginal cost curve presumes some knowledge of alternative production processes. Recall, too, that the **efficiency decision** requires a producer to choose that production process (and its associated cost curve) that minimizes costs for any particular rate of output.

FIGURE 16.1 PROFIT MAXIMIZATION IN ELECTRIC POWER PRODUCTION

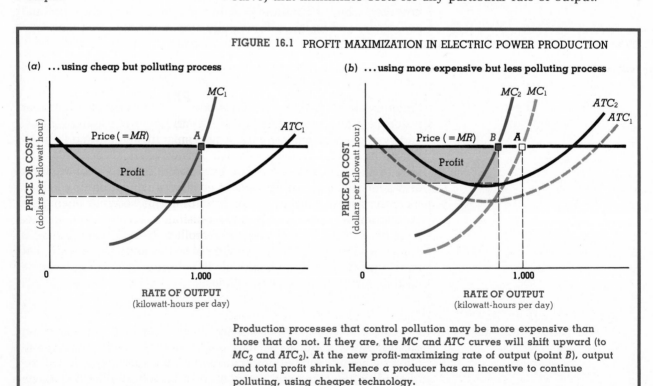

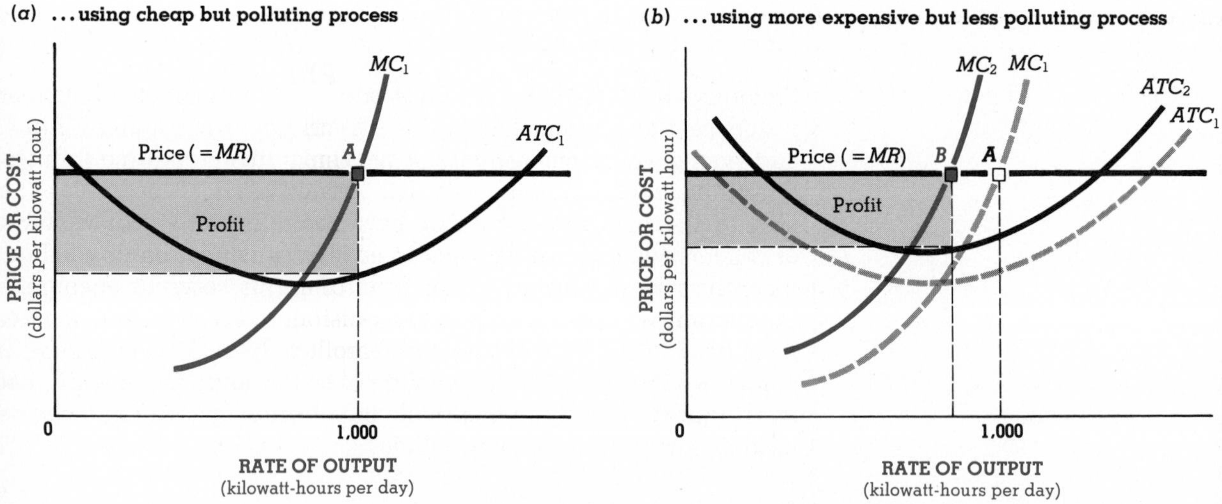

Production processes that control pollution may be more expensive than those that do not. If they are, the *MC* and *ATC* curves will shift upward (to MC_2 and ATC_2). At the new profit-maximizing rate of output (point *B*), output and total profit shrink. Hence a producer has an incentive to continue polluting, using cheaper technology.

Unfortunately, the efficiency decision in this case leads to the use of high-sulfur coal, the prime villain in SO_2 and particulate pollution. Other fuels, such as low-sulfur coal, fuel oil, and nuclear reactors, cost considerably more. Were you to switch to one of them, both the *ATC* and *MC* curves would shift upward, as in Figure 16.1*b*. Under these conditions, the most profitable rate of output would be less than before (point *B*), the total profits would decline (note the smaller profit rectangle in Figure 16.1*b*. Thus pollution abatement can be achieved, but only at significant cost to the plant.

The same kind of cost considerations lead the plant to engage in thermal pollution of adjacent waterways. Cool water must be run through an electric utility plant to keep the turbines from overheating. And once the water runs through the plant, it is too hot to recirculate. Hence it must be either dumped back into the adjacent river or cooled off by being circulated through cooling towers. As you might expect, it is cheaper simply to dump the hot water in the river. The fish don't like it, but they don't have to pay the construction costs associated with cooling towers. Were you to get on the antipollution bandwagon and build those towers, your production costs would rise, just as they did in Figure 16.1*b*. The fish would benefit, but at your expense.

The big question here is whether you and your fellow stockholders would be willing to incur higher costs in order to cut down on pollution. Eliminating either the air pollution or the water pollution emanating from the electric plant will cost a lot of money; eliminating both will cost much more. And to whose benefit? To the people who live downstream and downwind? We don't expect profit-maximizing producers to take such concerns into account. The behavior of profit-maximizers is guided by comparisons of revenues and costs, not by aesthetic concerns or the welfare of fish.

EXTERNALITIES: SOCIAL VS. PRIVATE COSTS

externalities: Costs (or benefits) of a market activity borne by a third party; the difference between the social and private costs (benefits) of a market activity.

The moral of this story—and the critical factor in pollution behavior—is that people tend to maximize their personal welfare, balancing private benefits against private costs. For the electric power plant, this means making production decisions on the basis of revenues received and costs incurred. The fact that the power plant imposes costs on others, in the form of air and water pollution, is irrelevant to its profit-maximizing decision. Those costs are *external* to the firm and do not appear on its profit-and-loss statement. Those **external costs** are no less real, but they are incurred by society at large rather than by the firm itself.

Externalities in production

Whenever external costs exist, a private firm will not allocate its resources and operate its plant in such a way as to maximize social welfare. In effect, society is permitting the power plant the free use of valued resources—clean air and clean water. Thus the power plant has a tremendous incentive to substitute those resources for others (such as high-priced fuel or cooling towers) in the production

"Gentlemen, we have polluted the environment of this community long enough. It's time we moved our plant to a new location."

process. The inefficiency of such an arrangement is obvious when we recall that the function of markets is to allocate scarce resources in accordance with consumers' expressed demands. Yet here we are, proclaiming a high value for clean air and clean water and encouraging the power plant to use up both resources by offering them at zero cost to the firm.

social costs: The full resource costs of an economic activity, including externalities.

private costs: The costs of an economic activity directly borne by the immediate producer or consumer (excluding externalities).

The inefficiency of this market arrangement can be expressed in terms of a distinction between social costs and private costs. **Social costs** are the total costs of all the resources used in a particular production activity. They are to be distinguished from **private costs,** which are the resource costs incurred by the specific producer.

Ideally, a producer's private costs will encompass all the attendant social costs, and his production decisions will be consistent with our social welfare. Unfortunately, this happy identity does not always exist, as our experience with the power plant illustrates. When social costs differ from private costs, external costs exist, and are, in fact, equal to the difference between them.[5] In such cases, the market mechanism will lead us to an undesirable allocation of resources, and thus to less social welfare than might otherwise be obtained.

The distinction between social and private costs is illustrated in Figure 16.2, which again depicts the cost situation confronting the electric power plant. Notice that we use two different marginal cost curves this time. The lower one, the *private MC* curve, reflects the private costs incurred by the power plant when it operates on a profit-maximization basis, using high-sulfur coal and no cooling towers. It is identical to the *MC* curve of Figure 16.1*a*. We now know, however, that such operations impose external costs on others in the

[5] The term "externality" may be used to refer to either external costs or external benefits; here we are dealing only with external costs.

FIGURE 16.2 SOCIAL VS. PRIVATE COSTS

Social costs exceed private costs by the amount of external costs (externalities). Production decisions based on private costs alone will lead to more output (q_p) of a good than is socially desired (q_s).

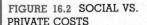

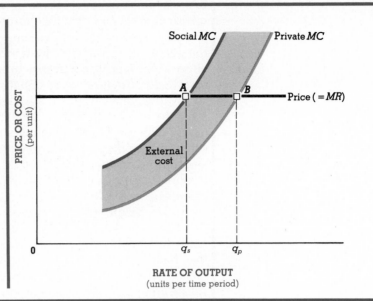

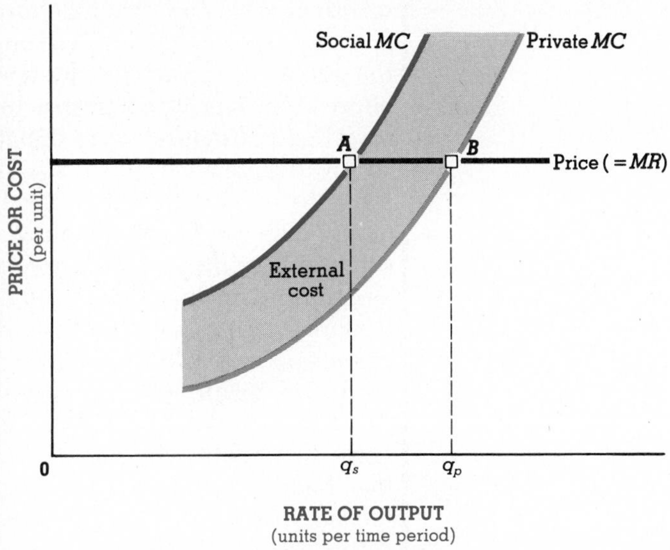

form of air and water pollution. Hence social costs are higher than private costs, as reflected in the *social MC* curve. Were we to maximize social welfare, we would equate social marginal costs with marginal revenue (point *A* in Figure 16.2) and thus produce at the output level q_s. The private profit maximizer, however, equates *private* marginal costs and marginal revenue (point *B*) and thus ends up producing at q_p, making more profit but also causing more pollution. As a general rule, ***if pollution costs are external, firms will produce too much of a polluting good.***

Externalities in consumption

The divergence between private and social costs that is apparent in the case of electric power plants can also be observed in many consumption activities. A consumer, like a producer, tends to maximize personal welfare. Among other things, we buy and use more of those goods and services that yield the highest satisfaction (marginal utility) per dollar expended. By implication (and the law of demand), we tend to use more of a product if we can get it at a discount—that is, pay less than the full price. Unfortunately, the "discount" often takes the form of an external cost imposed on neighbors and friends.

One familiar illustration of such a discount is automobile driving. The amount of driving one does is influenced by the price of a car and the marginal costs of driving it. As was convincingly illustrated during the energy crisis of the 1970s, people buy smaller cars and drive less when the attendant marginal costs (for instance, gasoline prices) increase substantially. But automobile use involves not only *private costs* but *external costs* as well. As observed earlier, auto emissions (carbon monoxide, hydrocarbons, and nitrogen oxides) have long been a principal cause of air pollution. In effect, automobile drivers have been able to use a valued resource, clean air, at no cost to themselves. Naturally, they tended to use more of that resource than they otherwise would, thus lowering their private marginal costs and driving and polluting more. Few motorists saw any personal benefit in installing exhaust-control devices, because the quality of the air they breathed would be little affected by their efforts. Hence private cost structures led to excessive pollution when social cost structures were dictating cleaner air.

A divergence between social and private costs can be observed even in the simplest of consumer activities, such as throwing an empty beer can out the window of your car. To hang onto the beer can and later dispose of it in a trash barrel involves personal effort and thus private marginal costs. To throw it out the window not only is more exciting but effectively transfers the burden of disposal costs to someone else. Thus private costs can be distinguished from social costs. The resulting externality ends up as roadside litter.

The same kind of divergence between private and social costs helps to explain why people abandon old cars in the street rather than haul them to scrapyards. It also explains why people use vacant lots as open dumps. In all of these cases, ***the polluter benefits by substituting external costs for private costs.*** In other words, market incentives encourage pollution.

SOME POLICY OPTIONS

In view of the strong market incentives that encourage pollution, we are lucky that our pollution problems are not worse than they are. Fortunately, only a handful of industries confront significant opportunities to substitute social costs for private costs in the production process, at least with respect to our air and water resources. On the consumer side of the market, such substitution possibilities are more widespread, but are held in check somewhat by social consciousness and frequent legal sanction. Nevertheless, our pollution problems are serious enough to require a public policy response. What can be done?

To begin with, we should realize that people will continue to respond to market incentives whenever they can. This suggests two general approaches for pollution-abatement policy:

- Alter market incentives in such a way that they discourage pollution.
- Bypass market incentives with some form of regulatory intervention.

Altering market incentives

Insofar as market incentives are concerned, the key to pollution abatement is to eliminate the divergence between private costs and social costs. As we have observed, it is the opportunity to shift some costs onto others that lies at the heart of the pollution problem. If we could somehow compel producers to *internalize* all costs—to pay for both private and previously external costs—the divergence would disappear, along with the incentive to pollute. Thus we have to find a way to make polluters pay for their pollution.

emission charge: A fee imposed on polluters, based on the quantity of pollution.

EMISSION CHARGES One possibility is to establish a system of **emission** (or effluent) **charges,** direct costs attached to the act of polluting. Suppose that we let you keep your power plant and permit you to operate it as your profit-maximizing calculations dictate. The only difference is that we no longer agree to supply you with clean air and cool water at zero cost. From now on, we will charge you in accordance with the amount of these scarce resources that you use. We might, say, charge you 2 cents for every gram of noxious emission you discharge into the air. In addition, we might charge you 3 cents for every gallon of water you use, heat, and discharge back into the river.

Confronted with such emission charges, you would surely be motivated to reconsider your efficiency and production decisions. Consider again the choice of fuels. We earlier chose high-sulfur coal, for the very good reason that it was the cheapest available fuel. Now, however, there is an additional cost attached to burning such fuel, in the form of an emission charge on noxious pollutants. This cost may change the efficiency decision in one of two ways. The increased cost of using high-sulfur coal may encourage you to switch to other, cleaner sources of energy. Or it may prove more economical to install "scrubbers" and other smokestack controls that reduce the volume of emissions from the burning of high-sulfur coal. This would entail additional capital outlays for the necessary abatement equipment, but would leave operating margins unchanged. The choice between these two options will depend on the relative costs involved. Of course, if emission charges are too low, neither option may be as profitable as continuing to burn and pollute with high-sulfur coal and simply paying a nominal fee. It is evident, however, that we could impose emission charges high enough to make the less polluting production alternatives appear more profitable.

The same kind of relative cost considerations would apply to the thermal pollution associated with the power plant. The choice heretofore has been between building expensive cooling towers (and not polluting) and not incurring such capital costs (and simply discharging the heated water into the river). The profit-maximizing choice was fairly obvious. Now, however, when the choice is between building cooling towers and paying out a steady flow of emission charges, the profit-maximizing decision is not so evident. The decisive factor will be how high we set the emission charges. If the emission charges are set high enough, the producer will find it unprofitable to pollute.

What works on producers will also sway consumers. Surely you've heard of deposits on returnable bottles. At one time the deposits were imposed by the beverage producer to encourage you to bring the bottle back so it could be used again. But producers discovered that such deposits discouraged sales and yielded very little cost savings. The economics of returnable bottles were further undermined by the advent of metal cans and, later, plastic bottles. Thirty years ago, virtually all soft drinks and most beer came in returnable bottles. Today, returnable bottles are rarely used. One result is the inclusion of over 30 billion bottles and 60 billion cans in our solid-waste-disposal problem.

We could reduce this solid-waste problem by imposing a deposit on all beverage containers. This would internalize pollution costs for the consumer and render the throwing of a beer can out the window equivalent to throwing away money. Some people would still find the thrill worthwhile, but they would be followed around by others who attached more value to money. The state of Oregon imposed a five-cent deposit on beverage containers in 1972 and soon thereafter discovered that beverage-container litter in Oregon declined by 81 percent! Since that time, several states and many communities have also imposed mandatory deposits as a mechanism for eliminating the distinction between social and private costs.

RECYCLING MATERIALS An important bonus that emission charges offer is an increased incentive for the recycling of materials, and thus a reduction in our solid-waste problem. The glass and metal in used bottles and cans can be recycled to produce new bottles and cans. Such recycling not only eliminates a lot of unsightly litter, but also diminishes the need to mine new resources from the earth, a process that often involves its own environmental problems. The critical issue is once again relative costs and market incentives. A container producer has no incentive to use recycled materials unless they offer superior cost efficiency and thus greater profits. The largest component in the costs of recycled materials is usually the associated costs of collection and transportation. In this regard, an emission charge such as the 5-cent container deposit lowers collection costs because it motivates consumers to return all their bottles and cans to a central location.

POLLUTION FINES Not far removed from the concept of emission charges is the use of fines or the imposition of cleanup costs. In some

EPA Ponders Letting Concerns Buy and Sell 'Right' to Pollute Air

Agency Studies Novel Ways to Clean Up Atmosphere But Hold Down the Costs

WASHINGTON—Douglas Costle, administrator of the Environmental Protection Agency, is looking into ways to peddle real filth.

The EPA chief talks about creating auctions and futures markets in which companies would buy and sell the "right" to spew pollutants into the air. His thesis: As long as all the companies in a specified area don't exceed strict emissions limits for that entire area, they could bid against one another to determine how much each could emit individually within the area. Mr. Costle even looks approvingly on the idea of private brokers arranging such deals.

Dirty-air transactions are among several novel, market-style ideas the EPA is seriously considering to help control pollution from industrial plants. Another notion is to allow companies to "bank," for future use, part of pollution savings they can achieve in an area. And the agency plans to test a "bubble concept" that would give manufacturers more leeway in deciding how best to reduce overall emissions from a single plant.

A Chance for Flexibility

The new approaches would be tested as possible alternatives to EPA antipollution regulations that tell companies how they must reduce plant emissions. Such rules frequently are sharply criticized both by industry and by government inflation-fighters as too rigid and too costly. "It may be that if you give (businessmen) some flexibility," Mr. Costle says, "they can find a more efficient way to control pollution than I could by coming in and doing the engineering for them."

—Douglas Martin

situations, such as an oil spill, the pollution is so sudden and concentrated that society has little choice but to clean it up quickly. The costs for such cleanup can be imposed on the polluter, however, through appropriate fines. Such fines would place the cost burden where it belongs. In addition, they would serve as an incentive for greater safety, for such things as double-hulled oil tankers and more efficient safety mechanisms on offshore oil wells. In the absence of pollution penalties, a producer has an incentive to avoid safety costs and take greater risks. The Water Quality Improvement Act of 1970 established financial liability for the cleanup costs involved in oil spills. It also required the producer to notify the government whenever such spills occurred.

The EPA acquired still greater authority to control oil and chemical spills with passage of the Comprehensive Environmental Response, Compensation, and Liability Act of 1980. That act establishes a tax on crude oil and an assortment of chemical products. The resulting revenues have created a "superfund" to be used to monitor and clean up hazardous oil and chemical spills. The act also allows the EPA to recoup *treble* damages from a firm that causes a spill but fails to help clean it up.

Bypassing market incentives

Although the potential benefits to be gained by using market incentives to encourage pollution abatement are substantial, they are not the only or always the best approach to the task. Consider again the case of automobile emissions. Were we to rely on emission charges as a mechanism for abating auto pollution, we might have to measure the amount of pollutants discharged by each vehicle and levy appropriate charges. But such a program would require tremendous effort and cost, because there are over 100 million cars on the road. In this case, the costs of monitoring emissions and levying charges might outweigh the benefits of reduced pollution. Certainly they would at least constitute a strong argument for seeking an alternative control mechanism.

In point of fact, public policy has relied almost exclusively on regulatory prohibitions. The federal government began regulating auto emissions in 1968 and got really serious under the provisions of the Clean Air Act of 1970. The act required auto manufacturers to reduce hydrocarbon, carbon monoxide, and nitrogen oxide emissions by 90 percent within six years of the act's passage. Although the timetable for reducing pollutants was later extended, the act did stimulate auto manufacturers to reduce auto emissions by 67 percent in a period of only five years.

Even stronger direct action against industrial polluters was initiated by the Environmental Protection Agency in 1977. For several years the EPA and the courts have been imposing fines on major polluters. In 1977, however, the EPA took advantage of a provision in the Clean Air Act that allows it to "blacklist" major polluters. A blacklisted firm is barred from doing business with the federal government. The first firm threatened with blacklisting was Kaiser Steel Corporation, which sells 20 percent of its output to the federal government. Once threatened with a loss of so much business, Kaiser stepped up its pollution-abatement efforts.

Public-sector behavior has also been affected by regulation. As we observed earlier (Chapter 3), most public-sector activity involves the production of goods and services with extensive externalities (both external benefits and external costs), and is not dictated by market prices and costs. Accordingly, changing market incentives would do little to reduce the pollution associated with public-sector activity (for example, highway construction). To remedy this situation, the National Environmental Policy Act of 1970 requires public agencies to give explicit consideration to environmental concerns in all major public actions. In particular, public agencies are required to formulate an environmental impact statement that discusses the environmental consequences of any contemplated action. Government agencies must also explore the environmental effects of alternative actions. In this way, the act provides some assurance that environmental considerations will become a routine feature of public-sector decision making.

THE ECONOMIC IMPACT OF POLLUTION CONTROL

If producers and consumers respond fully to altered incentives and regulations, the environment can be cleaned up dramatically. But such an antipollution effort will involve considerable cost. The EPA estimates that we shall have to spend an additional $518 billion in the period 1979–88 to achieve national air and water standards, while significantly reducing other forms of pollution (see Table 16.5). Such a huge outlay of resources will not only clean up the

TABLE 16.5 ESTIMATED MARGINAL POLLUTION-CONTROL EXPENDITURES, 1979–88
(billions of 1979 dollars)

The marginal cost of cleaning up pollution is substantial. This expense must be assessed in terms of its opportunity cost. Is a cleaner environment worth more than the goods and services forgone when resources are used to clean up pollution?

Kinds of pollution	*Costs*	
Air pollution		
Public	**$ 19.5**	
Private	**279.6**	
All air pollution		**$299.1**
Water pollution		
Public	**$ 84.3**	
Private	**85.4**	
All water pollution		**$169.7**
Solid-waste pollution		
Public	**$ 4.6**	
Private	**$ 10.8**	
All solid-waste pollution		**$ 15.4**
Noise pollution		**$ 6.9**
Land reclamation		**$ 15.3**
Toxic substances		**$ 8.2**
Drinking water		**$ 2.7**
Pesticides		**$ 1.2**
All forms of pollution		**$518.5**

Source: Council on Environmental Quality.

REVISING THE CLEAN AIR ACT: STANDARDS VS. CHARGES

The Clean Air Act of 1970 requires the EPA to set uniform standards for several air pollutants. "Primary" standards are intended to protect the public health; "secondary" standards are to protect property and general welfare.

In 1981 the Clean Air Act was scheduled for revision. As in earlier years, most of the debate was over the use of standards or charges as the mechanism for attaining cleaner air. Should the EPA require all producers (and consumers) to attain a uniform standard? Or should the EPA instead impose fines or other incentives to reach the same objective? Finally, should the EPA take greater account of the costs of meeting specific pollution controls and modify their enforcement accordingly?

The Reagan administration urged Congress to abandon the use of uniform national standards. It also urged the EPA to rely more on economic incentives (e.g., emission fees) than on the imposition of specific and uniform pollution-control standards and techniques. In this way, individual firms could operate more efficiently. Specifically, firms that could control their pollution at less cost would do so and avoid paying emission fees. By contrast, firms that faced high pollution-abatement costs would opt for less pollution control and higher fines. In the process, society would achieve the desired level of *average* pollution control at less total cost.

Opponents of the incentive approach offered several arguments. First, there is a strong ideological resistance to providing a "license to pollute." Environmentalists argue that everyone has a social obligation to control pollution. Second, it would be difficult to identify that fee which would exactly induce the desired level of pollution control. Even if it could be found, it would be politically tempting to raise or lower it as election circumstances dictated. Third, the use of pollution fines would necessitate high administrative and enforcement costs.

A survey of congressional, industry, and environmentalist participants in the Clean Air Act debate indicated that their views were worlds apart. Few understood the economic arguments for emission fees rather than uniform standards—and even fewer accepted them.* Ultimately Congress ducked the whole issue by simply extending the act another year (rather than explicitly renewing it).

* See Steven Kelman, "Economists and the Environmental Muddle," *Public Interest*, Summer 1981.

environment, but also affect more familiar economic outcomes. In this section we shall review a few of the anticipated effects.

Opportunity costs

Obviously, $518 billion is a lot of money, and the sum reflects enormous command over our productive resources. Although cleaning up the environment is a universally acknowledged goal, we must remind ourselves that those resources could be used to fulfill other goals as well. The $518 billion would buy a lot of subways and parks, or build decent homes for the poor. If we choose to devote those resources instead to environmental efforts, we shall have to forgo some other goods and services. This is not to say that environmental goals don't deserve that kind of priority, but simply to re-

opportunity cost: The most desired goods or services that are forgone in order to obtain something else.

mind us that any use of our scarce resources involves an **opportunity cost.**

Fortunately, the amount of additional resources required to clean up the environment is relatively modest in comparison to our productive capacity. GNP is expected to total nearly $30 trillion (in 1979 dollars) during the period 1979–88. On this basis, the environmental expenditures contemplated in Table 16.5 represent only 1.7 percent of total output.

The optimal rate of pollution

optimal rate of pollution: The rate of pollution that occurs when the marginal social benefit of pollution control equals its marginal social cost.

Whether 1.7 percent of GNP is too much or too little to spend on pollution control depends on the value we assign to other goods and services and to a cleaner environment. That is to say, the **optimal rate of pollution** occurs at the point at which the opportunity costs of further pollution control equal the benefits of further reductions in pollution. ***To determine the optimal rate of pollution, we need to compare the marginal social benefits of additional pollution control with the marginal social costs of additional pollution-control expenditure.*** If another dollar spent on pollution control yields no more than a dollar of social benefits, then additional pollution-control expenditure is not desirable. In such a situation, the goods and services that would be forsaken for additional pollution control are more valued than the environmental improvements that would result.

Who will pay?

Because clean air, water, and land are not market goods, the calculation of the marginal social benefits of pollution control is a formidable task. It is far easier to determine who will pay for the associated costs. Pollution-abatement efforts will not affect all producers and consumers equally. A relatively small number of economic activities account for the bulk of emissions and effluents. These activities will clearly have to bear a disproportionate share of the cleanup burden.

To ascertain how the burden of environmental protection will be distributed, consider first the electric power plant we discussed earlier. As we observed (Fig. 16.2), the plant's output will be reduced if production decisions are based on social rather than private marginal costs; that is, if environmental consequences are considered. If the plant itself is compelled to pay full social costs, in the form of either compulsory investment or emission charges, its profits will be reduced. Were no other changes to take place, the burden of environmental improvements would be borne primarily by the producer.

Such a scenario is unlikely, however. Rather than absorb all of the costs of pollution controls themselves, producers will seek to pass some of this burden on to their customers in the form of higher prices. Their ability to do so will depend on the extent of competition in their industry, their relative cost position in it, and the price elasticity of consumer demand. In reality, the electric power industry is not very competitive and its prices are subject to government regulation. In addition, consumer demand is relatively price inelastic. Accordingly, the profit-maximizing producer will appeal to the state or local power commission for an increase in electricity prices based on the costs of pollution control. Electric power consumers are likely to end up footing part or all of the environmental bill. This distribution of costs may be regarded as equitable because the increased prices will more fully reflect the social costs associated with electricity use.

In addition to the electric power industry, the automobile, paper, steel, and chemical industries will be adversely affected by pollution controls. In all of these cases, the prices of the related products will increase, in some instances by significant percentages. These price increases will help to reduce pollution in two ways. First, they will help to pay for pollution-control equipment. Second, they will encourage consumers to change their expenditure patterns in the direction of less polluting goods.

The same kinds of arguments apply to public-sector expenditures for pollution control. If a municipality wants to clean up the water, it will have to invest in better sewage and treatment facilities. If it finances these investments out of its existing budget, it will have to cut back on expenditures in other areas—schools, roads, public welfare. If it wants to maintain existing levels of those services, it will have to finance its pollution-control investments out of increased taxes, higher emission charges, or aid from Washington. Higher emission charges are the most efficient and equitable means of finance, especially if the pollution problem is localized and its sources easily monitored. Grants from the federal government are obviously the easiest method of local finance. They represent some equity to the extent that the beneficiaries of pollution control extend across state and local jurisdictions. In recent years, the federal government has assumed a large responsibility for such expenditures. In fiscal 1982, the federal government gave over $3 billion to state and local governments for pollution control.

TRANSITIONAL DISLOCATIONS Even though the resource requirements for environmental protection are relatively modest and the means for allocating them known, we should not conclude that our cleanup efforts will proceed painlessly. As we have already noted, some producers and consumers will end up paying a disproportionate share of the costs. Even though those large shares may be justified on the basis of pollution activity, they will inflict economic losses on specific individuals. Indeed, in some cases, the added costs of environmental protection may be so great as to force a plant to shut down. According to surveys by the EPA and the U.S. Department of Commerce, 107 plants were closed in the period 1971–77 as a result of pollution-control regulations and costs. Over 20,000 workers lost their jobs. Although these plant closings involved a very tiny proportion of the labor force, the affected workers and producers hardly welcomed their role in environmental progress. In general, affected firms and workers seek to postpone or avoid their losses through legal and political action. To reduce political friction and ease the transition to a cleaner environment, public policy has to respond to such microeconomic costs. The response may entail phasing out plants, retraining and relocating workers, or rebuilding a community's economic base.

SUMMARY

- Air, water, and solid-waste pollution impose social and economic costs. The costs of pollution include the direct damages inflicted on our health and resources, the expense of cleaning up, and the general aesthetic deterioration of the environment.
- Pollution is an externality, a cost of a market activity imposed on someone (a third party) other than the immediate producer or consumer.
- Producers and consumers generally operate on the basis of private benefits and costs. Accordingly, a private producer or consumer has an incentive to minimize his own costs by transforming private costs into external costs. One way of making such a substitution is to pollute—to use "free" air and water rather than install pollution-control equipment, or to leave the job of waste disposal to others.
- Social costs are the total amount of resources used in a production or consumption process. When social costs are greater than private costs, there are external costs. In this case, individuals will be motivated to produce and consume more of a product than is socially desirable, because they are not compelled to pay its full (social) cost. This motivation is readily illustrated with marginal cost curves and profit-maximizing production and efficiency decisions.
- One way to correct the market inefficiency created by externalities would be to compel producers and consumers to internalize all (social) costs. This result could be attained by the imposition of emission charges. Such charges would create an incentive to invest in pollution-abatement equipment, recycle reusable materials, or otherwise control pollution.
- An alternative approach to cleaning up the environment is to require specific pollution controls or to prohibit specific kinds of activities. The appropriate choice between the market and regulatory approaches depends on the feasibility and cost of monitoring pollution activity, as well as on ideological and political considerations.
- The opportunity costs of pollution control are the most desired goods and services given up when factors of production are used to control pollution. The optimal rate of pollution is reached when the marginal social benefits of further pollution control equal associated marginal social costs.
- In addition to diverting resources, pollution-control efforts alter relative prices, change the mix of output, and redistribute incomes. These effects are salutary from the perspective of environmental protection but cause losses for particular groups and thus require special economic or political attention.

Terms to remember

Define the following terms:

production decision
efficiency decision
externalities
social costs
private costs
emission charge
opportunity cost
optimal rate of pollution

Questions for discussion

1. Should we try to eliminate *all* pollution? What economic considerations might favor permitting some pollution?

2. Why would auto manufacturers resist exhaust-control devices? How would their costs, sales, and profits be affected?

3. Does anyone have an incentive to maintain auto-exhaust control devices in good working order? How can we ensure that they will be maintained?

4. Suppose we established a $10,000 fine for water pollution. Would some companies still find that polluting was economical? Under what conditions?

Problem

The following cost schedule depicts the private and social costs associated with the production of apacum, a highly toxic fertilizer. The sales price of apacum is $18 per ton.

Output (in tons)	**0**	**1**	**2**	**3**	**4**	**5**	**6**	**7**	**8**
Total private cost	**5**	**7**	**13**	**23**	**37**	**55**	**77**	**103**	**133**
Total social cost	**7**	**13**	**31**	**61**	**103**	**157**	**223**	**301**	**391**

Using the schedule:

(a) Graph the private and social marginal costs associated with apacum production.

(b) Identify the profit-maximizing private and social outputs and associated profits.

(c) On the basis of these curves, identify the pollution fee (fine) we would have to charge per unit in order to persuade the producer to produce the socially optimal rate of output.

CHAPTER 17

WORK AND WELFARE

The war on poverty is not a struggle simply to support people, to make them dependent on the generosity of others. It is a struggle to give people a chance. It is an effort to allow them to develop and use their capacities, as we have been allowed to develop and use ours, so that they can share, as others share, in the promise of this nation.

—LYNDON B. JOHNSON, 1964

[*Welfare is*] *a cancer that is destroying those it should succor and threatening society itself.*

—RONALD REAGAN, 1971

Public policy toward the poor has been plagued by a persistent dilemma. Should we provide poor people with enough income to buy "adequate" nutrition, housing, and clothing? Or should we instead provide them with improved opportunities to earn their own incomes? Quite simply, should we offer welfare or work to low-income families?

It is tempting to respond that *both* welfare and work are needed. In practice, however, the two policy options often conflict. The availability of welfare benefits reduces the need to work. All too often, welfare also lessens the *incentives* to work. On the other hand, not everyone who is poor has the ability or opportunity to earn an adequate income.

The trade-off between work and welfare is examined in this chapter. We start by looking at the scope of poverty in America. The "welfare system" is then described, with an emphasis on its work-inhibiting features. As we shall discover, there is no easy solution to the "welfare mess."

THE EXTENT OF POVERTY

To be counted as poor in America, an individual or family must be unable to provide for the essential needs of food, shelter, and clothing. Naturally, there is not going to be universal agreement about how little is not enough. Much effort has been expended in trying to establish an acceptable standard of poverty. Large families clearly have greater needs than do smaller families and thus could be regarded as poor even if they had slightly more income than a smaller, nonpoor family. A man and wife with six children and an annual income of $7,000 are demonstrably in greater financial straits than a childless couple earning $6,000 a year or a college student earning $5,000. In recognition of these differences in need, ***the official poverty index is based on a comparison of cash income and family size.***

Table 17.1 presents the official poverty standards for 1980. A single person was counted as poor in 1981 if he or she received less than $4,620 in cash income. A family of four, on the other hand, could have received up to $9,287 in 1981 (approximately $10,000 in 1983 dollars) and still been counted among the poor. A family of six with as much as $12,449 was included in the poverty count. Although there is some degree of arbitrariness in these "poverty lines," they are based on the costs of providing a subsistence food budget and other needs. They serve as a convenient yardstick for measuring the dimensions of poverty in the United States.

According to the Census Bureau, approximately 32 million Americans—nearly one in every seven people in the country—had cash incomes in 1981 that were smaller than the minimum standards shown in Table 17.1. Figure 17.1 indicates who all of these poor people were. In terms of sheer numbers, the poverty population is dominated by younger families with children. Indeed, the poverty population includes over 12 million children living either with two parents (6 million) or only their mother (6 million). Nearly one-third of all the poor are black, and a substantial proportion of the poor are over the age of 65. In general, these groups of the poor are located in all areas of the country, although the percentage of poor people in the South and in urban ghettos is slightly higher than elsewhere.

An exaggerated count

These official statistics on the extent of poverty in America paint a grim picture. Not only do they imply that one out of eight Americans is poor, but they also suggest that the number of poor people is growing. The number of people officially counted as poor in 1981 was

TABLE 17.1 FEDERAL POVERTY STANDARDS, BY FAMILY SIZE, 1981

The official definition of poverty relates current income to the "minimal" needs of a family. The poverty standard varies with family size and source of income (farm vs. nonfarm).

Number of family members	*Family income*
1	$ 4,620
2	5,917
3	7,250
4	9,287
5	11,007
6	12,449
7	14,110

Source: U.S. Department of Commerce, Bureau of the Census.

FIGURE 17.1 AGE AND FAMILY STATUS OF THE POOR, 1981

The poverty population is composed of three distinct groups: aged persons, two-parent families, and single-parent families. Almost all of the latter are headed by women.

Source: U.S. Department of Commerce, Bureau of the Census.

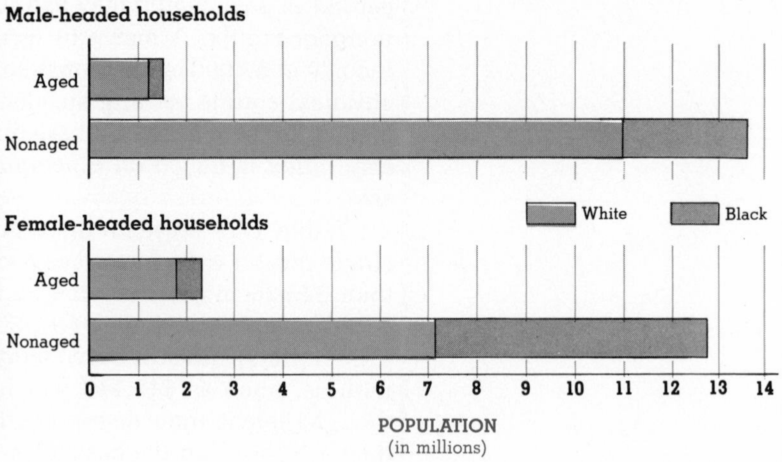

larger than in any year since 1966. Yet in that span of time a massive War on Poverty had been undertaken, and hundreds of billions of dollars had been paid out in income transfers.

One reason the official poverty count remains so high is that it neglects in-kind transfers. As we first noted in Chapter 15, the government not only provides *cash* transfers but **in-kind transfers** as well. These transfers include food stamps, Medicaid, and housing assistance.

in-kind transfers: Direct transfers of goods and services rather than cash; for example, food stamps and Medicaid.

FOOD STAMPS Food stamps are simply coupons ("stamps") that may be used to purchase food. Food stamps are given to poor families, who use them like regular money at the grocery store. The grocer, in turn, cashes the stamps in at a local bank, which redeems them at face value from the government. Thus food stamps increase the *real* income of poor families by increasing the amount of goods and services they can consume at any given level of *cash* income. In 1982 a poor family of four could receive a food-stamp allotment of up to $233 a month ($2,796 a year). The actual value of the stamps a family gets depends on its needs, as measured by family size and cash income.

MEDICAID Even larger than the food-stamp program is Medicaid, a program that provides medical services to the poor. Under Medicaid, an eligible person can use the services of a doctor or hospital just like anyone else. The difference is that the Medicaid patient simply passes the bill on to the government, rather than paying for it himself or submitting it to a private insurance company. Obviously, the amount of benefit a poor family gets from Medicaid depends on the amount of medical treatment it requires. In 1982 nearly all public-welfare recipients made some use of Medicaid, as did many others who had incomes just above the poverty standard. The average value of the services received exceeded $1,000 per family.

HOUSING ASSISTANCE In addition to food and medical services, a poor family can receive housing assistance. For the most part, such assistance is provided in the form of public housing, usually large housing projects owned and operated by the government. In a public housing project, the tenants enjoy cheap (subsidized) rents, although not a great deal more. Nevertheless, the fact that they are paying less than the market value of their apartments means that they are effectively receiving an income transfer. Although fewer than 3 million families receive such transfers every year, the average transfer works out to something like $1,000 a year. In addition to the public housing projects, there are housing assistance programs for low-income people who are renting or even buying their apartments and homes in the private market. In these programs, the rent or mortgage payment is reduced, with the government (the Department of Housing and Urban Development, or HUD) making up the difference.

Table 17.2 provides a summary of these major in-kind transfers. In 1981 alone, nearly $40 billion was spent on such in-kind transfers. None of this income was counted by the Census Bureau in determining who was poor. The Census Bureau counted only *cash* transfers and ignored *in-kind* transfers when computing people's incomes.

One reason the Census Bureau has ignored in-kind benefits is that their value is difficult to compute. Consider Medicaid, for example. The amount of Medicaid a person receives depends on how sick he or she is. If the full value of Medicaid services were counted as income, a serious illness would greatly increase a person's imputed income. By this measure, people would climb out of poverty by becoming ill or disabled!

Although there are difficulties in assessing the market value of in-kind transfers, such transfers clearly increase the real incomes of recipients. As a consequence, ***the official poverty count, based on cash incomes only, exaggerates the extent of poverty.*** The true count of poor people is probably 20 to 40 percent less than official estimates.

TABLE 17.2 IN-KIND TRANSFERS, 1981

The government transfers billions of dollars to the poor in the form of in-kind benefits. None of these benefits are counted, however, in census surveys of the poverty population. Hence the official count of poverty is too high.

Program	*Number of recipients (millions)*	*Average benefit per household (per month)*	*Total annual (billions of dollars)*
Food stamps	**23.0**	**$ 85**	**$11.3**
Medicaid	**22.0**	**100**	**16.8**
Housing assistance	**3.4**	**90**	**6.8**
Nutrition programs (including school lunches)	**25.7**	**20**	**5.0**
Total	**74.1**		**$39.9**

Source: Congressional Budget Office.

POLICY OPTIONS

Even after adjustments for in-kind transfers, there are still lots of poor people in the United States. Moreover, there appears to be a persistent public desire to aid the poor. The question is: What form should that assistance take? Should we encourage poor people to *earn* more income? Or should we simply provide them with income transfers?

More work

Encouraging poor people to work is a generally acceptable policy option. There are limits, however, to the effectiveness of this approach. Many poor people are too old or too sick to participate in the labor market. Others have full-time child-care responsibilities that make it difficult to hold a steady job. As Figure 17.1 indicates, 3.9 million poor people are over age 65 and another 12.8 million live in single-parent households.

We must also be careful to note that labor-force participation itself is no ticket out of poverty. In 1981 approximately 50 percent of the families in poverty participated in the labor force at some point during the year. Among poor families whose head was 25 to 64 years old, over 60 percent participated. Over a million of those families were headed by individuals who held full-time jobs all year long.

labor-force participant: Someone who is either employed for pay or actively seeking paid employment.

human capital: The bundle of skills an individual possesses.

One reason even **labor-force participants** remain poor is that they have inadequate *human capital.* **Human capital** is the bundle of skills and abilities that a person carries into the labor market. Such capital may include specialized vocational skills, a high level of general education, or simply raw talent. The impact of human capital on employment prospects is evident from our earlier discussion (Chapter 12) of marginal productivity. The more human capital an individual has to offer, the greater will be his or her **marginal productivity** in any given production process. By the same token, individuals with little human capital offer less productivity and are more likely to experience low wages and unemployment.

marginal productivity: The change in total output that results from employment of one additional unit of input (e.g., one more worker).

Having the "right" amount of human capital is itself no guarantee of job success, however. Such assets as education merely define the characteristics of the supply of labor. It is equally important to examine the nature of the *demand* for labor. Of particular concern in this regard is **cyclical unemployment.** When the demand for labor is inadequate, there aren't enough jobs to go around. Hence even people with "adequate" human capital discover that their earnings are too low.

cyclical unemployment: Unemployment attributable to a lack of job vacancies; unemployment that results from an inadequate level of aggregate demand.

Discrimination also precludes full use of human capital. Minority groups, women, and the offspring of the poor are generally not given an equal chance to acquire the "right" set of human-capital characteristics. Nor do they have an equal chance to use those characteristics in the labor market.[1] Hence race, sex, and class discrimination have significant impact on both the distribution and the extent of poverty. Even in a relatively prosperous economy, discrimination tends to create artificial barriers between workers and jobs.

[1] The nature and impact of discrimination are discussed in Chapter 18.

An Oversupply of College Graduates Forces Some into Lower-Level Jobs

In 1974, Anne Harbut went to Pennsylvania State University, at the age of 33, to earn a graduate degree because she wanted to run a social-services program. Today she is doing routine office work, and she is bitter.

"Basically, I shuffle a lot of papers across my desk, I fill out forms and interview people for low-level jobs," she complains. Unable to find a suitable post in her profession, she has worked since last summer as a personnel assistant at Philadelphia's Metropolitan Hospital.

"It's boring and at times it seems pointless," she says. "Once I had a job working on a construction gang in the Swiss Alps. It was more satisfying than this. At least we were accomplishing something. At the end of the day, we could see the road getting built."

Like Mrs. Harbut, large numbers of Americans are working at jobs for which their training has made them overqualified. They are the products of the nation's education binge over the last two decades, when colleges were churning out graduates at a far faster rate than the economy required. Government statistics show that while the proportion of college-educated members of the work force nearly doubled over that period, to 17.6% in 1979, there was more demand for service jobs than for general white-collar skills. This mismatch is exacerbated by the current recession.

Higher Education Oversold

As a result, the Labor Department predicts that during this decade one in four college graduates will take jobs in occupations that don't require a four-year college education. This is in sharp contrast to the booming 1960s, when "persons with college degrees could generally find the kind of professional, technical or managerial jobs they wanted," says Michael Pilot, who heads the department's occupation outlook program.

"In short, we've oversold the value of higher education," concludes Sar Levitan, an economist who specializes in employment problems. "It's a further tattering of the American dream."

—Robert S. Greenberger

The objective of "more work," then, entails several distinct policy approaches. First and foremost, it requires the attainment of full employment. Professor Harry Johnson summarized the point well: "In the absence of a policy of raising the demand for labor . . . , ad hoc policies for remedying poverty by piecemeal assaults on particular poverty-associated characteristics are likely to prove both ineffective and expensive. The most effective way to attack poverty is to attack unemployment, not the symptoms of it."[2]

If people are to work themselves out of poverty, they also need to acquire more human capital. The government, then, can further reduce poverty by providing increased education and training opportunities, particularly for low-income families.

More welfare

Although the work options for reducing poverty are straightforward, their success is not assured. Moreover, the work approach strikes many observers as unnecessarily roundabout and uncertain. If we really want to eliminate poverty, why not simply give people more money? Among others, economist Milton Friedman and urbanologist Irving Kristol have wondered aloud whether our public commitment to end poverty is sincere in the light of our failure to provide this obvious remedy.

income transfers: Payments to individuals for which no current goods or services are exchanged; e.g., social security, welfare, and unemployment benefits.

But the apparent simplicity of **income-transfer** solutions to poverty is deceptive. We could, of course, provide enough income transfers to close the poverty gap—the difference between what the poor now have and what they need to maintain minimum living standards. In 1981 that gap was only $37 billion, or just over 1 percent of

[2] Harry G. Johnson, "Poverty and Unemployment," in *The Economics of Poverty*, ed. Burton Weisbrod (Englewood Cliffs, N.J.: Prentice-Hall, 1965), p. 170.

total GNP. An expansion of income transfers to fill this gap, however, might create significant problems.

First of all, exclusive reliance on income transfers as a "solution" to poverty serves to perpetuate the poverty problem. Simply transferring income to the needy does little to improve their opportunities for employment and upward mobility. The added income makes life easier for the poor, of course, but otherwise leaves their circumstances unchanged. Thus income transfers are best viewed as an interim form of support, especially for those who are in a position to benefit from increased education or employment opportunities.[3]

Even on an interim basis, however, income transfers give rise to problems. Suppose we guaranteed everyone an income equal to the 1983 poverty standard of $10,000 for a nonfarm family of four. Any family earning less than this amount would receive an income-transfer payment to make up the difference, thus eliminating all existing poverty.

Unfortunately, this kind of program creates a strong incentive for persons just above the poverty line to leave the labor market. If offered an income transfer, people working at dead-end, low-paying jobs may abandon employment and join the ranks of the nonworking poor. Recall (from Chapter 11) that the decision to work is largely a response to the financial and psychological rewards associated with employment. People in dull, dirty, low-paying jobs get little of either. Hence by quitting their jobs, declaring themselves poor, and accepting a guaranteed income transfer, they would gain much more leisure at little financial or psychological cost.

People already counted as poor would have a similar incentive. By substituting public transfers for the meager employment income they already possessed, they would work less while still maintaining their incomes. Accordingly, ***the provision of income transfers may conflict with established work incentives.*** Hence both the size of the poverty population and the "need" for income transfers may be sensitive to the particular form our income-transfer policies take. The following section highlights this work–welfare dilemma.

THE WORK–WELFARE DILEMMA

The welfare system

Although many people tend to think of welfare as one big, centrally administered program, the realities of welfare are quite otherwise. As we noted earlier, the welfare system is composed of two distinct kinds of assistance. Some programs provide cash assistance to the poor. Other programs provide in-kind assistance—such things as housing, food, and medical services. Within each classification, there are a variety of programs, each with its own characteristics, regulations, and objectives. The programs are designed and administered by a changing mix of state, local, and federal governments.

Table 11.3 provides a summary of the major programs that pro-

[3] If the education and employment opportunities are slow in coming, however, the "interim" support may have to continue for a long time. In the interim, the children of the poor will at least benefit from improved nutrition and shelter.

TABLE 17.3 CASH-ASSISTANCE PROGRAMS, 1981

AFDC, the largest welfare program, provides cash assistance to families with children. SSI helps the aged and disabled. GA assists those poor people who aren't eligible for other cash-assistance programs.

Program	*Number of recipients*	*Average benefit per household (per month)*	*Total annual payments (billions of dollars)*
Supplemental security income (SSI)	**4 million**	**$185**	**$ 7.2**
Aid to families with dependent children (AFDC)	**11 million**	**300**	**13.2**
General assistance (GA)	**1 million**	**165**	**1.6**
Total	**16 million**		**$22.0**

Source: U.S. Department of Health and Human Services.

vide cash assistance to the poor. Each of the three programs listed in the table is directed toward a distinct population group. The federal supplemental security income (SSI) program aids the aged, the blind, and the permanently disabled. In 1981 it provided cash assistance to 4 million people at an estimated annual cost of approximately $7 billion. By contrast, the federal-state aid to families with dependent children (AFDC) program served 11 million people at an annual cost of roughly $13 billion. The third program, general assistance (GA), is operated solely under state and local auspices to provide help to those who are poor but do not fit one of the other two categories.

Who gets welfare

Although the cash assistance programs clearly help many people and cost a lot of money, they do not fully meet the needs of the poor. First, not all of the poor are helped. Of the 32 million people counted as poor in 1981, only 16 million received cash assistance. Second, even those who were helped did not receive enough income to stave off poverty. The typical AFDC family (mother and two or three children), for example, received less than half the cash income the government estimated it needed. Moreover, the amount of cash assistance provided varies tremendously from state to state. In 1981, average AFDC payments for a welfare family ranged from $1,000 a year in Mississippi to over $5,000 in California.

Conspicuously missing from the welfare rolls in nearly every state, regardless of the amount of cash assistance provided, are male-headed poor families. Being poor and in a family with children is not sufficient qualification for AFDC support. The presence of an able-bodied male adult in the home is taken as prima facie evidence that the family is capable of its own support. AFDC payments are largely reserved for fatherless homes. Male-headed poor families rarely receive welfare benefits, regardless of the needs such families may have.[4]

[4] An exception to this rule is the AFDC-UF program, which provides benefits to poor families with unemployed fathers. But the program is too small and restrictive to merit attention here. In early 1981 only 920,000 persons were receiving AFDC-UF benefits in 27 states.

Breaking Through the Welfare Myths

From remarks by Secretary of Health, Education and Welfare Joseph A. Califano Jr. before the Washington Press Club April 27:

Past debates about welfare have too often focused on pernicious myths about the poor in America. These myths have been perpetrated and perpetuated by ignorance, by incoherent and demagogic discussion by public officials, and inadequate reporting by the media. It is imperative that the forthcoming national debate on welfare not focus on phony issues, false choices or unrealistic expectations that have so clouded past discussions. . . .

Five myths have come to distort public understanding of the poor and welfare.

Myth No. 1—the most pernicious and most widespread—is that people are poor because they don't work and don't want to work, that the welfare rolls are replete with lazy loafers.

The facts are quite different.

Nearly 71 per cent of the 26 million poor Americans are people that we do not normally ask to work: children and young people under 16, the aged, the severely disabled, students or mothers with children under six. Another 19 per cent of the poor population works either full-time or part-time. Thus, 90 per cent of poor Americans either work full-or-part-time or are people no civilized society would force to work. . . .

Only 2 per cent of the 26 million poor people even resemble the mythical welfare stereotype—non-aged, non-disabled males who do not work. But census figures indicate that most of this group is between 62 and 64, ill, or looking for work. . . .

Myth No. 2 is that most of the poor are poor for life—that they represent a permanent stagnant group.

The fact is that the poverty population is extremely fluid—with sizable numbers of people moving in and out of poverty with remarkable frequency. Each year about 7.5 to 10 million people move above the poverty line, and a like number become poor.

Over the period 1967 through 1972, only 3 per cent of the American population was poor in every one of those 6 years. More than one-fifth—21 per cent—of the American population was poor in at least one of those 6 years. . . .

Most of the poor are poor, not because of some inherent character flaw or personal failing, but because of events they cannot control. And many of them do, in fact, regain higher incomes and climb back out of poverty.

Myth No. 3 is that the poor are mostly black and non-white. The fact is that 69 per cent of the American poor are white.

Myth No. 4 is that the poor don't know how to spend their money. The evidence we have shows that low-income people spend a somewhat greater proportion—about 88 per cent—of their income on food, clothing, housing, medical care and transportation than do people with higher incomes.

Myth No. 5 is that many welfare families receive payments that are far too high. The fact is that in 24 states, the combined benefits of Aid for Families with Dependent Children and food stamps total less than three-fourths of the official poverty-income level. And that poverty level was only $5,500 for a family of four in 1975. . . .

The Washington Post, Washington, D.C., May 1, 1977.

Our failure to provide welfare payments to male-headed families and our provision of very low benefits to eligible families is due in part to the fear that poor people wouldn't work if welfare benefits were higher. This is the work-incentive problem we noted earlier. We can see the problem in more detail by examining the way AFDC benefits are calculated.

The work-incentive problem

Until 1967, a family receiving AFDC payments had very little financial incentive to seek employment. This was not because welfare represented the "good life," however. Welfare benefits have always been below poverty standards. Rather, welfare regulations prohibited a family from improving its standard of living by working. Such a regulation might appear absurd, but it was simply the consequence of the way in which the amount of a family's benefits was calculated.

When a family applies for welfare, it is obliged to report any income at its disposal. A woman with small children, for example, might earn $50 a month by baby sitting and ironing for neighbors. Until 1967, the welfare authorities subtracted any such income from the family's needs (as determined by the local welfare department) and provided the difference. Suppose the welfare authorities concluded that Mrs. Jones and her three children needed $300 a month. They paid her only $250, knowing that Mrs. Jones herself could provide the rest. This procedure may have distributed welfare funds equitably among needy recipients, but it destroyed all motivation for self-improvement.

Imagine that Mrs. Jones was offered regular part-time employment as a nurse's aide at $4 an hour for ten hours per week. Now, Mrs. Jones may have been reluctant to leave her small children in the care of others, but she could certainly use the money. So she would have been inclined to accept the job, especially if transportation problems (she had no car) and child-care arrangements could be worked out. But what would have happened to her actual income if she had taken this step toward self-improvement? Absolutely nothing. The welfare authorities would simply have noted that she was now earning $160 a month and would have reduced her welfare payment to $140. Her family's income would have remained at $300 whether or not Mrs. Jones found employment and no matter how hard she strove for self-improvement.

The pre-1967 method of calculating benefits is illustrated in Figure 17.2. If she doesn't work at all, Mrs. Jones remains at point *A*, with $3,600 per year in welfare benefits and no wages. Now watch what happens when she takes a part-time job. If she works 500 hours a year (10 hours a week) she moves to point *W* on the wage line, with $2,000 of wages. But her gross income doesn't change. The welfare department cuts her benefits to $1,600 (point *X*) when she earns $2,000 on her own. Hence her gross income moves from point *A* to

FIGURE 17.2 WORK AND WELFARE: PRE-1967 OPTIONS

Before 1967, a welfare family's cash benefit was equal to the difference between state-determined needs and other income. As a result, benefits fell when other income increased. Gross income was thus unchanged. In this case, $2,000 of wages (point *W*) reduced welfare benefits to $1,600 (point *X*), leaving the family with its initial income of $3,600 (point *B*). A family stayed on welfare until its other income exceeded $3,600.

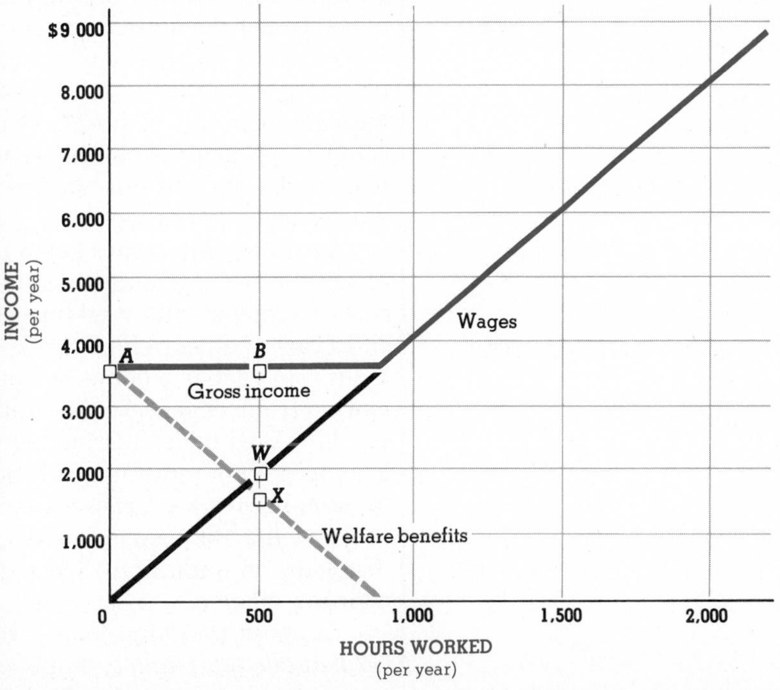

point *B*. She has no more money to spend after working 500 hours per year than she had when she stayed at home.

The "old" AFDC system clearly provided very little financial incentive to go out and find a job. In effect, any income earned was simply turned over to the welfare department through the mechanism of reduced cash assistance. The method of calculating welfare benefits on a residual basis—on the basis of the difference between needs and income—imposed a 100 percent tax on any wages a welfare recipient might earn.

marginal tax rate: The tax rate imposed on the last (marginal) dollar of income.

marginal utility of labor: The change in total utility derived from another hour's work; includes the utility associated with the extra goods and services that can be purchased with another hour's wages, as well as any intrinsic satisfaction derived from additional labor.

Clearly, not many people would be eager to work if they confronted a **marginal tax rate** of 100 percent. As we saw in Chapter 11, the decision to work is based on a comparison of the marginal utility of labor with the marginal utility of leisure. The **marginal utility of labor** consists of the satisfaction obtainable from the goods and services that can be purchased with one's wages plus any enjoyment derived from the job itself. In this case, labor provides no net increase in income. Thus a person would have no incentive to work unless leisure were actually burdensome (yielded *negative* marginal utility) or the job provided a lot of personal satisfaction.

IMPROVED INCENTIVES This glaring failure of the AFDC program to reinforce work incentives prompted some improvements in the welfare system. In 1967 Congress adopted a new procedure for calculating benefits.

Take again the case of Mrs. Jones. In the absence of any work effort, Mrs. Jones again starts out with $3,600 in welfare benefits. This is illustrated by point *A* in Figure 17.3. Now suppose she decides to accept the job as a nurse's aide, working 500 hours a year (10 hours per week). Under the old AFDC system, she would move from point *A* to point *B*, working more but with no change in total income. Under the revised system, however, she moves to point *C* and increases her income by working. Point *C* is obviously a more desirable place to be than point *B*, because it represents more income for the same amount of effort. Hence, whatever Mrs. Jones' feelings about work, she is more likely to take a job under the new system than under the old one. In this sense, the new system provides a greater incentive to work.

How does Mrs. Jones get to point *C* under the new system? First of all, the welfare authorities now recognize that there are certain costs associated with working—transportation expenses, additional child care, clothes, added meal costs, and so on. To ensure that Mrs. Jones' spendable income is not reduced by the amount of these work-related expenses, the welfare department "disregards" that much income in calculating her welfare benefits. Hence her welfare benefits are not reduced until she is earning at least enough income to cover her work expenses. To give Mrs. Jones still greater incentive to work, the 1967 amendments also required welfare authorities to disregard an *additional* $30 per month, *plus* one-third of any remaining income.

Suppose that Mrs. Jones' work expenses total $170 per month ($2,040 per year). She can now earn this much income without los-

FIGURE 17.3 WORK AND WELFARE: 1967–81 CASH OPTIONS

To encourage more work effort, welfare authorities have disregarded some income in computing a family's benefits. Until 1981 a welfare mother could earn $30 per month plus enough income to cover work expenses before her benefits were reduced. In this case, wages of $2,000 (point *W*) do not reduce welfare benefits at all, so gross income rises to $5,600 (point *C*). The family stays on welfare until its income exceeds $7,800.

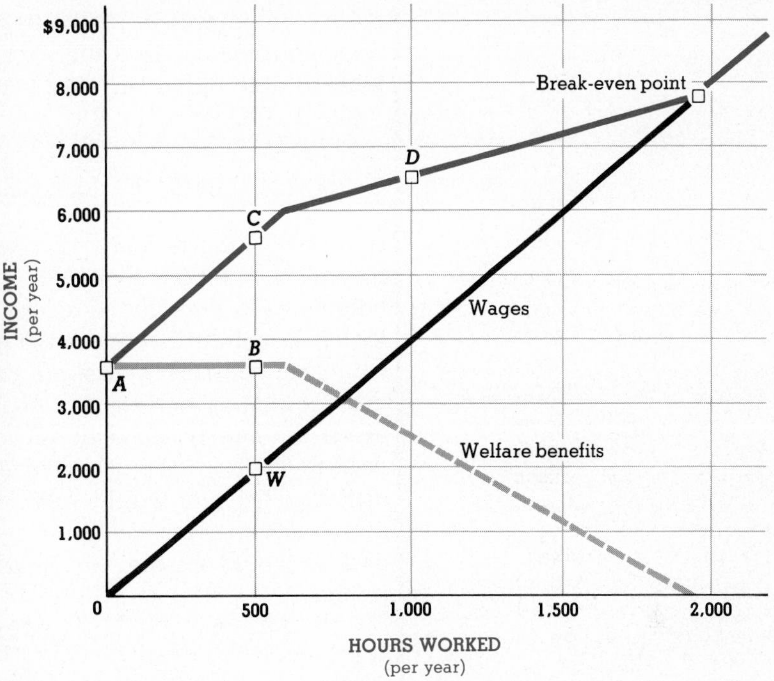

ing any welfare benefits. She can also earn an additional $360 per year without losing any welfare benefits, thanks to the $30-per-month "disregard." Hence Mrs. Jones can now earn as much as $2,400 per year without losing any welfare benefits. In other words, the marginal tax rate on her first $2,400 of earnings is zero. By working 500 hours per year, Mrs. Jones now moves from point *A* to point *C*, keeping $3,600 in welfare benefits *and* $2,000 in wages. This contrasts sharply with the pre-1967 system, which left Mrs. Jones at point *B*, with only $1,600 in welfare benefits and $2,000 in wages.

The welfare department begins to "tax" Mrs. Jones' earnings (reduce her welfare benefits) only after her wages exceed the "disregard" of $360 per year plus work expenses. Even at that point, however, the marginal tax rate is "only" 67 percent, rather than 100 percent. Hence Mrs. Jones has an economic incentive to work more than 500 hours per year. She will get to keep 33 cents out of every additional dollar she earns. The incentive is still modest, to be sure, but nevertheless greater than the one (nothing) that existed earlier.

Suppose now that Mrs. Jones wants to increase her work effort to 20 hours per week. If she worked 1,000 hours per year she could earn $4,000. What would happen to her welfare benefits? The formula for calculating her benefit is:

Welfare benefits
= \$3,600 − ⅔ (wages in excess of work expenses and disregard)
= \$3,600 − ⅔ [\$4,000 − (\$2,040 + \$360)]
= \$3,600 − \$1,067
= \$2,533

Hence by doubling her work effort, Mrs. Jones would move from point *C* to point *D* in Figure 31.3. At point *D* she receives $4,000 in wages plus $2,533 in welfare benefits. By her own efforts, then, Mrs. Jones is able to increase her family's income.

CONFLICTING WELFARE GOALS

It is comforting to know that Mrs. Jones can increase her family's income from $3,600 to $6,533 a year by working as a nurse's aid 20 hours a week. It might be nicer still if the welfare department would let her keep a little more of the money she earns from making beds, emptying bedpans, and sterilizing bandages. After all, the life of a nurse's aide is not exactly glamorous, and Mrs. Jones obviously needs the money. So why not lower the marginal tax rate from 67 percent to, say, 25 percent, or even zero? Such a reduction in the marginal tax rate would solve two problems. First, it would give Mrs. Jones an even greater incentive to work (see Figure 17.4). Second, it would enable Mrs. Jones to achieve a higher standard of living.

Incentives vs. costs

Unfortunately, a reduction in the marginal tax rate would also increase welfare costs. Suppose that we actually eliminated the marginal tax rate on Mrs. Jones' earnings, thus allowing her to keep everything she earned. Her total income would then rise to $7,600 ($3,600 in benefits plus $4,000 in wages). Terrific. But should we

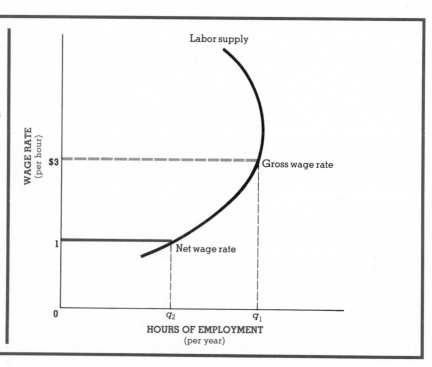

FIGURE 17.4 THE EFFECT OF WELFARE BENEFITS ON LABOR SUPPLY

The reduction in welfare benefits that accompanies an increase in earnings effectively reduces net wage rates. As a consequence, we expect the quantity of labor supplied to diminish when high marginal tax rates are imposed. A marginal tax rate of 67 percent implies that a worker gets to keep only $1 (net wage) out of every $3 earned (the gross wage). At the lower net wage, fewer hours of labor (q_2 vs. q_1) are supplied.

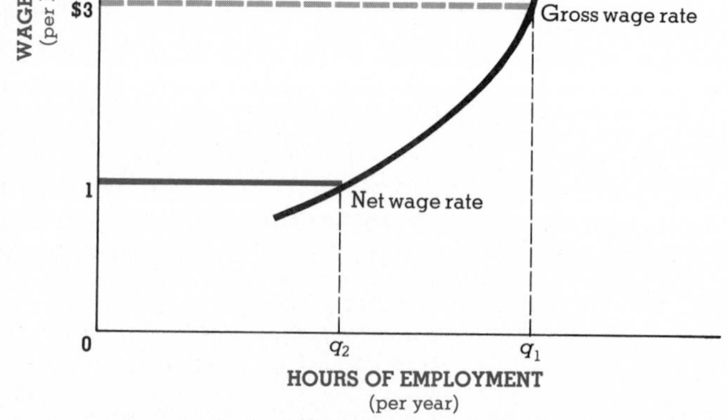

still be providing $3,600 in welfare payments to someone who earns $4,000 on her own? How about someone earning $8,000? $10,000? To make a long story short, where should we draw the line? Clearly, ***if we don't impose a marginal tax rate at some point, everyone will be eligible for full welfare benefits.***

While the thought of giving everyone a welfare check might sound like a great idea, it would turn out to be incredibly expensive. In the end, we would have to take those checks back in the form of increased taxes in order to pay for the vastly expanded program. We must recognize, then, a basic dilemma:

- Low marginal tax rates encourage more work effort but make more people eligible for welfare.
- High marginal tax rates discourage work effort but make fewer people eligible for welfare.

The conflict between work incentives and the desire to limit welfare costs and eligibility can be summarized in a neat little equation:

$$\text{Break-even level of income} = \frac{\text{basic benefits}}{\text{marginal tax rate}} + \text{earnings disregards}$$

The break-even level of income is the amount of income a person can earn before losing all welfare benefits. In Mrs. Jones' case, the annual income disregard was $2,400 ($2,040 for work expenses plus $30 per month) and the basic welfare benefit was $3,600 per year. Hence she could earn as much as $7,800 per year before losing all her welfare benefits. In other words, she could virtually hold a full-time job and still collect some welfare benefits. In this case, we encouraged work but made it difficult for Mrs. Jones to work her way off of welfare.

If the marginal tax rate were 100 percent, as under the pre-1967 system, the break-even point would be $3,600 ($3,600 ÷ 1.00). In that case, people who earned $3,600 on their own would get no assistance from welfare. Fewer people would be eligible for welfare, but those who drew benefits would have no incentive to work. Under our aborted proposal to lower marginal tax rates to zero, the break-even point would rise to infinity ($3,600 ÷ 0), and we would all be on welfare.

As this arithmetic makes apparent, ***we can achieve a lower break-even level of income only by sacrificing a high income floor, earnings disregards, or low marginal tax rates.*** Hence welfare costs can be minimized only if we sacrifice income provision or work incentives.

In-kind benefits

The conflict between work incentives and welfare costs was further intensified by the provision of in-kind benefits. People on welfare are also eligible for food stamps, Medicaid, housing assistance, and other direct benefits. Moreover, cash benefits are not reduced by the value of in-kind benefits. Hence *real* incomes of welfare recipients are typically higher than their cash incomes imply.

DO WORK INCENTIVES MATTER?

The potential disincentives associated with cash and in-kind welfare benefits are substantial. Debate continues, however, on just how large an impact these disincentives actually have on the labor supply of poor people. Do welfare recipients work less as a result of high marginal tax rates and income guarantees? If so, by how much?

To answer these questions, the U.S. Department of Health and Human Services funded several income-maintenance experiments. In these experiments, one group of poor people was provided with income guarantees and high marginal tax rates, while another group received nothing. The behavior of both groups was then observed for several years to determine whether the "welfare" group worked less than the "nonwelfare" group.

Income-maintenance experiments were conducted in New Jersey, North Carolina, Gary, Indiana, Denver, and Seattle. In general, the results indicate that high marginal tax rates *do* reduce the quantity of labor supplied, just as our theory predicts. In one experiment (Denver and Seattle) the labor supply of husbands declined by 5 percent as a result of income transfers. The labor supply of wives fell by 22 percent.

The implications of in-kind benefits for the work–welfare dilemma are illustrated in Figure 17.5. AFDC cash benefits still start out at $3,600 (point *A*). But now Mrs. Jones gets $1,000 in food stamps, $1,000 in housing assistance, and $1,000 worth of Medicaid services. Her *real* income jumps to $6,600 (point *A**), even if she doesn't work at all.

Once Mrs. Jones starts working, she will begin to lose some food stamps, since their value is based on family income. But she will keep her full Medicaid benefits so long as she is on welfare, and probably her housing assistance as well. Hence a *real* break-even level of income will be $2,000 higher than it was before. As Figure 17.5 reveals, Mrs. Jones can now enjoy a real income of $9,799.99 and still be on welfare! This level of income not only exceeds her family's poverty standard, but also surpasses the income of many working families not on welfare. Hence Mrs. Jones is not likely to leave the welfare rolls.

Figure 17.5 highlights another barrier to Mrs. Jones' exodus from welfare. Notice the drop in real income that occurs at the break-even point. If Mrs. Jones earned $7,800 or more in wages, she would lose all cash welfare benefits. At the same time, she might lose her Medicaid eligibility. Hence the last dollar earned at the break-even level results in a $1,000 loss of real income. Clearly there is a tremendous incentive *not* to earn that last dollar.

THE REAGAN REFORMS

President Reagan, among others, felt that the welfare system depicted in Figure 17.5 was far too generous. The combination of high disregards and "low" tax rates permitted too many people to receive

FIGURE 17.5 WORK AND WELFARE: 1967–81 REAL OPTIONS

The provision of in-kind benefits to welfare families increases their *real* incomes above their cash incomes. With food stamps, Medicaid, and housing assistance, plus AFDC benefits, Mrs. Jones would have $6,600 of real income (point *A**) without working. By working 500 hours per year, she would increase her income to $8,000 (point *C**). In this case, a welfare family could command a real income of nearly $9,800 before losing welfare eligibility. There would be a strong disincentive to earn that last dollar, however, since the family might then lose Medicaid benefits.

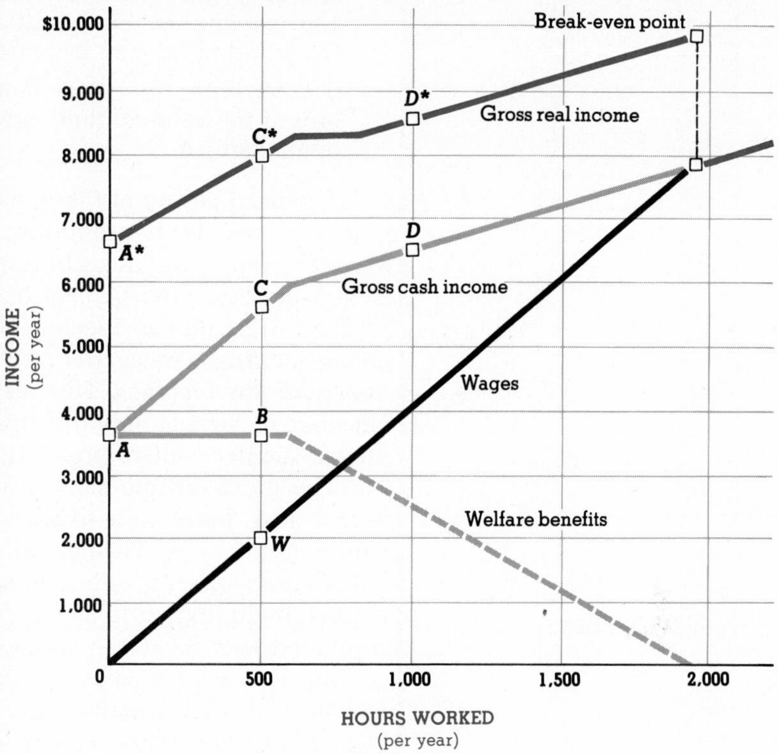

welfare. Moreover, once on welfare, a family was likely to stay on for years, because the break-even level was too high. Also, the discretionary nature of "work expenses" invited fraud and abuse. In the example we have studied, the real break-even level of income was $9,800. If Mrs. Jones had claimed more work expenses, her break-even level of income would have been still higher.

President Reagan felt that these income limits were far too high. A person on welfare could easily end up with more income than a person who was working. Moreover, the welfare recipient could enjoy an income in excess of the poverty standard. Reagan argued that this was inequitable and wasteful. He proposed to focus the welfare system more narrowly on the "truly needy." He also sought to encourage people to move off of welfare and into jobs.

In 1981 the Reagan administration succeeded in changing the rules for welfare eligibility and benefits. The major changes were:

- *Limit on gross income.* A family can receive welfare benefits only if its total income is less than 150 percent of the state's standard of need (itself usually less than the federal poverty standard). This rule sets an upper limit on the break-even level of income.
- *Limit on work expenses.* Recipients can no longer itemize work-related expenses. Uniform deductions of $75 per month for work expenses and $160 for child care are now to be used.
- *Time limit on work incentives.* The "30 and a third" rule for computing welfare benefits applies only to the first four months

of welfare receipt. After four months, the recipient confronts a 100 percent tax rate on all earnings in excess of standardized work and child-care expenses.

□ *Asset limitation.* Poor families are eligible for AFDC benefits only if the value of their assets is less than $1,000, exclusive of home and car.

The most severe of these changes is the income ceiling. In the case we have been examining, the state standard of need was $3,600.[5] Hence the Reagan-imposed ceiling on cash income is $5,400 per year (150 percent of $3,600). The cash ceiling also implies a ceiling on *real* income. Hence ***the immediate impact of the income ceiling is to restrict welfare eligibility more tightly to families with low incomes.*** This restriction is consistent with Reagan's objective of serving only the "truly needy." The restriction also implies a smaller welfare population and therefore lower costs.

The gross-income ceiling also lessens work incentives, however. If Mrs. Jones were to work 500 hours per year, as before, she would earn $2,000. Theoretically, this amount of wages would not reduce her welfare benefits, since it does not cover all her work expenses (including child care). However, the $2,000 in wages, when combined with $3,600 in welfare benefits, exceeds the new income ceiling. Hence Mrs. Jones cannot keep both $2,000 in wages and $3,600 in welfare benefits. Any wages in excess of $1,800 will be "taxed" at 100 percent. This means that Mrs. Jones will not enjoy a higher cash income until she is able to work at least 1,351 hours a year. By working that much, she would earn $5,404 in wages (at $4 per hour), just above the welfare ceiling. Hence Mrs. Jones has no incentive to take a job that pays between $1,800 and $5,400 in wages. Indeed, were she to earn $5,400 or more and move off of welfare, she might lose Medicaid and thus suffer a real income loss.

The net effect of the Reagan reforms is to discourage welfare recipients from taking part-time jobs, or even full-time jobs. In this sense, the reforms again reflect the basic conflict between holding down welfare costs and providing work incentives. The 1981 rule changes reduced the size of the potential welfare population but discouraged recipients from seeking employment.

Workfare

To overcome the disincentive features of the new welfare rules, President Reagan proposed that the "carrot" of low marginal tax rates be replaced by the "stick" of compulsory employment. The administration proposed that welfare recipients be required to "work off" their benefits by doing community-service work. With such compulsory "workfare," a welfare recipient could not choose between some work and no work. Rather, the choice would be between a public "work-experience" job (at the minimum wage) and any private-sector job that was available. In this case, the issue of work incentives, as measured by marginal tax rates, would be secondary.

[5] In many states the maximum welfare benefit is less than the need standard. In Mrs. Jones' case, we have assumed they are equal.

Governor Approves Welfare Cuts, Workfare Project in Pennsylvania

HARRISBURG, PA.—Republican Gov. Richard L. Thornburgh yesterday signed into law his proposal to cut off welfare checks to at least 64,000 Pennsylvanians, about one-third of those receiving cash grants from the state.

The legislation, approved by the Republican-controlled legislature last week, halts maximum $172-a-month state grants to childless, "able-bodied" recipients between the ages of 18 and 45, effective Jan. 1.

It also establishes Pennsylvania's first "workfare" program, under which an estimated 140,000 welfare recipients will be required to work at community service jobs to earn cash grants.

Thornburgh proposed the cuts in October, 1979, contending that Pennsylvania had become "a welfare haven" that burdened taxpayers.

"With 5.2 percent of the nation's population, Pennsylvania has nearly 20 percent of the nation's general assistance welfare recipients," he said. "This has placed an increasing burden on Pennsylvania taxpayers over the past decade."

He said savings from the cutoff would be used to provide a 5 percent increase in the cash grants for welfare families of three or more. For a family of three, that would amount to $16 more a month.

The Washington Post, Washington, D.C., April 9, 1982.

Welfare, Workfare, Warfare

Some welfare recipients in Siskiyou County, Calif., will be required to try to join the military, the AP reports. The county's board of supervisors unanimously adopted a policy that both men and women between the ages of 18 and 35 who receive general welfare assistance would be required to try to enlist on the theory that the military is a job like any other. Those who actually go to the recruiting office and get turned down can continue on welfare. Those who don't want to take the chance—well, we assume that's the idea.

Congress refused to adopt a national workfare plan but did allow states to experiment with their own versions of workfare. The primary objections to workfare were that many recipients simply could not work, that such jobs were nonproductive and costly to supervise, and that they obstructed welfare recipients' efforts to find regular jobs.

SUMMARY

- On the basis of cash incomes, 29 million people are officially counted as poor. In-kind transfers, however, substantially reduce the true poverty count.
- Welfare benefits are provided to many, but not all, poor people. Cash benefits are largely restricted to female-headed families with children.
- A reduction in welfare benefits that occurs when a recipient takes a job is an implicit tax. The rate at which welfare benefits are reduced when recipients earn wages represents the marginal tax rate.
- Marginal tax rates illustrate the work–welfare dilemma. High tax rates discourage work but restrict welfare eligibility. Low tax rates encourage work but enlarge the potential welfare population.
- The 1981 welfare reforms restricted welfare eligibility but also lessened work incentives. Compulsory jobs were proposed as a substitute for incentives.

Terms to remember

Define the following terms:

in-kind transfers
labor-force participant
human capital
marginal productivity
cyclical unemployment
income transfers
marginal tax rate
marginal utility of labor

Questions for discussion

1. Negative income tax (NIT) plans are distinguished by their promise of universal eligibility, based only on income standards (without regard for "employability" or other demographic factors). How would such plans differ from our current welfare system?

2. What compromise of the three welfare goals do you regard as most appropriate? How high would you set marginal tax rates?

3. What incentives would a father have under the AFDC system to desert his family if he were unable to find and retain a job that provided enough money to support them? How should we correct this situation?

Problem

Using the rules of the post-1981 (Reagan) welfare system, complete the following table relating income to hours worked. Assume the welfare recipient can earn $6 per hour and receives $1,000 each of Medicaid, food stamps, and housing aid so long as she is on welfare. She loses Medicaid when welfare benefits cease.

Hours worked	*Wages*	*Welfare benefits*	*Total cash income*	*Total real income*
0				
500				
1,000				
2,000				

CHAPTER 18

DISCRIMINATION

I have a dream that one day this nation will rise up and live out the true meaning of its creed: "We hold these truths to be self-evident, that all men are created equal."

—MARTIN LUTHER KING, JR., 1963

Discrimination has been identified as the source of substantial disparities in socioeconomic status. Blacks, Hispanics, and other minorities suffer from poor housing, limited educational opportunities, and lack of access to good jobs. The disadvantages imposed on women are less apparent, owing to the fact that they commonly share in the socioeconomic status of their mates. Nevertheless, women participate in the labor force much less extensively than men. When women do work, they usually command jobs and incomes markedly inferior to those available to men. These status disparities, plus a more general denial of opportunities for self-fulfillment, help to explain why the charges of racism and sexism persist and why they are important.

To understand how racism and sexism operate to create status disparities, we shall focus primarily on the labor market. We shall ask how and why minorities and women tend to get fewer rewards for their labor-force participation than do white men.

DIFFERENCES IN JOBS AND INCOMES

That minority groups and women generally occupy less attractive jobs and receive lower incomes in the labor market than do white males is beyond dispute. In 1980, the average white male worker earned an income of $16,657. By contrast, the average black male worker earned $10,979 and the average female worker received only about $8,500 (see Figure 18.1), Contributing to these enormous ine-

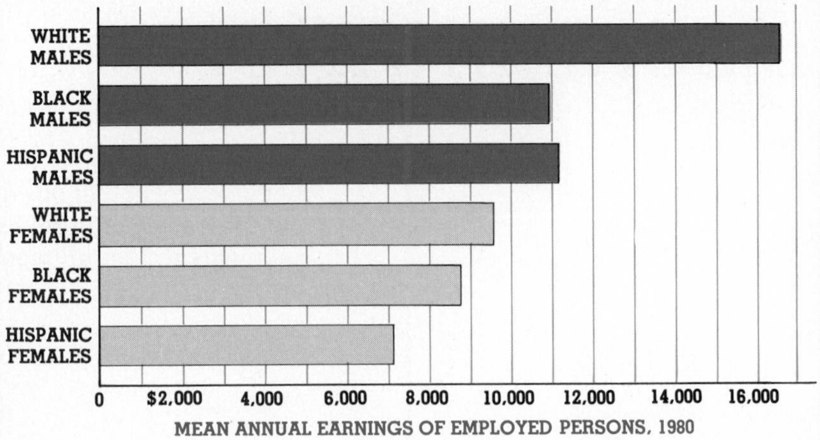

FIGURE 18.1 EARNINGS INEQUALITIES IN THE UNITED STATES

White males command much higher earnings than do minority males or women. Many, perhaps most, of these differences are due to discrimination, in both educational and employment opportunities.

Source: U.S. Department of Labor.

qualities in earnings is the fact that white males tend to hold jobs markedly different from those held by minorities and women. White males are far more likely to be employed as doctors, engineers, and college professors than are women or minority males. White males are seldom secretaries, file clerks, or private household workers. Minority males, on the other hand, are heavily concentrated in blue-collar occupations, particularly as operative and unskilled laborers. Women tend to hold jobs as clerks and secretaries but are also predominant in the ranks of schoolteachers (noncollege) and private service workers (maids, for instance).

Not only do white males tend to hold different kinds of jobs from those of either minority males or females; they also have a much easier time finding work. In early 1982 7.3 percent of adult white males were officially counted as "unemployed"—that is, seeking work. By contrast, the unemployment rate among minority males was a staggering 16.9 percent. Unemployment rates for women in 1982 fell between these two extremes, at 8.3 percent.

How much inequality is due to discrimination?

discrimination: **Inequality of treatment; denial of opportunity on the basis of characteristics unrelated to performance.**

The arguments about racism and sexism are not over the existence of these status disparities, but over their causes. To what extent are the job and income disparities due to underlying differences in talent or personal aspiration? And to what extent do they arise from an inequality of opportunity—from **discrimination** based on race or sex?

What makes the controversy so intense is that it is seldom easy to determine why a particular person did or did not get a particular job. Consider a situation in which a white worker and a black worker apply for the same job. The white applicant is accepted and the black applicant claims that he was unfairly discriminated against. What grounds do we have for accepting the charge of discrimination as opposed to, say, the charge that the black applicant is simply a poor loser?

The easiest cases of discrimination to prove are those that involve blatant discrepancies in treatment. In the example above, if only the black applicant had been required to take special tests or had possessed identifiably superior qualifications, the issue is readily resolved. The same kind of simplicity exists when black children are confined to dilapidated schools. Or when a prospective black home buyer is turned down after offering to pay the full retail value of a house. But the practice of discrimination is not always so apparent. Indeed, with the public eye focused on discrimination, those who engage in discriminatory practices are likely to develop great subtlety. Accordingly, evidence of discriminatory treatment may have to rest on the observation of end results. If a company has 4,000 employees, none of whom is black, a strong presumption exists that its hiring procedures are not impartial. So it is with the schools. If blacks and whites go into the educational system comparatively equal but come out with gross disparities in ability, it may be concluded that they were treated differently somewhere along the line. In other words, evidence of discriminatory treatment may be gathered by direct observation of treatment or by inference from results. Both types of evidence are used in formulating public policy and deciding court cases.

The acquisition and use of human capital

To identify more clearly the nature and impact of discrimination, we may return to the concept of marginal productivity. As we have noted in earlier chapters (particularly Chapter 12), a worker's employment opportunities and wages are directly related to his or her marginal productivity. In particular, we noted that a person's stock of **human capital**—one's skills and abilities—are a basic determinant of the contribution a person can make to output.

human capital: The bundle of skills that an individual possesses.

The level of marginal productivity actually attained will depend on one's human capital and the way it is employed. The amount of other resources (such as plant and equipment) that one has to work

OPINIONS ON DISCRIMINATION

A Harris poll taken in 1977 asked Americans about the extent of discrimination in schools, jobs, and housing. The responses revealed sharply different perspectives between whites and blacks. For example,

□ *Schools:* 61 percent of all blacks believe there is racial discrimination in public schools. Only 19 percent of all whites agree.

□ *Jobs:* 73 percent of all blacks feel they are discriminated against in access to white-collar jobs. Whites don't agree; 68 percent see no discrimination.

□ *Wages:* 66 percent of blacks feel they are unfairly paid lower wages; 72 percent of whites disagree.

□ *Housing:* 74 percent of blacks believe they lack equal access to decent housing; 61 percent of whites see no racial discrimination in housing.

A 1981 *Washington Post*/ABC News poll revealed much the same pattern. Sixty-seven percent of all blacks attributed their lower economic status to discrimination, but only 38 percent of all whites saw discrimination as the main cause of disparities in jobs, income, and housing.

marginal revenue product (MRP): The change in total revenue associated with one additional unit of input.

with are important determinants of marginal productivity. Finally, the *value* of a worker's output, **marginal revenue product,** will depend on the market worth of the goods and services produced. Thus discrimination can reduce an individual's income by:

- Denying a person the opportunity to acquire human capital.
- Denying a person the opportunity to use all of the human capital he or she has acquired.

The distinction between the acquisition and the use of human capital is important in measuring the full impact of discrimination. Suppose we found that the black worker who was denied a job had actually been rejected because he was unqualified; that is, on the basis of a human capital deficiency. Can we then conclude that he has not been the target of discrimination? No, at least not in any comprehensive sense. All we would know is that there appeared to be no discrimination *in the labor market* with respect to the utilization of human capital. The black job applicant might still have been denied an equal opportunity to acquire needed human capital, and in that respect he suffered economically from discrimination.

Many black workers, for example, are excluded from high-paying union jobs because they have been denied access to union apprenticeship programs that develop the required skills and experience. In such cases, the control over human-capital acquisition effectively translates into control over who gets which jobs. The same kind of relationship exists between acceptance at medical school and doctors' jobs, between admission to business school and corporate management, and between college admission and a broad assortment of highly paid jobs. One reason there are so few women in business management and professional positions is that business and professional schools have historically denied them admission. Hence to evaluate the full force of discrimination, we must ask two related questions: (1) Does everyone have an equal opportunity to acquire human capital? (2) Does everyone have an equal opportunity to employ it?

DISCRIMINATION IN EDUCATION

Much of the human capital that people bring to the labor market is developed in school. In effect, going to school represents an investment in one's own human capital. Such an investment is typically rewarded with more interesting jobs and higher pay. Hence we can begin to gauge the impact of discrimination by looking at the way educational opportunities are distributed in the United States.

Racial discrimination

The history of racial and other minority discrimination in education is well known. For most of our history, black and other minority children have confronted a situation of separate and unequal education. It was not until 1954 that the Supreme Court unanimously decided (*Brown* v. *Board of Education*) that separate schools are inherently unequal. Before that decision, little was done to upgrade

TABLE 18.1 SCHOOL INTEGRATION, 1980

Segregation is still prevalent in American schools. Most minority children attend schools in which at least half of the students are members of minority groups. Only one-third of minority children attend schools in which (Anglo) whites outnumber minority pupils.

	Percentage of minority students in schools where minority enrollment is:		
Region	*80–100 percent*	*50–79 percent*	*Less than 50 percent*
U.S. total	41	24	35
Northeast	57	19	24
Midwest	45	20	35
South	36	25	39
West	37	29	34

Source: U.S. Department of Health and Human Services.

the quality of black schools, much less to bring white and black children together in the same schools. It was not until the Civil Rights Act of 1964 that the 1954 Supreme Court decision began to be enforced with any sense of urgency. And it was not until the court-ordered busing plans of the early 1970s that black and white children began to approach equality of educational opportunity. That equality has still not been achieved but is considerably closer than it was two decades ago.

Table 18.1 summarizes the extent of racial integration in U.S. schools. In 1980 41 percent of all minority pupils (in elementary and secondary grades) were still attending schools in which nearly all the students were minority members. Only one-third of all minority pupils attended schools that were predominantly nonminority. Although there were large variations across regions—and interestingly enough, less segregation in the South than elsewhere—it is fair to conclude that segregated educational facilities prevailed everywhere. Whether in the North or in the South, in a city or on a farm, a minority child is very unlikely to attend a truly integrated school. Racial isolation in the schools is still a distinguishable feature of American educational systems.

INEQUALITY OF FACILITIES The statistics of Table 18.1 provide a sobering view of our efforts to furnish equal opportunity "with all deliberate speed." In the light of that background, we may argue that many minorities and whites still attend school separately. How equal, then, are their separate opportunities?

In the only comprehensive survey of our educational facilities ever undertaken, the U.S. Office of Education employed 67 separate measures of school quality, ranging from the number of books in the school library to the education of a teacher's mother. The Office of Education discovered that minority and white schools differed on a multitude of separate measures, but that such individual differences were relatively small. Only one clear pattern emerged from the mountain of statistics: minority schools tended to be most deficient in those facilities that were primarily academic in nature (science labs, textbooks, debate clubs).

In assessing these results, the Office of Education recognized many limitations in their approach. They reported:

EQUAL OPPORTUNITY?

A Harris survey asked a national cross-section of 1,497 adults: "As a matter of principle, do you favor or oppose desegregation of the public school system in the United States?"

DESEGREGATION OF PUBLIC SCHOOLS

	Favor (percent)	Oppose (percent)	Not sure (percent)
Nationwide	**56**	**35**	**9**
By region			
East	**57**	**33**	**10**
Midwest	**48**	**41**	**11**
South	**58**	**32**	**10**
West	**64**	**32**	**4**

In every region of the country desegregation of public education is favored in principle—but by only a slight majority.

The Harris survey then asked: "Would you favor or oppose busing school children to achieve racial balance?"

BUSING TO ACHIEVE RACIAL BALANCE

	Favor (percent)	Oppose (percent)	Not sure (percent)
Nationwide	**20**	**74**	**6**
By region			
East	**20**	**70**	**10**
Midwest	**19**	**74**	**7**
South	**18**	**77**	**5**
West	**27**	**70**	**3**

Although a slight majority of people in every region favor desegregation of schools in principle, they adamantly oppose busing as a means of achieving it.

Source: Harris survey, October 2, 1975.

The school environment of a child consists of many things, ranging from the desk he sits at to the child who sits next to him, and including the teacher who stands in front of his class. Any statistical survey gives only the most meager evidence of these environments, for two reasons. First, the reduction of the various aspects of the environment to quantitative measures must inherently miss many elements, tangible and more subtle, that are relevant to the child. . . .

Second, the child experiences his environment as a whole, while the statistical measures necessarily fragment it. Having a teacher without a college degree may indicate an element of disadvantage; but in the concrete situation, a schoolchild may be taught by a teacher who is not only without a college degree, but who has grown up and received his schooling in the local community, who has never been out of the State, who has a 10th-grade vocabulary, and who shares the local community's attitudes.

For both these reasons, the statistical examination of difference in school environments for minority and majority children will give an impression of lesser differences than actually exist.[1]

[1] U.S. Office of Education, *Equality of Educational Opportunity* (Washington, D.C.: U.S. Government Printing Office, 1966), p. 37.

We are left, then, with a very incomplete assessment of the school facilities available to whites and minorities. All we can say with certainty is that both everyday observation and the government survey lead one to conclude that tangible differences exist in the educational facilities available to minorities and whites. We have no summary measure, however, of the extent or the significance of those differences.

INHERENT INEQUALITIES The Supreme Court provided a way out of this statistical ambiguity when it determined in 1954 that segregated facilities were *inherently* unequal. The Court declared that "to separate [black children] from others of similar age and qualifications solely because of their race generates a feeling of inferiority as to their status in the community that may affect their hearts and minds in a way unlikely ever to be undone." The Court thus relegated the issue of tangible facilities to one of distinctly secondary importance. Even ostensibly "equal" schools for blacks and whites could never generate equal educational opportunity.

The Supreme Court justices were led to their landmark decision by several specific considerations. They recognized that black pupils in segregated schools would have low self-esteem, derived from the knowledge that they were surrounded by failures and in schools regarded as inferior. Moreover, they would acquire a personal sense of futility. They would know that regardless of their individual attainments, they would always be identified as members of a group viewed as less able, less successful, and less acceptable than whites. Hence individual black children would perceive little incentive to develop their individual talents. Community views would affect the attitudes of teachers also. Aware of (and probably sharing) the white community's low regard for blacks, teachers attached to black schools would tend to accept and transmit low expectations. They would not teach as much or as well to children deemed less teachable.

COLLEGE COMPLETION The disadvantages of a minority education accumulate. In general, minority students drop out of school earlier than whites. The cumulative disadvantage may be gauged by the low rate of college completion among minority groups. As Table 18.2 reveals, one-fourth of all white males aged 25 to 29 has completed four years of college. By contrast, the college graduation rate among minority males averaged only about 10 percent. A similar discrepancy exists between white and minority women. The implication of these statistics is that ***minority groups enter the labor market with much less human capital than whites.***

Sex discrimination

The educational handicaps of black and other minority groups are reasonably easy to document. The disadvantages that women confront in the educational system are more subtle, at least in the early grades. For the most part, the sex barriers that characterize primary and secondary educational systems consist of the sex-typing of certain kinds of curricula. Girls are encouraged to take home economics, foreign languages, and typing. They are gently discouraged from

TABLE 18.2 COLLEGE COMPLETION BY RACIAL OR ETHNIC GROUPS

Relatively few minority-group members complete four years of college. As a consequence, minority groups enter the labor market with less human capital than whites.

Racial or ethnic group	*Persons aged 25–29 who have completed at least 4 years of college (percent)*
Men	
White	**24.3**
Black	**12.1**
Hispanic	**8.6**
Women	
White	**20.5**
Black	**11.1**
Hispanic	**6.5**

Source: The National Center for Education Statistics.

taking manual crafts, business courses, and science. Some barriers are erected by school counselors who want to be "realistic" about occupational goals. Even higher barriers are erected by parents and peers, who are attuned to certain kinds of expectations with respect to male and female roles in society. As the Carnegie Commission on Higher Education has noted:

> Almost from the moment of birth, boys and girls are subject to a wide variety of cultural influences that tend to prepare them for differentiated roles in life. Little girls are typically given dolls or miniature cooking utensils for toys; boys are generally given trucks and electric trains and mechanical toys. School readers show pictures of father going off to work and mother waving good-bye at the window, or of father playing baseball with his sons while mother bakes cookies. Girls play jump rope or tag on the school playground, while boys play ball. At about the seventh or eighth grade, boys take a course in manual training, while girls are taught cooking and sewing.
>
> We are not suggesting that matters ought to be reversed, or that little girls should be forbidden to play with dolls, but rather that there ought to be more freedom of choice. Girls who show signs of a mechanical bent should be given an opportunity to play with mechanical toys and to enter the course on manual training. Boys should not be barred from courses on cooking and sewing if they are interested.[2]

This kind of acculturation tends to restrict the educational aspirations of female students and to frustrate them when they challenge those restrictions.

More explicit manifestations of sex discrimination in education have been apparent at the postcollege level. As suggested earlier, female college graduates have had a difficult time gaining access to the professional schools that confer the necessary credentials for many desirable jobs. Secretarial schools have always been easy to get into, but law schools, medical schools, and business schools have often been a different story. Figure 18.2 depicts the proportion of various academic degrees awarded to women.

[2] Carnegie Commission on Higher Education, *Opportunities for Women in Higher Education* (New York: McGraw-Hill, 1973), pp. 42–43.

FIGURE 18.2 WOMEN IN EDUCATION

Men and women graduate from high school in equal numbers. Thereafter, their educational experiences vary considerably. While relatively few women go on to law, medical, or engineering schools, women receive a preponderance of graduate degrees in education.

Source: National Center for Education Statistics.

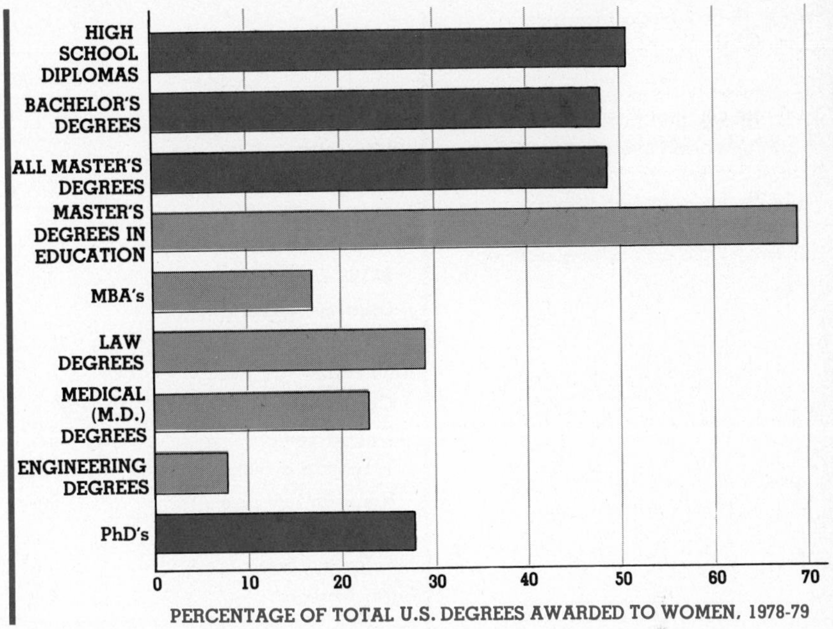

DISCRIMINATION IN THE LABOR MARKET

The discrimination confronting minorities, low-income children, and women obviously constrains their ability to acquire human capital and thus puts them at a disadvantage in the competition for jobs. The handicaps imposed in the educational system are only part of a continuing story, however. Once these groups enter the labor market, they cannot even anticipate the opportunity to employ fully the human capital that they have managed to acquire.

Racial discrimination

That minority workers are not treated equally in the labor market is now generally recognized. One needn't go back to the days of slavery to observe that black workers are undervalued and underutilized in the labor market. Nor need one go back to 1927, when a clothing manufacturer in New York advertised for help with the following wage offer: "White Workers $24; Colored Workers $20."[3] Such examples are not only outdated, but far too blatant and unsophisticated for labor markets that are monitored by government agencies and the courts.

Racial discrimination today rarely takes the form of paying unequal wages for equal work. More commonly, minority workers are simply denied access to a variety of occupations, jobs, and industries that happen to offer higher pay and better working conditions. Garbage collection and bus driving are regarded as appropriate occupations for minority workers. Retail salesmanship, management, and

[3] Cited by Orley Ashenfelter, "Changes in Labor Market Discrimination over Time," *Journal of Human Resources*, Fall 1970.

TABLE 18.3 OCCUPATIONAL STATUS, BY RACE AND SEX, 1981

Minority workers of either sex are underrepresented in white-collar occupations and overrepresented in blue-collar and service occupations. White males enjoy the greatest advantage in managerial-administrative and skilled-craft jobs.

	Male workers		*Female workers*	
Occupation	*White (percent)*	*Minority (percent)*	*White (percent)*	*Minority (percent)*
White collar				
Professional and technical	**16.3**	**11.7**	**17.3**	**15.4**
Managers and administrators	**15.5**	**7.0**	**7.8**	**4.1**
Sales workers	**6.5**	**2.7**	**7.3**	**3.2**
Clerical workers	**6.1**	**8.2**	**35.5**	**29.5**
Total	**44.4**	**29.6**	**67.9**	**52.2**
Blue collar				
Craft workers	**21.2**	**16.4**	**1.9**	**1.5**
Operatives	**10.6**	**15.0**	**9.1**	**14.2**
Transport drivers	**5.2**	**8.5**	**0.7**	**0.7**
Nonfarm laborers	**6.5**	**11.5**	**1.2**	**1.3**
Total	**43.5**	**51.4**	**12.9**	**17.7**
Service workers	**8.0**	**16.4**	**17.9**	**29.6**
Farm workers	**4.1**	**2.6**	**1.2**	**0.5**

Source: U.S. Department of Labor, Bureau of Labor Statistics.

even teaching are not regarded by whites as equally appropriate. And only in the most dire of circumstances could most whites imagine trusting themselves to the services of a black doctor or lawyer. Accordingly, blacks and other minorities are largely excluded from more pleasant and remunerative employment. Table 18.3 indicates the general nature of existing occupational patterns.

The professional, managerial, clerical, and craft occupations embrace most of the better-paying and pleasant jobs in the economy. Two-thirds of all white workers are in those positions now. Yet only 50 percent of all minority workers has gained access to these occupations. The situation is further aggravated by the fact that minority workers who do gain access to the better occupations often end up in the lowest and least desirable jobs *within* each occupational group. Within the professional, technical, and managerial class, for example, white workers tend to be lawyers, doctors, engineers, and accountants. Minority workers, on the other hand, are more likely to be recreation directors, welfare workers, and teachers in segregated schools. The same situation exists in the other occupational categories, sometimes in even more extreme form.

At the bottom of the occupational ladder, the respective concentrations of blacks and whites are, of course, reversed. As Table 18.3 reveals, one-half of all minority workers are concentrated in the lower occupational categories. And again, the disparities in actual jobs are great. Minority women are more likely to be maids in private homes, hotels, and office buildings. Minority men are more likely to be porters and janitors. The better service and laboring jobs (fire fighters, police officers, bartenders, and teamsters) are still largely reserved for whites.

THE ROLE OF EDUCATIONAL DIFFERENCES To some extent, of course, the occupational disparities between whites and minorities are attributable to the human-capital differences that they bring with them into the labor market. Very few universities, for example, are prepared to hire Hispanic high-school dropouts as professors, however "liberal" their claims for an equal-employment-opportunity policy. Hence Hispanics are underrepresented in that occupational category partly as a result of prior discrimination in the educational system. Thus we would be remiss if we blamed the entire occupational disparity on discriminatory employment practices.

The interesting question, then, is what kinds of employment differences persist *after* we take into account the initial handicaps imposed by human-capital differentials. Table 18.4 provides a tentative answer to this question by showing the comparative earnings of blacks and whites with equal educations. If there were no racial discrimination in the labor market, blacks and whites with equal education should command approximately equal wages. When this adjustment is actually made, however, the gap in wages between whites and blacks is only partially closed. The wages of black males are generally only 80 to 90 percent of the amount earned by white males with equivalent years of schooling.

The same kind of earnings differential applies to other minority groups. In 1981 the median wage of male Mexican-American high-school graduates was only $7.54 per hour. By contrast, white high-school graduates earned a median wage of $8.61 per hour.

These earnings differentials underscore the fact that ***the human capital of minority groups is generally undervalued in the labor market relative to white capital.*** Much but not all of this difference is due to discrimination. The 10 to 20 percent earnings differential that persists between minority and white workers with equal schooling overstates the degree of labor-market discrimination. It does not adjust for the *quality* of minority and majority schools. As we have already observed, a year of school for a minority student does not have the same educational value as a year of school for a white student. Minority educations are generally inferior. Hence comparisons of years of schooling, like those in Table 18.4, overstate the relative human capital possessed by black workers. On the other hand, we

TABLE 18.4 HOURLY WAGES, BY RACE, SEX, AND EDUCATION, 1981

The human capital of minority groups is generally undervalued in the labor market. Black males, for example, earn 10 to 20 percent less than white males with equal years of schooling. Part of this difference reflects disparities in the quality of education of blacks and whites. But some of this difference also reflects continuing discrimination in the labor market.

Years of schooling	*Male*			*Female*		
	White	*Black*	*Hispanic*	*White*	*Black*	*Hispanic*
High-school dropout	**7.65**	**6.16**	**6.59**	**4.24**	**3.98**	**3.92**
High-school graduate	**8.61**	**7.05**	**7.54**	**4.71**	**4.71**	**4.46**
Some college	**8.78**	**7.74**	**8.48**	**5.47**	**5.70**	**4.73**
College graduate	**8.21**	**7.58**	—	**5.92**	**6.22**	—

Source: U.S. Department of Labor, Bureau of Labor Statistics.

GPO Women Win $16 Million in Sex Bias Suit

A U.S. District Court judge yesterday ordered the federal government to pay an estimated $16 million to 324 women who successfully charged the Government Printing Office with sex discrimination—one of the largest awards ever made in a bias case brought against an employer, public or private.

Judge Charles R. Richey, who set the amount yesterday, had ruled last October that the GPO paid men higher wages then women for the same jobs in its bindery and that the agency deliberately maintained a job classification system that perpetuated sex discrimination. . . .

The judge's award yesterday means that [28] women who operated sewing machines at the bindery in May 1973 will each receive up to $110,000 in back pay, based on Richey's ruling that they were deliberately paid less than men for jobs that required the "same skill, effort (and) responsibility. . . ."

In his ruling last October, Richey also said that the GPO bindery's job classification system kept women . . . out of better "craft" jobs as bookbinders. Those jobs, Richey said, paid higher salaries and provided promotion opportunities. A four-year apprenticeship program, required for employes who wanted to become bookbinders, was virtually closed to 324 women who . . . were classified as "journeymen bindery workers," Richey said.

Those actions, Richey said, amounted to a pattern of sex discrimination, violating Title VII of the Civil Rights Act of 1964.

As a result, Richey yesterday ordered that the government pay 296 other women, working in other low-paying jobs at the bindery, about $3 million in back wages.

Moreover, Richey said, the GPO must continue to pay the women additional money until 50 percent of all bookbinder and supervisory jobs are filled by women.—Laura A. Kiernan

The Washington Post, Washington, D.C., May 21, 1980. Copyright © 1980 The Washington Post.

must recognize that minority educational achievements are themselves influenced by labor-market discrimination. That is to say, minority students will have less incentive to remain in school if they foresee little reward for their efforts. This kind of negative feedback makes labor-market discrimination that much more oppressive.

Sex discrimination

The same forces that tend to constrain the earnings of minority men also limit the employment and income opportunities of women. Here again, of course, we must take into account the fact that women enter the labor market with less human capital than men do, especially when measured in terms of advanced degrees. And they tend to be trained for different kinds of work, as a result of both social pressures and overt discrimination in the educational system. The consequence, as might be expected, is less labor-force participation, inferior occupations, and lower pay.

The tendency of women to work in different occupations from those of men has already been illustrated in Table 18.3. Those statistics are only a crude index to the actual disadvantage of women in the labor market, however. The occupation categories depicted in Table 18.3 are extremely broad and summarize an incredible variety of job experiences. The U.S. Department of Labor itself claims to have identified over 40,000 separate occupations. As we noted in our discussion of racial employment patterns, occupational statistics sometimes mask more differences than they reveal.

Table 18.5 attempts to provide a bit more insight into the segregation by sex that exists in the labor market. Within each of the major occupational categories of Table 18.3, there are thousands of more detailed occupations and literally millions of jobs. The statistics in Table 18.5 provide a clue as to the height that sex barriers reach when one begins to examine the labor market in some detail. Within the "professional and technical" occupational category, for

TABLE 18.5 A NONLIBERATED LABOR FORCE

There are still "women's jobs" and "men's jobs." Even within the same occupational category, men and women tend to perform different jobs. Among professional workers, for example, 84 percent of all elementary school teachers but only 4 percent of all engineers are women.

Occupational categories	The jobs that women hold	Proportion of jobs held by women (percent)	The jobs that women don't hold	Proportion of jobs held by women (percent)
Professional and technical	**Librarians**	**86**	**Engineers**	**4**
	Registered nurses	**97**	**Lawyers and judges**	**13**
	Elementary teachers	**84**	**Dentists**	**2**
	Dieticians	**94**	**Clergy**	**5**
Managers and administrators	**Food service**	**39**	**Public agencies**	**6**
Sales workers	**Demonstrators**	**95**	**Sales representatives**	**13**
Clerical and kindred workers	**Secretaries**	**99**	**Mail carriers**	**16**
	Bank tellers	**94**	**Shipping clerks**	**22**
	Telephone operators	**93**	**Dispatchers**	**38**
Craftworkers	**Bookbinders**	**56**	**Electricians**	**2**
	Decorators	**72**	**Telephone line and service workers**	**5**
Operatives	**Dressmakers**	**97**	**Taxicab drivers**	**9**
	Laundry and dry cleaning	**66**	**Truck drivers**	**3**
Service	**Waiters and waitresses**	**90**	**Police officers**	**6**
	Household service	**98**	**Bartenders**	**47**

Source: U.S. Department of Labor (1981 data).

example, we discover that there are clearly "female jobs" and "male jobs." Ninety-seven percent of all registered nurses are women, while only 2 percent of dentists are women. The same kind of imbalance is evident throughout the list.

Nor is this the end of the story. Even within the more detailed occupations of Table 18.5, men and women tend to be employed at different kinds of jobs, in different industries, and in different work settings. Consider just one example, that of waiters and waitresses. Women comprise a whopping 90 percent of that category, but how many of them are employed in the best restaurants (where prices and tips are highest)? Very few. Is it because they don't speak French as well?

BUT WOMEN HAVE BABIES! Perhaps it is because they have babies. Not on the job, of course, but 84 percent of all women do bear children at

"COMPARABLE WORTH": A NEW AND PERPLEXING MEASURE OF DISCRIMINATION

The Equal Pay Act of 1963 requires employers to pay men and women equal wages for equal work. In recent years, however, many women have argued that this measure of equality is too restrictive. Most women, after all, do not hold jobs identical to men's (see Table 32.5). Hence, there is seldom a basis for assessing "equal" pay.

To remedy this situation, it has been argued that women should get "comparable" pay, that is, equal pay for jobs *comparable* to men's in importance, skill, and responsibility. This concept has been the basis for a rash of new discrimination suits. In San Jose, California, comparable worth was a major demand in a 1981 strike by municipal workers. The strike was settled after the city agreed to pay $1.4 million in bonuses to "undervalued" female-dominated positions.

Although the concept of comparable worth has obvious appeal, it suggests a radical departure from market economics. In a competitive market, the "worth" of a job is measured by the prevailing wage. To assess "comparable worth," someone has to assign nonmarket values to each job, based on subjective judgements of "importance, skill, and responsibility." In the San Jose case, a consulting firm was hired to make these judgments. But many critics questioned the qualifications of that firm—or anyone—to substitute their judgments for those of the market.

The ultimate proof of sex discrimination

For years economists have been documenting the case that women have been discriminated against in the work place. The most direct decisive evidence yet of systematic sex discrimination in labor markets emerges not from an economic study but from a survey by Dr. Norman M. Fisk, a Stanford University psychiatrist. His questionnaire, sent to 170 people involved in sex-change operations, showed "that each person who changed from female to male earned more after the change."

Reprinted from the January 25, 1982, issue of *Business Week* by special permission.

some time in their lives. The job interruption that typically accompanies childbirth translates into lost job experience and thus less human-capital development, at least from a labor-market point of view. Can't this "natural" barrier to female productivity explain occupational and income differentials?

Partially, but only partially. As the president's Council of Economic Advisers has observed:

> One important factor influencing the [earnings] differential is experience. The lack of continuity in women's attachment to the labor force means that they will not have accumulated as much experience as men at a given age. The relatively steeper rise of men's income with age has been attributed to their greater accumulation of experience, of "human capital" acquired on the job. . . .
>
> . . . [But] a differential, perhaps on the order of 20 percent, between the earnings of men and women remains after adjusting for factors such as education, work experience during the year, and even lifelong work experience.[4]

Accordingly, we cannot dismiss occupational and earnings differentials between men and women on the basis of "natural" responsibilities of motherhood. Discrimination is clearly at work here. Moreover, we must take care to note that the same kind of negative feedback that constrains the human-capital development of minority men affects women, too. Why should a woman postpone childbirth or pursue a lengthy and difficult course of study if it appears that she will not receive commensurate rewards in the labor market? Role differentiation and labor-market discrimination tend to reinforce each other.

[4] *Economic Report of the President*, 1973, pp. 104–06.

THE IMPACT OF DISCRIMINATION

That discrimination continues to exist both in the educational system and in labor markets is beyond doubt. Rather obvious, too, is the fact that minority men and all women suffer real and tangible losses from such discrimination. But who gains? And what kinds of benefits do they reap? How are our principal economic outcomes affected?

Micro gains and losses

It is tempting to conclude that the prime beneficiaries of discrimination are white males, particularly those of the white, Anglo-Saxon, Protestant (WASP) type. And such a conclusion would not be entirely wrong. We should also recognize, however, that not all males, or even all WASP males, benefit from discrimination and, more important, that we all suffer in the aggregate.

With respect to educational facilities, there is a clear economic gain to whites. If minority students are relegated to inferior schools, then the better schools end up being white preserves. In a world where resources are limited—and the supply of good teachers is definitely limited—whites gain by expropriating a larger share of those resources. White children of lesser ability are also released from the necessity of competing with more able minority children in the quest for admissions. These are clear economic gains. Unfortunately, not all whites share in the spoils. Indeed, many whites suffer from racial discrimination. Not all whites can flee the inner city. Those left behind, primarily the poorest, are trapped in increasingly inferior educational systems, unable to enjoy the white monopolies held elsewhere, typically in the suburbs. They, like their minority neighbors, find their human-capital potential underdeveloped. Thus some whites gain while others lose.

The same kind of benefit distribution is apparent in the labor market. In general, racial discrimination in the labor market takes the form of confining minority workers to particular kinds of occupations, industries, and jobs. Two distinct groups of whites gain from this racial segregation of the labor market. White workers gain by being immunized against competition from blacks and other minorities in "white only" jobs. Employers (for instance, operators of laundries and hotels) who actually hire black workers in "black only" jobs gain by getting higher quality labor than they are in fact paying for. These economic gains are illustrated in Figure 18.3.

Not all whites gain directly, however, from such discrimination. Some, in fact, actually lose. White workers who cannot escape menial occupations suffer from increased competition from minority workers. The wages of white laundry and hotel workers, for example, are held down by the large number of blacks and other minority workers who are excluded from other occupations. These are the workers trapped in Market B of Figure 18.3, either by skill deficiencies or by geographical location. Some employers, too, suffer losses. In a segregated labor market, some employers often have to incur high labor costs through the use of poorly qualified whites. Some employers may even be driven out of business because they cannot afford to pay the higher wage, W_W.

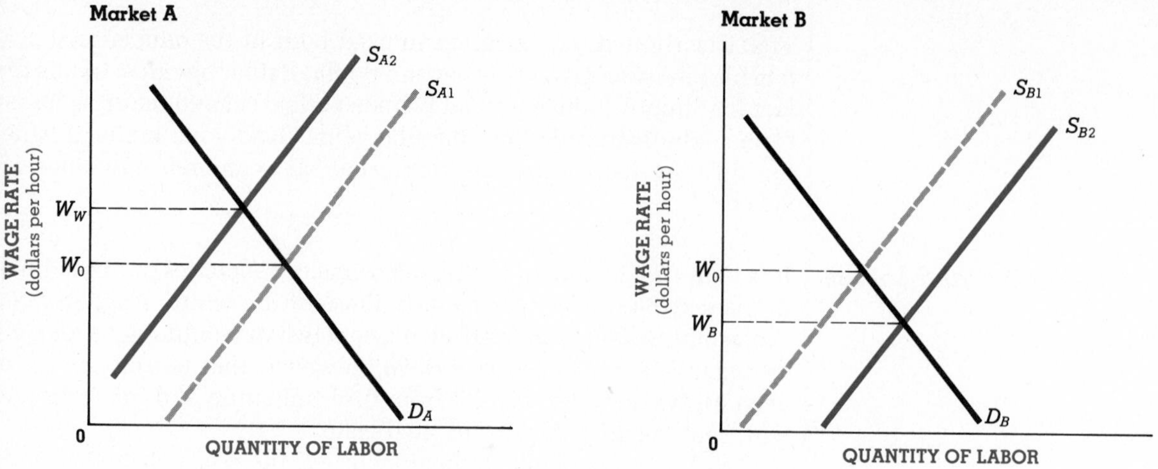

FIGURE 18.3 THE IMPACT OF JOB SEGREGATION

Suppose there are only two kinds of jobs, those in Market A and those in Market B. If everyone is allowed to move freely from one market to another, the equilibrium wage will end up at W_0 in both markets. Why? Because if wages were higher in A than in B, people would move out of B and into A. Such movements would lower the marginal revenue productivity in A while raising it in B. Hence freedom of movement between Markets A and B ensures an equality of average wage rates.

But now suppose black workers in Market A are kicked out and sent to Market B, making A a "whites-only" preserve. This has the effect of shifting the labor-supply curve in A to the left (to S_{A2}) and the labor-supply curve in B to the right (to S_{B2}). The net result, indicated by the new supply and demand intersections, is an increase in wages in Market A (to W_W) and a reduction of wages in Market B (to W_B).

Market incentives

The fact that some whites lose as a consequence of racial discrimination is especially noteworthy because it suggests the existence of market forces that seek to eliminate discrimination. Consider an employer in Market A of Figure 18.3. As we have observed, racial discrimination ends up raising his costs of production by requiring him to pay higher wage rates. Were he a true profit-maximizer, he would strive to break the racial barrier and hire more cost-effective workers. He could then attain greater **cost efficiency**, expand production, and increase his profits.

cost efficiency: The amount of output associated with an additional dollar spent on input; the *MPP* of an input divided by its price (cost).

Although the financial incentive for the producer in Market A to break the racial barrier is evident, it may be held in check by a variety of forces. He may himself harbor racial prejudices and be willing to subvert the profit motive for the sake of dissociating himself from blacks. As Professor Gary Becker has shown, such a posture may satisfy him psychologically, even if it costs him financially. Or he may fear reprisals from his white employees, fellow producers, or customers if he were to hire blacks. Professor Duran Bell has suggested that the white employees may turn out to be especially troublesome, because they are the prime beneficiaries of existing racial segregation. They may respond to integration of the workplace by

REVERSE DISCRIMINATION: THE UNSETTLED ISSUE

The patterns of discrimination practiced against minorities and women have inflicted significant economic losses on these groups. To compensate in part for these losses, the federal government and the courts have required schools and employers to take "affirmative action" to end discrimination. Schools and employers are required to make special efforts to recruit, admit, employ, train, and promote minorities and women. In almost all cases, affirmative action has meant some form of preferential treatment for minorities and women. In the more extreme cases, it has meant outright quotas for the admission or employment of these groups.

The preferential treatment associated with affirmative action implies discriminatory treatment of previously favored groups, particularly white males. This charge of "reverse discrimination" reached the U.S. Supreme Court in 1978 on the basis of a complaint by Allan Bakke. Bakke, a white male, argued that he had been denied admission to the University of California (Davis) medical school at the same time that less qualified minority applicants were being admitted. The Court agreed with Bakke, and ruled that rigid minority quotas were unconstitutional, although race could be considered as one of many factors in admissions decisions.

In essence, the courts have recognized a fundamental conflict between the desire to compensate the victims of past discrimination and the desire to uphold the principle of equal opportunity. Without affirmative action, the legacy of past discrimination will persist for decades. With affirmative action, however, white males and others will suffer some discrimination. Not surprisingly, over 80 percent of the public favor "selection on the basis of ability" but only 11 percent favor "preferential treatment." Congress and the courts have been attempting to strike an acceptable compromise between these two principles.

reducing their own productivity or impeding the efforts of minority workers.

"Radical" economists take an even dimmer view of the prospects of achieving equality through the market mechanism. From a Marxian perspective, discrimination against black workers functions to "divide and conquer" the laboring class. By dissipating energy and power on the maintenance of segregated job opportunities, the laboring class weakens its bargaining position. As a consequence, capitalists become the primary beneficiaries of continued discrimination.

Macro losses

Because some whites gain while other whites lose as a direct result of discrimination, it is difficult to calculate the net gain or loss to the white community on a microeconomic level. The same may be said of sex discrimination. Those men who want to be college professors or accountants clearly gain, while those who want to be elementary school teachers or bank tellers lose.

No such ambiguity attaches to the indirect losses that are incurred on an aggregate or macroeconomic level, however. When discrimination against minorities is pervasive, society as a whole loses potential human capital. The abilities and creativity of minority

HAVE WE GONE TOO FAR?: VIEWS ON AFFIRMATIVE ACTION

Question: A number of efforts have been made to help certain groups in this country improve their opportunities. . . . What about blacks and job opportunities—do you think that we in this country have gone too far, not far enough, or have done about the right amount in making job opportunities for blacks?

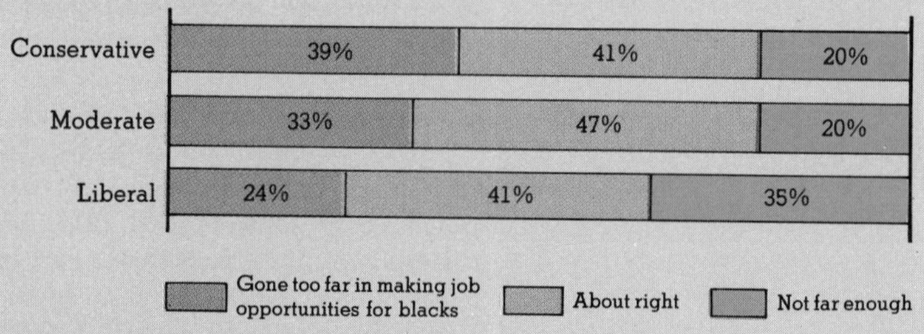

Answer: In the national sample, 33% said "gone too far . . . ," 43% said "about right," and 24% "not far enough."

Source: Survey by the Roper Organization (Roper Report 80-3), February 9–23, 1980, as reported in *Public Opinion*, February/March 1981.

workers remain underdeveloped and underemployed. The same may be said of discrimination against women or low-income families. ***Discrimination serves to shrink society's production possibilities and reduce total output.*** Estimates of the size of this loss in GNP run as high as $30 billion a year. In addition, much of the output we do produce is directed to such relatively unattractive uses as the surveillance of homes, streets, jails, and welfare case loads. This is clearly an undesirable shift in the mix of output. Finally, the practice of discrimination—the erection of artificial race, sex, or class barriers—undermines the efficiency of labor markets, thereby making prices higher than they would otherwise be (see Chapter 13 in *The Macro Economy Today*). Thus any direct gains or losses to individual whites, males, or upper-income persons are overwhelmed by the very large indirect losses suffered by the economy as a whole.

SUMMARY

- Discrimination is still a fact of life in both the educational system and the labor market. The effect of such discrimination is to deny people an opportunity to develop their human capital and to utilize fully the human capital they possess.
- Within the educational system, discrimination takes many forms. For minority students, discrimination frequently means segregated and inferior schools. For women, it means both subtle and overt pressures to pursue distinctive kinds of curricula and to constrain educational aspirations. For all those discriminated against, discrimination means less human capital with which to enter the labor market.

- In the labor market itself, minority groups and women do not have an equal opportunity to make the best of their restricted human-capital investments. Prejudice and institutional employment practices combine to handicap them still further. Thus blacks and whites with equal educational attainment end up getting different incomes. The same is true of men and women, even after we adjust for the fact that women typically interrupt their careers to bear children.
- Discrimination in the labor market may take many forms, but the most common is segregation by occupation, industry, or specific job responsibilities. A broad assortment of jobs tends to be "white only" or "male only," just as a great many jobs are filled largely by minorities or women. This segregation of jobs tends to depress the wages of those discriminated against and raise the wages of those who are in favored jobs.
- Although those discriminated against clearly lose in the quest for status, not all others gain. In particular, many employers are burdened with higher wage rates than would otherwise prevail as a result of job segregation. This situation creates an important market incentive for employers to break down race and sex barriers, thereby increasing both efficiency and profit.
- On a microeconomic level, discrimination translates into lower incomes for those discriminated against. On a macroeconomic level, discrimination results in reduced output, a less desirable mix of output, greater unemployment, and higher prices.

Terms to remember

Define the following terms:

discrimination
human capital
marginal revenue product
cost efficiency

Questions for discussion

1. Suppose a man gets a job in a steel plant while another man with identical abilities (human capital) ends up working in a textile mill. The man in the steel plant earns twice as much as the man in the textile mill, although both work the same number of hours. How can you explain this difference?

2. In the example above, the steel worker obviously has a good thing going. What would happen to his wages if everyone suddenly wanted to work in steel plants? How could he prevent that from happening?

3. Continuing the same illustration, suppose the owners of the steel mill decided that more competition for available jobs would increase their profits. What risks would they be taking in hiring new workers?

4. What basis does an employer have for evaluating the potential productivity of a job applicant? Why might employers, especially large ones, adopt rigid hiring criteria, even if those criteria discriminated against minorities and women? How could public policy overcome such obstacles?

Problem

Suppose that the initial demand and supply for labor are identical in two industries, construction and bus driving. In each of these industries the initial conditions are:

Wage rate (per hour)	**$1**	**$2**	**$3**	**$4**	**$5**	**$6**	**$7**	**$8**
Quantity of labor demanded (workers per week)	**19**	**18**	**17**	**16**	**15**	**14**	**13**	**12**
Quantity of labor supplied (workers per week)	**11**	**12**	**13**	**14**	**15**	**16**	**17**	**18**

(a) Graph the market conditions in each industry.

(b) What is the equilibrium wage in each industry?

(c) Illustrate what happens to supply conditions when four workers are excluded from the construction industry (at all wage rates) and forced to become bus drivers.

(d) What is the resultant equilibrium wage rate in each industry?

(e) Who gained and who lost as a result of this discrimination?

SECTION III

INTERNATIONAL ECONOMICS AND COMPARATIVE SYSTEMS

CHAPTER 19

INTERNATIONAL TRADE

The 1982 World Series between the Milwaukee Brewers and the St. Louis Cardinals was played with Japanese gloves, Korean baseballs, and Mexican bats, making baseball something less than the "all-American" game. In that same year, consumers spent a lot of their income on French racing bikes, Japanese stereo equipment, Italian sweaters, Swiss chocolates, Colombian coffee, Scotch whiskey, and Venezuelan oil. Most of these goods could have been produced in the United States, and many were. Why did we purchase them from other countries? For that matter, why did the rest of the world buy computers, tractors, electronic calculators, airplanes, and wheat from us rather than produce such products for themselves? Is there some advantage to be gained from international trade? If so, what is the nature of that advantage, and who reaps the benefits?

In this chapter we shall first survey the nature of international trade patterns, then examine the motivation for such trade. We shall also explore potential restrictions on trade and consider who might gain or lose from them.

U.S. TRADE PATTERNS

exports: Goods and services sold to foreign buyers.

imports: Goods and services purchased from foreign sources.

The United States is becoming increasingly dependent on international trade. In 1981 our merchandise **exports** totaled over $236 billion. This represented nearly 8 percent of total output. In addition, we had service exports (e.g., tourism, investment income) of nearly $100 billion. Our **imports** of goods and services were comparable.

FIGURE 19.1 EXPORTS IN RELATION TO GNP

Merchandise exports account for 7.8 percent of total U.S. output. Although substantial, this trade dependence is relatively low by international standards. Germany, for example, exports 26 percent of its total output.

Source: U.S. Department of Commerce, 1981.

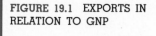

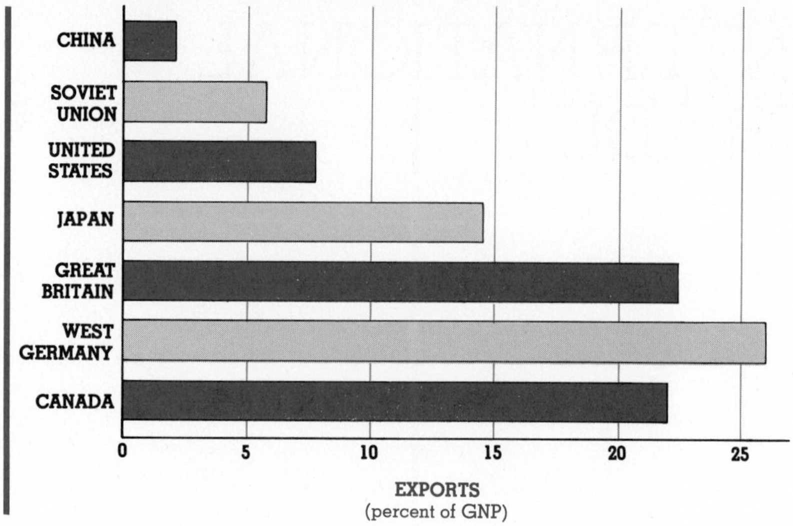

Although we depend on international trade much less than other countries (see Figure 19.1), our exports and imports are extremely important. Exports, for example, are part of the *aggregate demand* for goods and services. Hence an increase in exports reflects more demand for domestic goods and services. On the other hand, imports represent a form of leakage from the circular flow of income. A change in the volume of exports or imports will directly affect domestic production, employment, and prices. Moreover, the effects will tend to be *multiplied* as the initial change in trade makes its way around the circular flow.

The importance of trade for the domestic economy is even more apparent when specific goods are considered. True, there probably would have been a World Series in 1981 even without imported equipment. But Americans might have been asleep if we hadn't imported coffee (or tea). Likewise, there would have been no aluminum if we hadn't imported bauxite, no chrome bumpers if we hadn't imported chromium, no tin cans without imported tin. Just how vital imports of basic resources can be to our accustomed patterns of economic activity was dramatized when the OPEC countries reduced oil sales to us in 1973 and 1979. These supply interruptions and later price increases caused significant inflation and unemployment in the United States (see Chapter 16 in *The Macro Economy Today*).

The export situation is similar: the relatively low ratio of exports to total sales disguises our heavy dependence on exports in specific industries. Over 60 percent of our rice, corn, and wheat production was exported in 1981, as was half of our soybeans. Clearly, a decision by foreigners to stop eating American agricultural products could have devastated a lot of American farmers. Such companies as Boeing (planes), Caterpiller Tractor (construction equipment), Weyerhauser (logs, lumber), and Hewlett-Packard (electronics) sell over one-fourth of their output in foreign markets. Pepsi and Coke

FIGURE 19.2 U.S. TRADE PATTERNS

Most U.S. merchandise exports and imports consist of manufactured goods. However, agricultural exports and oil imports are growing rapidly. About 40 percent of all U.S. trade is with developing countries, including OPEC (oil-exporting) nations.

Source: U.S. Department of Commerce.

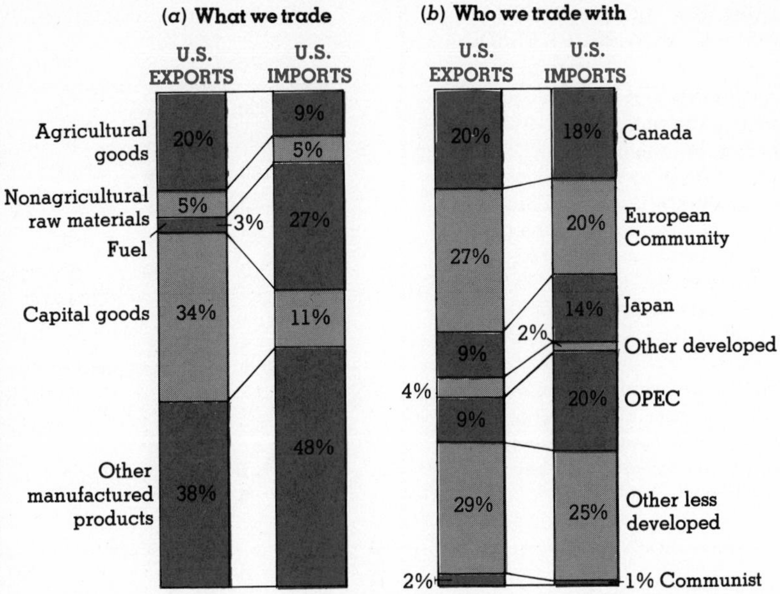

trade deficit: The amount by which the value of imports exceeds the value of exports in a given time period.

trade surplus: The amount by which the value of exports exceeds the value of imports in a given time period.

are battling it out in the soft-drink markets of such unlikely places as Egypt, Abu Dhabi, and the Soviet Union.

Figure 19.2 provides a quick summary of the trading we do in goods, and with whom. In 1981 we imported over $264 billion worth of merchandise. We exported a smaller amount ($236 billion), giving us a **trade deficit** of $28 billion. Had we exported more than we imported we would have had a **trade surplus.**[1]

Most of our imports came from Europe and Canada, although oil imports have accounted for an increasing share of our total imports. Trade with such planned economies as China and the Soviet Union is currently very small, but growing rapidly.

MOTIVATION TO TRADE

Our extensive trade with other countries of the world is motivated by the recognition that ***specialization increases total output.*** In other words, our decision to trade with other countries arises from the same considerations that motivate individuals to specialize in production, satisfying their remaining needs in the marketplace. Why don't you become self-sufficient, growing all your own food, building your own shelter, recording your own songs? Presumably because you have found that you can enjoy a much higher standard of living (and better music) by producing only a few goods and buy-

[1] Traditionally the trade deficit (surplus) refers to merchandise only. Imports and exports of services are added to compute the "current account" balance. In 1981 the current account was in surplus, since service exports (e.g., air travel) exceeded service imports by $41 billion.

FIGURE 19.3 CONSUMPTION POSSIBILITIES WITHOUT TRADE

In the absence of trade, a country's consumption possibilities are identical to its production possibilities. The assumed production possibilities of the United States and France are illustrated in the graphs and the corresponding schedules. Before entering into trade, the United States chose to produce and consume at point *D*, with 40 zillion loaves of bread and 30 zillion barrels of wine. France chose point *I* on its own production-possibilities curve. By trading, each country hopes to increase its consumption beyond these levels.

U.S. production possibilities

	Bread	+	*Wine*
A	100	+	0
B	80	+	10
C	60	+	20
D	40	+	30
E	20	+	40
F	0	+	50

French production possibilities

	Bread	+	*Wine*
G	15	+	0
H	12	+	12
I	9	+	24
J	6	+	36
K	3	+	48
L	0	+	60

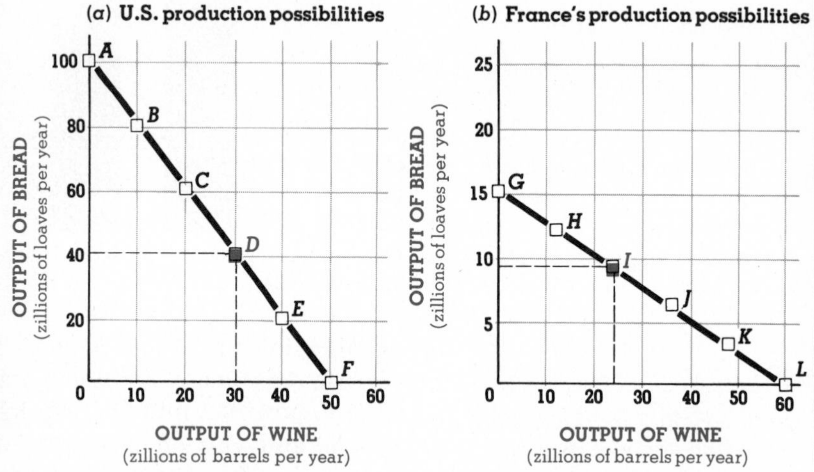

ing the rest in the marketplace. When countries engage in international trade, they are expressing the same kind of commitment to specialization, and for the same reasons.

To demonstrate the economic gains obtainable from international trade, we may examine the production-possibilities curves of two countries. We want to demonstrate that two countries that trade can together produce more output than they could in the absence of trade. If they can, ***the gain from trade will be increased world output and thus higher standards of living in both countries.***

Production and consumption without trade

Consider the production and consumption possibilities of just two countries—say, the United States and France. For the sake of illustration, we shall assume that both countries produce only two goods, bread and wine. We shall also set aside worries about the law of diminishing returns and the substitutability of resources, thus transforming the familiar **production-possibilities** curve into a straight line, as in Figure 19.3.

production possibilities: The alternative combinations of final goods and services that could be produced in a given time period with all available resources and technology.

The "curves" in Figure 19.3 and our own intuition suggest that the United States is capable of producing much more bread than France is. After all, we have a greater abundance of labor, land, and other factors of production than France does. We shall assume that the United States is capable of producing up to 100 zillion loaves of bread per year, if we devoted all of our resources to that purpose. This capability is indicated by point *A* in Figure 19.3*a* and the accompanying production-possibilities schedule. France (Figure 19.3*b*), on the other hand, confronts a *maximum* bread production of only 15 zillion loaves per year (point *G*) because it has little land available, less fuel, and fewer potential workers.

The capacities of the two countries for wine production are 50 zillion barrels for us (point *F*) and 60 zillion for France (point *L*), largely reflecting France's greater experience in tending vines. Both countries are also capable of producing alternative *combinations* of bread and wine, as evidenced by their respective production-possibilities curves (points *B*–*E* for the United States and *H*–*K* for France).

consumption possibilities: The alternative combinations of goods and services that a country could consume in a given time period.

In the absence of contact with the outside world, the production-possibilities curve for each country also defines its **consumption possibilities,** because neither country can consume more than it produces.[2] Thus the burning issue in each country is which mix of output to choose—WHAT to produce—out of the infinite number of choices available.

Assume that Americans choose point *D* on their production-possibilities curve. At point *D* we would produce and consume 40 zillion loaves of bread and 30 zillion barrels of wine each year. The French, on the other hand, prefer the mix of output represented by point *I* on their production-possibilities curve. At that point they produce and consume 9 zillion loaves of bread and 24 zillion barrels of wine.

Our primary interest here is in the combined annual output of the United States and France. In this case (points *D* and *I*), total world output comes to 49 zillion loaves of bread and 54 zillion barrels of wine. What we want to know is whether world output would increase if France and the United States abandoned their isolation and started trading. Could either country, or both, be made better off by engaging in a little trade?

Production and consumption with trade

In view of the fact that both countries are saddled with limited production possibilities, trying to eke out a little extra wine and bread from this situation might not appear very promising. Such a conclusion is unwarranted, however. Take another look at the production possibilities confronting the United States, as reproduced in Figure 19.4. Suppose that the United States were to produce at point *C* rather than point *D*. At point *C* we could produce 60 zillion loaves of bread and 20 zillion barrels of wine. That combination is clearly possible, even if less desirable (as evidenced by the fact that the United States earlier chose point *D*). Suppose further that the French were to move to point *K*, producing 48 zillion barrels of wine and only 3 zillion loaves of bread.

Two observations are now called for. The first is simply that output mixes have changed in each country. The second, and more

[2] If a country has inventories of consumer goods, consumption can exceed production for a brief period. The option is short-lived, however.

FIGURE 19.4 CONSUMPTION POSSIBILITIES WITH TRADE

A country can increase its consumption possibilities through international trade. Each country alters its mix of domestic output to produce more of the good it produces best. As they do so, total world output increases, and each country enjoys more consumption. In this case, trade allows U.S. consumption to move from point *D* to point *N*. France moves from point *I* to point *M*.

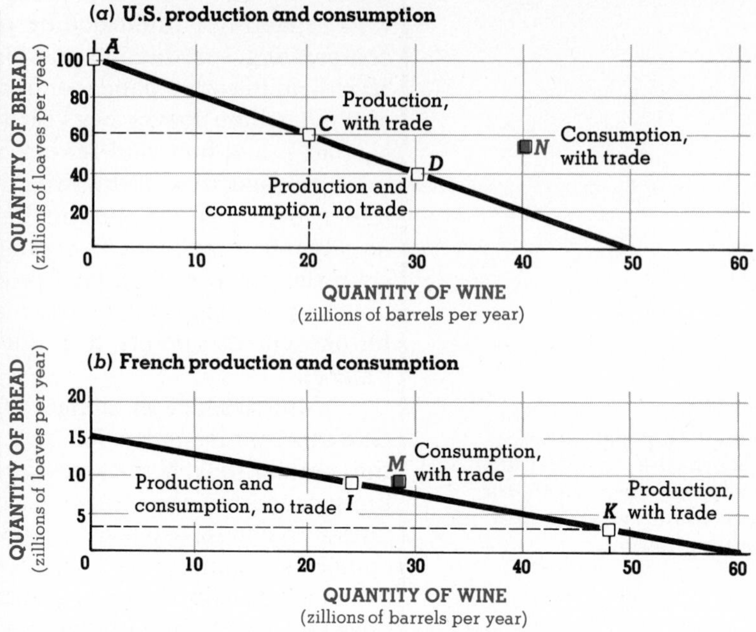

interesting, is that total world output has increased. When the United States and France were at points *D* and *I*, their *combined* annual output consisted of:

	Bread (zillions of loaves)	*Wine (zillions of barrels)*
U.S. (at point *D*)	40	30
France (at point *I*)	9	24
Total	49	54

Now world output includes:

	Bread (zillions of loaves)	*Wine (zillions of barrels)*
U.S. (at point *C*)	60	20
France (at point *K*)	3	48
Total	63	68

Total world output has increased by 14 zillion loaves of bread and 14 zillion barrels of wine. Clearly there is the potential here for making both countries better off than they were in the absence of trade.

The reason the United States and France weren't producing at points *C* and *K* before is that they simply didn't want to consume those particular combinations of output. The United States wanted a slightly more liquid combination than that represented by point *C* and the French could not survive long at point *K*. Hence they chose points *D* and *I*. Nevertheless, our discovery that points *C* and *K* result in greater total output suggests that everybody can be happier if we all cooperate. The obvious thing to do is to trade, to start exchanging wine for bread and vice versa.

Suppose that we are the first to discover the potential benefits that result from trade. Using Figure 19.4 as our guide, we suggest to the French that they move their mix of output from point *I* to point *K*. As an incentive for making such a move, we promise to give them 6 zillion loaves of bread in exchange for 20 zillion barrels of wine. This would leave them at point *M*, with as much bread to consume as they used to have, plus an extra 4 zillion barrels of wine. At point *I* they had 9 zillion loaves of bread and 24 zillion barrels of wine. At point *M* they can have 9 zillion loaves of bread and 28 zillion barrels of wine. Thus by altering their mix of output (from point *I* to point *K*) and then trading (point *K* to point *M*), the French end up with more goods and services than they had in the beginning. Notice in particular that the new consumption possibility made available through international trade (point *M*) lies outside the domestic production-possibilities curve.

The French will obviously be quite pleased with their limited trading experience, but where does this leave us? Do we gain from trade as well? The answer is yes. By trading, we, too, end up consuming a mix of output that lies outside our production-possibilities curve.

Note that at point *C* we produce 60 zillion loaves of bread per year and 20 zillion barrels of wine. We then give up 6 zillion loaves to get 20 zillion barrels of wine from the French. Hence we end up consuming at point *N*, enjoying 54 zillion loaves of bread and 40 zillion barrels of wine. Thus by first changing our mix of output (from point *D* to point *C*), then trading (point *C* to point *N*), we end up with 14 zillion more loaves of bread and 10 zillion more barrels of wine than we started with! Clearly international trade has made us better off.

There is no sleight of hand going on here. Rather, the gains from trade are due to the specialization that occurs when countries begin to exchange goods and services. When each country goes it alone, it is a prisoner of its own production-possibilities curve and must makes its production decisions on the basis of its own consumption desires. When international trade is permitted, however, each country can concentrate on the exploitation of its production capabilities. Each country then trades to acquire the goods it desires to consume. In other words, international trade allows each country to focus on what it does best, with the resultant specialization increasing total world output. In this way each country is able to escape the confines of its own production-possibilities curve, to reach beyond it for a larger basket of consumption goods. ***When a country engages in international trade, its consumption possibilities always exceed its production possibilities.*** This excess of consumption possibilities is demonstrated by the fact that points *N* and *M* lie outside the production-possibilities curves in Figure 19.4. If it were not possible for countries to increase their consumption by trading, there would be no incentive for trading, and thus no trade.

PURSUIT OF COMPARATIVE ADVANTAGE

Although international trade can make everyone better off, it is not so obvious what goods should be traded, or on what terms. In our previous illustration, the United States ended up trading loaves of bread for wine on terms that were decidedly favorable to us. Why did we choose to export bread rather than wine, and how did we end up getting such a good deal?

The basis for our decision to export bread lies in our comparative advantage in producing bread rather than wine. Recall that we can produce a maximum of 100 zillion loaves of bread per year or 50 zillion barrels of wine. Thus the domestic opportunity cost of producing 100 zillion loaves of bread is the 50 zillion barrels of wine we forsake in order to devote our resources to bread production. In fact, at every point on the U.S. production-possibilities curve of Figure 19.4*a*, the **opportunity cost** of a loaf of bread is one-half barrel of wine. That is to say, we are effectively paying half a barrel of wine to get a loaf of bread.

opportunity cost: The most desired goods or services that are forgone in order to obtain something else.

Although the opportunity costs of bread production in the United States might appear outrageous, note the even higher opportunity costs that prevail in France. According to Figure 19.4*b*, the opportunity cost of producing an additional loaf of bread in France is a staggering four barrels of wine. The production of additional bread entails giving up too much wine.

A comparison of the opportunity costs prevailing in each country unveils the nature of what we call comparative advantage. The United States has a **comparative advantage** in bread production because less wine has to be given up to produce bread in the United States than in France. In other words, the opportunity costs of bread production are lower here than in France. ***Comparative advantage refers to the relative (opportunity) costs of producing particular goods.***

comparative advantage: The ability of a country to produce a specific good at a lower opportunity cost than its trading partners.

Naturally, a country should specialize in what it is relatively efficient at producing, as reflected in the opportunity costs of production. Were you the production manager for the whole world, you would certainly want each country to exploit its relative abilities, thus maximizing world output. Each country can arrive at that same decision itself by comparing its own opportunity costs to those prevailing elsewhere and offering to trade to mutual advantage. World output, and thus the potential gains from trade, will be maximized when each country pursues its comparative advantage. It does so by exporting goods that entail relatively low domestic opportunity costs and importing goods that involve relatively high (domestic) opportunity costs.

Absolute costs don't count

In assessing the nature of comparative advantage, notice that we needn't know anything about the actual costs involved in production. Have you seen any data suggesting how much labor, land, or capital is required to produce a loaf of bread in either France or the United States? For all you and I know, the French may be able to produce both a loaf of bread and a barrel of wine with fewer resources than we are using. Such an **absolute advantage** in production might exist because of their much longer experience in cultivating both grapes and wheat, or simply because they have more talent.

absolute advantage: The ability of a country to produce a specific good with fewer resources (per unit of output) than other countries.

We can envy such productivity, and even try to emulate it, but it should not alter our production and international trade decisions. All we really care about are *opportunity costs*—what we have to give

REALLOCATING LABOR: COMPARATIVE ADVANTAGE AT WORK

Labor moved out of these industries:	*Jobs Lost*
Apparel	**−103,363**
Motor vehicles and parts	**−76,195**
Furnaces, steel products	**−46,502**
Shoes	**−37,745**
Motorcycles, bicycles, and parts	**−22,667**
Radio and television sets	**−20,405**
And into these industries:	*Jobs gained*
Aircraft	**+54,050**
Aircraft equipment	**+45,296**
Computing machines	**+38,483**
Logging	**+26,245**
Oil field machinery	**+20,505**
Construction machinery	**+17,626**

Source: C. Michael Aho and James A. Orr, "Trade-Sensitive Employment: Who Are the Affected Workers?" *Monthly Labor Review,* February 1981.

Between 1964 and 1975, imports displaced workers from some industries while growing exports created new jobs elsewhere. These figures depict some of the major trade-related job losses and gains. By reallocating our labor in this way, we altered the mix of output in the direction of comparative advantage.

up in order to get more of a desired good. If we can get a barrel of imported wine for less bread than we have to give up to produce that wine ourselves, we have a comparative advantage in producing bread. In other words, as long as we have a comparative advantage in bread production, as reflected in relative opportunity costs, we should exploit it. It doesn't matter to us whether France could produce either good with fewer resources. For that matter, even if we had an absolute advantage in both goods, our comparative advantage would still be in wheat, as we have already confirmed. The absolute costs of production were omitted from the previous illustration because they were irrelevant.

To clarify the distinction between absolute advantage and comparative advantage, consider this example. When Charlie Osgood joined the Willamette Warriors' football team, he was the fastest runner ever to play football in Willamette. He could also throw the ball farther than most people could see. In other words, he had an *absolute advantage* in both throwing and running that made all other football players look like second-string water boys. Without extolling Charlie's prowess any further, let it stand that Charlie would have made the greatest quarterback *or* the greatest end ever to play football. *Would have.* The problem was that he could play only one position at a time, just as our resources can be used to produce only one good at a time. Thus the Willamette coach had to play Charlie either as a quarterback or as an end. He reasoned that Charlie could throw only a bit farther than some of the other top quarterbacks but could far outdistance all the other ends. In other words, Charlie had a *comparative advantage* in running and was assigned to play as an end.

TERMS OF TRADE

terms of trade: The rate at which goods are exchanged; the amount of good *A* given up for good *B* in trade.

It is clear that it pays to pursue one's comparative advantage and trade with the rest of the world on that basis. It may not yet be clear, however, why we got such a good deal with France. We are clever traders, to be sure. But beyond that, is there any way to determine the **terms of trade,** the quantity of good *A* that must be given up in exchange for good *B*? In our previous illustration, the terms of trade were very favorable to us, as we exchanged only 6 zillion loaves of bread for 20 zillion barrels of wine. The terms of trade were thus 6 loaves = 20 barrels.

The limits to the terms of trade

The terms of trade with France were determined by our offer and France's ready acceptance. France was willing to accept our offer because the attendant terms of trade permitted France to increase its wine consumption without giving up any bread consumption. In other words, our offer to trade 6 loaves for 20 barrels was an improvement over France's domestic opportunity costs. France's domestic possibilities required her to give up 24 barrels of wine in order to produce 6 loaves of bread (see Figure 19.4*b*).[3] Getting bread via trade was simply cheaper for France than producing bread at home, as evidenced by the fact that France ended up with an extra 4 zillion barrels of wine.

Our first clue to the terms of trade, then, lies in each country's domestic opportunity costs. A country will not trade unless the terms of trade are superior to domestic opportunities. As Figure 19.4*a* illustrates, the opportunity cost of wine in the United States is 2 loaves of bread. Accordingly, we will not export bread unless we get at least one barrel of wine in exchange for every 2 loaves of bread we ship overseas. In other words, we will not play the game unless the terms of trade are superior to our own opportunity costs, thus providing us with some benefit.

We can confidently predict that ***the terms of trade between any two countries will lie somewhere between their respective opportunity costs in production.*** That is to say, a loaf of bread in international trade will be worth at least ½ barrel of wine (the U.S. opportunity cost) but no more than 4 barrels (the French opportunity cost). In point of fact, the terms of trade ended up at 1 loaf = 3.34 barrels (that is, at 6 loaves = 20 barrels). This represented a very large gain for the United States and a small gain for France. This outcome and several other possibilities are illustrated in Figure 19.5.

The role of markets and prices

Relatively little trade is subject to such direct negotiations between countries. More often than not, the decision on whether to import or export a particular good is left up to the market decisions of individual consumers and producers. There are exceptions, as is illustrated by much of our trade with centrally planned economies and frequent

[3] People sometimes use the term "domestic terms of trade" to refer to opportunity costs in production. In this case, we would say that France will trade only if the international terms of trade are superior to the domestic terms of trade.

FIGURE 19.5 SEARCHING FOR THE TERMS OF TRADE

Trade creates the conditions for increasing our consumption possibilities. Note in *a* that the United States is capable of producing 100 zillion loaves of bread per year (point *A*). If we reduce bread production to only 85 zillion loaves of bread per year, we could move down the production-possibilities curve to point *X*. At point *X* we could produce and consume 7.5 zillion barrels of wine per year and 85 zillion loaves of bread. On the other hand, if we continued to produce 100 zillion loaves of bread, we might be able to trade 15 zillion loaves to France in exchange for as much as 60 zillion barrels of wine. This would leave us producing at point *A* but consuming at point *Y*. At point *Y* we have more wine and no less bread than we had at point *X*. Hence consumption possibilities with trade exceed our production possibilities.

A country will end up on the consumption-possibilities curve only if it gets all of the gains from trade. It will remain on its own production-possibilities curve only if it gets *none* of the gains from trade. In reality, the terms of trade determine how the gains from trade are distributed, and thus at what point in the shaded area each country ends up.

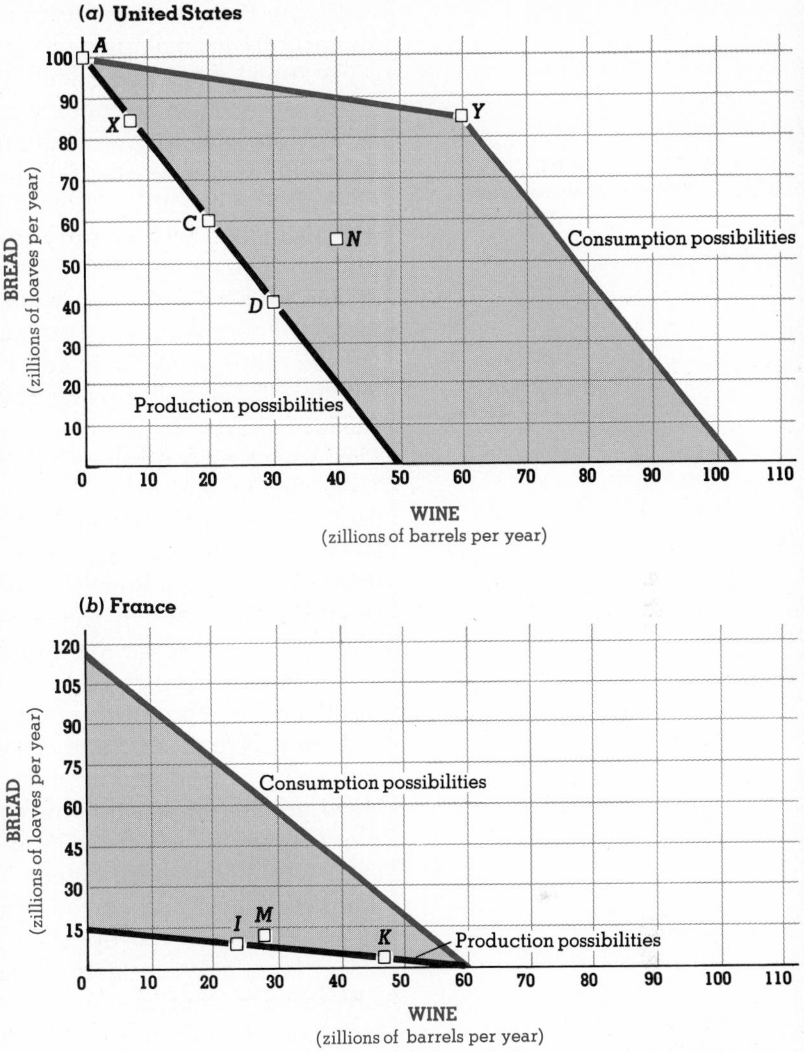

trade intervention by government agencies. But before we look at those exceptions, it is important to note the role that individual consumers and producers play in trade decisions.

Individual consumers and producers are not much impressed by such abstractions as comparative advantage and the gains from trade. Individual market participants tend to focus on market prices, always trying to allocate their resources in order to maximize profits or personal satisfaction. As a result, consumers tend to buy the products that deliver the most utility per dollar of expenditure, while producers try to get the most output per dollar of cost. Everybody's looking for a bargain.

So what does this have to do with international trade? Well, suppose that Henri, an enterprising Frenchman, visited the United States before the advent of international trade and observed our market behavior. He noticed that bread was relatively cheap while wine was relatively expensive, the opposite of the price relationship prevailing in France. These price comparisons brought to his mind the opportunity for making a fast buck. All he had to do was bring over some French wine and trade it in the United States for a large quantity of bread. Then he could return to France and exchange the bread for a greater quantity of wine. *Alors!* Were he to do this a few times, he would amass substantial profits.

Our French entrepreneur's exploits will not only enrich him but will also move each country in the direction of its comparative advantage. The United States ends up exporting bread to France and France ends up exporting wine to the United States, exactly as the theory of comparative advantage suggests. The activating agent is not the Ministry of Trade and its 620 trained economists, however, but simply one enterprising French trader. He is aided and encouraged, of course, by the consumers and producers in each country. The American consumers are happy to trade bread for his wines. They thereby end up paying less for wine (in terms of bread) than they would otherwise have to. In other words, the terms of trade Henri offers are more attractive than the prevailing (domestic) relative prices. On the French side of the Atlantic, Henri's welcome is equally warm. French consumers are able to get a better deal by trading their wine for his imported bread than by trading with the local bakers.

Even some producers are happy. The wheat farmers and bakers in America are pleased and eager to deal with Henri. He is willing to buy a lot of bread and even to pay a premium price for it. Indeed, bread production has become so profitable in the United States that a lot of people who used to grow and mash grapes are now starting to grow wheat and knead dough. This alters the mix of U.S. output in the direction of more bread, exactly as suggested earlier in Figure 19.4*a*. In France the opposite kind of production shift is taking place. French wheat farmers start to plant grapes so they can take advantage of Henri's generous purchases. Thus Henri is able to lead each country in the direction of its comparative advantage, while raking in a substantial profit for himself along the way.

Where the terms of trade and the volume of exports and imports end up depends in part on how good a trader Henri is. It will also depend on the behavior of the thousands of individual consumers and producers who participate in the market exchanges. In other words, trade flows depend on both the supply and the demand for bread and wine in each country. ***The terms of trade, like the price of any good, will depend on the willingness of market participants to buy or sell at various prices.***

PRESSURES FOR TRADE RESTRICTIONS

Although the potential gains from world trade are perhaps clear, we should not conclude that everyone will be smiling at the Franco-American trade celebration. On the contrary, some people will be very upset about the trade routes that Henri has established. They will not only boycott the celebration but actively seek to discourage us from continuing to trade with France.

Microeconomic pressures

Consider, for example, the winegrowers in upstate New York. Do you think they are going to be very happy about Henri's entrepreneurship? Recall that Americans can now buy wine more cheaply from France than they can from New York. New York winegrowers are apt to be outraged at some foreigner cutting into their market. Before long we may hear talk about unfair foreign competition or about the greater nutritional value of American grapes (which, incidentally, came originally from France).[4] The New York winegrowers may also emphasize the importance of maintaining an adequate grape supply and a strong wine industry at home, just in case of nuclear war.

Joining with the growers will be the farm workers and all of the other workers, producers, and merchants whose livelihood depends on the New York wine industry. If they are aggressive and clever enough, the growers will also get the governor of the state to join their demonstration. After all, the governor must recognize the needs of his people, and his people definitely don't include the wheat farmers in Kansas who are making a bundle from international trade. New York consumers are, of course, benefiting from lower wine prices, but they are unlikely to demonstrate over a few cents a bottle. On the other hand, those few extra pennies translate into millions of dollars for domestic wine producers.

The winegrowers in upstate New York (not to mention those in California) will gather additional support from abroad. The wheat farmers in France are no happier about international trade than are the winegrowers in the United States. They would dearly love to sink all those boats bringing wheat from America, thereby protecting their own market position.

If we are to make sense of international trade patterns and policies, then, we must recognize one central fact of life. There will always exist identifiable producer groups who have a direct and tangible interest in restricting or eliminating international trade. In particular, ***workers and producers who must compete with imported products—who work in import-competing industries—have an economic interest in restricting trade.*** Which helps to explain why GM, Ford, and Chrysler are unhappy about trade in Toyotas and Mercedes and why workers in Massachusetts want to end the importation of Italian shoes. It also explains why the textile producers in South Carolina think Taiwan and Korea are behaving irresponsibly when they sell cotton shirts and dresses in the United States.

Microeconomic resistance to international trade, then, arises from the fact that imports typically mean fewer jobs and less income for some part of the domestic population. At the same time, however, exports represent increased jobs and incomes for another part of the population. Producers and workers who are associated with export industries gain from trade. Thus on a microeconomic level, there are identifiable gainers and losers from international trade. ***Trade not only alters the mix of output but also redistributes in-***

Wine War

The European Common Market ordered an urgent explanation from France yesterday in an effort to head off a new flareup in the "wine war" which has soured relations with Italy.

The Executive Commission of the European Economic Community said it asked the French government why it imposed a temporary ban during the weekend on imports of Italian wine.

The wine war broke out last August when French winegrowers spoiled the cargo of an Italian wine tanker, protesting that the massive imports spoiled their market.

The Washington Post, Washington, D.C., February 2, 1982. Copyright © 1982 The Washington Post.

[4] In fact, the French had to re-import vines earlier sent to California after a grape blight destroyed the French vineyards in the late nineteenth century.

come from import-competing industries to export industries. This potential redistribution is the source of political and economic friction.

We must be careful to note, however, that the microeconomic gains from trade are greater than the microeconomic losses. It's not simply a question of robbing Peter to enrich Paul. On the contrary, we must remind ourselves that consumers in general are able to enjoy a higher standard of living as a result of international trade. As we saw earlier, trade increases world efficiency and total output. Accordingly, we end up slicing up a larger pie rather than just reslicing the same old smaller pie. Although this may be little consolation to the producer or worker who ends up getting a smaller slice than before, it does point up an essential fact. The gains from trade are large enough to make everybody better off if we so choose. Whether we actually choose to undertake such a distribution of the gains from trade is a separate question, to which we shall return shortly. We may note here, however, that restrictions on international trade designed to protect specific microeconomic interests have the effect of reducing the gains from trade. Trade restrictions leave us with a smaller pie to split up.

Additional pressures

Import-competing industries are the principal obstacle to expanded international trade. Selfish micro interests are not the only source of trade restrictions, however. Other arguments are also used to restrict trade.

NATIONAL SECURITY The national-security argument for trade restrictions is twofold. On the one hand, it is argued that we cannot depend on foreign suppliers to provide us with essential defense-related goods, because that would leave us vulnerable in time of war. The argument has some obvious merit, although it is easily subject to abuse. The oil industry, for example, used the national-security argument to persuade President Dwight Eisenhower to curtail oil imports. The result was that we used up our "essential" reserves faster than we would have in the context of unrestricted trade. The domestic oil industry, of course, reaped enormous benefit from Eisenhower's decision to protect our national security.[5]

The second part of the national-security argument relates to our export of defense-related goods. There is some doubt about the wisdom of shipping nuclear submarines or long-range missiles to a potential enemy, even for a high price. The case for limited trade restriction is again evident. But here also the argument can be overextended, as when we forbade the export to the Soviet Union of sugar-coated cereals and of machinery for making pantyhose.

DUMPING Another set of arguments against trade arises from the practice of dumping. Foreign producers "dump" their goods when they sell them in the United States at prices lower than those pre-

[5] The Mandatory Oil Import Program was terminated in 1973, when our domestic oil production could no longer satisfy domestic demand.

A LITANY OF LOSERS

Some excerpts from the Congressional Hearings on the Trade Reform Act of 1973:

In the past few years, sales of imported table wines . . . have soared at an alarming rate. . . . Unless this trend is halted immediately, the domestic wine industry will face economic ruin. . . . Foreign wine imports must be limited.
—Wine Institute

The apparel industry's workers have few other alternative job opportunities. They do want to work and earn a living at their work. Little wonder therefore that they want their jobs safeguarded against the erosion caused by the increasing penetration of apparel imports.
—International Ladies' Garment Workers' Union

We are never going to strengthen the dollar, cure our balance of payments problem, lick our high unemployment, eliminate an ever-worsening inflation, as long as the U.S. sits idly by as a dumping ground for shoes, TV sets, apparel, steel and automobiles, etc. It is about time that we told the Japanese, the Spanish, the Italians, the Brazilians, and the Argentinians, and others who insist on flooding our country with imported shoes that enough is enough.
—United Shoe Workers of America

We want to be friends with Mexico and Canada. . . . We would like to be put in the same ball game with them. . . . We are not trying to hinder foreign trade . . . [but] plants in Texas go out of business (17 in the last 7 years) because of the continued threat of fly-by-night creek bed, river bank Mexican brick operations implemented overnight.
—Brick Institute of America

vailing in their own country, perhaps even below the costs of production. Should the foreign producers continue this practice indefinitely, dumping would represent a great gain for us, because we would be getting foreign products on decidedly favorable terms. The problems over dumping arise from the fear that low prices will prevail only until the domestic import-competing industry is driven out of business. At that time we will be compelled to pay the foreign producer higher prices for his products. The fear of dumping, then, is analogous to the fear of predatory price cutting by powerful corporations, a practice we observed in Chapter 10.

The potential costs of dumping are serious and merit some policy response, but it is not always easy to prove dumping when it occurs. Those who must compete with imports have an uncanny ability to associate any and all low prices with predatory dumping. Thus responsible policy makers must take special care to confirm that dumping has occurred before attempting to restrict trade.

INFANT INDUSTRIES Dumping threatens to damage already established domestic industries. Even normal import prices, however, may make it difficult or impossible for a new domestic industry to develop. Infant industries are often burdened with abnormally high start-up costs. These high costs may arise from the need to train a whole work force and the expenses of establishing new marketing channels. With time to grow, however, an infant industry might ex-

> **Farmers to Rally**
>
> Thousands of Japanese farmers will rally in Tokyo today against proposals to lift restrictions on farm imports to ease U.S.-Japan trade friction.
>
> The farmers' campaign picked up momentum yesterday as a legislative panel passed a resolution warning the government of Prime Minister Zenko Suzuki against making the farmers the victims in U.S.-Japan trade wrangling.
>
> *The Washington Post*, Washington, D.C., April 23, 1982.

perience substantial cost reductions and establish a new comparative advantage. In such cases, trade restrictions are sought to nurture an industry in its infancy. Trade restrictions are justified, however, only if there is tangible evidence that the industry can develop reasonably quickly and expand the gains from trade.

IMPROVING THE TERMS OF TRADE One final argument for restricting trade rests on our earlier discussion of the way the gains from trade are distributed. As we observed, the distribution of the gains from trade depends on the terms of trade. That is, it depends on the quantity of exports that must be given up in order to get a given quantity of imports. If we buy fewer imports, foreign producers may lower their prices. If they do, the terms of trade will move in our favor, and we will end up with a larger share of the gains from trade.

One way to bring this sequence of events about is to put restrictions on imports, making it more difficult or expensive for Americans to buy foreign products. This kind of intervention will tend to cut down on import purchases, thereby inducing foreign producers to lower their prices. Unfortunately, this kind of strategem is available to everyone. Accordingly, our trading partners are likely to follow suit if we pursue such a course of action. Retaliatory restrictions on imports, each designed to improve the terms of trade, will ultimately eliminate all trade and therewith all of the gains people were competing for in the first place.

BARRIERS TO TRADE

The microeconomic losses associated with imports give rise to a constant clamor for trade restrictions. People whose jobs and incomes are threatened by international trade tend to organize quickly and air their grievances. Moreover, they are assured of a reasonably receptive hearing, both because of the political implications of good, well-financed organization and because the gains from trade are widely diffused. If successful, such efforts can lead to a variety of trade restrictions.

Embargoes

embargo: A prohibition on exports or imports.

The sure-fire way to restrict trade is simply to eliminate it. To do so, a country need only impose an embargo on exports, imports, or both. An **embargo** is nothing more than a prohibition against trading particular goods.

In 1973, for example, the Arab countries imposed an export embargo on oil destined for the United States in an effort to alter America's position on Israeli–Arab conflicts. And in 1959, when Fidel Castro became the prime minister of Cuba, the United States imposed an import embargo on Cuban goods. This embargo caused severe damage to Cuba's sugar industry and deprived American smokers of the famed Havana cigars.

Tariffs

tariff: A tax (duty) imposed on imported goods.

One of the most popular and visible restrictions on trade is the **tariff,** a special tax imposed on imported goods. Tariffs, also called "customs duties," were once the principal source of revenue for governments. In the eighteenth century, tariffs on tea, glass, wine, lead, and paper were imposed on the American colonies to provide extra revenue for the British government. The tariff on tea led to the Boston Tea Party in 1773 and gave added momentum to the independence movement. In modern times, tariffs have been used primarily as a means of import protection to satisfy specific microeconomic or macroeconomic interests. In 1982 U.S. tariffs added approximately 5 percent to the price of imported goods.

The attraction of tariffs to import-competing industries should be obvious. ***A tariff on imported goods makes them more expensive to domestic consumers, and thus less competitive with domestically produced goods.*** Among familiar tariffs in effect in 1982 were $0.51 per gallon on Scotch whiskey, $0.62 per gallon on Canadian whiskey, and $1.17 per gallon on imported champagne. All of these tariffs made American-produced spirits look like relatively good buys and thus contributed to higher sales and profits for domestic distillers and grape growers. In the same manner, imported-car prices are higher as a result of a 2.9 percent tariff, and Japanese stereos are burdened with tariffs ranging from 6.5 to 7.5 percent. In each of these cases, domestic producers in import-competing industries gain. The losers are domestic consumers, who end up paying higher prices; foreign producers, who lose business; and world efficiency, as trade is reduced.

Microeconomic interests are not the only source of pressure for tariff protection. As we have observed, imports represent leakage from the domestic circular flow and a potential loss of jobs at home. In the same way, exports represent increased aggregate demand and more jobs. From this perspective, the curtailment of imports looks like an easy solution to the problem of domestic unemployment. Just get people to "buy American" instead of buying imported products, it is argued, and domestic output and employment will expand. Congressman Willis Hawley used this argument in 1930. He assured his colleagues that higher tariffs would "bring about the growth and development in this country that has followed every other tariff bill, bringing as it does a new prosperity in which all people, in all sections, will increase their comforts, their enjoyment, and their happiness."[6] Congress responded by passing the Hawley-Smoot Tariff Act of 1930, which raised tariffs to an average of nearly 60 percent. The Hawley-Smoot Tariff effectively cut off most imports and contributed to the Great Depression.

Tariffs designed to expand domestic employment are more likely to fail than to succeed. If a tariff is successful in cutting down on imports, it effectively transfers the unemployment problem to other countries, a phenomenon often referred to as "beggar-my-neighbor." The resultant loss of business in other countries leaves them less able to purchase our exports and creates intense economic

[6] *New York Times,* June 15, 1930, p. 25.

and political pressures for retaliatory action. That is exactly what happened in the 1930s, as other countries erected barriers to trade to compensate for the effects of the Hawley-Smoot Tariff. World trade subsequently fell from $60 billion in 1928 to a mere $25 billion in 1938. In the process, all countries suffered from reduced demand (aggravated, of course, by foreign trade multipliers).

Quotas

quota: A limit on the quantity of a good that may be imported in a given time period.

Tariffs help to reduce the flow of imports by raising import prices. As an alternative barrier to trade, a country can impose import **quotas,** restrictions on the quantity of a particular good that may be imported. The United States maintained a quota on imported petroleum for a period of 14 years. Other goods that have been (and most of which still are) subject to import quotas in the United States are sugar, meat, dairy products, textiles, cotton, peanuts, and steel. According to the U.S. Department of State, approximately 12 percent of our imports are subject to import quotas.

Quotas, like all barriers to trade, reduce world efficiency and invite retaliatory action. Moreover, quotas are especially pernicious because of their impact on competition and the distribution of income. To see this impact, we may compare the market outcomes that result from no trade, free trade, tariff-restricted trade, and quota-restricted trade.

equilibrium price: The price at which the quantity of a good demanded in a given time period equals the quantity supplied.

Figure 19.6*a* depicts the supply-and-demand relationships that would prevail in an economy that imposed a trade embargo on textiles. In this situation, the **equilibrium price** of textiles is completely determined by domestic demand and supply curves. The equilibrium price is p_1 and the quantity of textiles consumed is q_1.

Suppose now that the embargo is lifted and foreign producers are allowed to sell textiles in the American market. The immediate effect of this decision will be a rightward shift of the market supply curve, as foreign supplies are added to domestic supplies (Figure 19.6*b*). If an unlimited quantity of textiles can be bought in world markets at a price of p_2, the new supply curve will look like S_2 (infinitely elastic at p_2). The new supply curve (S_2) intersects the old demand curve (D_1) at a new equilibrium price of p_2 and an expanded consumption of q_2. At this new equilibrium, domestic producers are supplying the quantity q_d while foreign producers are supplying the rest ($q_2 - q_d$). Comparing the new equilibrium to the old one, we see that the initiation of trade results in reduced prices and increased consumption.

Domestic textile producers are unhappy, of course, with their foreign competition. In the absence of trade, the domestic market equilibrium would provide more sales and higher prices to domestic companies. Once trade is opened up, the willingness of foreign producers to sell unlimited quantities of textiles at the price p_2 puts a limit on the price behavior of domestic producers. Accordingly, we can anticipate some lobbying for trade restrictions.

Figure 19.6*c* illustrates what would happen to prices and sales if the United Textile Producers were successful in persuading the government to impose a tariff. Let us assume that the tariff has the effect

FIGURE 19.6 THE IMPACT OF TRADE RESTRICTIONS

In the absence of trade, the domestic price and sales of a good will be determined by domestic supply and demand curves (point *A* in part *a*). Once trade is permitted, the market supply curve will be altered by the availability of imports. With free trade and unlimited availability of imports at price p_2, a new market equilibrium will be established at world prices (point *B*). Tariffs raise domestic prices and reduce the quantity sold (point *C*). Quotas put an absolute limit on imported sales, and thus give domestic producers a great opportunity to raise the market price (point *D*).

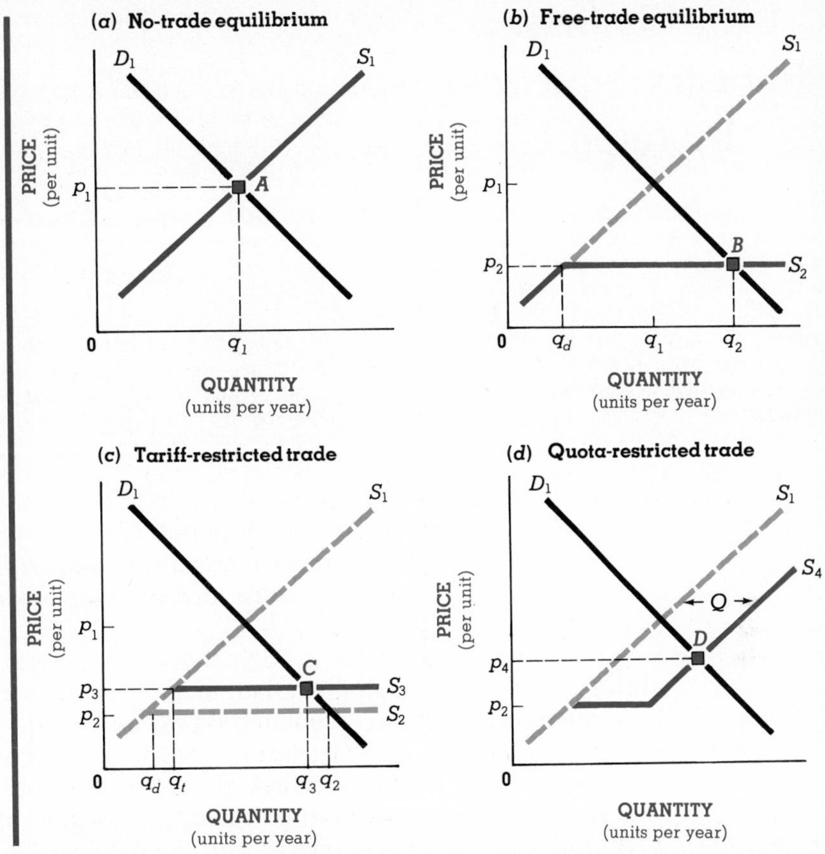

of raising imported textile prices from p_2 to p_3,[7] making it more difficult for foreign producers to undersell so many domestic producers. Domestic production expands from q_d to q_t, imports are reduced from $q_2 - q_d$ to $q_3 - q_t$, and the market price of textiles rises. Domestic textile producers are clearly better off, whereas domestic consumers and foreign producers are worse off. In addition, the U.S. Treasury will be better off as a result of increased tariff revenues.

Now consider the impact of a textile quota. Suppose that we eliminate tariffs but decree that imports cannot exceed the quantity Q. Because the quantity of imports can never exceed Q, the supply curve is effectively shifted to the right by that amount. The new curve S_4 (Figure 19.6*d*) indicates that no imports will occur below the world price p_2, and that above that price the quantity Q will be imported. Thus the *domestic* demand curve determines subsequent prices. Foreign producers are precluded from selling greater quantities as prices rise further. This outcome is in marked contrast to that of tariff-restricted trade (Figure 19.6*c*), which at least permits foreign

[7] Import prices will not necessarily rise by the full amount of a tariff, as foreign producers may lower their export prices somewhat to maintain sales. Thus the impact of a tariff on import prices depends in part on the price elasticity of foreign supply. In this case, we have assumed that foreign supplies are perfectly elastic, so that the difference $p_3 - p_2$ measures both the tariff and the ultimate price change.

U.S. Clothespin Industry Squeezed by Imports

The four major American manufacturers of wood spring clothespins want the government to stem the flow of rising imports from China, Romania, Poland and Czechoslovakia.

In case you believed the wood spring clothespin had been sent to oblivion by the gas and electric clothes dryer, consider these figures:

Last year, the United States imported 446.1 million clothespins with a total value of $2.8 million. . . .

The big gainers in sales were China, which rose from zero in 1974 to $447,000 worth in 1977, and Romania, which climbed from $11,000 in 1973 to $167,000 last year. Poland, always ahead of the rest on clothespins sales, remained the leader last year at $513,000.

As these countries were gaining, the four U.S. firms—three with plants in Maine, one in Vermont—were falling behind in holding their share of the market, according to statistics they gave the U.S. International Trade Commission, which is investigating the firms' complaints. . . .

"The money figures and the number of people are not fantastic, compared to what the American public hears every day. But if you stop the U.S. industry, you've ruined the economy of small towns and cut off workers' incomes," said Frederick C. McAlpin III, whose Washington law firm is handling the companies' petition.

—Ward Sinclair

The Washington Post, Washington, D.C., June 3, 1978.

producers to respond to rising prices. Accordingly, ***quotas are a much greater threat to competition than tariffs, because quotas preclude sales increases (of imported goods) at any price.***

Orderly marketing agreements

A slight variant of quotas has been used in recent years. The worldwide economic slump of the mid-1970s had two important effects on world trade. First, falling incomes reduced both export and domestic sales. Second, producers became more aggressive in foreign markets, trying to make up for their domestic losses. In the American shoe, textile, and color television industries, these developments were further aggravated by a lack of comparative advantage. As a consequence, sales in these industries slumped significantly, and industry spokesmen clamored for trade restrictions. President Carter responded by negotiating **orderly marketing agreements** (OMAs) with foreign governments (Japan, South Korea, Taiwan). The essence of these agreements was a promise by those governments to reduce the volume of television, shoe, and textile exports to the United States. Korea, for example, agreed to reduce its annual shoe exports to the United States from 44 million pairs to 33 million pairs. Taiwan reduced its shoe exports from 156 million pairs to 122 million pairs per year. For their part, the Japanese agreed to reduce sales of color television sets in the United States from 2.8 million to 1.75 million per year. All of these agreements represented an informal type of quota. The only differences were that they were negotiated rather than imposed, and they made provisions for later increases in sales. But these differences were lost on consumers, who ended up paying higher prices for these goods.

orderly marketing agreement (OMA): An agreement to reduce the volume of trade in a specific good; a "voluntary" quota.

Other barriers

Embargoes, export controls, tariffs, and quotas are the most visible barriers to trade, but they are far from being the only ones. Indeed, the variety of protectionist measures that have been devised is testimony to the ingenuity of the human mind. At the turn of the century, the Germans were committed to a most-favored-nation policy, a policy of extending equal treatment to all trading partners. The Germans, however, wanted to lower the tariff on cattle imports from Denmark without extending the same break to other countries, particularly Switzerland. But such a preferential tariff would have violated the most-favored-nation policy. Accordingly, the Germans created a new and higher tariff on "brown and dappled cows reared at a level of at least 300 meters above sea level and passing at least one month in every summer at an altitude of at least 800 meters." The new tariff was, of course, applied equally to all countries. But Danish cows never climbed that high, so they were not burdened with the new tariff.

Today most industrialized countries are likewise committed to a most-favored-nation policy, according to the General Agreement on Tariffs and Trade (GATT). That agreement, first signed in 1947, commits the world's trading partners to pursue free-trade policies. In pursuit of that objective, GATT signatories have negotiated agreements to lower tariffs and broaden quotas. In 1979, after six years of negotiation, the GATT countries agreed to reduce tariffs an average of 30 to 35 percent and to eliminate many of the 900 nontariff barriers to trade that exist. However, nontariff barriers to trade continued to grow. Italy, for example, has long discouraged auto imports by imposing a road tax based on weight and axle width. Not surprisingly, the tax resulted in increased levies on imported cars. The Japanese use complex and time-consuming licensing regulations and standards to keep out imports, thus sheltering domestic producers from competition. The United States is no less imaginative than most of its trading partners when it comes to nontariff barriers to trade. For example, we tax all distilled spirits entering this country as though they were 100 proof, thus effectively raising the tariff on an 86-proof bottle of Scotch. Domestic producers are thereby sheltered a bit from competition while the rest of us pay more for a drink.

Bat Men Strike Out in Japan

It may be a brand new baseball season, but they're still playing the same old game in the Japanese leagues.

U.S. bat manufacturers continue to strike out in Japan where they are pitched curves and sinkers by Japanese baseball groups preventing them from getting a handle on that big league baseball bat market.

After futilely slugging away, U.S. bat makers are calling a foul on the Japanese baseball leagues for refusing to certify foreign baseball equipment for use in their highly popular games.

The issue has been discussed by the Reagan administration and the Japanese government for several months. When the Japanese government announced this year that it was taking 99 steps to open its markets to foreign goods, the Japanese Ministry of Education issued guidance to all of the private sports associations to approve foreign products, according to the U.S. Trade Representative's Office.

But the U.S. sporting goods manufacturers said they have yet to make it to first base because they haven't made a single sale. The Japanese are balking and using delaying tactics such as sending certification papers to the American firms written in Japanese. . . .

What's at stake is scoring in the $30 million Japanese baseball bat market, which consists mostly of aluminum bats used to hit rubber balls in the Japanese-style game. . . .

Several years ago, American bat manufacturers such as Hillerich & Bradsby Co. Inc., which produces the Louisville Slugger and which has annual sales of $38 million, started making the lightweight bats, which retail from $18 to $40. About six months later, the Japanese began manufacturing their own aluminum bats.

A Japanese Embassy spokesman said the certification process was started after a spectator at one of the games was injured by a metal bat that broke during play. However, [a U.S. industry spokesperson] said the bat was Japanese-made. The embassy spokesman said he didn't know what kind of bat it was.

—Jane Seaberry

The Washington Post, Washington, D.C., April 15, 1982.

THE NUT WARS

The U.S. Department of Agriculture is responsible for establishing quality standards for filberts (hazelnuts) sold in U.S. markets. Typically, however, the federal agency has simply adopted the standards developed by the state of Oregon, the nation's number one filbert-producing state. On August 1, 1980, Oregon tightened its standards for shelled filberts. The new standards reduce permissible "decay" to 1 percent of volume from the earlier standard of 5 percent. The new standard had no effect on Oregon filberts, which are uniformly machine-dried. But it effectively eliminated imported filberts (most of which come from Turkey), which are air-dried in the traditional way. Turkey protested the new rule, as did American candy manufacturers, consumer groups, and even the Office of Management and Budget. Domestic growers, however, led by the Filbert Control Board, argued that "decayed" nuts were both unpleasant and potentially toxic.

The GATT countries started a new round of discussions on trade barriers in November 1982. The focus of this round is on trade in services (e.g., air transport, insurance, banking), which is particularly sensitive to nontariff barriers.

POLICY IMPLICATIONS: TRADE ADJUSTMENT

The microeconomic pressures for trade barriers arise from the economic losses inflicted on import-competing industries. If those losses could be avoided or compensated for, no such pressures would arise. The strategy to pursue in this case is some form of **adjustment assistance.**

adjustment assistance: Compensation to market participants for losses imposed by international trade.

The objective of trade, we should remember, is to reallocate resources in such a way as to increase world output and domestic consumption. To this end, each country is expected to shuffle its capital and labor from one industry to another, in the direction of comparative advantage. As we observed in Figures 19.4 and 19.5, this simply entails a move from one point on the production-possibilities curve to another point. Unfortunately, such shuffling from one industry to another is more difficult in practice than it is along the dimensions of a textbook graph.

In our previous illustration of Franco-American trade, vineyards were transformed instantaneously into wheat fields, vats into ovens, and grape pickers into wheat threshers. A nice trick if you can manage it, but few people can. Indeed, were such instantaneous resource reallocations possible, there would be no microeconomic resistance to international trade. Everyone would be able to share in the jobs and profits associated with comparative advantage. ***The resistance to trade arises from the fact that resource reallocations are difficult and costly in practice,*** both in human and in financial terms. The nature of resistance to trade is evident in a few grim statistics. In a recent survey of workers who lost their jobs as a result of import competition, it was found that 26 percent had gone for at least a year without work. Those who had found jobs had worked, on the average, only 50 percent of the time.

Worker assistance

The objective of adjustment assistance is to speed up the reallocation of resources and to make the transition less painful for affected workers. For this purpose, workers may be taught new skills, assisted in finding new jobs, aided in moving to new areas, and provided with interim income maintenance. In the case of older workers whose skills are not easily transferred, early retirement and pension benefits may be the most efficient kind of adjustment assistance.

All such assistance is expensive, of course. The Trade Expansion Act of 1962 permits displaced workers to receive 70 percent of their previous wages for a period of up to 18 months, plus training and relocation allowances. Between 1975 and 1981 over 1 million workers received nearly $3 billion in such assistance. Nevertheless, many labor unions have dismissed the program as "burial insurance." They argue that benefits are too low, and that in any case many workers can neither retrain nor relocate without considerable hardship. As John Mara, head of the Boot and Shoe Workers' Union, put it after seeing ninety shoe factories shut down in Massachusetts in the early 1970s: "Retraining for what? I want the economists to tell me what alternatives are available. Picking tomatoes in California?" ***The critical issue in trade adjustment is whether alternative jobs do exist and whether we are prepared to help workers get them.***

Industry subsidies

Not only workers but employers as well are adversely affected by import competition. When the competition from abroad is too great, a plant may have to shut down and its owners absorb a loss on their investment. Even though the owners may not need adjustment assistance as badly as do the displaced workers, they are going to be a source of protectionist pressure. Furthermore, their loss may leave an entire community without a major source of economic support. For both of these reasons, some adjustment assistance may be necessary or appropriate.

"Don't be childish, man! Kicking Toyotas is no answer to our balance-of-trade gap."

INDUSTRIES WORRIED BY GROWING IMPORTS

	Percent of total industry sales	
Imported products	*1960*	*1979*
Shoes	2	37
Autos	5	21
Steel	4	14
Textile machinery	7	45
Apparel	2	10
Consumer electronics	16	51
Machine tools	3	26
Industrial chemicals	2	19
Farm machinery	7	15

Source: Data from *Business Week*, June 30, 1980, p. 60.

The most common form of adjustment assistance to import-competing firms is a subsidy, a direct payment from the public treasury to the affected firm. Ideally, such a subsidy will be provided for the purpose of converting a plant to more profitable lines of production. When the plant cannot be easily converted, the subsidy should be temporary, with the explicit intent of simply slowing, not obstructing, the process of adjustment to comparative advantage. The Trade Act of 1974 provided for loans of up to $1 million for affected companies and another $3 million in loan guarantees, but few companies accepted such aid. They argued that it was both inadequate and too encumbered with red tape.

The Reagan administration, too, concluded that trade-adjustment assistance was not effective, but for different reasons. The administration concluded that special benefits to trade-impacted workers and industries slow the adjustment process more often than they facilitate it. It proposed to treat trade-displaced workers just like other unemployed workers. Only after regular unemployment benefits were exhausted would trade-displaced workers get explicit "adjustment assistance." Even then, their assistance would be no more generous than regular unemployment benefits. Firms, too, would have a more difficult time obtaining special trade-adjustment assistance. In this way, the Reagan administration hoped to encourage greater competition in domestic markets and to speed the move toward comparative advantage.

SUMMARY

- International trade permits each country to concentrate its resources on those goods it can produce relatively efficiently. This kind of productive specialization increases world output. For each country, the gains from trade are reflected in the fact that its consumption possibilities exceed its production possibilities.

- In determining what to produce and offer in trade, each country will exploit its comparative advantage—its *relative* efficiency in producing various goods. One way to determine where comparative advantage lies is to compare the quantity of good *A* that must be given up in order to get a given quantity of good *B* from domestic production. If the same quantity of *B* can be obtained for less *A* by engaging in world trade, we have a comparative advantage in the production of good *A*. Comparative advantage rests on a comparison of relative opportunity costs.
- The terms of trade—the rate at which goods are exchanged—are subject to the forces of international supply and demand. All we can say with certainty is that the terms of trade will lie somewhere between the opportunity costs of the trading partners. Once established, the terms of trade will help to determine the share of the gains from trade received by each trading partner.
- Resistance to trade emanates from workers and firms that must compete with cheap imports. Even though the country as a whole stands to benefit from trade, these individuals and companies may lose jobs and incomes in the process.
- The means of restricting trade are many and diverse. Embargoes are outright prohibitions against import or export of particular goods. Quotas merely limit the quantity of a good imported or exported. Tariffs, on the other hand, discourage imports by making them more expensive. Other nontariff barriers make trade too costly or time-consuming.
- Trade-adjustment assistance is a mechanism for compensating people who incur economic losses as a result of international trade, and thus represents an alternative to trade restrictions.

Terms to remember

Define the following terms:

exports
imports
trade deficit
trade surplus
production possibilities
consumption possibilities
opportunity cost
comparative advantage
absolute advantage
terms of trade
embargo
tariff
quota
equilibrium price
orderly marketing agreement (OMA)
adjustment assistance

Questions for discussion

1. Suppose a lawyer can type faster than any secretary. Should the lawyer do her own typing? Can you demonstrate the validity of your answer?
2. How much adjustment assistance should a displaced worker receive? For how long?
3. In what sense does international trade restrain the exercise of domestic market power?
4. Suppose we refused to sell goods to any country that reduced or halted its exports to us. Who would benefit and who would lose from such retaliation? Can you suggest alternative ways of ensuring import supplies?

5. Domestic producers often base their claim for import protection on the fact that workers in country *X* are paid substandard wages. Is this a valid argument for protection?

Problem

Alpha and Beta, two tiny islands off the east coast of Tricoli, produce pigs and pineapples. The following production-possibilities schedules describe their potential output in tons per year:

Alpha		*Beta*	
Pork	*Pineapples*	*Pork*	*Pineapples*
0	30	0	20
2	25	10	16
4	20	20	12
6	15	30	8
8	10	40	4
10	5	45	2
12	0	50	0

(a) Graph the production and consumption possibilities confronting each island.

(b) What is the opportunity cost of pineapples in each island (before trade)?

(c) Which island has a comparative advantage in pork production?

(d) Demonstrate that both islands will be better off by trading.

CHAPTER 20

INTERNATIONAL FINANCE

The essential role of money, whatever its appearance, is to provide a generally accepted unit of exchange and standard of value. Money enables markets to function with some reasonable degree of efficiency. Where money is widely used and accepted, people are willing to exchange their goods and services for paper currency. They know that they can later use that paper to acquire desired products. It doesn't really matter what kind of paper is used or whose picture is on it. As long as everyone is in agreement that the paper has a distinct value in the market, it will serve its essential function.

Money is important for international economic relations as well, and for many of the same reasons. Imagine that you are wandering through the ancient village of Layopia and come upon a solid quartz statue of Homo economicus, the god of economics. Overcome with desire, you offer $400 in U.S. currency to the Layopian monk who owns the statue. But the monk merely smiles a quizzical smile and declines your offer. He points out that although he thinks the pictures of George Washington framed in green are very pretty indeed, he has no use for such paper. Obviously, the monk has never seen American money and doesn't know its worth. American Express travelers' checks, maybe? No, no success with that either. Either you have to offer the monk something that is of value to him or you go home without Homo economicus. As it turns out, Layopians do have a monetary system, denominated in the wisdom teeth of porpoises. This won't help you, however, unless you have some porpoise teeth with you or can convince him that your own money is even more valuable than his.

Imagine that you are now in France, trying to cut into the wine and bread trade that Henri demonstrated (in Chapter 19) could be so profitable. As you recall, all you have to do is buy some wine in France, bring it back to the United States for sale, and use the proceeds to buy bread. Then you take the bread back to France for sale and add up your handsome profits. Easy enough. But you will discover a possible flaw in your plans to exploit comparative advantage as soon as you reach the vineyards. The French winegrowers are just as unreceptive to your dollars and travelers' checks as were the Layopian monks. As one grower explains, "*Je regrette, monsieur,* but what use have I of American dollars? I buy my meats and vegetables from Monsieur Pedot, and he accepts only French francs. Monsieur Sordoux, the cheese man, behaves the same way. So what am I to do with your dollars? I cannot buy groceries with them. Nonsense! Come back when you have groceries or French francs and we shall make a deal. Until then, *au revoir.*"

A few experiences like this and you will quickly perceive the importance of money for international trade. Unless trade is to be confined to clumsy and inefficient barter deals, some unit of exchange that is accepted as a standard of value in all trading countries is necessary. With such a medium of exchange, you would have no problem buying wine in France or quartz statues in Layopia. The problems of international finance generally revolve around this basic requirement of formulating an international standard of value. The difficulties of formulating such a standard arise from the fact that each country has created and maintains its own units of exchange—its own money.

EXCHANGE RATES: THE CRITICAL LINK

We do in fact buy Japanese cars, French wines, and other goods from abroad. That we can do so suggests that some international unit of exchange has been established, that some common form of money exists. But we also know that the French still use francs, the Japanese use yen, and we use dollars in everyday market transactions. How is it, then, that extensive international trade is possible?

What makes international trade so easy is that we are able to exchange dollars for francs, for yen, or for any other national currency we may desire. If you want to buy French wines from the growers, you can exchange your dollars for francs at the Bank of France or almost any commercial bank in France. With your newly acquired francs, you can proceed to the vineyards. There you may dicker with the growers over the price of their Beaujolais and buy as much wine as your income permits.

In fact, if you have no great desire to visit the vineyards but still enjoy Beaujolais, you can stay in the United States and simply go to the local liquor store. In this case, you pay for the wine in dollars. The person who imported the wine attends to the problems of exchanging your dollars for French francs and dickering with the growers.

No matter who actually haggles with the growers or brings the

exchange rate: The price of one country's currency expressed in terms of another's; the domestic price of a foreign currency.

wine back to the United States, however, someone is going to have to exchange dollars for francs. The critical question for everybody concerned is how many francs we can get for our dollars—that is, what the **exchange rate** is. If we can get five francs for every dollar, the exchange rate is 5 francs = 1 dollar. Or to express the whole thing in another way, we could note that the price of a French franc is 20 cents when the exchange rate is 5 to 1. Thus an exchange rate is simply the price of one currency in terms of another.

FOREIGN-EXCHANGE MARKETS

Most exchange rates are determined in foreign-exchange markets. Stop thinking of money as some sort of magical substance and view it instead as a useful commodity that can facilitate market exchanges. From that perspective, an exchange rate—the price of money—is subject to the same influences that determine all market prices: demand and supply.

The demand for foreign currency

With the possible exception of coin collectors and speculators, few people have much demand for foreign currencies per se. Foreign currencies, including French francs and Layopian porpoise teeth, are demanded not for their intrinsic value but for what they can buy. Hence ***the demand for foreign currency is primarily an expression of the demand for foreign goods and services.***

The demand for foreign currency originates in many ways. First and foremost, there is a demand for imported products, such as French wines, German cars, and Japanese stereo equipment. To acquire these things, we need foreign money. Table 20.1 indicates that we demanded over $264 billion worth of foreign currency for this purpose in 1981.

Foreign travel by Americans also generates a demand for foreign currency ($27 billion in 1981). When you are traveling, you need foreign currency to pay for transportation, hotel rooms, food, and anything else you wish to buy and can afford. Even if you are able to use U.S. dollars or travelers' checks on occasion, the recipients of such money will ultimately exchange them for local money, thereby reflecting your demand for foreign currency.

TABLE 20.1 U.S. DEMANDS FOR FOREIGN CURRENCY, 1981 (billions of dollars)

Our demand for foreign currency originates in our demand for foreign goods and services. Foreign producers want to be paid in their own currency. Hence to buy imported goods or services (including travel), we must first buy foreign currency.

Item	*Value*
Merchandise imports	$264.1
Travel expenditures	27.6
U.S. direct investment	8.7
Return on foreigners' investments	7.8
Private remittances and miscellaneous services	5.8
Military expenditures	11.3
Foreign aid, net	6.6

Source: U.S. Department of Commerce.

U.S. corporations demand foreign exchange, too. General Motors builds cars in Germany, Coca-Cola produces Coke in China, Exxon produces and refines oil all over the world. In nearly every such case, the U.S. firm must first build or buy some plant and equipment, using another country's factors of production. This activity requires foreign currency, and thus becomes another component of our demand for foreign currency.

Investment opportunities work both ways. Foreign producers often make direct investments in the United States. Shell and BP gas stations are a familiar example of direct foreign investment here, as are foreign auto plants, such as Volkswagen in Pennsylvania and Volvo in Virginia. In making such investments, foreign firms must first demand U.S. currency that can be used to buy our factors of production. Sooner or later, however, the foreign firms will want to reverse the flow of money, taking some of their profits back to their own banks and stockholders. In doing so, they create a demand for foreign currency as they convert the dollars they have earned in the United States into the currencies their stockholders and creditors can spend at home.

The other sources of the U.S. demand for foreign currency include transfers (typically by foreign workers who send home some of their U.S. income), U.S. military installations abroad (which are fed and housed with foreign goods and services), and foreign aid (which is often used to buy foreign goods).

The supply of foreign currency

Foreigners have the same kind of demand for U.S. dollars that we have for foreign currencies. They buy our merchandise (our exports, their imports), travel in the United States, and invest in productive resources located within our borders. Such ***demands for U.S. dollars also represent a supply of foreign currencies.*** That is to say, foreigners offer to exchange (supply) foreign currency when they desire (demand) U.S. dollars. The supply of foreign currencies generated by these foreign demands for U.S. dollars is summarized in Table 20.2.

Of particular note in Table 20.2 is the large amount of money involved in repatriated profits from direct American investments abroad. As we observed earlier, a company that invests in a foreign country wants to get some of its profits out sooner or later. U.S. firms have accumulated a tremendous investment in foreign countries,

TABLE 20.2 SUPPLIES OF FOREIGN CURRENCY, 1981
(billions of dollars)

The supply of foreign currency reflects a demand for American goods and services. To buy American goods and services, foreigners need U.S. currency. They offer to buy U.S. dollars with foreign currency. Such offers comprise the supply of foreign currency.

Item	*Value*
U.S. merchandise exports	**$263.3**
Travel income	**27.4**
Foreign direct investment in U.S.	**21.3**
Foreign purchases of U.S. securities, net	**5.0**
Return on U.S. foreign investments	**31.9**
Military exports	**9.7**

Source: U.S. Department of Commerce.

over $133 billion in book value by 1978.[1] These investments now generate a steady flow of profits and dividends back to the United States. This flow requires the conversion of foreign currencies into U.S. dollars (supply of foreign currencies, demand for U.S. dollars). Indeed, the current flow of profits exceeds the flow of new investments, as a comparison of Tables 20.1 and 20.2 will confirm.

Also noteworthy in Table 20.2 is the relatively large volume of net foreign purchases of U.S. securities. Foreign investors have tended to acquire limited participation in U.S. corporations by purchasing shares of stock rather than buying or building whole companies.[2]

Supply and demand curves

Tables 20.1 and 20.2 provide a reasonably complete view of the quantity of money that flowed through foreign-exchange markets in 1981. But such summary statistics can be misleading, because they don't convey how much those flows would have changed had exchange rates been different. Americans surely would have bought more imported goods in 1981 if foreign currencies had been less expensive. In other words, we should anticipate that the quantity of foreign currency demanded or supplied, like the quantity of any good traded in markets, depends on its price.

supply of foreign exchange: The quantities of foreign currency supplied (offered) in a given time period at alternative exchange rates (*ceteris paribus*).

demand for foreign exchange: The quantities of foreign currency demanded in a given time period at alternative exchange rates (*ceteris paribus*).

What this means is that both the demand for and **supply of foreign exchange** (foreign currencies) should be represented as curves, not as single points. In particular, we should recognize that the **demand for foreign exchange** is likely to have the familiar downward slope, while the supply of foreign exchange will have the usual upward slope. These two curves are illustrated in Figure 20.1.

THE DEMAND CURVE The explanations for the shape of the curves in Figure 20.1 should sound familiar. Consider the U.S. demand for any foreign product—say, Volkswagens.[3] Even people who have

[1] That is, the original cost less accumulated depreciation. Actual market values would be substantially higher, as a result of inflation.
[2] Whenever a foreign investor owns less than 25 percent of a U.S. company's stock, the investment is considered a *portfolio* investment rather than a *direct* investment.
[3] Two-thirds of all Volkswagens sold in the United States are now manufactured here. This decision was motivated in part by changing exchange rates, as we shall see.

FIGURE 20.1 THE FOREIGN-EXCHANGE MARKET

The foreign-exchange market operates like other markets. In this case, the "good" bought and sold is money (foreign exchange). The price and quantity of foreign exchange are determined by market supply and demand.

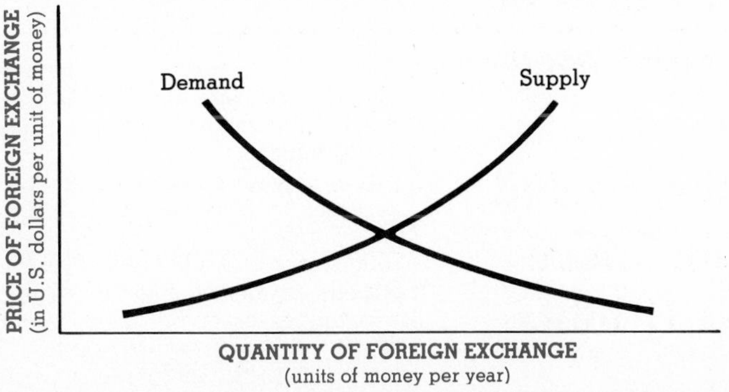

law of demand: The quantity of a good demanded in a given time period increases as its price falls (*ceteris paribus*).

never heard of foreign-exchange markets, or haven't the vaguest idea of what a deutsche mark is, buy VWs. All they know and care about is that they are willing to pay so many dollars for a Volkswagen and will buy something else when VWs are too expensive. Hence the U.S. demand curve for VWs will slope downward, reflecting **the law of demand**—the fact that the number of people willing and eager to buy a VW increases as VW prices drop.

Once we know the U.S. sales price for VWs, we can use the demand curve to determine how many VWs will be purchased and thus how much foreign exchange will be demanded. Two factors influence the U.S. price of VWs. The first is the willingness of the Volkswagen company to sell VWs for various amounts of deutsche marks. Remember that the VW producer and his workers want to be paid in their own currency—in deutsche marks (DM), the German monetary unit. The second factor is the number of deutsche marks that can be purchased for a dollar; that is, the *exchange rate* between deutsche marks and dollars. Hence the U.S. price of VWs is:

$$\text{Dollar price of VW} = \text{mark price of VW} \times \text{dollar price of German mark}$$

Suppose that the Volkswagen company (Volkswagenwerk) is prepared to sell a VW for DM10,000, and that the current exchange rate is DM2 = $1. At these rates, a VW will cost you $5,000. If you are willing to pay this much for a shiny new Volkswagen, you may do so at current exchange rates.

Now suppose that the exchange rate changes from DM2 = $1 to DM1 = $1. ***A higher dollar price for German marks will raise the dollar costs of German goods.*** In this case, the dollar price of a mark increases from $0.50 to $1. At this new exchange rate, the Volkswagen company is still willing to sell VWs at DM10,000 apiece. And German consumers continue to buy VWs at that price. But this constant mark price now translates into a higher *dollar* price. Thus a VW now costs you $10,000.

As the U.S. price of a VW rises, the number of VWs sold in the United States will decline. As VW sales decline, the quantity of German marks may decline as well. Thus the quantity of foreign currency demanded declines when the exchange rate rises because

U.S. Prices of Most Volkswagens Boosted for the Second Time Since Last October

ENGLEWOOD CLIFFS, N.J.—For the second time in two months, the prices of most Volkswagens sold in the U.S. are being raised. The latest increases average out to $155 a car, or 3.1%, and follow a $145-a-car boost last October.

The announcement of the latest increases by Volkswagen of America Inc., importer of German-made Volkswagens, Audis and Porsches, extends an almost nonstop string of price increases being made recently on foreign autos in the U.S. The flurry of price increases is being caused by the continued decline of the value of the U.S. dollar in comparison with overseas currencies. . . .

It isn't clear whether these latest increases, as they start to show up on cars currently being shipped to dealers, will dampen buyer enthusiasm for imports. Some Detroit auto men predict that foreign-car shoppers soon will begin to flinch at the sharply higher price tags.

Stronger Dollar

The stronger dollar prompts more Americans to travel abroad.

Advance bookings for European travel are up about 20% from a year ago for Mid-South Travel Service, Memphis, Tenn., which cites recent gains in the dollar's buying power. In Tyler, Texas, Jackson Tours says business is up more than 15% from last year, largely because of increased travel to Mexico, which devalued its peso 30% in February. And in the Cleveland area, Berea Travel Bureau is seeing more college students. "Now they can afford to take vacations in Europe," says a Berea manager.

foreign goods become more expensive and imports decline.[4] When the dollar price of the German mark actually increased in 1978, the Volkswagen company expressed considerable alarm.

THE SUPPLY CURVE The supply of foreign exchange can be explained in similar terms. Remember that the supply of foreign exchange arises from the foreign demand for dollars. If the exchange rate moves from DM2 = $1 to DM1 = $1, the mark price of dollars will fall. As dollars become cheaper for Germans, all American exports effectively fall in price. Thus we anticipate that Germans will want to buy more American products and therefore demand a greater quantity of dollars. In addition, foreign investors will perceive in a cheaper dollar the opportunity to buy American stocks, businesses, and property at fire-sale prices. Accordingly, they join foreign consumers in demanding more dollars and supplying more marks. Not all of these behavioral responses will occur overnight, but they are reasonably predictable over a brief period of time.[5]

MARKET DYNAMICS

equilibrium price: The price at which the quantity of a good demanded in a given time period equals the quantity supplied.

Given a neat and orderly demand curve and an equally neat and orderly supply curve, we can predict the **equilibrium price** of any commodity; that is, the price at which the quantity demanded will equal the quantity supplied. This prediction requires very little effort, since nearly anyone can figure out where the two curves cross in Figure 20.1.

shift in demand: A change in the quantity demanded at any (every) given price.

The interesting thing about markets is not their character in equilibrium but the fact that prices and quantities are always changing in response to shifts in demand and supply. The American demand for Volkswagens shifted overnight when Japan introduced a new line of competitively priced cars (Datsun, Honda, Toyota, Mazda). This **shift in demand** threw the demand curve in Figure 20.1 out of place and sent foreign-exchange specialists, GM executives, and worried VW managers back to the drawing boards. When wheat harvests in China and elsewhere turned out poorly in 1978,

[4] The extent to which imports decline as the cost of foreign currency rises depends on the *price elasticity of demand* (see Chapter 4).

[5] If the demand for our exports is relatively price inelastic, the percentage change in quantity demanded will be smaller than the percentage change in price. In this case, the quantity of foreign exchange supplied may actually decline as the dollar becomes cheaper. In such a case, the supply curve in Figure 20.1 would bend backward at higher exchange rates.

FIGURE 20.2 SHIFTS IN FOREIGN-EXCHANGE MARKETS

When Japan started selling Hondas, Toyotas, and Datsuns in the United States, the demand for Volkswagens shifted to the left (from D_1^* to D_2^* in *b*), while the demand for Japanese yen shifted to the right (from D_1 to D_2 in *a*). The dollar price of marks fell from p_1^* to p_2^* in *b*; the dollar price of yen rose from p_1 to p_2 in *a*.

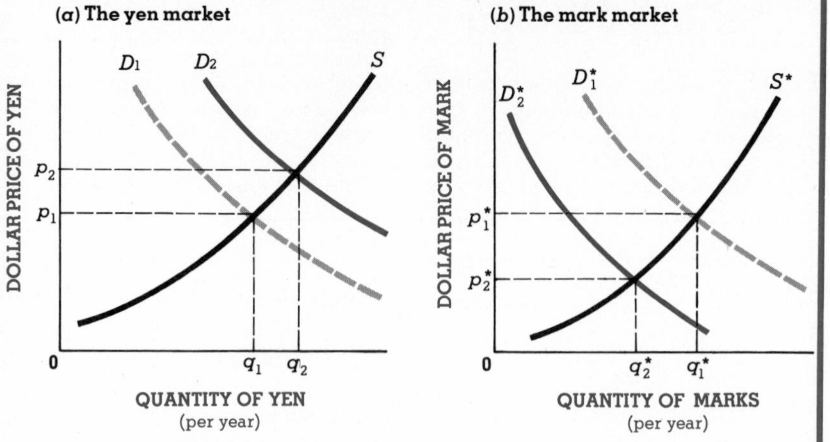

the demand for American wheat increased significantly. This increased demand shifted the supply of foreign exchange to the right (the demand for U.S. dollars to the left). Such shocks to the foreign-exchange market are illustrated in Figure 20.2.

Depreciation and appreciation

depreciation: A fall in the price of one currency relative to another.

appreciation: A rise in the price of one currency relative to another.

Exchange-rate changes have their own terminology. **Depreciation** of a currency refers to the fact that one currency has become cheaper in terms of another currency. In our earlier discussion of exchange rates, for example, we assumed that the exchange rate between deutsche marks and dollars changed from DM2 = \$1 to DM1 = \$1, making the price of a dollar cheaper. In this case the dollar depreciated with respect to the mark.

The other side of depreciation is **appreciation,** an increase in value of one currency as expressed in another country's currency. ***Whenever one currency depreciates, another currency must appreciate.*** When the exchange rate changed from DM2 = \$1 to DM1 = \$1, not only did the mark price of a dollar fall, but the dollar price of a mark rose. Hence the mark appreciated as the dollar depreciated.

Figure 20.3 illustrates actual changes in exchange rates since 1973. During the 1970s the German mark and Japanese yen appreciated substantially relative to the U.S. dollar. At the same time, the British pound depreciated. Hence German and Japanese goods got more expensive, while the dollar price of British goods fell. These trends were reversed in the early 1980s.

Also shown in Figure 20.3 is the trade-adjusted value of the U.S. dollar. This is the (weighted) average of all exchange rates for the dollar. In general, the dollar lost value in the late 1970s, but recovered in the early 1980s.

Market forces

Exchange rates change for the same reasons that any market price changes: either the underlying supply or demand (or both) has shifted. Among the more important sources of such shifts are:

- Relative income changes. If incomes are increasing faster in country *A* than in country *B*, consumers in *A* will tend to spend

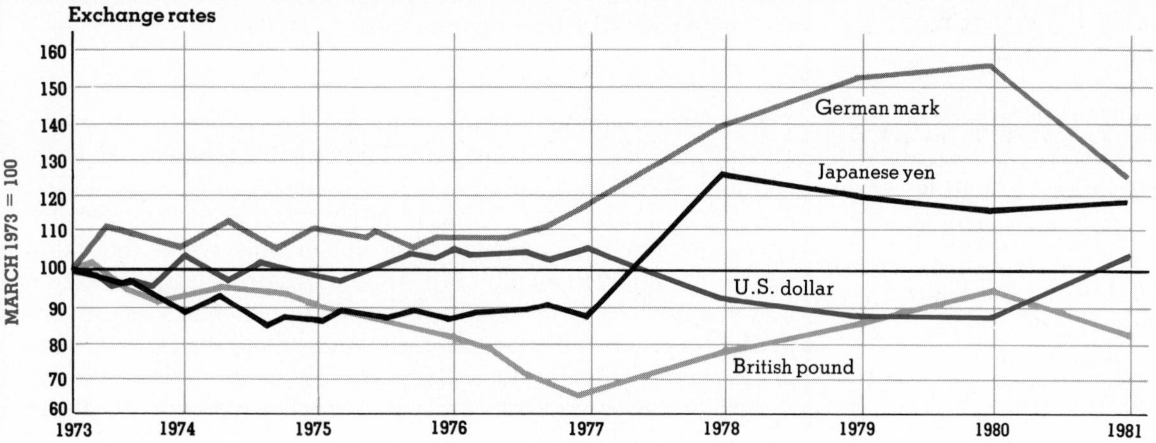

FIGURE 20.3 CHANGING EXCHANGE RATES

Since 1973, exchange rates have been flexible (not fixed). As a result, exchange rates have reflected differences between countries in unemployment, inflation, and economic growth. In general, a country's currency tends to appreciate if its rates of domestic inflation and growth are lower than those of its trading partners.

Source: *Economic Report of the President*, 1982.

more, thus increasing the demand for *B*'s exports and currency. *B*'s currency will appreciate.

- Relative price changes. If domestic prices are rising rapidly in country *A*, consumers will seek out lower-priced imports. The demand for *B*'s exports and currency will increase. *B*'s currency will appreciate.
- Changes in product availability. If country *A* experiences a disastrous wheat-crop failure, it will have to increase its food imports. *B*'s currency will appreciate.
- Relative interest-rate changes. If interest rates rise in country *A*, people in country *B* will want to move their deposits to *A*. Demand for *A*'s currency will rise and it will appreciate.
- Speculation. If speculators anticipate an increase in the price of *A*'s currency, for the above reasons or any other, they will begin buying it, thus pushing its price up. *A*'s currency will appreciate.

foreign-exchange markets: Places where foreign currencies are bought and sold.

All of these kinds of changes are taking place every minute of every day, thus keeping **foreign-exchange markets** active. Significant changes occur in currency values, however, only when several of these forces are moving in the same direction at the same time.

RESISTANCE TO EXCHANGE-RATE CHANGES

Exchange-rate changes are resisted by a broad assortment of microeconomic and macroeconomic interests. This resistance to exchange-rate changes is analogous to the resistance to trade flows based on comparative advantage and, in fact, typically derives from the same concerns (see Chapter 19).

Micro interests

The microeconomic resistance to foreign-exchange-rate changes arises from two general concerns. First, people who engage in international investment and trade flows like to have some basis for forecasting future costs, prices, and profits. Forecasts are always uncertain, but they are even less dependable when the value of money is subject to change. An American firm that invests $20 million in a tire factory in Brazil expects not only to make a profit on the production there, but also to return that profit to the United States. If the Brazilian cruzeiro depreciates sharply in the interim, however, the profits amassed in Brazil may dwindle to a mere trickle, or even a loss, when the cruzeiros are exchanged back into dollars. From this perspective, the uncertainty associated with fluctuating exchange rates is an unwanted and unnecessary burden.

Even when the direction of an exchange-rate move is certain, those who stand to lose from the change are prone to resist. ***A change in the price of a country's money automatically alters the price of all of its exports and imports.*** When the United States dollar appreciated in 1982, for example, the foreign price of all U.S. exports rose and the domestic price of all U.S. imports fell. U.S. importers were pleased, but U.S. exporters were upset.

In general, exporters are hostile to appreciations of their domestic currency, that is, exchange-rate movements that make their products more expensive in export markets. The workers associated with such exports are equally hostile to such exchange-rate movements, because their very jobs are at stake.

Even in the country whose currency becomes cheaper, there will be opposition to exchange-rate movements. When the U.S. dollar appreciates, Americans buy more foreign products. This increased U.S. demand for imports may drive up prices in other countries. In addition, foreign firms may take advantage of the reduced

The mighty dollar slams U.S. trade

Hobbled by an overvalued dollar, U.S. manufacturers and farmers are taking one of the worst drubbings they have ever suffered in world markets. Price-conscious foreign customers, battered by a business slowdown that is virtually worldwide, are turning elsewhere for the kind of manufactured goods—petrochemicals, aircraft, and computers, for example—that are the traditional source of U.S. competitive strength. And growers in countries with cheaper currencies are "just cutting us to pieces" in agricultural export markets, according to Burton M. Joseph, chairman of I.S. Joseph Co., a Minneapolis grain and agricultural-byproducts trader.

The declining ability of U.S. producers to compete was reflected in last year's U.S. trade deficit of $27 billion, the biggest since 1978. This year the deficit is expected to balloon to a record $35 billion, despite a sharp drop in the volume and cost of oil imports. Much of the trade erosion has occurred in manufactured goods, expected to show a surplus of only $8 billion this year, down from $19 billion in 1980.

The U.S. predicament is the mirror image of strong performances by West Germany and Japan, the chief industrial competitors of the U.S. Both have depressed currencies: The Deutschemark is currently worth 42¢, down from a 1978 peak of 58¢, and the yen is trading at 0.41¢, down from 0.56¢ in 1978. The competitive advantage of a cheap currency is spurring export booms in both nations. For Germany, a dramatic upswing in exports is expected to yield a trade surplus of $21 billion this year, up from $12 billion in 1981.

American competition by raising their prices. In either case, some inflation will result. The consumer's insistence that the government "do something" about rising prices may turn into a political force for "correcting" foreign-exchange rates.

Macro interests

Any microeconomic problem that becomes widespread enough can turn into a macroeconomic problem that requires major changes in domestic economic policies. Consider the problems confronting German industries after the 1978 appreciation of the deutsche mark. As we noted in Chapter 19 (Figure 19.1), West Germany exports a staggering 26 percent of the goods it produces. When German export industries are in trouble, the whole country is in trouble. Thus upward movements in the foreign price of German money threaten German economic planners and politicians with increasing unemployment. It is the kind of problem they could happily do without.

On the other side of foreign-exchange markets, a very different problem arises. As we have observed, a fall in the value of the U.S. dollar increases import prices, as well as the foreign demand for American products. Both of these factors contribute to inflationary pressures at home. That could present an awkward dilemma, especially if the administration is seeking to achieve full employment in a context of price stability.

In general, then, a country whose currency rises in value (appreciates) will have to contend with reduced aggregate demand and the threat of increased unemployment. On the other hand, a country whose currency falls in value (depreciates) will have to contend with increased aggregate demand and the threat of greater inflation. These problems are the core of macroeconomic (and political) resistance to exchange-rate movements.

POLICY ALTERNATIVES

Given the potential opposition to exchange-rate movements, governments may welcome institutional arrangements that can eliminate or restrain exchange-rate fluctuations. Governments have in fact embraced an assortment of measures to ensure exchange-rate stability. But such stability may itself give rise to undersirable micro- and macroeconomic effects, may even compound rather than solve economic problems. We will explore these issues as we review the major policy alternatives that countries confront.

Fixed exchange rates

gold standard: An agreement by countries to fix the price of their currencies in terms of gold; a mechanism for fixing exchange rates.

One way to eliminate fluctuations in exchange rates is to fix their value. To fix exchange rates, each country may simply proclaim that its currency is "worth" so much vis-à-vis that of other countries. The easiest way to do this is for each country to define the worth of its currency in terms of some common standard. The standard that has been most popular is gold. Under a **gold standard,** each country determines that its currency is worth so much gold. In so doing, it implicitly defines the worth of its currency in terms of all other currencies, which also have a fixed gold value. In 1944, for example, the major trading nations met at Bretton Woods, New Hampshire, and agreed that each currency was worth so much gold. The value of the U.S. dollar was defined as being equal to 0.0294 ounces of gold, while the British pound was defined as being worth 0.0823 ounces of gold. Thus the exchange rate between British pounds and U.S. dollars was effectively fixed at $1 = 0.357 pounds, or 1 pound = $2.80 (or $2.80/0.0823 = $1/0.0294).

BALANCE-OF-PAYMENTS PROBLEMS It is one thing to proclaim the worth of a country's currency; it is quite another to maintain the fixed rate of exchange. As we have observed, foreign-exchange rates are subject to continual and often unpredictable changes in supply and demand. Hence two countries that seek to stabilize their exchange rate at some fixed value are going to find it necessary either to eliminate or to compensate for such foreign-exchange market pressures.

Suppose that the exchange rate established by the United States and Great Britain is equal to e_1, as illustrated in Figure 20.4. As is apparent, that particular exchange rate is consistent with the then-prevailing demand and supply conditions in the foreign-exchange market (as indicated by curves D_1 and S_1).

Now suppose that Americans suddenly acquire a great taste for British ale and song and start spending more income on imported brew and records. As U.S. purchases of British goods increase, a U.S. **trade deficit** is likely to emerge: we will be spending more on their goods than they are spending on ours.

trade deficit: The amount by which the value of imports exceeds the value of exports in a given time period.

The emergence of a trade deficit implies a net increase in our demand for British currency, as reflected in the *shift* from D_1 to D_2 in Figure 20.4. Were exchange rates allowed to respond to market influences, the dollar price of a British pound would clearly rise, in this case to the value of e_2. But we have already noted that it is official policy to maintain the exchange rate at e_1. Unfortunately, at e_1 American consumers want to buy more pounds (q_D) than the British are willing to supply (q_S). The difference between the quantity de-

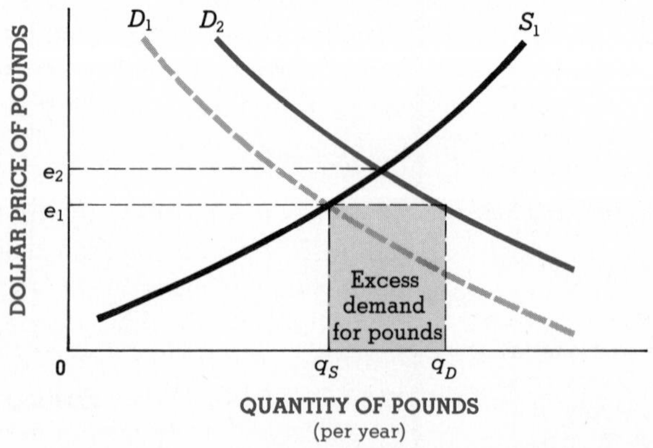

FIGURE 20.4 FIXED RATES AND MARKET IMBALANCE

If exchange rates are fixed, they cannot adjust to changes in market supply and demand. Suppose the exchange rate is initially fixed at e_1. When the demand for British pounds increases (shifts to the right), an excess demand for pounds emerges. More pounds are demanded (q_D) at the rate e_1 than are supplied (q_S).

market shortage: The amount by which the quantity demanded exceeds the quantity supplied at a given price; excess demand.

balance-of-payments deficit: An excess demand for foreign currency at current exchange rates.

balance-of-payments surplus: An excess demand for domestic currency at current exchange rates.

foreign-exchange reserves: Holdings of foreign exchange by official government agencies, usually the central bank or treasury.

manded and that supplied in the market at the rate e_1 represents a **market shortage** of British pounds.

The excess demand for pounds represents, first, a potential **balance-of-payments deficit** for the United States, because it implies that more dollars are flowing out of the country than into it. Second, it represents a **balance-of-payments surplus** for England, because its outward flow of pounds is less than its incoming flow. Both kinds of imbalance can cause real problems for policy makers.

Basically, there are only two solutions to balance-of-payments problems brought about by the attempt to fix exchange rates:

- Allow exchange rates to rise to e_2 (Figure 20.4), thereby eliminating the excess demand for pounds.
- Alter market supply or demand so that they intersect at the fixed rate e_1.

Since fixed exchange rates were the initial objective of policy, only the second alternative is of immediate interest.

THE NEED FOR RESERVES One way to alter market conditions would be for someone simply to supply British pounds to American consumers. The U.S. Treasury could have accumulated a reserve of foreign exchange at times when market conditions resulted in an excess supply of rather than an excess demand for British pounds. As we have noted, the market supply of and demand for foreign exchange are subject to frequent shifts. Although there is an excess demand for pounds today, there may have been an excess supply yesterday. Such a surplus would have enabled the U.S. Treasury to accumulate reserves. By selling some of those reserves now, the Treasury could help to stabilize market conditions at the officially established exchange rate. The sale of accumulated British pounds **(foreign-exchange reserves)** by the U.S. Treasury is illustrated in Figure 20.5 by the rightward shift of the pound supply curve.

Although foreign-exchange reserves can be used to fix exchange rates, such reserves may not be adequate when they are needed. Indeed, Figure 20.6 should be testimony enough to the fact that today's deficit is not always offset by tomorrow's surplus. One of the princi-

FIGURE 20.5 THE IMPACT OF MONETARY INTERVENTION

If the U.S. Treasury holds reserves of British pounds, it can use them to buy U.S. dollars in foreign-exchange markets. As it does so, the supply of pounds will shift to the right, to S_2, thereby maintaining the desired exchange rate, e_1. The Bank of England could bring about the same result by offering to buy U.S. dollars with pounds.

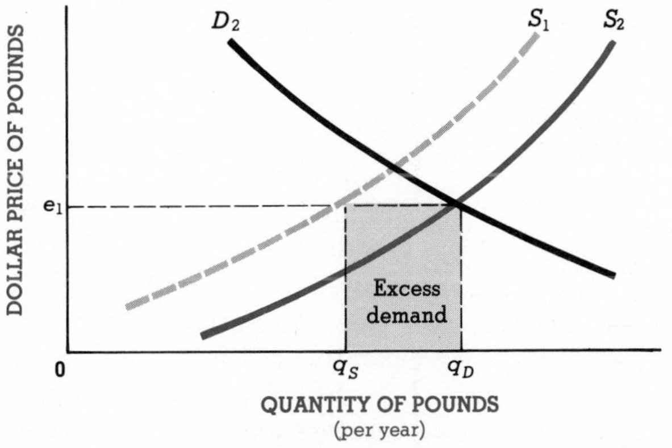

FIGURE 20.6 THE U.S. BALANCE OF PAYMENTS, 1950–73

The United States had a balance-of-payments deficit for 22 consecutive years. During this period, the foreign-exchange reserves of the U.S. Treasury were sharply reduced. Fixed exchange rates were maintained by the willingness of foreign countries to accumulate large reserves of U.S. dollars. However, neither the Treasury's reserves nor foreigners' willingness to accumulate dollars were unlimited. In 1973, fixed exchange rates were abandoned.

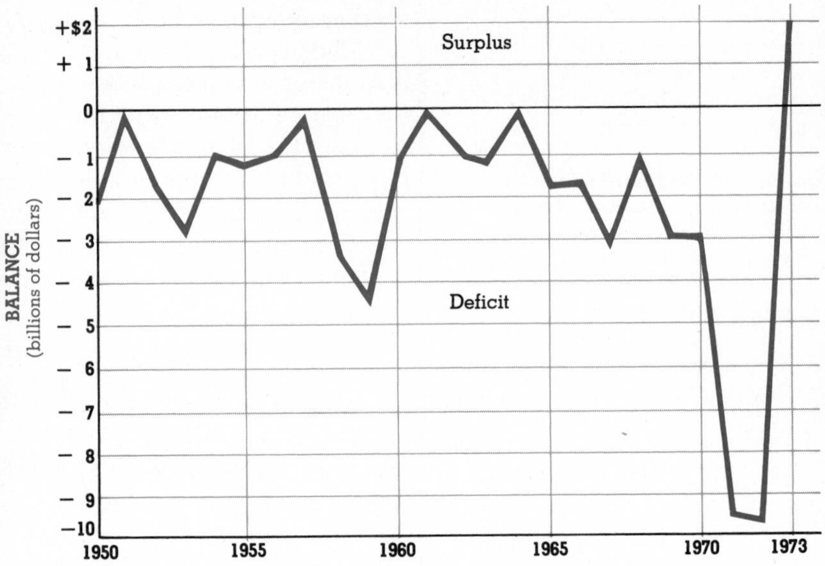

pal reasons that fixed exchange rates have not lived up to their expectations is that the United States had balance-of-payments deficits for 22 consecutive years. This long-term deficit overwhelmed our stock of foreign-exchange reserves and led to a search for other measures to balance foreign-exchange markets at officially fixed rates.

THE ROLE OF GOLD Gold reserves represent a potential substitute for foreign-exchange reserves. As long as each country's money has a value defined in terms of gold and is available at that price, we can use gold to buy British pounds, thereby restocking our foreign-exchange reserves. Or we can simply use the gold to purchase U.S. dollars in foreign-exchange markets. In either case, the exchange value of the dollar will tend to rise. However, we must have **gold reserves** available for this purpose. Unfortunately, the continuing U.S. balance-of-payments deficits recorded in Figure 20.6 exceeded even the hoards of gold buried under Fort Knox. As a consequence, our gold reserves lost their credibility as a potential "guarantee" of fixed exchange rates.

gold reserves: Stocks of gold held by a government to purchase foreign exchange.

DOMESTIC ADJUSTMENTS The supply and demand for foreign exchange can also be shifted by changes in basic fiscal, monetary, or trade policies. We could eliminate the excess demand for pounds (Figure 20.6), for example, by imposing quotas and tariffs on British goods. Such trade restrictions would reduce British imports to the United States and thus the demand for British pounds. Such restrictions on international trade, however, violate the principle of comparative advantage and thus reduce total world output.

Fiscal policy provides another way out of the imbalance. An increase in U.S. income-tax rates will reduce disposable income and have a negative effect on the demand for all goods, including imports. A reduction in government spending will have similar effects. In general, deflationary (or restrictive) fiscal policies can help correct a balance-of-payments deficit by lowering domestic incomes and thus import demands.

Monetary policies in a deficit country could follow the same restrictive course. A reduction in the money supply will tend to raise interest rates and slow aggregate spending. The balance of payments will be benefited in two ways. The slowdown in spending will help to reduce import demands and may induce domestic producers to focus more attention on export possibilities. In addition, the higher

BALANCE-OF-PAYMENTS ACCOUNTING

Most foreign-exchange transactions are related to imports and exports of goods and services. But foreign-exchange demands and supplies arise from a variety of other transactions as well. As a result, several different "balances" are computed for foreign-exchange markets.

TRADE BALANCE
equals merchandise exports minus merchandise imports.

CURRENT-ACCOUNT BALANCE
equals trade balance,
plus receipts from foreign travelers in the U.S. and receipts from U.S. investments abroad
less travel expenditures abroad and income payments to foreigners for their investments in the U.S.

CAPITAL-ACCOUNT BALANCE
equals foreign investment in the U.S. and other private capital inflow
less U.S. direct investment abroad and other private capital outflow.

Under a system of fixed exchange rates, the "balance of payments" equaled the sum of the current- and capital-account balances. If current and capital outflows exceeded inflows, a "deficit" existed in the balance of payments. This deficit (imbalance) between the quantities of foreign exchange demanded and supplied was "paid" for with official foreign-exchange reserves. The deficit country would transfer foreign exchange or gold to surplus countries.

Flexible exchange rates eliminate any residual "balance of payments." If foreigners demand more dollars than we supply, the price of dollars will rise. As a result of such exchange-rate movements, the quantity of dollars supplied and demanded is brought into equality. No overall residual "balance" remains; official "payments" are not required.

In fact, most countries still intervene in foreign-exchange markets to limit exchange-rate movements. The value of such official purchases and sales of foreign exchange are often regarded as an approximation to the "balance of payments." The "official-settlements balance" equals the change in foreign-exchange reserves held by the government.

interest rates may induce international investors to move some of their funds out of other countries into the deficit country. Such moves will provide immediate relief to the payments imbalance.

A surplus country wishing to help in solving the balance-of-payments problem could pursue expansionary—even inflationary—fiscal and monetary policies. By putting more money into the hands of its consumers, a surplus country could stimulate the demand for imports. As prices rose at home, the relative attractiveness of imports would be increased. Moreover, any inflation at home would reduce the competitiveness of exports, thereby helping to restrain the inflow of foreign demand. Taken together, such efforts would clearly help to reverse an international-payments imbalance.[6]

Even though domestic economic adjustments are capable of improving balance-of-payments problems, there are obvious costs involved, particularly in terms of full employment and price stability. In effect, ***domestic adjustments to payments imbalances require a deficit country to forsake full employment and a surplus country to forsake price stability.*** These are sacrifices few countries are willing to make. Accordingly, balance-of-payments problems typically lead to protracted arguments about who should adjust, repeated hopes that the imbalances will go away, and frequent "crises" ending in exchange-rate adjustments. It is important to realize that foreign-exchange imbalances brought about by fixed exchange rates must be overcome with either abundant supplies of foreign-exchange reserves or deliberate changes in fiscal, monetary, or trade policies. The accompanying news clipping on Mexico's

[6] Before 1930, not only were foreign-exchange rates fixed, but domestic monetary supplies were tied to gold stocks as well. Countries experiencing a balance-of-payments deficit were thus forced to contract their money supply and countries experiencing a payments surplus were forced to expand their money supply by a set amount. Monetary authorities were powerless to control domestic money supplies except by erecting barriers to trade. The system was abandoned when the world economy collapsed into the Great Depression.

Mexican Peso Plunges 28% Against Dollar

Nation's Economic Troubles Touch Off the Decision to Let Currency Float

MEXICO CITY—The Mexican peso dropped 28% against the U.S. dollar yesterday following the Mexican government's decision late Wednesday to let the currency float.

Shortly before the devaluation, the peso traded at about 27 to the dollar, and by late trading yesterday it had fallen to about 37.70 to the dollar, or about 2.6 cents. Economists said it was too early to tell where the peso would eventually settle. . . .

Apparently, capital flight forced the government to act, as Mexicans are flocking to the U.S. to travel and invest. The government has tried to stop the wave—by exhorting Mexicans to invest at home, raising passport fees, and prohibiting advertisements by U.S. real estate developers—but it wasn't enough.

Last year, Mexico had an $11.5 billion deficit in its current international payments account, which includes trade in goods and services as well as certain unilateral transfers. That was almost twice as wide as the $6.6 billion deficit of 1980.

"The government had little choice," said a Mexican banker. "Its reserves were getting low."

The peso float should bring down Mexican interest rates. To keep money in pesos, the government has kept interest rates at more than 20 percentage points above the interest on dollar accounts. But that policy was beginning to choke investment. The devaluation should allow the government to bring interest rates down to a level that will spur local investment.

—Lawrence Rout

1982 devaluation indicates what happens when these domestic adjustments are exhausted.

Flexible exchange rates

flexible exchange rates: A system in which exchange rates are permitted to vary with market supply and demand conditions.

Balance-of-payments problems would not arise in the first place, of course, if exchange rates were allowed to respond to market forces. Under a system of **flexible exchange rates** (often called "floating" exchange rates), the exchange rate moves up or down to choke off any excess supply of or demand for foreign exchange. Notice again in Figure 20.4 that the exchange-rate move from e_1 to e_2 prevents any excess demand from emerging. With flexible exchange rates, the quantity of foreign exchange demanded always equals the quantity supplied, and there is no imbalance. For the same reason, there is no need for foreign-exchange reserves.

Although flexible exchange rates eliminate balance-of-payments and foreign-exchange-reserves problems, they do not solve all of a country's international trade problems. ***Exchange-rate movements associated with flexible rates alter relative prices and may disrupt import and export flows.*** As we noted before, depreciation of the dollar raises the price of all imported goods. The price increases may contribute to domestic, cost-push inflation. Also, domestic businesses that sell imported goods or use them as production inputs may suffer sales losses. On the other hand, appreciation of the dollar raises the foreign price of U.S. goods and reduces the sales of American exporters. Hence someone is always hurt (and others are helped) by exchange-rate movements. The resistance to flexible exchange rates originates in these potential losses. Such resistance creates pressure for some form of official intervention in foreign-exchange markets.

"Damn it! How can I relax, knowing that out there, somewhere, somehow, someone's attacking the dollar?"

The United States and its major trading partners abandoned fixed exchange rates in 1973. Although exchange rates are now able to fluctuate freely, it should not be assumed that they necessarily go through wild gyrations. On the contrary, experience with flexible rates since 1973 suggests that some semblance of stability is possible even when exchange rates are free to change in response to market forces. In 1979 the Council of Economic Advisers concluded that the first five years of flexible exchange rates had worked reasonably well. Flexible rates had been particularly successful "in permitting the industrial economies to absorb shocks that were unprecedented in the post-war period."[7]

SPECULATION One force that often helps to maintain stability in a flexible-exchange-rate system is speculation. Speculators often counteract short-term changes in foreign-exchange supply and demand. If an exchange rate temporarily rises above its long-term equilibrium, speculators will move in to sell foreign exchange. By selling at high prices and later buying at lower prices, speculators hope to make a profit. In the process, they also help to stabilize foreign-exchange rates.

Speculation is not always stabilizing, however. Speculators may not correctly gauge the long-term equilibrium. Instead, they may move "with the market" and help push exchange rates far out of kilter. This kind of destabilizing speculation sharply lowered the international value of the U.S. dollar in 1978, forcing the Carter administration to intervene in foreign-exchange markets, borrowing foreign currencies to buy U.S. dollars.

Managed exchange rates

managed exchange rates: A system in which governments intervene in foreign-exchange markets to limit but not eliminate exchange-rate fluctuations; "dirty floats."

Governments can intervene in foreign-exchange markets without completely fixing exchange rates. That is to say, they may buy and sell foreign exchange for the purpose of narrowing rather than eliminating exchange-rate movements. Such limited intervention in foreign-exchange rates is referred to as **managed exchange rates,** or, more popularly, "dirty floats."

The basic objective of exchange-rate management is to provide the stabilizing force that some people hope private speculators will provide. In this regard, governments use their foreign-exchange reserves to buy domestic currency when it is depreciating too much. Or they will buy foreign exchange if domestic currency is appreciating too much. From this perspective, exchange-rate management appears as a fail-safe system for the private market. Unfortunately, the motivation for official intervention is sometimes suspect. Private speculators buy and sell foreign exchange for the sole purpose of making money. But government sales and purchases may be motivated by other considerations. A falling exchange rate increases the competitive advantage of a country's exports. A rising exchange rate makes international investment less expensive. Hence a country's efforts to "manage" exchange-rate movements may arouse suspicion and outright hostility in its trading partners.

[7] *Economic Report of the President,* 1979, p. 149.

Accordingly, although managed exchange rates would seem to be an ideal compromise between fixed rates and flexible rates, they can work only when some acceptable "rules of the game" and a condition of mutual trust have been established. As Sherman Maisel, a former governor of the Federal Reserve Board, has put it: "Monetary systems are based on credit and faith: if these are lacking a . . . crisis occurs."[8]

SUMMARY

- Money serves the same purposes in international trade as it does in the domestic economy—namely, to facilitate productive specialization and market exchanges. The basic problem of international finance is to create acceptable standards of value from the various currencies maintained by separate countries.
- Exchange rates are the basic mechanism for translating the value of one national currency into the equivalent value of another. Thus an exchange rate of $1 = DM3 means that one dollar is worth three German marks and can be purchased at that price in foreign-exchange markets.
- Foreign currencies have value because they can be used to acquire goods and resources from other countries. Accordingly, the supply of and demand for foreign currency reflect the demands for imports and exports, for international investment, and for overseas activities of governments.
- The equilibrium exchange rate is subject to any and all shifts of supply and demand for foreign exchange. If the relative incomes, relative prices, or relative interest rates of two countries change, their respective demands for foreign exchange will be affected. A depreciation is a change in market exchange rates that makes one country's currency cheaper in terms of another currency. An appreciation is the opposite kind of change.
- Changes in exchange rates are often resisted. Producers of export goods do not want their currencies to rise in value (appreciate), because the foreign price of exports will then rise and sales will fall. Importers and people who travel dislike it when their currencies fall in value (depreciate) because imports and foreign travel become more expensive.
- Under a system of fixed exchange rates, changes in the supply and demand for foreign exchange cannot be expressed in exchange-rate movements. Instead, such shifts will be reflected in excess demand for or excess supply of foreign exchange. Such market imbalances are referred to as balance-of-payments deficits or surpluses.
- To maintain fixed exchange rates, monetary authorities must enter the market to buy and sell foreign exchange. In order to do so, deficit countries must have foreign-exchange reserves. In the absence of sufficient reserves, a country can maintain fixed exchange rates only if it is willing to alter basic fiscal, monetary, or trade policies.

[8] Sherman Maisel, *Managing the Dollar* (New York: W. W. Norton, 1973), p. 196.

■ Flexible exchange rates eliminate balance-of-payments problems and the crises that accompany them. But complete flexibility can lead to excessive changes. To avoid this contingency, many countries prefer to adopt managed exchange rates—that is, rates determined by the market but subject to government intervention.

Terms to remember

Define the following terms:

exchange rate
supply of foreign exchange
demand for foreign exchange
law of demand
equilibrium price
shift in demand
depreciation
appreciation
foreign-exchange markets
gold standard
trade deficit
market shortage
balance-of-payments deficit
balance-of-payments surplus
foreign-exchange reserves
gold reserves
flexible exchange rates
managed exchange rates

Questions for discussion

1. How would rapid inflation in Mexico alter our demands for travel to Mexico and for Mexican imports? Does it make any difference whether the exchange rate between pesos and dollars is fixed or flexible?

2. Under what conditions would a country welcome a balance-of-payments deficit? When would it *not* want a deficit?

3. In what sense do fixed exchange rates permit a country to "export its inflation"?

4. In 1979 U.S. exports rose significantly while the value of imports rose slowly. How did the dollar depreciation contribute to this development?

5. Under a managed exchange-rate system, exchange rates can vary by small degrees. When should more significant rate changes be permitted or encouraged?

Problem

The following schedules summarize the supply and demand for trifflings, the national currency of Tricoli.

Triffling price (in U.S. dollars)	*0*	*$4*	*$8*	*$12*	*$16*	*$20*	*$24*
Quantity demanded (per year)	**40**	**38**	**36**	**34**	**32**	**30**	**28**
Quantity supplied (per year)	**1**	**11**	**21**	**31**	**41**	**51**	**61**

Using the above schedules:

(a) Graph the supply and demand curves.

(b) Determine the equilibrium exchange rate.

(c) Determine the size of the excess supply or excess demand that would exist if the Tricolian government fixed the exchange rate at $22 = 1 triffling.

(d) How might this imbalance be remedied?

GLOSSARY

Numbers in parentheses indicate the chapters in which the definitions appear.

absolute advantage: The ability of a country to produce a specific good with fewer resources (per unit of output) than other countries. (19)

adjustment assistance: Compensation to market participants for losses imposed by international trade. (19)

appreciation: A rise in the price of one currency relative to another. (20)

average fixed cost (*AFC*): Total fixed cost divided by the quantity produced in a given time period. (5)

average total cost (*ATC*): Total cost divided by the quantity produced in a given time period. (5) (7) (8)

average variable cost (*AVC*): Total variable cost divided by the quantity produced in a given time period. (5)

balance-of-payments deficit: An excess demand for foreign currency at current exchange rates (20)

balance-of-payments surplus: An excess demand for domestic currency at current exchange rates. (20)

barriers to entry: Obstacles that make it difficult or impossible for would-be producers to enter a particular market (e.g., patents). (7) (8) (10)

bilateral monopoly: A market with only one buyer (a monopsonist) and one seller (a monopolist). (13)

bracket creep: The movement of taxpayers into higher tax brackets (rates) as nominal incomes grow. (3)

categorical grants: Federal grants to state and local governments for specific expenditure purposes. (3)

ceteris paribus: The assumption of "everything else being equal," of nothing else changing. (1) (2) (4) (6)

collective bargaining: Direct negotiations between employers and unions to determine labor-market outcomes. (13)

collusion: Explicit agreements among producers to limit competition among them. (9)

comparative advantage: The ability of a country to produce a specific good at a lower opportunity cost than its trading partners. (19)

competitive firm: A firm without market power, with no ability to alter the market price of the goods it produces. (6) (7)

complementary goods: Goods frequently consumed in combination; when the price of good X rises, the quantity of good Y demanded falls (*ceteris paribus*). (4)

concentration ratio: The proportion of total industry output produced by the largest firms (usually the four largest). (10)

conglomerate: A firm that produces significant quantities of output in several industries. (10)

constant returns to scale: Increases in plant size do not affect minimum average cost; minimum per unit costs are identical for small plants and large plants. (5)

consumption possibilities: The alternative combinations of goods and services that a country could consume in a given time period. (19)

cost efficiency: The amount of output associated with an additional dollar spent on input; the *MPP* of an input divided by its price (cost). (12) (18)

cyclical unemployment: Unemployment attributable to a lack of job vacancies; unemployment that results from an inadequate level of aggregate demand. (17)

demand: The ability and willingness to buy specific quantities of a good at alternative prices in a given time period (*ceteris paribus*). (2)

demand curve: A curve describing the quantities of a good a consumer is willing and able to buy at alternative prices in a given time period (*ceteris paribus*). (2)

demand for foreign exchange: The quantities of foreign currency demanded in a given time period at alternative exchange rates (*ceteris paribus*). (20)

demand for labor: The quantities of labor employers are willing and able to hire at alternative wage rates in a given time period (*ceteris paribus*). (12) (13)

demand schedule: A table showing the quantities of a good a consumer is willing and able to buy at alternative prices in a given time period (*ceteris paribus*). (2) (4)

depreciation (tax): The tax deduction allowed for the cost of using capital and equipment in production. (6)

depreciation (currency): A fall in the price of one currency relative to another. (20)

derived demand: The demand for labor and other factors of production results from (depends on) the demand for final goods and services produced by these factors. (12)

discrimination: Inequality of treatment; denial of opportunity on the basis of characteristics unrelated to performance. (18)

economic cost: The value of all resources used to produce a good or service; opportunity cost. (5) (6) (14)

economic growth: An increase in output (real GNP); an expansion of production possibilities. (1)

economic profit: The difference between total revenues and total economic costs. (6) (7) (9) (14)

economics: The study of how best to allocate scarce resources among competing uses. (1)

economies of scale: Reductions in average costs that come about through increases in the size (scale) of plant and equipment. (5) (8)

efficiency: Maximum output of a good from the resources used in production. (5) (7)

efficiency decision: The choice of a production process for any given rate of output. (12) (16)

embargo: A prohibition on exports or imports. (19)

emission charge: A fee imposed on polluters, based on the quantity of pollution. (16)

equilibrium price: The price at which the quantity of a good demanded in a given time period equals the quantity supplied. (2) (7) (19) (20)

equilibrium wage: The wage rate at which the quantity of labor supplied in a given time period equals the quantity of labor demanded. (13)

exchange rate: The price of one country's currency, expressed in terms of another's; the domestic price of a foreign currency. (20)

exports: Goods and services sold to foreign buyers. (19)

externalities: Costs (or benefits) of a market activity borne by a third party; the difference between the social and private costs (benefits) of a market activity. (1) (3) (16)

factor market: Any place where factors of production (e.g., land, labor, capital) are bought and sold. (2)

factor share: The proportion of total income received by a factor of production. (14) (15)

factors of production: Resource inputs used to produce goods and services; for example, land, labor, capital. (1) (5)

fiscal year (FY): The twelve-month period used for government accounting purposes; begins October 1 and ends September 30. (3)

fixed costs: Costs of production that do not change when the rate of output is altered; for example, the cost of basic plant and equipment. (5) (14)

flexible exchange rates: A system in which exchange rates are permitted to vary with market supply and demand conditions. (20)

foreign-exchange markets: Places where foreign currencies are bought and sold. (20)

foreign-exchange reserves: Holdings of foreign exchange by official government agencies, usually the central bank or treasury. (20)

free rider: An individual who reaps direct benefits from someone else's purchase (consumption) of a public good. (3)

functional distribution of income: The division of income among factors of production, especially between capital and labor. (15)

gold reserves: Stocks of gold held by a government to purchase foreign exchange. (20)

gold standard: An agreement by countries to fix the price of their currencies in terms of gold; a mechanism for fixing exchange rates. (20)

human capital: The bundle of skills an individual possesses. (17) (18)

imports: Goods and services purchased from foreign sources. (19)

income effect of wages: An increased wage rate allows a person to reduce hours worked without losing income. (11)

income elasticity of demand: The percentage change in quantity demanded divided by the percentage change in income. (7)

income share: The proportion of total income received by a particular group. (15)

income transfers: Payments to individuals for which no current goods or services are exchanged; for example, social security, welfare, and unemployment benefits. (3) (17)

in-kind transfers: Direct transfers of goods and services rather than cash; for example, food stamps and Medicaid. (17)

interest: Payments made for the use of borrowed money. (3)

interest rate: The price paid for the use of money. (14)

intermediate goods: Goods or services purchased for use as input in the production of final goods or services. (3)

investment decision: The decision to build, buy, or lease plant and equipment to start or expand a business. (6) (8) (12)

labor-force participant: Someone who is either employed for pay or actively seeking paid employment. (17)

labor supply: The willingness and ability to work specific amounts of time at alternative wage rates in a given time period; the quantities of labor that would be supplied at alternative wage rates (*ceteris paribus*). (11) (13)

labor-supply curve: A curve depicting the quantities of labor supplied (offered) in a given time period at alternative wage rates (*ceteris paribus*). (11)

laissez faire: The doctrine of "leave it alone," of nonintervention by governments in the market mechanism. (2)

law of demand: The quantity of a good demanded in a given time period increases as its price falls (*ceteris paribus*). (4) (6) (9) (12) (20)

law of diminishing marginal utility: The marginal utility of a good declines as more of it is consumed in a given time period. (4) (11)

law of diminishing returns: The marginal physical product of a variable factor declines as more of it is employed with a given quantity of other (fixed) inputs. (5) (6) (12)

law of increasing opportunity costs: In order to get more of any good in a given time period, society must sacrifice ever-increasing amounts of other goods. (1)

long run: A period of time long enough for all inputs to be varied (no fixed costs). (5) (6)

long-run competitive equilibrium: $p = MC =$ minimum ATC. (7)

Lorenz curve: A graphic illustration of the cumulative size distribution of income; contrasts complete equality with the actual distribution of income. (15)

macroeconomics: The study of aggregate economic behavior, of the economy as a whole. (1)

managed exchange rates: A system in which governments intervene in foreign-exchange markets to limit but not eliminate exchange-rate fluctuations; "dirty floats." (20)

marginal cost: The increase in total cost associated with a one-unit increase in production. (5) (6) (7) (14)

marginal cost of labor: The change in total wage costs that results from a one-unit increase in the quantity of labor employed. (13)

marginal cost pricing: The offer (supply) of goods at prices equal to their marginal cost. (7) (8) (9)

marginal physical product (*MPP*): The change in total output associated with one additional unit of input. (5) (12)

marginal productivity: The change in total output that results from employment of one additional unit of input (e.g., one more worker). (17)

marginal revenue: The change in total revenue that results from a one-unit increase in the quantity sold. (6) (8) (9)

marginal revenue product (*MRP*): The change in total revenue associated with one additional unit of input. (12) (13) (14) (18)

marginal tax rate: The tax rate imposed on the last (marginal) dollar of income. (15) (17)

marginal utility: The change in total utility obtained from an additional (marginal) unit of a good or service consumed. (4)

marginal utility of labor: The change in total utility derived from another hour's work; includes the utility associated with the extra goods and services that can be purchased with another hour's wages as well as any intrinsic satisfaction derived from additional labor. (11) (17)

marginal wage: The change in total wages paid associated with a one-unit increase in the quantity of labor employed. (13)

market: Any place where individuals buy or sell resources or products. (2)

market demand: The total quantities of a good or service people are willing and able to buy at alternative prices in a given time period; the sum of individual demands. (2)

market economy: An economy that relies on markets for basic decisions about WHAT to produce, HOW to produce it, and FOR WHOM to produce. (2)

market mechanism: The use of market prices and sales to signal desired outputs (or resource allocations). (1) (2) (3) (7) (11)

market power: The ability to alter the market price of a good or service. (7) (8) (13)

market share: The percentage of total market output produced by a single firm. (9) (10)

market shortage: The amount by which the quantity demanded exceeds the quantity supplied at a given price; excess demand. (2) (19)

market supply: The total quantities of a good that sellers are willing and able to sell at alternative prices in a given time period (*ceteris paribus*); the combined willingness of all market suppliers to sell. (2) (7)

market surplus: The amount by which the quantity supplied exceeds the quantity demanded at a given price; excess supply. (2) (7)

microeconomics: The study of individual behavior in the economy, of the components of the larger economy. (1)

mixed economy: An economy that uses both market and nonmarket signals to allocate goods and resources. (1)

monopolistic competition: A market in which many firms produce similar goods or services, but each maintains some independent control of its own price. (9)

monopoly: A firm that produces the entire market supply of a particular good or service. (7) (8)

monopsony: A market in which there is only one buyer. (13)

natural monopoly: An industry in which one firm can achieve economies of scale over the entire range of market supply. (8)

oligopoly: A market in which a few firms produce all or most of the market supply of a particular good or service. (9) (10)

opportunity cost: The most desired goods or services that are forgone in order to obtain something else. (1) (2) (3) (4) (5) (7) (14) (16) (19)

opportunity wage: The highest wage an individual would earn in his or her best alternative job. (12)

optimal consumption: The mix of consumer purchases that maximizes the utility attainable from available income. (4)

optimal rate of pollution: The rate of pollution that occurs when the marginal social benefit of pollution control equals its marginal social cost. (16)

optimal work effort: That amount of work at which the marginal utility of an hour's labor is just equal to the marginal utility of another hour's leisure. (11)

orderly marketing agreement (OMA): An agreement to reduce the volume of trade in a specific good; a "voluntary" quota. (19)

perfectly competitive market: A market in which no buyer or seller has market power. (7)

personal income (*PI*): Income received by households before payment of personal taxes. (15)

predatory price cutting: Temporary price reductions designed to alter market shares or drive out competition. (10)

price discrimination: The sale of an identical good at different prices to different consumers by a single seller. (8)

price elasticity of demand: The percentage change in quantity demanded divided by the percentage change in price. (4) (6) (7) (8)

price elasticity of supply: The percentage change in quantity supplied divided by the percentage change in price. (14)

price fixing: Explicit agreements among producers regarding the price(s) at which a good is to be sold. (10)

price leadership: An oligopolistic pricing pattern that allows one firm to establish the (market) price for all firms in the industry. (9) (10)

price costs: The costs of an economic activity directly borne by the immediate producer or consumer (excluding externalities). (16)

product differentiation: Features that make one product appear different from competing products in the same market. (9) (10)

product market: Any place where finished goods and services (products) are bought and sold. (2)

production decision: The selection of the short-run rate of output (with existing plant and equipment). (6) (7) (8) (12) (16)

production function: A technological relation expressing the maximum quantity of a good attainable from different combinations of factor inputs. (5)

production possibilities: The alternative combinations of final goods and services that could be produced in a given time period with all available resources and technology. (1) (3) (7) (19)

production process: A specific combination of resources used to produce a good or service. (12)

productivity: Output per unit of input; for example, output per labor hour. (5)

profit: The difference between total revenue and total cost. (6) (See also economic profit.)

profit-maximization rule: Produce at that rate of output where marginal revenue equals marginal cost. (6) (8) (9)

profit per unit: Total profit divided by the quantity produced in a given time period; price minus average total cost. (7)

progressive tax: A tax system in which tax rates rise as incomes rise. (3) (15)

public good: A good or service whose consumption by one person does not exclude consumption by others. (3)

quantity demanded: The amount of a product a consumer is willing and able to buy at a specific price in a given time period (*ceteris paribus*). (4) (9)

quantity supplied: The amount of a product offered for sale at a specific price during a given time period (*ceteris paribus*). (6)

quota: A limit on the quantity of a good that may be imported in a given time period. (19)

regressive tax: A tax system in which tax rates fall as incomes rise. (3) (15)

rent: Payments to a factor of production in excess of the amount required to call forth a given quantity of the factor. (14)

revenue sharing: Federal aid to state and local governments without stringent restrictions on its use. (3)

shift in demand: A change in the quantity demanded at any (every) given price. (2) (4) (12) (20)

shift of supply: A change in the quantity supplied at any (every) given price. (7)

short run: The period in which the quantity (and quality) of some inputs is fixed, that is, cannot be changed. (5) (6)

short-run competitive equilibrium: $p = MC$. (7)

shutdown point: That rate of output where *AVC* equals price. (6)

size distribution of income: The way total personal income is divided up among households or income classes. (15)

social costs: The full resource costs of an economic activity, including externalities. (16)

substitute goods: Goods that substitute for each other; when the price of good X rises, the quantity of good Y demanded increases (*ceteris paribus*). (4)

substitution effect of wages: An increased wage rate raises the marginal utility of an hour's labor, thereby encouraging people to work more hours (to substitute labor for leisure). (11)

supply: The ability and willingness to sell (produce) specific quantities of a good at alternative prices in a given time period (*ceteris paribus*). (2) (5) (6) (13)

supply curve: A curve describing the quantities of a good a producer is willing and able to sell (produce) at alternative prices in a given time period (*ceteris paribus*). (6)

supply of foreign exchange: The quantities of foreign currency supplied (offered) in a given time period at alternative exchange rates (*ceteris paribus*). (20)

tariff: A tax (duty) imposed on imported goods. (19)

terms of trade: The rate at which goods are exchanged; the amount of good *A* given up for good *B* in trade. (19)

total cost: The market value of all resources used to produce a good or service. (5) (6)

total revenue: The price of a product multiplied by the quantity sold in a given time period; $b \times q$. (4) (6)

total utility: The amount of satisfaction obtained from entire consumption of a product. (4)

trade deficit: The amount by which the value of imports exceeds the value of exports in a given time period. (19) (20)

trade surplus: The amount by which the value of exports exceeds the value of imports in a given time period. (19)

union shop: An employment setting in which all workers must join the union within 30 days after being employed. (13)

unionization ratio: The percentage of the labor force belonging to a union. (13)

user charge: Fee paid for the use of a public-sector good or service. (3)

utility: The pleasure or satisfaction obtained from a good or service. (4) (11)

variable costs: Costs of production that change when the rate of output is altered; for example, labor and material costs. (5) (6)

wage rate: The amount of money paid for an hour's work; the price of labor. (11)

INDEX

ABOUT THE AUTHOR

Dr. Bradley Schiller has over a decade's experience teaching introductory economics, at American University, the University of California (Berkeley and Santa Cruz), and the University of Maryland. Dr. Schiller's unique contribution to teaching is his ability to relate basic principles to current socioeconomic problems, institutions, and public policy decisions. This perspective is evident throughout *The Economy Today*.

Dr. Schiller derives this policy focus from his extensive experience as a Washington consultant. He has been a consultant to most major federal agencies, many congressional committees, and political candidates. In addition, he has evaluated scores of government programs and helped design others. His studies of discrimination, employment and training programs, reindustrialization, pensions, welfare, and Social Security have appeared and been cited in both professional journals and popular media. In addition, Dr. Schiller has explained and evaluated "Reagan Economics" at numerous seminars and on radio shows.

Dr. Schiller received his Ph.D. from Harvard in 1969. His B.A. degree, with great distinction, was completed at the University of California (Berkeley) in 1965. He is now a professor of economics in the School of Government and Public Administration at The American University. In that capacity he is teaching basic economics to government workers, a job he hopes will have some visible impact one day.